The Anthropology of Latin America and the Caribbean

Harry Sanabria
University of Pittsburgh

Boston   New York   San Francisco
Mexico City   Montreal   Toronto   London   Madrid   Munich   Paris
Hong Kong   Singapore   Tokyo   Cape Town   Sydney

Series Editor: *Dave Repetto*
Development Editor: *Jennifer Jacobson*
Editorial Assistant: *Jack Cashman*
Senior Marketing Manager: *Kelly May*
Production Editor: *Roberta Sherman*
Editorial-Production Services and Electronic Composition: *WestWords, Inc.*
Composition Buyer: *Linda Cox*
Manufacturing Buyer: *Megan Cochran*
Photo Researcher: *Naomi Rudov*
Cover Administrator: *Joel Gendron*

For related titles and support materials, visit our online catalog at www.ablongman.com

Between the time website information is gathered and then published, it is not unusual for some sites to have closed. Also, the transcription of URLs can result in typographical errors. The publisher would appreciate notification where these errors occur so that they may be corrected in subsequent editions.

Library of Congress Cataloging-in-Publication Data

Sanabria, Harry.
    The Anthropology of Latin America and the Caribbean/Harry Sanabria. —1st ed.
        p. cm.
    Includes bibliographical references and index.
    ISBN 0-205-38099-9
        1. Ethnology—Latin America. 2. Ethnology—Caribbean Area. 3. Indians—History.
    4. Indians—Social life and customs. 5. Latin America—Social life and customs.
    6. Caribbean Area—Social life and customs. 7. Latin America—History. 8. Caribbean
    Area—History. I. Title.
    GN564.L29S36 2007
    305.80098—dc22   2006043035

Printed in the United States of America

10 9 8 7 6 5 4 3 2 1   RRD-VA   10   09   08   07   06

Photo Credits
p. 8, Harry Sanabria; p. 11, Bill Gentile/Corbis; p. 32, Jeremy Horner/Corbis; p. 33, Wolfgang Kaehler/Corbis; p. 34, AP Wide World Photos; p. 35, Fulvio Roiter/Corbis; p. 36, Beth Wald/Aurora & Quanta Productions; p. 37, Charles O'Rear/Bettmann/Corbis; p. 38, Jon Larson/SuperStock; p. 39, Joel Sartore/National Geographic Image Collection; p. 41, AP Wide World Photos; p. 42, Karl Kummels/SuperStock; p. 62, Courtesy of Museo de Antropologia de Xalapa, Mexico; p. 63, Mike Peters/Pearson Education; p. 65, Charles Lenars/Corbis; p. 67, Pearson Education Corporate Digital Archive; p. 90, Harry Sanabria; p. 102, AP Wide World Photos; p. 117, Art Resource; p. 134, Courtesy of Patrick C. Wilson; p. 155, Bill Gentile/Corbis; p. 166, AP Wide World Photos; p. 193, Harry Sanabria; p. 194, Harry Sanabria; p. 196, Harry Sanabria; p. 237, AP Wide World Photos; p. 243, Colin Jones/NewsCom; p. 261, Michael Moody/D. Done Bryant Stock Photography; p. 273, Sergio Dorantes/Corbis; p. 287, Courtesy of Patrick C. Wilson; p. 306, Herve Collart/Sygma/Corbis; p. 328, Sergio Moraes/Reuters/Corbis; p. 332, David Mercado/Sygma/Corbis; p. 345, Diego Giudice/Corbis; p. 353, Horacio Villalobos/Corbis; p. 363, Reuters/Corbis; p. 367, Carlos Carrion/Sygma/Corbis

Dedication

Para mis padres, Luis Manuel y Adelaida, quienes me enseñaron en el diario vivir que sin una apreciación del pasado y la cultura corremos el riesgo de deambular por la vida sin sentido.

Y a mi hija Katarina Sophía, para que nunca corra ese riesgo.

For my parents, Luis Manuel and Adelaida, who taught me in the course of everyday life that without an appreciation of the past and culture we run the risk of straying aimlessly through life.

And to my daughter Katarina Sophía, so she will never run that risk.

CONTENTS

l

ACKNOWLEDGMENTS AND THANKS

It is often said that writing is a lonely undertaking. Yet, while in many ways true, this book would not have been possible without the assistance and encouragement of numerous people.

To my friend and colleague Patrick C. Wilson, my deepest thanks and gratitude for agreeing to write Chapter 5, and, more importantly, staying in touch when I most needed emotional support. My appreciation also to my friend John Stevenson for every so often calling and checking up on me.

For providing me with useful bibliographic citations and permissions to reproduce photos, I am indebted to Andrea Cuellar, Robin Cutright, Rob Kruger, Kent Mathewson, Edmundo Morales, and Michael K. Steinberg. Becky L. Eden produced the initial drafts of the maps that appear in this book.

In Pittsburgh, Megan Rooney and the parents of *La Escuelita Arcoiris* generously allowed me to include a photo of their children in this book.

Throughout the years, the University of Pittsburgh been a wonderful setting for thinking and writing about Latin America and the Caribbean. My thanks to Rich Scaglion (then chair of the Department of Anthropology) and N. John Cooper (dean of the Faculty of Arts and Sciences), who approved the sabbatical during which the final draft of this book was written. Like all Latinamericanists at "Pitt," I will fondly remember Eduardo Lozano's passion and tireless efforts at building one of the finest Latin American library collections in the United States. Eduardo, who passed away shortly before this book was published, would have liked to have read it. At the Center for Latin American Studies, I particularly thank Shirley Kregar, John Frechione, and Rosalind Eannarino for their unending encouragement and for helping out in so many more ways than they can possibly imagine. George Reid Andrews, John Beverly, Robert D. Drennan, Hugo Nutini, and Elayne Zorn generously shared with me some of their publications. Crystal Wright meticulously tracked down, photocopied, and organized many of the reading materials for this text.

I would like to thank the reviewers who read the drafts at various stages and offered invaluable comments and suggestions: Brad M. Biglow, University of North Florida; Mark Bonta, Delta State University; Maria R. Garcia-Acevedo, California State University; Charles W. Houck, University of North Carolina, Charlotte; Cymene Howe, Cornell University; Debarun Majumdar, Texas State University, San Marcos; Jeffrey W. Mantz, California State University, Stanislaus; Steven L. Rubenstein, Ohio University; Marjorie Snipes, State University of West Georgia; and Anne C. Woodrick, University of Northern Iowa. Although I have not been able to address all the issues they raised, this text benefitted enormously from their input.

I am especially grateful to Jennifer Jacobson of Allyn and Bacon, who early on recognized the need for this book, marshalled excellent reviewers, furnished important insights, and prodded me to keep thinking and writing when I felt discouraged.

And my daughter Katarina Sophía has unknowingly been an unending source of pride, encouragement, and inspiration.

PREFACE

Several years ago, it occurred to me to teach a course that I titled "The Cultural Anthropology of Latin America and the Caribbean." I had previously taught a specialized course on the Andean region, but became increasingly convinced that a new and broader course focusing on Latin America and the Caribbean would enrich the undergraduate curriculum at the University of Pittsburgh. Part of this perceived need was prompted by students themselves, who often asked provocative and well-justified questions on how issues in the Andean context were different from or similar to those in other parts of Latin America and the Caribbean.

Developing and teaching this course was a formidable challenge, primarily because there was not in my mind an adequate, comprehensive, up-to-date, single-authored textbook for an undergraduate student audience. A few edited volumes on the anthropology of Latin America do of course exist. Yet, all have serious drawbacks:

1. Some are circumscribed to a specific region (e.g., the Caribbean, Mesoamerica).

2. Others are woefully outdated.

3. Most lack even basic data on how many people currently live in Latin America and the Caribbean or the languages spoken.

4. Virtually none provides a solid introduction to and visual depictions of landscapes, so important for understanding the physical and cultural habitats of Latin American and Caribbean peoples.

5. Almost none problematizes what "is" Latin America and the Caribbean, and how these regions emerged as legitimate foci of research and study.

6. Most either entirely omit or minimize archaeology or the European Conquest and ensuing colonial experience, crucial for understanding the contemporary experience of Latin American and Caribbean peoples.

7. Others fail to include readings and perspectives on themes—such as gender, and food and cuisine—that most instructors would attempt to cover in many cultural anthropology survey courses.

But thematic issues and coverage were only some of the shortcomings I ran into as I surveyed existing edited volumes with an undergraduate student audience in mind. Equally important, I was searching for a broad, analytically cohesive, and well integrated text that would shed light on the varied experiences of Latin American and Caribbean peoples through a unified theoretical prism or framework. I was also interested in a volume that would provide significant insights on contemporary trends and debates within Latin American cultural anthropology, such as those on sexuality, the anthropology of the body, mass violence and genocide, and the diasporic experiences of Latin American and Caribbean peoples in North America. I also had in mind a volume that furnished an up-to-date bibliography reflecting recent research trends as well as a comprehensive list of relevant films and film resources. I was, finally, also seeking a text that drew attention to and underscored the relevance of Latin American and Caribbean anthropology to Hispanic/Latino, Caribbean (including Afro-Caribbean), and African American students and peoples in North America.

Given these almost insurmountable drawbacks in what I perceived in existing volumes, I embarked on the task of writing the kind of textbook that I thought was so urgently needed. The present book is the result of this effort and quest.

Analytical Approach

All texts are implicitly or explicitly written with an analytical or theoretical framework through which authors seek to understand and communicate to others the world around them. This intellectual and philosophical prism, or paradigm (Kuhn 1962), filters or informs what sorts of questions to ask, a sense of why these may be important, and the range of possible answers to these questions. An analytical approach also shapes how and why some and not other themes, readings, and concepts are raised, and how these are interpreted and presented.

This book is no exception. The range of issues and interpretations raised in the following chapters are informed by a political–economic approach or framework. There are, of course, not one but several political–economic approaches, reflecting diverse intellectual traditions within cultural anthropology.[1] Nevertheless, I believe that most anthropologists working within this framework (and worldview) would generally agree that this perspective:

1. Recognizes and gives proper weight to the pervasiveness of power, inequality, and conflict in the social, cultural, and material worlds within which people live out, make sense of, and try to change their everyday lives.

2. Assumes that a sharp distinction between the cultural/symbolic and material spheres distorts reality, for both are continuously shaping and molding each other in different ways and with diverse, often unanticipated outcomes.

3. Posits that meanings, symbols, and social relationships at the local or community level are better understood by also interpreting and placing them within larger frames of reference—regional, national, or international.

4. Acknowledges that history matters a great deal—that an adequate interpretation of culture and social practices entails anchoring them in time and place.

5. Assumes that although all contemporary societies and cultures studied by anthropologists have been impacted in one way or another by wider events, connections, or processes often not of their own choosing (such as the spread of capitalism or colonialism), their members are not and have not been mere pawns to such impersonal forces, but active agents in mediating, interpreting, and shaping culture and social relations at the local level.

Strengths and Features

This book provides a comprehensive overview of contemporary anthropological research in and on Latin America and the Caribbean. Readers will encounter many more direct quotations than in other textbooks, reflecting a concerted attempt to convey "voices" of both authors as well as the peoples they study. *In Their Own Words* textboxes are designed to convey people's views in their own words, language, and cultural categories. This book also highlights important contentious issues. *Controversies* sections at the end of each chapter focus attention on important contemporary debates within the anthropology of Latin America and the Caribbean, thus allowing readers the opportunity to reflect on how theoretical and methodological differences lead to varying interpretations and debates. One important approach adopted in this book, and further justified in the following chapter, is that Latin America and the Caribbean ought to conceptually also include areas of North America (but particularly areas in the United States) where millions of Latin American and Caribbean peoples are forging new lives in novel circumstances. This approach is reflected in sections at the end of each chapter titled *In the United States.* In these sections, important issues raised in each chapter are further explored from the vantage point of the Latin American and Caribbean experience in the United States.

A thorough effort has also been made to furnish an array of reference and research tools. The almost 1,100 bibliographic citations provide an especially useful resource to further delve into the wide range of issues and debates in each chapter. The instructor's manual that accompanies this book lists more than 100 relevant Web sites, allowing students the opportunity to explore themes raised in the following chapters. Further, convinced as I am of the pedagogical importance of conveying to students a visual impression of Latin American and Caribbean landscapes and peoples, the instructor's manual also lists 300 recent films and videos, complete with a short summary and the relevant countries or regions that each alludes to. It also includes Web sites of film producers and/or distributors, and of recent Latin American and Caribbean film festivals. A test bank, prepared by Marjorie Snipes, University of West Georgia, who was a reviewer throughout the development of this text, includes questions in four question types for each chapter: true-false, multiple choice, short answer, and essay. Professor Snipes also assisted with preparation of the instructor's manual.

Organization and Themes

Chapter 1 (Anthropology, Latin America, and the Caribbean) starts off the volume by raising the question of why studying the anthropology of Latin America and the Caribbean is important. It then turns to a brief overview of anthropology and cultural anthropology, including key methods and concepts. The last section then introduces students to the cultural anthropological enterprise by comparing two powerful ethnographic works: Oscar Lewis' *La Vida: A Puerto Rican Family in the Culture of Poverty—San Juan and New York,* and Nancy Scheper-Hughes' *Death Without Weeping: The Violence of Everyday Life in Brazil.*

Chapter 2 (Introducing Latin America and the Caribbean) begins by focusing on the often inconsistent criteria used to circumscribe Latin America and the Caribbean, and then examines how this region or space emerged as a conceptual category. This is followed by an overview of countries and population dynamics, and languages spoken. Attention then shifts to landscapes, including their transformations before and after the European Conquest. The final section reassesses the culture area concept and suggests new ways that this concept can be more relevant to the contemporary Latin American and Caribbean context.

Chapter 3 (Society and Culture Before the Europeans) charts the archaeology of the region, emphasizing current research on the emergence of societal complexity throughout the Paleo-Indian, Archaic, Formative, and Horizon periods. The focus then shifts to the rise and expansion of the Inca and Aztec states so as to understand how these were unable to muster successful resistance to Europeans. The ongoing controversies on the peopling of the Americas are explored in the last section.

Chapter 4 (Conquest, Colonialism, and Resistance) centers on the European Conquest and its aftermath. How and why Europeans so quickly subdued most organized indigenous resistance, as well as the consequences of the Columbian Exchange, are first examined. Emphasis then turns to mechanisms of colonial control, and the importance of landed estates, plantations, and slavery in the colonial economy. Subsequent sections explore ways that indigenous societies resisted and adapted to colonial rule, as well as the process of ethnogenesis that resulted in the emergence of new social groups and identities. The chapter ends by examining how and why the 1992 Quincentennial was marked by considerable controversy.

Chapter 5 (Cultural Politics of Race and Ethnicity), written by Patrick C. Wilson, University of Lethbridge, focuses on the variety of cultural constructions of race and ethnicity (e.g., Black, Mestizo, Indian) and what these mean. The chapter begins by first emphasizing the fluidity of racial boundaries, stressing their cultural and social underpinnings, and contrasting these with those prevalent in North America. Race as a colonial construct is taken up in the next section, followed by an analysis of the role of mestizaje in nation-building efforts. Attention then turns to the rise of indigenous movements, the links between ethnicity, gender, and nationalism, and debates on intellectual property rights and indigenous peoples. The last section focuses on how race, ethnicity, and class structure the life experiences of Puerto Ricans in New York City.

Chapter 6 (Cultural Constructions of Gender and Sexuality) provides an overview of the cultural shaping of gender ideologies, relationships, and sexualities. It first examines these in Mesoamerica and the Andes prior to the European Conquest. Emphasis subsequently shifts to colonial efforts at reshaping gender and sexuality, and the crucial role of gender ideologies in nineteenth-century attempts at consolidating nation-states. The following two sections provide a critique to marianismo and machismo as dominant models of gender identities, relationships, and sexualities. The theme of gender and violence in Amazonian societies is taken up next. Finally, the chapter concludes by shifting attention to novel forms of marriage, gender, and sexual ideologies emerging in Mexico and among Mexican-American migrants living in Atlanta.

Chapter 7 (Religion and Everyday Life) turns to the multi-faceted role of religious beliefs and practices. It begins with an overview of major attributes of popular Catholicism, emphasizing the important roles of the Virgin Mary, the Devil, and All Saints and All Souls Day (Todos Santos). The chapter then focuses on how and why Protestantism is rapidly spreading, followed by a detailed scrutiny of the major tenets of Afro-Latin religious systems. The chapter next examines the controversies concerning the emergence and socio-economic significance of Mesoamerican civil-religious hierarchies. The final section emphasizes the importance of Vodou beliefs and rituals among Haitian migrants in Brooklyn, New York City.

Chapter 8 (Striving for Health and Coping with Illness) focuses on health and illness. A key thrust explores the links between poverty, marginality, and disease, paying particular attention to tuberculosis and HIV/AIDS. The folk or emic illnesses of susto, mal de ojo, and nervios are then examined in their social contexts. The focus then turns to how healthy bodies are construed cross-culturally; the relationships between religion and healing; and controversies surrounding the consumption and medicinal properties of marijuana and coca. The final section explores the prevalence of susto and mal de ojo among Mexican-American farm workers in Florida.

Chapter 9 (Food, Cuisine, and Cultural Expression) centers on the cultural and social significance of food and cuisine. It begins by stressing the importance of food and cuisine for cultural expression and identity, and social relationships. This is followed by a historical and cultural sketch of Latin American food, and then by an analysis of the relationships between food and ritual. Ways that gender and sexuality are related to food preparation, consumption, and sharing are then examined. The following section emphasizes the role of food and cuisine in the emergence of nationalism and the construction of nation-states. The last two sections highlight some debates on the "hot" and "cold" dichotomy, and on the symbolic and social roles of the preparation and consumption of tamales among Mexican-American migrant workers in Texas and Illinois.

Chapter 10 (Perspectives on Globalization) takes up the theme of globalization and some of its consequences. The first section reviews the cultural and economic dimensions of globalization. How global tourism in spurring cultural changes is then examined. This is followed by an analysis of cultural, social, and gendered dimensions of transnational flows of capital; in this section, the North American Free Trade Agreement is examined from the vantage point of migration, and labor and production in maquiladora plants. The subsequent section focuses on the environmental impact of globalization, emphasizing sustainable development, bioprospecting, and deforestation. Attention then shifts to controversies on how in Amazonia ethnographic representations of indigenous peoples may be endangering their well-being in a context in which powerful global interests vie for this region's resources. This chapter ends by focusing on the lives of Mexican-American domestic workers in California.

Chapter 11 (Manifestations of Popular Culture) first grapples with the concept, and then turns to some major dimensions or facets, of popular culture. The first section examines the many-sided roles of soccer and baseball to illustrate the social and cultural significance of sports. The historical and contemporary importance of Carnaval is surveyed next. The third section turns to music and dance—and specifically to tango, salsa, and reggae. The powerful cultural impact of television and soap operas is then examined. Focus then shifts to the controversy surrounding the relationship between tango, gender, and sexuality.

The final section explores the meanings of the quinceañera ritual marking a young girl's fifteenth birthday.

Chapter 12 (Violence, Memory, and Striving for a Just World) ends the book by examining and reflecting on examples of mass violence and social conflicts so as to understand some of their causes and explore their future legacies. One goal is to highlight how through memory individuals interpret and make sense of past traumatic events. Case studies include the Central American civil wars, the 1973 coup in Chile, Argentina's "dirty war," the ongoing violence in Colombia, the Zapatista rebellion in Mexico, and Peru's Shining Path insurgency. These case studies are followed by a critical overview of the controversy surrounding Rigoberta Menchú's autobiography. Finally, the chapter ends by shedding light on ways that Guatemalan Mayas are attempting to rebuild their lives in Los Angeles, and Morgantown, South Carolina.

E N D N O T E

1. The literature on this topic is huge. Some of the works that have informed my thinking over the years, many alluded to in this book, include: Said 1979; Scott 1985, 1990; Marcus and Fischer 1986; Kellog 1991; Nash 1981; Wolf 1997 [1982], 1999; Mintz 1985b; Roseberry 1988, 1989; Comaroff and Comaroff 1993; Gordon 1993; Rogers 1992; Silverman and Gulliver 1992; Dirks 1992, 1996, 2001; Dirks et al. 1994; Cohn 1996; McDonald 1996; Cooper and Stoler 1997; Stern 1988, 1993; Stoler 1995, 2002; Pels 1997; Blim 2000; Gledhill, 2000.

1 Anthropology, Latin America, and the Caribbean

This chapter introduces readers to some demographic, cultural, economic, geo-political, and transnational reasons why the study of the anthropology of Latin America and the Caribbean is important in today's contemporary world. It then turns to a brief overview of anthropology and cultural anthropology, including key methods and concepts. The third section introduces students to the cultural anthropological enterprise, including methods and theory, by comparing two powerful ethnographic works on the every-day lives of the poor in urban slums or shantytowns in Puerto Rico, New York City, and Brazil.

Why Study the Anthropology of Latin America and the Caribbean?

Is the study of Latin America and the Caribbean tantamount to privileging—intellectually, politically, or culturally—Latin America over other regions of the world? Of course not. But it *is* a question of recognizing the intense and manifold ways in which the destinies of North American and Latin American and Caribbean peoples have become so interwoven over the past 150 years, and *also* a question of being cognizant that Latin America and the Caribbean—and their peoples—have had (and will continue to have) a decisive impact on the culture, society, and politics of the United States, and vice-versa.[1]

There are at least five reasons why the study of the anthropology of Latin America and the Caribbean is relevant in our ever-interdependent world:

1. *Demographic*. Hispanics/Latinos are the largest and fastest growing ethnic group or category in the United States, in what some are calling the Latin-Americanization or "Latinization" of the United States (Stephen et al. 2003:3–4).[2] According to the U.S. Census Bureau, between 1980 and 1990, the Hispanic/Latino population rose from almost fifteen to more than twenty-two million, or 9 percent of the U.S. population, an increase of 60 percent (Gibson and Jung 2002). Between 1990 and 2000, Hispanics/Latinos increased another 58 percent (to almost thirty-six million), or almost 13 percent of the population of the United States, slightly surpassing the number of African Americans. The Hispanic/Latino population rose to be almost four times as large as those classed as Asians. During this time, Hispanics/Latinos also accounted for more than half of all foreign born U.S. citizens, and almost 60 percent of these are of Mexican descent (U.S.

Census Bureau 2000 a, b, c). This is also a relatively young population: by 2000, more than 35 percent were under the age of eighteen, compared with almost 24 percent among non-Hispanic Whites (U.S. Census Bureau 2001:2–3) and with higher fertility than other ethnic groups (U.S. Census Bureau 1993:4). In recent decades, new immigrants have opted for novel "gateways," especially in the southern United States. In Georgia, for instance, the Hispanic/Latino population increased four times between 1990 and 2000. And in Alabama, South Carolina, and Tennessee, it surged between 200 and 400 percent. Other recent gateways include the Midwestern states. Stephen et al. perceptively note that "If the number of Latinos in the United States from the 2000 census . . . is compared with the populations of the largest Latin American countries [Brazil, Mexico, Colombia, and Argentina] the United States would rank fifth" (2003:4). In Canada, there are about 250,000 Spanish speakers and an equal number of speakers of Portuguese (Stephen et al. 2003:4).

2. _Cultural._ This demographic importance is closely paralleled by a pervasive and ever-growing presence of Hispanic/Latino culture. For example, in many parts of the United States (especially in states such as Florida, New York, Texas, California, Colorado, Arizona, and New Mexico), Spanish is the most important lingua franca (general language of communication). Indeed, Hispanics/Latinos account for at least 60 percent of the almost forty-seven million United States citizens who speak a "language other than English" on a regular basis. And of these, less than half are reported to speak English "less than very well" (U.S. Census Bureau 2000d).

Members of small southern towns and cities are awakening to the presence of Spanish-language newspapers, the sounds of Mexican music on local radio channels, and the sight and smell of _taquerías,_ or taco restaurants (Hirsch 2003:18–9), all hard to imagine a few decades ago. Spanish-language newspapers and radio stations are also an ubiquitous and expanding presence in many small and large cities outside of the southern United States, and recent years have witnessed a phenomenal growth of television/media conglomerates—such as _Telemundo_ and _Univisión_—catering to a daily audience of millions of dedicated viewers (Ballvé 2004). Spanish-speaking media not only transmit news and events from the United States but also from Latin America. In this way, it performs important cultural functions, such as the forging of a pan-Latino identity or sense of belonging, as well as the fashioning—a constant recreation—of Hispanic/Latino culture in the United States. These issues are explored in Chapter 11.

The spread of Hispanic/Latino culture and language has also spilled into the realm of cultural politics, or of the so-called "culture wars" in the United States. Examples include ongoing debates over the value of bilingual and bicultural education, as well as fierce disputes over whether to ban the use of Spanish in government offices and public spaces, especially in New York, Texas, Pennsylvania, Arizona, and California, states with especially large Hispanic/Latino populations. Heated controversies surrounding the meaning and importance of historic markers and events—such as the Alamo in Texas and what "really" happened there—are another vivid reminder of how the politics of culture in the United States is tightly interwoven with the growing cultural and political weight of the Hispanic/Latino population (Trouillot 1995:9–11).

One noteworthy example of how the current culture wars in the United States seem fueled by the ever-growing importance of Hispanics/Latinos is the recent controversial claims by Harvard political scientist Samuel P. Huntington. He has argued that the fact that so many Hispanics/Latinos (Huntington is particularly casting his sight on "Mexicans") are (seemingly) refusing to completely "assimilate"—in other words, that apparently so many refuse to suddenly abandon their language and culture once in the United States—actually poses a dire political challenge by threatening to divide the United States into two peoples, cultures, and languages (Huntington 2004). This "challenge to America's traditional identity" (quoted in Carlson 2004), although never clearly defined, apparently manifests itself in the refusal to adopt "Anglo-Protestant culture" (Huntington 2004:32). Therefore, Hispanics/Latinos—as previous immigrants apparently have done—should assimilate "totally and successfully" (quoted in Solomon 2004). Such nativistic views, sentiments, and prejudices—which reached their extreme in the late 1800s and early 1900s (and are vividly portrayed in the Hollywood film *Gangs of New York*)—remarkably assume that cultural variability in and of itself is divisive, destructive, and the root cause of poverty; ignore the vast scholarship on ways in which European immigrants also valued aspects of their culture and identity; and overlook the large corpus of anthropological studies that demonstrates the multitude of ways in which Latin American and Caribbean immigrants are productive members of U.S. society, even if many appear to shun "Anglo-Protestant culture"—which, incidentally, remains for Huntington (and this author) a nebulous concept.[3]

The demographic and cultural importance of the Hispanic/Latino population has also been paralleled by—and has partly fed into—its crucial and growing political importance. Local and national level elections, for example, provide a perhaps unique reminder of not only how important "getting out" the Hispanic/Latino vote has become in recent years (Aizenman 2002, 2003), but also how other debates—on, for example, proposals to legalize the status of millions of Mexican and other Latin American undocumented workers in the United States—also feed into local and national level election issues (Christian Science Monitor 2004; Stevenson 2004; Washington Post 2004).

3. *Economic.* The intense volume of trade and commercial contacts between the United States and Latin America is also a key reason for studying Latin America and the Caribbean. As a block, Latin America is the United States' most important trading partner and is certain to remain so, particularly after the North American Free Trade Agreement (NAFTA) was signed between the United States, Canada, and Mexico in 1994 (see Chapter 10).

The volume of trade between the United States and Latin America is enormous. Latin America is the largest consumer of U.S. goods (and the United States is the most important source of Latin American imports), and virtually all Latin American exports are destined for the United States. Recent estimates of the volume of U.S. trade to and from nineteen of the twenty "core" Latin American countries, as defined by *The Statistical Abstract of Latin America* (Cuba was not included in these calculations), bear out these assertions; more than 20 percent of all U.S. exports are destined for Latin America, while Latin American goods make up almost 16 percent of all U.S. imports (Wilkie et al. 2001:785).

Furthermore, during most of Latin America's history—with perhaps the exception of England in Argentina, Chile, and Uruguay—the United States has been the source of most capital invested in Latin America, a historic trend that shows no sign of diminishing. One consequence of the massive capital flow is that most Latin American countries are heavily indebted to U.S. banks or multinational financial entities (such as the Inter-Development

Bank or the International Monetary Fund) that are backed by primarily U.S. capital (Green 1995; Watson 1994). As a result of this sheer volume of trade (and debt), there is a great deal of economic integration between the United States and Latin America. (There are, of course, some Latin American countries such as Mexico, Brazil, Venezuela, and Chile that, in terms of volume of exports and imports, are more tightly integrated to the United States.)

This high degree of economic integration has a multitude of obvious political consequences. Witness, for example, ongoing debates between labor groups, business interests, and U.S. and Mexican officials on who is reaping the greatest rewards from NAFTA (see Chapter 10); the political shockwaves in Washington when countries such as Mexico, Argentina, and Brazil either default or threaten to default on their foreign debt; or the strategic economic and political importance of class conflicts, political instability, and threats to oil production in Venezuela (La Franchi 2003; Chinni 2004; Phillips et al. 2002; Blustein and Faiola 2002). The public call for the United States to assassinate Venezuela's president Hugo Chávez that the evangelist Pat Robertson made is an extremely disturbing example of the complex interplay between politics and economic integration and dependence (Cooperman 2005; Goodstein and Forero 2005). It is also but one example of the consequences of ignoring historical and anthropological research on how the political economy of oil production has shaped Venezuela and the emergence of populist currents that Chávez represents (Coronil 1997).

4. *Geo-political.* The United States has been politically and economically involved in Latin American affairs since the Monroe Doctrine of the 1860s—which essentially placed Latin America within the strategic economic and political security interests of the United States, and which ideologically justified many military interventions. This strategic positioning of Latin America within U.S. foreign and economic policy ambit has led to a long history of unfortunate political and economic interventions in the internal affairs of Latin America, and a concomitant deeply-entrenched animosity toward the United States (although not necessarily toward U.S. citizens).

These involvements—repeatedly couched in the rhetoric of "national security" concerns—have almost always entailed interventions (some involving the military directly, others including U.S. support of coups favoring the entrenchment of "friendly" but internally dictatorial regimes) that have almost invariably favored the interests of U.S. multinational corporations (such as the United Fruit Company in Central America) and of the wealthy elite over the interests of the vast majority of Latin America's poorer sectors (generally referred to in Spanish-speaking Latin America as the *clases populares* [popular classes]). Some examples of these interventions include the presence of U.S. Marines in Nicaragua in the 1930s and the entrenchment of the Somoza dynasty; the overthrow (with overt Central Intelligence Agency [CIA] support) of Guatemalan president Arbenz in 1952; the U.S. invasion of the Dominican Republic in 1916 and the overthrow of its president, Juan Bosch, in 1964; the infamous coup against Chile's leftist President Salvador Allende in 1973; and the U.S. involvement in the Central American civil wars of the 1980s (O'Brien 1999; Langley 1989).

5. *Transnationalism.* The fifth major reason for studying Latin America has to do with the ongoing, constant cultural intermingling of lives in and between Latin America and the

United States, part and parcel of the intense migration between these two regions, as well as the growing cultural and political importance of Hispanics/Latinos in the United States, as previously discussed.

Consider, for example, the case of the Quispe family illustrated in the film *Transnational Fiesta,* which portrays the life history of the Quispe extended family from the interior highlands of Peru. The youngest members of the family started migrating to Washington, D.C. in the 1970s. Over a period of about fifteen years, the first migrants were joined by other family members, including brothers, sisters, cousins, and parents. Further, the Quispe family members have not severed their contacts with their home community in Peru but in fact continue to travel to Peru and participate in their home community's rich social and cultural life. They do so, for example, by sponsoring a lavish fiesta (community-wide celebration) in honor of their community's Virgin—an especially important facet of Latin American popular Catholicism that is also widely practiced in the United States (see Chapter 7.) For this fiesta, the Quispes marshal vast quantities of food and drink, which, according to their own estimates, cost them more than US $20,000. By sponsoring this fiesta, as well as videotaping it and periodically viewing their participation in this fiesta in their Washington homes, they are making a powerful statement that their cultural heritage is important to them as they forge their new lives in the United States.

Or consider, as well, the community of San Jerónimo, in the Mexican state of Oaxaca, described by Kearney (1996:15–21), which displays numerous cultural features that many would ascribe to a "traditional" Mexican peasant community. Economically, members of this community have access to communally owned farmland; farming tools are simple and seem to be ancient; the greater part of what is produced is consumed locally and not sold in marketplaces; and intracommunity labor exchanges are widespread. Culturally and socially, this community has a "rich ceremonial life" (Kearney 1996:16). Most marriages are between community members (i.e., there is a high level of marriage endogamy); the use of ponchos and sandals is widespread; and most speak Mixtec (a pre-Hispanic indigenous language) in everyday interactions. An unsuspecting visitor (or ethnographer) to this community might very well reach the conclusion that its members had limited contacts with the outside world. Yet, this view would be mistaken. Very little of what is actually consumed is produced locally, and San Jerónimo is continuously sending migrants to other parts of Mexico—and to the United States, especially California. Community members temporarily living in and constantly moving back and forth between San Jerónimo and California, send back home remittances, which help not only in raising the living standards of those remaining behind but also, paradoxically, help forge an image of San Jerónimo as a "traditional" community. It was apparent to Kearney that San Jerónimo "was maintained as a seemingly 'traditional' community precisely because of the high degree to which migrants from the town penetrated into distant and diverse socioeconomic niches elsewhere in Mexico and California" (1996:17).

Subsequent chapters of this book explore the manifold ways in which Latin American and Caribbean peoples are struggling to forge productive and meaningful lives in their home communities and countries, as well as in North America, in times of vast and rapid changes that so often work against them—and how culture is a crucial anchor of such efforts. This is, perhaps, the most important message of this book and of cultural anthropology as a discipline.

Doing Cultural Anthropology and Documenting Everyday Life

What in North America, and parts of Latin America and the Caribbean, is known as cultural (or socio-cultural) anthropology is part of a broader academic discipline (anthropology or **general anthropology**) comprised of four fields. **Physical** or **biological anthropology** is primarily concerned with the evolution of the human species (*homo sapiens sapiens*) and the relationship between biology and cultural behavior. This is the field within anthropology with the closest links to the natural and medical sciences. **Archaeology** centers attention on two main themes. The first documents the appearance, spread, and disappearance of social groups over long periods of time. The second major theme within archaeology focuses on the causes and consequences of the transition from small-scale and egalitarian to large, stratified societies, a process known as social or cultural evolution. (This concept is addressed more fully in Chapter 3.) **Linguistic anthropology** is concerned with learning about societies and their cultures from the vantage point of language. Some key questions include: How and why do languages change through time, and why do some become extinct? And what can be learned about the culture of a group of people or society by study-ing their language and how they communicate with themselves and others?

Cultural or **socio-cultural anthropology,** the anthropological cornerstone of this book, focuses primary attention on the study of the culture of contemporary social groups. Cultural anthropologists have two goals. The first is to understand how and why dissimilar peoples—members of other societies and cultures—think and behave differently from oth-ers. This emphasis on **cultural diversity** or **variability** is paralleled by the equally important goal of documenting and understanding **cultural similarities,** or what diverse peoples around the globe share, or have in common, *despite* their seeming differences. What daily issues do they face? What common aspirations, hopes, fears, and experiences do they share? What makes *all* peoples throughout the global cultural beings worthy of respect and dignity?

With these two goals in mind, cultural anthropologists typically go about their work by engaging in long-term, personal, face-to-face contact—and living with—the peoples they study, engaging in what is known as **participant observation.** The result of fieldwork (also called ethnographic research) is typically the publication of an **ethnography**—a description or portrait of the culture and everyday life of the people studied.

As noted in the Preface, the work that anthropologists do is always informed by dif-ferent theoretical frameworks. This explains why by the 1950s, anthropologists had gath-ered more than 160 definitions of culture (Miller 2005:9), one of cultural anthropology's key guiding concepts. By the early 1970s, Keesing (1974) had identified the major theoret-ical frameworks or positions within cultural anthropology that partly underpinned such dis-parate meanings attached to the concept of culture; Ortner did likewise a decade later (1984). Perhaps most anthropologists would agree that **culture** stands for the symbolic and material repertoire with and through which people in a given historical context make sense of the world around them—how the world ought to be, that is, notions of what is right and wrong, proper and improper, just and unjust; claim a certain distinctiveness or sense of identity; and provide themselves with the symbolic and materials tools with which to adapt to and cope with changing circumstances. Most anthropologists also acknowledge **intra-cultural variability**—that few social groups share a totally homogenous culture, especially in complex societies (see Chapter 3). A political-economic approach—such as the one that underpins this book—recognizes that the cultures of most (if not all) human groups studied by cultural anthropologists in the field have been anything but homogenous, *and* that these cultures have been pervaded by social, political, and economic inequality.

Similar difficulties underlie the notion of **cultural relativism,** perhaps the second most important concept in cultural anthropology. By cultural relativism anthropologists mean that beliefs, behaviors, and practices in other cultural contexts ought not be judged from the standards of one's own culture (or prejudices), and that to do so would be to inappropriately engage in **ethnocentrism.** Yet, even this seemingly straightforward idea—a linchpin in the development of cultural anthropology as an academic discipline—is fraught with difficulties and debates (Geertz 1984; Spiro 1986). Does cultural relativism mean that anthropologists in the field (or those who read what anthropologists write) ought to take on a neutral, "bias-free" stance toward whatever they encounter? How does the concept of cultural relativism dovetail not only with intolerance toward others but also with basic human rights issues (Renteln 1988)? What of cultural relativism in what appears to be extreme male-upon-female violence in some Amazonian societies, genocide in Central America during the 1980s, or Maya peasants killing each other during Guatemala's civil war (all explored in subsequent chapters)? If, as appears to be the case, cultural relativism—like culture—is a sliding, slippery concept, the meanings of which vary according to theoretical or ideological viewpoints, what to do? Perhaps once again recognizing cultural heterogeneity and inequality helps. Miller (2005:19), for example, makes a distinction between cultural relativism and **critical cultural relativism,** which "poses questions about cultural practices, and ideas about who accepts them and why, and who they might be harming or helping . . . Critical cultural relativism avoids the trap of adopting a homogenized view of complexity. It recognizes internal cultural differences and winners/losers, oppressors/victims."

There are of course no easy or "packaged" answers to the issues and questions raised here, and this book does not propose any. What this book *does* do is invite readers to explore these and other concepts, issues, and debates from the vantage point of the Latin American and Caribbean experience. In ending his review of theories of culture, Keesing suggested that it might be more important to think about questions and issues than definitions:

> Conceiving culture . . . within a vastly complex system, biological, social and symbolic, and grounding our abstract models in the concrete particularities of human social life, should make possible . . . deepening understanding. Whether in this quest the concept of culture is progressively refined, radically reinterpreted, or progressively extinguished will in the long run scarcely matter if along the way it has led us to ask strategic questions and to see connections that would otherwise have been hidden. (Keesing 1974:94)

Controversies: The Culture of Poverty and Perspectives on the Poor

The fact that all scholarly research is informed by often divergent theoretical perspectives (see the Preface) explains why cultural anthropologists often generate different and often contrasting views on similar themes or groups of people—and why cultural anthropology is frequently pervaded by controversies. The following two examples of research on the poor in urban slums or shantytowns (see also Chapter 2) illustrate how cultural anthropologists go about carrying out research, and how contrasting theoretical lenses lead to different interpretations and results.

Oscar Lewis and the "Culture of Poverty"

In and outside of anthropology, Oscar Lewis is best known for his idea that poverty, marginality, and oppression generate a **culture of poverty** shared by and reproduced intergenerationally among the poor. He developed this idea in *The Children of Sánchez* (1961), based on work in Mexico City. Yet, it was in *La Vida* (1965)—one of the most influential and controversial ethnographies to ever appear—that Lewis fully elaborated his theory. Lewis worked in New York City and in San Juan, Puerto Rico, in the shantytown he called La Esmeralda (La Perla), located just outside the old walled city (see Photo 1.1).

Some of the more characteristic traits of the culture of poverty are:

The lack of effective participation and integration of the poor in the major institutions of the larger society . . . Low wages . . . unemployment and underemployment lead to low income . . . [and] . . . absence of savings . . . People with a culture of poverty . . . have a low level of literacy, and education, usually

PHOTO 1.1 *La Perla, in San Juan, Puerto Rico.*

do not belong to labor unions, are not members of political parties . . . and make very little use of banks, hospitals, department stores, museums or art galleries . . . [At] . . . the . . . community level we find poor housing . . . crowding, gregariousness . . . On the family level the major traits . . . are the absence of childhood as a specially prolonged and protected stage in the life cycle, early initiation into sex, free unions or consensual marriages, a . . . high incidence of abandonment of wives and children, a trend toward female- or mother-centered families . . . [There is] a strong disposition to authoritarianism . . . verbal emphasis upon family solidarity . . . is only rarely achieved . . . (Lewis 1965:xlv–xlvii)

Further, Lewis underscored some rather dark dimensions of Puerto Rican culture in La Esmeralda, such as rage, aggression, psychopathology and, in general, a "poverty of culture" (1965:xxvi–lii). *La Vida* became a sensation and center of public and academic controversy because it dealt with the lives of U.S. citizens on U.S. soil and not of some faraway, "exotic" peoples. Further, it appeared in the midst of the politically important War on Poverty and civil rights movement of the 1960s. Indeed, Lewis' fieldwork in San Juan and New York City was funded by the U.S. Department of Health, Education and Welfare (Rigdon 1988:84). The cultural context was also significant for propelling *La Vida*'s popularity, for it surfaced on the heels of the immensely popular 1961 Broadway musical and film *West Side Story,* which depicts the lives of young immigrants from Puerto Rico, including the importance they attach to being members of Puerto Rican gangs, in New York City's Upper West Side borough of Manhattan.

Portraying the culture of poor and marginal Puerto Ricans as "pathological" partly accounts for the ire and scathing critiques that Lewis received. Yet, his research was pioneering in several ways. Lewis emphasized "the positive adaptive function" (1965:li) of shantytown culture. In fact—and anticipating other scholars by decades—Lewis suggested that despite its "pathology," the culture of poverty has "a high potential for protest and for being used in political movements against the existing social order" (1965:xlxi). In this respect, Lewis was also one of the first anthropologists to formally suggest a correlation between culture and social class. He also pioneered the use of the tape recorder during fieldwork, and his ethnographies were the first to contain vast amounts of verbatim transcripts. Again anticipating by decades other, more recent anthropological trends, he was convinced of the need to give "voice to people who are rarely heard" (1965:xii). As such, his books consisted of a short introduction in which he laid out his conceptual model, followed by verbatim transcripts interspersed, here and there, with field notes. The introduction to *La Vida* (the longest of Lewis' books), for example, consists of forty-two pages, while the volume's bulk spans almost seven hundred pages of family biographies.

Lewis' critics targeted methodological and theoretical issues. One had to do with his narrative mode—the presentation of a short, abstract model followed by hundreds of pages of sparsely edited data that lacked systematic analysis and interpretation. This textual strategy left "all the problems of interpretation . . . to the reader" (Valentine 1968:51). Further, this approach also made it difficult to discern how representative his family biographies were of a wider cultural pattern. Some authors have suggested that most people Lewis and his team interviewed were social deviants and not typical of other shantytown residents (Valentine 1968:51; Rigdon 1988:97).

Further, although Lewis was clearly arguing that the culture of poverty emerged in contexts of poverty, marginality, and oppression, he became increasingly convinced of the importance of family dynamics. The problem, of course, as Valentine early recognized, was that the more Lewis focused on the family, the more distant the broader explanatory context became, and "[T]he social system as a whole . . . [became] . . . little more than a shadowy backdrop for personal and household intimacies" (1968:63–64). One lasting and unfortunate legacy of this methodological and theoretical dilemma was that the culture of poverty was largely and ultimately viewed by many as intrinsic to Puerto Rican culture, while Lewis' more vital message—the importance of poverty and marginality—was mainly overlooked.

For years, Lewis himself had serious doubts about the fit between his theory and the family biographies he gathered, although he rarely admitted it openly. In a 1960 letter sent to the editor of *The Children of Sánchez*, he stated that " 'The Culture of Poverty' is a catchy phrase . . . [but] . . . the Sánchez family is *not* the best example" (quoted in Rigdon 1988:60; italics added). Lewis finally acknowledged that the theory he had defended for decades was difficult to sustain. In 1967, he wrote to Manuel Maldonado-Denis, a Puerto Rican historian and political scientist at the University of Puerto Rico:

> The more urban slum families I study, the more I am convinced of the wide range of adaptations, reaction patterns, values, etc. that are found . . . [and] . . . to condense it all within a single abstract model like the subculture of poverty is inevitably to distort the lives of these people. (Rigdon 1988:90)

Forty years after the publication of *La Vida,* the "culture of poverty" is still viewed by U.S. domestic policy makers as one important "cause" of numerous social ills. A vivid reminder, as Ortíz and Briggs (2003) point out, of the powerful role of ideology and politics in underpinning theory and the production of ethnographic texts.

Dying and Weeping in Brazilian Favelas

In *Death Without Weeping: The Violence of Everyday Life in Brazil*—a powerful ethnographic study of shantytown life in northeastern Brazil—Scheper-Hughes emphasizes "the role of pernicious class relations in the social production of child morbidity and mortality . . . [and] of . . . the macroparatism of uncontained 'market forces' that has fed and preyed on the bodies of the young, the vulnerable, and the powerless . . . sometimes at the price of child survival" (1992:280). In such a context of scarcity, deprivation, and violence, the likelihood that most infants will survive is in fact quite low and, hence:

> . . . in the absence of a firm grounding for the expectancy of child survival, maternal thinking and practice are grounded in a set of assumptions (e.g., that infants and babies are easily replaceable or that some infants are born "wanting" to die) that contribute even further to an environment that is dangerous, even antagonistic, to new life . . . [What] is created is an environment in which death is understood as the most ordinary and most expected outcome for the children of poor families. (Scheper-Hughes 1992:20)

Scheper-Hughes carried out fieldwork in Alto do Cruzeiro, a shantytown located on the outskirts of a small town in northeastern Brazil, a region characterized by recurring droughts; chronic hunger, malnutrition, and disease; and rampant and grinding poverty. It also has one of the highest infant mortality rates in the world. In Alto do Cruzeiro, most people are desperately poor, jobs are extremely lacking, and essential services such as clean running water, sewage facilities, and health services are virtually nonexistent. This is a site where violence—interpersonal violence and violence by the state against shantytown dwellers—is widespread (see also Goldstein 2003); interpersonal relationships are fleeting; marital unions do not endure; and the key family unit consists of women and their children. In this community, where survival is literally quite unpredictable, what *is* quite likely is that about half of all infants will not live to celebrate their fifth birthday (see Photo 1.2).

There are important similarities between Oscar Lewis' *La Vida* and Nancy Scheper-Hughes' *Death Without Weeping*. Both, for example, focus on poor, marginal groups in shantytowns; provide considerable voice to those they worked with and, as a result, furnish gripping accounts of their everyday lives; place considerable attention on poverty and its role in the emergence of violence; are written in an engaging style; and both are well-known and extremely controversial.

PHOTO 1.2 *A Brazilian teenager holds her young child in a Brazilian Shantytown. Recife, Brazil.*

There are also crucial methodological and theoretical differences. Unlike Lewis' strategy of deliberately stepping back—an approach in which the anthropologist (and interpretation) literally disappears from the text being read—Scheper-Hughes' voice is ever-present, qualifying and contextualizing for readers statements ushered by her (mostly female) informants. If the bulk of *La Vida* overwhelmingly consists of family biographies, *Death Without Weeping* centers on major domains of culture through which poor women attempt to construct meaning in their everyday lives. While in *La Vida,* Lewis circumscribes his theoretical framework in the introduction—never again to be raised—Scheper-Hughes both introduces her theory in the introductory chapter and contextualizes it throughout the text, thereby achieving a tighter integration between theory and method. Whereas Lewis' theory centers on the relationship between poverty and culture, viewing the latter largely in terms of personality and family dynamics, Scheper-Hughes focuses on how a political-economy of deprivation, scarcity, hunger, and violence inscribes itself on the bodies of women, structures their interpersonal relationships with others, and, most importantly, decisively impacts on the ability of mothers to care for their children and on mothers' emotional responses when some children die.

Scheper-Hughes is a medical anthropologist whose research was guided by three theoretical frameworks: critical medical anthropology, which emphasizes the political economy of inequality in the study of health; the anthropology of the body, centering attention on the somatic and psychosomatic manifestations of inequality; and the anthropology of the emotions, focusing on the emotional responses to and consequences of deprivation and poverty. Although her book deals with the impact of deprivation on many dimensions of Brazilian life—such as politics, interpersonal relationships, Carnaval, health, and illness—three objectives guided her fieldwork. The first was to suggest that infant and child mortality was not merely the *direct* result of poverty and malnutrition but *also* an outcome of indirect infanticide by mothers who neglected some of their infants and children so that others might survive. Second, she wanted to explain how and why women and mothers withdrew support, care, and nurturing from their infants and children, thereby speeding up their death. Finally, Scheper-Hughes sought to understand how these shanty-town mothers explained or provided an ideological justification (to themselves and others) for this form of child neglect. Scheper-Hughes' overriding argument is that motherhood—what is assumed to be a "mother"—is not, as so many have assumed for so long, an "innate" quality or predisposition, but one powerfully molded by the political-economic and cultural milieu within which Alto do Cruzeiro women find themselves.

Death Without Weeping is a polemical ethnography because it questions the validity of a deeply held assumption that many believe in—that of an innate "motherly love." Dealing with indirect infanticide and child neglect, Scheper-Hughes' ethnography vividly illustrates the tough life and death choices that the desperately and marginalized poor—especially women and mothers—sometimes have to make, and how they go about grappling with and justifying to themselves and others their choices. *Death Without Weeping* also represents the best of socially committed, activist cultural anthropology, which reminds us of the discipline's long tradition of advocacy. Her book is about

> . . . mother love and child death. It is about culture and scarcity, both material and psychological, and their effects on [maternal] thinking and practice . . . What, I wondered, were the effects of chronic hunger, sickness, death,

and loss on the ability to love, trust, have faith, and keep it in the broadest sense of these terms? If mother love is, as some bioevolutionary and developmental psychologists as well as some cultural feminists believe, a "natural," or at least expectable, womanly script, what does it mean for women for whom scarcity and death have made that love frantic? (Scheper-Hughes 1992:15)

Convinced that most of their children would not survive if all received equal attention, Alto do Cruzeiro mothers directly or indirectly neglect some infants so that others may live. In this tragic milieu, mother love is best expressed by an unwavering (if often unsuccessful) commitment to those infants who might have a prospect at surviving, and by "understand[ing] a baby's life as a provisional and undependable thing—a candle whose flame is as likely to flicker and go out as to burn brightly and continuously" (Scheper-Hughes 1992:275). This is not to suggest that mothers were the direct or indirect "cause" of most infant and child deaths in this community. Chronic malnutrition, rampant parasitic infections (due to the lack of clean water), and contagion were the principal causes of infant and child mortality, a fact that Alto do Cruzeiro mothers were painfully aware of when they explicitly named diarrhea as the main killer of their children (Scheper-Hughes 1992:314).

How *do* mothers know which infants have a chance at surviving? They find out by seeking visible somatic clues that point to their infants' chance at making it. An infant born pale, sickly, or without much energy ("weak" or "quiet") is believed to be already afflicted by some incurable illness or condition. Further, not only do these infants not display a "will" to survive, but also in dying they are transformed into "angels" who are eagerly embraced by God. By contrast, infants born with the "power" to survive life—"conceptualized as a *luta,* a power 'struggle' between large and small, strong and weak" (Scheper-Hughes 1992:315)—stand a far better chance at receiving their mothers' attention. Such infants are born with "force"—playful, loud, energetic, and far from pale. How *do* women contribute to the deaths of some of their infants so that others may live? Women frown upon abortion (children, mothers told Scheper-Hughes, are a "gift" from God), and infanticide—the direct, conscious killing of an infant—is shunned. Thus, the neglect of sickly infants is carried out through other, less visible, obvious ways. Some women would simply not feed their infants correctly, "forget" to feed them at all, or provide them with the least nutritious foods. Others with little money to spare did not take their infants to a doctor.

Alas, mothers' attempts to save some of their children often failed, not because of neglect but as a result of the concrete material and cultural contexts within which they were embedded. For example, breastfeeding—in a healthy context the best way of providing nutrition for an infant—was not a viable option (Scheper-Hughes 1992:316–26). In the daily struggle to earn income by working in the nearby sugarcane fields, women were often separated from their infants; malnutrition combined with exhausting work often debilitated ("wasted") women's bodies so that they could not produce enough milk; and sometimes infants were not left long enough on their mother's breast or were too weak to stimulate her production of milk.

The enormous symbolic weight attached to commercialized powdered milk—considered by women more nutritious and healthy—also worked to the disadvantage of infants. The importance of powdered milk also intersected with prevailing gender relations and notions of parenthood, marked by brittle marital unions where "The definition of father . . . is the man who arrives at least once a week bearing the prestigious purple-labeled can of Nestlé or, when relations are strained, who has the can of milk sent to the household through a friend or intermediary" (Scheper-Hughes 1992:323). Small wonder, then, that bottle feeding was preferred. Contaminated water—what most mothers had available—was an easy source of infection. Further, powdered milk was expensive—its purchase alone could consume 20 percent of a woman's weekly income. Unable to afford the amount of powdered milk needed, mothers nourished their infants primarily with bottle-fed *mingau* or *papa d'agua,* greatly diluted concoctions of flour and/or powdered milk.

Infants dying, mothers failing to weep . . . Hard to understand and perhaps much harder still to feel empathy. But in this shantytown, as Scheper-Hughes powerfully reminds us:

> Day-to-day moral thinking is guided by a "lifeboat ethics" . . . The central dilemma . . . concerns the decisions as to who among the shipwrecked is to be saved when it would spell certain disaster to try saving all. Infants and toddlers first? Women and children? The young and the strong? . . . The brave and the beautiful? . . . The sick and the vulnerable? In emergency situations the morality of triage—the rudimentary pragmatics of saving the salvageable—often supersedes other, more aesthetic or more egalitarian ethical principles." (1992:405)

Death Without Weeping is powerful reading indeed but, like any ethnography, is not without its drawbacks, many summarized by Lassalle and O'Dougherty (1997). One of their major points is that the specific chain of events leading to the deaths of infants and children are sometimes unclear, and Scheper-Hughes' statements on this issue are at times contradictory. For example, although malnutrition and infection were viewed by Scheper-Hughes and mothers as the ultimate causes of infant and child death (see previous discussion), Scheper-Hughes also states that women's "own neglect sometimes plays a final and definitive part" (1992:157). Further, Lassalle and O'Dougherty question whether "neglect" is the appropriate gloss for expressions conveyed by mothers trying to explain the death of their children. While the term *míngua* may be correctly translated as lack or scarcity, neglect may not be the best gloss for the expression *morrer à míngua* (literally to die of want, lack, or scarcity). If Lassalle and O'Dougherty are correct, then this translation "slip" is crucial for Scheper-Hughes' argument, for it "convert[s] situations of 'scarcity' into ones of 'neglect' in discussions of child death" (1997:246). Do, then, infants and children die because of scarcity—in which case women are hardly to blame, even if they practice moral triage—or because of their mothers' conscious neglect?

In producing an ethnography, anthropologists often have to walk a fine line between emphasizing external, structural forces (such as inequality or discrimination) and privileging informants' accounts and narratives. If too much attention is placed on the former, real people and their stories and explanations fade from view; if too much emphasis is placed on people's own words and voices, the broader contexts within which these make sense and can be explained disappear into the background (as was the case with Lewis' *La Vida*). This issue is important because despite Scheper-Hughes' repeated attempts to underscore the deprivation, scarcity, and hunger faced by women in the Brazilian *favelas,* Lassalle and

O'Dougherty suggest that she has not done enough to explain and contextualize how specific external forces or contexts impinge on women's decisions. The unfortunate result, Lassalle and O'Dougherty claim (1997:257), is that "one predictable reading is that of classic culture-of-poverty theory" because "By variously omitting or separating off analysis of political and economic conditions from the discussion of child survival . . . the women become (if inadvertently) the sole agents endangering the family's survival. Whereas much First World literature has represented Third World women as trapped by various cultural determinisms, this work retains that fatality" (1997:250).

Summary

This chapter explored some of the different yet complementary reasons why studying the cultural anthropology of Latin America and the Caribbean is important, *both* for the United States and Latin American and Caribbean peoples. Attention was also placed on highlighting some key methodological aspects of ethnographic research in cultural anthropology, as well as some important guiding concepts. The third and final section focused attention on how method and theory often generate contrasting or controversial ethnographic accounts.

ISSUES AND QUESTIONS

1. *The Anthropology of Latin America and the Caribbean.* In our increasingly interdependent world, why might studying the anthropology of Latin America and the Caribbean be so important? Can you think of reasons in addition to those raised in this chapter?

2. *Anthropological Methods and Concepts.* What are some important methods and concepts of cultural anthropology, and why are these so often controversial? Based on your interpreta- tion of the research by Oscar Lewis and Nancy Scheper-Hughes, would you say that cultural anthropology is a science, a form of art, or perhaps a combination of both?

3. *Life and Culture in Shantytowns.* Why is the study of shantytowns important? Why are the works by Oscar Lewis and Nancy Scheper-Hughes so controversial? In what ways are their arguments different and similar, and why?

KEY TERMS AND CONCEPTS

Archaeology   p. 6
Physical/biological anthropology
   p. 6
Critical cultural relativism
   p. 7
Cultural diversity   p. 6

Cultural relativism   p. 7
Cultural similarities   p. 6
Culture   p. 6
Culture of poverty   p. 8
Ethnocentrism   p. 7
Ethnography   p. 6

General anthropology   p. 6
Intracultural variability   p. 6
Linguistic anthropology   p. 6
Participant observation   p. 6
Cultural/socio-cultural
   anthropology   p. 6

ENDNOTES

1. A cultural caveat is in order. Most citizens of the United States allude to themselves as "Americans" and to the United States as "America." This is a practice that many Latin American and Caribbean peoples find ethnocentric and offensive, for many of those people also view themselves as "Americans"—inhabitants or citizens of the Americas—albeit "Latin" ones (Latinoamericanos). In this text I, therefore, follow the widely accepted practice to (generically) refer to citizens of the United States as North Americans (Norteamericanos), and to the United States as North America (Norteamérica). Most Latin Americans distinguish between Canada and North America (i.e., the United States).

2. "Hispanics," "Hispanic Americans," "Latinos," or (less commonly) "Spanish" are the most widely circulating terms referring to Spanish-speaking Latin American and Caribbean peoples in the United States. These terms are also culturally contentious identifiers, reflecting efforts by the U.S. Census Bureau to lump together (and thereby indirectly erase cultural differences between) peoples of different origins and identities, who often oppose such classifications. Also, "Hispanic" and "Latin" are ethnic/racial categories meaningless in most Latin American countries (Stephen et al. 2003). Although Hispanic and Latino are classifications coexisting with other self-ascribed ethnic identifiers (such as Puerto Rican or Dominican), these may be replacing other identities, such as among different Maya groups in California (Chapter 11). In this text, I have opted for the compound construction "Hispanic(s)/Latino(s)."

3. Indeed, after reading Huntington's statements, the author of this book—son of Puerto Rican immigrants to New York City, who has consistently refused to "totally . . . assimilate" (to use Huntington's unfortunate words)—now once in a while wonders whether he is, unknowingly, a perfect exemplar of "Anglo-Protestant culture."

2 Introducing Latin America and the Caribbean

This chapter provides readers with a brief yet comprehensive overview of Latin America and the Caribbean. It reviews various criteria used to delimit Latin America and the Caribbean, explores how this area emerged in the imagination of Europeans and Latin American elites in the nineteenth century, and then provides this book's rationale for considering this area as a single space of teaching and research. A brief survey of countries, population, languages, and migration patterns then follows. The bulk of the chapter surveys major landscapes, structural zones, and physiographic regions, and it considers debates on pre- and post-European landscape transformations. The final section critically re-examines how the concept of culture area—long wedded to landscapes—may still be useful in today's rapidly changing world.

Delimiting and Imagining Latin America: Ideas, Spaces, and Places

Dozens of countries and territories with half a billion citizens; hundreds of languages spoken; millions of people concentrated in huge megacities, many others living in rural communities; every imaginable ecologic niche spread over eight million square miles of land and sea; diverse historical trajectories, some pointing to Africa, some to Europe, and others firmly rooted in the New World; a long history of movement (diasporas) within and across national boundaries; hundreds or thousands of groups with their own self-ascribed, ethnic identity; a multiplicity of overlapping racial types and classifications, far from stable and rooted in biology; widely diverse notions of sexuality and gender relations; dozens of religious traditions and hundreds of diverse rituals, both secular and religious; widely dissimilar ways of construing health and classifying and treating illness; hundreds of different foods and cuisines; dozens of musical and dance traditions; a wide array of secular and religious popular celebrations with African, European, and New World influences—*this* is Latin America and the Caribbean, the focus of this text. Yet, what makes this a space or area of study and research? On the basis of which criteria or ideological positions do scholars delimit what is and what is not "Latin America" and the "Caribbean"?

Given this social, cultural, economic, and historical mélange, small wonder, then, that despite the crucial importance of Latin American and Caribbean peoples to and in North America (the United States and Canada), the proliferation of Latin American studies programs at major universities, and the thousands of books written, scholars continue to disagree which landscapes, nations, and territories are (or should be) included as part of Latin America and the Caribbean. Many scholars agree that Latin America is that part of the New World conquered and colonized by the Spanish, Portuguese, and French during the sixteenth and seventeenth centuries, and that therefore shares a common "Latin" culture partly evidenced by the predominance of a Romance language (Clawson 2004:7). On this criteria alone, the majority of *islands* in the Caribbean would be excluded, although most of the Caribbean's *population* (in Cuba, Puerto Rico, the Dominican Republic, and Haiti), ought to be included. Large parts of northern South America—for example, Suriname, until recently a Dutch colony—would also be excluded on language criteria alone. Yet, if "Latin" culture and the speaking of a Romance language are important defining criteria, then, as Moran (1987:3) suggests, Latin America should also include portions of the southwestern United States that were originally part of Mexico. Yet, Clawson (2004:7–8) disagrees "owing to the area's political status as part of the . . . United States and to the social and economic characteristics of the region that resemble more closely those of the technologically advanced industrialized nations than those of the Latin American and other developing countries."

The inconsistencies and ambiguities continue. The influential *Statistical Abstract of Latin America (SALA)* lists twenty countries in its "standard" category (Wilkie et al. 2001).[1] Cultural criteria seem crucial, since all appear undeniably Latin in that most of their citizens speak a Romance language. Yet, although Cuba and the Dominican Republic are included, Puerto Rico—an obviously "Latin" country—"is excluded from Latin America . . . because it has never been independent" from the United States. At the same time, "Haiti is included *not* because of its Latin-based French language but because of its interaction with the Dominican Republic (which it ruled between 1822 and 1844)" (Wilkie et al. 2001:ix; emphasis added).[2] In another example of *SALA*'s conflation of cultural and political criteria, Puerto Rico and Martinique are placed into the category of "Non-Traditionally Defined Latin America Adds," a category that includes "Former non-Spanish colonies . . . [which] . . . are excluded . . . [from Latin America] . . . because they have had little or no interaction in dialogue and events in Latin America" (Wilkie et al. 2001:xii–xiv).[3] Yet, historians and anthropologists focusing on the widespread ramifications of the African slave experience and emergence of maroon societies (Chapter 4) would sharply disagree.

Anthropologists too wrangle over boundaries and connections. Thus, a reader on the anthropology of Latin America "limits treatment of Latin America to the mainland, excluding the Caribbean islands that are so varied in terms of their colonial history that most of them share little with the legal, political, and historical traditions of Mexico [and] Central and South America" (Heath 2002:2). The historical trajectory of the Caribbean was indeed different than that of Mexico and Central and South America, which is why it is often conceptualized as a separate entity or region (Horowitz 1971a). Separate and different yes—but neither unrelated nor inconsequential. There have always been economic, cultural, and social connections between the Caribbean and the mainland—flows of peoples, ideas, goods, labor, and the like—especially along the Atlantic coastlines of Mexico, Central America, and northern South America (Richardson 1989; Mintz 1971, 1989, 1996a; Olwig 1997). So intense has been this cultural interaction across time and space that these latter areas are sometimes viewed by some anthropologists as part of the same culture area (see the following discussion on the culture area concept). This is also why despite distinguishing between the Caribbean and the mainland, most geographers study both together: "Although not all of the Caribbean . . . is . . . part of Latin America in the fullest cultural sense, this volume studies the Caribbean with Latin America owing to the close historical ties between the regions" (Clawson 2004:8; he lists forty-two "nations and territories" in Latin America and the Caribbean). Those excluding the Caribbean from the scope of Latin America privilege certain kinds of relationships and contributions over others, downplaying, for example, the important role of Cuba and Puerto Rico in music and dance (see Chapter 11). Further, Latin American studies centers in major U.S. universities invariably include the Caribbean as part of their scope in research and teaching.

These ambiguities are partly because **Latin America and the Caribbean are concepts,** or cultural constructs, the content or scope of which are informed by a particular view of the world, which in turn privileges certain criteria over others. And, like all concepts and ideas, they are conceptual prisms through which reality is grasped and are also products of specific histories. Spaces and spatial categories—the Caribbean, Middle America, or Latin America—are cultural, historical, and social constructions. Prior to 1492, the Caribbean did not exist as a spatial cultural category—which does not mean that the islands were not there (they of course were). What this approach *does* mean is that the "Caribbean" was not a meaningful category for indigenous societies—nor for anyone else for "Before 1492, the Americas were not on anybody's map" (Mignolo 2005:2).

What this perspective also means is that culturally and conceptually Latin America and the Caribbean are products of the sixteenth century European Conquest, the coalescence of the colonial social order a century later, the emergence of nation-states in the nineteenth century, and the global geopolitical rivalry between Western powers also during the nineteenth century. During the colonial period, Spanish colonies in the New World were administratively referred to as the *Indias Occidentales* (West Indies), although the term "America"—referring to the fourth continent into which the world was divided (after Asia, Africa, and Europe)—had surfaced on European maps by 1542 and was also widely used. After the wars of independence from Spain, "América" won favor by Creole elites (descendants of Spaniards raised in the colonies) (Mignolo 2005:22–34).

The adjective "Latin" (as in "Latin America") creeps into the political vocabulary and imagination, as well as onto maps, during the nineteenth century geopolitical struggles between European countries and the United States:

> The idea of "Latin America" that came into view in the second half of the nineteenth century depended . . . on an idea of "Latinidad"—"Latinity," "Latinitée"—that was being advanced by France . . . In the Iberian ex-colonies, the "idea" of Latin America emerged as a consequence of conflicts between imperial nations; it was needed by France to justify its civilizing mission in the South and its overt conflict with the US for influence in that area . . . "Latinidad" was used in France . . . to take the lead in Europe among the configuration of Latin countries involved in the Americas (Italy, Spain, Portugal, and France itself), and allowed it to also confront the United States' continuing expansion toward the South—its purchase of Louisiana from Napoleon and its appropriation of vast swaths of territory from Mexico. White Creole and Mestizo/a elites, in South America and the Spanish Caribbean islands, after independence from Spain adopted "Latinidad" to create their own . . . identity. Consequently . . . "*Latin*" America . . . [was a] . . . political project of Creole-Mestizo/a elites. (Mignolo 2005:58–59)

Debates surrounding the boundaries of Latin America and the Caribbean are also related to the concepts of space and place, which anthropologists, geographers, and sociologists have debated at length in recent years (Appadurai 1988; Harvey 1990; Butzer and Williams 1992c; Harley 1992; Rodman 1992; Merrifield 1993; Coronil 1996; Jacob 1996; De Genova 1998; Proctor 1998; Gieryn 2000; Unwin 2000; Chase 2002; Stephen et al. 2003). In North America, Basso's research on language and landscape among the Apache was a pioneering effort (1988).

Most scholars agree that both space and place have geographic or territorial referents (boundaries can be placed around them), but they often make distinctions between these two terms, however tenuous. **Space,** sometimes glossed as region, is a construct with spatial (i.e., geographic) coordinates or boundaries with which a landscape is set apart from others based on assumed commonalities or differences. The "Caribbean" is such a space; "Middle America," sometimes construed as including the Caribbean (Dow and Van Kemper 1991), is another.

Space and spatial constructs come into being, acquiring a "lived reality" meaningful to different people for dissimilar reasons. For example, for analytic purposes, volumes on the Caribbean (Horowitz 1971a; Mintz 1989) invariably include Puerto Rico. Yet, Puerto Ricans hardly identify themselves as a Caribbean people (*Caribeños*), although they do recognize that their island is *in* the Caribbean, and that in many ways Puerto Rico and Puerto Rican culture also exist in and extend to the mainland United States (Géliga Vargas 1996; Pérez 2002; Zentella 2003). Thus the Caribbean is a spatial construct in some ways more meaningful to academics than to peoples in that region. And even the Caribbean can be divided into yet other spaces—such as the Hispanic and non-Hispanic Caribbean (Hoetink 1985).

There are two ways that spaces and spatial coordinates and boundaries emerge and acquire a life of their own: one is through speech—the repeated use of terms and concepts that eventually become widespread and dominant; the other is through the production of maps. Both were crucial in forging Latin America as an imaginary (but no less real) space (Mignolo 2005), for both "involve the use of shared spatial imagery that [has] the strange effect of producing a consistent mental picture . . . an almost tangible and inescapable image of the world" (Coronil 1996:52). Harvey agrees, noting the twin roles of naming and the production of geographic images:

> The very act of naming geographic entities implies a power over them, most particularly the way in which places, their inhabitants, and their social functions get represented . . . by outsiders. (1990:419)

Mapmaking is particularly crucial because it reflects a vision of reality projected onto space (that is, a projected space). Commenting on the powerful role of mapmaking before and during the European Conquest of the Americas, Harley, alluding specifically to the New World, states that "cartography is part of the process by which territory becomes" (1992:532). Cartography—the academic discipline devoted to the production of maps—has a "cultural history" often and unfortunately ignored, for "The power of maps lies in the way they communicate knowledge and implicitly reinforce the social and political order through their efficiency as symbols" by projecting a certain view of spatial reality (Jacob 1996:194–195). And Harvey has called for a historical geography with an "imagination," critical reflection that "locates the history of ideas about space and time in their material, social, and political setting," and that also uncovers "a certain conception of space and time [as a] political decision" (1990:432).

Place is sometimes, though rarely, used instead of space. More often place refers to what some call a "lived" as opposed to an "empty" space. Often place is used in lieu of the anthropologists' locale, locality, area, or ethnographic setting, characterized by dominant cultural images or traits. Thus, for Appadurai (1988) all of India is a place (largely constructed by anthropologists) because it has long been associated in anthropological writings and the popular imagination with caste hierarchy. Rodman (1992) claims that places are locales with a spatial dimension through and in which people's cultural lives and identities are grounded—the "lived world in physical form" (1992:94). De Genova, in emphasizing the locales in Chicago in which Latin American culture is constructed on a daily basis, and advocating for a "Chicago that belongs to Latin America" (1998:90), invokes a similar idea. Gieryn, calling for a sociology more sensitive to place (or better "grounded" others might suggest), says that place has a geographic location (it has a "here and there"), and material form ("place is stuff"), and it is invested with meaning and values. There is a definite distinction between place and space:

> Place is not space—which is more properly conceived as abstract geometrics . . . detached from material form and cultural interpretation . . . Space is what place becomes when the unique gatherings of things, meanings and values are sucked out . . . Put positively, place is space filled up by people, practices, objects and representations. In particular, place should not be confused with the use of geographic or cartographic metaphors (boundaries, territories) that define conceptual or analytical spaces. (2000:465)

A place is a meaningful physical setting in and through which "values, morality, class, gender, deviance, power, change, culture, politics" are learned and "emplaced" (Gieryn 2000:467)—an idea that will resonate with anthropologists and social historians. Reminding geographers of the importance of "place meaning" and "place experience," and insisting that place really "matters," Merrifield stresses that "place is not merely abstract space: it is the terrain where basic social practices—consumption, enjoyment, tradition, self-identification, solidarity, social support and social reproduction, etc.—are lived out" (1993:522).

This book on the anthropology of Latin America and the Caribbean draws significantly on the ideas and debates just presented. Specifically, it identifies Latin America and the Caribbean as ideas (to hark back to Mignolo's suggestion); as spaces across which significant interactions have historically taken place; as well as a multiplicity of places in which culture is constructed on an ongoing basis and connected in multiple ways to other places or locales. As an *idea*, this volume recognizes the historical (and power-laden) backdrop through which Latin America and the Caribbean were conceptually and politically constructed. As a *space*, it acknowledges the multitude of relationships in the present and in the past that have connected and transformed an array of different peoples across time and distance—and without privileging one kind over another, for all have been important in their own ways. And, finally, as a *multiplicity of places*, this book draws attention to the cultural variability and specificity played out and constructed on an ongoing basis and in everyday life. The view adopted in this book is analogous to what Stephen et al. (2003)

have called *Las Américas*, and therefore includes Mesoamerica, Central and South America, the Caribbean ("Latin" or not), as well as significant sites of cultural production in the United States and (less so), Canada.

Countries and Population

The perspective underlying this book parallels the United Nations' comprehensive classification of Latin America and the Caribbean (2002), which identifies forty-seven countries or "political units" (see Figure 2.1). The land area of Latin America and the Caribbean totals eight million square miles, about 2.5 times the land mass of the continental United States (Moran 1987:3).

FIGURE 2.1   Latin America and the Caribbean.

In Figure 2.1, the Caribbean archipelago includes the Greater Antilles (Cuba, Jamaica, Hispaniola [divided between the Dominican Republic and Haiti], and Puerto Rico) and the Lesser Antilles (the West Indies or Leeward Islands in some of the older literature)—the countries and territories stretching from south/southeast of Puerto Rico to the northern tip of South America.[4] Central America includes the mainland countries between Mexico and Colombia (Belize, Guatemala, El Salvador, Honduras, Nicaragua, Costa Rica, and Panama). South America encompasses all countries south of Panama (Venezuela, Colombia, Ecuador, Guyana, Suriname, French Guiana, Peru, Bolivia, Brazil, Paraguay, Chile, Argentina, and Uruguay).[5]

The United Nations has calculated the population of Latin America and the Caribbean at more than 540 million (see Table 2.1).

The five most populated countries, in rank order, are Brazil, Mexico, Colombia, Argentina, and Peru. Latin America's population is extremely young, with more than one-third less than fifteen years old, and more than 50 percent under twenty-four years of age. The median age is twenty-three. With few exceptions (Argentina, Uruguay and, perhaps, Chile), until recently most Latin American countries were dubbed by demographers as

TABLE 2.1   Latin American Countries/Political Units and Population

Country/Political Unit	Population	Country/Political Unit	Population
1. Anguilla	12,000	25. Guatemala	12,347,000
2. Antigua and Barbuda	73,000	26. Guyana	765,000
3. Argentina	38,428,000	27. Haiti	8,326,000
4. Aruba	100,000	28. Honduras	6,941,000
5. Bahamas	314,000	29. Jamaica	2,651,000
6. Barbados	270,000	30. Martinique	393,000
7. Belize	256,000	31. Mexico	103,457,000
8. Bermuda	82,000	32. Montserrat	4,000
9. Bolivia	8,808,000	33. Netherlands Antilles	221,000
10. Brazil	178,470,000	34. Nicaragua	5,466,000
11. British Virgin Islands	21,000	35. Panama	3,120,000
12. Cayman Islands	40,000	36. Paraguay	5,878,000
13. Chile	15,805,000	37. Peru	27,167,000
14. Colombia	44,222,000	38. Puerto Rico	3,879,000
15. Costa Rica	4,173,000	39. St. Kitts and Nevis	42,000
16. Cuba	11,300,000	40. St. Lucia	149,000
17. Dominica	79,000	41. St. Vincent & The Grenadines	120,000
18. Dominican Republic	8,745,000	42. Suriname	436,000
19. Ecuador	13,003,000	43. Trinidad and Tobago	1,303,000
20. El Salvador	6,515	44. Turks and Caicos Islands	21,000
21. Falkland Islands (Malvinas)	3,000	45. United States Virgin Islands	111,000
22. French Guiana	178,000	46. Uruguay	3,415,000
23. Grenada	80,000	47. Venezuela	25,699,000
24. Guadeloupe	440,000	TOTAL	543,327,000

Source: Adapted from World Population 2002 Data Sheet, United Nations (2002). (Bermuda was originally classed as part of North America.)

"pretransitional" societies—that is, largely young, with high fertility and mortality rates, and predominantly rural. In the past decades, however, both fertility and mortality have dropped dramatically. For example, between 1970 and 1975 and between 1990 and 1995, the crude birth rate dropped from 35.4 to 25.1, a decline of 30 percent, while the crude death rate fell from 9.9 to 6.7, a 32 percent wane. (These rates measure the number of births or deaths for every one thousand persons in a given year. They are "crude" because all ages and both sexes are included.) Although mortality has declined more rapidly than fertility, the overall population continues to grow, although not as quickly as two or three decades ago (United Nations 1999). Despite the fall in mortality, more than half of all Latin Americans live in extreme poverty and unsanitary health conditions (Chapter 8).

Migration and Cities

Fifty years ago, most Latin Americans lived in rural communities—Argentina, Uruguay, and Chile are significant exceptions. Today, between 66 and 78 percent of Latin American and Caribbean peoples live in urban centers. In 2004, the urban populations of the four most populous countries—Brazil, Mexico, Colombia, and Argentina—equaled more than half of all people in Latin America and the Caribbean. In only a handful of countries do most people live in rural areas (Economic Commission for Latin America 2005:77). This migration to urban areas has been paralleled by a decline in the number of people engaged in agriculture. For example, between 1980 and 1998, the percentage of Brazil's population that made a living from agriculture decreased by more than 20 percent while in the Dominican Republic it declined 38 percent (Wilkie et al. 2001:351).

The seven largest cities (including their metropolitan areas), all with a population of at least three million people, are Mexico City (fifteen million), Buenos Aires (eleven million), São Paulo (ten million), Lima (six million), Bogotá (five million), Santiago (four million), and Caracas (three million) (Wilkie et al. 2001:100–101).

Processes underpinning the mass migration to urban areas include population growth; the stagnation of agriculture and of agricultural incomes; unequal distribution of land; the proliferation of tiny plots of agricultural fields (minifundia); declining terms of trade of agricultural crops; environmental degradation; and the desire to avail oneself of jobs and government services, such as education and health facilities (Portes 1972, 1989). The mass civil strife of the 1970s and 1980s also pushed many to the cities (see Chapter 12). Further, many who remain in the countryside often supplement their income through craft production, domestic employment, occasional wage work, and petty commerce largely outside of state surveillance—activities that make up the **informal economy** (Portes et al. 1989; Cook and Binford 1990). These changes have been accompanied by cultural transformations. Partly due to better communications—such as roads, television, cable and satellite service, and, more recently, the Internet—contemporary rural peoples are being exposed to a great deal of national and transnational information, messages, and symbols that would have been unimaginable to their forbearers just a few decades ago (see Chapter 11).

Rural to urban migration has spurred the growth of "mega-cities" (Gilbert 1996) and the spread of shantytowns (or urban slums) that ring their peripheries. This process of urbanization has important implications, for whereas in the past the cultural anthropology of Latin America and the Caribbean largely focused on rural areas and small-scale agricul-turalists, today anthropologists are paying increasing attention to life ways in urban areas.

Shantytowns, perched on hillside outskirts of most cities, are stunning features of Latin American urban landscapes. In Spanish-speaking countries, they are referred to by many terms (e.g., *barriadas, caseríos, villas miserias, arrabales, pueblos jóvenes, asen-tamientos*), while in Brazil they are called *favelas*. Often first- or second-generation migrants from rural areas, shantytown dwellers are overwhelmingly poor and marginal-ized by the state, and often have minimal access to government services such as electric-ity, running water, and health care. Shantytown life is extraordinarily hard and violence a facet of daily life (see Chapter 1). These settlements have also been important loci of social movements against elites and elite state policies. For example, shantytowns were important sites of resistance against the dictatorship of Augusto Pinochet in Chile, and Peru's Shining Path (*Sendero Luminoso*) guerrillas found strong support in Lima's shanty-towns (Schneider 1992; Burt 1998; see Chapter 12). As the previous chapter demon-strated, anthropological research has generated different interpretations of the everyday lives and cultures of shantytown residents, sparking fierce debates on methods, theory, and policy.

Languages

Speaking a Romance language may be important for some scolars as they go about delimit-ing Latin America, but in fact hundreds of different languages are spoken in addition to Spanish, French, and Portuguese.

Linguists consider mutually intelligible speech varieties (dialects) part of the same language and group similar languages into "families." Although this approach appears rel-atively straightforward, it is in fact difficult to determine the exact number of languages currently spoken in Latin America. This is because some have not been fully studied, and how they may or may not be related to other languages or dialects has not been completely ascertained. Further, the distinction between languages and dialects is not always clear-cut, and the criteria used to class a dialect as part of one language vary considerably from one linguist to another. A good example is from Mexico, where there is a cluster of related lan-guages of the Zapotec (or Zapotecan) language family: some linguists have identified more than fifty Zapotec languages while others believe this number is too high and that some are mere dialects. Further, national censuses are notoriously unreliable in determining the number of speakers of indigenous languages (Archive of the Indigenous Languages of Latin America n.d. [c, d]).

Latin America is one of the most linguistically diverse areas of the world. Prior to the sixteenth century European Conquest, more than 1,700 languages may have been present, and even today, 500 to 700 languages are still spoken, almost 200 of these in Mexico (Archive of the Indigenous Languages of Latin America n.d. [a]); Garza Cuarón and Lastra 1991). Hundreds of languages are also spoken in South America, mostly in lowland Amazonia, the most linguistically complex region of Latin America. At least 300 lan-guages, belonging to at least twenty language families, are spoken in Amazonia (Dixon and Aikhenvald 1999:2). See Table 2.2 for more details.

TABLE 2.2   Indigenous Languages Spoken in South America, Select Countries

Country	Number of Languages
Argentina	16
Bolivia	39
Brazil	162
Colombia	67
Guyana	12
Paraguay	20
Peru	105
Venezuela	33

Source: Adapted from South American Languages, Archive of the Indigenous Languages of Latin America n.d. (b).

Many languages are spoken by only small clusters of people, and as a result their languages will soon disappear—linguists call these **endangered languages.** Some examples are telling: about 70 percent of Brazil's indigenous languages (again, mostly located in Amazonia) are spoken by less than 1,000 people (Dixon and Aikhenvald 1999:7); by the late 1980s, there were only thirty speakers of Tehuelche in southern Argentina and, in Colombia's Amazonian region, a mere fifty speakers of Leuama (Adelaar 1991:55, 69). Other languages are far from disappearing in the foreseeable future. With several hundred thousand speakers, Mapudungu (also known as Mapuche or Araucano), spoken by the Mapuche, is the most important indigenous language in Chile and Argentina (Grinevald 1998:130–131). Others—such as Guaraní, Quechua, and Mayan—are spoken by millions and have been elevated to the rank of national languages, thereby recognizing the pluriethnic and cultural makeup of these countries. This is the case in Paraguay, where half of the population (three million) speak Guaraní, which is also spoken in Argentina, Bolivia, and Brazil; in Ecuador, Peru, and Bolivia, where nine to twelve million people speak different Quechua languages (Aymara is the second most important indigenous language in Peru and Bolivia); and in Guatemala, where half of its ten million citizens speak about twenty Mayan languages. In Mexico, some important languages and language families are Maya, Mixteco, Zapoteco, and Nahua or Nahuatl (Adelaar 1991; Albó 1995; Richards and Richards 1997; Grinevald 1998).

Indigenous language loss—the either complete or near-complete extinction of languages, or a decrease in the number of people who habitually speak a language—has been documented for decades. Demographic dynamics are not solely to blame for this state of affairs. Spanish and Portuguese have typically enjoyed tremendous status and prestige, and have also played a dominant cultural and political role in major realms of life. By contrast, indigenous language speakers have often been identified as "Indian" and discriminated against. Both the importance of Spanish and Portuguese as well as discrimination are responsible for the progressive loss of indigenous language use (Albó 1981; Garza and Lastra 1991; see also Chapter 5). Hence in the Andes, less than half of Peruvians or Ecuadorians are monolingual or habitual speakers of Quechua or Aymara (Bolivia may still be an exception), opting instead for Spanish on a regular basis. The same process is taking place in Mexico, where less than 14 percent of Mexicans are regular speakers of the Nahuatl and Mayan languages (Wilkie et al. 1999:139). Similar language loss has been documented elsewhere. For example, in the Cakchiquel Maya community of San Antonio Aguas Calientes (Guatemala), bilingualism is widespread, Spanish is more widely spoken than Cakchiquel Mayan, and Spanish is the first language of most children (Annis 1987:27–128). In Bolivia, Quechua and Aymara have come to be spoken by fewer people over time, and in progressively narrower domains of life (Albó 1981).

Yet the tide against indigenous languages may be changing—in no small way due to grassroots organizing and cultural and political shifts. The rise of indianist or indigenous movements and a surge in ethnic pride and consciousness (see Chapter 5) is accompanied and bolstered by a broad spectrum of attempts at enhancing pride and value in indigenous culture and language. This is being accomplished in different ways, such as the spread of Quechua radio programs and bilingual education efforts, and incorporating "alphabetic literacies into their own languages and ways of knowing" (Hornberger 1997a:9), partly through innovative multilingual education and literacy strategies. One example is from Peru, where Hornberger (1997b,c) has documented how individuals from different Quechua-speaking communities have regained their pride in and promoted the use of the Quechua language. One context is the shift to Protestantism, which is closely related to the resurgence of indigenous languages (see Chapter 7).

The case of Centeno, a young woman who was raised by her (Quechua/Spanish) bilingual parents is illustrative. Centeno, who admitted never speaking Quechua much as a child, joined the Evangelical Church of Peru when she was thirteen. She was soon prompted by missionaries to spread the "Word of God" in Quechua. A turning point in her language consciousness and sense of empowerment was when she was asked to deliver a formal address. Instead of writing first in Spanish and then translating the text into Quechua, she wrote the text directly into the latter. From the Quechua New Testament, she learned how to read and write Quechua, and she discovered the importance of teaching the word of God with "*cariño misk'i simi*, 'the tender language of the home'" (i.e., Quechua) (Hornberger 1997c:224–226).

In Guatemala, there is a strong and widespread support of "Mayan Language Revival and Revitalization," a movement led by formally trained indigenous linguists who have achieved key goals in promoting Mayan languages (England 2003). Richards and Richards (1997) note that in Guatemala, hundreds of pamphlets, grammar books, and dictionaries have been published in several Mayan languages since the mid-1980s. Whether this trend toward cultural and linguistic revival in Guatemala can offset increasing bilingualism, an intergenerational shift in the greater use of Spanish, and the difficulties children have in learning a Mayan language from ever fewer monolingual speakers has yet to be seen (Garzón 1998a, b, c). These are questions and issues relevant not only to Guatemalans and Mayas.

Landscapes, Culture, and Society

Latin American and Caribbean peoples have historically inhabited extraordinarily diverse environments—and also have left a deep imprint on them. What may appear as an unspoiled environment is, upon closer inspection, often anything but "natural" or pristine.

Landscape is a key and useful concept in cultural geography with which to examine and appreciate the diverse environments that for millennia have provided a habitat for Latin American and Caribbean peoples. The term **landscape** stems from the medieval German word *landschaft*, which had multiple meanings, one of which referred to a delimited piece of land (Olwig 1996:630–631). Carl Sauer—one of the founders of North American cultural geography—wrote that landscape ought to be viewed as "a land shape, in which the process of shaping is by no means thought of as simply physical." Human agency is intrinsic to a landscape, and "it is a forcible abstraction, by every good geographic tradition *a tour de force*, to consider a landscape as though it were devoid of (human) life" (Sauer 1969 [1925]:321–325; cited by Olwig 1996:644). Landscape is, then, part of a seemingly "natural" environment that nevertheless has been profoundly shaped by culture as well as physical processes. Landscapes "are both material and conceptual, constitute both physical infrastructure and symbolic communication" (Sluyter 2001:413). The concept of landscape directs attention to features of the environment that result from the mutual interplay of physical and human (cultural) activity. This approach from within cultural geography overlaps with how many archaeologists and cultural anthropologists have conceptualized relationships between the environment and culture (Hirsch and O'Hanlon 1995).

Landscapes are laden with symbolism and meaning. Specific landscape features— from seemingly "natural" characteristics such as hills and mountains, to more clearly cultural constructs like irrigation ditches, planted fields, landmarks, or a myriad of boundary markers—evoke a sense of place, belonging, and rootedness. Thus, culturally construed landscapes are often an important springboard from which societies pivot social relationships and construct oral traditions and historical narratives of themselves and others. This process of remembering—in which landscapes evoke and anchor memory as well as bolster and justify claims to ethnic distinctiveness and territorial claims—occurred innumerable times in Latin America and is still important. For example, among the Cumbe in the Ecuadorian Andes, landscape markers such as ditches (*zanjas*, Spanish) or remains of pre-Columbian terraced fields (*gradas*, Spanish) remind the Cumbe of their history, surface in narratives in which core plots often revolve around defending their territory against encroaching landowners, and legitimize Cumbes' claims to an indigenous ethnic identity. These landscape markers often make their way into both oral and written traditions (Rappaport 1994). Landscapes also loom important in Amazonia, historically marked by remarkable cultural and linguistic heterogeneity and intense processes of cultural change resulting in the emergence of new cultural groups and identities. Indeed (as will become clearer in Chapter 4), landscapes were (and are) "a critical basis for ethnogenesis itself" (Whitehead 2003:xv).

Major Landscapes

Geographers employ various and only partly overlapping criteria (such as climate, vegetation, soil types, elevation, and surface or topographic features) to classify and study the extraordinarily diverse Latin American and Caribbean landscapes. A focus on one or more criteria yields slightly different "pictures" or perspectives. For example, Denevan (1980:218–219) divides Latin America into seven "biomes" or ecosystems, a classification analogous to Clawson's eight "natural regions" (2004:70–85). Other classifications are proposed by Blouet and Blouet (2002).

Structural Zones

Clawson (2004:14–44) divides Latin America and the Caribbean into three **structural zones,** overarching swaths of distinctive landforms sharing analogous topography, climatic, altitudinal, and geological characteristics: (1) The Eastern Highlands; (2) The Central Lowlands; and (3) The Western Alpine System (see Figure 2.2). Clawson's structural zones are analogous to, but only partially overlap, with what Moran (1987) calls "three major surface divisions"—the Andean mountain chain, the Brazilian and Guiana shields, and the river basin lowlands.

The **Eastern Highlands,** lying entirely within South America, are high altitude, weathered, eroded tablelands between 2,000 and 5,000 feet above sea level (asl), punctuated by mountain ranges, plateaus, and narrow valleys. Major vegetation types include savannas and patches of forest. These highlands are rich in minerals, especially gold and iron ore. The northern segment overlaps with the northernmost tip of Brazil, large parts of Venezuela, Guyana, Suriname, French Guiana, and northcentral Colombia. This segment corresponds to the physiographic region that Clawson calls the Guiana Highlands (not shown in Figure 2.3), also sometimes called the Guiana Shield. At its southern edge lie Venezuela's Angel Falls, which at 3,200 feet asl are the highest waterfalls in the world. To the south, and separated by part of the Amazon River basin, lies the second segment of the Eastern Highlands, overlapping with the Brazilian Highlands physiographic region (not shown in Figure 2.3).[6] Between 2,000 and 3,000 feet asl, these highlands extend from northern Uruguay and eastern Paraguay to the Amazon River in the north, covering a full one-third of Brazil's territory. An important feature is the massive mountain range (the Great Escarpment) to the east along Brazil's Atlantic coast, which reaches elevations as high as 9,000 feet asl. Many of Brazil's largest cities are located along the narrow coastal plains wedged between the Great Escarpment and the Atlantic Ocean. The third segment, further south and almost entirely within southern Argentina, extends southward from the southern edge of Argentina's Pampas (see the following discussion of physiographic regions) to the tip of South America. These southern highlands overlap with the Patagonia physiographic region (see Figure 2.3), some rising 5,000 feet asl.

The **Central Lowlands** are low-lying areas of plains and plateaus that have extraordinary climatic and vegetative diversity. They are between the Guiana and Brazilian Highlands to the east and the Western Alpine System to the west. Altitude ranges from near sea level to several thousand feet asl. These mostly moist lowlands, extending from northern South America to Argentina, comprise large segments of northeastern Venezuela; almost all of Colombia; large parts of north and northwestern Brazil; eastern Ecuador, Peru, and Bolivia; most of Paraguay; and from northern Argentina south to Patagonia.

The **Western Alpine System** is a huge mountain mass originating at the southern tip of South America and extending northward along its western edge. At the northern tip of South America, this system branches into two directions: one swerves west through Central America and southern and central Mexico; the second system, partly submerged in the Atlantic, reappears as the land masses of the Lesser Antilles and as the central mountain chains of the Greater Antilles islands. Most of this mountain system lies within the tropical latitudes. Because climate is also a function of altitude, a noteworthy characteristic of this mountain system is the presence of scores of attitudinally tiered and ecological niches or "life zones" varying in climate, soil types, and vegetation (Tosi 1964; Troll 1968). This

FIGURE 2.2   Structural Zones of Latin America and the Caribbean. *Source:* Adapted from Clawson (2004:15).

FIGURE 2.3 Physiographic Regions of South America. *Source:* Adapted from Clawson (2004:16).

zonation or "verticality" of ecological niches—which also occurs less markedly in Central America and southern Mexico—has historically been important in the Andean region. Research has emphasized that flexible and nonspecialized subsistence activities, an elastic form of household organization in which household members do not always congregate together, the importance of wider kin networks through which resources flow, and the significance attached to reciprocity (especially reciprocal flows of labor) reflect attempts by Andean villagers to respond to and take advantage of this distribution of resources across diverse ecological niches located within and between different altitudinal zones (Orlove 1977; Orlove and Custred 1980; Orlove and Guillet 1985).

Physiographic Regions

Within each of Latin America's structural zones are **physiographic regions** (or provinces), sizeable terrains exhibiting distinctive and circumscribed topographic, climatological, altitudinal, soil, and vegetative features. Geographers rarely agree on the number, boundaries, and precise characteristics of these lower-scale regions, and the terminology used to describe them also varies considerably (Clawson 2004:14–44; Moran 1987; Denevan 1980; James 1950 [1942]). The following classification highlights important regions alluded to in the following chapters.

South America.   The following ten major South American physiographic regions are emphasized throughout this book (see Figure 2.3).

   1. *Llanos.* The *llanos,* also called plains or *campos,* are vast stretches of slightly undulating grasslands and savannas. Thinly populated, the llanos barely reach 700 feet asl and display marked dry and rainy seasons, often flooding during periods of intense rains. Since early colonial times, cattle ranching has been the most important economic activity in this region (see Photo 2.1).

PHOTO 2.1   *Herding long-horned cattle on the Llanos of Colombia.*

The northern dry llanos are centered mainly in northern Venezuela and southeastern Colombia, where they "reach to their highest elevations along the foothills of the Andes where braided river valleys are separated by intervening alluvial terraces of moderate relief. The land then descends ever so gradually toward the base of the Guiana Highlands where the Orinoco River follows a 2,600-kilometer (1,600 mile) course to the sea" (Clawson 2004:20). The second most important llanos terrain—the *Llanos de Mojos* in northeastern Bolivia—are principally wet, seasonally inundated savannas. Pioneering research in the Llanos de Mojos on raised field or mound agriculture, cultivated platforms above the countours of the land surface, was carried out by Denevan (1966).

2. *Amazonia.* Amazonia, also called the Amazon basin, is a huge expanse of mainly tropical forests primarily drained by the Amazon river (see Photo 2.2). It consists of large segments of north, central, and western Brazil (40 percent of Brazil's territory); eastern sections of Peru, Bolivia, and Ecuador; the southern and southeastern portions of Venezuela and Colombia; and the southern sections of Guyana, Suriname, and French Guiana. With more than two million square miles, the Amazon basin accounts for almost one-third of the world's tropical rain forests. Significant portions of low-lying tropical and subtropical forest terrain are also located in the coastal lowlands, especially along the Atlantic shores.

Scholars divide Amazonia into two distinct areas: (1) an interior, upland, and slightly elevated area called **terra firme** (firm or solid ground; Portuguese) that comprises 98 percent of Amazonia's land mass; and (2) a narrow strip (less than fifty miles at its widest point) of seasonally flooded alluvial plains called the **várzea**. Major features of the *terra firme* include heavy rainfall, nutrient-poor soils, wide dispersal of plant and animal species, lush vegetation, and high humidity.

For years, the predominant view was that the terra firme was a thinly populated region marked by the presence of small, seminomadic societies that practiced horticulture and hunting and gathering (Steward and Fanon 1959; Meggers 1971). Some scholars have

PHOTO 2.2 *A Caboclo hut, built on stilts, sits along Amazonia River, Brazil. Caboclo means "copper-colored" and is a reference to mixed Caucasian-Indian ancestry.*

recently suggested that such a view is mistaken, and that economically and politically complex societies were indeed widespread in large parts of the upland, interior Amazon prior to the European Conquest (Whitehead 1994; see also Chapter 3). Although terra firme soils are often nutrient-poor (most nutrients are stored in the lush vegetative cover and not the soil), *várzea* soils by contrast are extraordinarily productive because the annual seasonal flooding deposits thick layers of minerals and other rich nutrients that originate in the Andean mountains. The várzea is the only part of Amazonia in which intensive, permanent agriculture can be practiced without degrading the soil. It is near these seasonally rejuvenated soils with close access to maritime (river) resources that most of the larger, sedentary, and more complex Amazonian societies historically emerged. The várzea comprises only 2 percent of Amazonia, but it "is an area comparable in size to that of many European countries in total land area" (Moran 1987:8).

3. *Sertão.* This Brazilian region is renowned for its severely eroded and arid landscape. The *sertão* (bush, backwoods, or wasteland; Portuguese) overlaps with what in Brazil is know as the interior Northeast (*Nordeste*), famous for its constant droughts, periodic famines, and the poverty of most of its inhabitants (see Chapter 1). It is, in the words of James, "A land of . . . calamities" (1950 [1942]:392). The sertão is mostly located in the Brazilian northeastern states of Pernambuco, Bahia, Río Grande do Norte, and Ceara.

4. *Chaco.* Also called the *Gran Chaco,* this is a large expanse of primarily arid and very hot tropical savannas, scrub vegetation, and scattered grasslands southeast of the Brazilian Highlands (see Photo 2.3). Most of the *Chaco* is located in western Paraguay,

PHOTO 2.3   *Members of the Maka indigenous people dance during Paraguay's "Indigenous Day" celebrations in Mariano Roque Alonso, in the outskirts of Asunción, Paraguay on Monday, April 19, 2004. Originally from the Chaco Region, the Maka are part of over 80,000 indigenous peoples living in Paraguay.*

southeastern Bolivia, northern Argentina, and western Brazil (James (1950 [1942]:283; Clawson 2004:22). During the summer rainy season, large parts of the Chaco become flooded, especially its eastern side. The climate, soils, and vegetative cover of this region have historically worked against the development of large-scale complex societies. To this day, the Chaco is sparsely populated, inhabited primarily by small clusters of nomadic, foraging peoples (Hill and Hurtado 1996). This is a region, though, with oil deposits, and oil had much to do with the bloody 1932–1935 war between Bolivia and Paraguay.

5. *Pampas.* The Pampas are almost treeless flat plains and grasslands with a moderate, Mediterranean-type climate and extraordinarily rich soils. They extend for several hundred miles in an arc-like direction around the present day city of Buenos Aires, and also include part of southwestern Uruguay (see Photo 2.4). Prior to the European arrival, this region was populated by small-scale nomadic societies, whose way of life centered on the hunting of South American camelids, especially the *guanaco*. After the European Conquest, the Pampas quickly became the core of the cattle and agricultural industries of Argentina and Uruguay. It is also in this region that the famous Argentine cowboy culture—the gauchos, memorialized in the famous epic poem *Martín Fierro*—flourished during the eighteenth and nineteenth centuries. This cowboy culture has become one symbol of Argentine national identity (Slatta 1983).

6. *Patagonia.* This region, overlapping with the third of Clawson's Eastern Highlands, is a far more arid, desertlike landscape in central and southeastern Argentina extending in

PHOTO 2.4 *Gauchos roam the Pampas of Argentina as horsemen and cowhands. Gauchos also breed sheep and process their wool.*

PHOTO 2.5   *Herding sheep in Patagonia, Argentina. Wool and mutton production is the oldest industry of the Argentine Patagonia.*

an eastern and southeastern direction from the Pampas to the western Andean mountains (see Photo 2.5). (Analogous environmental conditions exist along smaller and narrower stretches of the Chilean side of the western Andes south of the Central Valley.) The cool, windswept Patagonia constitutes one-fourth of Argentina's territory. Prior to the European Conquest, the Patagonia was sparsely populated by societies analogous to those in the Pampas. Since colonial times, the principal economic activity has been the grazing of sheep; small pockets of irrigated agriculture appear near its three major rivers (Colorado, Negro, and Chubut).

  7. *Coastal plains.* (Not shown in Figure 2.3.) Because of the direction of cold Pacific Ocean streams, the western coasts are much drier than the eastern ones. Along the Pacific coast from the southern tip of the continent to mid-Peru are some of the driest coastlines in the world. Peru's Pacific coast is, however, crossed by numerous rivers originating in the Andes and flowing into the Pacific. Historically, these river valleys, close to the Andean foothills to the east and the Pacific shores to the west, have been sites of intensive agriculture, dense settlements, and large, complex societies. Precolonial indigenous peoples built extensive water canals and irrigation works in thirty of these valleys (Denevan 2001:139–140). Generally, aridity decreases from south to north, so the Pacific coastlines of Ecuador and Colombia are characterized by high rainfall and lush vegetation (Moran 1987:6).

8. *Atacama Desert.* The desert of Atacama, on Chile's Pacific coast, is one of the most distinctive South American landforms, starkly contrasting with Peru's coast further north. James' description is worth noting:

> No part of the Western Coast of South America is more forbidding, more utterly desert-like in aspect, than the stretch of about six hundred miles between Arica and Caldera. . . . The Atacama is . . . one of the driest places on earth. For years at a time no rain falls, so that the average figures of rainfall are quite meaningless. Over a period of twenty years, for instance, fourteen years passed at Iquique without a drop of rain, and during the six years in which some rain did fall the total amount was only 1.1 inches. Back of the Coastal Range, at Calama, no rain has ever been recorded. (1950 [1942]:197–199)

The barrenness of the Atacama belies, however, the presence of rich resources. Large deposits of copper have been mined near Calama since colonial times, and the mining company and town of Chuquicamata is one of the oldest and historically significant. (See Photo 2.6) Further, control over rich nitrate deposits—first used as fertilizer, then in the manufacture of explosives—precipitated the War of the Pacific (1879–1883), during

PHOTO 2.6 *Smoke rises from a smokestack at Chuquicamata, the world's largest open cast copper mine near Calama, Atacama, Chile.*

PHOTO 2.7   *High angle view of terraced field, Andean Mountains, Peru.*

which Chile wrested control over the northernmost part of the Atacama from Peru and Bolivia.

9. *Andean Mountains.* The highest mountain ranges of the Western Alpine System are present in Chile, Bolivia, and Peru. Barely 200 miles wide—except in the Altiplano—the Andes (along with the Himalayan mountains) are one of the highest mountain systems in the world (see Photo 2.7). Many peaks are as high as 18,000 to 20,000 feet asl, and Chile's Mount Aconcagua, at almost 23,000 feet, is the highest mountain in the Western hemisphere (Clawson 2004:27–28). For thousands of years, this high mountain region has been the core of intensive, irrigated agriculture, as well as the cradle (along with the Mesoamerican highlands) of large, highly complex, state-level societies—such as the Inca state that confronted the Europeans in the early sixteenth century.

10. *Altiplano.* In southern Peru, the Andean mountains split into two parallel chains (the eastern and western Cordilleras), which come together once again in southern Bolivia. Between the eastern and western branches of the Andes, and situated almost entirely within Bolivia, lies the Altiplano (see Photo 2.8). This is a high, semi-arid plateau, virtually devoid of trees, at about 13,000 feet asl. At its maximum, it is about 400 miles wide (James 1950:175). Bordering the Altiplano to the north is Lake Titicaca, South (and Latin) America's largest (and the world's highest navigable) fresh water lake. Prior to the European Conquest, this plateau was the center of large-scale Aymara-speaking chiefdoms,

PHOTO 2.8   *Aymara woman and her llama herd on the Altiplano. Adapted to thin air, many Aymara people subsist as high-plains herders and farmers.*

whose principal mode of subsistence was intensive, irrigated agriculture and pastoralism that revolved around the native South American camelids (such as the *guanaco, llama, vicuña,* and *alpaca*).

Mexico.   Mexico, " . . . like Central America, consists of an interior highland core bordered on the east and west by coastal lowlands" (Clawson 2004:34). From north to south, at least four physiographic regions are usually distinguished (see Figure 2.4).

1. *Central Plateau.*   At an altitude between 3,000 and 7,000 feet asl lies the enormous Central Plateau or Mesa Central, comprised of volcanic basins and ringed by two mountain ranges, the Western and Eastern Sierra Madre. The northernmost segment of the Central Plateau, the arid and hot **Mesa del Norte,** was populated by nomadic peoples who successfully resisted Aztec rule. Further south lies a more humid and cooler region, also called the **Mesa Central.** Tenochitlán, the Aztec capital, was located in the valley basin of present day Mexico City, at the southern part of the Mesa Central.

2. *Southern Highlands.*   Historically, this rugged and volcanic area, interspersed by deep valleys with rich soils, has been the center of intensive, high-yielding agriculture,

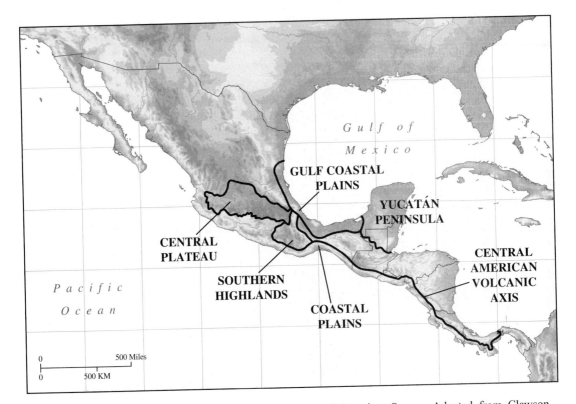

FIGURE 2.4 Physiographic Regions of Mexico and Central America. *Source:* Adapted from Clawson (2004:35).

and large, densely settled, and highly complex societies (see Photo 2.9). Many of the soils in this enormous mountain region are "some of the best found in the tropical world" (Whitmore and Turner II 2001:10). Structurally, the southern highlands are part of the **Neovolcanic Range** or Eje Volcánico (Volcanic Axis), a massive string high-altitude volcanic ranges and intermontane basins extending from the southeastern edge of the Central Plateau through most of Central America (Clawson 2004:38–39; Whitmore and Turner II 2001:8–10). The southern Mexican and, to the southeast, central Guatemalan portions of this region constitute a principal core of contemporary highland Maya culture. This area roughly corresponds to what James has called the Highlands of Chiapas, "the northwestern end of the mountainous region which extends through Central America" (1950 [1942]:559), including the Guatemalan highlands and those in southwestern El Salvador. Within the volcanic range and southern highlands of Mexico and parts of Central America, sharp differences in elevation give rise to three broad climatic zones: *tierra caliente,* or hot land, below 2,500 feet asl; the *tierra templada* (temperate land), between 2,500 and 6,000 feet asl, and the *tierra fría* (cold land), above 6,000 feet asl. Most of the tierra fría is located in Mexico and Guatemala (Whitmore and Turner II 2001:13).

PHOTO 2.9 *Quiche Indian farmers prepare the land as the rainy season begins in the highlands of Guatemala near the town of Santa Catarina Palapó, about 80 miles west of Guatemala City.*

3. *Gulf Coastal Plains/Gulf Region.* These include stretches of tropical forest terrain and low-lying coastal plains facing the Caribbean Sea, Gulf of Mexico, and the Atlantic Ocean, extending from central Mexico through most of Central America. Of particular importance is a wide and sizeable portion of north and northeastern lowlands called the Gulf Region. This area constitutes more than 12 percent of Mexico's territory; includes the states of Vera Cruz, Tabasco, Campeche, Yucatán, and Quintana Roo; and extends to northeastern Guatemala (i.e., the Petén lowlands) and virtually all of Belize. Large segments of these coastal areas are humid, receive a great deal of rainfall, and, with the exception of the northernmost part of the Mexican state of Yucatán, the predominant vegetation consists of tropical forest (James 1950 [1942]:579–585). Well-known Mesoamerican societies—the Olmec and the lowland Maya, for instance—prospered in this region prior to the European arrival; their "cultivated landscapes . . . consisted of a patchwork of different cultivation types interspersed with forests and scrub land" (Whitmore and Turner II 1992:406). What is often referred to as the Maya Lowlands includes

> The entire lowland limestone shelf of the Yucatán Peninsula as far south as the highlands of Chiapas and Guatemala, from the western border of the Gulf Coast lowlands to . . . northeastern Honduras . . . Other than its mountainous southern

PHOTO 2.10   *Harvesting Agave Plants (the Source of Henequen or Sisal Fiber), Yucatán, Mexico.*

borders, the only major elevation . . . are the Maya Mountains of Belize and the lower Lancandón range in Guatemala." (Whitmore and Turner II 2001:33)

4. *Yucatán Peninsula.* The northernmost segment of the Yucatán Peninsula is a very flat, arid plain, and much of the vegetation consists of scrub forest (see Photo 2.10). This area is also "a superb example of karst topography . . . Two of the most characteristic indicators of karst topography are the absence of surface streams and the presence of sinkholes or, as they are called in Yucatán, *cenotes*" (Clawson 2004:41). Humidity increases southward, so that less than one hundred miles south of Mérida, the state capital, the landscape quickly changes to slightly elevated rolling hills covered mostly by tropical forest vegetation. This southern segment of the Yucatán peninsula, which Whitmore and Turner refer to as the central and southern uplands, was "once the heart of the Classic Maya civilization" (1992:409). A key economic transformation took place in the Yucatán Peninsula at the turn of the twentieth century, when large estates planted in henequen (a plant used for the manufacture of strong twine) appeared.

Central America.   In Central America (see Figure 2.4), two broad regions are important to mention:

1. *Central American Volcanic Axis.* This axis (Clawson 2004:38–39) consists of a massive string of volcanic ranges, plateaus, and valleys that make up the greater part of

Central America. This "interior highland region . . . consists largely of densely populated, ash-filled valleys nestled among emerging volcanoes, most of which range from . . . 7,000 to 12,000 feet above sea level" (Clawson 2004:34).

   2. *Coastal plains.* Facing the Pacific, the coastal plains are narrow and relatively arid, while in the Caribbean they are wider and more humid.

Caribbean.   Most of the smaller Lesser Antilles are mainly comprised of the uppermost peaks of a partially submerged volcanic range. The larger Greater Antilles islands exhibit two distinct physiographic regions:

   1. The *interior mountain ranges,* *cordilleras* in Spanish, are a prolongation of the Western Alpine System. In the Greater Antilles, these appear as interior mountain ranges, such as Puerto Rico's Cordillera Central, Cuba's Sierra Maestra, and Jamaica's Blue Mountains. At the moment of the European Conquest, most of the islands in the Caribbean had been settled by primarily small-scale, semisedentary societies practicing horticulture and intensive agriculture in the interior plateaus and mountains, as well as taking advantage of coastal, maritime resources.

   2. *Coastal Plains.* After the European Conquest, many of these sparsely populated, narrow coastal areas were transformed into large-scale sugar cane plantations worked primarily by African slave labor.

Landscape Transformations Before and After the Europeans

For years, some scholars believed that Latin American landscapes prior to the European Conquest were primarily natural or pristine, relatively untouched by indigenous peoples. One corollary of this view was that devastating impacts to landscapes occurred only after the European arrival. In recent years, many geographers and archaeologists have criticized the assumptions of this view of a pre-European "Eden" landscape first and irrevocably spoiled by the European arrival. This "Pristine Myth" suggests that

> in 1492 the Americas were a sparsely populated wilderness, "a world of barely perceptible human disturbance." There is substantial evidence, however, that the Native American landscape of the early sixteenth century was a humanized landscape almost everywhere. Populations were large. Forest composition had been modified, grasslands had been created, wildlife disrupted, and erosion was severe in places. Earthworks, roads, fields, and settlements were ubiquitous. (Denevan 1992b:369)

Vast areas of Amazonia and the Andes had been turned into "cultivated landscapes" before 1492, with indigenous societies constructing extensive irrigation networks, terraced fields, and agricultural platforms, all which evolved over millennia (Denevan 2001). And, in the valley of Mexico, the Spaniards encountered what could only be described as a sculptured landscape. Well-manicured, terraced hillsides, some with irrigation gardens, cascaded towards the valley below. Neatly partitioned farms and orchards in the bottom lands were punctuated by villages and towns. A lacustrine system, controlled by dikes and sluices, separated saline and fresh waters and sustained a vast network of *chinampas* . . . rivaling in area the polders of the Netherlands. Impressive cities ringed the lakes, but aqueducts, causeways, and canoes led all eyes to the island capital of Tenochitlán, a Venice in the New World. (Whitmore and Turner II 2001:2)

Landscape transformations after the European Conquest were partly the outcome of the interplay of indigenous and European land use strategies. Depopulation was particularly important because it impaired the ability of indigenous societies to sustain their cultivated landscapes (Whitmore and Turner II 2001:3; Denevan 1992b). There is evidence that some savannas and grasslands were carved out of tropical forests and maintained through burning. Natural regeneration often intersected with these indigenous land use strategies as well as other post-1492 changes, so that the vegetative cover often went through several distinct cycles. For example, in parts of northern Colombia, some savannas observed by Europeans in the early 1500s "had reverted to rainforest by about 1750 following Indian decline, and had been reconverted to savanna for pasture by 1950" (Denevan 1992b:373). An analogous process occurred in the lowlands of Vera Cruz, Mexico (Sluyter 2001). Arnold's ethnohistorical research discusses the contrasting Aztec and European views of and relationships with their landscapes (1999).

In Amazonia, "much of what has been considered to be primary, natural, or undisturbed forest . . . may be the product of millennia of indigenous resource management and conservation as well as coevolution" (Sponsel 1992:245). Other evidence suggests similar changes in the Yucatán's forest cover, which had been significantly removed prior to 1492. Long before the European arrival, Yucatán's forests had rapidly recovered after the Maya collapse (Denevan 1992b:3478). Whitmore and Turner II talk of "a massive transformation of the central Maya Lowlands" prior to the European Conquest (2001:237), especially as a result of deforestation, resulting in "hybrid landscapes" after 1492 (Whitmore and Turner II 1992:416–418).

Whether, how, and when the introduction and subsequent expansion of European livestock, especially cattle and sheep, deeply transformed indigenous landscapes is the subject of lively debate. Although wild cattle thrived after being introduced into the llanos of Venezuela and Colombia, and the Pampas of Argentina, Gade (1992:467) reminds us that it was sheep and not cattle that were "the single European introduction most valuable to [Andean] native people." Yet sheep were also quite important elsewhere. Melville (1992) claims that by the mid-sixteenth century, at least four million sheep grazed in the valley of Mezquital, northeast of the valley of Mexico, which led to overgrazing and land erosion. Others are less certain. "For Mexico," Butzer writes, "it is popular to point to the introduction of Spanish livestock as an agent of ecological deterioration, but here again the evidence is far from convincing, at least for a general indictment," and that widespread, European-induced changes were probably not widespread or entrenched before the middle of the eighteenth century (1992:363). For their part, Whitmore and Turner II suggest that the number of sheep in central Mexico in the early seventeenth century may have been greatly exaggerated. Further, they claim that singling out European livestock as the cause of the widespread degradation in central Mexico is consistent with the unsubstantiated *leyenda verde* (green legend), which "has Amerindians sculpturing landscapes carefully designed to preserve and conserve nature" (2001: 228–234).

Controversies: Is the Culture Area Concept Still Useful?

A key idea in anthropology has been that natural environments have broadly shaped the contours of cultural development by providing different "constraints" and "opportunities" for the emergence of distinct types of societies (Moran 1987:3; Moran 2000:5). This link between environment and culture lies at the root of the **culture area** concept that, in the United States, dates to 1895 when anthropologists noted that culturally analogous societies clustered over areas sharing broad environmental features. A culture area was then construed as an assemblage of cultural, social, and economic traits associated with a geographic or environmental region. For example, anthropologists classed pre-European societies in the Pampas and Patagonia as either part of the Guanaco or Nomadic Hunters and Gatherers culture area (Dow and Van Kemper 1991). How many culture areas anthropologists proposed, as well as their boundaries (and, by implication, the kinds of societies within each), partially depended on the scale and unit of analysis employed. Thus, a higher scale and unit of analysis led to broader culture areas, with the result that internal cultural differences between societies within each were played down; conversely, lower-level units of analysis and, by implication, a more minute focus on cultural differences, led to other, smaller culture areas. As noted previously, other approaches have emphasized the importance of a mosaic of smaller ecological niches or "life zones."

The popular culture area concept underpinned the organization of highly influential Latin American ethnographic collections, such as the seven volume *Handbook of South American Indians* (Steward 1946–1959), and, years later, the sixteen volume *Handbook of Middle American Indians* (Wauchope 1964–1976). The popularity of this concept had to do with "the extreme simplicity of the concept. Nothing is more obvious than the prospective utility of an ethnographic map which groups tribal entities in relationship to some geographically delineated aspect of the environment" (Harris 1968:374). Yet popularity notwithstanding, the culture area concept was (and has been) riddled with conceptual difficulties. One pitfall was the danger of **environmental determinism,** the idea that geography "*in and of itself*" contributes to an understanding of cultural differences and similarities" (Harris 1968:374; italics added). As a way of avoiding determinism—postulating linear causal links between the physical environment and culture—most anthropologists focused on how specific aspects of the environment (e.g., types of soils, precipitation, or structural features of the terrain) in conjunction with key aspects of culture (especially technology, economic arrangements, and political organization), led to the emergence of distinct societies in specific historical moments. Further, anthropologists centered attention on broad differences and similarities across time and space, such as major archaeological pot-tery traditions; language families; key ways of extracting a living from the environment (e.g., intensive agriculture, foraging [hunting and gathering], or pastoralism); and main types of political and economic organization (e.g., egalitarian and mobile societies versus sedentary and stratified ones).

Most cultural anthropologists and archaeologists think of themselves and allude to others as, for example, Caribbeanists, Andeanists, or Mesoamericanists, and graduate stu-dents pursuing doctoral degrees are often required to pass area examinations on, for exam-ple, the Caribbean, Andes, or Mesoamerica. These classifications communicate expertise on a geographic and cultural landscape (e.g., knowing the language and culture of the area where the future anthropologist will eventually carry out fieldwork), and also assume that societies and their respective cultures are and have been historically related. Yet, because of contemporary globalization and transnationalism that often blur political, geographic, and cultural boundaries (examples are discussed in subsequent chapters), cultural anthropolo-gists (but less so archaeologists) are increasingly skeptical of the usefulness of the culture area concept. For example, writing on Guatemala, Goldin stresses that

> Many of the communities that we see today are essentially transformed com-munities in that they are global and transnational in nature. The boundaries, real or imagined, that anthropologists described in the 1940s, 1950s and 1960s were boundaries that held the township and the nation-state as the organizing categories. The boundaries (meaningful contexts) that we find today extend to the fields, cities and refugee camps of Mexico and the United States and the factories of Korea and Japan. (1999:107, quoted by Chase 2002:13; see also Alvarez 1995:450; Kearney 1991)

These critiques have much merit, and by highlighting examples of cultural flow and fluid-ity, this book also indirectly questions the analytic utility of the culture area concept, at least the way it was originally conceived. For example, to what extent is the idea of an "Andean" culture area helpful when Peruvian Andean peoples are as likely to participate in and identify with "traditional" community fiestas as live in Washington, D.C. in a fully "modern" context (see Preface), or when Ecuadorian Otalaveños are just as likely to main-tain a strong sense of ethnic and cultural identification while living and selling their handi-crafts in Amsterdam (Chapter 10)? Is a "Mesoamerican" culture area concept useful in understanding how and why a Mexican Mixtec from the state of Oaxaca can and is willing to display a "traditional" life way as well as spend a great deal of time in California, and what does this diasporic experience mean culturally (see Preface)? Why and how might a "Maya" area concept be important at all if, as the result of civil war and genocide, hundreds of thousands of Guatemalan Mayan speakers now live in California, South Carolina, and half a dozen other U.S. states (Chapter 12)?

There are, of course, no easy or straightforward answers to these questions. Yet, some anthropologists (including this author), while cognizant that culture areas are inher-ently problematic the way they were originally formulated, are not quite ready to totally do away with them. Lederman suggests that culture areas are useful "not as geographical mappings . . . but as situated disciplinary discourses," that is, common frameworks or understandings within which similar kinds of questions and issues are shared, cross-checked, and debated among a "specialized community of readers" who focus (but are not necessarily limited or bounded by) their attention on a specific region of the world (1998:442–443).

Hill and Santos-Granero provide a different perspective. They note that the Arawak language has been long associated with a particular culture area. But, in adopting an analytic approach stressing historical processes and transformations, they also acknowledge that Arawak-speaking peoples have historically engaged in long-range migrations to, and experienced diasporic-like conditions in, far flung places within Amazonia. Further, many contemporary Arawak-speakers have long been in intimate contact with and heavily influenced by Western outsiders, so much so that "most Arawakan peoples long ago adopted Western clothes and material culture through missionaries and trade with national societies" (2002:14). How can the culture area concept—which has so often implied boundedness, stability, and essentialism—still be useful? They suggest a "comparative historical approach . . . across separate regions" that are not geographically delimited but historically generated, shifting spaces over given physical landscapes, enabling anthropologists to "identify cultural practices that are widely shared by contemporary Arawakan peoples" across time and space (2002:13–15).

Lederman, Hill, and Santos-Granero's insights provide a useful way of reconsidering the potential usefulness of the concept of culture area, especially given the contemporary interest of many cultural anthropologists in historical processes and globalization. First, rather than viewing a culture area as a region wedded to particular environmental features, it ought be largely disengaged from its original physical geographic underpinnings. Second, rather than viewing it as relatively bounded—either in space or time—it would be more productive to conceptualize a culture area as a constantly shifting space with rapidly changing boundaries within which significant cultural, social, economic, and political interactions take place. Third, a culture area or space ought to be construed as inherently discontinuous—at least geographically—as "islands" of cultural interaction, some of which may be closer to each other than others. Take, for instance, the diaspora of Guatemalan Mayas following the civil war of the 1970s and 1980s (see Chapter 12): given the approach suggested here, the Maya culture area would include places and spaces in the United States where significant numbers of Mayas are currently concentrated *as well as* the principal highland departments of western Guatemala, and areas in neighboring Central American countries that were and still are the historic bastions of Maya culture. Fourth and lastly—and following Lederman (1998)—a given culture area could more productively be viewed as an intellectual arena within which significant issues surface and are debated.

Summary

The forty-seven countries and territories comprising Latin America and the Caribbean have more than half a billion inhabitants speaking hundreds of languages. These peoples are spread over extraordinarily diverse landscapes. More than half of the population today is concentrated in huge cities, most living in shantytowns or urban slums. Despite this marked demographic, cultural, and environmental diversity, most scholars consider Latin America and the Caribbean as a distinct region or space within which significant cultural, social, economic, and political interactions have historically taken place. Although the physical environment was profoundly altered and sometimes degraded prior to the European arrival, widespread environmental change and degradation was one of the most important consequences of the European Conquest. Anthropologists have long debated the usefulness of the culture area concept. Although some consider it outdated, others believe culture areas might be relevant if conceptualized in ways that take into account contemporary cultural flows across national and geographical boundaries.

ISSUES AND QUESTIONS

1. *Delimiting Latin America and the Caribbean.* Most readers of this textbook are at least intuitively aware of what "is" Latin America and the Caribbean. Yet, scholars disagree on which countries ought to be included as part of "Latin" America. Why is this so and why are these disagreements important?

2. *Imagining Latin America and the Caribbean.* One key theme in this chapter is that Latin America is partly an "idea," partly a cultural/social construct. What exactly does this notion mean, and to whom has it been relevant and why? Why might the notion of the social/cultural construction of Latin America and the Caribbean be marred in debate?

3. *Landscapes and Culture.* A central assumption of this chapter is that the culture of Latin American and Caribbean peoples cannot be fully grasped without learning about their landscapes. What does the concept of landscape allude to? Drawing on examples from this chapter, explain how and why landscapes are important.

4. *Culture Areas.* What are some of the assumptions underpinning the idea of culture areas and what are some of their drawbacks? In what ways might a reconceptualized culture area approach be relevant in the contemporary world?

KEY TERMS AND CONCEPTS

Altiplano   p. 38
Amazon   p. 33
Andean mountains   p. 38
Atacama desert   p. 37
Central American Volcanic Axis   p. 42
Central Lowlands   p. 29
Central Plateau   p. 39
Chaco   p. 34
Coastal Plains   p. 43
Culture area   p. 45
Eastern Highlands   p. 29
Endangered languages   p. 26

Environmental determinism   p. 45
Gulf Coastal Plains/Gulf Region   p. 41
Informal economy   p. 24
Interior mountain ranges   p. 43
Landscape   p. 28
Llanos   p. 32
Mesa Central   p. 39
Mesa del Norte   p. 39
Neovolcanic Range   p. 40
Pampas   p. 35
Patagonia   p. 35

Physiographic regions   p. 32
Place   p. 21
Sertão   p. 34
Shantytowns   p. 25
Southern Highlands   p. 39
Space   p. 20
Structural zones   p. 29
Terra firme   p. 33
Várzea   p. 33
Western Alpine System   p. 29
Yucatán peninsula   p. 42

ENDNOTES

1. These are Argentina, Guatemala, Bolivia, Haiti, Brazil, Honduras, Chile, Mexico, Colombia, Nicaragua, Costa Rica, Panama, Cuba, Paraguay, the Dominican Republic, Peru, Ecuador, Uruguay, El Salvador, and Venezuela.

2. The Population Reference Bureau, a nonprofit research organization, emphasizing political criteria, lists thirty-nine countries that make up its "Latin America and the Caribbean" region (2003:5–6).

3. This includes twenty-six independent and "dependent" countries. With the exception of Suriname, all independent countries are in the Caribbean and achieved independence from Great Britain between 1962 and 1981. The countries and territories included in *SALA*'s standard and add ons categories total forty-six.

4. These are Anguilla, Antigua and Barbuda, Aruba, Bahamas, Barbados, Bermuda, British Virgin Islands, Cayman Islands, Dominica, Grenada, Guadeloupe, Martinique, Montserrat, Netherlands Antilles, St. Kitts and Nevis, St. Lucia, St. Vincent and The Grenadines, Trinidad and Tobago, Turks and Caicos Islands, United States Virgin Islands.

5. Some authors refer to Mexico, Central America, and the Caribbean as part of Middle America (Denevan 1980:217; Clawson 2004:7–8). Mesoamerica is sometimes viewed as including areas of Mexico and Central America (especially in Guatemala, Honduras, Belize, and El Salvador) heavily influenced by Maya and Aztec civilizations (Carmack et al. 1996:1–39). For others, segments of the Caribbean are properly part of Mesoamerica (Moran 1987).

6. South America's three major river systems are the Orinoco, centered mainly in Venezuela and Colombia; the Amazon, whose more than 1,000 tributaries are located primarily in Brazil; and the Paraguay-Paraná-Río de la Plata in Paraguay, Uruguay, Argentina, and Brazil.

CHAPTER

3 Society and Culture Before the Europeans

T his chapter provides a synopsis of the historical development of Latin American and Caribbean societies. It surveys the emergence and transformations of egalitarian band and complex chiefdom and state societies, emphasizing when and how these emerged in specific environmental and political contexts. Particular importance is placed on the emergence and expansion of the Aztec and Inca empires in Mesoamerica and the Andes—areas in which significant numbers of indigenous peoples survived the European Conquest. The last section of this chapter focuses on the peopling of the Americas, one of the most significant and highly charged debates in current Latin American and Caribbean archaeology.

Anthropological Perspectives on the Evolution of Social Complexity

A great deal of anthropological—especially archaeological—research in Latin America and the Caribbean (and elsewhere) has centered on what is called the emergence of **societal** or **cultural complexity,** the process through which societies increased their capacity to harness resources from their environments to sustain larger populations and also achieved a greater degree of political and economic integration. This research is important for clearly discerning the kinds of societies that Europeans encountered in the sixteenth century as well as for understanding how these different types of societies fared after the Conquest. This section centers attention on and briefly summarizes the major attributes of what cultural anthropologists and archaeologists call band, tribal, chiefdom, and state societies. Where, when, and how these, as well as state-level societies, emerged in Latin America and the Caribbean prior to the European Conquest of the sixteenth century is the subject of the following section.

The major attributes of band, tribal, chiefdom, and state societies that archeologists and cultural anthropologists generally agree on were originally proposed by Service (1962) and are summarized by Miller (2005:234–240). See Figure 3.1 for more detail.

Bands are small-scale and highly mobile societies, typically numbering several dozen households related through kinship ties. Bands engage in a **foraging subsistence mode** (also called hunting and gathering) centered on the gathering and consumption of edible wild (undomesticated) plants, as well as occasional reliance on hunting. These are

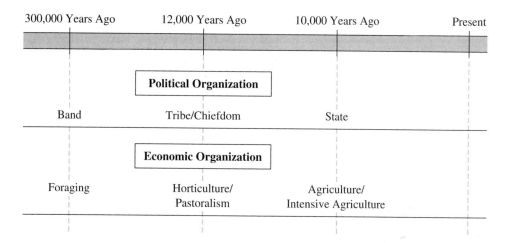

FIGURE 3.1   Economic and Political Organization of Band, Tribal, Chiefdom, and State Societies. *Source:* Adapted from Miller (2005:234).

egalitarian societies, which means, first, that all members have an equal right to avail themselves of resources in their territories, and, second, that there is an absence of political and coercive power, and of institutionalized political offices and leadership. For the greater part of history, most human societies were organized into bands. At the moment of the European Conquest, some bands or foraging societies were present in northern Mexico, but more were in Amazonia, southern Chile, and southern Argentina (Scheinsohn 2003:349). The Sirionó in eastern Bolivia, Araucanians in southern Chile, and the Ona and Tehuelche of southern Patagonia, Argentina, are historically well-known examples of South American band societies (Stearman 1987; Rivera 1999).

   Tribes are demographically larger, and, with the exception of some pastoralist societies, are often less mobile. Tribes are typically comprised of distinct groups, whose members claim a kinship or genealogical link to each other. In some contexts, tribes have surfaced with the advent of the **domestication** of plants and animals—their active and conscious supervision and control by social groups—yielding the possibilities of engaging in agriculture and pastoralism/animal husbandry, the two major subsistence modes of tribal societies. Unlike bands, tribes display signs of incipient inequality. Although a concentration of political power and the ability of some to coerce others is typically absent, tribes display formal political positions and clearly recognizable political leaders, whose major role is to mediate disputes. Unlike bands, tribal societies exhibit clear markers of economic differentiation, such as the ability of some groups to gain access to (and transmit to their own members) land or other resources. Many tribal groups still exist in Latin America, especially in Amazonia. Among some of the better-known examples are the Jívaro (also called Shuar) in eastern Ecuador, first studied by Harner (1973), Brazil's Kayapo, and the Yanömamo of Venezuela and Brazil (see also Chapters 6 and 10).

   Although methodologically difficult to distinguish from tribes, **chiefdoms** are much larger societies—sometimes numbering in the hundreds or thousands of households—with higher population densities and control over wider, larger landscapes. Higher population densities mean that the chiefdom mode of subsistence is predicated on a more intense extraction of resources from the environment through a concentrated exploitation of marine/coastal resources, a greater reliance on domesticated plants (a transition from incipient domestication to horticulture, to sustained agriculture), or full-scale domestication of herds of animals (pastoralism), or a combination of all three. The transition to political and economic concentration and inequality is also far more complete. Typically, there are formal, clearly named political positions and hereditary leadership and/or political offices ("chiefs"). And, for the first time, coercive power (i.e., the ability to coerce others) surfaces, sometimes coupled with the emergence of a warrior class aligned with politically powerful individuals engaged in ongoing conflicts/warfare with neighboring polities. Economic inequality—partly marked by the ability by some to exercise control over the labor of others—is also far more clearly marked and present. Chiefdoms were widespread in Latin America and the Caribbean at the moment of the European Conquest (Drennan and Uribe 1987c; Redmond 1998).

Finally, **states** represent the extreme end of a process of deepening political and economic inequality (Scarre and Fagan 2002). Compared to chiefdoms, states often have huge populations divided into many culturally distinct groups, and they exercise rule over much larger, far-flung territories. For example, prior to the European Conquest, the Andean Inca state had millions of inhabitants differentiated into a multitude of ethnic polities, and it spanned, north to south, more than 2,000 miles. States, which almost always have emerged in contexts of conflict and warfare, display an extreme concentration of political and coercive power, highly formalized and institutionalized political hierarchies and standing armies. Paralleling political inequality is the presence of stark and deeply entrenched social and economic differentiation, manifested by the appearance of unequal social classes and/or hierarchically ranked ethnic or culturally distinct groups. Religious changes—specifically the emergence of hierarchical imperial religions or state cults—also accompany and ideologically underpin the process of social and cultural complexity and inequality. Another key attribute of states is monumental architecture—a clear indication of an elite's ability to wrench labor from large segments of the population. An intensive exploitation of resources, exemplified by terraced and irrigated fields in the Andes, or raised platform agriculture (the "floating gardens" or chinampas in Mexico)— which persisted well into the colonial period (Cline 2000:208)—also suggest a state-level form of organization.

Phases in the Emergence of Societal Complexity in Latin America and the Caribbean

Archaeologists studying what is sometimes (and perhaps misleadingly) called Latin America's **prehistory** (that is, the historical development of Latin American societies prior to the European Conquest) typically specialize in distinct regions (e.g., Mesoamerica, Caribbean) and time periods or phases within which significant changes and/or regularities occur. This section surveys significant characteristics of the major periods into which Latin American archaeology has been generally divided. Readers should be aware that the

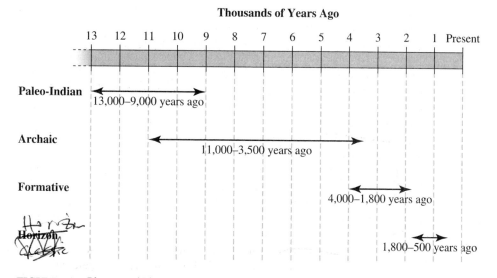

FIGURE 3.2 Phases and Time Spans in the Development of Social Complexity.

following synopsis is challenging because of the use of different classificatory schemes across Latin America. This means, for example, that there is considerable lack of consistency in naming (labeling) conventions, and that often the beginning and end points of the different periods only partially overlap. Both partly have to do with the fact that in Latin America there are "many approaches to archaeology, and few tendencies toward terminological consistency" (Lynch 1999:237), and also because "we are dealing with processes of cultural change rather than with discrete events" (Zietilin and Zietilin 2000:48) that operated in different ways in diverse landscapes. Bearing in mind these caveats—and especially that the outer limits or dates of each period blend into each other—the prehistory of Latin America and the Caribbean can be generally divided into four broad phases: Paleo-Indian, Archaic, Formative, and Horizon (see Figure 3.2).

Paleo-Indian

Despite the ongoing controversy on when the peopling of the Americas took place (discussed in greater detail in the "Controversies" section at the end of this chapter), there is little doubt that the **Paleo-Indian period** or adaptation was widely and firmly entrenched in Mesoamerica, and Central and South America between 13,000 and 9,000 years ago (Zietilin and Zietilin 2000:62; Lynch 1999:238; Roosevelt 1999:313).[1] A significant exception is the Caribbean, settled much later by peoples from Central America and northern South America.

In South America, some of the earliest known Paleo-Indian sites, dated to at least 10,000 years ago, have been found on the Andean Pacific coasts of Peru, Ecuador, and Chile. These sites reveal the presence of small foraging groups with a **maritime coastal adaptation,** a subsistence strategy heavily focused on the exploitation of marine/sea resources. An analogous subsistence strategy has been documented for Brazil's Atlantic coast (Scheinsohn 2003:350).

Meanwhile, deep in Brazilian Amazonia at the confluence of the Amazon and Tapajós rivers near the current city of Manaus, the Paleo-Indian site of Monte Alegre has been dated between 11,000 and 10,000 years ago. Excavations in caves and rock shelters have uncovered wall paintings and an abundance of plant and animal remains, as well as stone (lithic) and wooden tools. The archaeological analyses reveal an interesting portrait of these foragers:

> The Paleoindian culture . . . had . . . chipped stone tools, stylized rock art, and an economy of tropical forest and floodplain foraging . . . Paleoindians visited the cave periodically for more than 1200 years. While there, people ate tree fruits and a wide variety of river and land game, painted the cave, made stone tools, and cut wood. (Roosevelt et al. 1996:380; see also Roosevelt 1999:272, 313)

Current research therefore suggests that human groups relying on a wide spectrum of resources branched out into and adapted to different environmental niches, a hypothesis that makes especially good sense if one accepts multiple entry points into Mesoamerica, and Central and South America (see "Controversies" section later in this chapter). The only significant exceptions were the Andean highlands and altiplano, and the southern Pampas and Patagonian plains, where "open-ground hunting specialization" was a way of life partly dependent on the hunting of camelids (such as guanacos and vicuñas), deer, large rodents, and other small mammals (Lynch 1999:240). Some archeological sites in southern Patagonia appear to date to at least 13,000 years ago, and they are clearly associated with low population densities and a hunting strategy targeting camelids, especially the guanaco. Some coastal sites also demonstrate the importance of fishing. Andean camelids (namely, the llama and alpaca) were probably domesticated about 6,000 years ago (Scheinsohn 2003:347–354).

In Latin America, big-game hunting was never as important as in North America, and it makes more sense to view early Latin American Paleo-Indian societies as unspecialized foraging bands subsisting on a wide spectrum of maritime resources and undomesticated edible plants, occasionally supplemented by the hunting of wild game (Dillehay 2000:5–9). Even Lynch, who staunchly believes in a uniform culture of Paleo-Indians making their way into South America, agrees that "it would not be surprising if the classical western North American, big-game hunting, definition [of Paleo-Indians] no longer works" (1999:238). Indeed, the abundance of jackrabbit remains in some Mesoamerican Paleo-Indian sites, such as in Tehuacán (in Mexico's Eastern Sierra Madre mountain range), "should caution against an assumption that Mesoamerica's Paleo-Indian population depended on just a few large animal species" (Zietilin and Zietilin 2000:93), while in the Amazon and Andes

> Paleoindians appear to have adapted to seasonal humid tropical habitat by broad-spectrum hunting and collecting. Such a generalized subsistence adaptation was also characteristic of coastal and highland Peruvian Paleoindian cultures. Thus neither Amazonia nor the Central Andes provide empirical support for the hypothesis of a migration of big-game hunters from North America down the Andes. (Roosevelt 1999:314)

In South America, "There are no convincing signs that Paleoindians lived in closed forests" (Lynch 1999:244). Paleo-Indian societies were, then, small-scale egalitarian and highly mobile band societies. Their mode of subsistence centered largely on hunting and gathering; others who settled along coastlines also relied heavily on marine resources. Additional characteristics of these Paleo-Indian societies included the absence of permanently settled villages and of pottery.

Archaic

The **Archaic period,** between 11,000 and 3,500 years ago, broadly corresponds in the Andes to the Middle to Late Preceramic, and in Mesoamerica to the Incipient Agricultural phase (Richardson 1994:27; Conrad and Demarest 1984:14). It is during this period (6,000 to 5,000 years ago) that the Caribbean islands were first populated. Virtually all of the earliest archaeological sites in the Caribbean are found in the Greater Antilles, especially in Cuba, Hispaniola, and Puerto Rico.

The peopling of the Caribbean took place through several migratory waves. The first migrants may have reached the Greater Antilles 6,000 years ago, and an analysis of stone tools suggests that these early migrants may have originated in present-day Honduras and Belize. A subsequent (but still preceramic) migratory wave, originating in northern South America and almost certainly the mouth of the Orinoco river system, occurred 2,000 years later. These early foragers relied primarily on hunting and fishing (Weeks and Ferbel 1994:xxxviii). Subsequent migrations to the Caribbean are discussed in the Formative phase later in this chapter.

During the approximately 7,500 years of the Archaic period, social groups experienced at least six significant and related transformations that worked hand in hand and sharply set their world apart from that of their predecessors: (1) an increasing sedentary lifestyle; (2) a rise in population; (3) a reliance on a broader resource base; (4) the emergence of pottery; (5) the domestication of plants, or incipient agriculture; and (6) the rise of complex, chiefdom-level societies. Caribbean societies are, again, a significant exception, because most of the transformations mentioned above occurred much later.

1. *Sedentism.* Evidence of a more sedentary lifestyle—of semipermanent villages—is one of the most important developments during the mid-to latter Archaic period. This is especially the case along the Chilean, Peruvian, and Caribbean coastlines, suggesting the importance of a maritime coastal adaptation better suited to a less mobile life way (Lynch 1999:240–242; Shimada 1999; Lumbreras 1999; Allaire 1999:678). There is also some evidence of semipermanent settlements on the Amazonian floodplains at about the same time (Roosevelt 1999:310).

The fact that this sedentary lifestyle preceded and was not contingent on the prior existence of agriculture is extremely important, because it runs counter to a long-standing theory that the emergence of full-fledged agriculture was a precondition for sedentism. Some evidence suggests the emergence of sedentary or semisedentary lifestyles by foraging societies that did not practice full-fledged agriculture but lived in resource rich areas. Hence, "Sedentism should not be seen merely as a consequence of the shift to food production. Indeed, quite the opposite could be the case." And, at least for the Mesoamerican lowlands—and probably on the coastlines and the Amazonian floodplains—"where abundant wild plant and animal resources were available, the development of settled village life and merging social ranking need not have been dependent on . . . intensified . . . agriculture" (Zietilin and Zietilin 2000:95, 103). It appears that in many parts of Mesoamerica, and Central and South America, "plants were cultivated and domesticated early in the Archaic sequence, and that sedentism, population concentration, class-structured society, and communal work projects . . . came much later" (Lynch 1999:251).

2. *Increase in population.* The trend toward more sedentary residential patterns—which seem to have increased in size through time—was also accompanied by a rise in population (Lynch 1999:239). The increase in population, and in size and density of settlement patterns, was especially noticeable on the coastlines, especially where narrow river valleys cut through the coast and empty their waters into the Pacific (Roosevelt 1999:283; Lumbreras 1999). An increase in the size and density of settlement sites in Mesoamerica and other regions of South America is also well documented.

3. *Broader resource base.* Archaic groups would eventually rely on a broader spectrum of resources than did Paleo-Indian societies (Lynch 1999:239). This has been viewed as a consequence of initial specialized hunters' need to quickly adapt to novel ecological conditions perhaps not conducive to big-game hunting, as they made their way south. Such a broader resource base would include, for example, the consumption of a wide array of wild plants, such as nondomesticated beans eaten by early Archaic foragers in the Mexican region of Oaxaca (Zietilin and Zietilin 2000:98), or, in Amazonia, the hunting of a wide array of land and aquatic mammals coupled with fishing. Along the Andean Pacific coasts, this broad-based subsistence adaptation included fishing coupled with camelid hunting and incipient plant cultivation in the nearby foothills of the western Andes (Lumbreras 1999).

4. *Emergence of pottery.* Archaeologists have traditionally attached a great deal of importance to the appearance of pottery (ceramics) as a marker of societal complexity, presumably because a willingness and ability to manufacture ceramics indicates the presence of certain conditions (e.g., a secure resource base, a less mobile lifestyle) not usually associated with transient foragers.

Pottery was independently invented in different regions throughout the Americas. Some archaeologists believe that the earliest firm evidence of pottery lies in Ecuadorian and Colombian coastlines dating to 5,000 years ago (Allaire 1999:679), while other evidence points to pottery in the interior of Brazil at least 6,000 years ago (Roosevelt 1999:316). In Mesoamerica, the earliest pottery remains date to about 4,300 years ago (Zietilin and Zietilin 2000:47). Yet, exactly when and where pottery making emerges may not be as important as the possibility that *some* appearance of ceramics can be traced to semipermanent lowland societies that did not fully rely on agriculture as their major subsistence mode (Roosevelt 1999:310). This is a possibility that runs counter to previous views that pottery, sedentary lifestyles, and agriculture could only have emerged first in or adjacent to regions of "high" culture (e.g., the Andean and Mesoamerican highlands where vast states emerged prior to the European Conquest).

5. *Plant domestication.* A major hallmark of the Archaic period is an "intensification of food-gathering techniques, and perhaps of incipient cultivation" (Allaire 1999:678). It is during this period that some of the most important crops that sustained Latin American and Caribbean societies for millennia—such as manioc, beans, maize, potatoes, squash, chili peppers, and coca—were domesticated. The domestication of and full reliance on plant crops is important because it clearly signals an evolutionary move to societal complexity.

How, when, and why agriculture first appeared has been the subject of considerable controversy, tightly wedded to theories regarding the emergence of complex (chiefdom and state-level) societies. At least three controversial and related issues have centered on the relationship between the emergence of agriculture and societal complexity: (a) the origins of agriculture; (b) the agricultural potential of lowland environments; and (c) the importance of agriculture versus the role of the concentration of subsistence resources.

a. *The origins of agriculture*. Partly because of the so-called bias against the lowland tropics (see below), for many years the predominant view among archaeologists was that the two major centers of plant domestication were in or near the semi-arid mountainous regions of Mexico and the Andes (Meggers 1979:29–33). Although this may have been true of some important cultigens, recent research places the origins of plant domestication not in or near the core Andean or Mesoamerican regions—nor as a result of contact with these regions—but in the lowland tropics. This is in fact a theory first proposed by cultural geographer Carl Sauer in the 1950s and later by archaeologist Donald Lathrap in the 1970s.

Piperno and Pearsall (1998) have recently mustered considerable data suggesting that tropical forest and lowland environments are neither as hostile to or ill-suited for crop domestication as many originally thought. Further, they claim that plant domestication in lowland areas was underway earlier than in the Mexican and Peruvian highlands, and that by at least 9,000 years ago the cultivation of numerous plants and tubers was common in house gardens and larger plots of land. Piperno and Pearsall locate the origins of plant cultivation not in Amazonia—because of poor soils of the terra firme, and also partly because major river valleys subject to constant flooding would not have been attractive to incipient agriculturalists—but in "southwestern Ecuador/northern Peru, northern South America (Colombia/Venezuela/the Guianas/northern Brazil), and southwestern Mexico" (1998:29). Indeed, in these regions plant domestication may have begun much earlier than otherwise theorized, possibly 10,000 to 11,000 years ago—or at the onset of the Archaic period (Piperno and Pearsall 1998:4). There is now considerable evidence, for example, that two basic staples of Mesoamerican societies—maize and beans—were independently domesticated in several low-lying tropical environments from Mexico to the Andes at least 5,000 to 7,000 years ago (Piperno and Pearsall 1998:109–166; Roosevelt 1999:271; Zietilin and Zietilin 2000:105; Eubanks 2001). The oldest agricultural systems, though, may have been based on lowland manioc and highland Andean root crops, including the potato (Lynch 1999:252).

b. *The agricultural potential of lowland environments.* In South America at least, an enduring and heated controversy revolves around what Roosevelt (1999:167) has called the **geographical bias** against the lowland tropics, which views tropical ecology as not being conducive to sustained agricultural practices and, therefore, hampering the emergence of societal complexity. Until recently, therefore, an almost-dominant view had been that the shift toward sedentary lifestyles, the conditions necessary for the emergence of pottery, the initial domestication of plants, and the early emergence of complex societies could not have taken place in South American tropical lowland environments.

Several reasons accounted for this bias. One was the difficulties of uncovering ancient organic materials in lowland tropical environments. This has skewed research toward the highland Andes and Mexico, where organic materials stand a better chance of remaining preserved. Another was the long-held idea—popularized by Meggers' depiction of Amazonia as a "Counterfeit Paradise"—that the lushness of the tropical vegetation masked the "remarkable infertility of Amazonian soil[s]" (1971:12) in the upland forest areas (terra firme). According to this view, weathering, leaching, and other ecological processes, coupled with the scattered dispersal of edible plants and wild animals, meant that only the narrow várzea floodplain had the necessary ecological potential for sustained agricultural activity and cultural development.

But some question the widely held view that Amazonian soils were inadequate for sustained food production, and that the only ecologically sound way to practice agriculture is through slash-and-burn, which by definition implies a not fully sedentary population. Roosevelt (1999:311), for example, agrees that the quality of terra firme soils vary greatly, but claims that there are indeed some good soils, and that "in areas with richer soils, permanent agriculture has long been practiced, and even on poor soils, slash-and-burn cultivation has been widely used." The long-standing belief of the inherent infertility of upland Amazonian soils also often sidestepped the potential human (and therefore cultural) impact on landscapes, including soils. Research on what are now called anthropic or anthropogenic soils—that is, soils purposely altered to increase yields—now suggests that "the basic assumption made by earlier archaeologists, that Amazonia is an environment that cannot sustain intensive agricultural exploitation or dense human settlement, would seem to be wide off the mark" (Whitehead 1996a:247). It is nevertheless the case that many—if not most—of Amazonian chiefdom societies emerged on or near the várzea floodplains.

The controversy over the suitability of tropical lowlands for sustained agriculture and cultural complexity—centered mainly on South America, but especially Amazonia—has been largely absent in other regions. Indeed, for thousands of years large swaths of the Gulf Coast, Caribbean, and Pacific Mesoamerican lowlands (including the Yucatán peninsula) sustained large populations and urban centers, such as the Olmec and Classic Maya (Diehl 2000; Hammond 2000). Gasco and Smith (1996:47–49) note that some of the earliest Mesoamerican archaeological sites pointing to sedentism, large populations, and cultural complexity are in lowland areas. These furthermore display evidence of **primary state formation**—that is, "when a first-generation state evolves in a context of nonstate societies, without contact with other preexisting states" (Spencer and Redmond 2004:174). The ability of the Mesoamerican lowlands to sustain large populations and provide the potential for considerable cultural complexity may have much to do with the relative proximity of quite distinct environmental landscapes—highland mountains, coastal plains, and the sea—which would have furnished human groups a wide spectrum of year-round resources.

c. *Agriculture and the concentration of subsistence resources.* As noted previously, the rise of hierarchical, complex societies was not the result of one single process, but rather of the interplay of multiple factors working together in different ways in distinct regions and time periods. Although the emergence of and reliance on agriculture as a major subsistence strategy may have been an important process underpinning societal complexity in some regions, in others it was not. For example, some of the earliest hierarchical, ranked societies in South America emerged on the Pacific coast (Richardson 1994; Stanish 2001), where the continuous, year-round availability of diverse resources concentrated in relatively small areas enabled people to practice diverse subsistence strategies—fishing, hunting, gathering wild plants, and incipient domestication—that allowed for sedentism and increasing population. Analogous conditions appear to have surfaced along parts of the Amazon and Orinoco river systems, where "intensive agricultural economies were created by late prehistoric complex societies, not the other way around" (Roosevelt 1999:266).

At the same time, agriculture was almost certainly necessary to feed the increasing numbers of people who populated the big urban centers associated with the largest state-level societies. For example, the complex societies that initially surfaced on the high Andean altiplano relied on a wide array of camelids and other wild game, in addition to the cultivation of a wide range of tuber crops (especially different varieties of potatoes) and highly nutritious grains, such as *quinoa* (*Chenopodium quinoa*) and *tarwi* (*Lupinus mutabilis*). Yet, soon afterward, Andean peoples turned to intensive agricultural practices—such as hillside terracing and platform or mound agriculture—both of which dramatically increased the amount of food available (Colette 1986; Denevan 2001).

6. *Rise of complex societies.* The emergence of more settled village life, the appearance of pottery, and the intensification of production—either by a more intensive exploitation of coastal marine resources, or incipient plant domestication in combination with occasional hunting—all point to increasing social, political, and economic complexity and differentiation. It is from the mid to late Archaic and early Formative periods that archaeologists have mustered the greatest amount of evidence on the rise and consolidation of chiefdoms and the subsequent appearance of full-fledged regional states. The transition from chiefdoms to states entailed "intensified centralization of power, greater inequality between population sectors, expanded scale of labor appropriation by elites, increased administrative and labor specialization, codification of laws, and a formal juridical system" (Villamarín and Villamarín 1999:582).

When Spaniards and other Europeans began their conquests in the early sixteenth century, they encountered two basic types of societies: politically acephalous (noncentralized) societies and those that displayed varying levels of political centralization. Spaniards referred to the former as *behetrías* (what anthropologists would now call bands or tribes), and the latter as *señoríos* (from Spanish *señor*), *curacazgos* (from the Quechua word *c/kurakas* [chief or leader]), *cacicazgos* (from the Arawak word *cacique* [chief or leader]), or *reinos* (Spanish for *kingdom*) (Villamarín and Villamarín 1999:579).

In South America, the earliest chiefdoms appear to have surfaced in coastal Ecuador about 5,000 years ago, or during the middle Archaic period. They emerged on Peru's northern and central coastlines, and in the nearby highland regions (i.e., the foothills of the western flanks of the Andes) about 500 years later. By the end of the Archaic period—roughly 3,000 years ago—chiefdoms were widely present in the Bolivian altiplano, the

Peruvian highlands, northwest Argentina, the northern coastal and southwestern portions of Colombia, the north Chilean coast, portions of the Amazonian várzea, the eastern flanks of the Andes (the so-called *montaña*), the southern llanos of Venezuela and other regions (Villamarín and Villamarín 1999:583-619).

In fact, chiefdom societies appear to have been "more widespread and of longer duration on the South American continent" than many archaeologists had previously assumed (Drennan and Uribe 1987b:145). This is especially the case in Amazonia, where for many years some archaeologists had dismissed the idea that complex societies could ever have emerged. During the past several decades, new and better archaeological research, coupled with a more intensive tapping of historical and ethnohistorical sources (Whitehead 1996a), has clearly shown the prevalence of numerous chiefdoms along the Amazon floodplain. These chiefdoms were characterized by large and dense settlements, political hierarchies, clear political and economic inequality, and intensive food production. Interestingly enough, maize and not manioc appears to have been the major food staple (Roosevelt 1987). According to Whitehead (1994), the mistaken belief that the Amazonian landscape was antithetical to the rise of complex societies was also the result of a misguided use of **ethnographic analogy**—whereby contemporary societies are thought to be representative of those that existed in past times. These analogies were profoundly mistaken, for they sidestepped the widespread havoc that Europeans inflicted on Amazonian societies, especially those along the banks and floodplains of the major rivers.

Chiefdoms were also widespread throughout Mesoamerica (Zietilin and Zietilin 2000:91) and, in Panama, they may have emerged 3,000 years ago (Drennan and Uribe 1987a:61). In the Caribbean, there seems to have been a sharp distinction between the Greater and Lesser Antilles (see Chapter 2), with chiefdoms widespread in the former but not in the latter (Allaire 1999).

The size and complexity of chiefdoms varied considerably. Some of the largest Taíno chiefdoms that the Spaniards encountered in Cuba and Puerto Rico numbered perhaps no more than several hundred households (Keegan 1992; Rouse 1992), while Aymara-speaking *altiplano* chiefdoms in present-day Bolivia (which emerged much earlier than in the Caribbean) had thousands of households, and their scale and level of organization placed them much closer to state societies. There was indeed "a great deal of demographic variability within the (chiefdom) class" (Drennan 1987:319). Some Amazonian chiefdoms, such as the Tapajós/Santarém, were so large and politically and economically complex that they resembled state societies. With "a total population possibly as large as 250,000," it is difficult to neatly distinguish these chiefdoms from states (Roosevelt 1999:336–338).

Although Amazonia may not have been as adverse to the development of social complexity as was previously thought, it is nevertheless the case that, at least in South America, chiefdoms

> may have appeared earlier in the Andean coastal and highland valleys than in the lowland forests or riverine regions . . . [because] . . . where productive land that could provide a refuge was limited, 'population pressure' or social conflict may have led to organizational changes that did not develop in regions where the discontented could easily leave to homestead elsewhere in the forest. (Roosevelt 1999:265)

In addition, some states also emerged in a context of "competition over the more circumscribed and limited resource base of the cool, arid environment" (Roosevelt 1999:343), which suggests the continuing usefulness of Carneiro's long tested environmental circumscription theory for the origins of the state (1970). Unfortunately, these were also the societies that displayed the least ability to survive the Spanish and Portuguese onslaught, at least compared to inland terra firme groups (see Chapter 4). It is in the terra firme that native Amazonian societies best survived by retreating deeper and deeper into the forests.

Formative

The relatively short **Formative period**—roughly between 4,000 and 1,800 years ago—more or less overlaps with the Andean Initial, Early Horizon, and Early Intermediate periods (Richardson 1994:27; Zietilin and Zietilin 2000:48) and the Mesoamerican Preclassic or Formative periods (Conrad and Demarest 1984:14; Gasco and Smith 1996:43). This is a phase of economic, political, and social consolidation, in which the major processes set in motion during the previous Archaic period became firmly entrenched. This period is indisputably marked by sedentary lifestyles indicated by permanent settlements, the rise of large population settlements, intensive forms of agricultural production, and the presence of large and powerful chiefdom societies across much of Latin America. It is also during this period—perhaps toward its latter part—that states emerged which were characterized by the presence of large-scale and monumental architecture. In many parts of Latin America, it is difficult indeed to mark the clear boundary between this Formative period and the following Horizon period.

During this period, "the original migration of agricultural and pottery-making peoples into the Caribbean islands through the Lesser Antilles is known to have taken place" (Allaire 1999:704), a process still underway when Europeans first arrived in the Caribbean. This period is also when "the most sophisticated cultures of lower Central America" emerged, especially in Panama and Costa Rica (Allaire 1999:710–715). An important wave of migrants from the Orinoco region of South America—collectively called the Saladoid culture—reached the Caribbean during this period about 2,200 years ago. Making their way through the Lesser Antilles, then Puerto Rico, and eventually reaching the eastern tip of Hispaniola, the Saladoid maintained extensive trade networks with the northern South American mainland (Weeks and Ferbel 1994:xxxix–xlii; Allaire 1997; Watters 1997). The Saladoid peoples were almost certainly the immediate precursors of the agricultural, sedentary Arawak-speaking Taíno peoples widely present in the Greater Antilles (and, in the southeast, through the island of Guadeloupe) at the end of the fifteenth century who "Greeted Columbus" (Rouse 1992). *Taíno* derives from the Arawak word *nitaino*, meaning noble or elite (Weeks and Ferbel 1994:xxxiv; Keegan 1997:114), a linguistic clue suggesting long-standing differentiation and inequality in Caribbean societies by this time. **Matrilineal descent** was almost certainly characteristic of Taíno societies, with rights and obligations passed through the female line (Keegan 1992, 1997). At the moment of the European Conquest, a final migratory stream—this time of a people who the Spaniards called Caribs (*Caribes*)—was making its way north through the Lesser Antilles.

In Peru, Ecuador, and Chile, Archaic coastal settlements "were superseded by more complex riverine communities, in which the economy revolved around the raising of plants and animals with Andean or trans-Andean, not coastal, origins—as well as maize from Central America" (Lynch 1999:256). This indicates another important feature of this Formative period—the emergence of regional and even transregional economic ties and flows. These regional exchanges may have been important in the advent of what is known as the Chavín culture—possibly the first regional state to have developed in the Central Andean coast, or anywhere else in the Andes, for that matter (Roosevelt 1999:295). Other regional polities that emerged during this period and gained considerable influence throughout the Andes include Tiwanaku, on the Bolivian altiplano bordering Lake Titicaca, and Huari, in the Peruvian highlands (Bermann 1994; Lumbreras 1999; Shimada 1999).

The Formative period ushered in many important yet varied developments in Mesoamerica. On some coastlines facing the Gulf of Mexico and the Caribbean Sea—but especially proximate to the coast of Belize—the first permanently settled villages and early chiefdoms appeared (Allaire 1999:688); the earliest and distinctly Maya urban centers in Belize date to about 2,700 years ago. One of the best known and most spectacular archaeological cultures of Mesoamerica include, in the low-lying mountainous foothills and nearby coastal areas in what is now Vera Cruz, Mexico, the enigmatic Olmec, the most visible marker of which are massive stone head carvings (Diehl 2000; see Photo 3.1). Large ceremonial centers are also a hallmark of the Olmec, who prospered some 3,000 years ago.

PHOTO 3.1   *Olmec Stone Carving, Xalapa, Mexico.*

PHOTO 3.2   *The enormous Pyramid of the Sun towering into the cloudy sky over Teotihuacán, Mexico. A few tourists mill around in the bare flat space before the pyramid.*

From the vantage point of monumental architecture, perhaps far more impressive—and perhaps better known to many who have traveled to Mexico—are the massive pyramid structures of Teotihuacán, about an hour from Mexico City (see Photo 3.2). This indisputably regional state surfaced about 2,100 years ago, dominated central Mexico, interacted with Maya states for six centuries, and collapsed about 1,300 years ago. At the time, Teotihuacán was one of the largest cities on earth. By the time the Aztec state emerged on the scene, Teotihuacán's pyramids had been abandoned for at least 600 years.

The important Zapotec state in Oaxaca, Mexico, emerged during this period about 2,500 years ago. Monte Albán is important because it may be "the strongest candidate for a primary state in Mesoamerica" (Spencer and Redmond 2004:193). At about the same time as Monte Albán, the first settled villages of what later would become the spectacular Maya city-states appeared in the southern Mesoamerican highlands and Pacific coastal areas. In time, Maya culture would extend over "the southeastern extremity of Mexico, including the whole of the Yucatán peninsula and most of the modern states of Chiapas and Tabasco, to the west, and much of northwestern Central America, to the east, including . . . Guatemala and Belize and the western parts of Honduras and El Salvador" (Sharer 1994:19). Some Maya states prospered through the subsequent Horizon period.

Horizon

The **Horizon period**—the briefest of all—spans from about 1,800 to 500 years ago (i.e., up to the European Conquest). The Andean chronological periods known as Middle Horizon, Late Intermediate, and Late Horizon overlap with what is termed here the Horizon period, as do the Mesoamerican Classic and Postclassic periods (Richardson 1994:27; Conrad and Demarest 1984:14; Sharer 1994:48). The last one hundred or so years of this period—which witnessed the quick rise and almost sudden (in historical time) demise of the two most powerful states in the Americas, the Inca and Aztec—are called the Late Horizon or Late-Post Classic periods (Richardson 1994:27; Conrad and Demarest 1984:14). The term Horizon is used to denote a time frame characterized by the spread of a culture across and control over diverse ecological and cultural areas (Lumbreras 1999:518). It is also known as an "era of integration" (Shimada 1999:350).

An important characteristic of the 1,300 years of the Horizon period is the presence of large-scale, regional states that achieved control over far-flung regions and, often, over numerous ethnic polities. Some of the better known polities—Chavín and Huari in the Andes, and Teotihuacán in what is now Mexico—surfaced in the latter part of the previous Formative period and disappeared during the Horizon period. Other states—the Chimú on Peru's northern coast, the Inca in the Peruvian highlands, and the Toltec and, later, the Aztec in the Central Valley of Mexico—quickly rose to prominence. The achievement of spectacular cultural and technological advances—comparable to and often surpassing those in other world regions at the time—is the second most important feature of the Horizon period. For example, Inca engineers constructed the longest and most elaborate road system anywhere in the Americas (parts of this road system—the so-called Inca Trail—are still in existence), while Aztec engineers directed the reclamation of swamplands and the construction of **chinampas** in the Valley of Mexico. Both Incas and Aztecs excelled in astronomy, and ruling elites constructed elaborate bureaucracies.

Maya city-states achieved spectacular accomplishments in hieroglyphic writing, engineering, astronomy, calendrics, and mathematics, including the mathematical concept of zero, "apparently the earliest known instance of this concept in the world" (Sharer 1994:557). Maya city-states, such as Tikal (see Photo 3.3) in the tropical lowlands, with their magnificent pyramids, palace complexes, and elaborate burial sites that still awe visitors thousands of years after their construction, flourished and disappeared during these 1,300 years.

Several hundred years before the Spanish Conquest, most Maya city-states in the southern lowlands were suddenly abandoned, their magnificent structures eventually overrun by dense tropical vegetation growth. How and why the famous Maya "collapse" occurred is still disputed by archaeologists, although commonly accepted reasons include natural catastrophes (such as earthquakes or hurricanes), overpopulation and food shortages, foreign invasions, and ecological degradation accompanying the shift from swidden to more intensive forms of agriculture (Sharer 1994:340–348). It is no longer thought to be the case that the southern Maya totally collapsed while the northern Maya states endured for several hundred more years. Recent research suggests that some smaller southern lowland states may have survived the collapse while most of the northern Maya urban areas were abandoned less than a century after most of the southern states had disappeared.

Overarching state polities with centralized political control did not develop in the Yucatán peninsula or the Maya highlands during the Horizon period. When the Spaniards began their conquest of the Maya in 1529, they confronted more than a dozen warring polities or city-states, sometimes organized into loose confederations. As will become clearer in the next chapter, this factionalism and absence of overarching centralized political control paradoxically worked *against* the Spanish invaders.

PHOTO 3.3   *Temples surround an acropolis at a set of Mayan ruins within the Guatemalan jungle. Tikal, Guatemala.*

The Inca and Aztec States

The Inca and Aztec states that confronted the European conquerors were the most recent chapter—a culmination—of a long process of state formation that resulted in huge, densely populated, ethnically and linguistically diverse, and highly stratified state societies. The legacy of this history of state-building efforts spanning thousands of years prior to the European Conquest is still very much alive, as both regions currently exhibit the highest number and concentration of indigenous peoples, languages, and cultures in all Latin America. This section sketches some common characteristics of these two regions and states prior to the European Conquest, provides an overview of the state of affairs in the Andes and Mesoamerica during the fourteenth and fifteenth centuries, and finally outlines the dynamics of state expansion just prior to the European arrival.

The Andean and Mesoamerican Highlands: Fourteenth and Fifteenth Centuries

In the fourteenth and fifteenth centuries, the demise of powerful regional states during the mid- to late Horizon period created a power vacuum in the Andean and Mesoamerican highlands, resulting in intense competition and conflict among dozens of chiefdoms. These densely populated and conflict-ridden regions were marked by the presence of intensive and highly complex agricultural practices, such as hillside terracing, raised fields, and irrigated agriculture in the Andes, and, in the Valley of Mexico, the construction of chinampas.

There was also a great deal of linguistic and cultural diversity—so much so that there might in fact have been hundreds of ethnic groups or cultures throughout the Andean and Mesoamerican highlands, as well as in the adjoining lowlands and coastal areas. For example, on the eve of the European Conquest, there were at least three major language families spoken in the Andean highlands—Quechua, Aymara, and Puquina—as well as multiple languages and dialects within each. And it is almost certain that other languages were spoken by members of the numerous chiefdom polities who inhabited the coastal areas.

Most members of Andean and Mesoamerican ethnic polities and chiefdoms lived in small rural, agriculturally-oriented communities. The core social unit in the Andes was the *ayllu* and in Mesoamerica the *calpulli*—landholding groups or corporations comprised of individuals related through kinship, with a strong sense of self-identity. Within these groups or corporations, the greater part of local level politics, culture, and social relations were played out. Ayllus and calpulli also had their own pantheon of supernatural deities that populated the natural landscape, took care of households and communities, and with whom human beings engaged in ongoing social relationships (for the Andes see Stern 1982:3–26; Spalding 1984:27–34; for Mesoamerica see Conrad and Demarest 1984:22–25). Many Andean ayllus and Mesoamerican calpulli survived the aftermath of the Conquest and have endured until the present day. The Quechua-speaking Incas and Nahuatl-speaking Aztecs achieved rule over these enormous, rugged, ethnically and politically diverse, and highly conflictive landscapes in less than one hundred years.

The Inca and Aztec Expansions

What is known about the social, cultural, and political worlds of the Andes and Mesoamerica a century prior to the European Conquest stems mainly from ethnohistorical sources. These are detailed histories and documents compiled by both Spaniards and elite members of indigenous societies during the first three to four decades after the Conquest. Although the proper interpretation or "reading" of these sources is contingent on understanding why they were produced in the first place—and by whom and for whom—these testimonies have nevertheless yielded detailed insights into the culture and social organization of the Andean and Mesoamerican landscapes of more than 500 years ago (Salomon 1999). These sources have also formed the core of research into how Andeans and Mesoamericans (and other Latin American and Caribbean peoples) fared after the Conquest and during the colonial period (see Chapter 4).

The resemblance between the Inca and Aztec expansions is remarkable (Conrad and Demarest 1984; Richardson 1994; Weaver 1993). Both, for example, quickly expanded and reached their zenith in less than one hundred years. Ethnohistorical sources suggest that by the late 1300s, the Incas were but a small ethnic polity or chiefdom among many others in the Peruvian highlands near Cuzco. In 1438, they began to successfully subdue their neighbors, and in four successive waves ending in 1525 during the reign of (Inca) Huayna Capac, imperial armies extended Inca control from southern Colombia to the Maule river in southern Chile, between the eastern flanks of the Andes to the Pacific coast. This vast territory—more than 2,000 miles from north to south—exceeded the Roman Empire in length, and without a doubt was the largest and most complex empire that emerged in the Americas.

PHOTO 3.4   *The ancient fortress city of Machu Picchu below a range of towering Andes Mountains in Peru.*

The magnificent site of Machu Picchu in Peru (see Photo 3.4), originally thought to be one of many Inca fortifications along the eastern Andes, is now believed to have been a sort of "vacation retreat" for Inca royalty (Wilford 2003).

The Aztecs were also quite successful. By the late 1300s, the Mexica (one of three ethnic groups or polities who would be collectively called the "Aztecs") were one of many competing chiefdoms or city-states in the Valley of Mexico, as well as subjects of a more powerful neighboring polity. In alliance with two other polities, the Triple Alliance (i.e., Aztecs) began in 1428 to spread out from Tenochtlán, the Mexica capital, in what is now the center of modern-day Mexico City. Under six rulers (*tlatoani*), the Aztecs succeeded by 1520 during the reign of Mochtezuma II to extend their reach through central and southern Mexico, and some northern portions of Central America.

Thus, in less than one hundred years the Incas and Aztecs succeeded in forging their empires. Yet, how were they able to do so? How were the Incas and Aztecs—certainly not the most powerful polities in the Cuzco region of the Peruvian highlands and the Valley of Mexico—able to successfully achieve varying levels of control over most of the Andes and Mexico in a short time and against seemingly overwhelming odds? The bottom-line answer to these questions is that the Incas and Aztecs used multiple strategies to extend their rule, depending on the military, organizational, and political strength of their opponents (Guilmartin 1991; Hemming 1970; Hassig 1994; Clendinnen 1987).

Although it would be a mistake to think that force alone was the key to imperial success, military campaigns proved crucial when opponents refused to surrender. Many polities or ethnic groups (such as the Chimú on the Peruvian coast) were destroyed in protracted battles while many others succumbed after a few skirmishes. Yet, there were limits to military force. The Incas were unable to extend their reach far beyond the foothills of the eastern Andes and dominate the smaller and more mobile societies there, an array of still-autonomous chiefdoms in northern Ecuador and southern Colombia kept imperial troops at bay, and most of the Mapuche (Araucanian) peoples in southern Chile never succumbed to Inca rule.

The Aztecs confronted similar difficulties. For example, they were unable to extend their reach deep into the northern arid plateau (the Mesa Central), which was populated by seminomadic, foraging peoples, whom the Aztecs called barbarians (*teochichimeca*). Likewise, Aztec armies were incapable of militarily subduing at least six major ethnic polities, such as the well-known Tlaxcalans, who provided the Spaniards with the bulk of native troops who allied themselves with the invaders during the Conquest.

Far more effective than military force was the ability of Incas and Aztecs to establish alliances with and indirect rule over many potentially competing ethnic polities. The possibility of doing so was partly contingent on persuading opponents that they would fare poorly in open combat, and that it would be in their best interest to submit to imperial rule. Incas and Aztecs also pursued a divide-and-rule strategy, pitting their neighbors against each other and allying themselves with one party or the other. These strategies were extremely advantageous to the expanding Incas and Aztecs. They largely respected the territorial integrity of those who agreed to submit, and they altered the subsumed political and economic organization as little as possible. In turn, imperial overseers demanded tribute—especially labor and crops—which was crucial for the success of imperial expansion. Indeed, Inca and Aztec armies were largely comprised of either members of defeated polities or of those that had "voluntarily" agreed to submit to imperial rule.

Yet, and as will become clearer in the following chapter, the Incas and Aztecs were far from successful in consolidating their rule over the numerous ethnic polities within their empires. Both Inca and Aztec empires consisted of an unstable, fluctuating mosaic of areas, in which effective imperial control was always tenuous—there was no China-style "Great Wall." These were inherently unstable imperial polities, constantly expanding, often engaged in outright warfare, and continuously putting down rebellions by conquered groups. Such a state of affairs worked amazingly well for the Spanish conquerors.

What propelled the Incas and Aztecs to almost literally overrun the Andes and Mesoamerica? Why did they do that? The question of why the Incas and Aztecs expanded is very much linked to understanding which processes have spurred the development of social complexity, a search that many archaeologists have been engaged in for decades. Most agree that social complexity—including the eventual rise of state societies—is the outcome of a combination of environmental, technological, and demographic conditions.

Yet, one rather different yet related argument has been proposed by Conrad and Demarest, who suggest that by paying too much attention to environment, technology, and demography, archaeologists have overlooked the central role that religious ideas or ideology played in enabling the Aztecs and Incas to transform themselves into "the most efficient war machines in New World prehistory" (1984:2). In the highly conflictive world of the thirteenth and fourteenth centuries, the Aztecs and Incas were able to draw on some broad social and cultural features of Mesoamerican and Andean societies, and subsequently drastically alter them to forge an **imperial religious cult,** or state religion, that provided them with the motivation and legitimacy to expand their boundaries.

Mesoamerican religion pivoted around two major dimensions. One was devotion to an array of amorphous deities associated with specific features of the landscape, and with almost humanlike desires and needs. These were capricious beings who took care of their mortal devotees if reciprocated with offerings, but who could wreck havoc on them if they did not. The second, related dimension was human sacrifice, "one of the most ancient aspects of Mesoamerican culture" (Conrad and Demarest 1984:19). The manipulation of these two expressions of Mesoamerican religious thought proved crucial to the Aztecs' expansion. One major deity—Huitzilopochtli—originally a protector and the patron of Mesoamerican warriors, was elevated to the centerpiece of the religious pantheon and identified with the Sun. Likewise, human sacrifice, originally a broad-based belief, was transformed into Huitzilopochtli's basic need. The result was that Aztec rulers—by this time Aztecs had become sharply differentiated into elites and commoners—convinced themselves and others that Huitzilopochtli continuously demanded human sacrifice (and ritualized cannibalism), lest destruction come among them. This

> imperial cosmology held that the Mexica must relentlessly take captives in warfare and sacrifice them; the spiritual strength of the sacrificed enemy warriors would strengthen the sun and stave off its inevitable destruction by the forces of darkness. Thus it was specifically the Mexicas' sacred duty to pursue a course of endless warfare, conquest, and sacrifice to preserve the universe from the daily threat of annihilation. (Conrad and Demarest 1984:38)

Such a "divine quest" (Conrad and Demarest 1984:42) also arose in the Andes, where an astonishingly analogous process of refashioning basic features of pan-Andean religious life to the benefit of imperial expansion also took place. Like in Mesoamerica, the Andean supernatural world was populated by a host of needy humanlike beings who required devotion and offerings in exchange for looking after the welfare of the human world by, for example, insuring good harvests. The failure to abide by such reciprocal relationships could quickly translate into unfortunate and potentially tragic events. (The need to engage in ongoing and beneficial reciprocal relationships with supernatural beings is still a basic dimension of Andean and Mesoamerican religious thought [see Chapter 7]). Unlike in Mesoamerica, human sacrifice was only rarely practiced in the Andes and may have emerged late during Inca imperial times. Far more significant was the practice of ancestor worship—a pan-Andean religious tradition with deep historical roots that centered on the cult of dead ancestors (Conrad and Demarest 1984:89–94; Salomon 1995).

Among the Incas, the deeply rooted institution of ancestor worship intersected with other religious and political-economic changes that enormously enhanced the empire's imperial designs. One was the transformation of Inca rulers into divine personages descended from the Sun—one of the Incas' most important deities. (The Inca queen—the *Qolla*—was said to be descended from the Moon.) The other important change, according to Conrad and Demarest, was the appearance among early Andean states of split inheritance, whereby political power was transmitted to one heir while the personal wealth of former rulers was passed on to his descendants:

> By this term [split inheritance] we mean a mode of bequeathal based on two dichotomies: state versus personal wealth and principal versus secondary heirs.

In a fully developed pattern of split inheritance one principal heir receives the governmental position, plus the attendant rights and duties, of a deceased functionary. The latter's personal possessions and sources of income are assigned to his other descendants as a corporate group. These secondary heirs are not granted actual ownership of a dead man's estate. Instead, his holdings remain his own, and his secondary heirs serve as trustees for him. (1984:91)

By linking split inheritance to the widespread Andean notion of ancestor worship—and thereby assigning the personal wealth of dead Inca rulers (who nevertheless continued to demand devotion, tribute, and offerings via their private estates) to their kinsmen organized into royal corporations—Inca elites set up the ideological conditions of relentless state expansion:

The elaboration of royal mummy worship was a minor cultural change, a slight reworking of traditional Inca institutions. However, application of split inheritance to the royal estates produced a vast increase in the material demands of ancestor worship. The local ayllu could support all of its ancestors by reserving a small portion of its fields for them, but this inexpensive principle of "one for all" would not do for imperial leaders. If a deceased ruler's lands were tied up in maintaining him, and if his successor could inherit none of them, then each emperor would have to obtain his own estates. (Conrad and Demarest 1984:121; but see Paulsen 1981 for a dissenting perspective)

Controversies: The Peopling of the Americas

The peopling of Latin America and the Caribbean—when and how the North and South American continents were first inhabited and by whom—has been hotly contested by archaeologists for decades. Dozens of monographs, journal contributions, and Internet sites have appeared in recent years on "Archaeology's Greatest Mystery" (Adovasio 2002; see also Fagan 2000). This section focuses on four related issues that archaeologists have centered their attention on: (1) the mode of entry into the Americas, (2) how initial migrants made their way to different parts of Latin America, (3) the dates or periods of entry and (4) key characteristics of the initial migrants (i.e., what kinds of people were they?).

   1. *Mode of entry into the Americas.* Most archaeologists have believed for decades that the initial peopling of the North American continent occurred through a land connection—a land bridge—between Siberia and Alaska, and that therefore the first migrants to the Americas originated in northern Asia/Siberia. This land connection across the Bering Straight between Siberia and Alaska/North America was probably already in place at least 50,000 and perhaps 75,000 years ago during periods of intense glaciations, which had the effect of lowering the sea levels and thus exposing dry land that is currently hundreds of feet below present sea levels. This bridge—a huge landmass that was perhaps 500 miles wide and 1,000 miles from north to south, also called Beringia—opened and closed three or four times during the ebb and flow of glaciers, each time for several thousand years. For at least the past 12,000 years, Beringia has been covered by the sea (Lavallée 2000:58; Adovasio 2002:44–48). Despite the importance often attached to Beringia as a conduit facilitating entry into the Americas, it bears noting that even in contemporary times, indigenous groups in this area can transverse the Bering Straight with various types of boats even when the sea freezes. This suggests the possibility that many initial migrants may not have needed such a land bridge at all.

An alternative theory for the initial peopling of the Americas has initial migrants from Asia entering North America via the Pacific coastline, in the vicinity of what is now British Columbia and the Aleutian Islands (Lavallée 2000:59–60). According to Lynch (1999:189), this idea, although not totally implausible, has been substantiated by little solid evidence. Others entertain the possibility of an Atlantic crossing to North America, that is, that "people also could have migrated by boat along the edges of ice sheets extending from northwest Europe to the Atlantic side of North America. . . . the possibility of such a crossing requires attention" (Dillehay 2000:68). Although it is possible that some migrants may have arrived in the Americas via this route, there is negligible archaeological evidence for this hypothesis, largely because the ancient coastlines are today submerged below hundreds of feet of water. As Meltzer notes, this means that the hypothesis of coastal migratory routes is "safely untestable" (1995:38). Dixon (2000) argues for the peopling of North America through sea migration routes.

A related controversy has to do with whether the initial peopling took place in one migratory wave, or whether several successive migrations (with people coming from different parts of Asia) occurred. Linguistic, genetic, and dental research (e.g., the reconstruction of aboriginal North and South American languages and attempts to trace linguistic affinities to Asian languages; research on mitochondrial DNA [passed down only from mothers to daughters], and studies of dental morphology) have been used in this debate but have yielded different interpretations and results (Lynch 1999:213–220; Lavallée 2000:64–67; Dillehay 2000:2–3). Although archaeologists are still divided on this issue, the leading interpretation appears to be that the vast majority of Native Americans are linguistically and genetically related to northern Asian/Siberian peoples.

2. *How did migrants get to different parts of the Americas?* The fact that most migrants may have made their way into the North American continent by crossing Beringia does not necessarily mean that the first peoples to Mesoamerica, and Central and South America made their way south through a straight, land-based trajectory across the North American continent. Some archaeologists suggest that many migrants opted for moving south through the coastlines/coastal areas, which would have presented fewer physical barriers to movement, and which would have allowed them the opportunity to exploit rich maritime resources, moving "southward along the Pacific shelf and, later, perhaps along the Caribbean and Atlantic shelves as well" (Dillehay 2000:67). The fact that some of the "earliest, well-documented human traces" are found along South America's Pacific coast (Roosevelt 1999:272; see also Zietilin and Zietilin 2000:52–53; Dillehay 2000:63) lends some credence to this theory. Definitive conclusions and solid evidence are nonetheless still lacking.

3. *Dates or periods of arrival.* When the peopling of the North and South American continents took place is the subject of some of the fiercest debates in archaeology, and is partially related to the previously mentioned issue of the means through which the first migrants made their way into North and South America. On this issue, archaeologists fall into two camps: those who favor the theory that the first wave of humans entered the Americas perhaps tens of thousands of years ago, and those who claim that the initial entry into the Americas could not have taken place much before 12,000 to 13,000 years ago. (Most archaeologists who believe in far earlier dates advocate a coastal sidestepping of the Bering land bridge, as mentioned previously.)

Some archaeologists believe that the strongest case for an earlier (i.e., prior to 12,000 years ago) peopling of the Americas is based on the discovery of primarily stone (and presumably human-made) artifacts from South America, many of which have been dated much earlier (Lavallée 2000:42). One picture that emerges from the retrieval of earlier remains is that "Much cultural diversity existed throughout the Americas, but especially in South America, by 11,000 years ago" (Dillehay 2000:2–3), and the related idea that this diversity would have taken at least several thousand years more to fully coalesce. Further, since "the oldest generally accepted sites in North and South America are virtually contemporaneous," to advocate against a much earlier peopling means making the argument that the first migrants "must have traversed the hemisphere in a matter of centuries" (Meltzer 1995:26; see also Scheinsohn 2003:345). Unless the argument is accepted that those who reached southern South America 12,000 years ago did so through the coastlines or came from the Pacific or Europe (as discussed previously), it "strains credulity," Adovasio states (2002:196), that they could have traveled 10,000 miles in just several hundred years. Dillehay, one of the most vocal proponents for a much earlier peopling of the Americas, claims that humans could have entered the New World as early as 50,000 years ago (2000:67; Lavallée 2000), and Mesoamerican archaeologists Zietilin and Zietilin (2000:53) claim "In principle there is no reason why the earliest human migrations from northeastern Asia could not have occurred 40,000 to 60,000 years ago." Nevertheless, Zietilin and Zietilin quickly and clearly point out that "Claims for New World human occupation dating before 35,000–40,000 years ago remain highly speculative" (2000:55)—a view staunchly defended by many other archaeologists (Meltzer 1995).

Thomas Lynch is an outspoken advocate of the view that the peopling of the Americas could not have taken place a lot earlier than 13,000 years ago for, he maintains, there "is no compelling evidence of human occupation" anywhere in the Americas prior to this period (1999:191). His claim is based on four arguments. First, he is not convinced of the reliability of archaeological remains/sites dated tens of thousands of years ago, arguing that the excavations were done at sites in which a conflation of the remains of different cultures had occurred (i.e., that the original stratigraphic levels had been disrupted). Second, he argues that the artifacts (e.g., stone tools) dated prior to 12,000 years are not really human artifacts at all but were produced by natural process, such as weathering. More damaging still to those advocating a much earlier entry, his third claim, is that none of the earlier dated sites have yielded skeletal remains older than 12,000 years. Finally, dental, genetic, and linguistic evidence points to a later entry period (Lynch 1999:191–201).

Monte Verde in south-central Chile (near the Maule river) is extremely important because for most archaeologists it remains the earliest and most securely and extensively dated archaeological site in the Western Hemisphere (Meltzer et al. 1997). The site appears to have been occupied by a small band that had set up camp "on prime real estate, a day's walk or two from both the coast and the foothills of the [Andean] mountains" (Adovasio 2002:214). Excavations at Monte Verde yielded an impressive array of vestiges—plant and mastodon remains, stone tools, wooden spikes, and even footprints—most of which have been radio carbon dated to about 13,000 years. These dates "*might* imply an arrival in Beringia prior to 20,000 [years ago]" (Meltzer 1995:37; emphasis added).

   4. _Who (what kinds of people) were they?_ There is little doubt that the first inhabitants of the Americas were members of small, egalitarian band societies. For decades, the dominant story line was that these initial migrants who crossed the Bering land bridge were highly specialized big-game hunters following herds of big (and now largely extinct) game animals into North America. The discovery of archaeological sites in central North America yielding stone projectile points in association with remains of large mammals—indicative of the Clovis and Folsom cultures—lent credence to this theory, so much so that **big game specialization** (a lifestyle centered on the hunting of large mammals) was seen as the "hallmark" of this Paleo-Indian phase (Meggers 1979:13). This view is no longer widely accepted, for, as an anonymous reviewer of this text noted:

> Because kill sites are much easier to find than Paleoindian camps, our interpretation of their life way was skewed toward big game for many years. New data from Paleoindian camp contexts, however, suggest that, while limited by the sparse resources in the Ice Age environment, Paleoindians subsisted on a relatively wide range of flora and fauna. Like many hunting and collecting cultures, they made the most of what their environment offered . . . In more temperate/tropical zones, like much of Latin America, Paleoindians practiced a much more conventional hunting and gathering life way.

Adovasio agrees, emphasizing that

> today we know that at the time Clovis points appeared in North America, people in South America were already practicing many lifeways. Some chiefly hunted camelids (guanacos and llamas) in the Andean highlands, while others chased horses and other herbivores on the pampas and savannas of Argentina. Others still lived chiefly on shellfish and other marine foods along the coasts . . . Some people . . . did actively hunt Pleistocene megafauna, but it is highly unlikely that they could have survived only on those efforts without bagging smaller game and spending much time gathering fruit, nuts, and other plant foods. (2002:197–198)

Further, there might have been other reasons for the apparent bias toward big game hunting other than the higher likelihood of uncovering big game kill sites. Conkey and Gero suggest that deeply entrenched gender biases also played an important role, for "the exclusion of women from Paleoindian research has permitted a dominant paradigm to persist that focuses exclusively on hunting as the essential and definitional activity of early colonizers of the American continent" (1997:427).

Summary

Over the course of at least 12,000 years, human groups evolved from small, egalitarian, highly mobile, band societies subsisting through hunting and gathering, to more complex, stratified, and sedentary tribal, chiefdom, and state-level societies. These transformations took place through four partly overlapping phases: Paleo-Indian, Archaic, Formative, and Horizon. The culmination of this process of economic, and political complexity was the rise of the Inca and Aztec empires in the Andes and Mesoamerica less than one hundred years prior to the European Conquest.

When and through which routes the peopling of the Americas occurred is still the subject of considerable disagreement. Some archaeologists believe that the first migrants to North and South America crossed the Bering land bridge no more than 12,000 years ago and traveled south over land. Others think that the initial peopling occurred tens of thousands of years earlier, with many bypassing the Bering land connection, favoring instead a southern crossing along the Pacific coastlines.

ISSUES AND QUESTIONS

1. *Emergence of Complex Societies.* What do archaeologists and cultural anthropologists have in mind when they refer to "complex" societies? What are some of the most distinctive traits of the four phases into which the emergence or development of social complexity has been divided?

2. *Inca and Aztec Expansions.* What political, economic, or cultural conditions or strategies enabled Incas and Aztecs to expand their states so quickly and against so many enemies? Were they successful? How might answers to these questions also be relevant for understanding some of the consequences or legacies of the European Conquest?

3. *The Peopling of the Americas.* What are the major points of contention in this debate? Why is this debate important at all, and how might it explain how archaeologists go about generating and substantiating hypotheses?

KEY TERMS AND CONCEPTS

Archaic period   p. 55
Bands   p. 50
Big game specialization   p. 73
Chiefdoms   p. 51
Chinampas   p. 64
Domestication   p. 51
Egalitarian societies   p. 51
Ethnographic analogy   p. 60
Foraging subsistence mode   p. 50
Formative period   p. 61
Geographical bias   p. 57

Horizon period   p. 63
Imperial religious cult   p. 68
Maritime coastal adaptation   p. 53
Matrilineal descent   p. 61
Paleo-Indian period   p. 53
Prehistory   p. 52
Primary state formation   p. 58
Societal or cultural complexity   p. 50
States   p. 52
Tribes   p. 51

E N D N O T E

1. Archaeologists have several ways of alluding to past time periods: years ago; years before the present; B.C. (before [Jesus] Christ); B.P. (before the present); A.D. (present); B.C.E. (before Christian era, equivalent to B.C.); and C.E. (Christian era, similar to A.D.). For the sake of consistency and clarity, whenever possible (and with the exception of direct quotes), these conventions have been converted into years ago.

CHAPTER

4

Conquest, Colonialism, and Resistance

This chapter turns to the Spanish and Portuguese conquests of the sixteenth century and their immediate consequences. It first examines how so few Europeans rapidly undermined most organized resistance and subsequently explores the widespread ramifications of the exchange of plants and animals between the New World and Europe. Attention then shifts to the colonial period to understand how Europeans attempted to consolidate their rule, and ways that Latin American and Caribbean peoples actively resisted the colonial order. Emphasis is placed on the emergence of new societies within the context of colonial rule (ethnogenesis) and some of the lasting political, economic, social, and cultural legacies of European colonialism. The final section focuses on the Quincentennial controversy and how indigenous peoples have taken an active role in redefining the events of 1492.

The European Conquest

For Europeans and Latin American indigenous peoples alike, the fifteenth and sixteenth centuries were momentous milestones in their historical destinies. For Europeans, these centuries constituted the crucial age of exploration and conquest, vital for the kingdoms that spearheaded this undertaking and would later be called Spain and Portugal. For Latin American indigenous peoples, the encounter with and conquest by Europeans meant a radical, generally unwelcome, and profound transformation of their ways of life.

Voyages, Exploration, and Expeditions

On October 12, 1492, Christopher Columbus, sailing in search of a route from Europe to Asia, landed in what is now the Bahamas in the Caribbean. During this and three subsequent voyages, he claimed the New World for Ferdinand and Isabel of the kingdoms of Aragón and Castile, who had sponsored his voyage. In the following two decades, successive expeditions of Spanish and Portuguese explorers laid claim to and conquered what would later be known as the New World. (For excellent maps of the Spanish and Portuguese expeditions, see Lombardi et al. 1983:21–27.)

Beginning in 1508 (after Christopher Columbus' last 1502–1504 voyage), more than a dozen Spanish expeditions landed in the Caribbean, the main staging ground from which the conquest of Mexico, Mesoamerica, and South America was launched. In their initial forays into the Greater Antilles, Spaniards easily overwhelmed the small, Arawak-speaking Taíno chiefdoms in Cuba, Hispaniola, and Puerto Rico. (Indigenous societies in the Greater Antilles disappeared within the first three decades of the Conquest, while others in the Lesser Antilles fiercely resisted European encroachments for at least another two centuries.) After securing control, especially along the coastlines, and founding the key port cities of Havana and Santiago de Cuba (in what is now Cuba), Santo Domingo (present-day Dominican Republic), and San Juan (today's Puerto Rico), Spaniards fanned out, in successive and overlapping waves, in four major directions (Burkhart and Gasco 1996b; Clendinnen 1987:1–19; Hulme 1986:13–44; Elliott 1987).

One route was toward the coastal areas of what is now Belize and Guatemala, then skirting the Yucatán peninsula, and finally entering the Gulf of Mexico and establishing a beachhead in what is now Vera Cruz, Mexico. From these strategic points, the Cortés (also spelled Cortéz), Díaz del Castillo, and Córdoba expeditions first subdued the Aztec empire, and only decades later, after protracted struggles, most of the Maya city-states, along with perhaps dozens of smaller ethnic polities. A second general course led Spaniards to Central America (specifically to Panama, near the present-day border with Colombia). From there, smaller groups traveled west, into what is now Costa Rica and parts of Nicaragua. Much larger expeditions, such as those spearheaded by Francisco Pizarro, who confronted the Incas in 1532, traveled south/southeast, with offshoots eventually reaching southern Chile a few years later. A third wave of Spanish expeditions—the most prominent led by Jiménez de Quesada—entered South America through the northern Orinoco river system and vanquished the Chibcha chiefdoms in northern Colombia and Venezuela. The fourth and final general direction of Spanish expeditions was through the Atlantic, entering South America through and establishing the port city of Buenos Aires. From there, the Spaniards made their way south along the coast to the southernmost tip of the continent, although they did not venture far into the interior of the Pampas and Patagonia. (The 1519–1521 expedition by Magellan transversed the straights between Tierra del Fuego and the southern tip of the South American continent and then ventured into the Pacific.) From Buenos Aires, other groups traveled north—again via the major rivers—into Paraguay and southeastern Bolivia.

Meanwhile, the Portuguese were also busy laying claim to South America. Because of the Treaty of Tordesillas, they were restricted to lands in the New World up to 45 degrees longitude, that is, the easternmost sections of present-day Brazil. Between 1500 and 1544, Portuguese expeditions landed along and explored the Brazilian coastlines, eventually establishing important port towns such as Salvador and Río de Janeiro. From these, Portuguese explorers and missionaries moved into the Amazon Basin and its tributaries during the next one hundred years (Johnson 1987; Schwartz 1987).

Although Spain and Portugal eventually claimed most of Latin America and the Caribbean, they were not without serious rivals. Other European states—England, France, and Holland—also fiercely competed with Spaniards and Portuguese in the New World, especially over the Caribbean islands and the northern coastlines of Central and South America. Indeed, for more than two centuries after Columbus' arrival, the Caribbean region was intensely contested, particularly after the onset of the African slave trade and the rise of sugar as a major world commodity. Not one single European colonial power managed to establish either a political or economic monopoly over this region, so that by the end of the eighteenth century, the Caribbean islands and the Atlantic coastlines of Central and South America were shared among Spanish, Portuguese, English, French, and Dutch colonists. Important British colonies included Barbados, Jamaica, and Belize (formerly British Honduras) and, in the Lesser Antilles, Trinidad and Tobago. France secured control over strategic colonies such as Saint-Domingue (known as Haiti after its independence in 1804), Martinique, Guadeloupe, and French Guiana. And Holland secured a foothold in Suriname and some of the Lesser Antilles islands. This changing kaleidoscope of colonial control eventually resulted in a complex linguistic and cultural mosaic throughout most of the Caribbean region (Horowitz 1971a; Mintz and Price 1985; Mintz 1989; Trouillot 1992).

How Did (and Could) It Happen?

By 1580, Spaniards had colonized and secured tenuous indirect rule over vast stretches of the Caribbean, Mesoamerica, the Andes, northern South America, parts of Amazonia (especially along the major river systems), and the southern coastlines of Chile and Argentina. These enormous lands were inhabited by hundreds of societies, from small-scale foragers to huge, stratified empires, ranging in population from a few hundred to several million.

For decades after the arrival of the first Europeans, numerous indigenous peoples often retreated into hard-to-reach areas (such as the Lesser Antilles, the Pampas and Patagonia, and the Amazon Basin), thereby remaining outside the effective reach of Spaniards or Portuguese. Indeed, most indigenous societies in southern Chile and Argentina mounted such effective resistance to European advances that they were finally conquered (and forcibly placed into reservations) only in the nineteenth century (Paddon 1957; Faron 1968). Further, significant pockets of armed resistance (e.g., the Lesser Antilles, and among some Incas and Mayas) would continue for many years. Yet, by and large, Spaniards and Portuguese had effectively quelled most organized, large-scale resistance to the Conquest. More importantly, by the mid 1530s, Spaniards had smashed the two most important military threats confronting them: the mighty Inca and Aztec empires.

Although colonial rule would be repeatedly challenged along a number of fronts, the European Conquest was a monumental accomplishment, an unparalleled feat for the time. How did this happen? How were the Spaniards and, to a lesser extent, the Portuguese, able to so quickly carry out the Conquest? How were Spanish expeditions, often numbering no more than several hundred, able to defeat their Inca, Aztec, and Maya enemies who, if we are to believe the Conquest chronicles written by Spaniards, mustered tens of thousands of warriors against them? And what does all this tell us about the societies that resisted the European invaders?

At least four interrelated factors enabled the tiny Spanish expeditions to quickly overwhelm the Incas and Aztecs (how and why some Lowland Mayas were able to more effectively resist the Spanish invaders is discussed later). (1) lack of political consolidation of indigenous states; (2) tactical and military advantages; (3) cultural differences; and (4) disease (on the conquest of the Incas, see Hemming 1970 and Guilmartin 1991; on the Aztecs, see Todorov 1984; Cline 2000; Hassig 1994; on the Maya, see Clendinnen 1987; Sharer 1994:730-748; Collier et al. 1982 compare the similarities and differences between the Inca and Aztec states.)

1. *Lack of political consolidation of indigenous states.* Neither the Inca or Aztec states had achieved a significant degree of political consolidation prior to 1492. Both were politically fragile, continuously engaged in expanding their borders, subduing neighboring polities, and putting down rebellions. The Inca and Aztec rulers and elites had not managed to achieve **hegemony** over their territories—that is, they had not instilled consent, allegiance, and a sense of legitimacy in most of their subjects. As a result, their rule was constantly challenged throughout vast reaches of their empires. (See Williams 1977:108–114; Eagleton 1991:112–116; Crehan 2002 for different interpretations of this concept that is often associated with Antonio Gramsci.)

In 1531, Francisco Pizarro landed in Tumbes, on Peru's Pacific coast with fewer than 200 Spaniards. He then proceeded south through the western Andes. At that time, the Incas were especially vulnerable, having just emerged from a civil war between the two sons and contenders of the Inca throne, Huáscar and Atahualpa. The immediate spur of this conflict was the sudden death of the reigning monarch (Inca) Huayna Capac, who probably died from a European-introduced disease, and the lack of institutionalized means of succession in the absence of a living monarch.

The Spaniards had extraordinarily good luck in arriving at the end of this civil war, which bitterly divided Inca royal families and drew into the conflict many non-Inca peoples. Indeed, it was through non-Inca subjects that Pizarro received firsthand information about the conflict that ravaged the Inca state, and that the victorious Atahualpa was camped in nearby Cajamarca. Unopposed, Pizarro and his party proceeded to Cajamarca, where they roused Atahualpa and many of his nobles into a walled compound, seized Atahualpa, and slaughtered thousands of nobles and royal family members. Because Atahualpa was considered divine (he was thought to be a direct descendant of the Sun, a key Inca deity) and to be the embodiment of the power and moral authority of the state, his capture essentially paralyzed the state apparatus. For months, Pizarro ruled the empire through Atahualpa, despite the fact that the veteran Inca army, under the command of the feared Rumi Ñahui (Quechua for "eye of stone"), was camped only a few miles away. Pizarro later ordered the execution of Atahualpa, but not before receiving vast amounts of gold from all corners of the empire.

Pizarro then fought his way south to Cuzco, the Incas and their allies unable to stem the Spanish advance. He recruited allies from the ethnic groups who had opposed Inca rule or who had sided with the defeated Huáscar, and who therefore were bitter enemies of Atahualpa. Pizarro's indigenous allies provided supplies, intelligence reports, and thousands of soldiers. Further, Inca royal families were deeply divided (some Incas who had sided with Huáscar during the civil war allied themselves with Pizarro), and many of royal descent had died in this war. Thus, as an ethnic group the Incas were unable to muster a cohesive stand against the small group of Spaniards and their allies. In November 1533, just months after the death of Atahualpa, Pizarro lay siege to and captured Cuzco. Although some Incas retreated and held out in Vilcabamba, in the eastern Andes, for another forty years (see Hemming 1970), the capture of Cuzco effectively signaled the final defeat of the Inca state.

The conquest of the Aztec empire bore an uncanny resemblance to the Inca experience—and likewise favored the Spaniards. Cortés lands in Vera Cruz in April of 1519 and reaches Tenochtitlán, the Aztec capital, unopposed, just as Pizarro had encountered little resistance enroute to Cajamarca. Why the Aztec ruler Mochtezuma (also spelled Montezuma) did not immediately attack Cortés has been the subject of a great deal of speculation; one theory is that Cortés was viewed as an incarnation of Quetzalcoatl, the Serpent God, who, according to Aztec religious belief, would return from an eastward direction (Cline 2000:117). As discussed later in this section, other facets of Aztec culture might have played a role.

Arranging a meeting with Mochtezuma, Cortés then entrapped the leader and ruled the empire through him. After a massacre of thousands of Aztec nobles and royalty, and the death of Mochtezuma (he was probably killed by Pizarro), the Aztecs rose up and drove the Spaniards out of Tenochitlán. By May of 1521, Cortés regrouped and, with the assistance of tens of thousands of Tlaxcalan warriors (bitter enemies of the Aztecs), he lay siege to Tenochitlán. Politically divided and weakened, and facing rebellions by ethnic subjects while at the same time confronting the Spaniards and their indigenous allies, the Aztecs surrendered three months later.

2. *Tactical and military advantages.* In addition to taking advantage of political divisions within the Inca and Aztec states, and of support they received from countless indigenous allies, Spaniards also enjoyed superior tactical and military advantages (Guilmartin 1991). These included:

a. *Horses.* Horses provided crucial advantages in striking power, shock effect, and speed. Unknown to native societies, horses were bigger and more powerful than native Andean camelids and, at any rate, the latter were used as pack animals and never in waging war. (There were no Mesoamerican equivalents to the Andean camelids.) In commenting on the defeat of the Quiché Maya in present-day Highland Guatemala by vastly outnumbered Spaniards, Lovell (1992a:59) states that "The physical and psychological impact of cavalry on a people who had never before seen a horse and its rider in action was as devastating as the material superiority of steel and firearms over the bow and arrow." Incas and Aztecs may have felt similar awe at the sight of horses, which in any event were especially effective in providing Spaniards with the ability to strike harder, and more swiftly, and to reach further with the sword against foot soldiers. A preferred Inca and Aztec battlefield tactic—fighting in open, massed formations—proved especially vulnerable to cavalry charges by armored horsemen. The Incas did not master the art of the bow and arrow, which might have proved effective against cavalry, and Aztec weapons proved ineffective against Spanish armor.

b. *Superiority of Spanish weapons and technology.* Spaniards also enjoyed better weapons and technology of war, especially steel weapons such as long pikes and razor sharp swords. Pikes enabled Spaniards to strike at Incas and Aztecs almost at will, especially at close range. The Spanish double-edged sword in particular was extraordinarily lethal. For example, Inca weapons such as stone tipped axes and slings were crushing and not cutting or piercing weapons, and therefore Inca body armor, designed to avoid the shock of stone and not the cut of a blade, proved ineffective against the Spanish sword, especially in close combat. Spaniards also had superior body armor—steel—that provided better protection against Inca and Aztec projectiles. Spanish cannons, muskets, and crossbows, however inaccurate and clumsy, also had superior striking range than, for example, Inca slings and Aztec projectiles.

    c. *Higher level of social cohesion.* Spaniards displayed far greater discipline and ability to fight together as cohesive military units under trying circumstances. At least two factors undermined Inca and Aztec cohesion. The first was that although both the Incas and Aztecs had a professional warrior class, their armies were mainly recruited from members of tribute-paying societies organized along ethnic lines, and who paid primary allegiance to their own ethnic lords. Thus, Incas and Aztecs could not count on continued allegiance from their allies when ethnic lords died in battle, or when leaders switched their allegiance to the Spaniards. Further, most Inca and Aztec warriors were farmers, not professional soldiers. As such, their ability to sustain or resist long sieges was partly contingent on the ebb and flow of the agricultural cycle; some entire ethnic groups abandoned the battlefield and returned home at the onset of the planting and harvest seasons.

3. *Culture.* The role of ideas, beliefs, and world view in providing the Spaniards with an edge over Incas and Aztecs should not be underestimated. Although eager to enrich themselves and return to Europe as gentlemen (*caballeros*), Spaniards were also driven by a powerful ideology forged during the Spanish reconquest that centered on conquering and converting "pagans" to Christianity, and that impelled them to go on. The fact that so many Incas, Aztecs, and their allies were dying also probably convinced Spaniards that their God was indeed on their side and that they held the moral upper ground.

    By contrast, the polytheistic Inca (and Andean) and Aztec (and Mesoamerican) religious ideology and world view was predicated on reciprocity—on a constant give and take between mortals and supernatural deities. (As will become clearer in Chapter 7, this view is an important bedrock of contemporary popular Catholicism.) Hence, continued Spanish successes on the battlefield and the spreading death that engulfed Incas and Aztecs probably undermined the indigenous peoples' faith in their gods, and their belief in the ability of supernatural deities to provide assistance during such trying times. For example, during and after the fall of Tenochitlán, Cuautémoc (also spelled Chuauhtémoc), who became the Aztec ruler after the death of Cuitlahua, continued to sacrifice captives to Huitzilopochtli, the Aztec deity of war—to no avail. Indeed, the profound sense of disillusionment and shock that Incas, Aztecs, and Mayas almost certainly felt in the midst of such calamities—that their cosmic order was unraveling before their very eyes and their gods "dying" (Wachtel 1977)—may have also undermined their sense of purpose and ability to continue fighting.

    Todorov, in particular, has argued that cultural differences played a crucial role in the Aztec defeat (1984:63–97). He suggests that Aztecs primarily made sense of and reacted to events by privileging communication with the supernatural and the *meaning* of an event—not so much "what" was happening, but "why," and what it augered for the future. Communication with and advice from supernatural deities—and in particular the need to place the utterly alien Spaniards within a comprehensible framework—partly explains, according to Todorov, why Mochtezuma did not decisively move against Cortés before he had recruited large numbers of indigenous allies, that is, why Mochtezuma initially displayed hesitance or ambivalence. Todorov claims that other aspects of Aztec culture—from highly ritualized rules of battle to their cyclical view of time, in which the past was used to try to understand the present (i.e., the Spanish presence), likewise proved ineffective.

4. *Disease.* Europeans unwittingly brought with them to the New World pathogens, and in the process unleashed—possibly as early as Columbus' second landing in Hispaniola in 1493 (Guerra 1988)—an unparalleled wave of pandemics and mass mortality (Lovell 1992b; Lovell and Lutz 1995; Cook 1998; Crosby 1985; Newson 1986, 1991, 1995). Germs and disease were powerful European allies:

> Smallpox was the captain of the men of death in that war [the European Conquest], typhus fever the first lieutenant, and measles the secondary lieutenant. More terrible than the conquistadores on horseback, more deadly than sword or gunpowder, they made the conquest by the whites a walkover as compared to what it would have been without their aid. They were the forerunners of civilization, the companions of Christianity, the friends of the invader. (Ashburn 1947:98, quoted in Joralemon 1982:112. Cite appears in Miller 2005:162–163)

"These killers," as Crosby has aptly called them, "killed more effectively in the New [World], and the comparatively benign diseases of the Old World turned killer in the New" (1972:37). Striking populations without biological immunity, European-introduced diseases such as smallpox, measles, chicken pox, influenza, whooping cough, and typhus ravaged indigenous peoples with extraordinary speed and viciousness, killing huge numbers. A feeling of what can only be described as terror probably gripped most (see In Their Own Words 4.1).

By contrast, noncontagious local diseases, such as malaria, were spread by mosquitoes and skin boring insects and did not equally afflict Europeans. Malaria, though, would partly account for the reluctance of many Europeans to settle in low-lying tropical areas (Gade 1979; Gade and Escobar 1982). Also, European pathogens struck, in a particularly brutal way, the young and the elderly, undermining the ability of local societies to reproduce over time. Further, mortality was probably exacerbated by indigenous beliefs and customs concerning the treatment of the sick and dying. If contemporary ethnography is but a glimpse of cultural responses to illness that might have been present 500 years ago, then responses such as surrounding the sick with family and kin (Bastien 1992) almost certainly enhanced the speed and effectiveness with which pathogens spread.

A sustained defense against Europeans was especially difficult when disease weakened and killed off so many Incas, Aztecs, and their allies, and in doing so ravaged the empires' key leadership. For example, Cuitlahua, who succeeded Mochtezuma after his death, was himself thereafter quickly struck down by smallpox. The colossal mortality and havoc caused by war and disease also led to food shortages and famine that profoundly weakened native resistance. Finally, and perhaps at a more profound level, mass sickness and death probably shattered Inca and Aztec resolve in sustaining a successful resistance.

The number of people who died within fifty years of the Conquest is astonishing, regardless of which estimates on the size of the indigenous population prior to 1492 eventually become accepted. How many people inhabited pre-Conquest Latin America and the Caribbean has been the subject of lively disputes among geographers, historians, and

IN THEIR OWN WORDS 4.1

Indigenous Views of the Conquest

Early colonial documents written by native elites—such as *The Books of Chilam Balam*, of the Yucatán peninsula—provide dramatic depictions into how the trauma of conquest might have been interpreted and felt by those whose world was turned upside down:

> In those days all was good, and they (the gods) were struck down . . . There was no sin in those days . . . There was no sickness then, no pains in the bones, there was no fever for them, there was no small-pox, there was no burning in the chest . . . there was no wasting away . . . This is not what the white lords did when they came to our land. They taught fear and they withered the flowers . . . False are their kings, tyrants upon their thrones . . . Marauders by day, offenders by night, murderers of the world! . . . this was the beginning of begging, the cause of poverty out of which came secret discord, the

beginning of armed banditry, of sins committed, of looting, of enslavement for debt, the beginning of the yoke of debts . . . the beginning of suffering . . . (Wachtel 1977:31–32)

The *Annals of the Cakchiquels*, from Guatemala, provides a glimpse into the terror and despair felt by those who faced epidemics and mass death:

> First they became ill of a cough . . . It was truly terrible . . . Little by little heavy shadows and black night enveloped our fathers . . . when the plague raged . . . great was the stench of the dead . . . After our fathers and grandfathers succumbed, half of the people fled to the fields. The dogs and the vultures devoured the bodies. The mortality was terrible . . . We were born to die! (Burkhart and Gasco 1996:129)

archaeologists, and estimates have ranged from twelve to more than one hundred million. More specific regional estimates are also instructive: the population of central Mexico (roughly the area under the control of the Aztecs) has been calculated at between ten and twenty-five million; in the Andean region as few as three and as many as twelve million people could have been present; in the Caribbean island of Hispaniola (shared by present-day Haiti and the Dominican Republic), some estimates suggest more than one million inhabitants (Denevan 1992a; Lovell 1992b; Borah 1992; Wachtel 1977:86–98; Lovell and Lutz 1994).

Only a fraction of those present at the Conquest survived the ravages of war and epidemics, although these numbers, too, are controversial. Also unclear is the exact role that disease played in conjunction with other Conquest-related causes, such as war, disruption of native subsistence systems, or grueling work conditions imposed by Europeans. Nevertheless, most experts agree that about 90 percent of indigenous peoples perished, and that dozens (perhaps hundreds) of societies completely vanished (Casanueva 1991; Borah 1992; Cook 1998; Cook and Lovell 1991; Denevan 1992a; Dobyns 1993; Crosby 1985; Lovell and Lutz 1995). Some numbers are again illuminating: from a maximum of twenty-five million in the Central Valley of Mexico, perhaps no more than one million were still alive by the late 1500s; in what is now Peru, which might have had nine million people in 1520, less than 600,000 may have been present one hundred years later; by about 1560, there were probably less than two million inhabitants in the entire Andean region of the twelve million prior to the Conquest.

The consequences of mass death and depopulation were far reaching and profound. Indigenous landscapes were greatly altered because local societies were unable to muster the labor needed to maintain fields and irrigation earthworks (see Chapter 2). Depopulation was also an important factor in colonial attempts to group together remnants of different peoples, which in turn spurred the emergence of new ethnic groups and cultures.

Many of the factors that enabled the Spaniards to overwhelm the Incas and Aztecs, such as military superiority, disease, and assistance from native allies, also proved useful against the Maya. However, subduing the Maya proved far more difficult (Clendenin 1987; Sharer 1994:731–748; Lovell 1992a:37–66). The Maya appear not to have hesitated, as did the Aztecs, to confront the Spaniards. Spanish expeditions had reached the Mesoamerican coasts that were under Aztec and Maya control as early as 1517 (some shipwrecked Spaniards had made their way to the Yucatán peninsula in 1511), and the first systematic drive against the Maya began several years later. Yet, it was not until 1696 that Spaniards vanquished Itzá (in Guatemala's Petén region), the last stronghold of Maya resistance. One important factor that enabled some Maya to resist longer than other ethnic polities elsewhere in the Andes and Mesoamerica was that they were divided into more than a dozen rival (and quarreling) polities, and therefore did not form part of a unified, overarching political structure. The absence of unambiguous and enduring splits or cleavages between the Maya city-states in turn meant that, unlike the experience in the Valley of Mexico, where Cortés counted on the unambiguous assistance of the Tlaxcalans, Spaniards confronting the Maya were incapable of mustering a powerful-enough alliance of city-states to their side.

The Columbian Exchange

The European Conquest was much more than a military and political undertaking, and the ramifications of that endeavor were felt not only in the New World. Conquest linked two continents and two worlds not merely through the force of arms but also, and perhaps more importantly, through a two-way flow of plants and animals. It is this flow between and consequences in both the New and Old Worlds that is known as the **Columbian Exchange** (Crosby 1972). See Chapter 9 for more details about the Columbian exchange.

The cultural, economic, and political consequences of the Columbian Exchange were enormous, connecting European and native Latin American societies in manifold, unpredictable, and deeply irrevocable ways. Plants and animals that Europeans brought to the New World—such as wheat, sugarcane, bananas, olives, grapes, horses, chickens, goats, cattle, and pigs—would, in a drastically transformed colonial context, profoundly alter indigenous societies. First successfully planted in the Caribbean, sugarcane thrived in tropical and semitropical soils. As European, but especially English, demand for refined sugar increased in subsequent centuries (Mintz 1985b), sugarcane plantations (*ingenios*, Spanish; *engenhos*, Portuguese) spread relentlessly through the Caribbean and coastal areas in

Brazil, constituting a central pillar of the colonial economy. The spread of the plantation system centered on the cultivation of cane and its processing into sugar. This undertaking required vast amounts of labor that, given the post-Conquest demographic catastrophe and disappearance of most Caribbean native societies, spurred the coerced importation of millions of African slaves to the Caribbean and Brazil. In fact, many more African slaves ended up in the Caribbean than in the United States (Trouillot 1995:17). This slave trade left a lasting and deep imprint on the racial and cultural makeup of the region, especially in the Caribbean and Brazil (Andrews 2004).

Equally important in spurring cultural changes and decisively transforming indigenous societies were animals brought to the Americas. Cattle and sheep, for example, multiplied rapidly, especially in Mexico's Central Plateau, the Venezuelan and Colombian Llanos, the Bolivian Altiplano, and Argentina's Patagonia and Pampas. Horses were especially important, not only because they played such a crucial role in the European Conquest, but also because they multiplied rapidly in open temperate grasslands, such as in the Llanos of Colombia and the Pampas of Argentina, prompting the emergence of horse-based "cowboy" cultures analogous to those in the U.S. plains.

Native crops—manioc, beans, maize, potatoes, and chili peppers, for instance—also made their way to Europe, and in the process dramatically altered not only the diet but also the life chances and subsequent historical development of countless Europeans. Maize, for example, soon became an important crop in central Europe, although it was fed primarily to cattle. The potato—an Andean domesticate—was an especially crucial crop in the destinies of many European societies. When it first arrived in Europe, the potato was considered fit only for animal consumption. Yet, it eventually constituted a basic daily staple in countries such as Germany, Russia, and Ireland. In Ireland, especially, the potato would loom crucial: landlessness and poverty, coupled with a growing population and the ability of the potato to grow well in marginal soils, led most Irish peasants to not only plant but depend almost exclusively on this crop for their everyday subsistence. The overwhelming dependence on this crop was risky: the potato blight and ensuing crop failures between 1846 and 1849 eventually led to the death of at least one million Irish and spurred Irish mass migration to the United States at the turn of the nineteenth century (McNeill 1999).

The Colonial Period

The colonial period, which largely lasted from the Conquest until the early to mid–nineteenth century, is important for understanding contemporary Latin American societies. It is during these 300 years of colonial rule that the basic structure of Latin American economies—such as the primary focus toward and dependence on the export of key commodities and crops for the world market, and the entrenchment of the great Latin American landed estates—coalesced (Stein and Stein 1970; Wolf and Hansen 1972; Galeano 1997[1973]; Bethell 1987). These economic transformations in turn profoundly shaped societies that survived the Conquest. The colonial period was also important because what the ruling colonial elite needed to administer and rule over conquered native populations led to a profound restructuring of indigenous societies and cultures.

Mechanisms of Rule

Despite breaking mass rebellion by the late 1500s, Spaniards and Portuguese were nevertheless on decisively weak grounds, politically and economically: no more than several thousand colonizers were spread over millions of square miles populated by millions of culturally and linguistically distinct "Indians"—a quintessential colonial construction. Further, huge stretches of land, such as Amazonia, Pampas, Patagonia, and the Lesser Antilles, were populated by mobile and small-scale societies, which presented innumerable obstacles to effective control and rule. In densely populated areas in Mesoamerica and the Andes, Spaniards were in a decisively weak position vis-à-vis ethnic leaders who marshaled far more legitimacy, and Spaniards soon realized that alliances with these leaders were vital to consolidating colonial rule. For their part, native rulers and elites also stood much to gain by allying themselves with Europeans, so the entrenchment of colonial rule was also, in part, an indigenous creation (Service 1955; Gibson 1964, 1987; Stern 1982; Farriss 1984).

How to politically subjugate "Indians" and wrench from them the surpluses of labor, crops, and other goods essential to the colonial enterprise was perhaps the most important challenge for the new European rulers. Various means were deployed with varying success to consolidate and ensure colonial political, economic, and cultural control. This section centers on how five important mechanisms of rule profoundly altered indigenous societies during the colonial period and are still relevant in contemporary times. (1) establishment of encomiendas, repartimientos, and a variety of tribute obligations; (2) concentration of dispersed communities into urbanlike settlements; (3) expansion of the state bureaucracy; (4) reliance on indigenous elites as power and cultural brokers; and (5) public rituals and ceremonies.

Encomiendas, Repartimientos, and Tribute. Governing millions of culturally distinct peoples was a daunting challenge for European colonials. Spaniards overcame this difficulty in the early colonial period by awarding *encomiendas* to those Europeans who had participated in the Conquest. Essentially a spoil of war, an **encomienda** was a Spanish crown grant over indigenous labor, whereby "Indians" were entrusted and required to provide labor and tribute to an **encomendero.** The *encomendero* in turn pledged to the crown that he would ensure the Indians' economic well-being and their conversion to Christianity (the latter was an important ideological justification for the Conquest). Encomiendas, which were first tried out in the Caribbean, were often coupled with a land grant called **merced** or **composición** (Lockhart 1969, 1992; Gutiérrez 1991:101–108). In the densely populated Andean and Mesoamerican regions, some encomenderos enjoyed the labor and tribute from thousands of households (Stern 1982; Lovell 1992a). Encomiendas were sometimes awarded over entire ethnic polities which, in a strange twist of fate, "helped Indians maintain their identity" in Guatemala and elsewhere (Smith 1990a:14)..

The encomienda also served the political interests of the crown. It was useful for the colonial strategy of indirect rule—which had in so many ways also served the Incas and Aztecs—for encomenderos were directly responsible to the crown for the affairs of their encomiendas. Political and economic spearheads of the early colonial state, encomenderos administered their encomiendas through complex webs of reciprocal obligations and favors forged with indigenous leaders. Such an arrangement in turn bolstered the position and status of indigenous leaders who, by securing favorable treatment and resources from colonials, enhanced their own legitimacy and moral authority vis-à-vis their communities, as well as social mobility (Spalding 1985). Yet, alarmed by the growing political power of the encomenderos, the difficulty of providing additional encomiendas, and the growing abuses of Indians by the encomenderos (the latter chronicled by the well-known Dominican priest Bartolomé de las Casas), the Spanish crown enacted (1542–1543) what came to be known as the New Laws, which "prohibited slavery of Indians, regulated the tribute that could be paid by Indians to their encomenderos, and, most important, forbade the granting of any new encomiendas and prohibited the inheritance of those already in existence" (Burkhart and Gasco 1996a:156).

Encomiendas were eventually replaced by *repartimientos* toward the end of the sixteenth century. The term **repartimiento** comes from the Spanish verb *repartir,* to divide or redistribute. Through the repartimiento system, indigenous communities were grouped into administrative units (repartimientos) that provided labor to the state and other colonial elites, but under crown supervision. Forced labor was crucial in colonial thinking, "for it was widely held by the Spanish authorities that unless forced to work under such arrangements, the natives, being inherently slothful, would lapse into corrupt vagabondage" (Lovell 1992a:104). Repartimientos were assigned mandatory labor quotas which, in the Andes, were known as **mitas,** a term drawn from the Quechua *mit'a* (or turn), which expressed labor obligations provided to each other by Andean households and by ethnic polities to the Inca state.

Repartimiento labor was deployed to meet wide spectrum of needs. Some *mitas* were awarded for public works (such as maintaining highways), others to prominent colonials, who redeployed this labor on their own estates. Labor drafts were also assigned to the Catholic Church. The best known use of mita labor was that channeled to the great silver mines of Guanajuato in Mexico and Potosí in highland Bolivia, both major pillars of the colonial economy (Brading and Cross 1985; Bakewell 1987).

The extraction of labor and other tribute was fundamental to the colonial enterprise, but it would not work if indigenous societies could or would not produce wealth that could be appropriated by the colonizers. Above all, it was access to and appropriation of labor that was the linchpin of the colonial economy and state. Yet, coerced labor was also a key mechanism of political and economic control, and an intrinsic experience of the everyday lives of indigenous societies and African slaves on sugar plantations. Many coercive labor practices in different guises and contexts survived well after the end of the colonial period and were a key grievance underlying popular revolts and rebellions up until recent times.

Reducciones.   Disease, the ravages of Conquest, and pre-European settlement patterns meant that indigenous peoples were largely dispersed throughout the countryside and beyond the direct coercive control of Europeans. To consolidate its rule, the Spanish crown forcibly resettled indigenous peoples into villages, towns, and urban settlements surrounded by cultivated fields through a policy known as **reducciones,** sometimes also called *congregaciones* (from the Spanish to "reduce" or "congregate"). At times, culturally homogenous peoples were grouped together but, when this did not happen, one important, unintended consequence of this policy was to partially erase cultural differences and give rise to new ethnic identities. The policy of "reducing" indigenous peoples also enabled the colonial state and church to more effectively gather critical information on their new colonial subjects through censuses and administrative surveys, and therefore to enhance surveillance and control.

In frontier areas, missionaries often played a key role in reducing nomadic or seminomadic peoples into mission settlements. Missionaries and mission settlements performed an especially important task in consolidating colonial rule and in transforming local cultures (Langer and Jackson 1995; Burkholder and Johnson 2004:116). Such was the case, for example, among the Pueblo in New Mexico:

> At the missions the friars offered young men livestock, meat, and education in animal husbandry in return for baptism and obedience of God's laws, just as the hunt chiefs before them had taught young men hunting techniques and hunt magic in return for corn and meat payments . . . [E]ffective native hunt magic was always dependent on temporary sexual abstinence. This fact was not lost on the friars, who distributed livestock to men who promised to live monogamously. In precolonial times seniors had enjoyed the most meat because juniors were always indebted until they reached adulthood. Now obedient and pious junior men were the most favored by the friars. Thus in a few years, the introduction of European livestock eroded the hunt chief's authority, diminished the importance of hunting in Pueblo society, and totally transformed the age hierarchy on which meat distribution and consumption were based. (Gutiérrez 1991:77)

Yet *reducciones* also had the unintended effect of providing conditions for ethnic and cultural survival. Reducciones eventually ushered in the emergence of indigenous municipalities (*municipios*) or towns (*pueblos, pueblos de Indios* [Spanish] or *aldeias* [Portuguese]) that eventually formed the core of "traditional" communities in Mesoamerica, the Andes, and other parts of Latin America. One important outcome of this process of state incorporation was to instill a strong sense of ethnic or cultural identification among many present-day Mayan or Quechua-speaking peoples to their municipalities, *ayllus*, or pueblos.

Expansion of the State Bureaucracy.   One obvious way of ensuring control over conquered populations has been to extend the "reach" of the state by expanding its bureaucracy. During the colonial period, the ability of the state to "reach" most indigenous communities took hold only after administrative reforms in the 1560s. This reorganization had far-reaching consequences, especially in the heavily populated Mesoamerican and Andean hinterlands, and northern South America. One upshot was to expand the number and authority of local and regional political positions (such as the *corregidor, corregidor de Indios,* and *alcaldes*), with indigenous political organization modeled along the lines of the Spanish town government council (**cabildo**). Another important outcome was the emergence in many (but perhaps not all) Mesoamerican communities of civil-religious cargo systems, especially in Mexico and Guatemala. These are explored further in Chapter 7.

Political reorganization was in turn facilitated by the policy of reducciones discussed previously and a restructuring of indigenous political systems that would more directly intersect with and enhance the effectiveness of the colonial bureaucracy. For example, "In Guatemala, *corregimientos* or *alcaldías mayores* were made up of varying numbers of pueblos de indios—Indian towns or congregaciones governed (usually from a distance) by a *corregidor* or *alcalde mayor* represented in each community by native alcaldes (mayors) and *regidores* (councillors)" (Lovell 1992a:89). A similar structure was set up in the southern Peruvian Andes, where

> a revamped indigenous power structure, dependent upon the state's benevolence for its tenure and privileges, would serve as local agents of the corregidor and the colonial regime. The major kurakas, who retained their chieftainships subject to the consent of the state, would have to share authority with new native officials. Within the corregimientos, the principal towns of the repartimiento districts would seat Indian cabildos modeled after the Spanish municipal councils. The Indian *alcalde* (mayor), and other cabildo officials, would together with the kurakas oversee local life and represent the natives before state authorities. (Stern 1982:93)

Many paraphernalia, and political positions and rituals, that emerged during the colonial period are still relevant today, having formed part of "traditional" culture. For example, in some Andean communities, staffs of authority—elaborately adorned staffs made out of silver that signaled colonial-era indigenous political leadership—are still an overt expression of local political authorities (Rappaport 1994; Rasnake 1988). Further, some contemporary **rituals of rule** (Beezley et al. 1994a) publicly display political subordination to representatives of the nation-state and legitimize its rule. One contemporary example that can be clearly traced back to the colonial period is the New Year's procession of indigenous ayllu political leaders to local district headquarters in Pisaq, Peru (see Photo 4.1).

These are not mere examples of inert colonial "survivals" frozen in time—cultural practices with their original meanings unchanged that have little bearing on contemporary life—but, in fact, cultural artifacts of the colonial period that have been reinterpreted and culturally reframed to meet new challenges of the contemporary period. For example, authority staffs may have been one pathway through which colonial power structures operated, but in present-day southern Colombia, their use by indigenous groups, such as the Cumbe, is a powerful means through which the group is able to identify itself as "indigenous," establish claims to such an identity that hark back to the colonial period, and thereby take advantage of the Colombian legal system that awards certain advantages to colonial-era indigenous peoples. In turn, this appropriation of history and the past to revitalize and sustain ethnic identity has served to thwart claims against the group's communal lands by outsiders (Rappaport 1994).

Local Elites as Power and Cultural Brokers.   Indigenous political leaders (generally called *kurakas* or *caciques* in Spanish colonial America) were a crucial linchpin in the colonial strategy of indirect rule. Politically and culturally important brokers at the community level, it is they who first learned Spanish or Portuguese and adopted European values.

PHOTO 4.1   *Ayllu Political Authorities, Pisaq, Peru.*

It is they who early on learned to straddle both European and indigenous cultures—to serve as a cultural "bridge" between the European and native worlds—and it was largely through their strategic position that local cultures were transformed during the colonial period. These political leaders were drawn from pre-Conquest native elites, such as members or descendants of Inca, Aztec, and Maya royal families. Many were often eager to ally themselves with and benefit from the European colonial project. It is from within their privileged ranks that these "Hispanicized," or "acculturated Indians" (Stern 1982), played pivotal roles in the colonial political economy. They did so by participating in far-flung commercial networks, mobilizing labor on behalf of the colonial elites, or often shielding fellow community members from census takers (and thereby enabling them to evade forced labor drafts).

Godparenthood (also called coparenthood; *compadrazgo*), a colonial cultural and religious ritual complex with deep European roots that quickly flourished in most of Latin America and the Caribbean, also sustained colonial rule. The core of this ritual was the sponsorship of an infant's baptism—or of a couple to be married—in the course of which the sponsors became godparents (*padrinos*, Spanish; *padrinhos*, Portuguese) of their godchildren (*ahijados*, Spanish; *afilhados*, Portuguese) and coparents (*compadres*) of the baptized infant's or the groom or bride's parents.

This ritual, generating networks of fictive kin bound to each other through mutual rights and obligations, almost certainly had pre-Conquest analogues in many indigenous societies. Although this may partly account for the speed with which this custom became solidly entrenched in local cultures, another, more important reason had to with its intrinsic social malleability. It was compadrazgo's capacity to continuously generate wider social networks and rights and obligations—often between social unequals—in a seemingly endless variety of contexts far removed from its original religious foundation that underpinned its popularity. As a result, compadrazgo ties thrived across the colonial class and ethnic spectrum—between, for example, indigenous and colonial elites, ethnic lords and community members, and estate owners and tenants. (An important exception, at least in Brazil, was the reluctance of plantation owners to establish such bonds with their slaves [Gudeman and Schwartz 1984].) By generating dense webs of reciprocal (although fundamentally unequal) obligations and relationships morally justified in religious and spiritual terms, godparenthood served well the needs of many and indirectly bolstered the legitimacy of the colonial order's social and economic inequality. Compadrazgo is a key and visible feature of contemporary Latin America (Mintz and Wolf 1950; Deshon 1963; van den Berghe and van den Berghe 1966; Osborn 1968; Gudeman 1975; Charney 1991).

Social k [handwritten margin note]

Finally, indigenous elites also played a prominent role in writing (using the Spanish alphabet) accounts of local worlds prior to the Conquest, and in compiling native language dictionaries and grammars. The famous *Yucatán Mayan Books* of Chilam Balam, the *Quiche Mayan Popol Vuh* of the highlands of Guatemala, the "Letter to the King" by Guamán Poma de Ayala, or the equally famous (and unique) Huarochirí manuscript of Peru, to take but a few examples—all of which continue to yield remarkable insights into pre-Conquest life ways and world view, and indigenous visions of the post-Conquest world—were written by or with the assistance of these indigenous elites (Salomon 1999; Sharer 1994:595–597). In their ambiguous and highly paradoxical position in the colonial social order, these Hispanicized elites also spearheaded rebellions that so often shattered the colonial world.

Rituals and Ceremonies. Beezley et al. (1994b) remind us that in addition to force and coercion, successful rule more often than not rests on a widespread acceptance of symbols and legitimacy of the existing social order. In the Spanish colonial world, sponsorship of secular and religious popular celebrations and public rituals often served as a key mechanism through which colonial elites attempted to convey and instill widespread acceptance of Spanish values and key symbols, and therefore reinforce the social, cultural, and economic hierarchy on which the colonial order rested. Rituals such as Corpus Christi in colonial Mexico City, and a myriad of songs and dances, are examples of such attempts to legitimize colonial rule through public ceremonies (Curcio-Nagy 1994; Rivera Ayala 1994). (An important variant of these public rituals and ceremonies is Carnaval, examined in greater detail in Chapter 11.) Many religious celebrations and Catholic holidays at the village or parish level were organized and sponsored by religious brotherhoods or sodalities called **cofradías,** which were especially entrusted with carrying out celebrations venerating village saints. Although *cofradías* were fundamentally a colonial construction established to "mediate between community and state" (Smith 1990a:15), Wolf (1959:216) and Carrasco (1961) suggested years ago that they may have had some pre-Hispanic antecedents. Cofradías often accumulated significant resources (Lovell 1992a:113–115) and some were led by indigenous elites (Stern 1982:169). Parish clergy also had an important stake in the cofradías, for these provided the parish with an important source of revenue (Rus and Wassertrom 1980:468). Far removed from centers of colonial control and densely populated indigenous areas, Catholic mission settlements often served similar goals (Langer and Jackson 1995). Cofradías still exist in some Mesoamerican communities (Annis 1987:61–63). Further, cofradía members participate in the political-religious *cargo* systems (a product of the colonial period as well), which also have the goal of sponsoring celebrations to village saints (see Chapter 7).

Pillars of the Colonial Economy: Haciendas, Plantations, and Mines

Haciendas, plantations, and mines were at the heart of the colonial economy, and all deeply structured the subsequent economic, social, and cultural history of Latin American and Caribbean societies. Indeed, it is difficult to imagine the history of Cuba, Jamaica, or Haiti without sugar, plantations, and slavery, or understand the cultural development of Mesoamerica or the Andes without acknowledging how landed estates competed with Indian communities for land and labor. The spread of huge estates in the southern Pampas and Patagonia was partly a result of the natural landscapes that proved amenable to cattle and sheep grazing, but was also due to the difficulties that European colonizers encountered in subjugating seminomadic societies and appropriating their labor.

Haciendas.   The possibility of quickly becoming wealthy and returning to Europe after the Conquest was dashed early on once it became clear that not enough gold or other precious minerals could be found. Hence, most Europeans opted for settling and availing themselves of two key resources that they could exploit and that would hopefully enable them to achieve a lifestyle far beyond that which they could aspire to in Europe: labor and land. The landed estate (**hacienda,** Spanish; **fazenda,** Portuguese) early emerged as a key social, cultural, and economic institution throughout vast parts of Latin America. Its zenith nevertheless occured after independence, and particularly in the course of attempts by liberally-minded national governments to transform indigenous peasants into small-scale, independent, yeoman-like farmers analogous to those in the United States (Wolf and Hansen 1972:145–150; Wolf and Mintz 1957; Taylor 1974).

Some *haciendas* surfaced early in the colonial period, but scholars disagree on the mechanisms that ushered in their emergence. Some studies have suggested that haciendas emerged directly out of the encomienda system, while others have noted the appearance of haciendas in underpopulated regions devoid of encomiendas (Wolf and Mintz 1957; Mörner 1973; Taylor 1974; Schwartz 1978). Most scholars nevertheless agree that some sort of functional relationship existed between encomiendas and the emergence of many haciendas. For example, many haciendas emerged within or near indigenous communities, and the labor systems that typically emerged in them were strikingly similar to those that characterized encomiendas (Larson 1988b).

Haciendas were of different kinds: some were relatively small, no more than several hundred hectares, while others were huge, consisting of hundreds of thousands of hectares; some specialized in the production of key crops—coffee or sugar, for example—while others had a much wider productive base; some produced goods for local markets while many others satisfied the consumption needs of far-flung economic poles, such as mines; some haciendas drew their labor from nearby communities, while others essentially engulfed entire indigenous communities. A slightly different variant of the agro-pastoral haciendas was the cattle and sheep ranches (**estancias,** Spanish) that emerged especially in Argentina and Uruguay, and which formed the productive context within which the famous "gaucho" cowboy culture emerged. *Estancias* are still an important and prominent feature of the economic and cultural landscapes of Argentina and Uruguay.

Despite these differences, most haciendas had at least three common characteristics. First, they had relatively low levels of technology and capital investments, which limited productivity. This partly explains why many supplied goods to local markets. Second, the bulk of their labor was provided by a dependent and indigenous workforce that spent most of its time working the lands of the hacienda owner (**hacendado,** Spanish; **fazendeiro,** Portuguese). This workforce was neither primarily slave nor fully proletarian, for most laborers were granted their own plots of land within haciendas in exchange for their work on estate lands, while others had some sort of access to land in their home communities. Third, in addition to providing labor, tenants were also obligated through a variety of exploitative relationships to provide a wide span of tribute payments (such as a percentage of crops harvested on their own land plots, or a percentage of domestic or grazing animals) to the estate owner. Many were also indebted to estate owners and bound to them through debt peonage and patron-client relationships. The origins of this dependent labor force were various: for example, many indigenous peoples simply lost their lands and independent livelihood as haciendas coercively engulfed Indian communities; others, fleeing the dreaded mining labor drafts, simply abandoned their home communities and "freely" decided to become resident estate tenants.

The profoundly unequal and exploitative economic, political, and social relationships of the hacienda system constituted defining characteristics of the rural worlds of most Latin American peoples until recent times. These hierarchical relationships also accounted for the landlessness and profound inequality in access to land that underpinned the Mexican and Bolivian Revolutions of 1910 and 1952, and they also were at the core of grievances, political instability, and massive violence in Central America decades after these revolutions.

Plantations and Slavery.   Plantations were a particular kind of landed estate, the archetype of which was the sugar plantation that played such a prominent role in the history and culture of coastal Brazil, the Caribbean islands, and Central American coastal areas. The typical (sugar) **plantation** differed from the agro-pastoral hacienda in at least three ways. First, plantations typically required higher levels of capital and technological investments, especially in machinery needed for the grinding and initial processing of sugarcane. As Mintz (1996a:295) reminds us, "These technical features . . . introduced more than just an aura of industrial modernity into what were operations which predated, in many cases by whole centuries, the Industrial Revolution." Second, quite unlike the typical hacienda, the plantations' resident labor force consisted primarily of either slaves or full-time wage laborers. Third, plantations produced commodities, such as semi-refined sugar, molasses, and rum, that were primarily geared toward European markets. These characteristics mark plantations as quasi-agricultural factories producing for and primarily oriented to the world market (Wolf and Mintz 1957; Mintz 1985a; Ortiz 1970; Moreno Fraginals 1976).

Spaniards were the first to plant sugarcane in the Caribbean, doing so by the early sixteenth century. Yet, it was the Portuguese who, taking advantage of their African colonies (especially Angola), took the lead in establishing large-scale plantations staffed by increasing numbers of African slaves, especially along the Brazilian coastal areas of Pernambuco and Bahia (Klein 1986; Burkholder and Johnson 2004:132–139; Schwartz 1987). In fact, it was not until the mid- to late-eighteenth century that most Caribbean island coastal areas were transformed into vast plantations worked by a predominantly slave population that provided sugar and its byproducts for an expanding urban working class in Britain and other European countries, and therefore drew Africans, Europeans, and Latin American and Caribbean peoples into global webs of economic, political, social, and cultural relationships (Mintz 1985b). In Puerto Rico, sugar plantation agriculture reached its peak in terms of capital investment, efficiency, and technological innovations after the U.S. annexation of 1898 and the massive inflow of capital from major U.S. corporations (Ayala 1999; Dietz 1986).

The expansion of sugarcane plantations went hand in hand with the intensification of the African slave trade. Between 1551 and 1810, almost one million Africans were enslaved and shipped to Spanish America, most to the Caribbean. During that same period, almost two million slaves reached Brazil (Burkholder and Johnson 2004:134). Hundreds of thousands of others (and perhaps as many as one million) were eventually shipped to the English and French colonies of Jamaica, Saint-Domingue, and Martinique. More African slaves eventually reached the tiny island of Martinique—less than one-fourth the size of New York City's Long Island—than the United States (Trouillot 1995:17). In fact, ten times as many African slaves reached the Spanish and Portuguese colonies than the United States, and more than one hundred million people of African decent currently live in Latin America and the Caribbean—three times as many as in the United States (Andrews 1994:363).

African slaves—legally no more than chattel—faced extraordinary levels of mortality and unimaginably difficult, grinding, and cruel labor conditions. Small wonder that a priest wrote from the Brazilian city of Bahia in 1627 that "A sugar mill is hell and all the masters of them are damned" (Schwartz 1987:67). Yet, slaves were able to carve out a degree of autonomy, a scope of "freedom" in their everyday lives far removed from the gaze and surveillance of plantation masters (Mintz 1996b; see Chapter 9 for a further discussion of the role of slaves in food preparation and cuisine). As such, they creatively forged novel and lasting Afro-Latin and Afro-Brazilian traditions based on an amalgam of African, indigenous Latin American, and European cultural elements. These lasting contributions in religion and ritual, dance and music, and popular celebrations are examined in subsequent chapters.

Mines.   Mining, especially silver mining in Mexico and Bolivia, was the second most important pillar of the colonial economy and royal coffers. The production and export of silver linked vast territories and peoples into complex fields of regional relationships by spurring the production of agricultural and other goods to supply the mines and the growing mining populations (Bakewell 1987; Larson 1988b; Larson and Harris 1995). Silver and later tin mining would especially consolidate Bolivia's position as an exporter of raw commodities, serve as a powerful symbol of dependency and exploitation, and, as such, be an important catalyst of the 1952 revolution and subsequent nationalization of the mining industry (Barrios de Chungara 1978; Dunkerley 1984; Nash 1992).

Early attempts to supply mines with African slave labor proved unsuccessful because most Africans eventually died off, and it was the forced labor drafts that supplied most mines with their laborers during the early colonial period. Eventually, though, most mine workers would be drawn from members of indigenous communities who, by trying to avoid the mita, eventually opted for settling in the mines as "free" wage earners and discarding their identity as "Indians." That this process went hand in hand with an accelerated decline of the Indian population registered in colonial censuses does not indicate the sudden shedding of indigenous culture and the uncritical adoption of "Spanish" values and norms. Rather than resulting in a process of cultural loss or displacement, the centuries-long process of adaptation to mine work ushered in the emergence of culturally distinctive and oppositional cultures in, for example, Bolivian and Chilean mining communities (Nash 1979; Klubock 1997).

Resisting the Colonial Order

The formal end of the Conquest, and the progressive entrenchment of the colonial system and its mechanisms of rule and exploitation, entailed anything but an acceptance of the legitimacy of the new social order—ever so tenuous in vast reaches of Latin America and the Caribbean. Members of indigenous and slave communities rejected colonialism and the plans that colonizers had for them in many ways, and how they contested the colonial order had profound effects. Resistance to colonial rule largely took two forms: (1) outright, organized rebellions and (2) more evasive, "everyday forms" of resistance.

Rebellions. The colonial period was sprinkled with many instances of rebellion against colonial rule. Most were highly localized—taking place in specific haciendas or plantations—some were more regional, and most were brutally suppressed. Some revolts had a wide geographic scope, entailed a wide participation of a cross-section of indigenous and/or slave communities, and represented a very serious threat to the colonial order. In order to explore what these rebellions reveal about indigenous (and slave) societies and cultures, and also some of their long-term consequences, this section focuses on three examples of these latter, mass rebellions that signaled a major breakdown of European colonial rule and legitimacy: (1) the Pan-Andean rebellions of the late 1700s, (2) the Yucatán Caste War of 1847, and (3) the Haitian slave revolt of the late 1700s.

1. The Andean Rebellions (Thompson 2002; Stern 1987a; Szeminski 1987). During the eighteenth century, waves of rebellions struck the Andean region, threatening the stability of Spanish governance. Of the one hundred revolts between 1720 and 1790, two stand out: the 1742–1752 insurgency in the eastern Andean slopes, and the massive insurrection in 1780–1782. The latter culminated in the 1781 siege of La Paz (Bolivia), which royal troops from Buenos Aires helped to break.

The rebellions bear several interesting resemblances, a brief examination of which permits a glimpse of Andean and indigenous society in the latter part of the colonial period. The vast number who rebelled were common, poor Andeans, many of them peasants, from a wide spectrum of ethnic, racial, cultural, and economic backgrounds. Further, key leaders were often wealthy, elite Andeans, many of whom had profited enormously from the colonial economy. For example, Juan Santos Atahualpa, the leader of the 1742–1752 revolt, claimed to be a direct descendant of Atahualpa, who was captured at Cajamarca by Pizarro. Two centuries after the Conquest, the Andean world was deeply divided by class and privilege, and anything but culturally or socially homogenous.

Culturally and socially, leaders of these rebellions straddled both the largely indigenous Andean and the Hispanic worlds. As such, their worldview was powerfully shaped by Spanish ideas and concepts, reflecting the extent and depth to which the colonial order had made a deep cultural imprint. For example, Juan Santos Atahualpa, who was literate and Jesuit-educated, claimed that he was leading a drive for the return of a redemptive Inca king, a claim and goal that he believed had the full support of (the Christian) God. Likewise, Túpac Katari, a key insurrectionist leader during the 1781 siege of La Paz, is said to have attended mass each day, celebrated by captive clergy. These examples illustrate not only how deeply entrenched in Andean culture Catholic deities had become but also how they were politically and ideologically mustered and refashioned by Andean rebels to legitimize their cause.

The insurrections were spurred by colonial economic policies that impoverished large numbers of nonelite Andeans, including many local leaders. One of the most notorious of these policies was the forced sale of goods (**repartimiento de mercancías,** sometimes just called *reparto*) which were, incidentally, not limited to the Andean region. The rebellions were also flamed by attempts of the colonial state to directly meddle in the internal politics of local communities, and undermine the political position and legitimacy of local leaders (caciques, kurakas) and their privileged status within their communities.

The Andean insurrections ultimately failed to accomplish their leaders' goals. This was only partly because the colonial state was politically and militarily stronger. Equally important was that profound economic and social divisions riddled Andean communities. Their leaders especially were culturally in a somewhat ambiguous, almost paradoxical position, having to rationalize revolt against the colonial order by simultaneously drawing on ideas and concepts from the colonial cultural world. A united economic, cultural, and social stand against the colonial state was difficult indeed.

2. The Yucatán Caste War (Reed 2001; MacLeod 2000:24–25; Jones 2000:374–379). This conflict, centered primarily in the Yucatán peninsula, began in 1847 and ended in 1901—but not before hundreds of thousands had died. It was brought about by the expansion of cattle ranches and sugar and henequen plantations (henequen is a cactus plant, the fiber of which was used to make rope or twine). Also important were attempts by non-Maya Mexican elites to undermine access to communal land and water supplies, policies that destabilized the political position and legitimacy of Maya elites and marginalized large sectors of the (predominantly Mayan-speaking) Yucatán. Although this half-century long conflict occurred after Mexican independence, many policies that sparked it had their roots in the colonial period and worked against non-Maya elites, who had sought to consolidate their own economic and political power independently of the central government in Mexico City, and who would also fight, alongside Maya peoples, against the Mexican army. Hence, although Mayan-speaking peoples were key protagonists of this struggle (and were the ones to suffer the most), the Caste War was not solely an ethnic conflict between Mayas and non-Mayas—the "Whites," "Mestizos," or "Ladinos" (see Chapter 5).

Like Andean indigenous peoples during the 1780–1782 uprising, Maya loyalties were deeply divided: some fought against the Mexican army while others fought alongside it, and some leaders (*batab*) fought against some members of the Yucatán non-Maya elites while others did not. Political factionalism and ethnic cleavages worked against the forging of a common ground against a mutual enemy. (The lack of clear-cut cleavages and unambiguous loyalties was also an important dimension of the Guatemalan civil war that racked the Maya highlands in the 1980s.) Maya leaders, like their Andean counterparts more than a century earlier, were often drawn from the literate, elite members of Maya society. As a result, they stood in a culturally ambiguous position between indigenous and non-Maya worlds, and they often legitimized their rebellion by drawing on various cultural repertoires, including the Catholic religion. For example, just before his execution, one captured rebel leader justified his actions by alluding to both *The Book of Chilam Balam*— a post-Conquest narrative written by Maya elites—*and* the word of Jesus Christ. Another poignant example of how an amalgam of pre- and post-Conquest religious ideologies surfaced among the Maya was the widespread deployment of the wooden cross—the Cult of the Talking Cross—through which "Christ" and the "Father" spoke to and guided rebel leaders. And there are examples of Maya rebels interrupting their offensive operations to take part in village religious celebrations, clearly indicating the extent to which popular Catholicism had become solidly entrenched in Maya culture.

3. Haiti's Slave Revolution (Trouillot 1995). The westernmost part of the island of Hispaniola was governed by a tiny French and French-speaking Creole elite. Teeming with highly profitable sugar plantations worked by enormous numbers of African slaves, by the late eighteenth century Saint-Domingue was France's most important colonial possession in the Americas. What began in 1791 as a local revolt in the northern part of the colony quickly mushroomed into waves of rebellions that successfully fought off French planters and drove French armies almost literally to the sea. In fact, in Saint-Domingue Napoleon lost more troops and generals than at the famous battle of Waterloo against the British. The importance attached to and knowledge of this extraordinary historic event has generally been downplayed in North American history books—in what the anthropologist Michel-Rolph Trouillot (1995) has called a "silencing" of Haitian and slave history.

The Haitian case is the only example of a truly successful African slave rebellion in the Americas, and it led to the first independent nation-state in Latin America. What is also striking about the Haitian revolution is that those who rose up against the French were far from a homogenous population. Indeed, rebels were deeply divided along a number of cleavages: black freemen versus slaves; racially-mixed (i.e., *mulattoes*) versus blacks, and Creole slaves (those born in the colony) versus African-born slaves (*congos* or *bossales*). Because of ethnic, cultural and linguistic cleavages, some fought against while others sided with the French.

Evasive, "Everyday" Forms of Resistance. Resistance to colonial rule was more often less dramatic, overt, and confrontational. The idea of evasive, **everyday forms of resistance** is based on the work of Scott (1976, 1985, 1990), who has suggested that mass, public, overtly confrontational challenges to colonial rule have been, historically and cross-culturally, rare given the ability of states and elites to ruthlessly suppress them. Far more common, claims Scott, have been less open, frontal challenges that question the legitimacy of the colonial order, attempt to interfere with the normal functioning of mechanisms of exploitation and rule, and that, precisely because they are less open and public, leave their participants less vulnerable to repression. One important idea of Scott's work—which has had an exceptional impact in cultural anthropology, history, and related disciplines—is that colonial rule and control is never totally absolute and all-encompassing, that subjugated peoples have some degree of autonomy and "space" within which they maneuver, and that ways of resisting colonial rule are often entrenched in everyday lives, routines, and cultures (Comaroff and Comaroff 1992; Dirks 1992, 2001; Cooper and Stoler 1997).

The Latin American experience provides many examples of such everyday resistence to colonial rule. One was to take advantage of and work within the colonial legal system that, although predicated on a fundamental inequality between conquerors and conquered, nevertheless provided indigenous communities—but not slaves—with some basic legal rights. For example, within a few decades after the Conquest, indigenous communities in what is now the region of Ayacucho, Peru, had become skilled at maneuvering their way through the Spanish legal system and adept at using lawsuits and appeals to stall colonial initiatives and policies. The ability of Andean communities to evade and undermine labor drafts to mining districts provides yet another example: because only those legally classed as "Indians" could be subjected to the mita, indigenous peoples relied on many ways to avoid being legally classed as "Indians" in colonial censuses. Gradually, the colonial state faced increasing difficulties in providing a reliable workforce at the mines and production waned. Because the colonial state imposed tax on the amount of silver produced, royal coffers suffered as well. The formal abolition of the state mita was largely a result of these ingenious strategies employed by Andean peoples (Stern 1982; Evans 1990; Wightman 1990; Tandeter 1991; Powers 1995; Zulawski 1995; Murra 1998).

A strikingly analogous example of working within the judicial system can be observed in contemporary southern Colombia. There, the Cumbe have a long trajectory of relying on written documents—many from the colonial period—to claim and retain their identity as "Indians" (*indígenas*). These documents enable them to take advantage of the Colombian constitution, which guarantees certain rights, especially over communal land, to those who can demonstrate such an identity harking back to the colonial period. Knowledge of judicial codes and documents has in turn encouraged a literary tradition—an importance attached to the written word—that has often aided the Cumbe to resist attempts by non-indigenous elites to appropriate their communal lands (Rappaport 1994).

Another way to resist colonial rule was to simply flee to vast stretches of unexplored, difficult-to-reach areas well outside the surveillance and effective reach of colonial officials (see also the discussion of "maroon" societies in the following section on Ethnogenesis). For example, the heavily forested Petén region southeast of the Yucatán peninsula often provided a temporary haven for many Mayan-speaking peoples, many of whom were still being referred to as "Wild Indians" during the eighteenth century (Schwartz 1990:33–46). Further south, Cakchiquel Mayas fled to isolated mountain areas and ravines to avoid tribute and labor obligations, forming dispersed settlements that Spaniards called *pajuides*, from the Cakchiquel term *pajuyu*, which meant "in the hills" (Hill II 1992:121–123). Quechua- and Aymara-speaking peoples likewise evaded the dreaded labor drafts to the mines by fleeing to urban areas, isolated semitropical regions in the eastern flanks of the Andean mountains, or to agro-pastoral haciendas, where they swelled the ranks of tenant laborers (Larson 1988b; Larson and Harris 1995).

Although fleeing was a tactic employed by many, it was an especially important strategy for African slaves who, unlike their indigenous contemporaries, had no legal rights. And although even under extreme hardship many slaves appear to have retained some autonomy over their lives, especially in the realm of food and cuisine (Mintz 1996b)—an important point more fully discussed in Chapter 9—many of them opted for an entirely different way of life. Remote and forested areas in the Lesser Antilles and the Central American and northern South American coastlines, especially in Belize, Honduras, Suriname, and the Guianas, gave many the opportunity to escape colonial surveillance and provided a haven from and an alternative to slavery—and to forge new forms of ethnic consciousness that have persisted until the present.

Ethnogenesis

In recent years, anthropologists have increasingly focused on **ethnogenesis,** that is, "historical processes of ethnic formation" (Whitehead 1996b:20) or "the rapid formation of entirely new societies and cultures when individuals of diverse backgrounds are suddenly thrown together by fate and forced to create societies afresh" (Bilby 1996:119). Ethnogenesis is a concept "encompassing peoples' . . . cultural and political struggles to create enduring identities in general contexts of radical change and discontinuity" (Hill 1996:1).

Ethnogenesis is hardly the sole outcome of European colonialism, because the emergence of new ethnic identities is part of the cultural history of any region. For example, the major upheavals spurred by the spread of the Inca and Aztec empires almost certainly resulted in multiple instances of ethnogenesis, and historical and ethnohistorical research suggests analogous processes at work deep in Amazonia prior to the European presence (Whitehead 1994). Nevertheless, the bulk of current research on Latin American and Caribbean ethnogenesis relates it to the tremendous effects of the European Conquest. That many anthropologists focus on how Europeans (often unwittingly) contributed to ethnogenesis stems partly from the availability of historical records and accounts produced by Europeans themselves, and partly from the fact that "Many of these new societies owe their existence to the major upheavals and displacements of persons associated with European conquest and expansion during the last five centuries, with the African slave trade playing a particularly prominent role" (Bilby 1996:119).

How European administrators, explorers, and missionaries spurred ethnogenesis varied considerably in time and place (Hulme and Whitehead 1992). Among indigenous groups in ethnically diverse Suriname, "The range of ethnic self-ascription increasingly narrowed into either Carib or Arawak identities" (Whitehead 1996b:21), because of how Dutch and English rivals categorized indigenous allies who they recruited to their cause. Elsewhere, European trade spurred the coalescence of new identities in northern South America:

> [C]lose historical investigation of Carib origins strongly suggests that the regional dominance achieved by their chieftains by the mid seventeenth century, a key moment in the creation of modern Carib ethnicity, was based, in economic terms, on their redistribution of European goods in the Orinoco Basin and the Guayana uplands. (Whitehead 1994:42)

Other processes were also at work. In Amazonia, one response to depopulation

> was for a number of tribes . . . to merge. The ethnologist Franz Caspar (1956:221) lived for a while among the Tupari tribe and was told by them that "in the days of their grandfathers and great-grandfathers several small tribes had merged.

Of every man and every women Topto was able to say without hesitation of what extraction they were. There was only one man left out of each of the 'Vaikorotá', 'Aumeh' and 'Mensiató' tribes. Five were real 'Tupari.' All the rest . . . were 'Vakarau' . . . Even the present language of the tribe, he said, was not the old Tupari, for the minorities had adopted the language of the Vakarau." (Dixon and Aikhennvald 1999:5–6)

A good example of ethnogenesis is the emergence of **maroon societies** forged through an amalgam of African, indigenous, and sometimes European cultures (Price 1979). The English term *maroon* comes from the French *marronage,* in turn borrowed from the Spanish *cimarronaje,* which primarily referred to **cimarrones,** or runaway slaves who forged new lives relatively free of European colonial control (Mintz 1996a:302). Free slave communities formed by runaway slaves were called **palenques** in some Spanish-speaking regions and **quilombos** (originally an Angolan African term) or *macambos* in Portuguese Brazil. Landers (2004) notes that Spanish complaints about runaway slaves date to as early as 1503 in Hispaniola, reminds readers that maroon societies were also present in Spanish possessions in what is now part of the United States, and that many of their members allied themselves with North American Indian tribes.

In Brazil, one of the best known, enduring, and powerful maroon societies was Palmares in the northeastern state of Pernambuco. Palmares, comprised of various settlements primarily populated by runaway slaves as early as the late sixteenth century, was finally defeated by the Portuguese in 1694. One diary of an expedition against Palmares drew attention to streets six feet wide and more than 200 buildings, including a church (Anderson 1996:551). In eastern Cuba, some *palenque* communities remained relatively free of colonial control for almost 200 years (La Rosa Corzo 2003).

In the Caribbean and Central America, the best examples of maroon societies are the **Black Carib,** a term denoting a wide spectrum of groups from the Lesser Antilles to the Central American and northern South American coastlines that emerged out of the fusion of runaway African slaves and Carib-speaking indigenous groups. Although virtually all larger and sedentary Arawak-speaking indigenous societies in the Greater Antilles perished within a few decades of the Conquest, many mobile Carib-speaking groups in the smaller and scattered Lesser Antilles not only survived but actively resisted European encroachments well into the eighteenth century (Solien 1971; Basso 1977). In 1796, the Black Caribs in St. Vincent and Dominica surrendered to the British, thus ending the last vestige of indigenous resistance to European colonial rule in the Caribbean. The British then deported the Blacks Caribs to Honduras, and many eventually made their way to Central America (Hulme 1986:227–263; González 1988, 1997).

The process of ethnogenesis that ushered in maroon societies during the colonial period is still relevant in contemporary Latin America and the Caribbean—underscoring how memory and the past anchor the present. For example, in Venezuela,

when invoking the concept of *cimarronaje* today, the Afro-Venezuelan refers not merely to past history but to a living tradition still determined to resist the domination of a European ruling class. It recognizes that Black Venezuelans remain marginalized, economically oppressed citizens . . . (Guss 1996:184)

Further, many maroon groups that maintain their own ethnic identity are scattered through-out Latin America and the Caribbean. In northeastern Venezuela, the (now Spanish-speaking) Aripaeño trace their roots to African slaves who escaped from Dutch plantations in Suriname during the mid-eighteenth century. An important component of Aripaeño identity is historical lore that recounts the exodus from Dutch plantations, a central feature of which

> entails Pantera Negra, the offspring of an upper-class Dutch white woman and a black slave foreman who worked at the Dutch colonial plantation owned by the father of Pantera Negra's mother. Upon the couple's discovery of the preg-nancy, they fled in the company of other blacks from the plantation and settled in the Caura region . . . Pantera Negra was born during this journey to freedom or *grand marronnage*. Upon the death of her parents, Pantera Negra became the ruler of . . . the maroon community founded by her father . . . Pantera Negra . . . demarcates and permeates Aripaeño's ancestral territory with mythic . . . features that are grounded in historical events and that serve as important markers of their heritage and identity. (Pérez 2003:88)[1]

In contemporary Suriname the Ndyukua—numbering more than 20,000—are one of the two largest maroon groups. Not far from the Colombian port city of Cartagena is Palenque de San Basilio, with a distinctive Spanish-based creole language. Between Suriname and French Guiana lie the Aluku and other groups. The emergence of an African-based reli-gious system was (and has been) crucial for the preservation of a distinct maroon identity. Music has played an equally important role. Indeed, one of the most famous reggae bands—the Wailing Roots—are in fact Alukus (Bilby 2000; see Chapter 11 for further dis-cussion of reggae music). When in the middle of the seventeenth century Jamaica—then a Spanish colony—fell to the British, many African slaves fled to the interior Blue Moun-tains. Over the course of time, they intermingled with other Africans fresh from the slave trade, as well as with Creole-born slaves. The result of this cultural miscegenation was the emergence of "the Windward and Leeward Maroons [who] have maintained separate iden-tities until today" (Bilby 1996:122).

The Garifuna, who trace their origins to the Black Caribs, are some of the ethno-graphically better-known maroon groups (see Photo 4.2).

In present-day Honduras, the Garifuna "identify with blackness and Black culture, but also perceive themselves as more authentic in comparison to other groups since they have managed to preserve their language and unique customs" (Kirtsoglou and Theodos-sopoulos 2004:137). More importantly, by continuing to speak the Garifuna language, per-forming musical and dance traditions with clearly African roots, and keeping alive oral lore pointing to their original diasporic experience, the Garifuna perceive themselves as quite different from Spanish-speaking Hondurans. Rust (2001) accompanies her brief sketch of contemporary Garifuna in Honduras with maps and photos. Kerns (1997) has underscored the important role of women in religion and ritual among the Garifuna of Belize. As in the case with many other Latin American and Caribbean peoples, contemporary Garifuna cul-ture is being shaped by migration to the United States and the mass media. For example, Los Angeles is the destination of many Garifuna migrants, and the availability in Belize of

PHOTO 4.2   *The dance group Nueva Estrella celebrates the 202th anniversary of the arrival of the black community, called Garifunas, from the Caribbean to Honduras, with a performance at Tegucigalpa's Central Park, Honduras.*

United States cable programming is having a significant impact on youths and teenagers, many of whom "listen to American rap music along with their own punta rock, wear the baggy jeans and shirts favoured by U.S. hip-hop artists and, it seems, anything else they can find emblazoned with the logos of companies like Nike and Tommy Hilfiger" (Matthei and Smith 2004:278).

Colonial Legacies, Independence, and the Coalescence of Nation-States

The end of the colonial period began in 1804 with the independence of Haiti from France. During the next two decades, most Latin American countries achieved their formal political independence; some in the Caribbean have yet to do so.

The long colonial period left a deep and lasting political, economic, social, and cultural imprint, so much so that many seemingly "traditional" facets of Latin American culture—from religious beliefs to gender relations to ways of organizing into family or kin units—are largely a product, an aftermath, of the Conquest and the colonial period. This heritage was not fundamentally altered by the nineteenth century wars of independence and the formation of modern Latin American nation-states.

Independence was of course important to most (nonelite) Latin Americans: many indigenous peoples and African slaves fought and died for independence, although scholars still dispute why they did so. And independence, to be sure, had sweeping impacts on Latin American peoples. For example, the decades following independence witnessed concerted drives by Creole elites to more effectively govern and extract resources from their largely rural populations. These attempts often translated into policies that further stimulated the expansion of haciendas, plantations, and cattle ranches, and the growth of large populations of dependent laborers. These efforts were also paralleled by policies that aimed at undermining the economic autonomy of peasant communities by, for example, attacking the foundations of communally-owned lands, or by stimulating the growth of economic enclaves geared toward the production of commodities for the world market.

Yet, the cultures of many societies and social groups that were forged during the colonial period and that cultural anthropologists began systematically studying and documenting in the 1930s and 1940s, are strikingly analogous to those of the colonial period. Indeed, a colonial-era Nahuatl- or Maya-speaking peasant in Mesoamerica attending a contemporary celebration of the Days of the Dead (see Chapter 7) would find a great deal of resemblance to how this celebration was practiced in his/her time; an Aymara- or Quechua-speaking Andean peasant in southern Bolivia 300 years ago would recognize and understand many rituals that punctuate the agricultural cycle today; 200 years ago, Quechua-speaking peasants in Pisaq, Peru, would understand the "rituals of rule" performed today at the beginning of the New Year (see Photo 4.1); and indigenous Amazonians centuries ago would fully comprehend the importance of using hallucinogens during contemporary healing practices (see Chapter 8).

What are some colonial legacies that are especially important for understanding the contemporary cultural anthropology of Latin American societies (Wolf and Hansen 1972; Stern 1982; Mallon 1992, 1995; Thurner 1997; Burkholder and Johnson 2004:349–390)?

1. *Emergence of syncretic cultures.* One important and enduring legacy is the emergence of syncretic cultures, blending elements of European, indigenous pre-Hispanic, and/or African ways of life in manifold ways. This creative amalgam of old and new—the result of a need and struggle to make sense of and forge new and meaningful life ways in the post-Conquest period—in fact lies at the root of much of the so-called "traditional" contemporary Latin American culture. There is not *one* aspect of the contemporary cultures of *any* Latin American society that has not been heavily inflected by the colonial experience.

2. *Enclave economies.* In virtually all Latin American countries, an economic system emerged that was marked by a small number of tiny enclaves of capital intensive and/or export oriented industries. These enclaves were deeply connected to and often surrounded by vast hinterlands settled by culturally distinct small-scale agriculturalists (peasants) or slave communities. Controlled by local and sometimes international elites who shared little with the vast majority of indigenous or slave communities, these enclaves would lie at the foundation of the deep political, economic, and cultural divide between elites and popular classes that exemplify Latin American and Caribbean societies to the present day.

3. *Political and economic inequality.* Deep and lasting political and economic inequality was a fundamental dimension of the colonial period that was further exacerbated after independence. This profound disparity in turn partly accounts for the difficulties post-independence Latin American elites faced in forging a unified national identity, often expressed in contending notions of citizenship and nationalism, as well as different and sometimes antagonistic visions of the nation-state. The result was fertile ground for contemporary large-scale popular movements, such as the Mexican revolution of 1910 and the Bolivian revolution of 1952. Indeed, the ongoing Zapatista rebellion in Chiapas, Mexico, and the Central American civil wars of the 1980s which, especially in Guatemala, pitted large numbers of Maya Indians against Hispanicized state elites in a ferocious and bloody conflict (see Chapter 12), is a clear reminder of this social, cultural, and political-economic legacy between the haves and have nots.

4. *Cultural and racial divisions.* The deep political and economic inequality mentioned previously had an equally important cultural and ideological counterpart: a profound divide, in virtually all Latin American societies, along the overlapping axes of culture and race—between "Whites," "Indians," "Blacks," and others. As (Stern 1982:186) argues for colonial Peru—and the argument is equally valid for much of contemporary Latin America—"the Indian countryside . . . became poor and 'backward' not simply in economic terms, but in a social and ideological sense as well . . . colonialism created 'Indians' and defined them as an inferior, degraded race" (see Chapter 5). That the bloody civil strife that rocked Peru in the 1980s surfaced in Ayacucho (see Chapter 12)—the most "Indian" region of Peru and where many colonial-era revolts and rebellions were also centered—should remind us that in many ways the colonial "script" is still being played out in the politically, economically, and culturally fragmented societies of Latin America and the Caribbean.

Controversies: The Quincentennial, or Remembering Columbus

When on October 12, 1492 Christopher Columbus sighted and landed on what is now the Bahamas, little did he dream that his arrival would spur such far reaching and lasting transformations in the New and Old Worlds. Neither was he probably cognizant that 500 years later, his landing and the tremendous worldwide consequences that it ushered in would be both remembered and commemorated—as well as marred in considerable controversy.

Public commemorations are highly visible, shared symbolic ritual mediums through which historical events are remembered. But they are much more than that, for public commemorations are also important channels through which different claims of the "truth"—of what "really happened"—as well as their consequences are crafted and eventually disputed. "What we often call the 'legacy of the past,'" Trouillot (1995:17) reminds us, "may not be anything bequeathed by the past itself," but is invariably appropriated and re-interpreted by social groups with an interest in claiming and legitimizing distinct and often conflicting versions of the past. Further, these renderings often reveal much more about the present than about the "facts" that occurred long ago. The famous and now legendary 1836 "Battle of the Alamo" in Texas—widely popularized by Hollywood and deeply entrenched in U.S. historical lore—provides a well-known example of how a historical event—what "happened" and why—is interpreted in radically different ways, and how these dissimilar interpretations reveal much more about contemporary society and culture. Trouillot asks:

> Is that battle a moment of glory during which freedom-loving Anglos, outnumbered but undaunted, spontaneously chose to fight until death rather than surrender to a corrupt Mexican dictator? Or is it a brutal example of U.S. expansionism, the story of a few white predators taking over what was sacred territory and half-willingly providing, with their death, the alibi for a well-planned annexation? (1995:9)

This heightened and continuous controversy surrounding what "really happened" at the Alamo has a great deal to do with the growing political, economic, and demographic importance of the Hispanic/Latino population in the southwestern United States (Chapter 1). But it is also very much related to growing ethnic consciousness and intense efforts by Hispanics/Latinos to revalidate their cultural heritage.

An analogous process of ethnic and cultural validation—and of symbolic appropriations and refashioning of the past—has underpinned responses to and memories of Columbus' landing in the New World (see In Their Own Words 4.2).

Trouillot (1995:108–140) reminds us that for hundreds of years Columbus' arrival in the New World was scarcely remembered, much less commemorated, and that it was only in the late 1880s that Spain began planning for a massive commemoration of what would soon be known as the Discovery. This seemingly sudden interest had much to do with attempts by the government to grapple with Spain's internal conflicts as well as shore up its position vis-à-vis the growing geo-political importance of rival states:

IN THEIR OWN WORDS 4.2
Remembering Columbus

In many indigenous societies, events that took place deep in the past are remembered—literally kept alive—but invariably they are transformed through oral traditions. The momentous impact of the Columbian Encounter is one such example. Among the Kuna of Panama, the conquest and its impact are embedded in traditional historical songs that not only serve as reservoirs of memory but also underpin a sense of ethnic distinctiveness. The following are some segments that surface in a contemporary chiefly chant (Sherzer 1994):

Christopher Columbus who doesn't like our grandfathers . . .

The Spaniards entered at the mouth of the Kanir river . . .

Our grandfathers and grandmothers were mistreated . . .

Our grandfathers were assassinated and they [the Spaniards] cut their stomachs open . . .

Finally, our grandparents arrived at the river which was called, and there they remained, in poverty . . .

The Spaniards mistreated our grandparents . . .

> Torn by factional feuds, outflanked in Europe by nearly all the Atlantic states, threatened in the Americas by the economic incursions of Britain, the influence of the United States, and the constant fear of losing Cuba, Spain was in dire need of a moral and political uplift. (Trouillot 1995:125)[2]

But the cuadricentennial celebration of 1892 was also widely popular in the United States, where large numbers of Italians and Irish had immigrated by the late 1880s, and where ethnic politics "gave Columbus a lobby, a prerequisite to public success in U.S. culture" (Trouillot 1995:123). Celebrating the Discovery was, of course, important to the Italian American sense of ethnic pride, while among Irish Americans, "Columbus played a leading role in making citizens out of these immigrants. He provided them with a public example of Catholic devotion and civic virtue, and thus a powerful rejoinder to the cliché that allegiance to Rome preempted the Catholic's attachment to the United States" (Trouillot 1995:123).

The cuadricentennial celebration was scarcely controversial—but not so the quincentennial. As Lunenfeld notes:

> Nations outgrow heroes, the way children must learn to live without Santa. Lenin is being toppled in Russia. The Federal government removed Custer's name from his national park. It is now Christopher Columbus' turn at the chopping block. (1992:137)

By the late 1980s, a multiplicity of other "voices" in Latin America and the United States had surged forward in public and academic arenas questioning many conventional interpretations of what "happened" on and after October 12, 1492, as well as how to remember that event. By the early 1990s, many Latin American indigenous groups—as well as Native Americans in the United States—convened to publicly and angrily denounce (and not celebrate) Columbus' arrival in the New World, an event that they viewed more in terms of conquest and enslavement rather than "discovery" (Brown 1992; Bernstein 1991; Nash 2001:121). And in Latin America, well-known indigenous leaders, such as Domitila Chungara and Rigoberta Menchú (from Bolivia and Guatemala, respectively), conveyed through published interviews their understandings of that fateful date (Chungara and Yañez 1992; Menchú and Yañez 1992).

In what would turn out to be an "ocean of print" (Block 1994), scholars, journalists, and others hotly debated how to best interpret the quincentennial remembrance of 1492. In one of the most comprehensive reviews on this issue, Axtell provides a cogent overview of some of the contentious debates:

> During the Quincentenary, teachers, scholars, and activists generally lined up on two sides . . . One camp blamed Columbus and his European successors for all the deaths and misery of America's natives (and African slaves) to the present. Indian spokespersons and their non-Indian supporters in this camp tended to speak in broad generalities about greed, racism and ethnocentrism as the root causes of alleged genocide and ecocide and to include virtually all Euro-Americans in their indictments. Their writings sought to short-circuit the expected celebratory character of the Quincentenary . . . less by making

disinterested scholarly analyses of the past than by connecting the grim past of their ancestors and their own far-from-satisfactory present with carefully selected, emotionally charged historical vignettes and images and often eloquent expressions of sadness, pain and anger . . . The other camp sought to complicate the moral and historical issues by distinguishing among Euro-American (and Indian) groups and even individuals, by contextualizing events to avoid anachronism, by emphasizing the impartial role of disease, and by seeking understanding before, if not rather than, judgment. A number of articles defended Columbus and "the West" against the historical attacks and "misperceptions" of the counter-camp, some in mass media publications. (1995:690–691)

Many others sought a more middle ground, recognizing the devastating aftermath of 1492 on Native Americans while at the same time recognizing some positive consequences:

Plainly there is something unhistorical—an abuse of truth—in glossing over the painful episodes in the long process of exploration, colonization and, yes, exploitation that began with Columbus' voyages. But it is no less unhistorical—no less an abuse of truth—to depict that experience in exclusively negative terms. (Shaw 1991, quoted in Lunenfeld 1992:139)

It is partly this search for a middle ground in an acrimonious and ideologically driven debate that has prompted many scholars to refer to October 12, 1492 as the Columbian Encounter. From this perspective, to allude to the Discovery is unacceptable, for it betrays an uncritical acceptance of a Eurocentric mode of understanding history, while to refer to Columbus' arrival in the New World solely in terms of invasion, enslavement, or genocide is to adopt an equally uncritical, and no less ideologically narrow, perspective. As Axtell notes:

Encounters are mutual, reciprocal—two-way rather than one-way streets. Encounters are generically capacious: there are encounters of people but also of ideas, institutions, habits, values, plants, animals, and micro-organisms. Encounters are temporally and spatially fluid: they can occur at any time in any place, before or after 1492, around the globe. And, although natives, critics and activists may not approve the idea, encounters are morally neutral: the term does not prejudge the nature of the contact or its outcome. In sum, encounter is a spacious description that jettisons normative baggage to make room for disinterestedness and parity. (1992:336, quoted in Axtell 1995:695–696)

Summary

Aided by political and ethnic divisiveness in indigenous societies, technological superiority, cultural differences, and disease pathogens, Europeans overwhelmed most organized resistance to the Conquest in a few decades. During the 300 years of colonial rule, Europeans devised numerous strategies for consolidating their rule but were often not entirely successful. Indigenous societies and African slaves continuously challenged the colonial order along multiple fronts, sometimes through frontal rebellions, but more often indirectly but refusing to pay tribute or fleeing forced labor drafts. Running away to isolated areas, one strategy followed by many (especially African slaves) to defy colonial rule, led to the emergence of maroon societies forged through an amalgam of indigenous, African, and European cultures. Resistance to the European Conquest—what it meant or achieved—still runs deep, as when indigenous societies took an active role in denouncing the Conquest and re-interpreting the 1492 events 500 years later.

ISSUES AND QUESTIONS

1. *Explaining the Conquest.* How were Europeans able to carry out the Conquest and extend their reach so quickly throughout much of Latin America and the Caribbean? In what ways did indigenous societies consciously or unconsciously aid in their own Conquest? Are there historic parallels with North America?

2. *Consolidating Colonial Rule.* Success on the battlefield was a relatively quick and easy undertaking compared with the protracted and difficult efforts at consolidating colonial rule. Which economic, political, and cultural mechanisms were employed by Europeans to consolidate their rule? Were some more successful than others? Why? Where?

3. *Contesting Colonial Rule.* In what ways did members of indigenous societies contest colonial rule? Were these strategies successful or futile? Why, why not, and where? In what ways did culture play a role or eventually loom important in these efforts?

4. *Remembering Columbus.* Was Columbus a hero or a villain—or is this perhaps the wrong question to ask? Why was the Quincentennial controversy relevant and to whom? In what ways might this controversy still be significant in a cultural anthropology course or textbook?

KEY TERMS AND CONCEPTS

Andean rebellions p. 95
Black Carib p. 100
Cabildo p. 88
Cimarrones p. 100
Cofradías p. 91
Columbian Exchange p. 84
Encomendero p. 86
Encomienda p. 86
Estancias p. 92
Ethnogenesis p. 99
Everyday forms of resistance
  p. 97

Fazenda p. 92
Godparenthood p. 90
Hacendado or fazendeiro
  p. 93
Hacienda p. 92
Haiti's slave revolution p. 97
Hegemony p. 79
Maroon societies p. 100
Merced, composición p. 86
Mitas p. 87
Palenques p. 100
Plantation p. 93

Public commemorations p. 104
Quilombos p. 100
Reducciones p. 87
Repartimiento p. 87
Repartimiento de mercancías
  p. 96
Rituals of rule p. 89
Yucatán Caste War p. 96

E N D N O T E S

1 As Pérez suggests, women often played important material and symbolic roles in maroon societies. The essays compiled by Gaspar and Hine (2004) poignantly illustrate how as slaves, runaway slaves, or former slaves, women of African descent were decisive in resisting colonial rule.

2 This "uplift" was not successful, for in 1898—just six years after the celebration of the cuadricentennial—Spain lost Cuba and Puerto Rico (and, in Asia, the Phillipines) to the United States in the Spanish-American War.

5 Cultural Politics of Race and Ethnicity*

Latin American and Caribbean societies were founded on the admixture of European, indigenous American, and African slave populations. Yet, while it seems, in theory, simple to separate members of these societies based on their respective racial/ethnic heritage as Indians, Europeans, or Blacks, in reality, such divisions are not nearly so transparent. Although North Americans make simple and rigid racial divisions based on skin color, these divisions are less meaningful in Latin America, where phenotype (overt physical characteristics) alone does not determine race or ethnicity. In fact, three individuals from Quito, the capital city of Ecuador, may look very similar in terms of skin color, hair color, and eye color, and yet may variously identify themselves (and each other) as White, Indian, or Mestizo based on a range of significant cultural differences (see the next section on Racial Categories and Racial Fluidity in Latin America for a discussion of these and other terms). This chapter examines what race and ethnicity mean in the Latin American and Caribbean context, how the racial and ethnic makeup of different regions have come to be historically constructed, and why race and ethnic typologies are best thought of in terms of culturally constructed differences between groups, rather than as biological differences between people.

Racial Categories and Racial Fluidity in Latin America

Race can be defined as the grouping of human beings based on the presumption (but not the reality) that biological differences separate people into distinct populations. The emergence of the concept of race is intimately tied to European colonial expansion and theories of social evolution. Although the notion of shared biological difference has typically resulted in the association of physical appearance (phenotype) with racial difference in North America, "biological race" is actually a social construct based on the association of cultural characteristics with different "racial" types. **Ethnicity,** on the other hand, is best understood as a shared group identity based on the common association of key cultural elements. As a concept, ethnicity emerged in the latter part of the twentieth century as an analytical tool of social scientists who critiqued the discrimination and prejudice that

---

*This chapter was written by Patrick C. Wilson of the University of Lethbridge, Canada, expressly for this book.

underpinned racial classifications, and who attempted to reconfigure understanding of cultural difference by employing this new concept as an alternative to race.

Since the earliest years of Spanish and Portuguese colonial rule in the Americas, Europeans struggled to explain the vast cultural differences they encountered in the new colonies, provide a justification for the domination of indigenous peoples and the enslavement and transport of Africans to the New World, and make sense (in socio-cultural terms) of children born through the union of European and indigenous or African peoples. Because colonial rule in the Americas relied largely on the exploitation of the labor of indigenous inhabitants and African slaves, determining and regulating who corresponded to the subjugated Indian and African slave classes was a key component of European colonial rule. Even as early as the second half of the sixteenth century, when the category "Indian" was created as an important element of tax and tributary systems in colonial Peru (Stern 1982), concepts of racial and ethnic difference were central to the creation and maintenance of hierarchies of power in Latin America and the Caribbean. They continue to be important in many of the same ways today. More recently, however, cultural difference has become politicized in new forms through the emergence of social movements that valorize cultural and ethnic difference and challenge cultural racisms that have historically situated indigenous peoples and Blacks toward the bottom of social hierarchies. In these movements, the expression of cultural difference is asserted as a right, and their strong culturalist statements challenge nation-state attempts to claim a common national identity rooted in invented myths of racial and ethnic homogeneity.

North Americans tend to recognize rigid racial categories, perhaps best illustrated by the distinctions between "Blackness" and "Whiteness," where an individual is either considered African American or White and there is little room for ambiguity within or between these categories. This is not the case in Latin America and the Caribbean, where a range of intermediate categories between Black and White, or Indian and White, are widely recognized.

In the early colonial period, pseudoracial categories including **Mestizo** (a highly complex and fluid intermediary category between Indian and White; Mestiço, Portuguese) and **Mulatto** (likewise a complex category between Black and White) were created, among many others, and served as intermediate categories between White and Black or Indian, seen to be located at the polar extremes of the emerging racial classification system. In the early colonial period, these intermediate categories were recognized as being the result of mixed biological ancestry. Therefore, a Mestizo (Mestiza for a female) was a child born to Indian and Spanish or Portuguese parents. Typically, the father was Spanish or Portuguese and the mother was Indian, reflecting both the demographics of the early colonial period where there were far fewer European women in the Americas, and the socially accepted patterns of marriage, concubinage, and sexual relations between members of different racial groups. In Latin America, the general rule of hypergamy applied to interracial unions, whereby it was generally more acceptable for women of the "lower" racial group (in terms of social status and power) to marry or engage in sexual relations with men of a "higher" racial group, but not the other way around.

As unions between Spanish/Portuguese men and Indian or African women produced large numbers of children of mixed ancestry, the categories of Mestizo and Mulatto, respectively, came to reflect the emerging racial diversity. Over time, however, racial classification became increasingly complex, as generations of mixing led to multiple intermediate categories in places like Brazil, Mexico, and Cuba, and in general it became more difficult

TABLE 5.1   Some Brazilian Racial Terms

Portuguese	English
Amarelo	Yellow
Branco	White
Branco Caboclado	White with Caboclo ancestry
Branco Mulatto	White Mulatto
Branco Sarará	White Sarará (see below)
Cabo Verde	Very dark skinned with "White" features (such as straight hair)
Caboclo	Copper color(ed) (also mixed African-indigenous or European-indigenous ancestry)
Caboclo escuro	Dark Caboclo
Claro	Light
Côr de canela	Cinnamon color(ed)
Côr de cinza	Gray/ash color(ed)
Côr de cinza clara	Light gray/ash color(ed)
Creolo	Creole
Escuro	Dark
Louro	Blond, very fair (skin color)
Moreno	Dark/very brown
Moreno claro caboclado	Light dark/brown (and of Caboclo ancestry)
Moreno escuro	Very dark Moreno
Mulatto bem claro	Very light Mulatto
Mulatto escuro	Dark Mulatto
Negro	Black
Pardo	Grayish dark brown
Preto	Black/very dark (and non-"White" phenotype)
Preto claro	Light/fair Preto
Roxo	Purple/violet
Roxo claro	Light purple/violet
Roxo de cabelo bom	Purple/violet with nice hair
Sarará	Fair/light
Sarára escuro	Dark/black Sarará
Vermelho	Red

Source: Adapted from Harris 1964:58. English translations by Harry Sanabria.

to readily distinguish members of different categories based on physical appearance alone. In anthropology, Charles Wagley (1952) was at the forefront of the study of race and class in Brazil. Harris (1964), in his research on racial classification in Brazil in the 1960s, found forty different racial terms used in the community he studied; these reflected not only skin color but also other physical characteristics in addition to ancestry (see Table 5.1). And when the Brazilian Institute of Geography and Statistics (IBGE) conducted its own study in 1976 to collect people's self-referential skin colors, it compiled a list of 134 types.

These examples point not only to the remarkable complexity of racial classifications in Brazil, but also to the fact that these are cultural and not biological classifications. This is true for several reasons: First, the simple recognition that systems of racial classification are different from society to society points to the social construction of racial difference. Second, and as will become clearer as this chapter progresses, how racial categories are recognized and the meanings attached to these categories change over time and in different social contexts. Third, racial classifications and identities are relational, and therefore emerge and are transformed in the course of social interaction. Finally, the markers of racial difference after the early colonial period are as much cultural as they are physical; therefore, one's identification as a Mestizo, for example, is as much a recognition of differences in dress, language, and occupation as it is a comment on the phenotypic characteristics of that individual.

This points to the situational and social nature of racial classification. Again in contrast to North American racial classifications based on a rigid color-line, racial classification is complicated in Latin America by occupational differences, wealth, and education, among other factors. As Kottak (1999) suggests about Brazil, racial difference falls along a continuum and combines physical with cultural difference in the classification of racial types, and phenotypic characteristics are recognized on a shifting and highly detailed scale. Therefore, as Kottak further suggests, racial classification is not rigid, nor does race appear to be given substantial weight in many social contexts.

That race in Latin America and the Caribbean is about comparison and not about rigid difference is perhaps best illustrated by the example of Pelé, the famous Brazilian soccer player. Pelé, described by the Uruguayan journalist and essayist Eduardo Galeano as "[playing] soccer the way God would play soccer, if God decided to seriously dedicate himself to the task" (1986:202), is a national hero of Brazil and a cultural icon throughout Latin America, and he would be readily classified as Black or African American in North America. Many Brazilians, however, as a result of his achieved social status and wealth, classify him as White. Although color is not insignificant in Latin America, it is not always determinate of race. Not only in Brazil, but also in parts of the Caribbean, color does not lead to the rigid distinctions between Blacks and Whites. In Venezuela, it is common to recognize the mixed ancestry of the Venezuelan people, and Venezuelans often refer to themselves as *café con leche* (coffee with milk). What concerns them is how much (white) milk versus how much (black) coffee is visible on their skin. In this context, it is not race that frames the socially meaningful distinctions, but rather the color of one's skin and a preference for whiteness (Wright 1990).

The example of Pelé and discussion of Brazil's flexible racial system also point to the issue of **racial passing.** Passing is a social process by which an individual comes to move from one position on a racial hierarchy to another. As Harris (1964) argues, this often involves the withdrawal of an individual from ties to family and friends that would mark that person as a "lower" racial type by association, and it is often accompanied by changes in dress or hairstyle that may accentuate a different social position. In Brazil, passing is very common, and given the great fluidity of Brazilian racial classification, it is relatively easy and often does not require a break from family and friends. In other parts of Latin America and the Caribbean, however, passing is much more contentious, and people may go to great lengths to try and assert their position in a "higher" racial category. For example, an Aymara peasant in Bolivia migrating to live in or around the city of La Paz may attempt to alter his or her appearance to avoid being categorized as an "Indian." A young man moving to La Paz may perm his hair (to avoid having straight, coarse hair often associated with Indians); he may abandon his poncho and rubber soled sandals in favor of slacks, a button-down shirt, and dress shoes; and he may reject the use of the Aymara language, at least in public, to avoid associations between language and racial classification.

The potential for racial passing and the fluidity of racial classification systems in Brazil and parts of the Caribbean have led some observers to classify those parts of Latin America and the Caribbean with the most flexible systems as being "racial democracies." In anthropological and sociological circles, there has been considerable debate about the validity of this claim. On the one hand, some scholars suggest that the categorization of Brazil, Cuba, or the Dominican Republic as racial democracies because of official statements denouncing the concept of racial difference has obscured the endurance of social, economic, and political prejudice rooted in racial difference (Sagás 2000). Furthermore, because ideologies of racial democracies tend to downplay—if not exclude completely—the validity of racial difference, these ideologies are sometimes said to preclude the possibility of Blacks constructing a sense of unity that could lead to a Black resistance movement (Hanchard 1994; Wright 1990).

On the other side of the debate, however, are scholars such as de la Fuente (1999), who suggest that despite the limitations of conceptualizing Latin America and the Caribbean as "racial democracies," the fluidity of these systems offer marginal Black populations avenues for social inclusion and a language with which to challenge for equal positions in society. Analyzing early twentieth-century Cuba, de la Fuente (1999:46) argues that categorizing the rhetoric of racial democracy by figures such as José Martí (a leader of the Cuban independence movement from Spain) as "elite-made tools of domination and exclusion" fails to recognize both the subversive nature of these discourses in Latin America and the potential that these be coopted by Black populations in the course of political struggle. On the one hand, when most Europeans and North Americans were developing concepts of scientific racism, some of the founders of Latin American independence movements were arguing against these exclusionary politics. Even if the dreams of nonracialized utopic independent states in Latin America were not achieved, the potential for some segments of the population to ascend socially along a flexible and more open racial classification system did enable many individuals paths to social advancement. Black Cubans in the early twentieth century appropriated official discourses on racial democracy and used them to their own political advantage to place demands on Cuban leaders.

Although race is a social construct, it is not constructed in the same way in all places. The vast diversity in the social construction of race is aptly illustrated through reference to the Caribbean region. The tendency to treat the Caribbean as a cultural area masks the wide diversity in the region in terms of colonial history, cultural makeup, political economy, and—as a result—social organization. The meanings of "race" and color are equally diverse in the region, shaped by colonial policies toward miscegenation, the nature of slave-master relationships on plantations and the local plantation histories themselves, and locally constructed social relationships between different segments of the population that give "race relations" their unique local flavor (Hoetink 1985). Generally throughout Latin America and the Caribbean, race is based on cultural difference more than on ancestry, and the foundation of racial classification is not the rigid color-line that defines North American racial hierarchies. Instead, race and racial classification in Latin America is flexible, often allows for a number of intermediate racial types, is situational and influenced by a range of other cultural factors like education and occupation, and can change repeatedly during the course of a person's lifetime.

Colonialism, Empire, and the Invention of Race

The concept of race is largely a result of colonial expansion. Attempts to explain the cultural diversity encountered in newly created European colonies, coupled with the need to justify exploitative relationships with indigenous peoples and imported African slaves, led to debate and discussion about the differences between different cultural groups. Over time, these differences were solidified into categorical schema that led not only to the identification of people based on cultural differences read as biological differences, but also the administration of the colonial population along these same lines. The organization of systems of slavery and taxation and the collection of tribute were all regulated according to supposedly racial differences. Indigenous peoples were not subject to slavery, the fate of the millions of Africans brought to work on plantations in the Caribbean, Brazil, and other parts of Latin America, but they were subject to tributary obligations. Identification as Indian or African was a key determinant of duties and limited rights for these people.

Through the sexual encounters between colonizers and colonized, new populations were born, and intermediate racial types were conceptualized to try and make social sense out of this diversity. Mestizos and Mulattos were but two of many intermediate categories to take on social meaning in the emergent colonial context. Importantly, these categories also took on legal significance. Mestizos, for example, were freed of tributary obligations, and this often served as a motivation to assert mixed parentage as a means of gaining legal recognition as Mestizo (see Chapter 4). Yet, one was not able to freely identify as one racial type or another; instead, racial ascription was a highly politicized process of negotiation between internal self-identification and external racial categorization. As one explores the significance of categories like Indian, Black, or Mestizo, it is crucial to make a distinction between **identification**—the meanings that these categories acquire in social settings and partly through a process of ascription—as compared to **personal identity**—the meanings that these categories acquire for the people who self-identify with them. As Ramos (1994) suggests in her example of the cultural creation of Brazilian Indians, this distinction points to how forms of identification have served a variety of ideological purposes, and have often carried more weight than just the ways indigenous peoples may choose to self-identify or the meanings they may wish to attach to racial or ethnic labels.

Marriage and Race in the Eighteenth Through Early Twentieth Centuries

Racial hierarchies entered the intimacies of the bedroom in important ways in Latin America and the Caribbean at the end of the colonial and beginning of the Republican period. Throughout the region, sexual politics were rooted in the intersection of class and race. Marriage was an important event in the honor of elite families, because it resulted in the union of two families. The appropriate constellation of class and racial background was necessary in the selection of an acceptable marriage partner, and finding a socially acceptable marriage partner had direct implications for the maintenance of family honor. Martínez-Alier's (1989 [1974]) study of marriage in nineteenth-century Cuba demonstrates that the socially accepted marriage practices among elite members of Cuban society were based on class and racial endogamy, meaning specifically that White elites should marry White elites. Marriage and the choice of an appropriate spouse were closely tied to family honor (see Chapter 6), and a socially unacceptable marriage could represent not only a blemish for the individual thought to be marrying down (in social terms), but also a stain on family honor more generally. A series of royal decrees were passed, the most significant being the "Royal decree on marriages between persons of known nobility with members of the castes of negroes and mulattos" (Martínez-Alier 1989:12), that attempted to regulate marriages between White elite and non-White, nonelite members of society and helped to ensure that class and racial endogamy were the norm for the Cuban elite. On the occasional instance when this norm was broken, Martínez-Alier recounts the legal struggle that parents would engage in, quite often successfully, to prohibit these unions from continuing. Concerned parents would approach the legal authorities to prohibit the union of their presumably elite son or daughter with a non-White partner, emphasizing (and attempting to verify) the purity of blood that existed in their family and their elite social status. As Martínez-Alier (1989:15) explains:

> When parents objected to a marriage they did so because they felt it was a menace to family integrity and status vis-à-vis other families of their group. It is without exception the white candidate's family that opposes the marriage. Again and again the dissenting parents talk of the "absolute inequality" of the couple, of their own "known purity of blood" and of the "remarkable and transcendental stain" on their reputation, of the "degradation of the offspring" and the "disgrace and discontent" the marriage will bring to the family . . . One son objects to his father's remarriage to a "light mulatto girl" because he "belongs to a family of pure blood on all sides . . . [and] the marriage would be a stain on all the family which is composed of respectable citizens, farmers and *hacendados* useful to the public, being white."

The ensuing legal battles were always discussed in terms of preserving the honor of the family and the family member who had (hopefully only temporarily) strayed from social norms. The penalty for continuing to pursue such a relationship was that the child marrying a nonelite partner would often lose inheritance rights and/or be ostracized from the family.

Among non-White commoners, the impacts of prevalent discrimination against them did not necessarily lead to a sense of racial solidarity or shared identity. Rather, in a form of **hegemonic racism** (de la Cadena 2000) where non-White peoples partially adopted and reproduced the racial hierarchies imposed upon them by the White dominant society, divisions emerged within the ranks of people of color and led to the reproduction of a similar regulation of marriage among lower caste individuals. Parental permission for marriage was also important in these contexts, although the nuances of racial hierarchy became infinitely more complex than the White/non-White divide elites were concerned with. In this context, shades of racial mixture were of great importance, and parents of potential brides and grooms were known to protest when their son or daughter stated their intention to marry someone considered to be of lesser racial stock. Social improvement hinged on the gradual "whitening" of one's family through favorable marriage choices, resulting in a complex calculus of race and class that led to the creation of numerous intermediate and ranked categories between Black and White.

PHOTO 5.1 Castas in Mexico, *eighteenth century painting, Museo Nacional del Virreinato, Tepotzotlán, Mexico.*

The complexities of these intermediate categories, and the social significance of them, are perhaps best expressed in a new art form that emerged in Mexico in the latter part of the eighteenth century called casta paintings. Casta paintings depicted the complex racial configuration of Mexico, reflected elsewhere in the Caribbean and Central and South America (see Photo 5.1).

Typically consisting of sixteen paintings (although occasionally more or fewer racial types were identified), sometimes on a single canvas, these portrayed dominant notions of racial mixing in colonial Latin America. Crucial here, and important for understanding later constructions of race in Latin America and the Caribbean, is that the different "racial" types are distinguished not simply by phenotype (or physical appearance in terms of skin color, eye color, or hair color and type), but also by a set of corresponding cultural traits depicted in these paintings through dress styles. In all of these paintings, the focus is on the process of racial mixing and the production of intermediate racial types through mixed unions (Carrera 2003; Katzew 2004). These paintings depict a conjugal couple of mixed races with typically one, and occasionally two, child(ren). A caption accompanying each painting explains the relationship between racial mixing and racial types. For example, the union of a Spaniard and an Indian would produce Mestizos; between Spanish and Black, Mulatto; or between Black and Indian, Zambo. Casta paintings represent attempts by elite Mexicans to create coherent social and racial categories to make sense out of the increasingly complex cultural diversity in the New World, as well as to reassert Spanish authority in the region. By making Spaniards the preferred "racial" type and using the mixing of Spaniards with non-Spaniards as the starting point for creating a hierarchical racial typology of the region, elites were attempting to maintain a colonial order rooted on racial exclusion and an assertion of White privilege and inherent superiority, but whose foundation was increasingly uncertain and shaky. This is revealed further by the lack of agreement on different labels or typologies, because the actual labels attached to "racial" types and the specific ways in which these types were ranked varied from context to context.

Significantly, concerns of race, "whiteness," and marriage have not disappeared in the twenty-first century. In the first half of the twentieth century, racial endogamy was still the norm in the Andes, where elite intellectuals who called themselves **indigenistas** (scholars, social theorists, politicians, and other social elites who argued that the redemption of the Indian race was to be found in a return to a pure, Indian past, uncorrupted by the negative impacts of Spanish colonialism) justified racial segregation—not just in marriage, but in many aspects of social life—based on their belief in the need to preserve the purity of the Indian and European races. Even today, marriages are often evaluated based on their acceptability in terms of race and class. For example, Goldstein (2003), in her research on Brazilian shantytowns, recounts how the marriage of a Black woman into a fairly elite White family led to conflicts between this woman and the family's Black domestic helper. The domestic helper sensed that this marriage did not correspond to the expected marital norms of elite endogamy and recognized in this woman a set of cultural characteristics, such as speaking style and body language, that she associated more with herself and her neighbors from the shantytown in which she lived than with the elite behavior of her White employer's family. As a result, she was often unwilling to serve this woman because of her sense of social closeness to her. In this example, the violation of elite endogamy led to a union between an elite White man, and a nonelite Black woman. The accompanying discomfort felt by the Afro Brazilian domestic worker reflects the sense of imbalance in social relationships caused by the violation of expected marriage patterns.

Scientific Racisms of the Late Nineteenth and Early Twentieth Centuries

Ultimately, the motivation behind casta paintings and the social and legal regulation of marriage provide but two illustrations of a prevailing preoccupation, intrigue, and often revulsion that Europeans and White colonial elites felt when confronted with the cultural variation that existed in the New World. The need to explain this variation coincided with the rise of scientific racisms in Europe and the Americas that attempted to measure and explain differences between European and non-European peoples based on now-debunked theories of unilineal social evolution and Lamarkian social evolution. In the late nineteenth century, social theorists such as Herbert Spencer, influenced by the growing popularity of Darwinian and Lamarkian theories of biological evolution, posited that the evolution of human societies followed the same basic principles of biological evolution in the natural world. Social evolution created a hierarchy of human populations based on presumed differential levels of evolution, falsely asserting that non-European populations were "less evolved" than their European counterparts. Coinciding with the rise of the scientific method, social evolution and scientific racisms led to the hierarchical ranking of human populations based on presumed degrees of evolution, and sought to create human taxonomies based on the premise that European civilizations were the most advanced, and situating non-Western populations at different subordinate positions on a unilineal ladder of human social evolution.

In Mexico during the late nineteenth century, proponents of social evolution believed that the progress of the nation was linked to the improvement of Mexico's racial stock through the promotion of European immigration. This would presumably lead to the "whitening" of the population and would contribute to the modernization of the nation (Stern 2003). Physical anthropologists in the mid-twentieth century attempted to repudiate these racial classifications by suggesting that different human populations represented "biotypes" that were differentiated by their presumed aptitudes and deficiencies in cognitive and physiological terms. This led to a wave of scientific measuring of different Mexican populations that ultimately reinforced, rather than dismissed, racial hierarchies:

> In 1939 a curious entourage of urban professionals appeared at Patzcuaro Lake, located high in the mountains west of Mexico City in the state of Michoacan. Led by Dr. José Gómez Robleda, the director of the National University's recently formed Institute of Social Research . . . this team of psychologists, anthropologists, and physicians came to study the region's Tarascan Indians, a majority of whom earned their livelihood in fishing or agriculture. Determined to classify the Tarascans according to the internationally recognized theory of biotypology, they literally brought their laboratory with them, carrying spirometers, stethoscopes, Rorschach ink-blots, intelligence and imagination tests, blood sampling kits, ergographs, and other apparatus designed to measure the physiological and mental traits of humans. (Stern 2003:187)

Ultimately the research of biotypologists like Gómez Robleda affirmed the stereotypes that dominant members of Mexican society held of Indians, because his test results almost invariably showed Indian peoples to be inferior to Whites in a range of measures. When this evidence was used in support of dominant racisms of the time, indigenous and Black peoples were argued to exist in a condition of truncated evolutionary development, where they lacked the cultural and cognitive refinement to fully embrace the values and goals of a modernizing nation. These views served as strong justification for the mistreatment of non-Western peoples through slavery or debt-peonage and similar to the casta paintings of a century earlier, this conceptualization of race saw hybridity through racial mixing as a danger to social order: Mestizo and other "mixed-race" peoples were thought to be racially and morally depraved and primitive.

Some early anthropological studies were at the forefront of critiquing these scientific racisms. *The Myth of the Negro Past,* by Herskovits (1958 [1941]), is one such study. Employing a Boasian perspective that attributes cultural differences not to innate, biological differences between human groups, but rather to different historical trajectories in different societies, Herskovits strongly argues against an innate concept of Black inferiority. The dominant notion of Black inferiority, which endured in scientific circles into the mid-twentieth century and still finds expression in the racist science of some fringe researchers in fields of sociobiology and evolutionary psychology, suggested that people of African descent were naturally childlike and simple in character, contributing to the "savage" qualities of African cultures in the diaspora. Refuting this viewpoint, Herskovits engaged in an ambitious social history of Blacks in Africa and the New World to suggest that divergent cultural attitudes were the result of historical differences and cultural syncretisms and not innate biological differences in racial stock.

Culture and Race

Scientific racism rooted in nineteenth century unilineal evolutionary theory was one dominant discourse for the articulation of racial hierarchies in the Americas, but not the only or the most enduring one. In fact, by the early part of the twentieth century elite intellectuals in different parts of Latin America, and most prominently in Peru and Mexico, were thinking about race in radically different ways than the false biological models forwarded by European and some Latin American social evolutionary theorists. These new theorists, who called themselves *indigenistas,* were primarily focused on the relationships between White and indigenous segments of society and called for the vindication of the "Indian race," albeit in partial and contradictory ways.

The context for the rise of **indigenismo**—a set of social theories relating to the relationships between Indian and White races, and the social redemption of the Indian race—in places like Peru and Mexico was related to debates about national identity, national unity, and the "Indian Problem." When Peru lost the War of the Pacific to Chile (1879–1883), many Peruvian intellectual and political leaders blamed the defeat on their country's large indigenous population, which was depicted as incapable of grasping the concept of the Peruvian nation, and therefore preventing the Indians from fighting with the necessary passion to lead Peru to victory (Vásquez 1996). Although evolutionists saw these limitations to be inherent and a result of truncated evolution, indigenistas offered an alternative explanation rooted in histories of subjugation and the lack of access to education that left indigenous subjects too ignorant to cultivate a sense of belonging to the nation. These kinds of arguments reframed the racial question in terms of culture and economics, rather than biology.

In fact, there were other motivating factors behind the indigenista shift from biology to culture as an explanatory racial framework. On the one hand, it was a philosophical position that countered the Eurocentric views of social evolution and *blanqueamiento* (or whitening), in that it attempted to construct a concept of race that valued, rather than denigrated, racial difference in the Americas. Second, the critical distinction of cultural rather than biological determinants of race allowed for the differentiation of "races" in terms other than those of phenotypic difference. Through generations of miscegenation, it became increasingly difficult to differentiate among the inhabitants of regions of Latin America with high indigenous populations, such as the Andes, Mexico, and parts of Central America, on the basis of physical differences alone. If "White" elites could not be readily differentiated from Indians based simply on phenotype, then how were these populations to be distinguished?

Cultural difference became the foundation of racial distinctions. As de la Cadena (2000) illustrates in her work on constructions of racial difference in twentieth-century Peru, indigenista intellectuals in Cuzco formulated a concept of race that attempted to solidify their own position on top of a racial hierarchy while reconciling regional prejudice and claiming to champion the Indian cause. Peruvian intellectuals in the capital city of Lima, located on the coast, employed a racial hierarchy that attempted to identify Indians based on a mix of phenotype and geographic location: Indians lived in the highlands, whereas Whites lived on the coast. This geographic racism was unappealing to Cuzco elites, because their location in the Andes tied them in terms of physical location with Indians. Instead, prominent Cuzqueño indigenistas, such as José Carlos Mariátegui, argued that "race" was a cultural condition resulting from the denigration of Indians through generations of oppression at the hands of some—but not all—hacendados. As such, indigenistas saw their project to be one of the vindication of the Indian race through purifying Indian culture, and leading intellectuals proposed and implemented a number of policies based on their concepts of racial purification.

First, they argued for the need to separate Indians from Whites, both spatially and racially. In essence, this was a critique of proponents of racial mixing, which indigenistas saw as racial pollution that led to the denigration of both Indian and White races. They argued that before the Spanish Conquest, the Indian race was a noble race, but that it was through the combination of oppression by the Spanish and racial mixing that the Indian race had deteriorated. One key to returning the Indian race to its noble past was to stop cultural and racial mixing. This was to be achieved by encouraging, and often coercing, indigenous peoples living in the cities to move to the countryside, reflecting the indigenista belief that the "proper place" for indigenous peoples was in the rural landscape, and by encouraging them to speak Quechua rather than Spanish. In one of the more dramatic moves to enforce the policy of racial segregation, houses of indigenous people in Cuzco were razed in the late 1920s in an attempt to force them back to rural areas (de la Cadena 2000).

The association of racial types with geographic space has been an enduring one in Latin America and the Caribbean. Even today, rural living is associated with Indians, and urbanites are thought to be "whiter." In places like Colombia, race is mapped on the national territory, as Afro Colombians for the most part live on the Atlantic and Pacific coasts of Colombia and in small patches of southwestern Colombia. In fact, the sight of people of indigenous or African descent in the capital city of Bogotá (which has become more common in recent years as massive numbers of displaced peoples have come to the city as a result of the ongoing civil war in that country) still evokes comments from local residents. Calling a displaced Afro Colombian war victim begging in the downtown sector a *costeño* (from the coast) is not simply making a comment on that person's place of origin. It is mapping the color of that person's skin with a particular region of the country, asserting that the "proper" physical space for that person to inhabit is not the cool, Andean city of Bogotá, but rather the hot, tropical climes of the coasts. Even recognizing these people as *desplazados* (displaced), in addition to recognizing their likely status as refugees of the armed conflict, is also marking them as outside of their racially inscribed territories.

Returning to Peru of the 1920s, indigenista policymakers during this period, such as Luis Eduardo Valcárcel, attempted to establish a dual education system—one for Indians and another for Whites—and argued for the use of a "pure" form of the Quechua language that they called Capac Shimi, in contrast to the more common Quechua, Runa Shima, that was thought to be polluted by Spanish influence. Their constructions of race were thought to vindicate Indians by placing the cause of their inferior social condition on generations of exploitation rather than on inferior biology, and this left open the possibility of racial improvement during the course of one's lifetime through proper education and the refinement of behavior. As part of the valorization of Indian culture, indigenistas organized and staged numerous cultural events that celebrated a glorious Inca past as an important component of the Peruvian present.

Ultimately, however, the defense of the Indian by indigenista intellectuals was only partial. Although they did valorize elements of indigenous culture, those elements were tied to a presumed glorious past, not to an Indian present. The negative associations of the Indian in the city—ragged, disease-ridden, and intellectually stunted from generations of denigration—created a social space for Indians in the countryside that was removed from contact with most White elites, and that was founded on the belief that race, geography, and occupation were intertwined. Indians were farmers who lived in the countryside and spoke Quechua, while Whites lived in the city as politicians, professionals, and intellectuals.

Decency, Hygiene, and Race

Cultural constructions of race in Latin America have endured long past the heyday of indigenismo. In fact, discourses of racial difference in Latin America today often hinge on the concept of "decency." Decency, or what it means to be a decent person, relates to a range of physical and behavioral traits that separate elites from commoners, or Whites from Indians and Blacks, in society. The way one dresses, the kind of occupation one has, where one lives, musical and food preferences, or choices for recreation can all be indicators of decency or the lack thereof. But concepts of decency are also embodied in other ways, through hair styles, mannerisms, or spoken dialects. Taken together, cultural racisms are embodied in intimate ways that are crucial markers of Whiteness or non-Whiteness, oftentimes irrespective of the color of one's skin.

In elite private schools throughout Latin America, in addition to a typical school curriculum, children learn how to behave properly. In Bogotá, Colombia, for example, some private schools train children in proper etiquette as a central component of forming a new generation of elite adults. Textbooks in urbanity are employed in these classes that teach children about the proper forms of holding one's body and behaving in a range of social and domestic situations. For example, the *Manual de urbanidad y buenas maneras* (*Manual of Urbanity and Good Manners,* Carreño 2004) is a commonly employed textbook that examines proper conduct for "decent people" inside and outside the household. It was written in the nineteenth century by Manuel Carreño, who was born in Caracas, Venezuela, but educated in Spain. The European education is important because it illustrates the extent to which elite Latin Americans look to Europe for their cultural models. The book covers a vast range of social behavior and personal hygiene, examining the condition and cleanliness of one's clothing, the inappropriateness of scratching one's head or under one's shirt, and the necessity of maintaining one's body impeccably clean, including washing one's face several times during an average day. Some of the most interesting elements of the *Manual de urbanidad* relate to relations between the sexes and the obligations of good gentlemen in the manner in which they care for female companions. For example, when the manual discusses the proper use of a narrow staircase it states:

> The gentleman who accompanies a lady on a staircase that is too narrow to walk at her side should proceed ahead of her when climbing the staircase, so as not to give the appearance that he is examining her legs, and also when descending the staircase, so as to be able to give her his hand in the event that she should misstep. (Carreño 2004:91; translated by Patrick C. Wilson)

In the manner of speaking with others, the manual explains that only the most refined language should be used, that one should avoid informal language, foul language, or the discussion of repugnant themes outside of the company of one's most intimate friends. Even then, one should make sure that one's tone of voice and use of language is inoffensive to those who hear it.

Recreation may present certain challenges to the maintenance of the norms of decency, especially when outings include excursions to the countryside. The countryside—according to dominant social and racial hierarchies, a place for peasants and Indians—is also a location of potential racial contamination, a reflection of long-standing beliefs that environment can shape race. These beliefs, which find their origins in colonial ontologies of racial difference and which are linked to Lamarckian theories of evolution that posited the influence of environmental factors on the development and inheritance of traits, make trips to the countryside potentially "dangerous," through the blurring of social boundaries between Indians and Whites, rural and urban, and the association of these people and places with indecent or decent behavior. Likewise, excursions to the countryside represent moments in which the norms of proper attire are temporarily relaxed, adding to the sense of possible racial and social transgression, but this does not represent an abandonment of the norms of proper urban etiquette. Again drawing from the *Manual de urbanidad,* Carreño says:

> Among people of good education, the liberty offered by the countryside should always be circumscribed by the limits of moderation and proper decorum; even though there is a certain degree of flexibility that is needed to harmonize with the countryside and to enjoy the enchantments of nature, it should never entirely substitute the etiquette that should reign in all situations of life. (2004 :321 translated by Patrick C. Wilson)

Decency is not simply a set of behavioral traits that should be abided in society. These traits take on a moral quality. The acts of speaking properly, dressing properly, or sitting properly are considered moral acts and a reflection of the human soul, and violations of these standards of behavior are considered morally repugnant (Pedraza 1999). Discussions of decency often are ultimately discussions about racial difference cast in behavioral terms. Speaking styles, dress styles, or mannerisms are cultural, but they also break down along racial lines. Goldstein (2003), in her discussion of race and class in Rio de Janeiro, Brazil, examines what she calls the "aesthetics of domination." Using Bourdieu's (1984) concept of the relationship between "taste" and power, she argues that culturally shaped attitudes and behaviors become symbols of social difference that act to maintain structures of power in society. Looking at the relationships between elite families in Rio and their domestic servants who are Afro Brazilians, many of whom live in extremely harsh conditions in Rio's shantytowns, she illustrates how social and economic differences are not simply marked by the obvious contrasts of Whiteness versus Blackness, or upper-class apartment versus shantytown dwelling, but are demonstrated through a range of mutually-recognizable behavioral traits. Black women in Rio are distinguishable by their lack of refinement in the spoken word or by the way in which they swing their hips when walking, as much as by their occupation or residential location. Elite families, on the other hand, are characterized by a "culture of incompetence" that sets them apart from nonelites. By "culture of incompetence," Goldstein is referring to the myriad manual tasks such as washing dishes or fixing plumbing that elite people cannot or will not perform. The ability to *not* do menial tasks, but to have someone do them for you, is an important marker of elite Whiteness in Brazil and throughout Latin America.

Colonial

These markers of difference are mutually understood by both elites and nonelites in Brazil. One Afro Brazilian woman, who worked as a domestic servant in Brazil, was so aware of the ways in which her speaking style marked her as low-class that she enrolled in night school and repeated each grade, in an attempt to erase this marker of difference. Yet, for Black people in Brazil or indigenous people in the Andes, language is but one cultural marker of racial difference. For example, Colloredo-Mansfeld (1999), writing about Ecuador, illustrates the ways in which beliefs about hygiene become racialized rather than being accepted simply as a reflection of occupational differences. The common slur "dirty Indian" (*Indio sucio*) equates hygiene with race, and the suggestion that an indigenous person from the countryside smells like a "wet dog" because of his wool poncho denigrates indigenous peoples through an association between them and the animal world.

In this way, race becomes associated with certain kinds of occupation (Orlove 1998). Reddened and wind-burnt cheeks; calloused hands with dirty, rough fingernails; mud-caked shoes and boots are all the result of agricultural labor in the cold Andean countryside of Bolivia or Ecuador. Yet, they also contrast with decency and urbanity as defined by urban elites, and they reflect the kinds of "contamination" that are associated with rural life. In the case of rural Ecuador, sights and smells of the countryside are associated with dirtiness and disease, as recounted by Colloredo-Mansfeld (1999). When a group of indigenous people was engaging in collective labor for the construction of a potable water system for the area's communities, the White engineers responsible for the project refused offers by the indigenous workers to share their food, citing the dirtiness of the ground upon which the indigenous people were eating. Yet, the dirtiness was not simply confined to the rural surroundings, but also to the indigenous bodies associated with it, and many White elites assume indigenous peoples to be carriers of disease. In the nineteenth and early twentieth centuries, public markets were recognized as sites of disease, as much because of the crowding of Indian bodies into these public spaces as because of the lack of proper conditions to carefully preserve food (F. Wilson 2004). When cholera, a waterborne disease, broke out in northern Ecuador in the early 1990s, local White residents blamed the disease on the lack of hygiene of the indigenous inhabitants, rather than on the failure of the Ecuadorian state to provide its inhabitants with clean drinking water.

In the end, decency and economic status are usually, but not always, associated. Although it can be generally stated that money whitens, money as a defining trait of social status and ultimately race is contextual and dependent upon how that money is acquired and how a person conducts him/herself. In the early 1900s, the death of an elite member of society often served as a moment to reinforce the moral values of eliteness. As de la Cadena (2000:55) demonstrates for the case of Cuzco:

> The values of decency for gentlemen were conveyed to all of urban society through two frequent street rituals: funerals and duels. These public performances confirmed that gentlemen held a high place in Cuzco society. The 1924 funeral of Romualdo Aguilar is an example. Aguilar was the owner of a large hacienda, a professor at the university of San Antonio Abad, and an attorney in the local court

... The orators [at his funeral] described the comfort of Romualdo Aguilar's residence in Chiñicara, where he personally directed the tasks that "his team of Indian workers performed." They stressed his "culture and gentleness," "austerity, tried-and-true honesty, and patriotic love," "erudition, integrity and justice," and "voluntary service on behalf of others." ... Besides functioning as manifestations of grief, such funerals were rites of passage in which the deceased was publicly recognized as a selfless modern intellectual who had promoted the moral well-being and progress of all cuzqueños.

Aguilar's education and long family history of prosperity contributed greatly to his image as a decent member of Cuzco society. Old money, money that can be traced back to the colonial period and the actions of gentlemen hacendados or plantation owners, is decent money. Nouveau riche engaged in occupations considered less respectful, such as running a slaughterhouse or distributing agricultural produce, despite often equaling or exceeding White elites in strictly economic terms, are not considered decent, White members of society. Eliteness and whiteness, in this context, is not confined to economic prosperity, but is instead more related to the nexus of occupation with behavioral traits that contribute to or detract from one's social standing in society.

Mestizos and Mestizaje: Class, Race, and Nation

Although Mestizos, if we use a strict biological definition rooted in the mixing of Spanish and Indian blood, have existed since the earliest years of the colonial period, who subscribes to Mestizo identity, and the exact nature of that identity, is and has been quite contested. In that sense, Mestizos are a biological reality, but Mestizo identity in terms of its being a culturally-defined racial category is more recent and is multiple in its signification. In early Republican Peru of the mid-nineteenth century, for example, it appears that self-identification as Mestizo was actually relatively uncommon Further, the difficulties associated with recognizing a "Mestizo" on the basis of phenotype alone left state administrators attempting to record racial data at the whims of peoples' preferred self-identification. It is possible that many chose to identify as Indian during this time period because such identification carried with it the right to land, albeit with certain tributary obligations attached (Chambers 2003).

What it meant to be Mestizo, and who was and was not a Mestizo was, and until quite recently continued to be, primarily an intellectual debate rather than a category of extensive self-identification. As discussed already, early twentieth-century indigenistas criticized the miscegenation of indigenous and Spanish blood as a degeneration of racial types. Yet, other intellectual trends, and particularly those gaining strength from mid-century embraced **mestizaje,** (mestiçagem, Portuguese) or the process of mixing blood, as a positive component of improving racial stock and modernizing the nation. Intellectuals such as Vasconcelos in Mexico or Freyre in Brazil celebrated the mixing of racial types as part of a process of positive eugenics, leading to the creation of a "healthy cross-breed" (Appelbaum et al. 2003). Vasconcelos and Manuel Gamio in Mexico in the post-revolutionary period saw miscegenation as resulting in the creation of a new Cosmic Race, a noble bronze race that would preserve the positive qualities of both the Spanish and the Aztecs (King 1990). Others, such as Ecuadorian proponents of mestizaje in the 1960s and 1970s, viewed the process of racial mixing as cleansing impure qualities of the Spanish race (conceived of in terms of its histories of abuses levied against indigenous peoples during the colonial period), and those of Indians (thought to be reflected in their stubborn, tradition-bound nature). These proponents of *mestizaje,* like the Peruvian intellectual Valcárcel, viewed themselves as indigenistas, but they disagreed on the positive or negative results of miscegenation. In both manifestations of *indigenismo,* there were shortcomings in the contemporary indigenous population that needed to be rectified, and in the case of those promoting mestizaje, the ultimate goal was assimilationist. Central to all discussions of mestizaje in Latin America is the belief that the creation of a "Mestizo race" is a central part of a more general process of whitening the population, both culturally and racially. As Weismantel and Eisenman suggest, "Andean racisms . . . agree that the fundamental problem in the Andes lies in the inability (or stubborn refusal) of the Indian to become white—or white enough" (1998:123).

Mestizaje, as an ideology of racial mixing, suggests that the creation of intermediate Mestizo racial categories is as much a process of cultural change as it is a result of biological mixing. The goals of mestizaje have been pegged to broad, elite plans of creating a homogenous national culture, or attempts to construct a modern nation. Both of these goals rest on a view of nation-building and modernity that is based on a European model. From the mid-twentieth century forward, in many parts of Central and South America, projects of nation-building have been couched in terms of attempting to create a homogenous Mestizo nation, founded on the mixing of indigenous and Spanish characteristics. This goal rests on Eurocentric notions of nationalism that have debated the importance of homogenous national culture for the indoctrination of national citizens or the formation of national consciousness. Departing from earlier indigenista thought, which argued for the separation of Indian and White populations, modernizing nationalists from mid-century instead began to seek the key to nation-building in the creation of an ethnically homogenous citizenry. Basing their theories on dominant ideologies of nationalism, and echoing concerns of the nineteenth century relating to the capacity of indigenous peoples to grasp the concept of the nation and forge an emotional attachment to it, these ideologies suggested that one key to forming a modern nation was the elimination of select "traditional" cultural traits that were thought to serve as barriers to the development of national consciousness.

At the same time, the post–World War II creation of an international development machine with its focus on the Third World led to an increase in attention paid to the cultural composition of these countries. Development specialists working in countries such as Mexico, Guatemala, and Nicaragua in Central America, and Bolivia, Peru, Colombia, and Ecuador in South America argued for the need to transform "traditional" Indians into "modern" Mestizos as a necessary part of the process toward economic (and cultural) modernization. They argued that indigenous peoples felt a primordial attachment to the land (echoing indigenista arguments that Indians were located in the countryside) and saw expressions of indigenous culture in language, clothing, food, music, and dance as signs of traditionalism that impeded indigenous peoples' ability to embrace modern ideals.

Tied to modernization theory and influential development specialists from the mid-1950s, mestizaje was an ideology that linked cultural practices with racial and economic ideals. Modernist development theory from the time, encapsulated in the neo-evolutionary schema of Rostow (1960), who argued that countries had to proceed through stages to achieve a modern condition, suggested that development was based on specific values and on cultural traits. The key to modernizing was thought to be linked to instilling capitalist economic motives in the lives of everyday people, and achieving this was linked to a cultural transformation rooted in a Western system of values.

The existence of large indigenous populations was a visible reminder for modernizing nationalists of the challenges they felt they faced in their nation-building projects. The same kinds of racially derogatory qualities were attached to indigenous peoples as in other moments of the nineteenth and early twentieth centuries: Indians as dirty, lazy, slow-witted, and so on. Land reform initiatives and bilingual education programs created during the 1960s reflected the desire to break the presumed traditionalism and dependency of indigenous peoples on their "patrons" and to help them become self-sufficient and market-oriented. Rural development programs that encouraged the adoption of cash-cropping to replace subsistence agriculture, and attempts to provide land and land titles to landless or marginally landed Indians in the rural countryside, also reflected the belief that these people needed to be incorporated into the national economy. In Ecuador, one condition of receiving land title under the national land reform act was that the title-holders of that land put it to productive use for market consumption. The modernizing goals of many of these regimes were also reflected in semantic changes made official by different Latin American states. In Bolivia in 1952 and Peru in 1968, campesino (peasant) replaced Indio (Indian) in all official pronouncements. Much earlier in Mexico, following the revolution, a similar shift in official discourse occurred. These shifts represent more than just word choice; they also illustrate an attempt by these states during an era of modernization to privilege class-based identities over other forms of cultural identities. In Peru, this shift was accompanied by a restructuring of the rural education program to promote bilingual education in the countryside, and ultimately—in a seemingly contradictory move—the recognition of the Quechua language as an official language of the state. Yet, this seeming contradiction is resolved by the recognition that those reforms were part of a broader move to incorporate these rural people into the nation and instill a sense of national belonging and patriotism in them (Devine 1999).

A third intellectual and political current of the mid-twentieth century was communist organizing. Even prior to the Cuban Revolution, communist parties were gaining in importance in different parts of Latin America and were pursuing cultural politics in many ways related to the nationalist or modernizing projects of mestizaje. Communist organizers in Latin America during this same time period likewise viewed indigenous culture as a deterrent to social and economic transformation, seeing it as an obstacle to the creation of class consciousness in the countryside. In the film *Entre Marx y una Mujer Desnuda,* Ecuadorian filmmaker Camilo Luzuriaga depicts a scene in which a group of young communist party organizers goes to a rural indigenous village to introduce the party platform. Communist party members such as those represented in the film were driven by goals of instilling a sense of class consciousness in the local residents and shaking them loose from their traditional cultures, which Latin American communist organizers of the time saw as the vestiges of times long past and a source of mystification in the present (de la Cadena 1996). Entering the town in the midst of a community celebration, where indigenous peoples are engaged in music and dance and seem impervious to the arrival of the guests from the city, the narrator (and one of the young communists) states:

> Were we invisible, or didn't they want to see us? We lived in the same space, but in different times. How could we talk to them about the revolution? We were traveling salesmen selling miracles, and the revolution we offered them kept being postponed for later, always for later, for when the famous social conditions were all set. (Grupo Cine 2004; translated by Patrick C. Wilson)

For development-minded modernizers, nation-building intellectuals and political elites, or communist organizers, the molding of cultural and racial homogeneity in the form of the creation of a Mestizo citizenry was thought to be a necessary goal for the advancement of the nation. Mestizaje was founded on a variety of origin myths and symbols of the Mestizo, as well as a set of political and economic practices. The town of Riosucio in the western Colombian Andes is spatially organized in such a way as to illustrate the historical separateness of Indian and Spanish races, while emphasizing how these two have come together in the founding of the Mestizo Colombian nation. The town has had two central plazas since colonial times, the "Plaza of the Indians" and the "Plaza of the Whites." For many years, a fence divided the two sides of town (the fence served as another physical marker of racial difference), but people would sneak across the fence at nighttime for forbidden sexual liaisons. The breaking down of these physical barriers and the pursuit of this forbidden love became symbols in microcosm of the Mestizo nation in Colombia (Applebaum 2003).

In Peru, one of the origin myths of the Mestizo nation relates back to its Inca past and the first days of the conquest by the Spanish. In this myth, the Inca princess Isabel Chimpu Ocllo is credited with giving birth to the first Peruvian Mestizo and is thought to be the mother of Guamán Poma de Ayala, the famous Mestizo chronicler of abuses of indigenous peoples at the hands of Spaniards. In this version of the story, she is depicted as the willing partner of a Spaniard, and is contrasted with another elite Inca woman, Kori Ocllo, who resisted the advances of Spanish men by covering her body in manure and eventually taking her own life rather than submitting to sexual conquest by the Spanish (de la Cadena 2000). Similarly, significance in Mexico is given to La Malinche, the indigenous woman who served as Hernán Cortés' translator during the conquest, as well as being his mistress and bearing him a son. She, like Isabel Chimpu Ocllo and Kori Ocllo, is a conflictive figure in Mexican cultural memory, depicted both as a traitor to the Mexican people for serving Cortés in the conquest and succumbing passively to his sexual advances (hence her nickname, *la chingada*), and as heroine as the mother of the Mexican Mestizo race (Paz 1985).

In Ecuador, elite pronouncements of mestizaje likewise try to draw connections between a mestizo present and an Inca past. In 1972, the president of Ecuador, Rodríguez Lara, during a visit to the rainforest city of Puyo, responded to requests on the part of indigenous peoples for the protection of their lands from accelerated colonization in the following manner:

> The President responded to this appeal far differently than when asked other questions about the economy of the Oriente [Amazon]. He did not address

himself to economic, political, or legal matters, but rather invoked his own legendary ancestry. For Ecuador, especially in the Oriente, his answer was most unusual. He stated that he had always maintained that all Ecuadorians were part Indian, all of them contained some blood of the Inca Atahualpa; that although he did not know where he had acquired such blood, he insisted that he, too, was part Indian. "There is no more Indian problem," he insisted, "we all become white when we accept the goals of the national culture." (Whitten 1976:7)

Claiming that he and all Ecuadorians shared blood of the Inca Atahualpa (who was himself from the city of Quito, Ecuador's capital city), Rodríguez Lara drew a common racial connection between all inhabitants of Ecuadorian national territory. At the same time, he suggested that not simply blood, but also culture and values, were crucial for the creation of an Ecuadorian Mestizo nation; he suggested that Ecuador would modernize when all people adopted the values of Mestizo national culture (Whitten 1976).

One final, and related, anecdote relates to the ways in which these modernizing discourses of mestizaje have, in fact, penetrated the lived experiences of indigenous peoples, shaping the way in which some perceive their social world and the goals that they pursue. In the main meeting hall in the offices of an indigenous organization in Amazonian Ecuador, one of the walls had been painted (until 1998) with a mural that adeptly depicted the process of mestizaje, with its stages of modernization. Looking at the mural from left to right, the viewer saw five images of a man at different stages along the transition from Indian to Mestizo. In the first frame, the man was depicted naked, with long hair and carrying a spear. As the frames progressed, the man slowly added pieces of clothing, cut his hair, and abandoned his spear. The final frame was an image of a man with short, parted hair, wearing a suit and glasses, with a watch on one wrist, and a day-organizer in hand—the modern Mestizo. Also noteworthy, as one gazed from left to right, the man increased in height. Bodies were physically transformed through the transition from Indian to Mestizo, but equally important were the cultural traits that accompanied racial improvement and modernization.

Race in Latin America and the Caribbean—as throughout the world—is a cultural construction. Although often backed by scientific discourses and explanations, racial typologies and hierarchies are ultimately cultural systems that attempt to explain differences in physical appearance or cultural attributes through reference to false assumptions about biological difference. Racial typologies and hierarchies have not been consistent in Latin America, and they change both across regions and over time. By the late-1970s, discourses of race began to give way to discourses about ethnicity. Yet, race has not disappeared as a meaningful category of social analysis in Latin America; rather, the overt focus on cultural and ethnic difference and the rejection of the term *race* by social scientists, due to its association with prejudice and its false claims of biological difference, have often obscured the extent to which people still frame their understanding of the social landscape in racially-defined terms. As we now turn to a discussion of the importance of ethnicity and ethnically-based social movements in Latin America, we should continue to question the extent to which ethnic identity has come to stand for—but perhaps not replace—racial typologies of the earlier part of the twentieth century.

The Rise of Ethnicity and Ethnic Movements

Evo Morales, an Aymara-speaking leader of Bolivia's coca leaf growers, was elected that country's first indigenous president in 2005. In the days leading up to his official inauguration in January 2006, he was blessed by an Aymara priest at the pre-Hispanic ruins of Tiwanaku, near the shore of Lake Titicaca, and he spoke of his presidency as a rebirth or re-awakening of the Bolivian nation. As he toured Europe prior to his inauguration in the casual sweaters commonly worn by the indigenous peasants of Bolivia (much to the scorn of the French press), his supporters back home celebrated his humbleness and commitment to helping the poorest Bolivians. Morales came to power amidst a wave of indigenous social movements that have been sweeping Latin America since the 1980s. These movements are based not only on economic and political demands, but also on cultural demands rooted in ethnic difference. This section examines the importance of ethnicity and ethnic politics for understanding social relations in Latin America.

The concept of ethnicity is really an invention of social scientists. In an attempt to move beyond a concept of race that appeared to not be salvageable due to its strong association with racism, racial hierarchies, and false associations between biology and cultural difference, social theorists such as Barth (1969) in the 1960s attempted to articulate a concept that would embrace shared cultural distinctiveness as the meaningful distinction to be made between populations. Accompanying this intellectual shift, and especially so since the 1980s, is the emergence of numerous social movements in Latin America based on ethnic difference. Part of a broader global trend in social movements that have begun to articulate demands in terms of cultural difference and the defense of cultural rights, rather than simply in terms of economic difference (Escobar and Alvarez 1992), indigenous and Black groups in Latin America have begun to assert their rights to express their cultural differences and to try to delineate a socially sanctioned space for this expression within national cultures that have often been historically hostile to these groups. Whether it be through the formation of ethnic organizations, as in the case of indigenous groups in parts of Mesoamerica and South America; the expression of cultural difference through popular culture, such as in music or dance; the global recognition of indigenous human rights and freedom of cultural expression; or debates about majority–minority relationships in these ethnically diverse Latin American countries, ethnicity has become centrally important for understanding how different people in Latin America today understand their social situation. Importantly, many of the same themes that were relevant for understanding racial hierarchies earlier in the nineteenth and twentieth centuries, such as dress, language, or geographic location, are still prominently featured in discussions of ethnicity, but are now recast to highlight rights or claims to cultural difference.

Indian versus Indigenous

Throughout this chapter, the terms *Indian* and *indigenous* have been used relatively interchangeably. Yet, this fails to recognize the significance and different connotations that these terms serve in different regions, at different moments in history, and from distinct social vantage points. For example, the use of Indian in daily conversation is much more common today in Guatemala than it is in Ecuador or Bolivia, where the use of the term indigenous is preferred. In spite of differences in use, Indian (*Indio* in Spanish) often carries racist overtones. Indigenous, on the other hand, has taken on significance more recently, in the context of the emergence of ethnic revitalization movements and global concern with the fate of historically-oppressed minorities. Although this brief section cannot do full justice to the regional and local complexities of these two terms, it will raise some issues that point to these complexities, and also will illustrate the ways that these terms are laden with social significance.

The term Indian traces its origin to Columbus' confusion upon his arrival in the New World. Having mistakenly assumed he had landed in the Indies, he dubbed the local inhabitants he encountered Indians. Although the confusion was soon resolved, the name stuck and became a name not only used to refer to the pre-Hispanic inhabitants of the region, but also as an administrative category with tributary obligations. Since then, and especially since the nineteenth and early twentieth centuries, this category has taken on social significance in the context of modernizing nationalisms, and ideologies of mestizaje and *indigenismo*. The term, Indian, in these contexts, carries connotations of backwardness, anti-progress, and retrogradation, as seen in the 1950s, and from a Marxist perspective was an epiphenomenal condition resulting from histories of class oppression. In parts of Latin America, like the central Andes, Indian is a highly derogatory and racist term, and would rarely be a term of self-identification. In other places, however, such as in Guatemala, **ladinos,** the Guatemalan landed-elite, still continue to employ the term in reference to the predominantly poor, rural Maya peasantry. These people, in turn, avoid the use of Indio because of its racist connotations (although this may be a more recent phenomenon linked to the rise of a global indigenous movement), instead referring to themselves as indigenous or *naturales,* a colonial-era category that makes an association between people as "first inhabitants" and as being close to the land (MacKenzie 2005).

While "Indian" has direct links to colonialism, "indigenous" in some ways is a term that emerged out of attempts to grapple with colonial legacies. Growing concern with the futures of non-Western peoples in the context of accelerating globalization, capitalism, and the legacies of colonial abuses, led to the growth of human rights nongovernmental organizations (NGOs) focusing on issues of "indigenous rights." The United Nations (UN) adopted a campaign for indigenous peoples, establishing the UN Working Group on Indigenous Populations (WGIP), giving indigenous activists the possibility to shape the policy agenda at the level of the UN. Other organizations, such as Cultural Survival and the International Working Group on Indigenous Affairs (IWGIA), have also served as important advocacy groups for indigenous peoples. In these contexts, "indigenous peoples" takes on quite different meanings than "Indian" does. In ongoing debates about how to categorize people as indigenous or not, the consensus that exists has revolved around an indigenous person being a member of a cultural group that was subjected to European colonization and that remains subordinate in social and racial hierarchies dominated by European descendents in the present; further, indigenous people must be able to make claims as descendents of "original inhabitants" (Béteille 1998; Karlsson 2003).

Indigenous consciousness gained momentum starting in the 1960s with North American and Australian aboriginal movements. This growing consciousness has led to a transnational indigenous movement (see the "Indigenous Movements and the Politics of Difference" section) that has argued for special rights and recognition based on cultural distinctiveness and legacies of colonial exploitation. As such, indigenous is a politicized category, because it positions those who occupy it as members of historically disadvantaged groups seeking rights and restitution from their states. The category of indigenous, like that of Indian, is not static. Instead, it is quite common for people to self-identify as indigenous in certain contexts, such as during protests, but perhaps in their daily lives they would more closely identify with their specific ethnic group, region, or community. Categories of Indian and indigenous are, like all elements of identity politics, complex, unstable, and historically-constructed. This brief discussion was intended not to cover the diversity of uses of these terms, but rather to raise the reader's awareness of this complexity and provide a brief discussion of some of the implications of the usage of these terms in different social contexts.

Ethnicity, Culture, and Class

A central and long-standing debate in the anthropology of Latin America and the Caribbean relates to the relationship between Indian ethnicity and socioeconomic status. Historically and generally remaining true through today, people identified as Indians in Mexico, Central America, and the Andes occupy the lowest rung of the socioeconomic hierarchy. The enduring question is how do we make sense of or explain the association between class and ethnicity?

One explanation, forwarded by Van den Berghe and Primov, among others, suggests that structural causes explain the association between ethnicity and class in places like Peru. They argue that structural determinants rooted in what they call "eco-geographical variables," and what we might refer to as an urban–rural divide, lead to severe structural constraints upon the ability of rural people, who are most likely to be Indians, to advance in socioeconomic terms:

> These three dimensions—urbanism, distance from the main road, and altitude—are not causal variables but merely close correlates and, hence, predictors of the political and economic structure that underlies the entire system of ethnic and class inequality. Mestizos are predominantly town dwellers, while Indians are rural, and the bigger the town the more power and wealth are concentrated in it. Except for wool production, which is concentrated in the *puna* [high Andean grassland] zone, proximity to the main road is directly linked with participation in the market economy and access to the occupational, entrepreneurial, and educational opportunities that make social mobility and capital accumulation possible. As for altitude, the best valley land was often virtually monopolized by the *haciendas* . . . While the population of the valleys became increasingly mestizoized . . . that of the *puna* remained more exclusively Indian. (1977:251–252)

Because Latin American and Caribbean societies do not employ a rigid racial classificatory scheme, it is possible for individuals to shift from being a member of one ethnic group to becoming a member of another. Van den Berghe and Primov (1977) generally see this shift as being upwards—from being Indian to becoming Mestizo—and associate the shift with individuals who migrate to the towns or cities and who come to have an occupation as merchant, professional, or teacher. In fact, residence and occupation are such important markers of ethnicity that these authors argue it to be impossible for an individual to live in an urban area, work as a teacher, and be identified as Indian. Therefore, in this conceptualization, class and other structural constraints that continually exploit rural peoples and keep them at the bottom of an economic hierarchy account for the association between Indianness and low socioeconomic standing.

In another view, cultural differences between Indians and Mestizos lead to cultural oppression of Indian groups, thereby resulting in class subjugation as well. This approach, which privileges cultural difference and systems of cultural prejudice over class and structural differences, argues that the economic subjugation of Indians is a result of the historical and contemporary cultural discrimination against them leading to a sense of cultural inferiority. In Friedlander's study of Hueyapán Indians in Mexico (1975), she notes the ways in which Hueyapeños, themselves, depict Indianness to be a negative cultural identity. It is this negative cultural identity, recognizable in attributes such as language, foods, and occupation, that leads to class subjugation. Similar to the structural model proposed by Van den Berghe and Primov, ethnic passing is possible in Mexico, and through education and the ability to speak Spanish fluently and without a Nahuatl accent one can become a Mestizo.

The difference between these two models is what is treated as primary. In Van den Berghe and Primov's model, to be Indian is predominantly the result of structural subjugation that has ethnic implications; while in Friedlander's view, being Indian means being a member of a subjugated cultural group, which also has class implications. Although this debate has not been fully resolved, the most promising explanations are those that tend to lie somewhere in the middle, recognizing both the importance of structural forms of power and oppression as well as cultural forms of discrimination in making sense of Indianness in Latin America. One example is Smith's (1990a) approach to studying social relations in Guatemala. In trying to bridge the gap between these two sides, she argues that structural forms are not devoid of culture, and equally important, cultural forms are not devoid of power. She demonstrates the ways in which Indian cultures and communities are both transformed by and act to transform the Guatemalan state and economy. Arguing that cultural expression is laden with power, and that the expression of power is also culturally-defined, she demonstrates that Indian communities and Indian cultural identities are not static (as does Friedlander for the case of Mexico), while also illustrating the ways in which these identities are framed by but also act to shape political economy. Importantly, Smith's treatment of Indianness in Guatemala leaves open the possibility that ethnic identities can serve as vehicles of protest and that cultural valorization can be a context of popular struggle, which is precisely what happened in places like Ecuador and Mexico in the late 1980s and 1990s.

Indigenous Movements and the Politics of Difference

In 1990, a massive indigenous uprising paralyzed the Andean region of Ecuador, as indigenous protestors blocked roads, occupied hacienda lands, and took some police and local officials hostage. Organized by Ecuador's national indigenous organization, the Confederación de Nacionalidades Indígenas del Ecuador (CONAIE), the size and scope of this uprising took many intellectuals and most Ecuadorians by surprise, and it ruptured the long-standing image of the passive and slow-witted Indian. Despite violent repression by the Ecuadorian military and police, the leaders of the indigenous uprising were successful at forcing the Ecuadorian government to negotiate an agreement with them. Indigenous leaders released a list of demands, many of which revolved around land conflicts and claims, because the distribution of land remains highly skewed in favor of large landowners at the expense of small indigenous farmers. Other demands included the creation of a credit agency to be managed by CONAIE, the conservation of water resources to ensure sufficient water for indigenous agricultural purposes, and a price freeze on agricultural raw materials and goods purchased for use by indigenous agriculturalists. Yet, the demands of the leaders were not simply limited to economic grievances, but instead took on a decidedly cultural tone: financing of bilingual (Quichua-Spanish) education, the respect of and support for indigenous medicinal practices, that CONAIE be able to oversee the protection and exploration of archaeological sites, and an amendment to the constitution to declare Ecuador a multinational state (Field 1991; see also Photo 5.2).

Similarly, the Mexican New Year's celebration to ring in 1994 was met with the unexpected news of a widespread armed uprising in the southern, largely rural province of Chiapas. Thousands of predominantly indigenous people coordinated attacks on several municipalities in the name of a long-deceased hero of the Mexican Revolution, Emiliano Zapata, timing their attacks with the initiation of the North American Free Trade Agreement (NAFTA; see Chapter 12). Tying their demands to a history of economic and political marginalization; a present in which economic liberalism would, in their opinion, only aggravate their marginal position; and rallying around the image of a past hero who fought for the well-being of the poor and the Indian, the Zapatista Army of National Liberation (EZLN) burst onto the national and international scene. Benefiting from a savvy leader and the adept use

PHOTO 5.2   *Indigenous people demonstrating in Tena, Ecuador.*

of Internet resources, international media, and a network of human rights organizations, the EZLN has pressed for the recognition of indigenous rights in Mexico, as well as the restructuring of unequal land tenure systems and other economic protections (Stephen 2002; see also Chapter 12). In Ecuador and Mexico, as in other parts of Latin America, ethnic revitalization movements rooted in indigenous identity are reshaping the political dynamics between states and historically oppressed peoples (Warren and Jackson 2002).

In some regards, the rise of indigenous movements in different parts of Latin America is related to the failure of ideologies and policy related to mestizaje to, on the one hand, improve the conditions of many peoples' lives, and on the other hand, convince them of their "new" identity as Mestizos. In the 1970s, it was common to talk of the disappearance of the Indian, sometimes with longing and remorse, and other times with hope and optimism. Seeing the disappearance of Indians as a natural outcome of modernizing projects in Latin American states, it was assumed that over time, Mestizos would come to replace them. And in some contexts, it appeared that this transition was, in fact, occurring. The participation of indigenous farmers in peasant rallies and the formation of peasant unions in different parts of Latin America seemed to point to the transition away from a culture-based identity toward one that was rooted in economic determinants. Yet, the active participation of many rural peoples in modernizing projects, such as land reform or new educational initiatives, largely did not lead to the fulfillment of promises of upward economic mobility made by political leaders of the 1950s, 1960s, and 1970s. In Bolivia, for example, the promises of integration into a newly minted Mestizo nation, and the social and economic mobility it was to entail, never arrived. Highlighting the flexibility and contextual nature of cultural identity, many people who formally self-identified as Mestizo or peasant in post-revolutionary Bolivia now began to adopt ethnic labels grounded in Indian identity. Many of those people who marched under peasant banners in the 1970s, by the late 1980s were marching behind the rainbow-colored whiphala flag—a symbol of multiethnic indigenous identity. One interpretation for this rise in indigenous activism in Bolivia and elsewhere relates to the failure of the modernizing regimes to significantly improve the lives of rural peoples, and therefore represents a rejection of ideologies of mestizaje (Roper et al. 2003; Strobele-Gregor 1994; Wilson 2003).

Land, Ethnicity, and Indianness

Indigenous peoples have been historically associated with rural landscapes. In the past, this was conceived of by many White intellectuals as a primordial attachment to land; since the 1980s, many indigenous communities have made land a central component of broader struggles for cultural rights. Linking ancestral claims to occupation of land with contemporary concerns for cultural survival, indigenous people have successfully placed demands for recognition of territorial rights, often in terms of collective rights, on their states. Part of the success of these movements has been the result of indigenous peoples' abilities to articulate their cultural struggles with a growing international awareness and concern with environmental conservation and the fate of the rainforest (Sawyer 2004).

In this broader global context, indigenous peoples have been especially successful at articulating demands for land recognition where socially recognized territories, some of which often have a spiritual or religious element, intersect with threats of environmental

Kayapo

destruction. In the Brazilian rainforest, for example, indigenous groups in the 1980s launched their concerns onto a global stage. In a successful struggle by the Kayapo Indians to stop the construction of a dam that would have flooded a large section of their ancestral territory, a key factor was the Brazilian government's recognition that the international community was watching these events unfold. Kayapo leaders, who went to the Brazilian Congress in full indigenous regalia to press their demands to stop dam construction, and who could speak eloquently of the historical and spiritual ties between indigenous peoples and their lands, also successfully spurred a great deal of international attention and advocacy for the plight of their people. As international media flocked to the Brazilian rainforest to cover confrontations and debates between the company building the dam and the indigenous inhabitants, and pop musician Sting arrived in support of the indigenous communities, international pressure mounted on the Brazilian government to step in and halt dam construction.

Although international pressure was a key factor in halting the construction of the dam, such pressure was possible as the result of a symbolically powerful strategy by the Kayapo to simultaneously represent themselves as defenders of the forest and integrate key cultural forms as central to their struggle. First, Kayapo leaders successfully employed a Western environmental discourse that linked the forest, the animals, and the indigenous inhabitants as interconnected parts, and that framed the indigenous inhabitants as key defenders and protectors of the rainforest. This legitimated their ability to speak on behalf of the forest. Second, in a highly symbolic move, the Kayapo, with support and involvement of a number of different Amazonian indigenous groups, constructed the Altamira village, an interethnic community located in the heart of the region that would have been flooded by the dam construction. The construction of this village contributed to the ties between social space and environmental space, because the Kayapo and other indigenous groups living in the community were countering the vision of Western environmental destruction with an image of indigenous environmental compatibility. Further, the multiethnic community represented a show of broad-based support for the Kayapo's struggle among other indigenous groups (Turner 1989). Finally, the Kayapo themselves appropriated media technology for self-representation in the context of their struggles. As Turner suggests, the use of video by the Kayapo provided them a medium of self-expression, and it became a crucial vehicle for cultural mobilization. Turner describes indigenous media as being a potential vehicle of cultural resistance because it can simultaneously assert and privilege certain cultural attributes that may serve current political contexts, as well as conserve cultural identity more generally (Turner 1992). In this way, the Kayapo appropriation of video in the context of the dam construction and other confrontations over the defense of their land from appropriation by illegal gold miners or loggers serves as both a local and global context of indigenous empowerment.

It is not simply the Kayapo who have struggled for recognition of territorial rights. In many parts of Latin America, indigenous peoples have organized themselves around the defense of territory, often in global form rather than on the basis of individual private property. The Mapuche Indians of Chile, for example, have a long history of land struggle that dates to the time of the Conquest. More recently, since the end of the Pinochet dictatorship in 1990, the Mapuche have successfully negotiated with the Chilean state the defense of parts of their territory from the advance of logging companies. For example, a protracted struggle between the Mapuche community of Quinquén and the Galletué timber company led the Mapuche to seek government intervention to stop the expropriation of community lands for timber contracts. In the end, the government came to a financial agreement with the lumber company, paid to protect the land in question as national forest, and ultimately purchased the land from its private owners to restore it to the Mapuche communities. One result of Mapuche activism was the creation of a special government agency to address indigenous concerns in Chile (Sznajder 2003).

Ethnicity, Nationalism, and Gender

This section first explores how heightened indigenous ethnic identities may sometimes clash with nationalisms promoted by state elites. It then turns to ways in which these ethnic identities are time and again profoundly gendered.

Nationalism

The preceding examples point to some of the challenges that indigenous peoples face in their negotiations with states. Whether indigenous peoples make up relatively smaller or larger percentages of the population of a country (e.g., in Nicaragua and Colombia, indigenous peoples make up very small percentages of total population; in Guatemala or Peru, depending on how census data are taken, they may account for the majority of those populations), they remain minority populations in terms of access to political and economic power. One of the challenges facing indigenous peoples in their expressions of cultural difference and their demands for cultural recognition is that these are often met by resistance and even hostility by political elites, many of whom are still proponents of the modernizing nationalisms championed from the 1950s through the 1970s and are still arguing for the creation of a homogenous national citizenry. Some political elites have argued that the official recognition of cultural difference, as called for, for example, as part of the plurinational indigenous movement in Ecuador, would lead to the break-up of the nation-state. Citing examples of ethnic violence in places like Yugoslavia and Rwanda, some Ecuadorians, including the powerful leaders of the Ecuadorian military, have strongly opposed the official recognition of cultural difference. In other contexts, such as Colombia and Venezuela, with small percentages of indigenous inhabitants, constitutional reforms in the early and late 1990s, respectively, led to official recognition of indigenous rights. In the case of Venezuela, the success of the indigenous movement in gaining official recognition through the results of the constitutional assembly in 1999 was an outcome of successful organizational strategies on the part of indigenous leaders, as well as Venezuela's recognition that its system of rights for indigenous peoples lagged behind its neighbor in Colombia, and broader international trends in Latin America and elsewhere that saw increasing legal recognition and defense of indigenous populations (Van Cott 2003).

In some places, ethnic conflict has turned violent. The civil war in Guatemala in the 1980s and early 1990s led to often indiscriminate violence against Maya villagers in the countryside (see also Chapter 12). Justifying such violence because of the (often false) assumption that Maya villagers were supporting the guerrilla forces, government forces enacted a genocidal campaign against them. Part of the hidden agenda in this violence was the goal of creating national homogeneity through the violent elimination of ethnic otherness. In the end, much of this violence against Maya civilians produced the opposite. A shared sense of pan-Maya identity began to emerge that cross-cut geographical and linguistic differences within the Maya population. Recognizing the violence against them as resulting from their cultural difference from mainstream society, many villagers began to articulate a sense of shared ethnic consciousness that helped the Maya nationalist movement to become prominent in the postwar context (Menchú 1984; Warren 1998). Accounts such as Rigoberta Menchú's autobiography of personal loss and struggle in the context of violence in Guatemala again, as in the context of Brazilian indigenous organizing, brought international attention to the plight of indigenous peoples, and was ultimately extremely influential in the outpouring of support from international human rights groups and even the United Nations.

The factuality of Rigoberta Menchú's account has come under question in an account by Stoll (1999a), where he suggests that certain details of her account are inaccurate and that some relating to her personal and family life are untrue (see also Chapter 12). Although Stoll's revisiting of Rigoberta Menchú (who in 1992 won the Nobel Prize for her autobiography and struggle against violence in Guatemala), her life, and her story is primarily focused on issues of representation, ethnographic authority, and the ways in which the international media picked up on Menchú's account and blessed it with authority, it also points to two general trends among indigenous leaders. First, many of the leaders of indigenous movements are individuals who possess many of the social advantages that in other contexts would enable them to pass as Mestizos in mainstream society: education, fluency in Spanish, and a degree (if minor) of economic means (Warren 1998). In the case of Menchú, her international fame has enabled her to live outside of Guatemala, becoming a spokesperson for Maya Guatemalans from abroad. Second, and perhaps more importantly, indigenous leaders have often been held accountable for the "objective" factuality of their accounts and have come under fire when those accounts are seen to be contradictory or inaccurate. This perhaps relates to a broader trend to romanticize indigenous peoples as "noble savages" (Chapter 10), thereby stripping them of their full subjectivity and capacity to be fallible like other humans.

These kinds of criticisms of indigenous leaders have more than occasionally led to further difficulties for the indigenous groups they are trying to advocate for, because the international community has occasionally abandoned these groups in the face of internal contradictions (Conklin and Graham 1995). Because what it means to be an "authentic" Indian is being partially constructed by the assumptions and beliefs of international observers, representatives of nongovernmental human rights and conservation organizations, among others, indigenous peoples are oftentimes held accountable for their actions in ways that nonindigenous peoples are not. When indigenous peoples act in non-environmentally friendly ways, or choose to abandon native dress in favor of Western clothing, or to speak Spanish or Portuguese instead of their native language, the romanticized notions of Indian peoples often come unraveled for the international viewer (Conklin 1997; Ramos 1998). Therefore, it is important to recognize how indigenous ethnic identities are situational and are a partial construction of the global production of images of indigenous peoples as well as being a local negotiation of beliefs, values, and desires.

Gender

Indigenous ethnicity, as with ethnic identity in many other contexts, is also highly gendered. Typically, it is the female members of an ethnic group that wear "traditional" dress and speak the indigenous language, even in contexts in which many of the men have abandoned traditional dress in favor of Western clothing, oftentimes migrate to the city in search of temporary or permanent employment, and are bilingual (and sometimes monolingual) Spanish or Portuguese speakers. Some of this relates to the gendering of education and work, where men have historically had greater access than women to education, and where gendered social roles give men greater flexibility to migrate to urban centers or other regions in search of employment. This results in women tending to more frequently be monolingual speakers of indigenous languages and being more closely confined to the contexts of their indigenous communities, as noted by Weismantel for the case of southern Ecuador (1988).

Yet, this seeming association of women to culture and homestead does not produce passive female subjects. Instead, women's movements throughout Latin America have been growing in strength, with indigenous women taking the lead not just in women's movements, but more broadly in indigenous movements. In part, because of their visible signs of "Indian authenticity," expressed through indigenous dress and language, these women have become equated with indigenous culture more generally, and therefore with legitimate claims for cultural respect. Indigenous women, like women elsewhere in Latin America, have also exploited their ability to protest in ways that men often cannot. These women have led marches that have confronted the military in Ecuador and Bolivia; in Chiapas, some women have been able to stand down the Mexican military, whose soldiers are more reluctant to open fire on groups of protesting women than they would be for their male counterparts. Therefore, although women in some contexts are represented as tradition-bound and the carriers of cultural traditions, in other contexts they have greater freedoms than their male counterparts to engage in acts of defiance to hostile state and military authorities.

Controversies: Intellectual Property Rights and Indigenous Peoples

Throughout the history of contact between Europeans and indigenous peoples of the Americas, social and economic relations have been framed by colonial and neo-colonial policies and practices. As discussed in Chapter 4, the colonial encounter entailed the economic exploitation of indigenous peoples, and these peoples have regularly suffered the consequences of land expropriation by dominant elites, the state, and multinational corporations. Therefore, resource exploitation is nothing new for indigenous peoples. More recently, however, indigenous minds and bodies have become a new frontier of interest for scientists, and some are asking if scientific forays into indigenous lives through quests to tap into "indigenous knowledge systems" or to map indigenous genetic material as part of the Human Genome Diversity Project serve the interests of indigenous peoples or simply continue historical patterns of social and economic domination.

A variety of actors are interested in what can be learned from indigenous peoples (see also Chapter 10). Pharmaceutical companies, for example, regularly seek local knowledge of medicinal plant use with the hope of possibly "discovering" new plant varieties with medical applications. Some conservation biologists in recent years have suggested that the key to rainforest conservation may lie in better understanding the mechanisms employed by indigenous inhabitants in their sustainable ways of living with their natural surroundings. Some questions that arise in these contexts are who owns this knowledge and if and how people should be compensated for the knowledge that they share with biological or pharmaceutical researchers. These considerations are important, as the actions of researchers in indigenous communities can often introduce sources of social conflict, or raise questions about who is reaping the rewards of the knowledge being extracted. The work of some pharmaceutical companies in the Amazon region, for example, has led the companies to seek international patent on plant species that are of religious significance and central in the healing practices of indigenous peoples. This (with clear reason) has led indigenous leaders to cry foul, and to demand that indigenous peoples be rewarded and compensated for their knowledge, as well as for the extraction and use of important plant species (Ramos, forthcoming; Brush 1993).

The extension of **intellectual property rights** (the legal control over raw materials/resources and their subsequent transformations as well as entitlement to any benefits as a result of these changes) to indigenous peoples has been posited as one possible solution to the dangers of the appropriation and use of knowledge without fair compensation (Brush 1993). This proposal offers certain advantages, because it would provide international support for the need to recognize the legitimacy of indigenous knowledge systems, the right of indigenous peoples to be compensated for their collaboration with scientific researchers, and a degree of control over the use of that knowledge. Yet, the issue is far from simple. As Brown (1998) suggests, a series of problems is associated with the extension of intellectual property rights to, for example, an ethnic group. Which individual, or group of individuals, is granted recognition as possessing the knowledge in question? Because, arguably, all members of society possess a degree of knowledge about plant species widely used in local medicinal practices, does that then mean that all members of the group "own" that knowledge? If that is the case, there are potential problems if the group is internally divided about sharing that knowledge with researchers. Further, the granting of rights to knowledge entails a range of complications related to attempts to control the flow or spread of that knowledge, making the containment of the spread of knowledge practically impossible.

Research with indigenous peoples has gone much further than simply mining local knowledge of plant resources, however. There is also a long history of bioprospecting in indigenous communities that involves extracting information from indigenous bodies themselves. This has included the collection of skeletal remains for tests in the early twentieth century that served the interests of racist scientific experimentation, the collection of blood samples for a range of experiments that still continue today, and the collection of DNA samples for the ongoing Human Genome Project and its offshoot, the Human Genome Diversity Project. Proponents of the collection of indigenous blood, other bodily fluids, and DNA suggest there is a range of practical applications for these materials in medical research that could offer possible cures to diseases suffered disproportionately by indigenous populations. Others suggest that DNA testing can allow for a definitive test of whether a particular individual is "really" indigenous. Still others have argued that as indigenous populations risk extinction, partly through what they see as the racially destructive forces of biological mixing with nonindigenous populations, DNA banks may be all that we will have left of indigenous populations in the near future (Ramos forthcoming).

These justifications, although weak in their own right, fail to address central questions about the ethics of performing these kinds of experiments on human subjects, and about the tricky issues of group consent. Not unlike the question of intellectual property rights previously discussed, if geneticists are claiming that the DNA of a given individual is representative of the group, then is group consensus required prior to using those materials? Further, once the samples are taken, they are quite regularly used by a variety of different research teams and for purposes that were not delimited in the original research plan. Some scientists suggest that once the blood leaves the body, that blood becomes property of the laboratory that possesses it, but that assertion clearly raises thorny issues of individual and group rights (Marks 2003). Responding to the individual justifications of genetic research on indigenous populations, Marks (2003) convincingly suggests that this research has limited medical value for the group as a whole, because of the massive amount of genetic variation within human populations, and the DNA samples would have to be accompanied by a vast array of other personal history to make them useful for medical research in any meaningful way. Further, the rationale that DNA testing would be useful for determining the validity of claims to membership in an indigenous group is clearly preposterous. As discussed throughout this chapter, identity is a social construction, not a biological one, so claims that DNA tests could "verify" if someone is indigenous fail to understand the social facts of indigeneity. Moving beyond indigenous identity as a social construction, rather than a biological one, is the additional problem of centuries of admixture between populations (Shelton and Marks 2001). These kinds of genetic tests are often guilty of disregarding the historical complexities of these populations and reifying cultural boundaries as if they were real biological or reproductive communities. These biological fallacies ultimately render genetic bases of racial difference untenable.

In the United States: Race and Respect in the Streets of New York City

This chapter has explored the importance of race and ethnicity for understanding social relationships in Latin America. For Latin American and Caribbean peoples migrating to the United States, the foundations of social organization that racial systems and ethnic identities represent are challenged and often transformed by living in North America, in a context with very different understandings of these social dynamics. On the one hand, and as mentioned at the beginning of this chapter, racial hierarchies are quite rigid in North America, and racial affiliation is based primarily on skin color and ancestry. For immigrants from Latin America and the Caribbean, who are used to the flexibility and fluidity of racial systems, who recognize the constructed and contextual nature of these systems, and who often employ a range of meaningful intermediate racial categories between Black and White, integration into the limiting and fixed North American racial system may be disconcerting. On the other hand, "Latino" is recognized as an ethnic category in the United States, a category that lumps together people of incredibly diverse cultural and historical backgrounds (see Chapter 1). It is not necessarily the case that an ex–sugar cane worker from the

Dominican Republic and a political refugee from an elite Peruvian family share much in common in terms of racial or cultural identity, yet upon arrival to the United States, both become members of the Hispanic/Latino ethnic group. Making sense of these new racial and ethnic dynamics is one of the challenges that Latin American and Caribbean peoples face upon arrival to the United States.

Bourgois

In his book *In Search of Respect: Selling Crack in El Barrio* Bourgois (1995) examines the dynamics of racial discrimination as they relate to economic marginalization in New York. He conducted his research in East Harlem, "El Barrio," home, during the time of his research, to a varied population that included mostly immigrants from Puerto Rico and other Latin American and Caribbean countries, as well as African Americans.

One of the most striking observations from this research has to do with the inability of this population to move up the social ladder outside of El Barrio due to the difficulties that they experience when attempting to join the legal labor force. Several factors account for this. First, there is outright racial discrimination in the hiring practices of potential employers. Second, consistent abuse at the workplace is common, such as improper verbal treatment or demeaning attitudes that often contain racist undertones and highlight the suspicions that many members of mainstream, White society harbor about Hispanics/Latinos. Third, and very important, there is often a lack of compatibility between expected performance and profound cultural values held by Puerto Ricans. As an example, Puerto Rican men typically feel offended when asked to perform tasks they believe are more appropriate for women. These include secretarial or cleaning tasks (a resemblance of women's domestic work), or fitting-room assistance (involving touching the bodies of other men). The performance of these types of tasks not only generates a tremendous amount of discomfort, but can put in jeopardy the gender identity of the person performing them in the eyes of members of his community. Additionally, many of the jobs available to these daughters and sons of Puerto Rican immigrants are among the most undesired in the United States, such as unlicensed asbestos remover or deep fat-fry cook.

As a consequence, people from El Barrio often have a difficult time finding and keeping jobs that would provide some degree of economic stability and the possibility of social mobility. Not surprisingly, some of them become involved in the dangerous underground and often self-destructive drug economy, a risky path that furthers their social and economic marginality. In this sphere, however, people can achieve a sense of personal worth that can never be found in the legal economy or when they mix with members from mainstream (White) society. This feeling of personal worth is what the author refers to with the title of the book (*In Search of Respect*). For example, a clever drug dealer can achieve status and become a highly respected figure in the local community while at the same time maintaining values fundamental for social success in his/her circle. In contrast, for people to succeed in the legal economy, they have to endorse hegemonic mainstream attitudes, prove their desire to adopt values they are not familiar with, but remain compliant members of low social and economic classes. The tradeoff seems convenient in the short term, a risk worth taking for someone desperate to earn money and preserve a sense of dignity. In the long term, however, in addition to the economic uncertainty of illegal activities, engagement with the underground drug economy frequently leads to drug addiction and incarceration, with the subsequent destructive psychological and economic consequences for individuals, families, and communities.

IN THEIR OWN WORDS   5.1

Brazil's Indigenous Peoples Speak Out

Marta Silva Vito Guaraní, president of the Kaguateca Association for Displaced Indians—Marçal de Souza—in a speech delivered before the U.S. House of Representatives in 1994 (quoted in Langer and Muñoz 2003:188–189).

The lands of my people were occupied by large landowners, who have lands that go as far as they eye can see, full of well-treated and well-fed cattle. On my land, cattle are worth more than Indians. Many Indians in Mato Grosso do Sul are leaving their communities and moving to urban centers. They go to live in the slums, and little by little they start losing their cultural identity and become "nobodies." In the villages they live surrounded by gunmen and by the ranchers' cattle. The cattle stomp on their gardens and tractors knock down their houses. The rivers are dirty with the waste from the large farms in the region: pesticides, mercury, etc. They finished with our forest, they are finishing with what is left of our savannahs. They killed our birds and our animals. And they say that we are no longer Indians because we wear clothes . . . Over seven thousand Indians are working

in the charcoal factories and the sugarcane processing plants. They live in a state of slavery. This is the integration that white society offers us. But we Indians, the first owners of this land, cannot accept this humiliating and inhuman integration!

For this reason, young Guaraní are killing themselves; they are searching for the end, hanging themselves. The women from the community of Jaguapiré told me that they will kill their children and kill themselves afterwards if they try to take their land away again. I cannot cross my arms before the massacre of my people. It is for them that I am here to tell the world that the Indians of Brazil do not see land as private property. Land is important for peoples to survive culturally and in their humanity. To populate an area is to give human value to a place, to complete a stage in our evolution—therefore taking away the [land] means to kill the people. For this, it is necessary to demarcate the indigenous land in Brazil. It is necessary to secure the land for our survival.

Land is culture and culture is life for us.

Bourgois argues that racialized visions of Puerto Rican people dominate the social imagination of mainstream society, which perceives the social disarray of immigrant communities to be simply a manifestation of their own dismal cultural patterns. The wider structural forces that produce poverty, psychological instability, family crises, and health problems among individuals in immigrant communities are not usually at the center of the debate. Rather, traits attributed to Puerto Ricans as a culture are held responsible for their situation. This is a form of racial determinism. For example, epidemics that were common during the early settling of Puerto Rican families in East Harlem were seen as a consequence of primitive notions of hygiene. Family violence is typically seen as an expression of a macho culture that despises women and goes along with dominant racisms toward African Americans in the United States. Drug trafficking and the accompanying crime and violence are also often depicted as "imported problems" rather than social problems that emerge from racial discrimination and segregation deeply embedded in the structure of U.S. society. In reality, the epidemics resulted from a combination of malnutrition, overcrowding, and poor public sanitary infrastructure, not poor personal hygiene. A closer look at family violence, in turn, shows that this is related to the gendered frustrations of men unable to adequately provide for their families. Under favorable conditions, neither epidemics nor family violence or drug dealing would be present, showing that these social phenomenon are not, in fact, related to racial difference, but rather to the structure of social inequality faced by many Latin American and Caribbean immigrants to the United States.

Summary

Expressions of race and ethnicity in Latin America and the Caribbean are complex and often contradictory. This chapter has explored the shift from biological to cultural expressions of race, followed by an abandonment of race in favor of ethnicity, or group cultural difference, as an explanatory model. Although explicit talk of race has been replaced by the language of ethnicity, many of the same characteristics attached to minority groups remain consistent. It is still the case that geography, occupation, dress, behavior, and language are important markers of difference. Such differences have been drawn upon as inspiration for indigenous movements in some parts of Latin America, but these also become contexts for social stratification and the sometimes violent repression of difference. In Costa Rica, plantation workers are stratified based on ethnicity, with different ethnic groups thought to be best suited for different kinds of jobs (Bourgois 1989). In this context, indigenous, Black, and Mestizo workers on a banana plantation use discourses of ethnic difference to explain their respective places on an occupational (class) hierarchy, yet these distinctions, although couched in the language of ethnicity, are remarkably similar to those of race. Although parts of the Caribbean and Brazil make claims of racial democracies, occupational opportunity and social status are still largely determined by the color of one's skin, and blackness—with its association with cultural and behavioral difference—continues to structure hierarchies of power. Far from being color-blind, these countries are still deeply marked by legacies of slavery, racial prejudice, and difference (Sagás 2000). Given the enduring importance of race in Latin America and the Caribbean, some have called for a return to race (Weismantel and Eisenman 1998). Ideas of race do, in fact, structure ways in which many people make sense of the cultural diversity around them, and therefore race remains a useful analytical tool for exploring the social meanings attached to these cultural differences. At the same time, one should not abandon an exploration of ethnic identities. Ethnicity has provided a language of opposition for minority groups, and it serves as an important means of self-identification. Ethnic identities are the result of contact and negotiation with dominant and neighboring ethnic groups. In this global climate, ethnic identities in Latin America are also formed through processes of negotiation and expression of identity shaped by exposure to international media, human rights organizations, and the United Nations, among others, as well as being formed locally through the selection and display of particular cultural traits. In this sense, race and ethnicity come together and overlap in complex and sometimes inseparable ways.

ISSUES AND QUESTIONS

1. *Racial Fluidity and Racial Passing.* Critical to the understanding of racial systems in Latin America are the ideas of racial fluidity and racial passing. How is it that racial systems in places like Brazil are fluid, and how does this leave open the possibility of racial passing? Why is racial passing more possible in parts of Latin America than in the United States?

2. *Indigenous Social Movements.* Indigenous movements, as discussed in this chapter, have become quite prominent in many Latin American countries. How do you think the rise of indigenous movements may be linked to the modernizing nationalisms in the 1950s, 1960s, and 1970s? How does the cultural content of these movements critique dominant ideologies of *mestizaje?*

3. *Indigenismo.* Many of the enduring racial hierarchies in Latin America are based on *indigenista* thinking. Would you argue that *indigenismo* in the early part of the twentieth century was redemptive and empowering for indigenous populations? Why or why not? What were some of the implications of *indigenismo* for understanding correlations between race, class, and culture in dominant constructions of racial hierarchies?

KEY TERMS AND CONCEPTS

Ethnicity   p. 110
Hegemonic racism   p. 116
Identification   p. 115
Indigenismo   p. 120
Indigenistas   p. 118

Intellectual property rights
    p. 140
Ladinos   p. 131
Mestizaje   p. 125
Mestizo   p. 111

Mulatto   p. 111
Personal identity   p. 115
Race   p. 110
Racial passing   p. 113

6 Cultural Constructions of Gender and Sexuality

This chapter charts some major attributes of gender and sexuality ideologies and relationships from the pre-Conquest period to contemporary times. It first focuses on the period prior to the European Conquest, emphasizing the role of state expansion in Mesoamerica and the Andes in shaping ideologies, practices, and relationships. The following two sections turn to the European Conquest and postcolonial era, emphasizing the clash between indigenous and European constructions of gender and sexuality, and how and why shaping these was crucial for efforts at consolidating colonial rule and nascent Latin American and Caribbean nation-states. The chapter then turns to a discussion and critique of *marianismo* and *machismo,* two widespread models of gender and sexuality. The subsequent section centers on the expression of sexual identities and how these underpin gendered notions of masculinity and femininity. This is followed by an assessment of the controversy surrounding gender and violence in Amazonian societies. The chapter ends by examining how gender, courtship, and sexuality are being redefined by Mexican men and women whose lives straddle both sides of the Mexico–United States border.

Pre-European Gender Systems

Gender—"the ways in which differences and similarities related to physical sexuality are understood, contested, organized and practiced" (Gutmann 1996:11)—is a fundamental and pervasive dimension of culture and social relations. As such, gender ideologies, norms, and practices influence everyday life in a myriad of ways. What kinds of roles—economic, political, social, or cultural—men and women should or should not, can or cannot occupy, are often largely contingent on prevailing norms that stipulate sanctioned spheres of action for males and females. Further, since gender is related but not irreducible to sexual/anatomical/ physiological differences, the possibility of taking on some roles and not others is also often the result of widespread, although not always fully accepted, notions of what constitutes appropriate "masculine" or "feminine" behavior. Gender is related to yet different from **sexuality**—how erotic and physical desires and practices toward others are shaped, internalized, challenged, and practiced by men and women. Culturally constructed notions of sexuality and sexual behavior—how men and women define themselves, or are defined by others, as sexual beings—are, like culture itself, highly malleable and diverse, and the result of historical forces played out in concrete social, economic, political, and cultural contexts.

It is in Mesoamerica and the Andes where more is known about pre-Columbian gender and sexuality. This is so because of the survival of large numbers of indigenous peoples after the Conquest and their crucial role in the fledging colonial economy, and therefore Spanish interest in documenting their life ways. Aztec, Maya, and Inca elites also produced their own histories (Chapter 3) that contain insights into pre- and postcolonial gender systems. Relevant sources are exceedingly rare in other locales, especially where—as in the Caribbean—most indigenous peoples perished, and with them the bureaucratic need for documenting their life ways, or where—as in Amazonia—many who did survive were only tenuously incorporated within the colonial orbit.

Despite their potential, the drawbacks of indigenous sources on gender are that they provide snapshots in time and few insights into historical changes, and they often emphasize elite and male perspectives. There is also the strong possibility that these sources convey gender through the worldview of European colonizers (Brumfiel 2001:61–62). As a result, these sources "cannot be used uncritically as 'windows' onto the pre-Hispanic past" because they sometimes transmit idealized and partial views (Klein 2001:372; Burkhart 2001b:88). Nevertheless, drawing on insights from the field of gender and archaeology and inspired by feminist scholarship, the archaeology of gender in Mesoamerica and the Andes has blossomed in recent years (Conkey and Gero 1997; Visweswaran 1997; Klein and Quilter 2001; Meskell 2002; Trevelyan and Gustafson 2002). Further, since indigenous peoples were allowed opportunities to contest policies and convey grievances in court (Stern 1982), judicial records furnish a useful prism through which to purview the intimacy of domestic lives and gender relations from the perspective of women's and men's own words and cultural categories, and these records also provide rich insights into "gender culture[s]" (Stern 1995:ix). These records are the cornerstone of most gendered social history for colonial Latin America (Stolcke 1988; Seed 1988; Twinam 1999). They also offer rich insights into precolonial gender systems.

Sexuality, Parallelism, and Complementarity

One line of work has centered on notions of sexuality and sexual identity. Joyce, for example, states that "conquest-era Mesoamerican deities were described as sexually fluid, sometimes male, and sometimes female," and mythical accounts also "place a dual-gendered being at the beginning of creation" (2001:109–110). Similarly, Wiraqocha, the Andean distant creator god, was neither male nor female, but an "unsexed" supernatural being (Dean 2001:148–149). An emerging consensus is that in Mesoamerica and the Andes "gender was not . . . inherently bipolar . . . and multiple variants of the masculine and feminine were clearly recognized" (Klein 2001:371). Further, some evidence suggests an emphasis on maleness and male sexuality. Many pictographs, figurines, and stone-carved images depict male (but not female) genitalia, suggesting a "phallocentric construction of the male body in Classic to Postclassic Maya societies . . . [and] . . . an almost homoerotic sensibility" (Joyce 2001:131). And, relying on Yucatec Maya-language documents written with the Roman alphabet, Sigal (2000) has suggested that bi- and homoeroticism was widespread in Maya culture and society.

Gender complementarity and parallelism were widespread in Mesoamerica. Among the Aztecs, both women and men held important roles in a wide spectrum of contexts, and it was not uncommon for women to hold prominent political, administrative positions. Women also played a significant role in key public life-cycle rituals—such as those associated with birth and naming, or marriage and household formation—and also held crucial roles as healers, midwives, spinners, and weavers. Mesoamerican gender parallelism also appears in religion, for supernatural deities responsible for fertility and sustenance were female, and women were often temple priestesses (Kellog 1995). Further, some "rulers of ancient Mayan states often considered themselves 'Two-Spirit Persons'—an individual whose persona is a blend of the feminine and masculine" (Trevelyan and Gustafson 2002:4–7).

Parallelism and complementarity were also important in the Andes. Women often wielded considerable prestige and authority, and they held political leadership positions. Parallelism was clearly evident in the religious sphere. For instance, Pachamama, the most important female deity linked to fertility, was paired with Illapa, the god of thunder and rain. **Parallel descent**—the transmission of rights, duties, and obligations from women to their female offspring and from men to their male offspring—meant that women could claim access to and use of productive resources independent of their male spouses (Silverblatt 1987). Some elements of matrilineal descent (defined in Chapter 3) continue to exist in contemporary Andean indigenous communities, where Pachamama is still invoked in agricultural rituals (Arnold 1988; Harris 2000).

Gender parallelism and complementarity does not mean that absolute equality pervaded gender relations. Archaeological research at the Maya site of Tikal (in current day Guatemala) suggests that gender hierarchy was especially pronounced among the elite ruling class (Cohodas 2002). Parallelism, complementarity, and hierarchy probably coexisted side by side among the Maya, and probably among the Aztecs and Incas as well. An example of the presence of diverse gender ideologies and relationships comes from the Codex Mendoza (a post-Conquest, early sixteenth century Aztec pictorial document named after Antonio de Mendoza, Viceroy of Mexico), in which men and women are depicted in an Aztec court litigating in equal numbers, as well as illustrations of fathers teaching boys and mothers teaching girls appropriate labor roles. Yet, gender hierarchy was also present—for all judges were male (Cohodas 2002:28).

Gender and State Expansion

In noncomplex (but especially foraging) societies, gender roles, practices, and relationships are typically complementary and egalitarian, with both women and men enjoying high status and standing. The intensification of production, sedentism, and stratification associated with complex societies such as chiefdoms and states historically have ushered in pronounced gender inequities and hierarchy (Meskell 2002; Silverblatt 1988; Conkey and Gero 1997; Myers 1988; Spielmann and Eder 1994). Cross-culturally, state formation is invariably accompanied by gender and sexual hierarchies (Miller 1993; Gailey 1987).

Nash (1980), an early proponent of this view for Latin America, suggests that the Aztecs' "predatory" economy, incessant warfare, and the rise of a class-based society undermined women's political, symbolic, and productive autonomy. Mesoamerican state expansion may have also led to "controlling adult sexuality" and attempts at constructing "dichotomous heterosexual adult genders" (Joyce 2001:111). The reshaping of sexuality may have deepened after the Conquest, for fledging Iberian kingdoms in the sixteenth and seventeenth centuries strove to stamp out male homoerotic sensibilities. "State building through violent sexuality," Trexler tells us, "was alive and well," during this period, as was the "gendering of political structures" (1995:58–59).

State expansion also resulted in a restructuring of the **gender division of labor,** the range of productive tasks typically ascribed to and undertaken by males and females. One example is cloth production and the use of spindle whorls under the Aztecs (Brumfiel 2001). Textiles, laden with a great deal of symbolic weight, were an important tribute category. (This was also true in the Andes.) Spinning and the production of cloth were exclusively female tasks. The expansion of the Aztec state led to an intensification of tribute in textiles. In some regions, this increased demand was associated with an increase in spindle whorls, suggesting that more women were devoting additional time and labor to manufacturing cloth. In other places, where the number of spindle whorls seems not to have increased (especially in prime agricultural regions), women may have engaged in other strategies—such as the direct purchase of textiles in marketplaces—to meet increasing tribute. Other evidence suggests a more profound change in the division of labor. For example, in Cholula, Mexico, in "a mass grave containing the remains of fifty individuals, spindle whorls were associated with both male and female skeletons, suggesting that both men and women engaged in textile production" (Brumfiel 2001:70).

Like in other Andean polities, gender parallelism was an important feature of Inca society and culture. For example, in Inca cosmology, the Sun—the supreme male deity—was paired with the Moon, the all-important female god. Pre-imperial Inca society was also marked by parallel descent and a considerable wielding of power, prestige, and authority by women (Silverblatt 1987).

Inca imperialism spurred deep changes in gender and religious ideologies and practices of conquered societies, legitimizing and rendering intelligible Inca domination—what Silverblatt (1987) called the **conquest hierarchy.** For instance, the Inca claim that they were the direct descendants of the Sun and Moon was important because many leaders of conquered polities soon viewed themselves as descendants of Venus, who in turn was a progeny of the Sun. In this way, Incas could claim that they were the "fathers" and "mothers" of subjugated ethnic groups leaders, while the *kurakas* (or ethnic lords) themselves were symbolically transformed into the "fathers" and "mothers" of their communities' members. The Incas also attempted to embed imperial deities—such as the female Moon Goddess—onto local religious universes. A hierarchical relationship also emerged between Inca and non-Inca women. The Inca Coya (Queen), for example, eventually played a considerable role in local-level women's religious organizations. Inca expansionism also meant that non-Inca women lost ground to males, for at the same time that the power and prestige of males increased as they engaged in warfare and conquest, the influence, status, and prestige of women declined markedly. One example of women's decline in status was the ability of Incas to distribute women in marriage with the objective of promoting political alliances. The emergence of a symbolically important class of young, virgin, and holy women (*aclla*), sacrificed to the (male Inca) Sun deity, illustrates how gender was refashioned to fit the ideological and political needs of state-building efforts.

The Conquest and Colonial Period

Colonialism—the political-economic, social, and cultural subjugation of one people under another—has historically been a deeply gendered process (Stoler 1995, 2002; Strobel 2002; Jolly 1998; McClintock 1995). This insight is relevant for understanding why the European Conquest and the long period of colonial rule necessarily wrought profound changes in Mesoamerican and Andean gender systems. In important ways, contemporary gender ideologies and practices are partially rooted in the Conquest and the entrenchment of European colonialism. Spanish colonizers made every effort to root out sexual and gender mores and relationships they considered abominable and threatening, and which the Spaniards often called *malas costumbres* (bad customs). Because women were viewed as legal minors, attempts to refashion indigenous gender systems also entailed a drive to undermine their economic, political, and social autonomy, and to ensure their subordination to males. Widespread violence by European males against indigenous women was one outcome of these efforts (Silverblatt 1995). In central Mexico, early colonial sources suggest "a new emphasis on chastity and virginity, a stress on domestic work and limitations placed on female activity outside the household, a revaluation of the marriage bond, and the demonizing of women who do not fit Christian patterns" (Burkhart 2001b:103). The campaigns against idolatry—systematic attempts at stamping out non-Christian beliefs and practices and at forced religious conversion (see Chapter 7)—also focused on eradicating indigenous sexual mores, such as marital cohabitation (so-called "trial marriages") and premarital intercourse (Silverblatt 1998:66–67). In the Andes (Silverblatt 1987) as well as in Mesoamerica (Behar 1987), women, especially unmarried women, were singled out because they were perceived as especially vulnerable to the influence of the Devil. Indeed, the Devil loomed significantly in male–female gender relations and as an important ally of women:

> From the 16th century, pacts with the Devil were important in Mexico; by the 18th century, they were an integral part of the magical domain of male/female relations . . . [P]acts with the devil were more extreme than . . . folk remedies . . . looked at earlier for taming and tying husbands and straying lovers. Women called in the Devil, it seems, as a last resort, when male dominance and the double standard could no longer be reconciled with God and the saints and all the other consolations the Church had to offer. (Behar 1987:43, 47; see also López 2002; Lipsett-Rivera 2002)

The fundamentally colonial construction of the Devil as an important gender-inflected mechanism of social control persisted well beyond the end of the colonial period, as will become clear in the next chapter.

As noted in Chapter 5, colonial (male) gender ideologies were wedded to the notion of **honor**, which emphasized premarital (female) chastity, church sanctioned marriages, and the siring of legitimate children. If women lost their virginity prior to marriage, or engaged in extramarital relationships, they brought shame and dishonor to their families and family names. This logic did not apply to men, who were *not* expected to be virgins prior to marriage, and whose masculinity rested partly on public displays of sexual virility, extramarital relationships, and the procreation of (illegitimate) children (Seed 1988; Gutiérrez 1991; Twinam 1999). The transmission, distribution, and legitimation of privilege in colonial society rested partly on the male defense of female chastity and family honor, and the promotion of legitimate heirs. In this way "gender conceptions [were] idioms for interpreting and manipulating social inequality" (Collier 1980:191). These views on sexuality and marriage were diametrically opposed to and meant very little in the context of indigenous cultural norms. In the Andes, women regularly engaged in sexual intercourse prior to marriage, bearing children was highly prized, and the European notion of illegitimacy made little if no sense (Silverblatt 1998:71, 82; Charney 2001). Colonial efforts to reshape gender also narrowed other dimensions of women's autonomy. Although Spanish and Portuguese colonial gender ideologies and jural norms granted women many legal rights, such as the ability to sign contracts, appear in court, and bequeath wills, these rights were highly restricted (Dore 2000a:12).

Colonial attempts at controlling and reshaping sexuality, marriage, and notions of womanhood were largely unsuccessful. For example, unrelenting concerns about rates of illegitimacy attest to the difficulties faced in instilling elite and dominant gender, conjugal, and sexual norms among large sectors of the indigenous and popular classes in virtually every corner of Latin America and the Caribbean (Calvo 1989; Socolow 1989; Potthast-Jutkeit 1991; Stavig 1995; Nazzari 1996). Latin America's ethnic and class heterogeneity—and the unequal distribution of material resources and privilege endemic to the colonial system—therefore resulted in an "anomalous and contradictory structure of gender relations" (Kuznesof 1992:269). Ethnographic fieldwork in the Andes has in fact documented widespread sexual intercourse and trial unions before marriage, as well as little stigma attached to illegitimate offspring (Sanabria 2001).

Gender and the Consolidation of Nation-States

After independence from colonial rule, national elites went about consolidating their nation-states, and in so doing often viewed "well-ordered" families and states as mirror images of each other (Scott 1986; Randall and Waylen 1998; Dore and Molyneux 2000). The construction of gender was intrinsic to state-making efforts and these in turn rested on a gendered (and unequal) view of social, political, and economic life (Deans-Smith 1994; Dore 2000a; Molyneux 2000b).

The colonial cultural and gender system legitimizing and sanctioning male privilege and authority may have been strengthened after independence. Political disarray after the wars of independence resulted in a perceived need by elites to bolster patriarchal authority as a way of restoring the state's ability to rule. As one Mexican politician believed, a woman's autonomy from her husband would "risk the continued mutiny of the population against the established authority, and undermine the stability of the Mexican state" (quoted in Dore 2000a:19).

The nineteenth century codification of private property laws, intensification of export crop production, and assaults on corporate indigenous lands—in which women often held extensive usufruct rights to land and other resources—all worked together to seriously undermine the status and autonomy of many women throughout vast sweeps of Latin America (Dore 2000b). Other legislation was equally pernicious. In many countries, time-honored, colonial-era codes on partible inheritance ensuring that all female and male legitimate offspring equally share their parent's holdings were overturned. Other laws criminalized female (but not male) adultery and infidelity, and even allowed husbands to kill their wives if the husband could prove in court that his wife had sexual intercourse with another man (Dore 2000a:23). These laws probably affected middle and elite sectors and classes the most, as well as those indigenous communities that lost most of their landholdings.

Femininity and Masculinity: Rethinking Marianismo and Machismo

Much research has underscored that Latin American and Caribbean gender systems are and have been for a long time profoundly unequal, and that they are predicated on the legal, socio-cultural, and economic subordination of women to men. Further, popular lore—and a not inconsequential body of scholarly work—has often portrayed Latin American women as enculturated into being passive and subservient to men. Their identity pivots around being a self-sacrificing mother and caring for children, and they are seemingly more than willing to accept the burdens thought intrinsic to womanhood and motherhood. This constellation of cultural ideals is known as **marianismo.** The counterpoint to marianismo is **machismo,** which refers to ideals and practices that—at least in the public and dominant sphere—purportedly determine male identity and masculinity, and which structures male interactions with women and other men. The ideal masculine (*macho*) man is fearless in the face of danger and willing and able to safeguard the well-being and honor of his family, over which he exercises unquestioned authority, especially over women. Our ideal macho is also thoroughly and publicly heterosexual and sexually virile, with a "natural" and uncontrollable sexual drive. Unlike the women whose honor he must defend, he can demonstrate his virility through extramarital affairs and the siring of illegitimate children. Machismo is also often responsible for domestic violence against women and associated with child abandonment.

Marianismo, first coined by Stevens (1973), alludes to a broad range of traits and expectations defining womanhood and femininity, what the "ideal" woman ought to believe, and how she ought to behave. Marianismo is modeled on, and draws its inspiration from, Catholic images of the Virgin Mary as a woman, and partly overlaps with the notion of honor mentioned previously. An ideal woman is one who is humble and self-sacrificing toward her children and family as, we are told, "No self-denial . . . is too great for the Latin American woman" (Stevens 1973:94–95). She is also submissive, profoundly sad, complacent, and deeply devoted to and submissive to her mother-in-law and husband. Sexual mores also come into play, for woman are not expected to enjoy or be active instigators of sexual intercourse. These ideals and norms are not "imposed on women by tyrannical men," for they may be as "liberated" as most really wish to be. As a result, most women would not opt to "work outside the home if they were given the opportunity to do so" (Stevens 1973:98), for their role provides them with a sense of continuity, identity, and, within the domestic domain, a sense of power. Marianismo quickly became a framework of gender relations and female personhood (Nash 1989), so much so that it "has evolved into a nearly universal model of the behavior of Latin American women" (Ehlers 1991:1).

The ideas touted by Stevens and many who helped popularize them have been criticized. Collier (1986) suggests that, in a Spanish Andalusian village, a general shift away from marianist thinking and behavior was propelled by the replacement of a rural, labor-intensive agricultural economy by an industrial economy and migration to urban areas, and that women

Areq chapter

enthusiastically adopted a different way of thinking when the opportunity arose. Others claim that Stevens' statements were not based on fieldwork but on stereotypes, popular images, and a faulty reading of the available scholarship (Navarro 2002). Stevens (1973:91) admits that marianismo is especially relevant to "mestizo social classes" and less important in indigenous communities as long as they retain their cultural "purity," and that most marianist traits are particularly germane to upper- and middle-class women. In other words, Stevens suggests the (very strong) possibility of the differential distribution of marianist ideology across class and ethnic backgrounds. Navarro claims that Stevens' argument nevertheless essentializes "the ideal Latin American woman [who] is everywhere the same" (2002:265).

According to Ehlers, marianismo ideologically condones male domestic violence and suggests that women "welcome abusive male behavior as the spiritual verification of their true womanhood" (1991:1). Not so, claims Ehlers, who tells us that "Rich or poor, in towns and villages across the [Guatemalan] highlands, rarely a day passes without another woeful tale of offenses, abuses, and bad habits of men" (1991:1). Central to Ehlers' critique of marianismo is that it overlooks the very real and painful asymmetry in power relations between women and men, plays down the extent of domestic violence (often linked to machismo ideology; see the sections of this text on "Real Machos" and "Contesting Machismo"), and ignores how asymmetrical gender relations are underpinned by differential access to productive opportunities. Gender is about a lot more than ideology.

Contesting Marianismo: Women and Gender in Revolutionary Settings

In principle, revolutions strive for restructuring culture and society, and achieving economic and social equality. Because "revolution in the real world has never been gender-free" (Kampwirth 2002:1), a focus on revolutionary settings provides an opportunity for understanding the difficulties in transforming unequal gender systems and questioning marianismo as a cultural construct. This section focuses on three prominent examples: the 1959 Cuban revolution; the aborted attempt at socialism in Chile under Salvador Allende's Unidad Popular (UP) government in 1973; and the unsuccessful effort at revolutionary change under Nicaragua's Sandinista movement in the early 1980s. The extraordinary participation of women in Peru's Shining Path insurgency during the 1980s is discussed in Chapter 12.

Cuba. Before 1959, many laws favoring women (e.g., decriminalizing divorce and the right to vote) had been passed but few had concrete consequences in daily practice, and customary gender inequities and expectations within the domestic domain remained largely intact. After the revolution, the Cuban government recognized the importance of incorporating women within the party and state by creating an organization linked to the state—the Federation of Cuban Women (Federación de Mujeres Cubanas, FMC). Although the FMC was viewed as a way of achieving "women's emancipation" (formal entry into the workforce, equality before the law, and the like), and despite the real opportunities offered to and strides made by women, the political system continues to be male-dominated (Molyneux 2000a:295–297). Significantly, the FMC was not set up to fundamentally transform gender, and the government has demonstrated ambivalence toward female and, more generally, gender equality. "Masculine" qualities are given far more symbolic weight over "feminine" ones, and many—including, it would seem, many women—believe that a woman's rightful place is the domestic domain. For example, *Mujeres* (Women), FMC's official publication, "devotes more space to children, health, cooking, sewing, and . . . motherly concerns [than to politics]" (McGee Deutsch 1991:285–286). Further, official publications have done little to alter time-honored ideas concerning motherhood and fatherhood, emphasizing "discreet femininity and motherhood for women" while stressing virility and lack of paternity for men. "Evidently," McGee Deutsch states, "female revolutionaries must be mothers, but . . . male revolutionaries need not be fathers" (1991:286–287). Despite its revolutionary zeal and the opportunities that the revolution has provided women, Cuba, says Padula, is "aggressively masculine" (1996:227). Recent reviews of gender and sexuality in Cuban society suggest deepening inequality within the domestic domain, as well as virulent undercurrents against feminism, female sexuality, and male homosexuality (Ocasio 2002; Nuñez Sarmiento 2003).

Chile.   Partly because of its historically high levels of urbanization, industrialization, and literacy, along with its strong labor and socialist movements, Chile represents an interesting comparison to Cuba. Further, like Cuba—but perhaps unlike Nicaragua, discussed in the following section—Chile had a long tradition of political organizations headed by and representing women which, however, often emphasized "feminine" issues (McGee Deutsch 1991:293).

As in Cuba and Nicaragua, the Allende government sought to incorporate women as active revolutionary participants to stave off growing conservative opposition. While calling for expanded child care, equal pay, and liberalization of divorce laws, among other progressive measures, it too displayed deep ambivalence and doubtful ideological commitment to gender change. For example, Allende appointed few women to top political positions, he "regarded men as the true subjects of revolution," and others used "traditional conceptions of manhood to explain and popularize" UP's goals (McGee Deutsch 1991:299–300). In the end, the September 1973 coup (see Chapter 12 for more details) quickly ruined any likelihood of an imminent transformation of gender in Chilean society, for

> when General Pinochet took office he immediately ordered women . . . to return to their homes. While he dismantled most of the UP reforms, he retained some of its programs for women and children, thus tightening the identification between womanhood and motherhood. At the same time, his government promoted the figure of the soldier as the male ideal and the patriarchal family as the model for the new political order. In this manner Pinochet's regime removed whatever creative ambiguity existed in the definition of masculinity and femininity in Allende's Chile. (McGee Deutsch 1991:304)

Yet in the long run, more often than not repression fails to achieve its desired ends. The early 2006 election of Michelle Bachelet as Chile's president—a single mother, who herself was tortured, imprisoned, and exiled during Pinochet's rule—is a clear and encouraging reminder.

Nicaragua.   In July 1979, the *Frente Sandinista de Liberación Nacional* (FSLN) toppled the dictatorial regime of Anastasio Somoza, whose family had been installed in power by United States Marines four decades earlier. Nicaragua is an interesting counterpoint to Cuba because of the high percentage of women who joined the revolution and engaged in combat, which partly accounted for their ability to convey gender concerns to top levels of the FSLN leadership (Chinchilla 1990; Kampwirth 2002:21–43; see Photo 6.1). It is also interesting because of the greater autonomy that women's organizations displayed vis-à-vis the state and their generally more favorable stance toward feminist issues. On the other hand, after the fall of Somoza, Nicaragua was besieged by an armed counter-revolution supported by the United States (i.e., the contra war), which undermined the ability of the FSLN to sway most women to their side (see Chapter 12 for more details).

The Sandinista women's organization (Association of Women Confronting the National Problem, AMPRONAC), tied to but not under the direct control of the FSLN, was able to mobilize large numbers of women to the Sandinista cause not because many who joined rejected conventional gender categories but, almost paradoxically, because of

> many women's identification with their role as self-sacrificing defenders of their families, especially their children, [which] seemed to give them the courage to violate traditional gender-role prescriptions against public activity (outside of work and church) and to march into . . . jails and military barracks to demand the release of sons, daughters, husbands, lovers, and other family members. (Chinchilla 1990:375)

PHOTO 6.1   *Sandinista soldiers during the Nicaraguan civil war.*

AMPRONAC was unable to define itself as a vehicle for gender transformation, for its members were ideologically deeply divided. For example, although some viewed themselves as feminists, others did not; although some members advocated abortion rights, others disagreed. Moreover, at the uppermost levels of the political hierarchy, women did not achieve equality with men (Chinchilla 1990:371; Kampwirth 2002:33). Equally significant, and like Cuba and Chile, a significant segment of the top (male) political leadership was unable or unwilling to break free of conventional gender categories, a condition exacerbated by the state of constant warfare. President Ortega, for example, equated motherhood with womanhood—a conventional script—and both to the political survival of the revolution:

> The ones fighting in the front lines against this aggression are young men. One way of depleting our youth is to promote the sterilization of women . . . or to promote a policy of abortion. The problem is that the woman is the one who reproduces. The man can't play that role . . . some women, aspiring to be liberated, decide not to bear children. A woman who does so negates her own continuity and [that of] the human species. (Jaquith and Kopec 1987, quoted in Chinchilla 1990:387)

By the late 1980s, women represented the largest percentage of laborers in critical areas of the economy, such as in agriculture, textiles, light manufacturing, and in the informal sector where they served as domestic workers and petty peddlers. Yet, Nicaragua's gender system was not radically transformed and, significantly enough, more than half of the women seeking assistance at the AMPRONAC's legal office for women were victims of domestic violence (Chinchilla 1990:386). The Sandinistas did not forge a coherent strategy to transform the country's gender system, and they paid dearly for it: in the 1989 elections—which the Sandinistas lost—the "largest block of sentiment" against them were women and not men (Molyneux 2000a:294).

Contesting Marianismo: Sexuality and Female-Headed Households

Sexuality.   As a model, marianismo posits that women acquiesce in their relationships with their spouses and also adopt a self-sacrificing stance toward their own sexuality and sexual desires. A parallel dimension of this gender ideology posits a gendered **house/street divide,** whereby women's roles and behaviors are supposedly confined to the domestic domain (house; *casa,* Spanish and Portuguese) while male behavior and roles properly belong in the "street" *(calle,* Spanish; *rua,* Portuguese). The following case studies of women in a rural Nicaraguan village, Brazilian favela, and Puerto Rican town belie this view and also demonstrate how sexual and conjugal behavior is deployed by women to challenge established gender ideologies and hierarchies, as well as the house/street divide. This gendered dichotomy (and the importance of marianist ideology) appears far less applicable and important in indigenous and popular rural communities, where women enjoy much higher status.

In Tule, a small community in southwestern Nicaragua, female and male sexual norms and expectations are closely identified with distinct yet partly overlapping private and public spheres (Montoya 2002b). As in other countries, the prevailing gender ideology maintains that women who are simultaneously involved with more than one man, or who have lost their virginity before marrying or establishing a sanctioned consensual union, are of ill-repute and "of the street" (*de la calle*), a social space inhabited by other lewd individuals—male or females—such as sex workers, petty criminals, or homosexuals (de Moya 2004). These "bad" or "spoiled" women contrast with those who follow (at least publicly) customary gender conventions. Whether married, in a consensual relationship, or simply dating, "good" women or "women of the house" have only one sexual/conjugal relationship at any given point in time. The prevailing gender ideology furthermore stipulates that once a woman becomes "spoiled," she cannot later become a "woman of the house." In this way, her tarnished reputation, closely wedded to her body, sexuality, and sexual behavior, thwarts the possibility of establishing a legitimate conjugal union in the future. Because the house is construed as a feminine space, men who spend too much time at home are often construed, as in the Dominican Republic, as not "real" or "true" masculine males (de Moya 2004).

This public/private dichotomy—the profane and disrespectable "street" and the sacred, respectable, decent "house"—is one understood and accepted by most men and women, and most women do indeed strive to become "good" women of the house. Yet, this dichotomy is not totally inflexible, and can be subject to multiple and potentially conflicting interpretations, and a "bad" woman can in fact become a "woman of the house"— sometimes with the help of her partner, spouse, or other men. Several examples illustrate how women in Tule demonstrate considerable agency in deploying "trangressive sexuality" (Montoya 2002b:67) to manipulate and juggle the statuses of "good" and "bad" to their own advantage, and to find suitable partners to both challenge and eventually bridge the street and house divide.

One is the case of Lorena who, while single, lost her virginity to her lover Emilio. Although she did so before Emilio publicly expressed his interest in formalizing their bond by stating that he wanted to "take her home" (i.e., live with her in a stable, long-term relationship), Lorena was not branded a "bad" women. This is because prior to her relationship with Emilio, Lorena's "clean" sexual past had earned her a solid reputation, because her loss of virginity was not too visible (she had not engaged in multiple and well-publicized sexual liaisons), and because Emilio was her "first man." This suggests "that it was not virginity itself that was of value, but rather the process of remaining a virgin until achieving . . . the status of wife and mother" (Montoya 2002b:75).

Luisa's example illustrates how an extramarital affair—a sure sign of a "bad" woman—can still allow a woman to maintain the status and prestige associated with being a "woman of the house." Married to but in a troubled relationship with Juan, Luisa began dating and having a masked relationship with Ricardo. Since extramarital affairs in a small village such as Tule are difficult to totally conceal, Luisa was warned by her father Justino, with whom she lived, that people were "talking" (i.e., gossiping), about her possible relationship. Because too much "talk" would eventually publicly confirm this affair and almost certainly bring about a tarnished reputation, and driven by the need to protect the honor of his daughter and family name, Justino threw his daughter out of the house. Luisa was now quite fearful of her reputation and future, for if she were publicly acknowledged as a "woman of the street" her father would not have her back, but neither would Ricardo, her lover, be willing to publicly accept her. Faced with these options, in less than two days Luisa managed to convince Ricardo to take her into his house, and both went to great lengths to openly display their relationship and allow neighbors and friends to see that she was now his "wife." In other words, Luisa engaged in an extramarital relationship without losing prestige and was able to move "directly from one position in the house to another" (Montoya 2002b:79).

Goldstein provides numerous examples of Brazilian shantytown women continuously engaged in attempts at "overturning the gender hierarchy" (2003:242), where the distinction between street and home is also significant. Women in this context are painfully aware of how male privilege puts them at a considerable disadvantage but, rather than acquiescing, they are constantly challenging males, as well as forging relationships with them to advance their own interests. And women work equally hard against the prevailing sexual double standard that construes male sexuality as animal-like and uncontrollable—and that thereby legitimizes male infidelity—while at the same time expecting women to be loyal partners lest their own sexual affairs tarnish their male partner's reputation.

Glória had had a long-term, ongoing relationship with Zezinho, who was married to Lucina. Tired of being beaten by Zezinho, Lucina moved out of the household, leaving Zezinho to care for their six children. Three of the children were taken in by Lucina's mother, but the remaining three were now Glória's responsibility, who moved in after Lucina's abrupt departure, and who was pregnant with a son sired by Zezinho. As in Brazilian (and other Latin American and Caribbean) shantytowns, theirs was an extremely poor household, barely making ends meet with Glória's income as an intermittent domestic worker and Zezinho's job as an occasional handyman. To make matters worse, Zezinho drank heavily, brought home very little money, and barely provided for Glória and the children. Glória and Zezinho eventually separated but, one night, found themselves next to each other at a bar. When Zezinho was asked by someone what kind of relationship he has with Glória, he responded, "I am eating her," a consumption metaphor used to describe an exploitative sexual relationship (see Chapter 9). Glória,

> incensed by Zezinho's claim and choice of metaphors, seized the opportunity and smacked him hard in the face, bloodying his nose. The use of this eating metaphor was insulting, especially since she considered Zezinho by that time to be a leech—all along "eating" her hard-earned wages without contributing much of his own earnings to their combined household. In this context, his power-invoking claim to be "eating" her was a humiliation and a sign of disrespect beyond what Glória could bear. (Goldstein 2003:239)

Soneca, Glória's daughter, also illustrates the extent to which women attempt to capitalize on sexual liaisons to reap advantages for themselves and their children, and thereby undermining a gender hierarchy that is predicated on male privilege. Further, in using "eating" metaphors, Soneca also illustrates how women can appropriate metaphors and idioms often used by men to call attention to their control over women. Soneca had an affair lasting several months with a married neighbor. In recounting this relationship to Goldstein,

Soneca emphasized, with pride, how she induced her lover to buy food for her rather than for his own children. Hence, he was not really "eating" *her* because by enticing him to provide food and other luxury goods for her and her sister, Soneca was inverting the balance of this exploitative relationship to her own advantage. And in the process, she felt "powerful."

Such examples of turning the tables on customary gender ideologies are probably far more common and widespread than many stereotypical accounts of gender in Latin America and the Caribbean would have most believe. It is also quite probable that such attempts at inverting gender hierarchy and privilege have deep historic roots. In the case of Puerto Rico, for example, Briggs (2002) and Suárez Findlay (1999) have shown how sexuality and sexual mores among early twentieth-century proletarian women were construed for many decades by United States colonial administrators and Puerto Rican elites as a social "problem" closely aligned, in their views, with high rates of "prostitution," undisciplined and lurid sexuality, serial sexual relationships, and the unwillingness of large numbers of women to formally marry. Because definitions of morality and sexuality lay at the heart of colonial power relations, the colonial state marshaled considerable resources to remold the reproductive and sexual behavior of poor women, whose unchecked sexuality and fertility were seen as the cause of many of the island's problems, especially widespread poverty. As a result, birth control campaigns were put into place, programs were created to instill "proper" childrearing practices and "suitable" forms of motherhood, and laws were passed to decriminalize birth control and encourage legal unions (Briggs 2002). These efforts were largely unsuccessful and, in refusing to fully internalize dominant gender ideologies and expectations, Puerto Rican working-class women "did not passively reproduce patriarchal social codes. Rather, they struggled with the men in their lives over the precise definitions of acceptable gendered labor and sexual conduct. Even while accepting the dominant tenets of honor and gender obligations, women often attempted to manipulate them to their own advantage" (Suárez Findlay 1999:20). That large numbers of women took advantage of the legalization of divorce in the early 1900s to contest and terminate their marriages in court. (Suárez Findlay 1999:110–134) suggests the lack of a widespread acceptance of marianismo among a significant proportion of working-class Puerto Rican women in the early decades of the twentieth century.

Matrifocality: Female-Headed Households. Previous pages have emphasized how the colonial period and postcolonial attempts at consolidating nation-states were partially grounded on attempts to redefine indigenous and popular gender systems as well as ensconce a male-centered and intensely hierarchical system of gender ideologies and privileges that attempted to circumscribe and undermine women's autonomy and status. These attempts assumed the political centrality of males and of male-headed households, and that the "patriarchal family . . . [was] . . . the centerpiece of social stability." Efforts at building this "gendered social order" often fell short of their goals, for the patriarchal family did *not* constitute a significant dimension of the lived experience of a large proportion of families and households. Depending on country, region, class, and ethnic group, anywhere between 25 to 50 percent of households in nineteenth century Latin America and the Caribbean were **matrifocal households** in that they were headed by women (Dore 1997:101–111).

"In the 1980s," Dore tells us, "sociologists discovered a high proportion of female-headed or matrifocal households in Latin America. With the prevailing stereotype of the family, they concluded that such households were a new phenomenon" (1997:102). Not so anthropologists, many of whom had reported on the widespread occurrence of female-headed, matrifocal households, especially in the Caribbean, Brazil, and parts of Central America at least two decades earlier (Safa 1974; Lewis 1968; Smith 1970, 1971, 1992; Horowitz 1971b; Lowenthal 1984). In fact, the term *matrifocal* was originally coined by the anthropologist Raymond T. Smith as early as 1956 to refer to the family structure he observed among working-class British Guyanese (Prior 2005:372).

Reliable survey data on percentages of female-headed households in contemporary Latin America and the Caribbean are difficult to come by, and often data from one source is at odds with data from another. In the mid-1970s, between 14 and 20 percent of households in six countries (Colombia, Costa Rica, the Dominican Republic, Mexico, Panama, and Peru) were headed by women (De Vos 1987:513). Slightly lower ranges are reported by Arias and Palloni (1999) for eleven countries, also in the 1970s. By 1999, the percentage of households headed by women in fifteen countries ranged from a low of 19 percent in Mexico to as high as 35 percent in Nicaragua (the fifteen countries are: Argentina, Bolivia, Chile, Colombia, Costa Rica, Ecuador, EI Salvador, Guatemala, Honduras, Mexico, Nicaragua, Panama, Paraguay, Uruguay, and Venezuela). In fact, the 1990s witnessed an across-the-board increase in female-headed households in all fifteen countries, probably as a result of the massive economic upheavals and grinding poverty spurred by free-market reforms. Even Argentina—often considered a solid bastion of Europeanized middle-class lifestyle—was not spared, as women headed 27 percent of its households in 1999 (Chant 2002:547). Although the proportion of female-headed households varies greatly within specific countries (Jelin 1991), it is probably correct to assume an inverse relationship between the prevalence of female-headed households, poverty, and class hierarchy. Indeed, virtually all anthropological fieldwork on matrifocal households has been carried out in marginalized and poverty-stricken slums or shantytowns (Bolles 1996; Handwerker 1989; Lewis 1968; Lowenthal 1984; Prior 2005; Safa 1974; Cardoso 1984; Clarke 1973; Goldstein 2003; Scheper-Hughes 1992).

Female-headed or matrifocal households have several interrelated characteristics in common. First, household boundaries are porous, in perpetual flux, periodically incorporating new members and losing others, especially children. Second, they are marked by brittle sexual liaisons and conjugal unions, in what Mintz (1956:375) in his study of proletarian sugar plantation workers in southern Puerto Rico called a "relative instability of marriage," or what Smith, referring to other Caribbean areas, subsequently described as "the prevalence of unstable mating" (1971:455). Third, the fundamental unit of family and household life, and socialization and social relationships, revolves around mothers and children—and other women. Adult males—especially male spouses—are only erratically present. Nancy Scheper-Hughes phrased this fleeting male presence in a Brazilian shantytown the following way: "Shantytown households and families are 'made up' through a creative form of bricolage in which we can think of a mother and her children as the stable core and husbands and fathers as detachable and circulating units" (1992:323). Fourth, such households and sexual and conjugal relationships usher in high rates of illegitimate offspring. Fifth, nuclear family members (such as fathers or siblings) are often dispersed, living in other households, often with extended family members. These were some of the cultural traits of "lower-class" families that Lewis and others viewed as "pathological" aspects of the culture of poverty (Chapter 2).

The prevalence of matrifocal households is significant for at least two reasons. First, it reveals the extent to which prevailing (and often stereotypical) ideologies are at odds with what actually occurs "on the ground" among many Latin American men and women. Second, the very structure of matrifocal households, as well as their ability to survive and persevere, rests precisely on a rejection of male authority and privilege, expectations of female submission and acquiescence, and elite (dominant/national) views and norms of sexuality and gender-specific roles wedded to marianismo as a model of behavior.

Although one must be careful to not idealize or romanticize agency or autonomy by those at the very bottom of the social and economic hierarchy, nor downplay the wrenching poverty and economic uncertainty that they face on daily basis, anthropologists have written much on how actual behavior and survival strategies by women clash with marianist ideology. Prior (2005) and Sobo (1993), for example, emphasize how Jamaican women, as mothers and household-heads, have considerable control over resources and make many key decisions that affect the survival of their households despite the fact that they rely on and cherish income and gifts they obtain through sexual liaisons with men. Others have underscored that women's dominance in marketing goods and services essential for household survival also provides them considerable autonomy vis-à-vis their spouses (Stephen 1992; Seligman 1993). Further, although many women are in fact subjected to physical violence, rather than acquiescing, they often fight back. Also, it is the women and not men who take the first step in agreeing to sexual relations, who have the most important say about whether a sexual liaison is worth developing into a long-term consensual union, and who exercise control over sexual favors and "services" to men. Moreover, notions of sexuality bear little resemblance to marianist ideology, because the sexual past of women is of little relevance in their ability to establish future relationships. These women have, in Prior's words, "power." These are important points also raised in Sobo's ethnography (1993).

Real "Machos" or Contingent Masculinities?

Partly as a counterpoint and counterpart to burgeoning feminist scholarship of the past two decades, anthropologists and others are paying increasing attention to ways in which masculinity—male identity and practice, or manhood—is understood and constructed within and between societies, and how it relates to other domains of culture (Gutmann 1997, 2003a; Viveros Vigoya 2003; Parker 1991, 2003b; Nurse 2004; Reddock 2004a, 2004b). As with other concepts, masculinity is anything but precise, and it has been understood and studied in at least four different ways:

> The first concept of masculinity holds that it is, by definition, anything that men think and do. The second is that masculinity is anything men think and do to be men. The third is that some men are inherently or by ascription considered "more manly" than other men. The final manner of approaching masculinity emphasizes the . . . importance of male–female relations, so that masculinity is considered anything that women are not. (Gutmann 1997:386)

Research on masculinity is grouped around several closely related, partly overlapping, domains (Lancaster 1992; Gutmann 1997, 2003b; Viveros Vigoya 2003).

1. One body of work continues the well-established foci in anthropology on the gendered division of labor, and the differential allocation of productive resources, status, and prestige between males and females.

2. A second research thrust focuses on the construction of masculinity within the family or domestic domain. The ways in which procreation and male parenting (fatherhood) shape and are fashioned by ideals of manhood, and how space is segregated to allow opportunities for intense all-male bonding and sociality—what some scholars refer to as **homosociality**—are two examples of this work.

3. A third area of scholarship centers attention on how masculinity is both expressed and experienced somatically. Different ways of understanding the body and its relationship to reproduction (such as the extent to which performing sexual intercourse is wedded to having offspring or to sexuality), and same-sex desires and practices (which ought not be confused with the North American concept of homosexuality), are but two examples of how the body and the sexualized body loom important in how males construe themselves as men. (Both homosociality and homosexuality are dealt with more extensively in Chapter 8 and Chapter 11.)

4. The ways in which the wielding of power over others is intrinsic to masculinity and public displays of masculine behavior is the fourth area of concern in the masculinity scholarship. The exercise of male power over women (including domestic violence) has been long studied, yet scholars have also attempted to understand how and why the exercise of power—including the control some men hold over other men—is so often crucial for masculine identity.

5. Other themes include how masculine identities and behavior are related to war, violence, and emerging forms of nationalism and national identity. The ways in which authoritarian regimes often ideologically rest on and construct highly aggressive and violent manifestations of masculinity is a case in point. Previous pages have noted, for example, how the Chilean coup of 1973 encouraged the image of the (male) soldier as a key attribute of Chilean manhood. In Bolivia, there is an obligatory military draft—but obligatory or not, most poor Bolivian males, of whatever ethnic or linguistic background, would probably volunteer anyway, because military service is viewed as an essential and symbolically powerful stage in forging their manhood. Gill aptly notes the paradox and deep contradictions of this deeply entrenched and pervasive rite of passage:

> Popular notions of masculinity emerge in part from the efforts of male peasants and poor urban dwellers to engage dominant institutions, such as the military, in order to prove their worth, find personal dignity, and establish claims to membership in the nation. But in so doing the oppressed may simultaneously become collusive with their very domination by participating in the creation of beliefs about masculinity, femininity, and citizenship that are destructive within their communities and households. (2000:117)

6. Finally, scholars have underscored that the forging of masculine identities is anything but a "man only" concern, and that in their relationships to men, women play a key and active role in defining what, at least ideally, constitutes a "real" man.

Four important and related ideas cross-cut and consistently surface in the masculinity literature surveyed above. The first is that it is time to abandon the stereotypical idea of a homogenous, uniform Latin American "man" or "male," or of a single conception of masculinity. Different, competing, overlapping, and sometimes contradictory masculinities may in fact exist across all of Latin America and the Caribbean. Such contradictions are apparent in the Dominican Republic (see In Their Own Words 6.1).

IN THEIR OWN WORDS 6.1
The Language of Masculinities

Language is a useful analytical tool with which to explore the multiplicity of masculinities, or masculine identities, in a societal context. Based on a continuum of prestige, power, and dominance, de Moya (2004) outlines five categories of masculinity in the Dominican Republic, each encompassing various masculine identities, not all reproduced below:

Category	Attributes	Subcategories/Labels
Hegemonic heterosexual	Heterosexual; sexually potent; powerful at home and in public	*macho proba'o* (proven male); *duro* (hard); *toro* (bull); *caballo* (stud)
Subordinate heterosexual	Fail to display ability to have children and form a family	*hombres incompletos* (incomplete men): *jamón* (literally "ham": singleton); *hombre casado sin hijos* (married man without children)
	Behave "like women," i.e., shy, passive, not aggressive, and of "weak" character	*hombres en apariencia* (men in appearance only); *medio hombre* (half-man); *payaso* (clown); *enano* (dwarf); *mi'jito* (my child)
	Extremely handsome, delicate, or dependent on mother or wife	*pollo* (chicken; chick); *señorito* (spoiled child/brat); *lindo* (pretty); *arrima'o* (loafer); *piojo* (louse)
Subordinate bisexual	"Closet" homosexuals, but with bisexual partners	*ambidiestro* (ambidextrous); *medio pájaro* (half bird); *bi-sexual* (bisexual); *tapados* (closeted)
	Has sex with female partners for pleasure, and may practice insertive sex to paying male clients	*hombre normal* or *macho* (normal man or macho); *bugarrón/bugato* (butch, hustler); *tíguere-rapta-tíguere* (tiger who penetrates a tiger)
Marginal homosexual	Open identification as homosexual; *declarados* (out of the closet)	*pájaro* (bird); *maricón* (queer); *afeminado* (effeminate); *marigarrón* (gay man who practices both sexual roles); *cambiada* (transgendered)
Residual	Masculine or masculinized women	*Marimacho* (butch, tomboy); *hombruna* (manly looking); *cachapera* (lesbian)

In addition to recognizing the heterogeneity of masculine identities and practices, the masculinity literature has emphasized, second, the prevalence of a vast disparity between masculinities that exist "on the ground" (what people actually think and do) and pervasive and dominant—but not hegemonic and idealized—conceptions of masculinity.

Third, scholars have repeatedly stressed how seemingly identical masculine idioms can have different meanings to different kinds of men *and* women. Although the semantic polyvalence of machismo—an overriding masculine idiom—is dealt with in the following section, one example here will serve to illustrate the point. In Mexico City, for men identifying themselves as heterosexual, *mayate* may have multiple meanings, but it is often used to refer to homosexuals. Yet, for some Mexicans in the United States, and others who have lived in the United States, mayate is often a disparaging term referring to African Americans in the United States (Gutmann 2003b:8–9).

Finally, the meanings that men and women attach to masculine idioms vary according to generation and historical context. For example, although abusive males and domestic violence may be one cornerstone of machismo and a macho identity, for others a macho may indicate "a man who is responsible for providing financially and otherwise for his family . . . [and] for older men, to be macho more often means to be *un hombre de honor* (an honorable man) . . ." (Gutmann 1996:221).

Gutmann has stated that in Latin America, "The dominant male ideological expressions of [hegemonic masculinities] . . . [are] . . . homophobia, machismo, and misogyny" (2003b:3). In many academic and popular writings, machismo—and the array of often disparaging traits associated with this idiom that have been outlined previously—is repeatedly thought of as the defining feature or essence of the ideal Latin American (and often Mexican) male. This is the "supposed cultural trait of Mexican men that is at once so famous and yet so thoroughly unknown," a "scourge," that, according to Gutmann, infects "all warm male bodies that speak Spanish" (1996:12, 220). Yet, "many men, and more than a few women, in Santo Domingo [the Mexico City working class neighborhood, or *colonia,* where Gutmann carried out his fieldwork] exhibit certain of these qualities and not others" (1996:15).

Despite connoting a seemingly ageless quality of Mexican maleness, the terms macho and machismo have relatively recent origins (Gutmann 1996:222–231). It was only in the 1940s and 1950s when these terms became widespread in Mexico and common in North American academic writings. Their wide usage and dissemination in Mexico during this period was very much tied to (male and urban) elite/Mestizo concerns about the lack of a uniform Mexican national identity and attempts to forge a more cohesive nation-state. The twin goals of instilling a uniform sense of nationalism and of constructing a stronger state in a country historically marked by profound regional, class, and ethnic divisions was, of course, no easy undertaking. As Mexican elites appropriated, redefined, and recast a gendered construction of male identity as a national and nationalist symbol, "Mexico came mean machismo and machismo to mean Mexico" (Gutmann 1996:224). Their ability to do so was facilitated and paralleled by the expansion of mass media, particularly cinema, and scholarly publications within Mexico itself that attributed the "problem" of national identity to a flawed and insecure male identity.

Contesting Machismo: Alcohol and Fatherhood

Alcohol. Machos are supposed to drink, drink a lot, and enjoy doing so. This is, at least, part of the popular image often associated with masculine behavior and the definition of machismo in Mexico and elsewhere in Latin America. Yet, Gutmann's fieldwork in Mexico City casts serious doubts on the validity of this claim and, he suggests, it is time to "subject to greater scrutiny the celebrated image of the Mexican proletarian male with a bottle of tequila in his hand and a silly, satisfied grin on his lips" (1996:174).

Among men and women in Santo Domingo, alcohol drinking is indeed widespread. Yet, there is a wide diversity in drinking patterns—some men drink only on weekends, few drink daily, and others, evidently alcoholics, drink regularly and heavily. Many males drink far less than they say they do, attempting in this way to (publicly) conform to idealized and dominant constructions of masculinity. Further, alcohol drinking is not by any means an exclusively male domain. "Far more women," Gutmann states, "today drink alcoholic beverages, and in far greater quantities, than they did in the past" (1996:178).

Ethnographic studies have also emphasized that coercion to drink, especially in all-male contexts, is an important feature of Mexican drinking patterns. Yet, even here Gutmann uncovers considerable diversity, as well as numerous instances in which abstention from drinking "was culturally sanctioned, respected, and encouraged" (1996:186). One especially interesting example is when men claim *estoy jurado:*

> Estoy jurado means "I'm pledged," as in "I'm pledged not to drink." . . . Don Timoteo told me that that he was drunk every day for fifteen years, but that (as of March 1993) he had been *jurado* for five years and eight months. . . . [He] had pledged to stay sober for a year to prove to his family that he could stop. He said that most people are *jurado* to the Virgin de Guadalupe, but that he had made his pledge to the lesser-known Virgin de Carmen . . . The state of being *jurado* is a clearly and widely recognized cultural category among men in Colonia Santo Domingo that exempts them from drinking, and indeed often brings the respect of others . . . I never heard anyone try to tempt a man with a drink if it was known that he was *jurado.* (1996:186–187)

Fathering. The image of the Mexican male as an irresponsible, detached, and distant father, far more interested in siring numerous children as a public display of virility and manliness, should also be seriously questioned. With "fathering, as with all other aspects of male identities and practices in Mexico, there is not one Mexican pattern of masculinity against which all men compare themselves or should be compared. The diversity of fathering practices in Mexico is in fact central to the ambiguous character of masculinity there" (Gutmann 1996:52; see Photo 6.2).

There appears to be a class divide around which different fathering expectations and practices coalesce. For example, the detached father rarely involved with his children, and leaving child-care responsibilities to his wife, may in fact be more common in middle- or upper-class households that, able to afford full-time nannies (*muchachas*), "free" the father to pursue other interests. By contrast, no households in Colonia Santo Domingo had

PHOTO 6.2 *Ana Espindola, left, with a Mexico tricolored soccer ball, and her father walk past the Aztec stadium in Mexico City, 2005. The following day, Mexico and the United States played at the stadium in the World Cup qualifying match.*

resources to employ nannies, many women had to work outside the household to make ends meet, and many extended family kin lived elsewhere. A Mexican banking official once told Gutmann that "Mexicans do not carry babies," yet when Gutmann circulated in Santo Domingo a photograph illustrating a man holding and cuddling his child, most residents of this Colonia viewed it as an entirely appropriate behavior on the part of fathers, and we learn that

> fathers in the colonia to a far greater extent [than elite classes] are integral in all stages of their children's lives . . . most of these men define their own and others' masculinity in part in terms of their active role in parenting. (1996:85)

Generational and class differences often intersect in complementary ways, so that active parenting roles are often accompanied by a far greater participation in household chores, and "it is not uncommon for husbands and fathers in their twenties and thirties . . . to wash dishes, sweep, change diapers, and go shopping on a regular basis" (1996:151).

Although previous pages have focused on "the diversity of fathering experiences" in Mexico—to use, once again, Gutmann's words—these types of experiences are not by any means exclusive to Mexico, or to only Mexican notions of masculinity or masculine identity and behavior. Olavarría, for instance, has documented how many fathers in Santiago, Chile, are increasingly taking it upon themselves to assume many roles and tasks—more child rearing, more housekeeping—that, until recently, ran counter to dominant notions of masculinity. As a twenty-one-year-old father stated: "I like doing housecleaning. This has nothing to do with being a man or a woman. I still have to do my share . . . What woman wouldn't want her man to help?" (2003:333).

There is currently a move away from an ideal model of family and domestic life that stipulates that fathers are mere providers and mothers should assume full responsibility for domestic chores and child rearing—another dimension of the public/private gender divide mentioned previously. This change has much to do with economic transformations that undermine the possibility of sustaining this model in actual practice, and that force women of working-class families to increasingly be engaged in full-time work outside the home. Although many, especially older, fathers appear uncomfortable with their new roles, Olavarría suggests that these changes in the Chilean economy and domestic domain have not had a significant impact on local conceptions of masculinity. Yet, this suggestion may need further corroboration. For instance, given the historic role of mining (especially copper mining) in Chilean society, and the subsequent formation of a highly masculinist and belligerent working-class mining culture (Klubock 1997; Hutchison 2001), it may very well be that current economic changes undermining the ideal nuclear family/male patriarch may have rather different effects.

Models of Behavior or Lived Experience?

Despite their ideological import as models of behavior, marianismo and machismo are not—and probably have not been—representative of the lived experience of many Latin American and Caribbean women and men. An important challenge is to aim for generalizations that make sense across the spectrum of Latin American societies and cultures without falling into the trap of stereotypes or clichés, while simultaneously acknowledging the tremendous changes that have been sweeping Latin America and the Caribbean in the past forty years as a result of migration and urbanization, globalization, and deep and lasting economic transformations.

Perhaps too much importance has been placed on normative statements—what people say ought be the case—which more often than not reflect dominant, national, and elite-level cultural expectations rarely practiced in everyday life. Further, an emphasis on normative, elite-constructed models has unfortunately led to essentializing models of gender and sexuality, overlooking the fact that seemingly identical gender and sexuality constructs and expectations—what an ideal "mother," "man," or "woman" ought to consist of—has had varying meanings to different kinds of women and men in diverse contexts and historical periods.

The disparate meanings and interpretations of marianismo and machismo also suggest that gender and sexuality ideologies and practices in ethnically diverse and class stratified societies are anything but monolithic, seamless wholes equally believed in and practiced by all; these ideologies and practices may be "dominant" in that they represent widely circulating and pervasive elite-centered norms and expectations, but they do not manifest hegemony. This idea of gender and culture itself as highly fragmented in turn has two important implications. First, broad models are only partially useful (and sometimes not useful at all) for understanding gender among indigenous and ethnically diverse peoples only partly assimilated, culturally or economically, to national-level (that is, dominant "White"/"Mestizo") norms and expectations. This is also probably the case in regions or countries—such as Brazil or parts of the Caribbean and Central America—that were heavily influenced by the slave experience and that retain to this day significant aspects of African culture. Neither do marianismo or machismo appear to be culturally significant in the non-Spanish or Portuguese-speaking regions of Latin America. Second, culture, gender, and sexuality will vary significantly across class lines, and dominant ideologies and models are often hotly contested and disputed by women and men at the bottom of the economic and social hierarchy (Goldstein 2003). Ferrándiz (2003) has also emphasized how men in a Venezuelan shantytown attempt to challenge dominant perceptions of them as predominantly *malandros*—dangerous thugs—and how such widespread and stigmatizing views of shantytown male identity result in what he calls a "wounded masculinity."

Shifting Contours of Masculinity, Femininity, and Sexual Identities

This section centers on the relationships between notions of masculinity and femininity, sexuality, and sexual identities. (Sex work and workers are dealt with in Chapter 8 within the context of AIDS research.)

Stereotypical depictions of machos, or highly visible masculine *men,* invariably portray them as unquestionably heterosexual—emotionally and sexually attracted to women—thereby implicitly contrasting them with homosexuals, who are attracted, sexually or otherwise, to other men. Yet, like all stereotypes, such portrayals conceal much more than they reveal. Further, and like all cultural terms, those alluding to erotic and sexual practices, preferences, and identities—such as *homosexual, heterosexual,* or *bisexual*—have multiple meanings within and across different Latin American and Caribbean societies. In sharp contrast to the North American sexual culture—wherein males who prefer intercourse with other males are invariably defined as gay—this equivalence does not hold for much of Latin America and the Caribbean. Further, sexuality and sexual practices play a far more decisive role in shaping gender identities (i.e., who are considered "men" or "women" regardless of biological sex) in Latin America and the Caribbean.

Anthropologists have carried out a great deal of research on the plurality of sexual identities and their shifting relationships to gendered notions of masculinity and femininity (Bliss 2001; Nesvig 2001; López-Vicuña 2004). In the case of Brazil, Parker (1995) reminds readers that terms and categories emerge in concrete historical contexts and with specific referents. He furthermore emphasizes that despite the widespread acknowledgement and importance of same-sex desires and practices in the Brazilian popular or "folk model of the sexual universe," until the late 1970s, terms such as homosexuality (*homossexualidade,* Portuguese),

> or the system of sexual classifications that is so familiar in Europe and the United States simply failed to play a significant role in Brazilian popular culture or to influence the lives and experiences of the vast majority of Brazilians. (1995:248; see also Parker 1991)

Indeed, as late as the 1980s, anthropologists noted that preventive HIV/AIDS public health policies and programs modeled after the United States' labeling of "homosexuals," "bisexuals," and "heterosexuals," simply did not make sense to most Brazilians because

> such sexual identities were uncommon among the local population . . . this classification . . . ignored the large number of Brazilian men who were married to women but who nonetheless maintained sexual relations with other men. Such persons were likely to see themselves simply as "men," not as bisexual, homosexual, or even heterosexual . . . Brazilians tended to describe their sexual lives in terms of broad social identities such as "man," "woman," or even "normal," rather than in terms that linked social identities to specific forms of sexual desire. (Larvie 2003:301; see also Chapter 8 in this book)

This shifting overlap between sexual and gender identities is widespread. In Guadalajara, Mexico, Carrillo (2002, 2003) has emphasized the deep gulf between notions of masculinity and femininity, and sexual desires and practices. He notes that although machismo and manhood (*hombría*) are often defined in reference and contrast to effeminate men (*maricones*), in fact this bipolar distinction does not apply to many men he interviewed, for there is

> a new and growing sense that manhood in Mexico has to be measured by more than masculinity, machismo, or a man's sexual attraction to women. It is in this sense that openly homosexual, masculine men force a redefinition of what being a man in Mexico means. (2003:353)

Carillo's work with masculine men who engage in sexual intercourse with other men also reveals the cultural specificity of terms such as homosexual, male, or gay. For example, one man called Eugenio clearly identified himself as *homosexual*, which to him meant that "I am *varón* [male], but my sexual preference is for other males, because I feel completely male. I don't believe I am effeminate, either in my looks or in my demeanor" (Carrillo 2003:356). Further, other Mexican men who regularly had sex with men made a clear distinction between being gay and homosexual:

> In characterizing what being gay is, they commonly emphasized the fact that they would not marry women or have children—signs of leading a double life. At the same time, however, they did not view their own double lives as necessarily contradicting their sense of being *gay* and not *homosexual*. (Carrillo 2003:364)

Others interviewed by Carrillo could entirely identify themselves as normal, heterosexual men while also engaging in frequent intercourse with other males—but only as long as the sexual partner was indisputably masculine *and* the recipient of sexual penetration. As in other Latin American and Caribbean countries, "sexual positions" (Lancaster 1997) are key in defining masculinity and sexual identity. Prieur's research among homosexual transvestites in a Mexico City working-class neighborhood complements Carrillo's work and offers additional insights into the dynamics of masculine and sexual identities (1996). Her work validates other research that equates a man's active sexual role (with either men or women) as an index of masculinity and expression of dominance. One interesting aspect of her work centered on the multiple, overlapping classifications and vocabularies of male sexual identities and practices (see Table 6.1). Kulick, drawing on his research with Brazilian transgendered prostitutes (*travestis*), further notes the importance of anal—as opposed to oral—intercourse in the construction of masculine identity:

> One of the defining attributes of being a *homen* (man) . . . is that a man will not be interested in another male's penis. A man . . . will happily penetrate another male's anus. But he will not touch or express any desire for another male's penis. For him to do so would be tantamount to relinquishing his status as a man and be reclassified as a *viado* (homosexual, faggot), which is how the travestis are classified by others and how they see themselves. Travestis want their boyfriends to be men, not viados. (1997:577; see also Kulick 1998)

Sexuality and gendered identity also have much to do with power and dominance. In Nicaragua (Lancaster 1992) and elsewhere, a man who penetrates or is the subject of penetration expresses statements of control over others, in turn an important attribute of masculine identity. In Martinique, for example, "Many self-identified homosexual Martinican men recognize and categorize themselves as men, simply making a substitution so that they can be men through the conquest of other men rather than women" (Murray 1999:169).

TABLE 6.1   Some Male Sexual Identities and Practices in a Mexico City Working-Class Neighborhood

Term	Meaning
Mayate	Masculine looking men who have sex with other men, and also sexual relationships with women
Tortilla	Man who during sexual intercourse penetrates and is penetrated by other men
Normal	Man who retains the active role during sexual intercourse with either men or women
Buga	Man who has sexual intercourse exclusively with women
Homosexual	Man who assumes the passive sexual role during intercourse with other men
Vestida	Homosexual transvestite who wears women's clothes
Joto/Jota	Refers to both homosexual (joto) and vestida (jota)
Heterosexual	Being a man, or normal
Bisexual	Masculine men who have sex with other masculine men *or* androgynous-looking men; are both active and passive during intercourse
Jotos Heterosexuales	Homosexuals who prefer to penetrate men

Source: adapted from Prieur (1996)

Research on males who have intercourse with other males therefore suggests that sexuality and sexual practices play an influential role in shaping gender identities—so powerful a role in fact that Kulick has gone so far as to state that

> gender in Latin America should be seen not as consisting of men and women, but rather of men and not-men, the latter being a category into which both biological females and males who enjoy anal penetration are culturally situated. (1997:575)

Examples of how women have challenged marianismo, machismo, and male-centered notions of "appropriate" female sexuality and identity surfaced in previous pages of this chapter. Yet, entrenched cultural frameworks are not easily cast aside, and sometimes the coalescence of alternate sexualities and sexual identities entails a temporary and conflictive overlap with dominant cultural notions.

One example is that of María Pérez, a Mexican woman originally from a small town in the state of Puebla, daughter of Mestizo peasants, and interviewed by Zavella (2003) in the United States. María was raised according to conventional female gender and sexuality canons that emphasized heterosexuality; sinfulness of sexual pleasure; importance of marrying, having a family, bearing children; submissiveness to a future spouse; and the like. When she was twelve, María not only realized that some women had relationships with other women in her town—they were vilified as *jotas* (lesbians; compare with *joto,* in Table 6.1)—but that she herself was attracted to women. She soon began sexually exploring and playing with other young women, yet perceived herself as a "popular boy" when surrounded by many "admiring girls." Further, when she began her first serious (yet still secretive) relationship with another woman, "their relationship was cast in a heterosexist mold, in the sense that María played the male and her lover the female when they made a commitment" to each other (Zavella 2003:236). Several years later, at age fifteen, she fell in love with Josefina, whom María called her "wife." In addition, Josefina embodied—at least from María's point of view—many cherished marianist qualities. As María stated to Zavella, Josefina

> had the most beautiful eyes and beautiful hair. She was all woman, in the sense that she was *the* woman, *la madre abnegada, la mujer sufrida* (the self-denying mother, the suffering woman) and all that. It was very appropriate for me to get in that relationship because I was the macho prototype, a macho man in the tradition of values. (Zavella 2003:237)

During the first two years of María's relationship with Josefina (it lasted nine years), both agreed to avoid vaginal penetration—in effect reflecting dominant views concerning the importance of virginity prior to marriage. Seven years later, the relationship fell apart because Josefina fell in love with a man and subsequently had an abortion. Yet, what really hurt María the most was not Josefina's relationship with a man but the abortion, because "María's own Catholicism and desire for a child that consummated their love made Josefina's . . . abortion unfathomable" (Zavella 2003:239). Despite acknowledging and feeling at ease with her sexuality and sexual identity, many more years passed before María was able to shed male-centered gender and sexual ideologies, an accomplishment she achieved when she migrated to the United States.

Controversies: Gender, Masculinity, and Violence
in Amazonian Societies

Many anthropologists have emphasized that gender relations are more egalitarian in foraging and many horticultural societies where women make crucial contributions to the livelihood of their households. This appears so despite the often-noted ritual and symbolic importance of males in the public domain (Mukhopadhyay and Higgins 1988; Kelekna 1994). Others have argued that stark gender inequality is often absent in peasant communities for, despite the public prominence of males, women play pivotal roles in the productive process (Buechler and Buechler 1996; Prior 2005; Rosenbaum 1996; Nash 1993; Handwerker 1989; Hamilton 1998; Harris 2000).

One implication of this research is that balanced gender relationships are predicated on access to resources and the undertaking of tasks that enhance the productive capacity and roles of women. A relevant example is Chanchaló, an Andean peasant community in northeastern Ecuador (Hamilton 1998). There, peasants often state that households have not one but two "heads"—emphasizing not merely complementarity but also a balance between the productive resources marshaled by both women and men for the well-being of their households. Households are considered two-headed partly because local (and not national) inheritance patterns and other forms of accessing productive resources enable women to accumulate land and other resources independent of their spouses. The reverse also holds—gender inequality tends to intensify when women's access to productive resources is either undermined or devalued. An example is Ehler's study (1991) of gender relations, economic strategies, and the division of labor in San Antonio Palopó, a Cakchiquel Mayan-speaking rural community in Guatemala. Prior to the introduction of commercial weaving opportunities, San Antonio Palopó was a mainly agricultural community where both men and women worked side by side. Women did most of the weaving at home. The appearance of a commercial weaving cooperative upset the division of labor, because men began joining the cooperative in greater numbers, devoting more and more time to weaving, and less time to agriculture. Hence, the complementarity characteristic of agricultural production has been undermined and gender relations are far less equal than in the past.

Generalizations, however, are often hotly contested, and this is especially the case in the considerable controversy on gender relations in Amazonian (and Melanesian) societies. (Melanesia usually refers to a sub-region of the Pacific islands that includes, among others, New Guinea, the Admiralty Islands, Fiji, the Solomon and Santa Cruz Islands, Vanuatu [formerly New Hebrides], and New Caledonia.) For example, Kelekna (1994:225–226) states that "Although it is true that female status remains high in some extensive horticultural, nonpastoral societies of temperate regions . . . this does not hold for the tropics," such as in lowland Amazonia, which is characterized by swidden (or slash-and-burn) agriculture, endemic warfare, and "marked gender asymmetry."

One of the most striking features of Amazonian societies is the pervasiveness of gender and sexuality. These are **gender-inflected societies** in that

gender roles and their attendant ideas about sexuality appear as templates for many other domains of culture. Human sexuality is projected upon nature so that flora, fauna, and natural objects have anthropomorphically sexual qualities.

Ritual systems, cosmology, leadership, warfare, self-concepts and images of the human body, kinship, and perceptions of the environment are genderized: thought of and conceived in terms that are linked to masculinity, femininity, and human sexuality. (Gregor and Tuzin 2001:8)

Reichel-Dolmatoff's research on the gender and sexualized religious universe of the Tukano (1971) is a classic in Amazonian ethnography. Descola's fieldwork among the Achuar (sometimes called Jívaro) in southern Ecuador and northern Peru underscores how subsistence activities are also profoundly gendered and sexualized. For example, fishing is an important subsistence activity, and one way of bagging many fish at a time is by stunning ("poisoning") them. This is done by building temporary levees and inserting into the slow moving water the ground leaves or roots of certain toxic shrubs. The act of poisoning fish, according to Descola,

> is symbolically expressed by constant reference to sexual themes . . . the equivalence between sexual relations and fish poisoning can . . . be seen in the men's standard play on the . . . expression that designates this technique, *entza nijiatin* ("to wash the river"), and *entza nijirtin* ("to copulate with the river") . . . Women may not touch the toxic plants, for the contact would make [the plants] impotent; women are especially forbidden to crush the leaves and roots, an operation that can be assimilated metaphorically to ejaculation. (1994:280)

A second important feature of gender in Amazonian societies is the widespread presence of male-centered and controlled ritual activities—variously called male initiation rituals, men's cults, or male-centered fertility cults—that appear to enhance male privilege and are fundamental in constructing a masculine identity (Gregor and Tuzin 2001:12–14; Hill 2001:47–52). Anthropologists have long debated the relationship between these "man making" rituals that stress the importance of either enemy and/or female menstrual blood and gender inequality (Conklin 2001:146). Hill (2001:46–47) posits that Amazonian societies can be placed along a continuum: at one end are those in which gender separation and antagonisms are marked and bolstered by male-controlled ritual hierarchies, while at the opposite extreme are those societies in which "men rely less on intimidation and threats of physical violence against women, and public recognition of the interdependency of men and women is given in ceremonial exchanges and nonritual contexts."

In fact, the relationship between masculinity, violence, and gender equality has been one of the most contentious issues in the study of Amazonian gender, and is related to contrasting interpretations of the extent and origins of warfare among Amazonian groups. In the 1980s, one important theme in Amazonian ethnography was the so-called **sex wars.** Two important issues loomed important in this line of work. The first was that male access to women was a catalyst for intervillage raiding and warfare. The second theme centered on the idea that gender relations were pervaded by deeply entrenched antagonisms, if not actual violence. Much of this research and the ensuing debates centered on the prevalence of rituals, male sexual anxieties vis-à-vis women, and power struggles between males and females expressed through sexual idioms, hypermasculine rituals, and male-upon-female physical violence (Knauft 1997:234–237; McCallum 2001:160–169).

Perhaps the best known and controversial example of an Amazonian society riddled by entrenched warfare, and male-upon-female violence surfaces in Chagnon's *Yanömamo: The Fierce People* (1997), one of the most popular ethnographic accounts to be written. The Yanömamo, who practice swidden cultivation coupled with hunting and fishing, and straddle both sides of the Venezuelan–Brazilian border, are the largest and best known Amazonian indigenous group. Chagnon consistently portrays the Yanömamo (also known as the Yanömama or Yanömami) as intrinsically "fierce." In fact, Yanömamo gender relations are marked by what appear to be remarkably antagonistic relations between men and women, and pervasive male-onto-female violence. The following captures the general tenor of male–female relationships:

> Yanömamo society is decidedly masculine . . . [Girls] . . . are largely pawns to be disposed of by kinsmen . . . Women must respond quickly to the demands of their husbands . . . Should the wife be slow . . . some irate husbands scold them or even beat them . . . Most physical reprimands . . . take the form of blows with the hand or with a piece of firewood, but a good many husbands are more severe. Some of them chop their wives with the sharp edge of a machete or ax or shoot them with a barbed arrow in some non vital area . . . Some men are given to punishing their wives by holding the glowing end of a piece of firewood against them, producing painful and serious burns . . . It is not uncommon for a man to injure his sexually errant wife seriously and some men have even killed wives for infidelity by shooting them with an arrow. (Chagnon 1997:122–125)

Male access to and control over women is by far *the* most important catalyst for high levels of violence and warfare according to Chagnon. Due to a marked sex imbalance, a cultural preference for and high status attached to polygyny, and the importance of trading women for solidifying marriage and political alliances, males violently compete and engage in endemic warfare for control over women. But why should this be so? The answer hinges on a socio-biological explanation that links access to women and the siring of offspring to evolutionary advantages, for there seems to be a

> Correlation between military success and reproductive success. . . . *Unokais* (men who have killed) are more successful at obtaining wives and, as a consequence, have more offspring than men their own age who are not *unokais* . . . *unokais* are socially rewarded and have greater prestige than other men and, for these reasons, are more often able to obtain extra wives by whom they have larger than average numbers of children. Thus, "cultural success" leads . . . to biological success. (Chagnon 1997:205)

In fact, Yanömamo violence is but one example of a much deeper and cross-cultural attribute of *male* responsibility—if not nature:

> Turning the other cheek on neighbors who are led by [violent] men . . . might not be the best strategy if your own—and your group's—survival is of any concern, and it usually is. Men who do these things are generally called warriors or

soldiers and, historically, those among them who survive seem to have been generously rewarded for their deeds by acquiring status, wealth, power. . . . We elect such men to Congress, or the Presidency, and give them medals. Among the Yanomamö . . . they just get more wives and have more children. (Chagnon 1997:206)

Others have disputed Chagnon's descriptions of the extent, intensity, and causes of Yanömamo violence. Tierney (2000:159–162) and Ferguson (1995:359–360) suggest that Chagnon may have overlooked other, far less violent, pathways through which Yanömamo men acquire wives and have many offspring, and they dispute the central idea that access to wives is a major catalyst for violence. Some anthropologists working with other Yanömamo groups suggest the presence of less violence and male-upon-female antagonisms (Smole 1976; Alés 2000; see also Chapter 10).

There are in fact many Amazonian societies marked by far more egalitarian gender roles and relationships. McCallum's ethnography of gender relations among the Cashinahua, at the border between Peru and northwestern Brazil, is a case in point (2001). The Cashinahua that McCallum studied on the Brazilian side of the border are a Panoan-speaking group living in a heavily forested region and subsisting on swidden (slash-and-burn) cultivation, hunting and fishing, and occasional rubber tapping.

All men and women are expected to marry young and polygyny is sanctioned and highly valued, although most marriages are monogamous. The Cashinahua view of marriage "emphasizes male-female cooperation and complementarity; assumes a good marriage to be an affectionate and lifelong partnership; and enshrines it as the only relationship that allows men and women to be complete persons" (McCallum 2001:59). In a pattern called matrilocal or uxorilocal postmarital residence, when young men marry, they move into their wife's house. It is in this same house that the women's married sisters and her mother, as well as their spouses and children, also typically live. A married women will eventually possess gardens near her mother's house.

The Cashinahua conception of gender is of an ongoing, complementary process related to the acquisition of knowledge and its eventual deployment in the productive sphere, so that "Only producing adults are completely gendered. What is more, only gendered adults are complete persons" (McCallum 2001:48). Female and male agency surfaces in the complementary division of labor. Spinning and weaving textiles is a highly valued endeavor that women undertake. With the possible exception of hunting—a distinctly male occupation—a rigid gender division of labor does not exist. The importance of both female and male agency surfaces in other realms. Although the "chief" or "main" leader who represents the Cashinahua vis-à-vis the outside world is always male, his wife is referred to as the "woman leader" (McCallum 2001:111).

McCallum argues that among the Cashinahua and the Sharanahua (another Amazonian group), rituals that imply gender antagonisms could be equally interpreted "as a celebration of sexuality and an incentive to engage in sexual relations, not a 'war'" (2001:170). Among the Cashinahua and other "Amazonian societies . . . social [including gender] inequality . . . is not institutionalized in economic or political terms," which may partly explain why male violence against women is "extremely rare" (McCallum 2001:158, 115).

In the United States: Courtship, Sexuality, and Love Across the Border

Like any other domain of culture, gender ideologies and practices are anything but static. This process of ongoing change is particularly evident in Mexican communities from which many members migrate back and forth between Mexico and the United States. Hirsch (2003) documents how Mexican single and married men and women in Mexico and the United States are redefining their views on gender, sexuality, and courtship, and in the process crafting novel "companionate" marriages that are ushering in declining fertility and smaller families. Such transformations have much to do with cultural and economic changes in Mexico as well as with the unique challenges and opportunities, and cultural influences, that both men and women—single or married—face in their attempts to construct new lives in the United States.

In an example of **multisited ethnography,** or carrying out fieldwork in multiple locations (Marcus 1995), Hirsch carried out research in two Mexican communities—Degollado (State of Jalisco), and El Fuerte (State of Michoacán)—and in the United States with migrant men and women in Atlanta. Ethnographic fieldwork focused on gathering life histories from thirteen informants from each field site. Important features of the women and men that Hirsch worked with were their intense mobility between their home communities and Atlanta, how Mexico and Atlanta are both important sites for crucial rituals and life events, and how migrants attempt to stay in touch with those back home. For example, many who migrate to Atlanta often return to their home communities to participate in and sponsor important village celebrations; some women may marry and live in Atlanta for a while and then return to Mexico for extended periods of time; others may marry and spend their formative years in Mexico and only later move to Atlanta; and virtually all migrants in Atlanta attempt in one way or another to re-create ties (and memories) with kin and friends back home through the exchange of presents, mail, and video recordings of important ritual events, and also through telephone conversations. It is this constant flow of cultural ties, memories, and ongoing social relationships that warrants, in Hirsch's approach, consideration of these migrants as well as those who do *not* migrate, as a single, transnational community.

Elder female informants that Hirsch interviewed in the Mexican field sites recall that thirty or forty years ago, women were expected to be "properly married" (*casarse bien*). Casarse bien entailed, among other things, a prohibition on premarital sex (which would "stain" the women's honor and that of her family) and a formal request by the future groom to the bride's father for her hand in marriage, to be celebrated in a Catholic church ceremony. Even casual physical contact between the future spouses in the course of dating—holding hands or, worse, kissing in public—was frowned upon. Further, the ideal and expected conjugal/marriage contract was one in which the casa/calle (home/street) divide was rigidly enforced, with the woman mainly staying home and assuming the lead role in domestic affairs and the rearing of children, while the male spouse working outside the home and enjoying a great deal of liberty "in the street." Husbands wielded a great deal of authority within the home—they were the ones who "gave the orders" (*quien manda*). And although it would be a mistake to think that women and wives were always submissive—Stern's study (1995) of gender relations in Mexico City, Morelos, and Oaxaca during late colonial times proves that often they were not—the women interviewed by Hirsch often claimed that consistent, open, and public challenges to male authority were rare. Male prerogative over the sexual rights to his wife's body—his insistence on engaging in sexual intercourse whenever he pleased—was also rarely openly challenged. Further, for women procreation was the ultimate and single most important motive for sexual intercourse. Emotional and sexual intimacy—expressing feelings or reservations about the marital bond or sexual intercourse, or worse, sexual pleasure—was often taboo, and in any event invariably subordinated to the overriding goal of procreating and rearing children, especially male offspring. Marital ideals and bonds were marked by the respect (*respeto*) of these prevalent norms. For some women, such a marital contract was part and parcel of the suffering (*sufrimiento*) that they felt destined to as women and wives.

Such gender and marital ideals are undergoing rapid changes, both in Mexico and among migrants in the United States. The most important change in gender ideology, especially among younger women and men in both Mexico and Atlanta, is conveyed in marital ideals linguistically expressed as a shift from respeto (respect) to *confianza* (trust). These linguistic constructs point attention to important changes in the meanings of intimacy, sexuality, gender roles and expectations, and shifting power relations between males and females within the domestic domain. The outcome of these shifts, which are foregrounded and make sense in the context of broad political–economic changes in the milieu within which younger males and females reconstruct their lives in Mexico and the United States, is the emergence of the ideal of a **companionate marriage.** In this type of marriage and marital ideal, gender ideologies, relationships, and expectations are far more balanced than they were among previous generations of men and women. For example, decision-making in many matters is now more often an outcome of joint negotiations (as opposed to important decisions made unilaterally by males); a less rigid gendered division of labor occurs (e.g., women working outside the household, and males willing to share in domestic tasks—with a corresponding redefinitions of femininity and masculinity); the classic home/street dichotomy is redefined; far more emphasis is placed on emotional and physical intimacy in the marital relationship, overshadowing the importance attached in previous generations (and in many households in Mexico today) to obligation and procreation as the ultimate goal of marriage; sexual pleasure and love, to be experienced by both women and men, is now considered a cornerstone of a happy and successful marriage; and, finally, more emphasis is placed on having a small family in which fathers and mothers have enough time (and emotional energy) to devote to their children.

In Mexico, this transformation in sexual and gender culture is related to cultural, social, economic, and technological changes. The increasing presence of television sets and spread and availability of mass media—cable programming and satellite dishes, the purchase of which is often possible because of migrant remittances from the United States—have made more widely available new images (and possibilities) of novel forms of sexuality and gender through *telenovelas* (soap operas) and cable programming (see Chapter 11 for more details). Rising rates of school attendance and literacy, coupled with the teaching of sex education in schools, have also been important, primarily because they have encouraged the frank discussion of sexuality, "Topics about which respectable people did not speak in public" in the not too distant past (Hirsch 2003:83). New views on the appropriate age at marriage—for example, the disapproval of young girls who marry when they are fourteen or fifteen years old—are both a reflection of and a major contributing factor to changing views of sexuality, gender, and marriage ideals. Migration to the United States is a third powerful force of cultural change:

> As growing numbers of married and single women have migrated north . . . slipping off to el norte has become firmly established as an option for women whose behavior does not conform to community standards. Female return-migrants parade their superior status as norteñas [living "in the North," that is, in the United States or Canada] by dressing less modestly, smoking in public, driving, and in general going out of their way to show townspeople how things are done al otro lado ["on the other side" in the United States or Canada]. A generation ago hand-holding was a stain on an unmarried woman's honor, but it is now widely regarded as innocuous. Women insist on sticking to all the old customs at their peril: most of the year there are many fewer young men than women in the town, and in fact the town is full of *quedadas* (literally, leftover women) in their thirties and forties. (Hirsch 2003:84)

Migration to and life experiences in the United States are therefore an important part of this story. Indeed, the economic, cultural, and social milieu in the United States makes it difficult for both males and females to uphold and legitimize past views on sexuality and gender, despite the fact that not all migrant women and men undergo identical life experiences. For example, although anonymity in the United States might contribute to feelings of loneliness, the positive upshot is that such a context relaxes social controls (through gossip) on women. As one woman told Hirsch,

> Here it's a totally different life. Nobody knows you. Here you can go wherever you want, with whoever you want . . . in Degollado where we live, everyone knows each other . . . so the whole town [would say] "Did you see Fulana's daughter going around with that guy's son?" . . . Here, who cares about these things? (2003:192)

Also, greater opportunities for and women's need to work outside the home invariably reconfigure traditional gender expectations and roles, among other things by enhancing women's economic independence. Further, social contexts contribute to the erosion of the casa/calle divide, and the ability or needs of males to adhere to past masculine notions and practices. For example:

> For men, the physical diffusiveness of . . . Atlanta lessens the . . . pressures to participate in a certain style of masculine leisure-time activities: many Mexicans in Atlanta work for gringo bosses who care more about whether they show up on time and work hard than whether they are suspect as homosexuals because they refuse to go drinking. For men who choose to be "family men," the lack of one public, central social space such as the plaza, makes it easier to

pick friends who share their masculinity ideals and avoid those who will push them to perform in other ways. (Hirsch 2003:195)

This shift toward a companionate marriage which, incidentally, is also a function of **neo-local residence** where couples establish their own independent households, is based on a new model of intimacy—sexual or otherwise—between women and their spouses. Unlike previous forms of marriages and underlying gender relations—which were primarily held together by a sense of obligation that spouses had to each other, their children, or community—the "glue" holding together companionate marriages is a new sense of intimacy and personal fulfillment. The corresponding linguistic shift is quite noticeable:

> The language women use to talk about sex reflects the shift to a paradigm of mutual desire. Many of the older women—even those who seem to have shared a pleasurable intimacy with their partners—employed the word *usar* (to use) to describe vaginal intercourse; for example, they might say *"cuando él me usa"* (when he "uses" me) to describe sexual relations. Usar is a mechanical, instrumental word, describing the utilization of an inanimate object—the word one might employ to talk about an iron, or a plow. Younger women describe intercourse using words like *hacer el amor* (making love) or *estar juntos* (being together) or *tener relaciones* (having relations). (Hirsch 2003:213–214)

All said, the emerging companionate marriage does indeed resemble the kinds of marriages and marital ideals among many "modern" (and middle-class) North Americans. Yet, herein lies, perhaps, a looming danger, for, as Hirsch herself notes, the social and cultural foundations of these new marriages are both narrow and potentially fragile, which may "presage further increases in rates of marital dissolution in Mexico" (2003:283).

Summary

The best sources on pre-European gender systems come from Mesoamerica and the Andean region. There, gender ideologies and relationships prior to the rise of the Aztec and Inca states revolved around the twin concepts of parallelism and complementarity. Aztec and Inca state expansion had a profound impact on gender, resulting in more hierarchical gender ideologies and relationships. Transforming gender and sexuality was an important objective of European colonizers for the consolidation of colonial rule. Like in other domains of culture, such efforts were widely resisted and only partially successful. Colonial efforts to reshape gender also loomed important after Latin American countries gained independence, because control over women's sexuality and undermining their status and autonomy were viewed as crucial for the consolidation of nation-states. Two widespread gender models—marianismo and machismo—were shown to have multiple meanings and often little association with the daily lives of men and women in many parts of Latin America and the Caribbean. This chapter also underscored how gender identities are profoundly molded by sexuality and sexual identities.

ISSUES AND QUESTIONS

1. *Studying Gender.* What does the study of gender entail and what does it not? What are some examples, drawn from any part of this chapter, that illustrate ways in which the study of gender provides insights into other aspects or domains of culture?

2. *Gender, Inequality, and Politics.* A central theme throughout this chapter is that gender ideologies and relationships are very much connected to inequality and politics. What examples drawn from both the pre- and post-European periods illustrate these connections?

3. *Contesting Dominant Gender Ideologies.* One feature of hierarchically structured state societies is that there are gaps and tensions between dominant, or elite, and popular cultural beliefs and practices. With this idea in mind, discuss at least two examples that illustrate dominant or elite gender expectations and how these are contested at the popular level by both men and women.

4. *Femininities and Masculinities.* Culture is far from uniform or homogenous, and gender is no exception. Drawing from material in this chapter, explain at least two examples of femininities and masculinities in Latin America and the Caribbean. Are there parallels with North America?

KEY TERMS AND CONCEPTS

Colonialism   p. 150
Companionate marriage   p. 177
Conquest hierarchy   p. 149
Gender   p. 146
Gender complementarity and parallelism   p. 147
Gender division of labor   p. 149

Gender-inflected societies p. 172
Homosociality   p. 162
Honor   p. 150
House/street divide   p. 156
Machismo   p. 152
Marianismo   p. 152

Matrifocal households   p. 159
Multisited ethnography   p. 176
Neo-local residence   p. 179
Parallel descent   p. 148
Sex wars   p. 173
Sexuality   p. 146

7   Religion and Everyday Life

This chapter emphasizes the central and multifaceted role of religious beliefs and practices in everyday life. It first centers on how popular Catholicism differs from formal Catholicism, and how it expresses popular aspirations and sentiments by focusing on three examples: the Virgin Mary, the Devil, and All Saints and All Souls Day. The chapter then turns to the spread of Protestantism, underscoring how and why this religious conversion is taking place so rapidly, and what might be some cultural and social consequences. The focus subsequently shifts to the enduring and significant presence of African-derived religious beliefs and practices in Brazil and the Caribbean. The controversy surrounding the origins and functions of Mesoamerican civil–religious hierarchies is discussed next. The final section takes readers to southern Brooklyn to understand and appreciate the relevance of vodou among Haitians in New York City. (Shamanism is discussed in conjunction with health and healing practices in Chapter 8.)

Popular Catholicism

As a system of beliefs and ritualized behaviors centered on supernatural beings and forces above and beyond nature and humankind, **religion** is key in understanding cultural differences. It is partly through religious beliefs and practices that members of social groups attempt to grapple with and make sense of the world, particularly during seemingly senseless or arbitrary events.

By the early to mid-colonial period, the medieval Catholicism brought to the New World by Spanish and Portuguese colonizers had become solidly entrenched but it had not replaced indigenous and African religious beliefs (Ingham 1986). There are several reasons why European religious beliefs formed part of Latin American and Caribbean daily life and culture just a few decades after the Conquest. One had to do with religious persecution through the **campaigns against idolatry.** European secular and religious colonizers engaged in widespread campaigns against what they considered idols and sacred worship places. Torture, coercion, forced indoctrination, and the destruction of temples and "pagan" icons and idols were pervasive during the sixteenth and seventeenth centuries. One symbolically important strategy was to erect churches over the ruins of pre-Conquest indigenous temples and shrines (Stern 1982:62–67; Clendinnen 1987: 45–71; Silverblatt 1987:169–181; Griffiths 1996).

That indigenous and African peoples had **polytheistic religious systems**—flexible enough to accommodate additional supernatural beings—was far more important than persecution in spreading Catholicism. By stressing incorporation and not exclusion, an array of European deities, such as God, Jesus Christ, the Saints, and the Virgin Mary, easily made their way into indigenous and African religious beliefs. This point is developed more fully later in this chapter.

Also, the celebration of many Catholic rituals coincided in an uncanny way with the timing and meaning of many indigenous celebrations, and Catholic deities had analogous indigenous counterparts, such as in Mesoamerica:

> Both religious traditions had a rite of baptism. In Catholicism the child was baptized and named . . . The Mexica similarly bathed and named the child in a religious rite, and the Maya celebrated with a ceremony the first time the child was carried astride the hip. Both religious traditions had a kind of confession. The Mexica and the inhabitants of the Gulf coast confessed their sexual transgressions to a priest of the earth goddess Filth-Eater; the Zapotec had annual public confessions; and the Maya confessed themselves either to priests or members of their families in case of illness. Both religious traditions possessed a ritual of communion. The Catholics drank wine and swallowed a wafer . . . the Mexica consumed images of the gods made with amaranth and liberally anointed with sacrificial blood. Both . . . used incense in their churches . . . fasted and did penance . . . went on pilgrimages to holy places; [and] both kept houses of celibate virgins. Both believed in the existence of a supernatural mother . . . [and both] . . . made use of the cross. (Wolf 1959:171–172)

In addition, Catholic clergy often astutely timed their religious rites to coincide with major tenets of indigenous religion, thereby usurping the powers of indigenous deities and religious leaders. Pardo (2004) has examined how Catholic clergy attempted to spread Christianity by focusing on Catholic sacraments that resembled Nahua rituals. Another example, drawn from Spanish chronicler accounts, comes from the northern reaches of the Spanish empire, in what is now New Mexico. There,

> one of the first functions the friars assumed what that of potent rain chiefs. Because the Pueblo cosmology was not very different from that of the Indians of central Mexico, the friars were well aware of the symbolic power in the Pueblo belief system. Thus the friars tried to time their arrival in New Mexico to coincide with the rainy season . . . [W]hen the friars entered San Juan Pueblo, they found the earth parched and the crops wilted for lack of rain. The friars constructed a cross, prayed for rain, and ordered the Indians to do likewise. Then, while the sky was as clear as a diamond, exactly twenty-four hours after the outcry had gone up, it rained . . . so abundantly that the crops recovered. San Juan's inhabitants rejoiced and presented many feathers, corn meal, and other gifts to the crucifix and to the friars. (Gutiérrez 1991:56)

In many ways, Latin American and Caribbean peoples who came under the sway of the Spanish and Portuguese have been largely Catholic since the early colonial period. Yet this truism does not shed light on what it means to be religious or Catholic, or how and why Catholicism has come to occupy such a central place in the everyday lives of Latin American and Caribbean peoples.

During the colonial period, a distinctive fusion of (medieval) Catholicism and local (indigenous and African) beliefs and practices emerged. There was, to be sure, a great degree of variability, a "creation of many Catholicisms at the level of ordinary people . . . ad hoc mixtures of belief and even, to a lesser extent, of ritual" (MacLeod 2000:18). Nevertheless, these different strands of Catholicism shared and continue to share much in common. It is this widely shared yet varied religious system that emerged from the fusion of medieval Catholicism and diverse indigenous and African traditions that is commonly called **popular Catholicism.**

Major Attributes of Popular Catholicism

Rowe and Schelling outline some key differences between formal and popular Catholicism:

> . . . popular Catholicism tends to lack a conception of salvation, and its idea of sin is at variance with orthodox theology; the sacraments receive little emphasis, and the priest is viewed principally as a functionary of the Church, not as a mediator with God, a role which is fulfilled by the cult of the saints who are often seen as being "effectively present" in the images and sculptures which represent them; domestic liturgies are given more importance than the formal rites of the Church. (1991:69)

The preceding statement is useful in understanding some differences between formal and popular Catholicism. Yet, it does not fully capture the deep continuities and breaks between formal and popular Catholicism, how such an amalgam took root, or the ways in which popular Catholicism is relevant to other dimensions of everyday life.

It is useful to think of at least six key attributes of popular Catholicism:

1. *Syncretism.* The Conquest and entrenchment of medieval European Catholicism did not completely replace the pre-European supernatural pantheon. Some deities were lost—especially several of the vague, over-arching creator gods—but many who were especially important for day-to-day physical and cultural well-being survived and have prospered to this day. As a result, anthropologists have often stressed the importance of **religious syncretism**—a "blending" or compartmentalization of supernatural deities drawn from the Catholic, indigenous, and African pantheons. Even present-day seemingly non-European (sometimes incorrectly called "traditional") beliefs and rituals are often a composite of European and indigenous elements. One especially poignant example is on display in an early colonial cathedral in Quito, Ecuador. There hangs a sixteenth-century painting of the Last Supper, but one in which a guinea pig—ritually important in Andean culture to this day—appears on the table in lieu of bread, so symbolically important in European culture (Morales 1995:100). This painting was no doubt conceived by an Ecuadorian Andean deeply influenced by European Catholicism but who nevertheless retained a significant share of his cultural heritage.

2. *Importance of public rituals and ceremonies.* To be religious or a devout Catholic entails private religious expressions, either individually or as participants in family devotions. Yet, a striking characteristic of popular Catholicism is also the active and visible participation in public household and community rituals that punctuate the year. Although these public rituals and ceremonies vary a great deal, they cluster into at least four major categories that:

    a. *Overlap with the Catholic Church liturgical calendar.* Some examples are the well-known liturgical periods of Easter, Christmas, and Lent, as well as specific ritual ceremonies—such as Corpus Christi—that loomed so important during the colonial period and are still meaningful in many contemporary contexts (Beezley et al. 1994a). All entail household or community-wide celebrations (*fiestas,* Spanish) of one kind or another.

    b. *Are sponsored in devotion to or in honor of deities of the Catholic pantheon.* These include rituals and public celebrations on behalf of saints who play a role in the spiritual and material well-being of communities and their members. In rural communities, many rituals and ceremonies honoring specific saints, as well as specific community patron saints, often overlap with crucial periods of the agricultural season, such as planting and harvest. Also in this category are the all-important community and national rituals sponsored on behalf of the Virgin Mary (see the "Facets of Popular Catholicism" section below for further details).

    c. *Are sponsored in devotion to or in honor of non-Catholic deities.* The Latin American and Caribbean ritual landscape abounds with examples of public celebrations and rituals on behalf of indigenous and African deities, many associated with features of the natural landscape. These include, for example, the variety of mountain spirits in the Andes (Bolin 1998), forest deities in the Yucatán Peninsula (Eiss 2002), and the African orishas and lwa that loom so important in the African-derived religious traditions of Brazil, Cuba, and Haiti. Afro–Latin religious traditions are discussed later in this chapter in the "The African Heritage: Candomblé, Santeria, and Vodou" section.

    d. *Hark back to pre-Hispanic and non-Catholic themes.* Many Latin American and Caribbean peoples often engage in rituals centered on themes that have strong preconquest and non-Catholic motifs. Examples include those marking and commemorating the life cycle of individuals and social groups (such as households), as well as the passing of agricultural seasons (Gose 1994).

3. *Symbiotic and reciprocal relationships between humans (mortals) and supernatural deities.* In popular Catholicism, there is the belief that humans need and ought to forge symbiotic and reciprocal relationships with deities inhabiting the supernatural world. This is the outcome of the encounter of two different yet structurally analogous religious traditions. On the one hand, indigenous and African religious traditions were highly pragmatic, instrumental, centered on everyday, mundane needs and practicalities. Their deities were anthropomorphic beings who, although more powerful than humans, also displayed humanlike needs, wants, vices, frailties, and strengths. Mortals could harness and manipulate the good will and powers of supernatural deities by propitiating rituals and offerings on their behalf, by satisfying their wants and needs.

4. *Presence of lay practitioners.* Often responsible for many rituals of popular Catholicism are an array of informal, lay religious practitioners. Some are known as *rezadores* or *rezadoras* (men or women who pray). They are in charge of various kinds of prayer ceremonies. One kind of ceremony, witnessed by this author in New York City as well as in Puerto Rico, is known as the *rosario* (rosary), marking and commemorating an anniversary of the passing of a deceased loved one. Another kind of lay practioner is the *espiritista* (spiritualist), who performs a vital role as a medium through which individuals can almost literally talk with their deceased kin (Pérez y Mena 1991; Fernández Olmos and Paravisini-Gebert 2003).

5. *Blurring of boundaries between living and dead.* A fifth attribute of popular Catholicism is that the boundary between "this" and "that" world, between the living and the dead, mortals and supernatural entities, is anything but clear-cut. This is, of course, partially a logical outcome of the sorts of relationships that mortals and supernatural beings strive to forge with each other. There are ritually delimited times and spaces in which the dead are very much alive or, to phrase it in a slightly different way, periods of the year in which the dead and the living are once again able to renew their relationships and share the same cultural and ritual space. An especially vivid example of the coexistence of, and the blurring of the boundary between, the living and the dead is *Todos Santos,* or All Saints and Soul's Day, discussed later in this chapter.

6. *A critique of the social order.* Popular Catholicism is very much tied to politics and critiques of the social order. Catholicism and the Catholic Church were important to the success (and ideological rationale) of the Conquest, and both historically have been allied to elites and the domination of the wealthy and powerful over the poor and not powerful: religion has often been a weapon of ideological domination. Yet, for nonelite groups, the structural features of popular Catholicism have often enabled it to work as a vehicle for the expression of social discontent. For example, Chapter 4 noted that leaders of Andean and Maya rebellions often invoked the assistance Catholic deities to their cause; other examples appear throughout this chapter. In fact, some anthropologists believe this to be *the* most important characteristic of Latin American popular religion:

> By popular religion, we mean religious or ritual activities consciously practiced outside or in opposition to dominant institutionalized religion or those religious activities which, although carried on within the framework of institutionalized religion, offer a critique of that framework and of larger political and economic inequities. (Stephen and Dow 1990:8; see also Lancaster 1988 for a Nicaraguan case study)

Related to the issue of popular Catholicism as a venue for social critique has been the emergence, since the 1960s, of a broad movement from within the Catholic Church known as **liberation theology.** This movement seeks a closer rapport or encounter between teachings of the Bible—especially the messages of social justice and equality—and the lived experience and reality of Latin American and Carribean peoples. Not only are the teachings of the Bible carried in a way that focuses on inequality and oppression, but liberation theology also encourages activist organizing at the local level in what are known as Christian base communities (Dodson 1979; Klaiber 1989; Levine 1992, 1993; Canin 1997; Norget 1997).

Liberation theology and Christian base communities proved crucial in the emergence of popular revolts and guerilla organizations in Central America during the 1970s and 1980s (see Chapter 12 for more detailed information).

Facets of Popular Catholicism

This section turns to three prominent examples of popular Catholicism: the central role of the Virgin Mary in Haiti and Bolivia; the prominent presence of the Devil in parts of Latin America; and the celebration of All Saints and All Souls Day (Todos Santos) in Mexico and Bolivia.

The Virgin Mary.   The Catholic and broadly Christian notion of saints—supernatural beings occupying an intermediate position and role between a supreme deity (God) and mortals—made a great deal of sense to indigenous New World and African peoples whose members also worshipped deities directly responsible for the well-being of household, community, and kin. In her study of the cult to the Virgin of Copacabana, the religious patroness of Bolivia, Salles-Reese states that

> toward the middle of the thirteenth century, the cult of the Virgin Mary grew significantly throughout Europe. Until then, only the worship of a distant, justice-seeking, fear inspiring God was prevalent. Because she represented a gentler and non threatening figure, many of the faithful were inclined to worship the Virgin; by the thirteenth century, Mary had became an integral part of Christian worship. (1997:158)

This European medieval concept of a powerful yet gentle and compassionate feminine deity was firmly entrenched by the sixteenth century in the religious ideology and worldview of Spanish and Portuguese conquerors. This belief also resonated with indigenous and, later, African peoples, for whom the supernatural pantheon was also populated by powerful feminine beings associated, above all, with fertility and prosperity. Such was the case, for example, of the Andean Pachamama (Earth Mother), who is still revered; the Aztec goddess Tonantzin; and Ezili, the West and Central African goddess of love, sensuality, and prosperity, who still looms important for many in Brazil and parts of the Caribbean that received large numbers of African slaves.

The cult to the Virgin Mary is widespread in much of Latin America and the Caribbean (Lafaye 1974; Taylor, W. 1987; Crandon-Malamud 1993; Platt 1993; Eiss 2002). Extraordinarily significant is the Virgin of Guadeloupe (*La Guadalupana,* as she is commonly and affectionately referred to), the patron saint of Mexico and a powerful icon of Mexican national identity. Significantly, she is said to have appeared in 1531 not to an elite Mexican but to the dark-skinned Indian Juan Diego. To this day, she is revered in Mexico, especially by women, and plays a key role in the everyday struggle of Mexicans for a better life (Brading 2001). Relying on Nahuatl language sources, Burkhart (2001a) has documented the rise of the cult to the Virgin Mary during Mexico's early colonial period.

In popular Catholicism, saints are actual personages, almost, as in the case of the mythical Greek gods, divine humans with real needs, desires, and temperaments. In contrast with Catholic or Christian doctrine, which places them in a somewhat secondary position vis-à-vis Jesus Christ and God, saints play a much more powerful, immediate, and decisive role in everyday life. Ever since the Conquest, the Virgin Mary was placed alongside saints in this category of powerful, intimate beings who decisively intercede on behalf of their mortal worshippers. Her decisive role has often had little to do with some of the qualities ascribed to her by formal Church doctrine. For example, the notion that Mary was a virgin probably mattered little—as it does today—and almost certainly was incomprehensible to most indigenous and African peoples for whom virginity contrasted with radically different gender and sexual ideologies (see Chapter 6).

Haiti.   Although from a religious standpoint Haiti is often associated with the constellation of African-derived beliefs and rituals called *vodou* (or *vodoun*)—discussed later in this chapter—in fact most Haitians are nominally Roman Catholic, a direct result of French colonialism. As such, the Virgin Mary also looms important in this nation comprised overwhelmingly of descendants of African slaves.

Rey (1999) notes that the widespread belief in vodou spirits (*lwa*) in Haiti (see also "The African Heritage: Candomblé, Santería, and Vodou" section) is paralleled by an equally striking devotion to the Virgin Mary, viewed by most Haitians as one of many spirits that inhabit the vodou pantheon. Mary is especially identified with but does not replace Elizi, the most important feminine/female vodou spirit. Elizi embodies, promotes, and demands—like most mortals would—sensuality, sexuality, wealth, prosperity, and the like. The Virgin Mary also fulfills some of the most important obligations the spirits have toward those who are faithful—to help them out in the daily struggle for survival:

> Historical and contemporary anthropological research reveals that Mary has been adopted and welcomed by Haitians as an important spiritual force, operating side-by-side with Ezili—each functioning in a complex mosaic among the many lwa and saints who may be invoked in the daily struggle to survive and the quest for health and the fullness of life. (Rey 1999:231–232)

One of Rey's major points is that devotion to the Virgin Mary is particularly pronounced among Haiti's poor and destitute, that is, most of Haiti's population; and that her role is virtually identical to and parallels the lwa actively engaged in the everyday, mundane lives of their devotees. Therefore, the belief in and devotion to the Virgin Mary is not only strongly linked to the struggle to survive but also to politics. For many poor Haitians, the Virgin Mary is often—as Rey appropriately subtitles his book—their "Lady of Class Struggle." This strategic positioning of the Virgin Mary onto the center stage of the everyday struggle to survive—and the critique of the social order that it potentially represents—is a key attribute of popular Catholicism.

The Virgin Mary was probably early on identified by Haitian slaves with important African feminine deities. In French colonial sources "there is no direct reference to the identification of Mary with any African spirit among the slaves, though it is reasonable to suspect that indeed they must initially have perceived the Virgin to be some peculiar manifestation of the goddesses of the homeland" (Rey 1999:217). For most contemporary Haitians, especially those (the majority) at the bottom of the social hierarchy, "Mary . . . [is] . . . a leading member of the spirit world, which consists of both African gods and Catholic saints" (1999:219).

Because vodou "spirits . . . usually reflect the lifestyles, sufferings, joys, and aspirations of the people who serve them" (Rey 1999:203) and the Virgin Mary has been placed alongside them for some time, it is possible to understand why she is so central to everyday, mundane issues of inequality, poverty, and politics. The following case study of Guertha illustrates this point quite well.

The life history of Guertha, particularly relevant to this discussion of popular Catholicism, spans between the fall of the long-standing dictatorship of François ("Papa Doc") Duvalier in 1971—one of the most lasting and repressive regimes in Latin American and Caribbean history—the presidency of his son Jean-Claude (1971–1986), the 1991 coup that ousted the popularly elected president Jean-Bertrand Aristide, and the 1992 intervention by United States Marines to reinstall Aristide to power. (Aristide was again forced into exile in 2004.) Guertha's recollections provide a glaring example of how popular Catholicism and the Virgin Mary are intertwined with personal tragedies in the midst of political turmoil and repression.

At the time of Rey's fieldwork, Guertha was a poor, thirty-four-year-old street vendor who, like most Haitian peasants, was devoted to the belief and practice of vodou. After paramilitary thugs (*attachés*) raped her, abducted and killed her husband (who was an Aristide supporter), and burned down their home, she fled with her three children to Port-au-Prince, Haiti's capital. There, she found housing with a cousin and entered into what Rey calls "conjugal contracts" with males in order to survive. After a while, she mustered enough cash to set up a small-scale street business peddling plasticware on the streets. Six months later, attachés abducted her cousin (also a pro-Aristide supporter) and ransacked their home. Guertha lost her savings and much of her merchandise in this attack. Further, the more generous of her two lovers, by whom Guertha was now pregnant, was also arrested. Guertha was destitute, homeless, pregnant, and taking care of three children.

If Haitian poor have historically looked upon the lwa in times of dire need, Guertha had a great deal of difficulty sustaining her belief in vodou in the face of tremendous personal calamities:

> The "language" of Vodou, which might have provided her with some empowerment in the face of less formidable, more familiar adversity, was now unintelligible. Guertha's darkening situation was entirely out of her control. While ever-respectful of the lwa, her distrust of the few Vodou priests and priestesses whom she had met in Port-au-Prince, along with the utter gravity of her quandary, resulted in feelings of spiritual angst and powerlessness that she had never known before. Guertha suddenly felt abandoned by the lwa. (Rey 1999:254)

Prior to these events, Guertha, like most Haitians, paid devotion to the Virgin Mary as well as to the lwa. Yet, after the tragic circumstances described previously, "The Virgin would come to eclipse Ezili in Guertha's religious life" (Rey 1999:255). She came to believe that it was really the Virgin and not the lwa who saved her and her children's lives when they arrived in Port-au-Prince. After her husband was abducted and murdered, she went every morning to Church and prayed to the Virgin, calling her *mami cherie* (dearest mother/mommie).

Not unexpectedly, her prayers also had a strong political content: "I pray to you to bring the American soldiers to Haiti to oust the forces of darkness who are crushing the people. Make the Americans come and return Titi [Aristide] to power so that we can live again" (1999:257). Her prayers were answered shortly thereafter, when United States Marines occupied Haiti to put an end to the political chaos and growing anarchy, and to back Aristide's return to power. One can only imagine what Guertha might have thought in 2004 when Aristide was ousted from office and forced into exile, with the tacit consent of the U.S. government.

Bolivia.   The active, vital presence of the Virgin Mary in Bolivia and most of the Andean region certainly goes back to the early colonial period (Salles-Reese 1997; Cahill 2002). The historical record abounds with apparitions of the Virgin Mary—by the early colonial period "the Virgin was (and still is) identified with *pachamama,* the earth mother" (Platt 1993:173)—while ethnographic research highlights her central role in everyday life. Historical accounts suggest, as in Haiti, how apparitions of the Virgin Mary have been intertwined with everyday needs and life contingencies. The following example is based on the author's fieldwork in Pampa (a pseudonym), a predominantly Quechua-speaking peasant community in the Cochabamba region of Bolivia. Until the Bolivian revolution of 1952, Pampa was a medium-sized hacienda worked by tenants.

The 1876 rainy season arrived late in Cochabamba and by early 1877, precipitation had all but ceased, marking the beginning of one of the most intense, prolonged, and devastating droughts in Bolivian history. Soon thereafter, harvests dwindled, food shortages became pervasive, and hunger widespread. Starvation, which quickly followed, was worsened by a wave of deadly epidemics. Massive mortality, mass migration, and other social dislocations in urban areas and rural communities appear to have been everyday events. Only three years later did rainfall reach normal levels in Cochabamba, and several more years passed before the full effects of disease began to wane.

The 1877–1880 crisis, while probably not unprecedented in Bolivian (or Andean) history, was nevertheless one of the worst to afflict this region since mid-to-late colonial times. It is, therefore, probably no historical coincidence that the Virgin Mary appeared in Pampa in 1879, precisely at a time in which—according to local accounts—so many community members were dying so quickly that they were buried in mass, makeshift graves. It was also during this time that Bolivia, allied with Peru, was engaged in the War of the Pacific against Chile.

According to local lore, Santos Rojas was on his way to tend his fields when, crossing a river, he stumbled. As he pulled himself up, he noticed an image of the Virgin Mary inscribed on a nearby large rock. When he approached and began to lift the rock, a glowing light emanated from within it. Santos immediately kneeled and made the sign of the cross. Seconds later, a soft, serene, and feminine voice from within the rock told him to take it home, for this would be a sign that her son Jesus would bless the humble of Pampa. Santos dashed to his household compound and alerted others to this miraculous apparition. Accompanied by family members, Santos returned to where he had stumbled and pointed out the rock with the engraved image. They placed it in a mantle (*aguayo*) and then proceeded back home, where they set up a makeshift altar. Word quickly spread that the Virgin Mary—affectionately referred to as *"la Virgencita"* (the little Virgin)—had appeared in Pampa, and during the next several days, streams of excited Pampeños visited the makeshift altar.

The commotion did not go unnoticed by Pampa's administrator, for many Pampeños, excited and awed by the appearance of the Virgin, had begun neglecting their chores on hacienda lands. Led by Santos, Pampeños requested permission to hold a celebration (fiesta) on the Virgin's behalf. Further, given the formidable expenses that they would have to incur, and the ongoing drought, they also requested that the administrator not only temporarily suspend the tribute payments customarily demanded of them, but that the hacienda also shoulder some of the costs for the fiesta. Yet, in a breach of the moral contract and reciprocal relationships that tied tenants and landowners (see Langer 1985 for a case study in southern Bolivia), the administrator refused their requests.

Several days later, the administrator was struck by a mysterious illness that blinded him. He quickly became convinced, as were Pampeños, that he was being punished by the Virgin for having stood in the way of her fiesta and for having neglected (by refusing to cease collecting tribute) the welfare of his tenants. A day or so later he convened an assembly of all tenant household heads and announced that he would in fact allow the fiesta to take place, provide potatoes and other goods to defray its costs, and also temporarily suspend the collection of tribute. Although it is unclear whether he eventually recovered his eyesight (some say he did, while others disagree), the first fiesta in honor of the Virgin of Pampa was celebrated shortly thereafter. Not only is the Virgin Mary still revered in Pampa, but this 1879 apparition sparked a regional celebration and ritual processions that each October draws thousands of participants from surrounding rural communities and urban centers.

That the Virgin Mary loomed as an important symbolic icon of resistance in this Bolivian community is not without many historic parallels elsewhere. One interesting example is the 1712 revolt of Tzetlal Mayas in Chiapas. There, the Virgin Mary is said to have appeared to a young Tzetlal girl, María López, who subsequently became an important rebel leader. One letter that circulated in the region encouraging neighboring communities to also revolt was signed by "The Most Holy Virgin Mary of the Cross" (Burkhart and Gasco 1996a:170–172). And Bolivian elites have attempted to instill acquiescence by reshaping the meanings of popular religious celebrations centered on devotion to the Virgin Mary (Crandon-Malamud 1993).

Working with the Devil. In popular Catholicism, one important supernatural deity often harnessed on behalf of human needs and aspirations is (and has been) the Devil. Although this belief in the ability of humans to forge meaningful and instrumental relationships with the Devil goes back to the colonial period and does in fact have some pre-Hispanic antecedents (see Chapter 4), this belief system is currently widespread. Whether in the Colombian lowlands (Taussig 1980), eastern Peru (Dobkin de Ríos 1972), Central America (Edelman 1994), Bolivian mining districts (Nash 1979), or highland Ecuador (Crain 1991; Miles 1994), narratives about the ever-looming presence of and pacts with the Devil abound. And despite historical and cultural differences in the content and meanings of these narratives and pacts, ethnographic and historical research seems to concur that these are fundamentally social commentaries about and attempts to grapple with—redress even—profound ethnic, social, economic, and gender inequities. As Edelman nicely summarizes:

> In rural Latin America devil-pact stories constitute a significant, nearly ubiquitous matrix through which to view relations of power and exploitation and

through which to express a variety of socially conditioned anxieties . . . The "cultural form" of the devil allegory needs to be conceptually broadened to include prerogatives exercised by dominant groups that are not related only to economic exploitation, such as the coercion of sexual favors. For subaltern groups . . . the devil is a marvelous metaphor for the conjunction of class and sexual oppression. (1994:60)

One powerful thread in Devil narratives, as Edelman points out, has to do with gender, sexual oppression and morally appropriate behavior. This is a point nicely illustrated by a Devil narrative gathered by Miles (1994:148–149) from Cuenca, Ecuador (see In Their Own Words 7.1).

IN THEIR OWN WORDS 7.1
Working with the Devil

"Once upon a time there were two sisters. The sisters lived unhappily because they did not share things between them. One sister married a man who soon after the wedding took up drinking . . . One night as he approached the house very late and drunk, the one sister told the other and said, 'I'm not going to marry a drunk and lazy man. I'm going to marry a rich one with gold teeth and expensive clothes.'

"Later the next day, as the greedy sister was at the river washing clothes, a dove passed over head . . . As she lifted her head . . . she saw a man standing before her. The man was very well dressed in white suit with a brilliant gold tooth and tremendous cowboys boots. . . . [S]he asked him, 'Are you my boyfriend/groom? [*novio*]' 'Yes,' he replied. 'Then we must go and meet my parents,' she said. So they did.

'Look,' she said to her parents, 'here is my boyfriend/groom. He's very handsome, a millionaire, and look, he has [a] gold tooth.' Her father only said, 'Well, daughter, marry him if you want to.'

"The day of the wedding came. They were married in a church and held a big party and dance afterward. Around midnight, everyone . . . fell asleep from so much food, trago [cane alcohol], and dancing. Later, one man awoke and saw the groom at the head of the table turn into a rat, run around the sleeping people on the floor, and flee out the back door. The man woke everyone and told them that the bride must have married the devil himself. By now it was dawn. The bride ran to the Church and begged the priest to help her. 'I can do nothing for you daughter,' he told her, 'you are already married.'

"As the woman fled the church, she was stopped by an old witch sitting outside the church. 'Get a dozen bars of soap, a dozen needles, a dozen skeins of fine thread, and a dozen rags,' said the old witch. 'Take these up into the mountains . . . Just behind her came the devil and his mother atop a burro made of gold. The bride started up the mountain, and as she passed across a stream, she threw the soap, needles, thread, and rags behind her. The devil and his parents were just crossing the stream, and as they reached out to grab her, they slipped on the soap, were stuck by the needles, their arms were bound by the thread, and the cloth rags covered their eyes. The woman looked behind her and as she turned to remount her burro, it turned into a horse. She fled back down the mountain and went straight to the church. She became a nun and never was a greedy and envious person again" (Miles 1994:147–148).

Todos Santos: The Days of the Dead.   One of the most colorful, distinctive, and cere-
monially important manifestations of popular Catholicism is the November 1 and 2 celebration of All Souls and All Saints Day. A widespread private and public ritual with deep
European medieval as well pre-Conquest roots, this ritual celebration is also called Día(s)
de los Muertos (Day[s] of the Dead), Día(s) de las Ánimas (Day[s] of the Souls), Día(s) de
los Difuntos (Day[s] of the Deceased) or, more commonly, **Todos Santos** (All Saints
[Day]). Todos Santos roughly coincides with—but is culturally *far* more significant than—
the celebration of Halloween in North America, which can be traced to ancient Celtic European spring festivals (Santino 1983). In Europe

> by the second half of the fifteenth century All Saints Day and All Souls Day
> were liturgical feasts celebrated as a unit and ranked among the three or four
> most important occasions in the yearly ritual cycle of Western Christendom . . .
> By the beginning of the sixteenth century . . . the combined celebration of All
> Saints and All Souls Day in Spain was commonly referred to as Todos Santos.
> (Nutini 1988:42–45)

Although Todos Santos is widely acknowledged in much of contemporary Spanish-
speaking Latin America and the Caribbean, the specific beliefs and practices of this celebration vary a great deal, even within specific countries. For example, in many parts of the
Caribbean and the southern cone countries (i.e., Argentina, Uruguay and, to a lesser extent,
Chile), few probably believe that the spirit or soul (*alma* or *ánima* in Spanish) of the
deceased actually return to partake of the same physical and ritual space as the living. Further, in these countries, this celebration is often limited to remembering the recently
departed through prayers and the lighting of candles at home, as well as a visit to the cemetery, where graves are washed.

By contrast, in much of Mexico, Mesoamerica, the Andes and, to a lesser extent,
Central America, it is widely believed that beginning on the afternoon or evening of October 31 and running through November 1, the souls or spirits of the recently departed *do*
return "home." They do so to share space and time with family members, who undertake
elaborate preparations to greet and honor them during their brief stay, until their departure
on November 2. It is precisely in these regions that the most elaborate ceremonies and paraphernalia surrounding Todos Santos are observed, creating a spectacle vividly captured in
the film *La Ofrenda*. The following account of Todos Santos centers on the Central Valley
region of Mexico (Nutini 1988; Brandes 1997) as well as in Pampa (Bolivia), this author's
ethnographic field site. As currently practiced in central Mexico, Todos Santos had become
deeply and widely entrenched by the beginning of the seventeenth century (Nutini
1988:110).

Todos Santos is about remembering and honoring the recently deceased, establishing
a ritual connection with the afterlife, narrowing the gap between life and death, and juxtaposing the living and the dead. It is above all a period of **liminality** (a solemn time when
ordinary, everyday expectations and behaviors are temporarily suspended and others undertaken), a time for reflecting on the meanings of life and death. Icons and images of death,
particularly the use of skull (*calavera,* Spanish) imagery, are prominently displayed in both

PHOTO 7.1   *Mexican paper maché figurines depicting female cadavers.*

rural and urban Mexican contexts (see Photo 7.1). In comparison, the Todos Santos celebrations in Pampa and other Andean communities display little if no skull imagery.

Although preparations for Todos Santos may begin one week earlier, these are certainly underway in earnest by the morning of October 31. Todos Santos is generally a two-day, two-pronged private (i.e., household) and public ritual; the first centers on preparing for the arrival and greeting of the deceased souls on October 31 and November 1, and the second on preparing for their departure from this world on November 2. Countless variations of this ritual of course exist: in the Yucatán peninsula, for example, many villagers believe that the souls of the deceased stay around for the entire month of November, and the final farewell takes place on November 30 (anonymous reviewer).

Preparations for the arrival of the souls and their incorporation into the social and cultural sphere of family and kin involve prayers, chants, and libations centered around the family or household altar. Although household altars are commonplace and not erected solely for the purpose of celebrating Todos Santos (see, for example, Figure 24 in Annis 1987:92), it is during this celebration that the altar serves as the quintessential medium through which the initial greeting of the souls takes place. What is displayed and offered to the souls at the altar and how it is arranged determine if the souls will feel welcome. Therefore, a great deal of time, care, pride, and joy go into the meticulous preparation of highly

PHOTO 7.2   *Todos Santos altar in rural Cochabamba, Bolivia.*

ornate and decorated altars. In Pampa, facing and surrounding the altars are arcs made of tree branches, often adorned with leaves, flowers, or other ornaments, symbolically representing the gateways through which the ánimas enter and leave the mortal world (see Photo 7.2). Altars are also displayed at gravesites.

The altar typically consists of a table in the living room or main greeting space. Candles, pictures, or other memorabilia of the deceased are placed on the table. Icons and other representations of Jesus Christ, the Virgin Mary, and the saints are often prominent. Yet, what truly converts the table into an altar suited for the greeting of the *ánimas* is the array of ceremonial foods and drinks that they will share with their kin. A properly assembled altar includes the array of foods and drinks that the deceased enjoyed in this world and that the ánimas too will delight in during their short visit. The ánimas themselves are believed to arrive (and start hovering around the altar) in the afternoon or evening of October 31, and they unquestionably arrive by midnight or the early morning hours of November 1.

Any slight noise, piercing sound of wind, or startling movement of tree branches or the ornaments that make up the arc surrounding the altar is believed to be clear indication of the active presence of the ánimas. The fading of food and drink placed on the altar is another way of confirming their arrival and presence. For example, if by the morning of November 1, food appears to have been chewed away, or there is less fermented corn beer in the gourds, then evidently the ánimas have enjoyed their food and drink and not, as non-believers might think, that the food was picked away by mice, or that less chicha is the result of evaporation.

Major ritual activities on November 1 also include a trip to the cemetery, where tombs are washed and decorated, candles lit, and ceremonial foods placed. The ánimas' favorite dishes—and hence the kinds of ceremonial foods that appear on the altars—vary, of course, according to region, ecological context, and/or historical period. For example, in contemporary Mexico, ceremonial foods include different assortments of tortillas, tamales, or moles dishes, while in Pampa and much of the Andean region, potato-based dishes loom especially important, as do other ritually significant offerings, such as guinea pigs (Morales 1995). In Mexico, favorite and ceremonial drinks include *pulque* (the alcoholic beverage made out of the agave cactus plant) and *atole* (a maize-based beverage), while in the Andes, fermented maize beer (*chicha* in Spanish; *aqa/aha* in Quechua) invariably makes its way onto the altar. In both regions, distilled alcohol (*aguardiente* in Mexico, *trago* in the Andes) are also offered. Unlike food offerings that appear in African-derived religious traditions in both Mexico and the Andes, the foods displayed at the altar are not eaten by those who have prepared them but are instead reserved for the visiting souls.

The ecological context also structures the scope of available foods. For example, crops harvested just prior to this period will invariably appear as ceremonial offerings. Likewise, in the altiplano, or in high mountainous communities such as Pampa, dishes based on freeze-dried potatoes (*ch'uño,* Quechua) consistently make their way to the altar, while these types of dishes are far less common in Quechua-speaking communities in the lower, sub-tropical or tropical climate of the eastern Andes. The sorts of ecological niches that different groups have access to will, of course, vary across time, and therefore also play a role in the kinds of dishes that ánimas enjoyed in this world and that they long for during their visit. In the 1950s, for example, Pampeños began migrating to the eastern Bolivian lowlands, where they began cultivating a variety of tropical and sub-tropical crops, such as rice, pineapples, and coca. These are foods that would not have appeared on an altar prior to the 1950s, but that surface today.

Similarly, the political-economic and historical context may explain the pervasiveness of sweet foods—candies, sweets, and the like—in the central Mexican Todos Santos celebration. Mintz (1985b) has argued that culturally entrenched patterns of taste and desire—he was focusing on sugar and sweets—can only be understood by situating them in the political, economic, and historical contexts within which these patterns emerged. Following Mintz's historical and political-economic perspective, both Brandes (1997) and Chollet (1998) have suggested that the pervasiveness of sweet foods during Todos Santos in some Mexican regions has a great deal to do with the nearby emergence of colonial sugarcane plantations and the incorporation of peasants into the plantation economy.

Baked, elaborately carved anthropomorphic figures made from flour are a ubiquitous presence on altars, and one of the most important ceremonial offerings to the ánimas. In central Mexico, this type of offering is called *pan de muertos* (Spanish for "bread of the dead"; the original Nahuatl term, *tamamixtli,* is rarely used). In Pampa as well as in most of the Quechua-and Aymara-speaking Andean world, these anthropomorphically shaped breads—which only surface during Todos Santos—look like (and are supposed to represent) babies, and are therefore called *t'anta wawas* (bread babies, Quechua). Other bread-based offerings, such as oval or round baked doughs called *rosquillas* in central Mexico and *rosquetas* in Pampa, also appear, but the t'anta wawas are symbolically far more significant.

Many ritual elements of the celebration of Todos Santos have their origins in the challenges faced by Mesoamerican and Andean peoples after the Conquest. For example, it

PHOTO 7.3   *Schoolchildren celebrating Todos Santos at the Escuelita Arcoiris, Pittsburgh, Pennsylvania.*

may be, as Brandes (1997) has hypothesized, that the ritual importance of bread—a European staple symbolically associated with life—can be traced to the early colonial period, particularly during periods of mass death and starvation that came at the heels of the Conquest. There is also unambiguous evidence of a cult of the dead (and ritualized food offerings) in both Mesoamerica and the Andes prior to the European Conquest (Gossen 1996; Salomon 1995).

The ánimas depart on November 2. Major ritual activities of this day center on preparing for their farewell—what is known in Mexico as *la despedida* (Spanish) and in Pampa as *k'acharpaya* (Quechua). These may include another visit to the cemetery and the washing of the gravesites, usually accompanied by a great deal of ritual intoxication. A large meal attended by kin and household members is always part of the November 2 festivities. In Andean rural communities such as Pampa, an important ritual step entails moving the arc that previously surrounded the altar indoors and placing it on open ground that faces the cemetery: it is through this portal that the ánimas will embark on their trip back to the afterlife. Todos Santos is also often celebrated in the United States (see Photo 7.3).

The Spread of Protestantism

Most Latin Americans probably identify themselves, in one way or another, as Catholic, practicing popular Catholicism. Nevertheless, Protestantism is rapidly spreading throughout Latin America and the Caribbean. Although it is difficult to estimate how many have converted during the past thirty years, most scholars agree that this religious conversion is widespread and expanding quickly. By the late 1980s, more than 10 percent of Latin America's population identified itself as *evangélico* (evangelical) or *creyente* (believer) (Stoll 1993:2). Protestantism is especially striking in Guatemala, which has had two Protestant presidents since 1982, and where more than 30 percent of the population had converted to Protestantism by the early 1990s (Green 1993:161). Twenty-five to 30 percent of all Chileans and Brazilians have turned their backs on Catholicism (Coleman et al. 1993:111). In Chiapas, Mexico, more than half of members of some indigenous municipalities are Protestant (Gros 1999:179).

When villagers in San Antonio Aguas Calientes, a bilingual Cakchiquel-Maya municipality in Guatemala, were asked by Annis (1987:80) what it meant to be Protestant, they emphasized the following major differences between Protestantism and Catholicism:

> Protestants do not drink, smoke, dance or gamble.
> Protestants do not venerate saints, and they flatly reject as idolatry all artifactual representations of saintly or demonic personages.
> They do not participate in any *cofradía*-related ritual.
> They reject *compadrazgo,* ritual godparenthood.
> They reject communal celebration of saints' days (fiestas), which involve the parading of religious images through the streets or the re-enactment of holy drama.

Maya Women in Mexico

Conversion to Protestantism is often a deeply gendered process, frequently spearheaded by women reacting against a domestic and broader social context often plagued by heavy alcohol drinking, especially by their spouses.

Many ritual celebrations are repeatedly marked by what may appear to outsiders to be an excessive drinking of alcohol, or what has been called **ritual intoxication**. Anthropological writings on ritual drinking or intoxication have long emphasized that what appears to be excessive drinking bordering on alcoholism is often culturally condoned ritual behavior; that it has a long history in Latin America, often preceding the Spanish Conquest (there is evidence of ritual intoxication prior to the Spanish Conquest, and countless examples during the colonial period); and that interpreting such drinking patterns as equivalent to problem drinking borders on ethnocentrism.

Allen, who addresses Andean drinking patterns in the context of coca chewing, says that

> it is difficult, if not impossible to live in an Andean community without drinking. As with coca, a willingness to drink and to share alcohol indicates a sociable attitude, and as with coca, it is important to drink according to prescribed ceremonial rules. Good drinking manners resemble coca chewing etiquette: both involve prescribed phases of invitation and thanks; both require an offering to the earth and the sacred places; and both begin in an unhurried, respectful atmosphere . . . in drinking as well as in coca chewing, the act of sharing takes on central importance. (1988:141)

Most anthropological research on ritualized drinking is guided by the idea that intoxication is not necessarily the same as alcoholism, and that it is not a social problem. This idea resonates with what Douglas (1987:3–8) called **constructive drinking:**

> From the wider comparative standpoint of anthropology, "problem drinking" is very rare and alcoholism seems to be virtually absent even in many societies where drunkenness is frequent, highly esteemed and actively sought . . . the general tenor of the anthropological perspective is that celebration is normal and that in most cultures alcohol is a normal adjunct to celebration . . . drinks also act as markers of personal identity and as boundaries of inclusion and exclusion.

There is nevertheless the possibility that many anthropologists have romanticized ritual intoxication and that, in their attempts to counter cross-cultural ethnocentrism, they may have neglected cases where excessive drinking may be dysfunctional. Allen herself points to the possibility of dysfunctional drinking:

> As long as opportunities to drink are limited, the situation contains its own check; when the booze runs out everything returns to normal. But as the availability of trago increases with improved transportation and access to cash, opportunistic drinking easily turns into chronic drinking. Alcoholism is not now a serious problem in Sonqo but the potential is there . . . often . . . hostilities, submerged under layers of praise and endearment, break out while runakuna are drunk. While this is hardly surprising, it is noteworthy that drinking provides one of the few contexts in which displays of grief and anger are even tolerable. (1998:148)

It is precisely the idea that the vast literature on ritualized intoxication in Mesoamerica has downplayed the dysfunctional aspects of alcohol drinking that guided Eber's (2000) fieldwork on the role and consequences of alcohol consumption in Pedrano, a southeastern Mexican Maya community. In Pedrano, where fully one-third of the population is now Protestant, conversion is tightly wedded to a broad gendered movement spearheaded by women against the consumption of alcoholic beverages. By focusing on the interplay of excessive drinking, domestic conflicts, and gender, Eber situates drinking within the contemporary context of poverty, marginalization, gender relations, and ethnic conflict:

> Compulsive drinking and its consequences are social problems everywhere . . . researchers have only begun to consider alcohol's effects on women and their families . . . The major questions that guided my research of women's experiences with ritual and problem drinking . . . were: how is women's relationship to alcohol changing . . . and how are Pedranos handling their own and others' drinking problems? . . . A central task of my research was to understand ideas of power and social relations in Pedrano society. . . . While women do not hold political offices, they obtain power through the highly charged relationships

they can forge with their deities or ancestors during communal rituals . . . In these rituals they interweave social and cosmic realms and control powerful symbolic substances, such as alcohol. (2000:10)

Ritualized drinking, Eber states, is important in Pedrano, enabling community members to communicate with supernatural deities and underpinning religious traditions and community identity. Yet, dysfunctional drinking is also widespread, which Eber attributes to a de-coupling of drinking from ritual, especially among young people for whom local traditions and values no longer hold sway:

> While I felt obligated to understand the sacred foundation Pedrano elders have laid, I also saw much casual drinking and disregard for traditions among young men and some women. Pedranos' rituals of renewal demand obedience to strict rules and a commitment to the group. Elders have been able to make their rituals with alcohol work for them because they have integrated these rituals into a whole that sustains their people and that they in turn sustain through ritual obligations . . . Pedrano elders still work tirelessly to sustain their vision of wholeness, but for centuries ritual support alone [has] not been enough to keep problem drinking at bay. Deepening economic inequalities involving alcohol as a medium of exploitation, and the rapid pace of social change in the highlands, put more and more men and women of all ages and traditions at risk for dependency on alcohol. (2000:244)

Problem drinking—especially male dysfunctional drinking—leads to many consequences that particularly affect women, in turn providing some of the practical rationales for religious conversion. For women, the breaching of gender expectations (e.g., that husbands should provide for their wives and children) and rising domestic violence are two of the most important consequences of problem drinking. "Women," Eber states, "openly describe ways men abuse them or their children as a result of drinking: scolding or criticizing them, being excessively jealous, accusing them of adultery, taking up with other women, hitting them and their children, not working enough in the milpa, and not providing them with corn, beans, and some cash" (2000:135; for parallel accounts of violence against women in the context of drinking and fiestas elsewhere, see Harvey 1994; Pérez 2000).

Pedrano women attempt to deal with problem drinking through culturally sanctioned ways. Praying and ritual offering to saints and local deities is one way through which women attempt to grapple with the plight of spousal drinking:

> To stop her own drinking problem Angélika [a Pedrano community member with whom Eber had established close rapport] sought direction from powerful invisible beings in dreams and prayer. Although Angélika serves rum in the fiestas in which she officiates, respecting its sacred power all the while, in her dreams the mother of the sky and God tell her that when she and her people drink too much, rum rises to the sky and makes the heavens reek. They have told Angélika clearly that if she and her people cannot drink rum respectfully, then it is better for them to give it up. (Eber 2000:142)

Some women also turn to shamans, who have the ability to ascertain whether the drinking problem is a result of witchcraft, and who can harness the good will of supernatural deities on their behalf.

For these Maya women, converting to Protestantism, and convincing their spouses to do so as well, is the most successful strategy to deal with problem drinking—excessive drinking that takes place outside ritually defined contexts—and the ensuing and seemingly rampant domestic violence. Protestants' "zero tolerance" of alcohol drinking, which may be more entrenched in some parts of Latin America and the Caribbean than in the United States, resonates with these Maya women and their quest for more balanced and equitable gender relations. Thus, the swift spread of Protestantism is not only a shift in religious ideology but also an important change in cultural values and social relations. Conversion to Protestantism entails a fundamentally different way of thinking about the relationship between personal salvation, poverty, and everyday life:

> In addition to promoting personal salvation, Protestants set themselves apart by stressing private capital accumulation. Protestants say their new prosperity is due to improved living conditions made possible by saving their money, rather than spending it on rum, candles, and chickens for healing ceremonies, or on lavish outlays of liquor, food, and other ingredients at traditional fiestas. (Eber 2000:217)

Andean Villagers in Highland Ecuador

The reasons expressed by Maya women for snubbing alcohol, turning their backs on Catholicism, and embracing Protestantism are echoed by many Aymara- and Quechua-speaking women and men in the Andes. In Ecuador, Protestants probably make up more than 15 percent of the population. As among the Maya, the trend against alcohol consumption in highland Ecuador is also related to how much of the household's budget gets siphoned away by problem drinking as well as the considerable expenses that sponsoring fiestas and other rituals (such as weddings and baptisms) entail (Muratorio 1981).

Two messages, also mentioned by Eber in her work about Maya women, resonate in Ecuadorian communities, especially with women. The first is that costly ritual celebrations are unnecessary, for believers can and should communicate with God directly. The second is that villagers are poor precisely because they attach so much importance to, and unnecessarily channel large sums of money toward, these celebrations. Because, villagers are told, they can communicate directly with God, costly ritual celebrations (that often benefit others, including Catholic clergy) are unnecessary. As a result, they can and ought to channel their monies and other resources toward improving their diet, local schools, health care, and the like. This is a message that has resonance elsewhere: in the Cakchiquel-Maya municipality studied by Annis in Guatemala, "San Antonio Protestants do not hesitate in explaining the practical advantages of a religion that venerates a god who is inexpensive to serve" (1987:85).

The empowering message that villagers can substantially improve their material well-being by converting to Protestantism is paralleled and backed up by deeds. In stark contrast to the Catholic Church, which historically has been far more interested in spiritual salvation, Protestant denominations are able and willing to undertake specific efforts aimed at directly raising the standard of living of their converts. They do so, for example, by funneling resources for schools and teachers, heath care, and literacy campaigns in Quichua. These efforts are part and parcel of a rather different worldview: one ought to attend to not only the spiritual but also the material and cultural needs of local communities.

Protestants have also succeeded in their conversion quest because of the cultural content of their messages and deeds. One key strategy has been to provide religious services and educational programs in, and translating the Bible into, Quichua, the local Quechua dialect. One response that missionaries received from Quichua-speakers encountering the Bible in their own language was that "This is our language, God is speaking to us. God actually loves the Indian as well as the Spanish" (Muratorio 1981:515). God's message is also couched in more meaningful ways than in a traditional Catholic ceremony, emphasizing the Quichua villagers' cultural framework and their understanding of the position they occupy in Ecuadorian society. Thus, Muratorio observed a ceremony in which

> the pastor read parts of Paul's Epistle to the Romans on the equality of divine punishment and interpreted it to the audience by saying: "Whites, Quichuas, Mestizos, Blacks, and Gringos will be judged equally before God's law." (1981:521)

Such an approach emphasizing the intrinsic worth of villagers and their culture, in a context in which Quichua and Quechua-speakers have historically been identified by nonindigenous "White" elites as "dirty," "brutish," and "ignorant," has led to a renewed sense of self-pride as "Indians." This ethnically and culturally charged sense of empowerment has much to do with the speed with which the Protestant creed has been received: a mere decade after Muratorio's research in the region of Colta, the "Catholic Church . . . [had] in effect disappeared completely" (Gros 1999:184).

The African Heritage: Candomblé, Santería, and Vodou

As noted in Chapter 4, during the colonial period millions of African slaves were forcibly transported to Latin America and the Caribbean, the vast majority settling in the Caribbean islands and Brazil. Two major and related cultural consequences of the almost three hundred years of the colonial and slave experience are worthy of note. The first is that over time, important cultural and linguistic differences between slaves from different parts of Africa disappeared, and the second is that colonialism and slavery did not totally erase their cultural heritage. Indeed, slaves and their descendants in plantations, haciendas, and urban settings forged novel and widely shared cultural traditions drawn from diverse African, European, and indigenous backgrounds. The result was the coalescence of a distinctive and vibrant Afro–Latin culture (Andrews 2004), especially noticeable in the religious sphere.

Candomblé, santería, and **vodou** are three prominent examples of Afro–Latin religions that resulted from colonialism and **syncretism**—the process whereby different cultural traditions come into contact and merge in different ways to form novel ones. (Other religious practices surveyed in previous pages are, of course, the result of the same process.) Herskovits was perhaps the first anthropologist to carry out detailed ethnographic research on Caribbean Afro–Latin religious practices, and on what he appropriately called (referring to Haiti) the "syncretization of African and Catholic gods" (1937a:636; see also 1937b).

The African beliefs and practices underlying these traditions are and have been varied, reflecting the diverse cultural backgrounds and geographic origins of slaves. Nevertheless, they had a great deal in common, which facilitated the emergence in the New World of a pan-African religious tradition. Harding has summarized some of these key features—many of which, incidentally, also surface in popular Catholicism—as consisting of

> the importance of communal worship; the cultivation and expectation of intense, pragmatic, physical communion with the representations of the forces of the universe (many deities or one supreme deity); the special role of drama, music, and dance in religious culture and expression; . . . rites of healing and purification; and the belief that natural forces can be manipulated by certain individuals to effect a variety of ends. (2000:22)

The following pages focus on some distinctive characteristics of candomblé in Brazil, santería in Cuba, and vodou in Haiti, relying on candomblé as an analytic prism through which to understand the differences and similarities between these religious traditions, and stressing the historical and political-economic contexts within which they emerged.

Candomblé, santería, and vodou are broad religious traditions of primarily African origins that in the New World coalesced during the eighteenth and nineteenth centuries. Historical and cultural products of the vicissitudes of the slave trade and the forced incorporation of diverse West African peoples into wider fields of relationships spawned by European colonialism, both in West Africa and Latin America and the Caribbean, candomblé, santería, and vodou are still widely practiced in contemporary Brazil (especially in the state of Bahia), Cuba, and Haiti (Harding 2000; Voeks 1997; Murphy 1994; Brodwin 1996). The most important African influence in candomblé and santería is and historically has been Yoruba—not a surprising fact because Yoruba-speaking peoples from West Africa, and specifically from what is now Nigeria and Benin, formed the last bulk of slaves transported to Brazil and Cuba.

Although devotees of each tradition believe in supreme creator gods, such as *candomblé's* Olórum, these are distant, almost inaccessible beings having little to do with the mundane aspects and struggles of daily life. As a result, they do not loom crucial in the everyday life and beliefs and ritual practices of most ordinary Brazilians, Cubans, and Haitians. Far more important are the dozen or so deities (*orishas* or *orixás* in candomblé and santería; lwa in vodou) who are intermediaries between the distant creator gods and mortals. Forging ongoing, mutually beneficial relationships with the orishas and lwa through worship rituals and ceremonies constitutes the core of the candomblé, santería, and vodou religious systems. The instrumental channeling of aggressive or malignant forces to the detriment of specific individuals—what in the popular imagination is considered "black magic"—is but one particular and highly exaggerated domain of vodou.

Service or devotion to the spirits requires assembling household altars (structurally analogous to those erected for Todos Santos), as well as undertaking ceremonies punctuated by chants, prayers, libations, dances, and the use of drums. These ceremonies often take place in specially designated sacred temples or houses of worship, such as the Brazilian *terreiros* or the *santería casas*. Music and dance, chants and incarnations form part of rituals in devotion to the orishas, and through which mortals attempt to communicate with them. Dance and music are particularly important mediums through which a communicative and ritual "bridge" is established between mortals and the deities. As Murphy emphasizes for Haiti:

> Vodou is, first and foremost, a dance, a system of movements which bring people and lwa together in a progressive and mutual relationship of knowledge and growth. . . . It is through the movement of dance that the lwa are able to fully present to the congregation. The ritual orientation of the initiates, the rhythms of the drums, the songs . . . work together to create a kinesthetic medium for the lwa to manifest themselves in dance. (1994:17, 27)

Orishas and lwa require of their devotees appropriate offerings during certain days of the week. For example, candomblé's Oxalá, the son of the supreme god Olórum, requires the sacrifice of chickens and doves on Friday, his day to receive worship and homage. What kinds of ritual offerings the spirits insist on are often structured by what they are likened to in this mortal world. For example, Danbala, one of the most important vodou lwa, is equated with a snake, and therefore demands the kinds of foods that appeal to snakes, such as eggs. Feisty and quite demanding, Haitian vodou lwa "are quick to resent what they consider to be stingy service" (Murphy 1994:27). The offering, consumption, and sharing of food is particularly meaningful and symbolically important in Haitian vodou, a fact very much related to the grinding poverty and appalling dietary and health conditions that most Haitians, now and in the past, have had to grapple with. As Murphy says:

> Finally, and most practically, the lwa comes to the service to eat. In a country where most people do not have enough to eat, the importance of sharing food cannot be overemphasized. The lwa are fed, and so the serviteurs are fed. The [followers] of the lwa benefit from the lwa's appetites, and those attending may share in the feast. The lwa are brought into a community of shared food, and thus shared responsibility. Vodou is a society that feeds its serviteurs. (1994:28)

In candomblé as well as vodou, important as well are possession trances, which also loom critical in divination and healing practices by folk healers or curandeiros.

Candomblé, santería, and vodou are traditions with clear ritual and power hierarchies. Especially prominent are those who have amassed ritual knowledge and can therefore communicate more effectively with the spirit world, such as the Haitian voudou's *mambo* or *oungan* (also *hougan*), or the Cuban santería's *santa* or *santo* (female and male spiritual leaders, respectively). Gender is particularly important in key leadership positions and ritual roles: the heads of most Brazilian candomblés are and historically have been women—the head of most Brazilian candomblés in Bahia is referred to as "mother" (*mãe* in Portuguese, *iya* in Yoruba)—and in Cuba, female santeras have usually been far more prominent and numerous than male santeros. Religion and ritual, and particularly the ability to communicate with potentially benevolent supernatural beings, has been one of the few arenas of cultural (and public) life where women have been able to assert themselves in a particularly effective way.

Candomblé, santería, and vodou are not monolithic traditions with identical practices and beliefs. For example, in 1980, at least 1,500 candomblés were registered in the Brazilian state of Bahia (Murphy 1994:51); not all worshipped the same orishas. There is also a great deal of variability within each of these traditions. This variation is expressed, for instance, in the few but distinctive "nations" (*nações* in Portuguese; *naciones* in Spanish) into which candomblé and santería congregations are organized. Identifying oneself (and one's religious community) as part of an ethnic collectivity dates to the early slave experience, suggesting how slaves and former slaves attempted to cling to their sense of identity and belonging. Sometimes the colonial context was conducive to the formation of these nations: in Cuba, for example, at least sixteen *naciones* were registered in Havana by the time of the slave emancipation in the late 1880s. Today, however, identification with a nation simply reflects participation in a specific candomblé, santería, or vodou organization with its own distinctive rituals and particular constellation of deities.

Candomblé, santería, and vodou are and have been for a long time true communities in the anthropological sense: clusters of people often related by kinship (or pseudo-kinship) ties; shared orientations and worldviews; mutual obligations and responsibilities to other community members, both living and deceased; and "spaces" within which a sense of self and identity is continuously forged and remembered. As Murphy tells us:

> Believers of a vodou community might be either family members connected by blood to a particular compound, or unaffined neighbors drawn to a ounfo or "temple" . . . For family members, vodou is a way or remembering the dead and the lwa which have incarnated themselves in their family. (1994:17)

One can surmise that membership in these communities—often spatially and culturally "hidden" from the gaze of elites—was an especially viable path or medium through which many slaves and their descendants constituted their social and cultural lives, including their religious traditions.

"Service" to the candomblé and santería orishas or the vodou lwa is sparked by a "call," often set off by a personal crisis, an unfortunate event, an unexplainable incident of potentially catastrophic consequences. Like Latin American popular Catholicism, with which they share many structural attributes, candomblé, santería, and vodou are an assemblage of practical, instrumental beliefs and practices centered on the here and now, on the contingencies and struggles of everyday life. As such, believers attach little importance to ethereal and abstract concepts, such as heaven, hell, salvation, purgatory, or damnation, and it is quite reasonable to assume that their slave forbearers, for whom the struggle to survive was a daily challenge, did likewise. Dealing with the practicalities and exigencies of every life—how to obtain a job, how to keep healthy, how to find and not lose significant relationships, how to avoid political persecution, and so forth—are the sorts of issues that one consults the orishas and lwa on. And, not unexpectedly, health and illness are a significant domain within which relationships with orishas and lwa are forged. Orishas and lwa are quasi-supernatural beings, yet they form part of this world, sharing—and understanding—

many of the humans' moral weaknesses and emotional needs. They are worshipped because they are powerful beings who understand the human condition and are able and willing—if their own needs and wishes are met in the course of ritual practices—to intercede on behalf their devotees. Orishas and lwa are in many ways potential allies in the quest for a better life but, if not served as they wish, potentially dangerous enemies as well.

Candomblé, santería, and vodou are believed in by primarily the poor, the destitute, the underclass. As Voeks (1997:67) says about Brazilian candomblé: "It is not a religion of celebrates . . . [it] . . . is very much a religion of common folk. Its rank and file are dominated by washerwomen, domestics, street hawkers and rubbish collectors, denizens of the favelas (shantytowns) that represent the Afro-Brazilians' heritage from slavery." And as Rey tells us about Haitian vodou:

> It is to the religious needs born of enslavement and poverty that the Vodou spirits respond. . . . Vodou is essentially not a religion of high-flung cosmology, but of practical assistance in getting by in this world as best one can. Yet this world is not entirely distinct from that of the spirits, which is precisely what allows the lwa to so routinely intervene in the lives of humans, fortifying them in the struggle to survive. (1999:203–204)

African religious beliefs and practices were forcefully persecuted, for the slaves' attachment to what appeared as diabolic, pagan practices of witchcraft and sorcery were always viewed with suspicion and fear by colonial authorities. In Brazil, for example, plantation owners were ever fearful of ritual gatherings of slaves and former slaves, believing that these emotionally and socially intense assemblies would forebear revolt. Analogous concerns were expressed elsewhere. Consider, for instance, the following statement from a French traveler in Haiti prior to the outbreak of mass rebellions in 1781:

> In order to quiet the alarms which this mysterious cult of Vandoux causes in the colony, the affect to dance it in public, to the sound of the drums and of rhythmic handclapping . . . nothing is more dangerous . . . than this cult of Vandoux. It can be made into a terrible weapon—this extravagant idea that the ministers of this alleged god know all and can do all. (quoted in Murphy 1994:11)

It appears that this French traveler was on to something, for popular lore has it that the slave rebellions that eventually led to independence erupted just shortly after slaves sacrificed a wild boar to African gods (Murphy 1994:11).

These beliefs and practices survived in the deeply personal and shielded spheres of home and community worship houses and traditions. Eventually, the widely shared and wrenching slave experience, coupled with the structural similarities between the different African religious traditions, resulted in shared religious traditions within and through which slaves could reconstitute and forge a unified sense of identity and common experience in opposition to colonial rule.

The reconstitution of novel, often Yoruba-dominated, religious traditions in the slave context resulted in the disappearance of many African deities, beliefs, and rituals; their transformation into new ones; and their merger with others from European popular

Catholicism. Which African spiritual beings would survive and blend with those of the dominant religion—and therefore be revered to this very day—was largely contingent on the specific circumstances of the slave experience in both Africa and Latin America. For example, the Yoruba orisha Xangó, a warrior god associated with thunder and lightning, survived the slave experience in Brazil, and is important in many contemporary candomblés and santerías. This is so partly because its priests and cult leaders were sold into captivity by rival and victorious West African kingdoms and almost certainly arrived in Bahia after being sold to European slave traders, but also probably because devotion to Xangó resonated well with slaves' need to forge a viable resistance culture.

The cultural and social relevance of African deities in the specific context of slavery would often determine their fate. "The spiritual survivors," Voeks tells us, "were those who empowered the captive population—who employed their powers to further the cause of their believers, not their oppressors" (1997:55). One candomblé example is Ogun, a Yoruba orisha of war which, symbolizing strength and resistance, was wholeheartedly embraced by Brazilian slaves. By contrast, Okó, a Yoruba god of agriculture, fared poorly and even today has few candomblé followers. For slaves toiling the land in brutally exploitative conditions on behalf of white slave masters, devotion to Okó would have been tantamount to ideologically legitimizing their own impoverishment and oppression.

A common structural feature of the African religious traditions that would later coalesce into candomblé, santería, and vodou was their inherent malleability (i.e., the possibility of incorporating and discarding specific deities) as well as reverence to a wide spectrum of quasi-supernatural beings who could be enticed—if not manipulated—to help mortals overcome moments of hardship and face everyday challenges. This too was a key feature of late medieval European Catholicism, especially in Spain and Portugal, where the proliferation of cults to saints and the Virgin Mary had reached new levels.

For Africans attempting to physically and culturally survive enslavement, popular Catholicism, especially the host of seemingly powerful beings such as the saints and the Virgin Mary, probably seemed strangely familiar and attractive. The functional equivalence between African deities and many European counterparts was one reason African deities were often identified with European ones, with European saints and the Virgin Mary eventually constituting a powerful complement to the African pantheon. Further, even as early as the seventeenth century, and no doubt due to colonial incursions, European religious deities were already making their way into the religious pantheons of many Central and West African peoples. For example, catechism classes in seventeenth century Dahomey allowed the name of one local deity to replace that of Jesus Christ. Such an experience probably underpinned the intrinsic familiarity with which slaves viewed Catholic deities.

Thus, in many parts of Brazil and the Caribbean, the important candomblé orisha Oxalá, identified with peace and love, was merged with Jesus Christ. Likewise, "Omolu, the feared Yoruba god of smallpox and contagious disease, became known in many parts of the neo-Yoruba landscape as Saint Lazarus, the disabled Catholic saint honored for his healing ability," and in some contemporary candomblé rituals, the "white Virgin Mary passes without notice for the maternal African goddess Yemanjá" (Voeks 1997:60–61). Indeed, many vodou rituals—so often mistakenly associated with "black magic"—actually begin with Catholic chants, prayers, and incantations evoking God, the Virgin Mary, and a host of Catholic saints.

Controversies: Mesoamerican Civil–Religious Cargo Systems

Perhaps no other aspect of Mesoamerican religion has received greater ethnographic scrutiny and has been equally shrouded in controversy as the **civil–religious hierarchies** (also known as cargo systems) in Mexico and Guatemala. For more than seventy years, anthropologists have debated the origins, differences, and cultural, social, and economic significance of this important facet of Mesoamerican life (Tax 1937; Wolf 1955, 1957, 1986; Carrasco 1961; Cancian 1965, 1990; Dow 1977; DeWalt 1979; Brass 1986; Friedlander 1981; Mathews 1985; Wasserstrom 1978; Rus and Wasserstrom 1980; Chance 1990). Although structurally equivalent political and/or religious hierarchies—the *varayuqkuna* (Quechua/Aymara for "staff holders"; see Chapter 4) are also present in some contemporary Andean communities (Van den Berghe and Primov 1977; Brass 1986; Rasnake 1988; Abercrombie 1998)—most ethnographic and historical research on these hierarchies has centered on Mesoamerica. **Cargo** is a useful keyword, usually translated as post, or office, alluding to hierarchically ranked political and religious positions that community members are expected to occupy in the course of their life cycle. By doing so, commitment to the community is reaffirmed, prestige is acquired, and sponsors become important leaders. Cargo is also semantically related to *carga,* or burden—alluding to the financial expenses that sponsors incur in obligatory and prestige-generating ceremonies or fiestas in honor of community and household saints.

Mathews emphasizes that although much ethnographic literature has stressed the importance of male sponsors (*mayordomos*), in fact sponsorship is a household affair in which all household members acquire prestige. She notes that community members in Oaxaca "persist in recognizing male/female couples as joint titleholders to religious office," and that male mayordomos are required to seek out (female) mayordomas to carry out the celebrations in honor of the saints (1985:290). This pattern has deep roots for, as Stern notes for other parts of Mexico, during the eighteenth and nineteenth centuries "women and men assumed joint responsibility for preparing the lavish propitiations of saints . . . and women were sometimes recognized as fiesta sponsors (*mayordomas*) in their own right" (1995:131).

These systems have varied considerably across time and space, reflecting the diversity of indigenous communities onto which Spanish crown and religious officials attempted to graft their own political and religious institutions to ensure colonial rule; attempts by community members to use colonial institutions to their own advantage; and the broader social, political, and economic forces with which indigenous peoples contended.

There are at least two basic types of cargo systems. In the first, the political and religious offices not only parallel but also intersect with each other, so that sponsors rotate between civil and religious positions. Strictly speaking, these are the civil–religious hierarchies. The second important variant is where ranked civil and religious positions parallel but do not formally intersect; here, individuals may "climb" the religious "ladder" without necessarily having to do the same in the civil sphere. One example is the system described by Cancian (1965:29) in Zinacantan, Chiapas, Mexico, comprised of four tiers and fifty-five cargo positions (see Figure 7.1).

These religious and political hierarchies are key facets of what Wolf called "closed corporate" communities (1955, 1957). Although Wolf later recanted some of his earlier

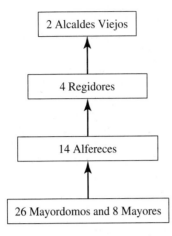

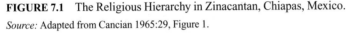

FIGURE 7.1   The Religious Hierarchy in Zinacantan, Chiapas, Mexico.

Source: Adapted from Cancian 1965:29, Figure 1.

generalizations (1986), his summary of the major features of these communities provides a backdrop to debates that have surfaced in the study of cargo systems. Such communities

> maintain a body of rights to possessions, such as land . . . put pressures on members to redistribute surpluses . . . preferably in the operation of a religious system, and induce them to content themselves with the rewards of "shared poverty" . . . they strive to prevent outsiders from becoming members of the community, and in placing limits on the ability of members to communicate with the larger society . . . they are corporate organizations, maintaining a perpetuity of rights and membership . . . and they are closed corporations, because they limit these privileges to insiders, and discourage close participation of members in the social relations of the outside world. (Wolf 1957:2)

Several related debates have consistently surfaced in the study of these religious and civil systems.

1. *When and how they emerged.* Some authors believe that cargo systems can be traced to the mid-colonial period when crown officials congregated dispersed settlements into urbanlike towns, created village-level political positions whose leaders would represent their communities vis-à-vis crown officials, and organized cofradías to honor Catholic saints. Focusing on the Aztec area, Carrasco (1961) emphasized that pre-Hispanic communities also had similar ranked political and religious prestige "ladders," suggesting that these pre-Hispanic antecedents facilitated the acceptance of the Spanish colonial political positions and cofradías, and were important in shaping how these eventually developed. For example, the Spanish political structure and offices (corregidores, alcaldes, and the like) coexisted for some time with local political positions, and it was only after colonial policies undermined native political elites that the Spanish system became entrenched.

In the religious sphere, an equally important coexistence and adaptation emerged. Aztec communities also honored and remembered their deities by engaging in public celebrations and feasts, rituals that paralleled the fiestas sponsored by the cofradías. Early on, cofradías and the fiestas they sponsored were financed through communal landholdings and resources, but through time, these were replaced by individual sponsorship by mayordomos or mayordomías (Carrasco 1961:493).

Although cognizant of links with colonial institutions, Rus and Wasserstrom (1980) believe that the more modern forms of civil–religious hierarchies (those that anthropologists began studying in the 1930s and 1940s) have their origins, at least in Zinacantan, in the nineteenth century. Guided by a political–economic perspective focusing on the relationships between migration and wage labor, they suggest that by the early to mid-1800s, many Zinacanteco men were migrating to lowland areas to work as wage laborers and sharecroppers. Poor health conditions and rampant disease took their toll, so that many (who were also members of cofradías) died, and the cofradía system (and its system of saintly celebrations) disintegrated. Nevertheless, two related developments ushered in the emergence of the more modern form of civil–religious systems. The first was that parish priests instituted new fiestas and festivals for other saints and ensured that municipal political leaders (alcaldes and regidores) would fill these offices. Second, lucrative wage labor and sharecropping arrangements by the late 1800s in Sonusco (a non-lowland region) reduced male mortality and allowed some Zinacanteco males to rebuild families and accumulate wealth. By the early 1900s, competition for mayordomías heightened and Zinacantecos had organized "the various cargos into a hierarchy of ranked office through which economic achievement might be measured" (Rus and Wasserstrom 1980:472).

Chance (1990) suggests that the earliest forms of the cargo systems were a civil hierarchy that emerged in the sixteenth century, comprised mainly of the Spanish-imposed political offices. Religious offices and celebrations were centered in and sponsored by cofradías, which mainly emerged in the seventeenth and eighteenth centuries. The fusion of the formerly separate yet parallel civil and religious hierarchies occurred a century later due to

> expropriations of *cofradía* property by the church and prohibition of communal support of religious fiestas by some Spanish officials. These pressures brought about a shift from collective to household fiesta sponsorship. At the same time, the colonial status differences between indigenous nobles and commoners were being dismantled and there was growing concern in the villages that each household should help shoulder the burden of maintaining the cult of the saints. (Chance 1990:29)

2. *Whether these hierarchies function as "shields" against the outside world.* Because only community members can occupy these civil and religious positions, and the sponsorship of religious celebrations is often on behalf of village patron saints, these hierarchies have been viewed as closely wedded to community boundaries and access to resources, membership, and ethnic identity and the continuity of cultural traditions (Wolf 1956). Further, religious and political hierarchies have been sometimes seen as a cultural "shield" limiting the kinds of relationships with and influences of the outside world. Carrasco (1961:494) was clear on this point when he stated that these systems block the community's "total assimilation into the greater society."

In fact, colonial and postcolonial elite policies largely shaped the form and content of religious and civil–religious hierarchies, undermining the claim that cargo systems form a type of protective shield around communities. In parts of western Guatemala, cargo systems have essentially disappeared due to ongoing political and economic intrusions of state and economic elites into Maya communities (Watanabe 1990). Elsewhere, other processes were at work. Rus and Wasserstrom (1980) have marshaled evidence that in the decades before and after the Mexican Revolution, state officials in the region of Chamula played important political roles within indigenous communities, and in the process profoundly shaped the civil–religious hierarchies. During the 1930s, state officials began to name politically-loyal scribes to community-level political posts. In time, and allied with some community elders or *principales* (i.e., those who had reached the top positions of the civil–religious hierarchy), these politically-appointed scribes gradually gained control of the civil–religious hierarchies by enthusiastically occupying religious and civil posts, a situation made possible by a 1937 law that allowed the selling of liquor in indigenous communities by those occupying religious posts. By the 1950s, these scribes themselves had become elders, and "their unorthodox political origins had been all but forgotten" (Rus and Wasserstrom 1980:474).

Further, Friedlander (1981) notes that in Hueyapan (in the state of Morelos), rather than isolating or shielding community members from the outside world, the cargo system has served as an effective bridge between the community and the Mexican nation-state. That is, rather than attempting to do away with "traditional" institutions, representatives of the Mexican state use them to forge a sense of national identity and Mexican nationalism. Indigenous school teachers have spearheaded these efforts by designating neighborhoods (*barrios*) with the names of national heroes (e.g., Benito Juárez) and prompting community members to sponsor celebrations in their honor as well as for national holidays (e.g., November 20, commemorating the Mexican Revolution).

3. *Whether civil and religious systems minimize internal conflicts by leveling wealth differences and hindering internal social and economic differentiation.* One former widespread view was phrased by Carrasco: "The ladder [i.e., prestige] system . . . has a survival value in that it holds the community together by checking the internal economic and social differentiation that tends to disrupt the community" (1961:493–494). The ideas here are that cargo participation entails considerable expense for obligatory ritual celebrations; that those who are wealthier are pressured to muster the most elaborate and costliest fiestas; and that consequently, wealth differences between and economic stratification of community members are reduced. This idea of cargos as "leveling-mechanisms" also has important cultural and social associations for, it is assumed, less economic stratification would lead to less suspicion and accusations of witchcraft (spurred by jealousy, envy, and the like)—in effect, it would lead to greater community harmony.

Cancian's research in Zinacantan (1965:136–140) suggests that the cargo system does not absolutely do away with economic stratification. Further, because greater prestige is associated with larger outlays of wealth in festival sponsorship, the cargo system legitimizes the accumulation of and sumptuous display of wealth—in effect, providing wealth differences and economic stratification with an ideological underpinning. Dow (1977:219) states that the main function of cargo systems is to redistribute surpluses within a community rather than level wealth differences between households. Cargo systems rarely if ever endanger the basis of economic stratification: a sponsor may accumulate and invest large amounts of food and drink in a fiesta, and maybe slaughter a cow, but not sell his/her land. Further, the idea that cargo systems are leveling mechanisms rests on two questionable assumptions: that most wealth is generated from within the community, and that the community is "closed" to outside forces. Nash (2001:65) notes that in some Mexican communities, cargo holders are also key political party representatives who accumulate wealth by monopolizing inflowing political funds and controlling liquor and soft drink franchises. And in a poignant example of the transformational impact of broader economic and political forces on indigenous communities and institutions, Steinberg (2004:177–178) notes that by generating new sources of wealth, marijuana cultivation in some Belizean Maya communities is undermining their cargo systems, and especially the standing and authority of community alcaldes.

In The United States: Re-Creating Vodou in Brooklyn

Almost half a million Haitians have fled their poverty-stricken homeland in recent decades, the vast majority settling in south Florida and the greater New York City area (Stepick 1998). New York City is one of the most culturally diverse cities in the United States, with Latin American and Caribbean peoples making up more than 50 percent of its almost three million foreign-born inhabitants (New York City 2000).

Along with many Puerto Ricans, Jamaicans, and other Caribbean peoples (or, as the colloquial expression goes, people "from the islands"), most Haitians have settled in New York City's southern borough of Brooklyn, transforming it into a rich cultural mosaic and hub of Latin American and Caribbean culture. Brown nicely captures the ethnic and cultural "flavor" of southern Brooklyn:

> As . . . I inched through . . . Nostrand Avenue on an intensely hot July afternoon , . . [our] . . . nostrils filled with the smells of charcoal and roasting meat and our ears with overlapping episodes of salsa, reggae, and the bouncy monotony of what Haitians call jazz. Animated conservations could be heard in Haitian French Creole, Spanish, and more than one lyrical dialect of English. The street was a crazy quilt of shops: Chicka-Licka, the Ashanti Bazaar, a storefront Christian church with an improbably long and specific name, a Haitian restaurant, and Botanica Shango—one of the apothecaries of New World African religions offering fast-luck and get-rich powders, High John the Conqueror root, and votive candles marked for the Seven African Powers. (1991:1)

If, as Brown (1991:5) tell us, "A well-worn joke claims, with some truth, that of Haiti's six million people 85 percent are Catholic, 15 percent are Protestant, and 100 percent serve the Vodou spirits," then this certainly appears to be the case with most Haitians in New York City, many of whom have retained and reconfigured vodou beliefs and practices to meet the novel challenges of their new life in the United States. (For the practice of vodou among Haitians in the East Harlem section of New York City, see McAlister 1998.)

Alourdes, who arrived in the United States in the mid-1980s, is a mambo, a vodou priestess. She is at the center of a network of vodou believers who, in her apartment, "serve" at least six major categories of spirits or lwa. As in Haiti, the lwa are also represented by Catholic saints and deities to such an extent that it might make sense to think of them as having double, complementary identities. Hence, the Virgin is equated with Elizi; Saint Patrick with Danbala, the serpent deity; and Saint Isidore, representing the peasant farmer, is identified with Azaka, the African deity representing cultivation and the farming way of life.

Ceremonial offerings are at the heart of vodou in Haiti and among Haitians in Brooklyn. As a "server" of the lwa, it is up to Alourdes to organize these events. She does this by annually sponsoring a "birthday party" for each lwa, the date of which roughly coincides with the saints' day set aside by the Catholic liturgical calendar. Some lwa, along with many attending these "parties," are referred to as *kouzen,* which although literally translates as "cousin," more generally connotes a family or kinlike connection. Lwa and their devotees are thus bound to each other through responsibilities and obligations that one would expect in any kin network.

The centerpiece of the "birthday party" is a decorated table structurally equivalent to the altar displayed during the celebration of Todos Santos discussed earlier in this chapter. On top of the table, covered with a white linen cloth, are candles, cardboard skeletons, shamrocks, and various icons depicting the lwa, who are invariably portrayed in the form of Catholic saints. The table is also laden with food and drink, such as fruits, vegetables, and dishes of local cuisines. Indeed, it is the offering of food—nourishment—that the lwa expect and that lies at the core of the ritual event, which Brown (1991:44) suggests is rooted in the Haitian experience of hunger and poverty. The sorts of foods offered to the lwa are also very much a product of the local context. Although the sacrifice of goats and chickens to lwa may be commonplace in rural Haiti, this would be difficult to do in urban Brooklyn. Hence, some lwa—such as Azaka—seem content to accept fancy cakes from local bakeries, including a frosted cake with the message "Happy Birthday P. [Papa] Azaka" (Brown 1991:41). Failure to offer a timely and appropriate party can bode disaster and ill-health. As Maggie, one of Alourdes' daughters, told Brown, "Kouzen [Azaka] just think we not going to do nothing for him this year. So he made Mommie sick" (1991:45). Virtually any kind of misfortune, including difficulties with immigration authorities, can be directly attributed to the lack of proper offering to the lwa.

These birthday parties are fundamentally healing rituals in which Alourdes embodies the lwa spirit and attempts to harness its power on behalf of those attending the ceremony. The lwa are said to posses or "ride" Alourdes, and to speak through her. These ceremonies typically begin with Catholic chants and prayers. Hence, "One of the first calls on Saint Peter (like Lazarus, a Catholic counterpart of Legba), [is to] 'open the door, the door to Paradise.' Others beg Mary, Jesus, and various saints for grace and forgiveness" (Brown 1991:52).

Summary

This chapter surveyed important expressions of religious beliefs and practices. From the early colonial period onwards, popular Catholicism emerged as a central manifestation of the interplay between European and indigenous and African religious systems, and as a key symbolic and pragmatic medium conveying the aspirations and lived experiences in Latin America and the Caribbean. In many ways the contemporary spread of Protestantism does not represented a significant departure in world views, intersecting and paralleling the symbolic and down-to-earth outlook that Latin American and Caribbean peoples imbued popular Catholicism with for 500 years. Religious beliefs and practices were also a crucial channel and means through and with which African slaves coped with their harsh circumstances and attempted to forge meaningful lives in the New World. The continued relevance of popular Catholicism, and of African-derived religious traditions in today's contemporary world points to the highly malleable and adaptive functions of culture.

ISSUES AND QUESTIONS

1. *Popular Catholicism.* What explains the emergence of popular Catholicism in the early colonial period and how does it differ from formal, institutionalized Catholicism? What specific examples suggest different ways in which popular Catholicism is interwoven in everyday lives, aspirations, and challenges?

2. *Spread of Protestantism.* How and why is Protestantism spreading throughout Latin America and the Caribbean? Can a parallelism be drawn between the rise of Protestantism in Latin America and the surge of evangelical Christian sects in the United States? Why? Why not?

3. *Afro–Latin Religions.* The African legacy in Latin America and the Caribbean is particularly pronounced in the realm of religion and religious ritual. Why might this be so? In what ways are Afro–Latin religious traditions similar to or different from popular Catholicism?

4. *Civil–Religious Hierarchies.* What are civil–religious hierarchies and what explains their presence in Mesoamerica? What kinds of social and cultural consequences do these hierarchies have at the local level? What might be some reasons these appear to be declining in importance in recent decades?

KEY TERMS AND CONCEPTS

Campaigns against idolatry
  p. 181
Candomblé   p. 201
Cargo   p. 207
Civil–religious hierarchies
  p. 207
Constructive drinking   p. 198

Liberation theology   p. 185
Liminality   p. 192
Polytheistic religious systems
  p. 182
Popular Catholicism   p. 183
Religion   p. 181
Religious syncretism   p. 183

Ritual intoxication   p. 197
Santería   p. 201
Syncretism   p. 201
Todos Santos   p. 192
Vodou   p. 201

8 Striving for Health and Coping with Illness

How people in Latin America and the Caribbean understand and grapple with health and illness is the focus of this chapter. The major concepts in medical anthropology, including the distinction between bio- and ethnomedicine, are first reviewed. Attention then turns to various indicators that underscore the region's poor health. The following section focuses on three examples of folk or popular illnesses, emphasizing how illness is often interpreted as an expression of dysfunctional social relationships. The anthropology of the body and how healthy bodies are culturally construed is then discussed. Attention then shifts to the relationship between religion, the diagnosis of illness, and healing practices, followed by a review of long-standing controversies surrounding health and the consumption of marijuana and coca. The last section brings readers back to the United States by focusing on the contemporary prevalence of susto and mal de ojo illnesses among migrant farm workers in Florida.

Medical Anthropology

All societies have a **medical system**—beliefs, values, practices, and knowledge that enables their members to understand, diagnose, and treat health and illness. Four premises underpin **medical anthropology,** which studies the social, cultural, and biological dimensions of health and illness from a cross-cultural perspective:

> First, that illness and healing are basic human experiences that are best understood holistically in the complex and varied interactions between human biology and culture; second, that disease is an aspect of human environments influenced by culturally specific behaviors and socio-political circumstances; third, that the human body and symptoms are interpreted through cultural filters of beliefs . . . ; and fourth, that cultural aspects of healing systems have important pragmatic consequences for the acceptability, efficacy, and improvement of health care. (Brown et al. 1998:12)

Ethnomedicine (also called traditional medicine), refers to the culturally-specific medical systems in non-Western societies. Ethnomedical systems and practitioners (healers) underscore social and cultural factors in diagnosing and treating culturally-specific **illness,** often a somatic manifestation of a fundamental imbalance, or lack of harmony, between humans, or between humans and the supernatural. This imbalance is the result of either strained social relationships (due to, for example, greed, envy, or jealously), or the failure to carry out prescribed obligations to other humans or supernatural entities with whom humans interact. Treatment typically centers on restoring harmony, balance, and good will. Ethnomedical anthropologists focus on describing culturally specific healing practices and categories of illness, and on understanding how these influence access to and acceptance of biomedical treatment.

Biomedicine is the medical system dominant in Western societies. Unlike ethnomedicine, to diagnose and treat ailments **(disease),** biomedical practitioners attach primary explanatory power to biological pathogens and physiological imbalances, largely downplaying the role of culture and social relations. Also unlike ethnomedicine, biomedicine makes the distinction—deeply rooted in European/Western thought—between ailments of the mind and body, relegating the former to the category of psychological, emotional, or psychosomatic illnesses, and the latter to disease. Medical anthropologists try to understand how these two medical systems intersect, and when, how, and why patients opt for either one or the other or both (Bastien 1992; Finkler 1998; Brown et al. 1998).

Critical medical anthropology, also known as the political economy of health, stresses how political and economic inequality affects the emergence and etiology of and responses to illness and disease (Joralemon 1999:45–46). An important critique is that "many . . . anthropologists have incorrectly attributed . . . disparities in health to local sociocultural differences without examining the influence of global political–economic inequality on the distribution [and emergence] of disease" (Brown et al. 1998:16). This approach is important in understanding the emergence, transmission, and entrenchment of infectious diseases such as tuberculosis and HIV/AIDS. Stebbin's research on health and smoking in Mexico and South America is also informed by a critical medical perspective (1998, 2001). Singer has been at the forefront in the study of the political economy of health among Hispanics/Latinos in the eastern United States (2001a, 2001b).

The Poor Health of Latin America and the Caribbean

To gauge the state of a population's health, the Pan American Health Organization (PHO) and the World Health Organization (WHO) periodically compile data on health indicators, and availability and distribution of biomedical health resources. These measures, while glossing over vast disparities between rural and urban communities, poor and wealthy, women and men, and ethnic groups, are useful for appraising overall trends.

Mortality, Access to Biomedicine, and Malnutrition

Adult and infant and child mortality rates are routinely used to measure health trends. High mortality rates clustered around the youngest and most vulnerable—infants and children—point to an inability of family and kin to adequately provide for household survival. Thirty of the thirty-three Latin American and Caribbean countries about which the World Health

TABLE 8.1   Male Adult, Infant, and Child Mortality Rates

Country	Male Adult Mortality[a] (U.S. rate = 140)	Infant/Child Mortality[b] (U.S. rate = 9)
Antigua and Barbados	195	22
Argentina	177	20
Bahamas	248	13
Barbados	189	17
Belize	189	44
Bolivia	260	78
Brazil	246	42
Chile	134	16
Colombia	236	27
Costa Rica	127	12
Cuba	138	8
Dominica	206	13
Dominican Republic	256	37
Ecuador	216	34
El Salvador	257	36
Grenada	261	25
Guatemala	283	57
Guyana	299	61
Haiti	493	138
Honduras	269	44
Jamaica	162	16
Mexico	170	30
Nicaragua	213	38
Panama	146	25
Paraguay	171	37
Peru	205	38
St. Kitts and Nevis	206	20
St. Lucia	211	14
St. Vincent and the Grenadines	238	25
Suriname	281	33
Trinidad and Tobago	246	24
Uruguay	182	18
Venezuela	182	23

[a]Number of male adult (15–59 years old) deaths per thousand live births

[b]Number of male infant and children (< 5 years old) deaths per thousand live births

Source: Adapted from World Health Organization (2001–2002)

Organization regularly compiles data on male adult mortality (which is typically higher than for women) have higher rates than the United States. Important exceptions are Chile, Cuba, and Costa Rica. Haiti has the highest male adult mortality rate, more than three times that of the United States (see Table 8.1).

Latin America also fares poorly in infant and child mortality. Cuba is the only country whose rate is lower than that of the United States. Once again, Haiti fared worst, with a rate fifteen times higher than the United States and Cuba. Some of the poorest countries with the largest percentages of indigenous peoples—Bolivia and Guatemala, for example—have some of the highest mortality rates. Cuba's health status is not only far superior to most Latin American countries, but it also compares favorably with the United States. "By 1992, Cuba had achieved a life expectancy rate within two years of that for the United States, an infant mortality rate within 1 percentage point of that in the United States, and had reduced low birth weight births to within 2 percentage points of the U.S." (Whiteford 1998:275). Cuba has achieved this success due to a concerted drive to provide free preventive care at the grassroots level through a system of community health centers, and to ensure clean potable water and adequate human and solid waste management (Feinsilver 1993).

Providing access to health resources is also a way of ascertaining health status, although these efforts are often skewed toward urban areas and concentrated among the well-to-do. The proportion of a country's gross domestic product (GDP; the value of all goods and services produced) channeled toward health spending is a rough measure of overall health. During 1995, government spending on health in Argentina, Costa Rica, and Nicaragua was more than 10 percent of the GDP, while the range for most other countries was between 4 and 9 percent. Between 1990 and 1996, only 5 percent of central government resources were channeled toward the health sector in all of Latin America and the Caribbean (United Nations 1998; Pan American Health Organization 2001b).

The ratio of physicians to the total population is also a proxy measure of health. There are about eleven physicians for every ten thousand people in Latin America and the Caribbean, yet their distribution is highly skewed. For example, Cuba has thirty-two times the number of physicians for every ten thousand people than does Haiti. With more than fifty-one physicians for every ten thousand people, Cubans enjoy the highest physician–patient ratio (Pan American Health Organization 2001b). Mexico provides a clear example of the highly skewed allocation of physicians, as well as the glaring inequality in the distribution of and access to basic health resources that can be found in much of Latin America:

> 11 million Mexicans (12.1% of that country's population) live in four states that have more than 16.5 physicians per 10,000 population, but 24 million (26.3%) live in four other states that have fewer than 8.6 physicians per 10,000 population. (Pan American Health Organization 1998:14)

Access to clean and safe drinking water and sanitation facilities is one important way good health can be attained. According to the United Nations (1998:105), more than 70 percent of people in Latin America have access to "safe water" and "adequate sanitation." However, these claims should be interpreted with some caution, because "safety" and "adequacy" standards vary from country to country and, as is often the case with country-level survey data, reliability is problematic. Research on outbreaks of cholera in Peru, Venezuela, and elsewhere in the early 1990s (Guthmann 1995; Briggs 2003; Cueto 2003) contradict suggestions that water and sanitation levels are adequate for most, and also show how such outbreaks are related to inequality and disastrous public health policies.

The United Nations typically uses various indicators to measure malnutrition, another way of gauging health. In Latin America and the Caribbean, between 1990 and 1994 the percentage of children with low birth weight was 10, compared to 16 in sub-Saharan Africa and 6 in industrialized counties. Between 1990 and 1997, 21 percent of children under five in Latin America and the Caribbean suffered from wasting and stunting, while in industrialized countries this rate was negligible. A closer look at variations is always revealing: as with most indicators, Haiti fared the worst. Between 1980 and 1990, more than half of all Haitian children between twenty-four and fifty-nine months were stunted, while the percentage of stunted children in Peru, Bolivia, and Ecuador ranged from 37 to 38 percent. At 10 percent, Chile's children fared better than most in Latin America and the Caribbean, with the possible exception of Cuba. Malnutrition rates for children less than five years old are particularly high in Haiti and Guatemala (27.5 and 24.2, respectively), while these rates average between 5.9 and 9.5 percent in Mexico, Peru, Bolivia, and the Dominican Republic (Lee and Bobadilla 1994; United Nations 1998; Pan American Health Organization 2001b).

Poverty, Inequality, and Disease

Ethnomedical beliefs and practices are neither the cause of poor health nor do they necessarily stand in the way of achieving and sustaining good health. Most anthropologists agree that poor health and susceptibility to disease are primarily an outcome of entrenched poverty and inequality, which also skew the distribution of biomedical resources toward those at the top of the social and economic hierarchies. This requires paying attention to "how relative social and economic positioning—inequality—affects risk for infection" (Farmer 1996:261). As Vinh-Kim and Peschard state in their review of anthropology, inequality, and health:

> The relationship between poverty and ill health is well established . . . The mechanisms by which poverty causes disease . . . include weakened immunity and neurophysiological development because of malnutrition, ease of spread of pathogens because of insalubrious living conditions, and the precariousness of social support networks . . . It is the material deprivation poverty entails that is unhealthy. (2003:449; for analogous arguments, see Krieger et al. 1993)

Latin America is "the world region with the worst income distribution indicators of all" (Economic Commission for Latin America 2004:5). Almost half of the population is poor and, of these, almost 50 percent are indigent, or desperately poor, especially in rural areas (see Table 8.2). Hoffman and Centeno (2003) echo this view, reminding us of the intersection of gender, culture, and race: those at the bottom of what they call the "lopsided continent" are primarily women, indigenous peoples, those of African descent, and the non-"White."

In the past two decades, much of Latin America and the Caribbean experienced an erosion of living standards, increased poverty, and the concentration of wealth in the top 10 percent of households. Ironically, this has been especially the case in Argentina and Venezuela, both of which have bountiful natural resources. If this increasing inequality—the gap between the haves and have-nots—has earned Latin America "the dubious distinction of being the most backward region on the planet in terms of distribution," then

TABLE 8.2 Poverty and Indigence in Latin America, 1990–2002

Year	Percentage of People in		Millions of People in	
	Poverty	Indigence	Poverty	Indigence
1990	48.3	22.5	200	93
1997	43.5	19.0	204	89
2000	42.5	18.1	207	88
2002	44.1	19.4	221	97

Source: Adapted from Economic Commission for Latin America (2004:7)

Brazil and Argentina stand out as the most unequal of all Latin American countries. In 2002, Brazil's gini coefficient of income distribution (a statistical measure of inequality) was more than sixteen times that of the United States, while Argentina's was fifteen times higher (Economic Commission for Latin America 2004:8–12).

Further, nutritional standards appear to be worsening—and not merely because of entrenched poverty and a widening gap between the wealthy and the poor. The growth of agribusinesses, the cultivation of export crops, and a decline in subsistence food crops are also responsible. Also undermining the nutritional status of many are cultural shifts in food preferences, with a growing penchant for processed "modern" foods (high in starch, sugar, sodium, and fats) to the detriment of more nutritious grains, vegetables, and root crops (Franke 1987; Orlove 1987; Weismantel 1988:113).

In line with the critical or political–economic approach to health, many medical anthropologists are paying increasing attention to the emergence and spread of infectious diseases (Barrett et al. 1998). Inhorn and Brown state that medical anthropologists should be concerned with infectious diseases, which often cause intense suffering and mortality in societies studied by anthropologists, and ought to be able and willing to work with biomedical specialists. This does not mean that anthropologists should downplay culturally-specific understandings of illness and disease, for "culture provides a . . . system for understanding—and attempting to manipulate through medicine—the diseases that cause human suffering and death" (1990:110).

The incidence of contagious and infectious diseases such as tuberculosis and HIV/AIDS provides another way to ascertain poor health. The Pan American Health Organization has compiled data on tuberculosis rates for thirty-one Latin American and Carribean countries (see Table 8.3). Only five (Barbados, Costa Rica, Jamaica, St. Kitts and Nevis, and Antigua and Barbados) have a rate lower than the United States' rate of 7.9. Cuba's rate of 14.3—or almost twice that of the United States—seems unusually high, given its relatively good track record in other health indicators. The three worst-off countries are Haiti, Bolivia, and Peru. Other countries average three to five times the United States' rate. Despite being very high, these rates are down sharply from previous decades (Haeduk and Bobadilla 1994:8). AIDS is the most rapidly spreading infectious disease in Latin America, which, as a region, has the second highest incidence rate in the world after sub-Saharan Africa. Brazil, with more than one-third of worldwide AIDS cases, has been especially hard hit. The second most important foci of AIDS is Haiti.

TABLE 8.3 Prevalence of Tuberculosis and HIV/AIDS

Country	Tuberculosis[a]	AIDS[b]
Antigua and Barbados	7.6	—
Argentina	38.0	6.4
Bahamas	20.8	0.28
Barbados	1.1	0.12
Belize	24.2	0.18
Bermuda	—	—
Bolivia	134.3	0.24
Brazil	54.2	32.51
Chile	28.0	1.28
Colombia	26.6	9.36
Costa Rica	4.6	0.59
Cuba	14.3	0.01
Dominica	14.1	—
Dominican Republic	75.4	4.33
Ecuador	54.1	1.03
El Salvador	29.1	1.43
Grenada	—	—
Guatemala	32.0	3.84
Guyana	37.5	0.54
Haiti	91.4	13.79
Honduras	71.8	3.10
Jamaica	4.9	1.08
Mexico	22.2	7.88
Nicaragua	70.9	0.32
Panama	41.1	0.79
Paraguay	43.3	0.74
Peru	174.3	4.04
St. Kitts and Nevis	7.3	—
St. Lucia	—	—
St. Vincent and the Grenadines	—	—
Suriname	12.3	0.26
Trinidad and Tobago	15.8	1.43
Uruguay	21.9	0.30
Venezuela	25.0	5.42

[a]Rate per 100,000 population in 1996. *Source:* Pan American Health Organization (1998:133). The U.S. rate is 7.9.

[b]Percentage of all adults and children living with HIV, Latin America and the Caribbean, end of 2003.

Source: Adapted from UNAIDS 2004b:202–203.

Tuberculosis. Tuberculosis (TB) is caused by the bacterium tubercle bacillus, which typically attacks the lungs. Crowding, along with poor sanitation and hygiene—conditions widespread in Latin America—are ideal for the spread of TB. Initial symptoms include lack of energy, weight loss, and coughing; more serious symptoms are sweating, chest pains, and the coughing up of blood. Declared by the World Health Organization in 1993 to be a global emergency, TB is a disease of poverty that "remains the world's leading cause of preventable illness and is now more prevalent than in any previous period of human history" (Gandy and Zumla 2002:385). Although great strides have been achieved in developing effective drug remedies, TB incidence has spread dramatically in recent decades.

Several factors are responsible for this spread. Some are biomedical, such as the emergence of drug-resistant strains of TB, as well as its well-known coinfection with the HIV virus. But political, economic, and cultural factors have also played important—some think more critical—roles, such as civil strife and mass migrations of refugees; stigmatization and a lack of integration between bio- and ethnomedical systems; and growing poverty, a widening gap between the haves and have-nots. An important political–economic factor accounting for the spread of TB (and, more generally, worsening health conditions) and a drastic reduction in health care expenditures by national governments is free-market economic reforms. Stillwaggon (1998), for example, has focused on dismal health conditions in Argentina due to neo-liberal economic policies and deepening poverty during the 1980s and early 1990s, with a specific focus on the health of children. (For a more recent analysis of Argentina's economic and political crisis at the beginning of the twenty-first century, see Dinerstein 2003.) Indeed, historical and epidemiological research suggests that

> issues of poverty, gender inequality, disease stigmatization and the adequacy of medical services are central elements in any full explanation of the contemporary resurgence of this disease . . . The principal motor behind the resurgence of tuberculosis has been the sharp rise in global poverty, which has undermined many of the public health advances of the twentieth century. (Gandy and Zumla 2002:391–393)

A frequent assumption is that culture-specific ethnomedical systems may present an obstacle for proper treatment of disease *and* that their understanding is key in providing better biomedical health care. This idea underpins most research done under the rubric of "patients and healers," and it is exemplified in the work on TB carried out by Bastien in Bolivia (1992) and Menegoni (1996) in the highland Chiapas region of Mexico.

A widespread illness in the Andes is *liquichado* (Spanish), which Bastien (1992) identifies with TB. The major symptom is a relentless and irreversible loss of weight, which Andean peoples interpret as a progressive loss of body fat. This illness is believed to be caused by a *kharisiri,* or "cutter" of fat, who is widely viewed "as a doctor, lawyer, or priest who travels at night to remove fat from peasants" (1992:183–184). Bastien tells the story of Marcelino, a twenty-five-year-old sick with liquichado for a year. Treated with antibiotics by a health technician, Marcelino stopped taking them once he felt better. After a serious relapse, Marcelino's mother asked for help from the village shaman/healer and refused to send Marcelino to a hospital. She did so because she was convinced that her son would die there alone, and because she agreed with the shaman/healer that he was suffering from liquichado. Marcelino died soon thereafter. One possible reason his mother refused to send him to a hospital, suggests Bastien, is because "she didn't want to put her son in the hands of someone who was associated with the attributed cause of his sickness," because doctors, especially surgeons, are also sometimes viewed as kharisiris (1992:183–186). Bastien suggests that one effective option would have been "to have the doctor visit and treat Marcelino with the shaman and members of the family present so that they could observe the treatment" (1992:185). However, his suggestion does not grapple with the question of what to do when physicians are culturally viewed as kharisiris, nor does it adequately take into account the possibility that Marcelino and his family might not have had the resources to continue purchasing the required medications.

Menegoni's work in highland Chiapas, Mexico, also stresses the interplay of biomedical and ethnomedical approaches to TB, especially "the influence of cultural beliefs on the Indians' response to TB control programs" (1996:383). Called *sak obal* (white cough) in the local Mayan language, TB is widespread in Chiapas, which has an incidence rate almost three times that of Mexico as a whole. Due to Protestant proselytizing, many Mayas no longer view illness as the sole result of the concerted actions of supernatural beings. Although some ethnomedical beliefs and practices have declined, they have not been swept away by biomedical ones, for Mayas have reinterpreted biomedical categories through their more familiar ethnomedical concepts. For example, the idea of "strength" or "force" used to interpret the effectiveness of herbal medicines is also used for biomedical ones (Menegoni 1996:388).

Although many Mayas in Chiapas would like to see a doctor, they rarely use the public health system in San Cristóbal, the nearest town and administrative center, because of high transportation costs. Yet, for those that Menegoni studied who *did* have access to treatment, several reasons were responsible for the inadequate TB treatment they received. One was poor attention and supervision by biomedical staff, especially their inability to "maintain continuous rapport with patients and provide them with the necessary information and support to develop more positive attitudes and continue treatment" (Menegoni 1996:395). Cultural beliefs were also responsible for the lack of treatment completion. For example, some patients were unaware of the biological causes of TB, most attributing it to an aggravation of bronchitis or a cough; others to getting wet or of inhaling volcanic ashes. Menegoni concludes that

> local medical beliefs do not represent an absolute obstacle for tuberculosis interventions. But . . . they can lead to delays in diagnosis and abandonment of treatment . . . Extensive research with patients . . . has shown that problems of adherence to medical regimes are not solely rooted in the cultural differences existing between lay and professional explanatory models. (1996:396–397)

Farmer's approach to understanding TB and the conditions most responsible for its ravages is different, stemming as it does from a critical/political economy perspective. Reviewing how the culture concept has been employed in TB research, especially the emphasis placed on noncompliance with treatment regimes, Farmer claims that social scientists (including anthropologists) have often viewed local beliefs as an intractable obstacle to TB treatment. Ethnomedical beliefs and practices have often been seen as the main reason why so many infected with TB—and other contagious diseases, such as AIDS—die. His critique is that social scientists have adopted a **culturalist approach,** in which beliefs, values, and attitudes—and not inequality and differential power relations—are seen as the chief culprit for the spread of tuberculosis and the lack of adequate treatment. As a result, "the poor have no options but to be at risk for TB, and are thus from the outset victims of 'structural violence'" (Farmer 1997a:349). The concept of **structural violence,** originally coined by Liberation theologists (Chapter 7), draws attention to the effects of broad and pervasive patterns of poverty, inequality, and oppression that cut across cultural, ethnic, class, and gender boundaries (Farmer 2004a, 2004b).

Farmer provides a detailed case study of Robert David, a nineteen-year-old Haitian who in 1986 was afflicted with TB. Farmer emphasizes the structural impediments—"violence," Farmer would say—that Robert was subjected to. Robert's family brought him to a hospital, which was, however, two hours away by truck. During the first treatment regime, Robert's family members sold more than half of the land they owned to pay for his medications. Despite 1.5 years of irregular treatment, by 1989 he had still not recovered and his condition worsened in 1993. By then he was unable to purchase most medications due to lack of money, and some that he did purchase produced serious side effects. By now he had developed drug-resistant TB, and the drugs that he needed were not available in Haiti; meanwhile, others were prescribed to him, with little or no effect. He died in 1995.

This brief sketch suggests the thrust of Farmer's argument: Far too much research—and probably a biomedical "reading" of Robert David's death—underscores individual patients while neglecting the wider contexts of inequality and poverty that impede access to basic resources as the ultimate causes of TB. Paluzzi has emphasized a similar point in early twentieth-century Chile, which at that time had one of the highest incidences of TB mortality. She argues that the development of biomedical TB treatment options was accompanied by a shift in medical discourse away from the social contexts of TB transmission to one emphasizing "individual behaviors that were seen as deficient . . . and used as explanations for increased susceptibility" (2004:763).

If biomedical researchers have paid too little attention to the structural conditions of poverty and inequality underpinning drug-resistant TB, so have social scientists. Culture—in terms of either health beliefs held by TB-inflicted patients, or the inability of medical personnel to understand these beliefs—is far too often, suggests Farmer, construed by social scientists working in Haiti and elsewhere as a chief culprit. He strongly disagrees, stating for the particular context of Haiti that:

> It could be more easily argued that TB-control programs . . . have failed not through cultural insensitivity but rather through a lack of commitment to the destitute sick . . . We found that patients' etiologic beliefs did not predict their compliance with chemotherapy . . . what *did* predict adherence to therapy? Among patients offered free and convenient care, compliance and outcome were strongly related only to whether or not patients had access to supplemental food and income . . . cultural, political, and economic factors, although inevitably important, cannot be of equal significance in all settings. (Farmer 1997a:351–352)

According to Farmer, by elevating the causal status of culture while simultaneously downplaying structural inequality, social scientists—and many anthropologists—have conflated "structural violence with cultural difference." They have unwittingly done so by minimizing the role of poverty; exaggerating the agency of patients ("Calls to change 'lifestyle and behavior' are often made to precisely those persons whose agency is most constrained"); engaging in a "romanticism" of the ability of "folk healing" to treat tuberculosis; and, finally, by displaying insularity ("often unwilling to learn the basics of infectious disease or epidemiology") (1997a:354–355).

AIDS.   AIDS—an acronym that stands for acquired immunodeficiency syndrome, the final and typically fatal stage of the disease of the immune system caused by the human immunodeficiency virus (HIV)—is no doubt the most catastrophic public health crisis in recent memory, and possibly one of the deadliest diseases to assail humankind. Since the late 1970s, more than nineteen million people have perished from AIDS, and most of the almost thirty-seven million currently infected with the HIV virus will also die from the disease. Medical anthropologists have played an important role in AIDS-related research by highlighting the different ways in which cultural understandings of the body, reproduction, and etiology impede or facilitate the spread of the HIV virus (Barrett et al. 1998; Inhorn 1990; Bolton 1991; MacQueen 1994; Schoeph 2001; UNAIDS 2004a, 2004b).

Latin America and the Caribbean is an important epicenter of the AIDS epidemic, with more than two million people infected with the HIV virus and a prevalence rate (the proportion of adults fifteen- to forty-nine-years-old living with HIV/AIDS) of 2.8 percent, second only to sub-Saharan Africa's rate of 8.8 percent. Intravenous drug use and men having sex with men are the two major routes of transmission. Most HIV/AIDS cases have occurred in Brazil, while Haiti's prevalence rate of 5.6 percent is the highest of any country outside of sub-Saharan Africa. In Brazil, men who have sex with other men— not to be confused with prostitution or homosexuality—is an important avenue through which the HIV virus has spread, while in Haiti it has proliferated primarily through heterosexual intercourse (UNAIDS 2004a; Pan American Health Organization 2001a; see also Table 8.3).

Brazil.   At least five hundred thousand and perhaps more than seven-hundred-fifty thousand Brazilians are infected with HIV, and those numbers are increasing rapidly. After years of public denial—HIV and AIDS were considered a problem "in a distant world of entertainment, sexual perversion, and scandal far from the day-to-day realities of life for most Brazilians" (Larvie 2003:297)—Brazilian public health officials finally and openly recognized the widespread and critical public health threat posed by HIV/AIDS (Griffin and Vermelho 2002; Parker 1997). In the early 1980s, the HIV virus was centered in Brazil's southeastern region, especially in the cities of São Paulo and Rio de Janeiro; a decade later it was prevalent in all Brazil. HIV was first detected among middle-class, urban, "White" Brazilians; ten years later large numbers of Brazilians of all social, ethnic, racial, and class backgrounds were infected. The pace at which HIV has spread to every corner of Brazil's huge and varied landscapes, and across its social, cultural, and economic strata, is remarkable. This swiftness has much to do with migration:

> Over the course of . . . a decade, the epidemic has rapidly become centered in the poorest and most marginal sectors of Brazilian society . . . It is in the *favelas* . . . which are largely abandoned by the police and other authorities, that drug traffic is concentrated, that marginalized and stigmatized populations such as transvestite prostitutes, drug users, or others who are simply down on their luck, can find places to live . . . Community health services are at best limited, where they exist at all, and a range of different infirmities (sexually transmitted and otherwise) go undetected or untreated. In short, all of the social and

medical "cofactors" associated with high levels of HIV infection are found in abundant quantity, and it is in these areas that the AIDS epidemic has taken hold most firmly. (Parker 1997:63)

The popular and scientific media has emphasized deep and lasting connections between Brazilian sensuality, sexuality, and HIV/AIDS. This presumed link is not new, for "representations of Brazil and Brazilians as both sexually overactive and diseased" can be traced to the early colonial period, suggesting that Brazil's underdevelopment was in many ways a result of such a sexually hyperactive and diseased population, and the "policing of sexual customs primarily target[ing] the lower and working classes of the country's urban areas" also became an important part of health and legal policies through most of the twentieth century (Larvie 2003:291–296). Virtually identical representations and policies linking seemingly uncontrollable sexuality, disease, and poverty surfaced in Puerto Rico after its annexation by the United States in 1898 (Briggs 2002).

Nevertheless, the spread of HIV/AIDS is probably related to sexuality *and* its intersection with class inequality. In the early years of the HIV/AIDS epidemic, more than half of all infection cases were related to male–male sexual intercourse, especially among urban, middle-class Brazilians. By the early 1990s, HIV infection was part and parcel of intravenous drug use, which was at that time relatively new in Brazil. By the late 1990s, the highest rates (and numbers) of infection were male–female sexual transmission.

One of the most relevant and culturally meaningful approaches to the study of HIV/AIDS in Brazil has been the concept of multiple sexual identities or subcultures (Larvie 1997, 1999, 2003; Parker 1997; Terto 2000; Griffin and Vermelho 2002; see also Chapter 6). One important focus of HIV/AIDS–related public health efforts in Brazil has centered on male prostitutes, the efforts guided by the assumption that this segment of the population is an important vector of transmission. Paralleling these efforts are public images representing Brazil as a mecca of sensuality and open and unabashed sexuality, with ample opportunities for male-to-male sexual encounters—what Goldstein has called the "carnavalization of desire" (2003:226–259). These representations are closely linked to Brazil's sex tourism industry, for "male prostitutes constitute a sub-proletarian workforce that is simultaneously managed as a resource for and as a threat to Brazil in a context of transnational tourism and public health programs" (Larvie 1997:160).

Anthropological research has provided valuable insights into the world of male sex workers (*michês*). This is a broad category that can be divided into "hyper-masculine michês (hustlers) and . . . ultra-feminine *travestis* (very roughly transvestites or drag queens)" (Larvie 1997:150; see also Klein 2002), groupings that do not neatly overlap with gay or homosexual identities. The widespread view that michês have a high number of regular sexual partners—and that by having so many (paying) sexual partners their sexual behavior is a principal spur to the spread of HIV/AIDS—may also be mistaken. Michês can be further differentiated into a group of professionals who derive most of their income from selling sex, and a much larger group ("part-timers") with other sources of income, for whom getting paid for sex is merely part of the context for engaging in sex with other men:

The idea of sex for money provides the context—but does not constitute the principal objective—for sexual relations between many of the *michês* . . . sex work operates as an institution that provides a ritualized exchange (materials or symbolic payment) that justifies otherwise stigmatizing sex acts . . . As one truck driver . . . told us, "I'm not really here to earn money. But I only get to Rio once a year and this is one of the few places I know where I can meet other men." . . . In this sense, the act of "prostitution" may actually be more akin to a ritualized form of sexual transgression than the kind of sex-for-money transaction that occurs commonly among female and transvestite sex workers. (Larvie 1999:168)

Haiti.   The stigmatization of marginalized groups in a context of widespread anxiety sparked by the spread of invisible and deadly pathogens has been a recurrent episode in the history of infectious diseases (Berger 2004). Such was the case with the onset of the AIDS epidemic in the United States during the early 1980s, paralleled by widespread fear, speculation, rumors, and misguided scientific research that attributed the "cause" of this incurable disease to gay men, and homosexual and heterosexual Haitians in Haiti and the United States. The popular media, and many biomedical and social scientists—"seduced by the call of the wild" (Farmer 1992:3)—depicted Haitians as a distant "other," closer to untamed beasts than full members of humankind. Widely circulated images of diseased (and very black) Haitians swarming onto the shores of the United States were accompanied by portraits of ostensibly bizarre and ghastly—almost sub-human—vodou rituals that, allegedly, facilitated the spread of the HIV virus. In these popular images, seemingly buttressed by scientific research, race, sexuality, and culture conspired to condemn Haitians to what appeared to be a wretched future. How Haitians were represented is of course not unique, though perhaps extreme. Puerto Ricans at the beginning of the twentieth century were also represented by U.S. colonial officials as "black," debilitated, and diseased people that needed to be kept at bay and closely supervised, especially since they could reach the United States without legal impediments (Briggs 2002). And just as in the late 1980s, facets of Haitian culture—sexuality and vodou, for example—were singled out as the cause of the diseased and potentially dangerous Haitian body, so too seventy years earlier Puerto Rican culture, especially unrestrained sexuality and conjugal arrangements, were singled out as a "cause" of the wrenching poverty and high mortality that afflicted the island. The deep relationships between colonialism, scientific discourses, racism, and conceptions of health and sexuality are of course not limited to Latin America and the Caribbean (Stoler 1995, 2002).

Returning to Haiti, in 1986 Moore and LeBaron wrote the following of vodou and its possible association with HIV:

In frenzied trance, the priest lets blood: mamal's [sic] throats are cut; typically, chicken's [sic] heads are torn off their necks. The priest bites out the chicken's tongue with his teeth and may suck on the bloody stump of the neck . . . [These offerings are] . . . infected with one of the Type C oncogenic retroviruses, which is closely related to HTLV . . . [and the animals'] blood is directly ingested by priests and their assistants . . . many [of whom] . . . are homosexual men . . . in a position to satisfy their sexual desires, especially in urban areas. (1986: 81, 84; quoted by Farmer 1992:3)

Subsequent research has shown that this hyperbole linking sexuality, race, and culture was deeply flawed and misguided, and that rather than positing a link between race, "exotic" beliefs and practices, and the spread of HIV/AIDS, it is far more useful to focus on "the complex relationships between power, gender, and sexuality" (Farmer 1997b:414). It is mainly through heterosexual encounters that HIV/AIDS has spread in Haiti, and it is important to stress the structural positioning of the poor and destitute—particularly women—in its transmission. Haiti has one of the highest HIV/AIDS rates in Latin America and the Caribbean, a state of affairs worsened by one of the lowest life expectancy rates and exceedingly high infant and child mortality. Abject poverty, massive unemployment, and an appalling lack of medical facilities and services are part and parcel of the life conditions of ordinary Haitian men and women (Comerford 2002).

The life history of Guylene Adrien underscores the interplay of marginality, poverty, gender, and political inequality and insecurity in the spread of AIDS (Farmer 1997b). Born into a poor rural family, she was no more than fifteen years old when her father apparently cajoled her into engaging into a *plasaj* (consensual union) with Occident, a well-off peasant twenty years her senior. After the relationship broke up, Guylene—now with two small children, a girl and a boy—left her daughter with Occident's wife and spent time at her parents' house in another village.

Guylene entered into a second conjugal relationship, this time with Osner, a frequently unemployed mechanic. They moved to Port-au-Prince (Haiti's capital) in search of better prospects, leaving Guylene's infant son in the care of her mother. Her few years in Port-au-Prince were also hard. Osner was unable to find work, and Guylene was forced to work intermittently as a maid and street vendor. Personal tragedies soon struck. She first heard that her infant son (the one under the care of her mother) suddenly died and, shortly thereafter, Osner was diagnosed with tuberculosis. Osner died soon thereafter, leaving Guylene a pregnant widow.

Guylene had the baby and moved to her home village to be with her mother and only sister. Hunger was pervasive, so Guylene then moved in with some cousins in a nearby coastal town, working as their servant. She did this until her baby fell severely ill, and then she decided to return to the village where Osner's mother lived and where medical facilities were more available. Guylene, also very sick by this time, left her baby with Osner's mother and travelled again to Port-au-Prince in an unsuccessful quest for work. Soon after arriving in Port-au-Prince, she learned that her "baby died quite suddenly of cardiac failure, presumed secondary to HIV cardiomyopathy" (Farmer 1997b:419). Upon returning to Osner's mother's village, Guylene herself tested HIV positive. Even in her condition, soon thereafter Guylene entered into a short-lived conjugal relationships with a soldier stationed nearby.

Guylene's life history provides deep insights into the vulnerability of poor women and their heightened risk of AIDS, as well the structural underpinnings of HIV transmission. Indeed, it is their quest for economic security and some sense of control over their lives that almost paradoxically makes poor Haitian women so vulnerable to HIV/AIDS. Poor women's gender inequality, poverty, and a generalized sense of powerlessness to control the quality of their lives are the most important roots of HIV/AIDS transmission in Haiti. These structural conditions are at the core of marital unions and sexual relationships (stable consensual unions as well as serial monogamy) that significantly heighten their risk to HIV. This in turn takes place in a context of poor health and nutrition, and an absence of culturally sensitive biomedical health care (Farmer 1997b:424).

Gender and Health

Farmer tells us that "of all the millions of persons on the losing end of the system, few are more trammeled by punitive constraints than are Haitian women living in poverty. For poor Haitian women, often enough, the structures are more like strictures" (1997b:424). Guylene's tragic life history highlights the fact that health is not "gender blind" (Macintyre 2001) and that Latin American and Caribbean women, especially poor and marginalized women, are far more likely than men to experience ill health.

Gendered discrimination and the differential allocation of food and nutrition within the domestic domain probably account for the fact that female infants and children (i.e., those under five years of age) are more likely to die than males. A Mexican proverb succinctly captures what is almost certainly a widespread pattern leading to malnutrition, ill-health, and subsequent susceptibility to a range of potentially fatal diseases: "Cuando la comida es poca, a la niña no le toca" (When there is little food, the little girl gets none) (Gómez 1993:26). Other data point to a similar gendered skewing of health, for women are more likely to be diabetic and suffer rheumatoid arthritis and osteoporosis than are men. Such inequities have not gone unnoticed, and the emergence of "gender and development" and "gender and health" as important research foci is a first step toward addressing these deeply entrenched inequities (Debert-Ribeiro 1993; de los Ríos 1993). The social context is also important, for in Mexico (and probably elsewhere) boys and girls are far healthier when immersed in wider networks of kin and relatives (Kanaiaupuni et al. 2005).

Yet, material deprivations and inequities, while obviously crucial, are not the sole causes of the gap between male and female health. The cultural and social context within which men and women live out their everyday lives—including the gender system of which it forms part—also plays an important role. Women, Finkler tells us, are far more prone than men to experience **life's lesions**—"The perceived adversity of existence, including inimical social relationships and unresolved contradictions . . . which gnaw at the person's being [and] become inscribed on the body" (1994:15–16). In Mexico City, these life's lesions strike women more often than men, making them more susceptible to experiencing psychosomatic ailments. These lesions are rooted in adverse, unresolved, and contradictory cultural and gender relationships and expectations, including women's lack of autonomy and power within the domestic domain, ideologies stressing female passivity and subordination (sexual and otherwise), male infidelity, and systematic lack of commitment to the economic well-being of women and their children (see In Their Own Words 8.1).

These and other reasons are also why women are more likely to experience the folk illnesses of susto, mal de ojo, or nervios (see the following section, "Folk Illnesses: Susto, Mal de Ojo, and Nervios"). Women's illness is often attributed to emotional releases in the form of anger, nerves, or susto. Yet it is the public and uncontrollable display of anger that is widely attributed to be the major cause or explanation for a wide range of illnesses. Although males also experience lesions, Finkler makes the point that the same gender system that generates illness among women shields males from some of the worst consequences of their own lesions:

> Men are shielded from sickness . . . in ways that women are not . . . The . . . contradictions men must face become attenuated or obliterated by the coherence

IN THEIR OWN WORDS **8.1**

Women in Mexico City and Life's Lesions

Margarita is a thirty-seven-year-old married woman. She views herself as a "sick person" and displays symptoms of depression. Her words illustrate life lesions that some women experience in Mexican society (Finkler 1994:91–113).

Growing Up: "I had the life of a dog in my parents' house because I was made to work unceasingly, and because my father beat my mother and my sisters . . . He even beat my brothers, particularly the one who was very dark . . ."

An Abusive Father: "When I was a child I noticed my father's strange conduct. When I was eleven years old, my father . . . looked at me out of the corner of his eye, and I had a terrible desire to have sex . . . and I became very tense . . . Since then whenever my father came close to me . . . I put my hands around my breasts . . . in the car . . . he always brushed around my breasts with his arm."

Relationship with Husband: "I could not live with this man . . . He was very jealous. I was locked up all day until he got home . . . My parents never stepped through the door of my house . . . I was eighteen years old then . . . and he went out with women thirty-five years old . . . But he wanted me to stay with him because he said I would be beaten if I went back to my father."

How Margarita Interprets Her Illness. "I am sick because of my situation as a woman, my mental norms and moral rules. My situation is not the way I wanted it. I could not do anything. If I wanted to work to earn money I would have had to leave the bosom of my family, and where would I go with my child, who would support me? They had me against the wall."

---

they encounter at home as the rightful heads of the household. In their households men are protected from external assaults, while women suffer sickness-producing affronts to their beings above and beyond those incurred by the world outside the home, owing to the dominant ideology of male superiority and the culturally accepted rights men have over them. Men's hegemonic superiority by virtue of their sex cushions them against assaults on their beings in the private and public domains. The ruling ideology supports male superiority and privilege, mitigating against life's lesions and protecting them from sickness. (Finkler 1994:46–47)

Folk Illnesses: Susto, Mal de Ojo, and Nervios

Susto, mal de ojos (*mau-olhado,* Portuguese), and *nervios* (*nervos,* Portuguese) are three of the better-known and widespread popular or folk illnesses in Latin America and the Caribbean, and among Hispanics/Latinos in North America. These three illnesses are often studied together because their symptoms, etiologies, and treatment modalities overlap considerably. For the past fifty years, anthropologists studying these illnesses have emphasized their occurrence across ethnic, linguistic, geographic, and class boundaries (Uzzell 1974; O'Nell 1975; Rubel 1977; Bastien 1992; Scheper-Hughes 1992; Baer and Bustillo 1993; Rebhun 1994; Guarnaccia et al. 1989, 1990, 1996). Further, these illnesses are almost always diagnosed and treated by ethnomedical healers (Huber and Sandstrom 2001). Biomedical practitioners—who often classify these illnesses as ill-defined psychosomatic disorders—are rarely sought out for help because few understand the social and cultural context, and the linguistic medium, through which these illness surface and are rationalized. In her review of herbal practices in folk medicine Alcorn (1990:259) states that "few subjects are debated as emotionally as the question of whether folk medicines prescribed to treat the litany of ailments from hemorrhoids to stomach aches really work or are simply the superstitious garble of ignorant peoples." Identical debates have surrounded the diagnosis and treatment of susto, mal de ojos, and nervios.

Susto (fright; sometimes also called espanto) is an illness characterized by the presence of one or more of the following symptoms: loss of appetite, listlessness, lack of interest or motivation in daily activities, apathy, nausea, diarrhea, irritability, weakness, and withdrawal. Men and women, young and old, and even infants and children may experience susto—although some are more susceptible than others.

Any number of seemingly unrelated events may spark susto—from falling off a ladder to a snake bite to engaging in a brawl—but all entail a sudden and unexpected event that startles, frightens, or produces anxiety. In some cases—especially in indigenous contexts—susto is associated with the temporary departure of the individual's soul. Further, many susto cases arise after a dispute, potential argument, violent encounter, unjust outcome, unhappy event, or life threatening situation that produces emotional pain, feelings of hostility, or outright anger, and that invariably draws in others. For example, Rubel (1977:199–201) writes about a woman in a small Guatemalan village who finds her husband in a relationship with another woman; when she proceeds to scold him, he hits her with a rock and she came down with susto. O'Nell (1975:59) discusses a case that took place in Mexico, in the middle of a house warming party. The brother of the hostess, quite drunk and raging with jealously, grabbed a machete and threatened guests. Unexpected death can also lead to susto, as when a woman in the Brazilian northeast suffered a miscarriage (Rebhun 1994:373), or when an Aymara-speaking Bolivian peasant lost his son (Bastien 1992:134–135).

Mal de ojo (evil eye) often presents symptoms similar to susto, but in the case of children may also include high fever, severe diarrhea, and constant crying (Baer and Bustillo 1993:92). In the Brazilian northeast, children suffering from *mal olhado* (Portuguese for evil eye) may also display symptoms of dehydration and ear infection (Rebhun 1994:371). The underlying cause of mal de ojo is more straightforward than with susto. Invariably, mal de ojo surfaces when a person experiencing envy or jealously unintentionally or (as is more often the case) deliberately gazes upon another person. Jealously, envy, anger, resentment, or illegitimate desires ignite a potential for mal de ojo. In such a context, those who are well-nourished are at risk of mal de ojo from the emaciated; the wealthy from the poor; fertile women from those who cannot bear children; those who feel betrayed from those who they think betrayed them; the lucky from the unfortunate.

Rebhun (1994) provides an example of mal olhado from the Brazilian northeast. The case concerns Nezinha, a thirty-five-year-old woman who, when much younger, ran away with and married her boyfriend, with whom she had three children. After her husband abandoned her, she moved into her parents' home. But this move shattered the hope that her brother had in moving into his parents' house after his own marriage. Tensions and resentments began to pile up between Nezinha and her mother (they never got along very well), and her brother and his fiancée. According to Nezinha, the situation worsened (and she became "sick" with mal olhado) when her

> brother had an affair with a friend of mine. So my mother liked it a lot, because she didn't like his fiancée and she hoped he would leave her. So she told the fiancée about the affair in hopes they would break up. But he left my friend. So then my mother . . . said to the fiancée that I was the one who arranged . . . the affair . . . but I didn't, it's a lie. So the fiancée had a fight with my brother. So now my brother is angry at me, thinking that I told his fiancée . . . The fiancée hates me because she believes my mother's untrue story. My friend is angry at me . . . because she thinks I told . . . Everybody is mad at me . . . And here I am without being able to sleep, with a headache, constantly sick. (Rebhun 1994:372)

Nervios, also called attack of nerves (*ataque de nervios,* Spanish; *ataque de nervos,* Portuguese), is primarily identified by a heightened sense of irritability, shakiness, dizziness, occasional fainting or loss of consciousness, crying, trembling, anger, rage, and bouts of violence. It is a combination of these symptoms, coupled with a loss of emotional and bodily control, that distinguishes nervios from susto and mal de ojos (Scheper-Hughes 1992:167–215; Rebhum 1994:368-369; Guarnaccia et al. 1996:345). Individuals experiencing *ataque de nervios* are unable to cope with the stresses and challenges of everyday life; loss of control is a key symptom. Emotional expressions include depression, screaming, anger. Trembling, convulsions, and seizures are some somatic sensations. Behavioral responses can include aggression toward others or suicidal feelings, and changes in consciousness (fainting, amnesia, dizziness, or hallucinations) are not uncommon (Guarnaccia et al. 1996:350). See In Their Own Words 8.2 for more details.

Most anthropologists would agree that those who characteristically suffer ataque de nervios are the poor, disenfranchised members of society, where class and ethnicity loom important, because for the most part, this illness has been "identified among people of poor, rural origins—people who either live in peripheral areas of developed countries . . . or who are poor migrants to major urban centers" (Davis and Guarnaccia 1989:10). Hence, ataque de nervios is a cultural and somatic "idiom of distress" (Davis and Guarnaccia 1989:5; Guarnaccia et al. 1989:47) that communicates, via bodily and emotional expressions, social tensions, disruptions in family support systems, deprivations, and other social pressures. In this context, the body signals personal and shared suffering, as well as an important culturally acceptable venue through which individuals and groups can remark on what they perceive to be the roots of their suffering (Lock 1993:142). Gender is also an important prism through which to understand nervios, for women are far more susceptible than men in experiencing an ataque de nervios (Rebhun 1994:369; Guarnaccia et al. 1996:361).

Ataque de Nervios Among Puerto Ricans

Listening to people's own words and commentaries is often the best way to fully understand the nature of an illness. The following commentaries by Puerto Ricans who have experienced—or seen others experience—an ataque de nervios is a case in point (Guarnaccia et al. 1996):

> An ataque de nervios is a person who loses total control of her/himself, and without having control, without having any control over her/his person, is aggressive towards others or towards her/himself.
>
> They burst out screaming, they cry out, they begin to break things. They become agitated, anxious. They feel desperate. I have seen people who even lose consciousness. They burst out crying.
>
> I have seen people . . . that . . . scream, maybe even fall to the floor. I have seen them foaming at the mouth even though they are not epileptic, they become very rigid. There are people whose eyes roll back (without being attacks of epilepsy, but of nerves), even their mouths become twisted.
>
> He "passed out" and he grabbed and pushed someone and then when he woke up he had no memory of having done it.

Scheper-Hughes (1992:167–215) reminds us that shantytown women experiencing nerves are not only poor, marginalized, and in a constant state of insecurity, but are also malnourished, sick, and hungry—and they probably die sooner than others. Her point is paralleled by Bastian's observation that after the closing of major mines in Bolivia in the late 1980s, many former miners who went to a clinic complaining of susto were diagnosed with anemia and tuberculosis (1992:182). And Baer and Bustillo (1993:91) cite studies that in Oaxaca, Mexico, susto is associated with higher rates of morbidity and mortality. Perhaps the message here is that cultural explanations and analyses of folk illnesses should be accompanied by a focus on the political–economic context within which they occur, and that susto, mal de ojos, and nervios are better approached at the crossroads of ethno- and biomedicine.

The Expressive and Healthy Body

Anthropologists have repeatedly shown that how the human body is perceived in non-Western contexts is usually at odds with naturalistic explanations and models shared by biomedical practitioners. Almost without exception, the human body's physiological processes and anatomical makeup are understood cross-culturally as mirroring and providing an analytical backdrop to social relationships and cultural expectations.

Anthropologists working in the field of the **anthropology of the body** have stressed that indigenous peoples do not share the view of the radical separation between mind and body, and nature and culture, that so deeply pervades Western thought and culture. Hence, many believe that the biomedical paradigm privileging the human body as a biological entity to the exclusion of the social and cultural borders on ethnocentrism and is limited in its ability to further the cross-cultural understanding of illness and health. Research has emphasized the importance of how "social categories are literally inscribed on and into the body" and how work on "embodied experience" can help in furthering knowledge of the diagnosis and treatment of illness and health (Lock 1993:133–137). Related work has centered on an **anthropology of the emotions** and how the body serves as a core metaphor through which to express personal and collective emotional states (Guarnaccia et al. 1996).

Bodies, Communities, and Mountains in the Andes

For the Aymara-speaking Qollahuaya of highland Bolivia, the anatomy and physiology of their bodies mirror the high mountain dwellings of the spiritual beings with whom the Qollahuaya engage in a variety of reciprocal relationships, and within which their kin-based communities (*ayllus*) are located. Their "topographical-hydraulic model" views the human body "as a vertical axis with three levels through which blood and fat flow from the center to the peripheral in centripetal and centrifugal motion" (Bastien 1985:595–596). This reflects the three ecological tiers into which the Qollahuaya divide their mountain landscapes, which also coincide with the geographic positioning of their three ayllus. The highest tier has a head (*uma*), eyes (*ñawi*), and a mouth (*wayra*); the stomach (*sixa*) and heart (*sonco*) are located in the second, lower tier; the lowest level displays the legs (*chaquis*) and toenails (*sillus*).

This ethnophysiology of the body also echoes how the Qollahuaya view their landscape, social world, and bodies in symmetrically corresponding ways. The physiology of the body depends on a constant flow and flushing of fluids and substances—blood, semen, urine, fat, and the like. Likewise, cross-cutting kinship ties, community-wide rituals at shrines dotting the three tiers, as well as an exchange of resources between the three ecological tiers, is what gives their mountains and communities a wholeness, in just the same way that the interdependence of body parts and flow of fluids imparts to the human body its overall integrity. These views have implications for their understanding and treatment of illness. Because the body, landscape, and social relations form a whole, the Qollahuaya view of illness privileges culturally inappropriate behavior or the breaking of social norms or sanctions. This view also holds toward the landscape, for if the Qollahuaya are careless during planting, or fail to carry out appropriate agricultural rituals, the mountains become ill and fail to provide them sustenance.

An important illness category entails the loss of bodily fluids. Liquichado, structurally equivalent to tuberculosis (see previous discussion of TB) is the result of the loss of symbolically important body fat, which is construed as the result of malignant actions of others. If they urinate in a cave at night, sometimes women may be the cause of diarrhea among children. Qollahuaya suffering from susto display symptoms such as melancholy, slight fever, and lack of appetite, as well as a loss of body fluids that ultimately are absorbed by the earth.

Healing practices—and the Qollahuaya are famous Andean ritual healers—are of two major types. The first is to engage in rituals in which healers "feed" the earth at shrines dotting the three landscape tiers by offering coca, blood, and fat. Second, healers center their therapeutic and healing practices on enhancing the restoration and circulation of bodily liquids and substances, and on eliminating noxious ones, especially through the use of a wide spectrum of therapeutic plants.

Body and Knowledge in Lowland South America

The Cashinahua of Amazonian Brazil and Peru have a different conception of the body. Yet, like the Qollahuaya, they too view body anatomy and physiology as an expressive medium and in primarily social ways (McCallum 1996). The developmental trajectory of the Cashinahua body is not simply a result of natural or biological processes. Neither do the Cashinahua make a sharp distinction between mind and body. Rather, the body is "made to grow" by an interaction with its environment, particularly its social context, and through the agency of humans (especially kin) and spiritual beings with whom the body comes into contact. As such, the body's development and well-being are construed in primarily social terms.

Central importance is attached to the role of knowledge in the body's proper biological and social development. This ongoing process of learning from others involves "the inscription of knowledge into body parts in a material sense . . . [and] . . . different parts of the body are the loci of different kinds of knowledge" (McCallum 1996:355). For instance, the body's skin can acquire "skin knowledge" through the direct intercession of one of the spirits inhabiting the body, as when certain root plants are rubbed onto a man's hands, an action that generates "hand knowledge" that enables him to be a good hunter. Acquisition of "knowledge" through the ears via, for example, speech and song, also aids in the development of sociality, a crucial dimension of normal development. Such a view is also very much related to one of the ways the Cashinahua and other Amazonian peoples such as the Barasana construe health and illness: because "the skin and the body orifices are thought of as organs that ought to allow the passage of beneficial knowledge into the body or else impede the entrance of destructive agents," diarrhea "means that life forces go out"—a potentially dangerous condition (McCallum 1996:356). Because "life forces" interact with kin and supernatural beings, illness is a socially produced condition:

> If health is a combination of accumulated knowledge and the ability to act on it socially, illness can be understood as *a disturbance in the body's capacity to know* . . . When ill, a person runs the double risk of loss of memory of (and desire for) kin, and a surfeit of capacity to know "others"—the dead or spirits. (McCallum 1996:363)

Jamaican Bodies: Health, Sexuality, and Gender

Sobo (1993) has researched how poor rural Jamaican women and men conceptualize the body and its relationship to health and illness. The body is an open, porous, permeable organism that should remain "equalized"—clean and thermally regulated. Eating is necessary to "build up" the body, especially the vitally important blood. Foods such as soups and tomatoes are especially good at building blood, yet cooked pork is especially prized as a builder of blood. A healthy person is one who is fat, happy, and generous; by contrast, unhappiness and a-social behavior drain or "melt" body fat, a situation that thin and emaciated people have gone through (Sobo 1993:32–35).

Health is also contingent on a proper balance between an intake of bodily fluids and substances through the "belly" and their discharge through the "tripe" (intestines). The proper discharge ("wash out") enhances the purity of the blood and helps keep the belly "clean." Other potential causes of illness include not maintaining an adequate temperature, that is, of being "cold" as opposed to "hot." One way the body becomes too hot is when a person engages in too much physical labor, although a constant state of physical inactivity can then make people (and bodies) too "cold," and therefore interrupt the healthy and necessary flow of bodily liquids and substances. Illness is metaphorically equated with the life cycle of fruits which, when too soft, decompose and must be disposed of.

Maintaining health means preserving the body's internal equilibrium by monitoring the intake and discharge of substances and protecting it from anti-social or evil beings. Ill-health can surface as a result of malicious actions of kin, community members, or evil spirits, who wreak havoc with the body's balance and its ability to incorporate healthy substances and release them before they rot. This in turn is a symbolic pointer to disruptive social relationships and a lack of equilibrium in the wider social world. Thus, people who are healthy and

> "live good" cannot, ideally, be caught by socially precipitated sickness: sickness instigated in response to perceived affronts by an animate being (a neighbor, a demon, God, or a duppy [ancestral ghost] sent by a . . . "grudgeful" villager). In an ideal world, a moral, sociable person could never anger anyone enough to attack . . . When sickness strikes, then, the moral and social well-being of the victim appears to others to be in a questionable state. (Sobo 1993:294)

These interpretations also provide insights regarding Jamaican views on sexuality and reproduction. A "hot" body—one in which the pores are "open" and able to incorporate and expunge internal substances before, like fruit, they rot—is also stimulated by sexual intercourse. Sex is referred as "work," and both promote overall health. Fertility is highly prized, for being able to conceive is a sure sign of health, as is sexual intercourse, although too much of the latter, like work, can turn a body too "cold." Sperm ("germs") accumulating in a man's scrotum ("seed bag") too long can be a health risk; as a result, intercourse involves "clearing the line" and avoiding "discharge" from accruing in the body. Root tonics are consumed by men, who believe that these "build" and "clean" blood, actions which swell sexual potency. For women, orgasm and menstruation are opportunities to discharge semen and other toxic matter. Sperm is believed to make women "fat," and thus sexually appealing. Men usually do not have intercourse with menstruating women, believing that such a practice puts their body into contact with decomposing (and therefore unhealthy) semen.

Religion and Healing

Religious and healing beliefs and practices overlap in manifold ways. This is partly because religion, especially in indigenous, non-Western societies, entails a broader view of the relationships between mortals and the supernatural, and a strong undercurrent of sociality. Concepts of good, evil, and the afterlife are made sense of during the exigencies of daily life, including grappling with illness.

Shamanism, Ritual Poetics, and Hallucinogenic Healing

Shamanism is a religious system marked by the belief that specific persons—shamans—have the ability to directly communicate with the supernatural through a trance or possession experience (Atkinson 1992). Sometimes overlapping with popular Catholicism and Afro–Latin religious traditions (discussed in Chapter 7), shamanism is widespread in Latin America (Taussig 1987; Reichel-Dolmatoff 1975; Langdon and Baer 1992; Jackson 1975:325; Crocker 1985; Furst 1987; Gow 1994).

The shaman's body is the medium through which spirit powers are mobilized, and the bodily experience of possession is crucial for the success of the shamanistic experience. The trance experience is usually viewed as a temporary departure of the shaman's soul, which embarks on a journey into the spirit world. Unlike death, the shaman's spirit returns to his/her body. Possession entails an almost literal invasion of the shaman's body, usually signaled by the onset of ecstatic and seemingly uncontrollable behavior. It is by allowing himself/herself to become a human receptacle of the spirits that the shaman is able to temporarily control and channel their powers.

Trance possession is often accompanied by the consumption of ritually significant mind and body altering substances, such as tobacco, hallucinogens, or alcohol. Such is the case of the Arawak-speaking Wakuéai peoples of Colombia, Venezuela, and Brazil in the northwestern Amazon region, whose shamans can muster the powers of influential and omniscient tobacco spirits. Shamanistic ceremonies are accompanied by highly ritualized, frenzied dancing and playing of music. Among the Wakuéai, as well as other Amazonian groups, songs and chants constitute an effective means of harnessing the powers of supernatural deities (Hill 1993). Vidal's summary of early nineteenth century European descriptions of some of these ceremonies among Arawak-speaking peoples in the Orinoco River basin of northern South America are reminiscent of some ceremonies still carried out today:

> These religious festivals could last for more than eight days and were described as ceremonies in which men, or men and women, danced and slashed each other with a whip . . . after the lashes, the men gathered together, smoking tobacco, snuffing *yopo* [a hallucinogenic drug], and drinking fermented beer. Rituals were accompanied by martial and festival musical instruments that included drums, trumpets, and flutes. (Vidal 2002:264)

Shamans are intermediaries between "this" and "that" world, harnessing the powers of supernatural beings for various ends. Shamans play a crucial role as guardians of the social order and mediators of inter-personal conflicts, and thereby an important political role. They are also invariably healers of some kind, diagnosing and treating illness, and inter-

PHOTO 8.1   *A seventy-eight-year-old shaman from the Inga tribe of Colombia's Amazon prepares a batch of a hallucinogenic drink called yage. Bogotá, Colombia.*

preting causes of death (Dobkin de Ríos 1972; Joralemon 1993; Bastien 1992: 72-104; Atkinson 1992; Winkelman 1990; see Photo 8.1).

There are many kinds of shamanistic healing practices and beliefs, but all rely on an intimate knowledge of the local flora and the transformation of plants into substances that are consumed and that allow healers to harness or redirect evil forces or beings. Many healing practices also involve the use of poetic chants—what Hill (1993:192) calls "curing music" and Gow (1991:236) labels "curing songs"—that channel spiritual forces for curing purposes. Ritualized poetic chants for healing purposes—that express what is known as **ritual power** (Comaroff and Comaroff 1993), or the ability to harness authority or legitimacy through ritual means—are especially prominent among the Wakuénai people of Amazonian Venezuela, where singing

> is the prescribed treatment for diseases of the genital organs, neurological disorders, nightmares, and children's behavioral problems (e.g., temper tantrums or frequent crying). In addition, there are several shorter . . . chants for treating specific diseases, such as severe headaches and skin rashes. . . . For the most part, curing rituals are brief events in which . . . songs are performed for only a few minutes. However, when a person suffers from severe, life-threatening illness, curing rituals become prolonged events in which both ritual curers, the chant-owner and the shaman, combine their powers in an effort to avert death. (Hill 1993:192)

We should be wary of viewing the shamanism and associated ritual lore and practice of Amazonian societies in isolation from broader historical forces, including the (often deadly) presence of Western peoples and economic webs that have in so many ways profoundly and irrevocably shaped Amazonian peoples' destinies (Tierney 2000; Taussig 1987; Roosevelt 1994). Thus, among the Carib-speaking Patamuna people of Guyana, the specific variety of shamanism involving chants, called alleluia, is a late nineteenth century invention sparked by contact with missionaries (Whitehead 2002:5), and it is probably related to encroaching trade networks. Similarly, the curing music and healing rituals of the Venezuela Wakuénai have much to do with the spread of eighteenth century European-introduced diseases, as well as more contemporary events, such as a 1980 measles epidemic (Hill 1993:162–187). In lowland Colombia, shamanistic knowledge and practices revolving around malignant beings and forces are an outcome of and response to wider political–economic intrusions, such as the violence, exploitation, and usurpation of land and undermining of livelihoods associated with expansion of sugar plantations and extractive rubber estates (Taussig 1987).

Health, illness, and death surface conspicuously in the relationship between shamanism, healing, and the consumption of hallucinogenic, consciousness-altering plants, especially in lowland Amazonia (Harner 1973; Jackson 1975:324–327; Furst 1987). Cross-culturally, the consumption of hallucinogenic and other consciousness-altering plants and substances takes place in highly ritualized and meaningful contexts associated with reaching out to the supernatural, striving for health, and grappling with illness and misfortune. The cultural importance attached to states of "altered consciousness" in highly ritualized and socially sanctioned settings has been succinctly stated by Davis:

> The Amerindian enters the realm of the hallucinogenic visions not out of boredom, or to relieve . . . restless anxiety, but rather to fulfill some collective need of the group. In the Amazon . . . hallucinogens are taken to divine the future, track the paths of enemies, ensure the fidelity of women, diagnose and treat diseases. The Huichol in Mexico eat their peyote at the completion of long arduous pilgrimages in order that they may experience in life the journey of the soul of the dead to the underground. The Amahuaca Indians of Peru drink yage that the nature of the forest animals and plants may be revealed to their apprentices . . . But whatever the ostensible purpose of the hallucinogenic journey, the Amerindian imbibes his plants in a highly structured manner that places a ritualistic framework of order around their use. Moreover, the experience is explicitly sought for positive ends. It is not a means of escaping from an uncertain existence; rather it is perceived as a means of contribution to the welfare of all one's people. (1985:193; for other important studies that have emphasized the important role of hallucinogenic plants in healing rituals, see Castañeda 1968 and Myerhoff 1974).

One of the most widespread and well-known hallucinogenic plants is *ayahuasca* (also *yajé, yagé,* or *yage*), a vine that when boiled and fermented produces a thick beverage (also called ayahuasca) with powerful hallucinogenic properties. (See Photo 8.1) It is especially consumed by lowland Amazonian groups in Colombia, Ecuador, Peru, and Venezuela, where it is used in religious rituals, divination and witchcraft, as an aphrodisiac, and in healing rituals (Dobkin de Ríos 1972; Taussig 1987; Gow 1991).

Ayahuasca healing rituals in Amazonian Peru have been studied by Dobkin de Ríos in Iquitos (1972) and Gow in nearby Bajo Urubamba (1991) Both areas are ethnically mixed and conflictive frontier regions. Shamanistic healing and the consumption of ayahuasca are widespread among all ethnic groups and social classes, but are particularly prominent among those at the bottom of the local social and economic hierarchy.

Two major categories of illnesses are known in Iquitos and Bajo Urubamba. The first, called "God-given" ailments in Iquitos and *cutipa* (Quechua) in Bajo Urubamba, point to conditions that are part and parcel of life routines, of the hazards of everyday life. In Iquitos, these God-given and seemingly treatable ailments, such as colds, infections, and bruises, are usually first treated by local healers (*curanderos, empíricos*), who often end up referring their patients to biomedical technicians (*sanitarios*) or, far less often, physicians. Treatment typically entails store-bought pharmaceutical remedies.

A second, more serious, category of illness consists of those caused by the purposeful actions of others. They often develop into life-threatening conditions. In Iquitos, the culprits are evil people (who are often neighbors or kin), or demons and jungle spirits whose powers have been harnessed by malicious human beings. These God-given ailments that unexplainably worsen, or that can come about when a patient is beset by a host of locally defined illnesses that defy biomedical treatment, are structurally analogous to the "sent" illnesses in the Haitian context (see the following section, "Medicine and Religious Pluralism," for additional details). (Interestingly enough, and in stark contrast to Iquitos, in the Bajo Urubamba region studied by Gow, illnesses "sent" by God are serious epidemics and seemingly incurable illnesses viewed as a retribution for sinful behavior.)

Diagnosis and treatment are carried out by local healers or shamans, "those who know" (*los que saben;* Gow 1991:237). Healers in Iquitos treat patients with a range of tonics, herbal preparations, and the like, often taking advantage of their detailed knowledge of the local flora and potentially useful medicinal plants. This intimate ethnobotanical knowledge and awareness of local biodiversity is not limited to eastern Peru: in the lowland Putumayo region of Colombia, for example, a shaman/herbalist has knowledge of the therapeutic properties of thousands of plants (Taussig 1987;285), and an equally impressive knowledge is well documented from Brazilian Amazonia (Wayland 2001).

Virtually all healers in Iquitos and Bajo Urubamba are *ayahuasqueros,* or shamans whose diagnosis and treatment repertoire pivot around the use of ayahuasca. Patients and healers alike attempt to understand why a condition (such as a bruise) has worsened or why an ailment (such as susto) has surfaced. This quest of understanding the "why" invariably requires seeking out and identifying underlying social referents. Most local people believe that serious illness originates in **witchcraft,** that is, the malignant use or deployment of supernatural powers. Envy, jealousy, revenge, grudges, and unresolved quarrels are some of the immediate causes of harm (*daño,* Spanish), which are inflicted by some on others through evil magic. Illness is above all a social phenomenon that points to disruptions in the social field. Ayahuasqueros consequently concentrate on ailments generated by evil magic and with social or interpersonal referents:

> Magical beliefs . . . are by no means limited to affairs of the heart, but rather are a general, persistent affirmation that people at the bottom are cruel and envious, and can cause harm to others in the form of a generalized malice. Found

among the poor and middle-income segments of the community, [are] beliefs
in evil-wishing as well as the varied illnesses that *ayahuasqueros* are called
upon to heal with the powerful potion of ayahuasca. (Dobkin de Ríos 1972:65)

Ayahuasca healing sessions usually take place at night in a jungle clearance, and they are
usually attended by small clusters of people who suffer related symptoms. Close to midnight, the healer distributes the ayahuasca beverage and is usually the last one to drink it.
Ayahuasca drinking is often accompanied by chants and songs in Quechua, although most
participants address each other in Spanish. Visions and hallucinations are a means through
which healers "reach" the afflicted area of the body (Dobkin de Ríos 1972:72).

Medicine and Religious Pluralism

Brodwin's ethnography (1996) exemplifies how in rural Haiti, **religious pluralism** (the
coexistence and complementarity of different religious systems), biomedicine, and ethnomedicine compete and complement each other in the diagnosis and treatment of illness. In
Haiti, biomedicine is widely accepted. In the streets and roads, and in urban and rural marketplaces, it is easy to find an array of peddlers selling a wide variety of pills, syringes, and
other biomedical supplies. Further, those who have the means to send the sick to clinics do
so, while at the same time relying on midwives, herbalists, and healers (Brodwin 1996:56).

But why have two complementary medical systems? The answer has to do with how
illnesses are classified and causality conceptualized, as well as the options available in the
event that biomedicine fails. Haitians distinguish between two broad illness categories. The
first is made up of illnesses that ought to be easily treated; these are "of" or "sent" by
"God." The second, potentially far more serious, category includes those illnesses that defy
biomedical treatment—those that clinics, hospitals, and physicians are unable to cure;
these are "sent" by "Satan" (see also Farmer 1992). As Brodwin explains:

A biomedical cure for an illness . . . means that it was caused by unremarkable
natural processes ("an illness of God"). But when biomedicine fails, people
classify the illness as "satanic," that is, caused by other humans. This diagnosis
endangers the moral status of the ill individual and inaugurates the search for
healing from Catholic, Protestant, and vodoun practitioners. (1996:23–24)

Brodwin provides a case study of a young man severely injured in motorcycle accident
who, despite repeated visits to hospitals, eventually died. His death "did not indict biomedicine . . . people considered the inability of biomedicine to cure . . . not as a marker of
biomedicine's weakness, but rather as a sign that [his] illness was an illness of Satan . . .
not . . . of God" (Brodwin 1996:95). The ultimate cause of a potentially life-threatening illness of Satan—which, again, is "sent" by someone—is, of course, social. Envy, jealousy,
and lack of social harmony are examples of contexts that spur the malicious sending of
sickness. But then who is most likely to experience such an illness? Most likely those who
stand out from the rest, who do not fit in, who break loose of social conventions, such as
those who succeed, unexpectedly become wealthy, or "capture" for themselves and/or their
immediate family resources that are outside the reach of most. This ideology obviously
points to how medical beliefs serve as mechanisms of social control. Women are especially

vulnerable to affliction by Satan's illnesses, especially those women trying to break free of conventional gender roles (Brodwin 1996:183).

Ethnomedical beliefs and practices are intertwined with the competition for what Brodwin calls "healing power" between popular Catholicism, Protestantism, and vodou. Competing therapies, especially the widespread recourse to supernatural deities who aid in healing or deflecting malicious attacks and sending sickness by others, are often couched in terms of therapies undertaken by Catholic, vodou, or Protestant healers. Although most Haitians claim a formal religious affiliation, and each religion is associated with specific healing practices, if possible most people will opt for more than one treatment modality. Catholic relatives of a sick person will not hesitate to engage the services of a vodou healer if they (and their ill relative) believe that vodou rites will be more effective than Catholic or Protestant healing rituals. This flexibility in healing modalities has much to do with the overlap of Haiti's religious systems. Although Catholic patients and healers may condemn the vodou spirits (lwa) in public, they may at the same time describe themselves as "serving" the lwa. As Brodwin states, "In fact, people continue to denigrate the lwa and hougan even when they admit to hougan's healing power and recount their own attendance in his consulting room" (1999:117). The absence of a rigid ideological and ritual divide between Catholicism, Protestantism, and vodou means that the average Haitian can understand the treatment modalities and rituals of each. Thus, the homes of hougans

> are the site of . . . rituals for the lwa involving animal sacrifice for a family's ancestral spirits as well as the embodiment of the lwa by their human devotees . . . these ceremonies are probably the most important of the hougan's religious tasks. Other major ceremonies take place according to a ritual calendar which overlaps with the cycle of Catholic holidays (these ceremonies are concentrated in late summer, coinciding with several patron saints' festivals, and from all saints' day until the new year) . . . the two most common techniques of divination involve ordinary playing cards and Catholic prayer books . . . most hougan . . . draw deeply from the Catholic symbolic and cosmological system. They incorporate its images and vocabulary in their divination practice . . . in ways familiar to any Catholic herbalist . . . the icons of saints staring down from the walls, the books of devotional prayers which the spirit interprets, and the ritual actions of crossing oneself and reciting Latin prayers all surround the . . . divination procedures with elements of village Catholicism familiar to most rural Haitians. (Brodwin 1996:132–141)

Controversies: Marijuana and Coca, Health and Politics

Few issues in the United States are laden with so much controversy, misinformation, ideologically opposed positions, and political divisiveness as the legalization of drugs, especially marijuana. For decades, social and medical scientists and policy makers have debated the pros and cons of legalizing marijuana, especially for medicinal purposes, and yet a consensus is far on the horizon. Opponents of legalization emphasize that marijuana is a "gateway" drug—meaning that smoking it significantly enhances the risk that smokers will turn to other, more dangerous drugs; that little solid scientific evidence supports marijuana's medicinal advantages; and that legalizing marijuana will increase drug trafficking and violence on the streets. Proponents of legalization argue that evidence pointing to marijuana as a gateway drug is slim, and that what really underpins the consumption of other, far more dangerous drugs is poverty, marginality, and domestic abuse; that studies of marijuana use in Europe (where drug laws are often far less stringent) offer no proof of marijuana use propelling smokers to opt for other drugs; that legalizing marijuana would in fact undercut much of the violence that is generated by illegal trafficking groups; that there is in fact some scientific evidence that smoking marijuana has some advantages for those who are critically ill (e.g., those suffering from cancer or AIDS); and that the social and economic costs of stringent drugs control policies far outweigh its benefits. The eleven U.S. states that have enacted laws allowing limited use of marijuana for medicinal purposes are now engaged in a legal struggle with the federal government after a 2005 Supreme Court decision declaring these laws unconstitutional (Inciardi 1999; Nahas 1999; Ford 2001; Rosenthal et al. 2003; Gerber 2004; Hurley 2005; Murphy 2005; Shohov 2003; Satel 2005).

In a brazen editorial, the *Washington Post* (2002) stated that the real problem is not pot but prohibition. It said that there are millions of productive, law-abiding citizens who, by smoking marijuana, can be cast as criminals; that there is in fact solid evidence that shows virtually no adverse neuropsychological effects of marijuana smoking; and that arresting almost one million citizens each year for possessing or smoking marijuana borders on the irrational. Significantly, this editorial reminded readers of federally-funded anthropological studies of intense marijuana consumption in Jamaica and Costa Rica that demonstrated virtually no adverse effects. It is to these two studies that the following pages now turn.

Marijuana in Jamaica and Costa Rica

A classic study on the social and cultural importance of marijuana (cannabis) was carried out by Rubin and Comitas during the mid-1970s in Jamaica. This was the first interdisciplinary study examining "the total environment of the marijuana smoker" (Rubin and Comitas 1975:3) in a Latin American and Caribbean context. Two research methodologies underpinned their study. The first was a social science perspective that included ethnohistorical, ethnographic, and sociological thrusts, entailing historical research, archival work, fieldwork, and informal and structured interviewing. The second was clinically-based, including medical, psychiatric, and psychological tests.

Marijuana (called ganja in Jamaica) was introduced during the nineteenth century by East Indian indentured laborers brought to work on English colonial sugar plantations. Although illegal, growing marijuana and consuming ganja quickly became entrenched in Jamaican society and culture. Until recently, marijuana was a major cash crop, most of it exported to the United States. Competition from other countries, such as Mexico and Belize, as well as intense eradication campaigns spearheaded by the United States, have devastated a once lucrative crop (Rosenberg 2001).

In the mid-1970s, Rubin and Comitas claimed that "among the working class, of both rural and urban areas, ganja use is pervasive" and that at the national level "ganja use . . . is extraordinarily widespread" (1975:3, 37). With at least 60 to 70 percent of the rural popula-

PHOTO 8.2   *A Rastafarian in Jamaica smoking marijuana, October 2005.*

tion (including children) ganja consumers, Jamaica has "undoubtly one of the highest rates of marijuana use for any population in the Western world" (Rubin and Comitas 1975:38; also see Photo 8.2).

Part of the reason for the widespread acceptance of ganja has to do with Jamaica's ecological and economic conditions. The marijuana shrub—like coca describe in the next section—thrives in nutrient-poor tropical soils, requires and receives a great deal of rainfall, and produces at least two harvests annually. It grows easily, "like a weed," as one local farmer said (Rubin and Comitas 1975:42). Further, unlike the market for consumption crops, the demand for and supply of ganja is far more stable, therefore providing a predictable, if small, source of cash.

Ganja's integration within local cultural patterns also accounts for its broad acceptance and consumption. Large numbers of intermittent and part-time vendors who market ganja are culturally similar to common, ordinary Jamaican consumers. Few important class, social, or cultural differences set ganja vendors apart from their clients. Jamaicans consume ganja in many meaningful ways. The communal smoking of a "spliffs" ("joints" in the United States) contributes to a strong sense of solidarity, community, and friendship, as well as a feeling of mutual trust among adults. In addition to being used as a spice and condiment in local cuisines, ganja appears in a wide variety of medicinal practices and preparations. Medicinal teas brewed with ganja leaves or sticks are popular; they are especially recommended for children, because ganja "branifies" them (makes them think better) and contributes to their well-being. Ganja also makes its way into health tonics prepared with rum or wine. Many topical preparations used for pain relief, or for treating skin irritations, insect bites, or open wounds are prepared or heavily laced with ganja. Ganja is also said to enhance appetite, boost sex desire, and increase an individual's ability to engage in strenuous physical tasks by "building" his/her blood and strength. Most Jamaicans also associate "the use of ganja with clear thinking, meditation and concentration, euphoria, feelings of well-being towards others and self-assertiveness" (Rubin and Comitas 1975:56). The smoking of ganja is also a key aspect of the Rastafari religious worldview, discussed in Chapter 11.

The medical, psychiatric, and psychological thrusts of Rubin and Comitas' research project did not uncover any noxious or harmful effects of concentrated ganja consumption. Smoking ganja does not lead to hallucinations, "'vivid ideas crowding the brain,' or tendencies to violence . . . and wild sex orgies. Such reactions would violate working-class mores" (Rubin and Comitas 1975:161). And, in a clear reminder of the important role of the social and cultural framework within which certain drugs are consumed, the authors conclude that the idea that marijuana is a gateway drug—that is, that consuming marijuana sparks the need or desire for other, more powerful substances—is one that

> do[es] not apply to Jamaica . . . [Further, the] . . . findings do not bear out any of the extreme allegations about the deleterious effects of chronic use of cannabis on sanity, cerebral atrophy, brain damage or personality deterioration. There is no evidence of withdrawal symptoms or reports of severe overdose reactions or of physical dependency. (Rubin and Comitas 1975:164–165)

These conclusions are also reinforced by the parallel study carried out by Dreher, who focused specifically on the smoking of ganja by males in rural households:

> The claims . . . that the consequences of routine smoking of cannabis include impairment of the ability to work, apathy, lethargy, unsound judgment, and detachment from reality simply are not supported by the evidence from rural Jamaica; in fact, the evidence indicates that ganja functions in just the opposite manner. (Dreher 1982:197)

Thus, for cultural and health-related reasons, ganja consumption is stubbornly entrenched in Jamaica, despite the decades-long campaign to eradicate marijuana. This stark reality may be why some Jamaican legislators have openly called for a partial legalization of marijuana use (González 2001).

About six years after the conclusion of the Rubin and Comitas research project in Jamaica, Carter's scientific team carried out in 1980 a study of "chronic" marijuana use among working-class Costa Ricans, a two-year study funded (like the research in Jamaica) by the U.S. government. Unlike the case of Jamaica, Carter's 1980 study found that in Costa Rica, marijuana was consumed almost exclusively by smoking, and that there were fewer uses of marijuana in healing practices, with most medical uses of marijuana restricted to treatment of coughs and asthma. Although illegal, the possession and smoking of marijuana seems to have been entrenched among working-class sectors from about the mid- to late 1800s. Further, about 10 percent of San José's male working-class population smoked marijuana on a regular basis, a percentage far lower than in Jamaica. Marijuana smokers varied a great deal in the number of cigarettes they smoked on a daily basis: the range was 2.5 to 25, with a mean of 11.8, leading Carter to conclude that "the users in our . . . sample thus represent a range of cannabis consumption quite comparable to that reported in other countries" (1980:31), such as India, Morocco, or Egypt.

One important conclusion of this study was that although smokers had a wider range of social and adjustment problems (e.g., poor school performance, difficulties with parents, alcohol drinking), marijuana use was *not* the cause of these problems but rather its *result.* The problems were the accumulation of negative childhood experiences that anticipated marijuana smoking:

> Circumstances and personal experiences, rather than drug use *per se,* were the primary cause of the marginal behavior of [some marijuana smokers] . . . [Further] . . . If marijuana use leads to poorer social adjustment, irresponsible behavior, and lack of motivation, one would expect that the heavier the use the greater such problems would be. The opposite, however, turned out to be the case. The heavier the use, the more stable the employment record was, the fewer the periods of unemployment were, and the more likelihood there was that the user was enjoying the benefits of a long-term, full-time job. (Carter 1980:197–199)

In addition, Carter's research team uncovered no evidence that smoking marijuana leads to the use of other "hard" drugs (e.g., cocaine, heroin, barbiturates):

> Very few subjectively perceived adverse effects were reported or observed over the two-year period . . . We found no . . . clear evidence of marijuana-caused interference in the normal functioning of adult, working-class males . . . Indeed, some of the physicians and psychologists on our team were sincerely disappointed at the lack of significant differences between our controlled population of users and nonusers. (Carter 1980:203–206)

Coca in the Andes

The coca issue in the United States is fundamentally different than that of marijuana, partly because of the pharmacological differences between marijuana and the two main derivatives of coca consumed in the United States (cocaine and crack), and because of the greater violence, in the United States and abroad, associated with the production and distribution of cocaine/crack. Unfortunately, few concerns in United States–Latin American relationships have been laced with so much controversy and bitterness—and few have been so sorely misunderstood—as the ongoing conflict centered on the cultivation and consumption of the coca leaf in South America, particularly in Bolivia, Peru, and Colombia, the three most important coca leaf–producing countries. Suppressing cocaine trafficking has been confounded, in Colombia especially, with combating long-standing guerilla movements, and the result is that many Colombians are subjected to systemic violence and terror (Taussig 2003, 2004; Kirk 2003; see also Chapter 12). United States–funded campaigns to eradicate coca cultivation have been met with widespread resistance and enhanced anti–United States sentiments. They also are viewed as a new form of colonial intrusion, and they have left in their wake violence and political instability (Sanabria 1997, 2004). Further, despite apparent successes by Colombian police against the Cali and Medellín drug cartels between 1995 and 1997—including the arrest or killing of major drug kingpins

such as Pablo Escobar—and intensified aerial pesticide spraying of coca fields, coca cultivation continues to increase and spread elsewhere in Colombia previously free of coca
(Tate 2000; Vargas Meza 2000; Crandall 2001).

Often lost in drug and foreign policy debates on the coca and cocaine "problem"
(unfortunately, coca and cocaine are often used interchangeably in these debates), is that
coca has been consumed in different ways in many Central and South American societies
for thousands of years, especially in Peru and Bolivia (Plowman 1984, 1986; Allen 1988;
Sanabria 1993; Léons and Sanabria 1997; Taussig 2004). In Peru and Bolivia, the consumption of coca is a "total social fact" (Spedding 1997), deeply entrenched in Andean society
and culture. Consuming and sharing coca is a superb medium of communication and social
interactions. Properly arranged marriages, for example, often require the presence and
sharing of coca leaves. Coca also looms important in agricultural rituals designed to insure
good harvests, ritualized communication and reciprocal relationships with supernatural
deities, and divination. Consuming coca is also an important aspect of Andean cultural
identity (Nash 1979; Allen 1988). This relationship in turn has partly underpinned the
strong links between sense of cultural identity, repression of coca cultivation and drug trafficking, and the rise of indigenous social movements, such as those represented by Bolivian
president Evo Morales.

Coca leaves are mainly "chewed." Typically, an Andean peasant holds a leaf in his/her
hand and with his/her teeth removes the petals from the stem, repeating the process until a
wad forms in the mouth. Lime or ash is then placed in the mouth that, when mixed with the
saliva, accelerates the chemical breakdown of the leaves. This entire process is repeated
every fifteen to twenty minutes. The nutritional and health value of coca is well known.
Coca leaves are amazing storehouses of nutrition. The impressive array of vitamins, minerals, and other beneficial nutrients they contain is especially important given the historically
poor diet of Andean peasants (Burchard 1992). For example, in one study

> the amounts of 15 nutrients in coca leaves were compared to averages of these
> nutrients present in 50 Latin American foods. Coca was found to be higher in
> calories, protein, carbohydrates, calcium, phosphorous, iron, Vitamin A and
> riboflavin. (Plowman 1984:96)

And yet, in an obvious example of how the politics of coca and the "coca wars" can unduly
influence foreign policy and ideologically obscure social and cultural reality, a 1984
congressional report by the influential House Select Committee on Narcotics Abuse and
Control stated that:

> the Committee could then begin developing appropriate programs to gradually
> eliminate coca chewing in Bolivia . . . The chewing of coca leaf is a primitive,
> antiquated, debilitating practice, harmful to the individual and the public health
> and has considerable genocidal overtones. (quoted by Henman 1985:188)

Coca has historically been a key component of Andean health (Bastien and Donahue 1981).
In high altitude mountain areas, where most Andean peasants live, oxygen levels are low,
resulting in *soroche,* or high-altitude sickness. Some evidence exists that chewing coca
leaves may relieve soroche by maximizing the body's oxygen intake. Coca leaves also
dampen hunger, thirst, and cold, and they relieve sensations of weariness and pain. Further,

coca forms an integral part of Andean peasants' health system in other ways. Coca is combined with a wide array of plants and herbs to diagnose and treat dozens of culturally-specific ailments. Some of these aliments can be easily recognized by biomedical practitioners, including headaches and stomach or intestinal problems. Other illnesses—such as *viento* (Spanish; *waira,* Quechua) (strong wind currents) or those caused by evil spirits such as the kharisiri, who cause tuberculosis (see the previous section, "Poverty, Inequality, and Disease") are typically Andean. To diagnose and treat these illnesses, coca leaves can be boiled, ground, toasted or used dry; used alone or mixed with other substances; drunk as a tea; used in ointments and bathing solutions; or, as in many healing rituals, rubbed against the body (Bastien and Donahue 1981; Bastien 1992:77).

In the United States: Susto and Mal de Ojo Among Florida Farmworkers

Research on susto, mal de ojo, and nervios among Hispanic/Latino groups in the United States dates back to at least the early 1950s. Anthropologists and not biomedically trained professionals carried out virtually all this early work on "culture-bound" syndromes, the assumption being that biomedicine was ill-equipped to understand, diagnose, and treat these folk illnesses. Further, they did most of the early research among Mexican Americans in the south and southwestern states, such as Texas and New Mexico (Rubel 1977).

A growing consensus is that an approach "integrating ethnomedicine and biomedicine" (Bastien 1992) is fruitful in studying and treating folk or culture-bound illnesses. The research by Baer and Bustillo (1993) on susto and mal de ojos among Florida farmworkers illustrates the potential and limitations of biomedicine in successfully dealing with these illnesses.

Baer and Bustillo carried out interviews among Mexican and Mexican American women (most from northern Mexico) waiting to be seen by a physician in a local clinic. The authors had three goals. The first was to gather women's statements on the prevalence of susto and mal de ojo (as well as other illnesses) in their children, along with what kinds of treatments the mothers prescribed for them. Their second goal was to share these statements with the clinic's physicians to elicit their views on whether the illnesses (especially susto and mal de ojo) reported by mothers were life-threatening. Finally, Baer and Bustillo's third goal was for physicians to offer a diagnosis and suggest treatment recommendations. Physicians only had available to them translations of mother's statements; they did not examine any children.

On average, mothers reported slightly more than two illnesses for their children (most of these illnesses occurred before their children's second birthday), and a total of forty-eight cases of susto. The mean age of children who experienced susto was one year, and more than 70 percent never again experienced it. For most (58 percent), the susto episode lasted from two to four days. Mothers reported typical symptoms that included vomiting, fevers, diarrhea, loss of weight, crying, or waking up at night. Almost 90 percent of the susto cases were treated either by the mothers themselves, by a *señora* (an older woman "who knows how to cure") or a *curandera* (female folk healer); only *one* mother referred a susto case to a physician. The most common treatments included the use of herbs, praying, providing the child with a combination of water and sugar, and taking the child to a priest. Although most mothers were convinced that a worsening case of susto could ultimately be fatal, only half said they would take their children to a physician in such a scenario—reflecting, of course, the fact that they believed that physicians were incapable of treating susto.

Just as the mothers were evenly split on whether severe cases of susto should be referred to biomedical personnel, so too physicians appeared to be deeply divided. Although physicians thought that 60 percent of the children who had susto should have been seen by a doctor, their opinions were far from consistent. For example, of the twenty-one cases of susto in which severe crying was the most important symptom, physicians thought only ten should have been treated at the clinic. Further, although physicians claimed that 20 percent of the susto cases could be fatal if not treated, they "found it difficult to suggest diagnoses for the majority of the children the mothers had diagnosed as having susto, and, based on the information given, were not able to do so for any of the cases. Hospitalization was not suggested in any of these cases" (Baer and Bustillo 1993:96).

Mal de ojo was a different scenario. Most children experiencing this illness were younger (mean age of nine months) than those suffering from susto and, unlike susto, mal de ojo appeared at least one more time in most children. Typical symptoms included crankiness, noticeable eye signs (such as sunken eyes or eyes with mucus), and, compared with susto, far more severe fevers and diarrhea. Like susto, treatment rarely included taking a sick child to a physician, although mothers thought that mal de ojo, like susto, could be fatal. Even if non-biomedical treatments failed, only a minority of women stated that they would take their children to a physician. Physicians were far less divided in their opinions on mal de ojo. Although only able to diagnose five cases (compared to no susto cases), they thought two of the children, who they diagnosed with sepsis or bacteremia (bacterial infections), should be hospitalized. Far more interesting is that most physicians believed that almost 90 percent of the mal de ojo cases displayed symptoms so severe as to require biomedical treatment.

Baer and Bustillo concluded that *both* mothers and physicians are right *and* wrong in their beliefs concerning the efficacy of ethno- and biomedical treatment. Mothers in this study were correct in assuming that some of their treatments were effective and that physicians cannot ultimately diagnose and cure most of these illnesses—but they were wrong in assuming that physicians are unable to treat many of the symptoms. The study also shows that physicians in this clinic correctly believe that they can diagnose some of the cases and treat some of the symptoms—suggesting that biomedical personnel who view these folk illnesses as not "real" medical problems are mistaken. What is needed, then—especially for vulnerable young infants—is

> having the services of sensitive biomedical practitioners . . . to address the symptoms and proximate biological cause of the illness. It is also necessary, however, to have available the services of folk healers to provide and create social and psychological support and address the emically determined, ultimate social cause of the illness. The persistence of the attitude among physicians that folk illnesses are merely old-fashioned superstitions will only increase morbidity and mortality among Mexican and Mexican American populations from a series of life-threatening conditions they have learned to recognize and label in their own fashion. (1993:99)

Summary

This chapter underscored the kinds of research on health issues that medical anthropologists undertake. Poor health, closely related to widespread poverty, is a distinctive mark of Latin America and the Caribbean. These conditions—affecting women more than men—are exemplified by high mortality and malnutrition rates, unequal access to medical resources, and rampant rates of tuberculosis and HIV/AIDS. The distinction in medical anthropology between disease and illness was illustrated by examining the causes and consequences of susto, mal de ojo, and nervios, three widespread illnesses. Attention then focused on the anthropology of the body and how healthy bodies are culturally understood. Attention was also placed on the relationships between religious and healing beliefs and practices. The chapter then turned to the contentious issue of marijuana and coca eradication campaigns, and the health benefits of these two substances. The final section underscored the prevalence of susto and mal de ojos illnesses in contemporary Florida.

ISSUES AND QUESTIONS

1. *Medical Anthropology.* What are the major issues or questions in the field of medical anthropology? Why do medical anthropologists make a distinction between disease and illness, what does this difference consist of, and what are two examples that illustrate the usefulness of this distinction?

2. *Poor Health.* This chapter emphasized that most Latin American and Caribbean peoples suffer from poor health. What are the reasons for this state of affairs and what are some key indicators? What reasons explain the spread of tuberculosis and HIV/AIDS?

3. *Gender and Sexuality.* In what ways is health related to gender and sexuality? What might be some examples in which gender and sexuality are especially important in understanding how people respond to or try to cope with disease/illness?

4. *Religion, Drugs, and Health.* Drawing from two or more examples, explain how religion and religious ritual, the consumption of mind-altering substances ("drugs"), and attempts to achieve and maintain good health are related. Might any of the examples mentioned in the text be relevant in North America?

KEY TERMS AND CONCEPTS

Anthropology of the body p. 232
Anthropology of the emotions p. 233
Biomedicine p. 215
Critical medical anthropology p. 215
Culturalist approach p. 222

Disease p. 215
Ethnomedicine p. 214
Illness p. 214
Life's lesions p. 228
Mal de ojo p. 230
Medical anthropology p. 214
Medical system p. 214

Nervios p. 231
Religious pluralism p. 240
Ritual power p. 237
Shamanism p. 236
Structural violence p. 222
Susto p. 230
Witchcraft p. 239

9   Food, Cuisine, and Cultural Expression

This chapter explores the cultural and social significance of food and cuisine. It starts with an overview of some significant themes in the anthropology of food. The next section provides a historical sketch of and backdrop to major Latin American and Caribbean foods and cuisines. The third section focuses on the relationship between food, ritual, and social relationships by first examining the significance of guinea pigs in the Andes and Ecuador, and then exploring ideas about food and pollution in Trinidad. The ways in which food and cuisine are important for gender identities and relationships in Ecuador, Jamaica, and Brazil are subsequently discussed. How food and cuisine loom important in the construction of national identities in Belize and Mexico is raised in the fifth section. Attention then shifts to the significance of the widespread cultural distinction between hot and cold foods. The last section focuses on the importance of preparing and sharing tamales for itinerant Mexican farm workers.

Food and Culture

What people cook and eat, what sorts of food they share, and how, why, and in which contexts they do so, constitute a powerful analytic window into understanding cultural expression and identity, as well as social relationships. Diet—the types, proportions, and nutritional values of foods eaten—and cuisine—the kinds of meals or dishes that are prepared and shared—all reveal important insights into history and the construction of culture. It is difficult to imagine Mexico without maize, or think of Mexicans (or Mexican Americans in the United States) shunning maize-based dishes such as tacos and tamales. It is likewise hard to envisage Caribbean and Central American peoples doing without rice and beans, or spurning the almost endless variety of banana and plantain-based dishes. If, as some have suggested, "we are what we eat" and if, as may certainly be the case, ". . . to eat is to live [and] to live must be to eat" (Mintz 1994:103)—then it likewise follows that we can learn a great deal about Latin American and Caribbean culture by focusing on diet and cuisine. (Indeed, throughout Spanish speaking Latin America and the Caribbean, it is in the sphere of agriculture, crops, and cuisines that an abundance of indigenous and African loan words, as well as enormous variability in Spanish lexical terms, exists.)

To reflect on and ask questions about food and culture—to inquire about the meanings of food in different societal contexts is, as Mintz (1994:104–105) suggests, tantamount to pondering ourselves as a culturally constituted human species:

> Eating habits . . . are not only acquired habits but also historically derived habits, uninscribed in our natures, except by early social learning. Though all peoples have ideas about what foods are good for them, in no culture do they eat everything. What is more, no people eats only what is thought to be good for them . . . This aspect of our behavior has to do with the uniquely human capacity to create a symbolic world, and then both to call it reality and to treat it as real.

But what does an **anthropology of food**—the field of cultural anthropology that centers attention on the social and cultural dimensions of food and cuisine (Mintz and Du Bois 2002)—specifically reveal? What is explicitly learned about domains of culture in specific social and historical contexts? In *The Anthropology of Food and Body: Gender, Meaning, and Power*, Counihan (1999:6–8) provides an elegant answer:

> Food is a many-splendored thing, central to biological and social life. We ingest food over and over again across days, seasons, and years to fill our bellies and satisfy emotional as well as physical hungers. Eating together lies at the heart of social relations; at meals we create family and friendships by sharing food . . . Similarly, when social relations are bad, eating can be painful and unpleasant. . . . An examination of foodways—behaviors and beliefs surrounding the production, distribution, and consumption of food—reveals much about power relations and conceptions of sex and gender, for every coherent social group has its own unique foodways . . . Class, caste, race, and gender hierarchies are maintained, in part, through differential control over and access to food. One's place in the social system is revealed by what, how much, and with whom one eats.

As Counihan notes, one important thrust in the anthropology of food has been the ways in which preparing and eating food reflect and make statements about class and other hierarchical differences. This point has been echoed by Mintz and Du Bois, who state that "like all culturally defined material substances used in the creation and maintenance of social relationships, food serves both to solidify group membership and to set groups apart" (2002:109). Analogous arguments have been made by Johnsson (1986) about Bolivian Aymara-speakers and Sandstrom (1991) in a Mexican Nahua-speaking community.

In the opening paragraph of his book *Remembrance of Repasts: An Anthropology of Food and Memory*, Sutton (2001:1) recalls the following:

> "Food and Memory? Why would anyone want to remember anything they had eaten?" This sardonic comment, made by an Oxford don, seemed to sum up the

response when I presented a paper on the topic in 1996 at the department of anthropology at Oxford.

Yet it now seems clear that food—its preparation, consumption, and sharing—also serves to incite memory, powerfully igniting past experiences. This is important because, as many anthropologists have long recognized, culture is both symbolically and historically constructed in the course of daily practice. Thus, the kinds of foods and cuisines, ways of preparing them, and contexts within which they are eaten and enjoyed function as **reservoirs of memory**—how the past is recalled; memories of common heritage spurred; and the past, present, and future interpreted (Mintz 1994:104; Pilcher 1998; Mintz and Du Bois 2002:100). In many ways, "the past is used as a resource for imagining an alternative future" (Rowe and Schelling 1991:52). This point poignantly comes across in ways that food, identity, and memory surface among Salvadoran immigrants in the United States (see In Their Own Words 9.1). In Washington, D.C., food preparations and displays during festivals have analogous consequences (Cadaval 1998).

IN THEIR OWN WORDS 9 . 1
Food, Sociality, and Identity Among Salvadoran Immigrants

For Latin American immigrants in the United States, cooking and sharing familiar meals is a powerful venue through which memories are kept alive, sociality is underpinned, and a sense of identity is continuously re-created. Stower's research and field notes among Salvadoran immigrants in the United States (2003) demonstrates the multiple contexts in which food and cuisine loom so important.

Celebrating Christmas
   It was the night of the *Celebración Navideña,* and the Salvadoran community converged at the local public school after hours to . . . claim this city space for their own to celebrate, to praise their children, and to reaffirm their culture and community . . . Although the evening was Salvadoran, little of what was happening on stage seemed to be traditional Salvadoran *folclórico* . . . In contrast to the

cumbia, which has subdued movements, the teenage performers acted out the sensuous movements of the *salsa* . . . I slipped out of the auditorium . . . curious to see what was occurring in the cafeteria . . . here in the kitchen . . . was the culinary stage of Salvadoran immigrant identity. Where by day ethnic Irish cafeteria ladies served the typical American school lunch fare of frozen pizza and chicken nuggets, this evening Salvadoran women claimed this culinary space. They had heaped the silver steam table pans, which usually held canned vegetables and mashed potatoes, with freshly made *carne guisada, arroz con pollo,* and *arroz curtido* . . . Salvadorans . . . on reprieve from a daytime of hard, low paying labor filled themselves with the conviviality of good food. They chatted in Spanish not only about their children here but also about those they left behind in . . . their homeland—a place distant and imagined because they could not return. Tonight, Salvadorans in Gateway City sat in the starkness of an American school cafeteria, transversing the political boundaries of immigrant status, dreaming and eating El Salvador, together. (187–189)

Dinner at Home

Tonight María was making *carne guisada,* a beef stew of vegetables infused with onion and tomato . . . She had three pans going on the stove at once, plus the *comal* for the *tortillas.* . . . "Why are you cooking so much, María?" I asked. It was a hot Wednesday night. María was obviously tired; she had only just returned from her long day at the foam factory. "My husband and brother-in-law expect a big meal when they get

home," she remarked . . . María set a large piece of meat on the plate and surrounded it with the aromatic vegetables and a mound of rice. She placed the dish on the kitchen table, in front of her weary husband, along with the warm stack of *tortillas.* Although he had to eat quickly, he savoured his dinner, eating it "Salvadoran style"—using a *tortilla* to scoop up each bite. With every mouthful of this ideal Salvadoran meal, he tasted mythical notions of his life in El Salvador and the hope of the life he wished to live here. In this chaotic kitchen in the middle of Gateway City's poorest neighborhood, for a few moments, he consumed "the good life" in Salvadoran terms; he could feel like he "had made it" and was king of his castle before rushing off to his night job cleaning offices. (230–231)

Mintz (1996b) adds a slightly different angle to questions about what food and cuisine mean. Two fundamental features of Caribbean societies, as previously emphasized (see Chapter 4), were sugar plantation agriculture and slavery. The economics of slave plantation agriculture encouraged and enabled slaves to grow subsistence crops and feed themselves on marginal lands, and thus not all aspects of the lives of slaves were under the constant surveillance of masters and overseers. In *some* (but certainly not *all*) ways, slave groups and communities resembled what are known as **peasants**—rural cultivators with a subsistence-oriented strategy based on agriculture (or agriculture with pastoralism/animal husbandry), and economic, political, and social subordination to elites, such as landowners (Wolf 1966; Silverman 1979). Kearney is one of many who believe that "whatever validity . . . [the peasant category] . . . may once have had, has been outdistanced by contemporary history," for "peasants are mostly gone and . . . global conditions do not favor the perpetuation of those who remain" (1996:1–3). The ethnographic vignette of the community of San Jerónimo in Chapter 1 (see the "Why Study the Anthropology of Latin America and the Caribbean?" section) exemplifies, according to Kearney, these changes.

Hence, not all aspects of the everyday lives of slaves were rigidly controlled by their masters/owners. In fact, despite their enslavement, Africans working on sugar plantations enjoyed a great deal of autonomy—freedom, according to Mintz—especially in the realm of food and cuisine. By growing their own crops and preparing their own meals and those of their owners, African slaves were able to forge distinctive cuisines (the bedrock of "traditional" dishes consumed today) and at the same time influence the tastes and cuisines of their masters:

> What the slaves got to eat, what they could produce or catch to eat, and how they came to create a cuisine of their own became building-blocks of slave culture . . . slaves not only had taste and canons of taste, but also . . . their taste in food influenced the tastes of their masters. Many of the foods the masters would come to eat and prize in so-called slave societies they would learn . . . from slaves. . . . In the act of creating a cuisine . . . slaves came to enjoy an unanticipated freedom of maneuver . . . the tasting of freedom was linked to the tasting of food. (Mintz 1996b:36–37)

Historical and Cultural Sketch of Latin American Food

Pre-Columbian peoples of Latin America and the Caribbean consumed a wide spectrum of abundant foods. Evidence from archeology and physical anthropology on the health and nutrition of Latin American and Caribbean peoples prior to the European Conquest remains spotty and, at times, inconclusive. Differential access to food inevitably accompanied social stratification and the evolution of political complexity, and indigenous peoples were not free of disease, warfare, or periodic famines. Nevertheless, broad reviews of the health, diet, and nutrition of pre-Columbian peoples have not uncovered widespread and systematic nutritional deficiencies (Merbs 1992; Dufour 1994; Hern 1994; Larson 1994; Ubelaker 1995; Steckel et al. 2002).

In Mexico and most of Mesoamerica, the four most important domesticated crops were maize, chili peppers, beans, and squash. These crops were quite nutritious. High in complex carbohydrates and proteins, maize and beans are an especially nutritious combination; when eaten together, they complement each other's deficiencies in essential amino acids so they become as nutritious as animal proteins (Super and Vargas 2000:1248). Squash and chili peppers were also a nutritional bonanza for Mesoamerican peoples, as Pilcher (1998:12) eloquently notes:

> Squash added trace minerals and water, important benefits in the arid climate. Rounding out the basic diet were the remarkably nutritious chile peppers. They supplied vitamins A and C as well as various forms of B, aided digestion, inhibited intestinal disease, and even helped lower body temperatures by causing sweating, which cools by evaporation. Pre-Columbian peoples also recognized the chile's pharmacological uses . . .

It is not surprising that a great deal of symbolic importance was attached to maize because it was the centerpiece of the Mesoamerican diet. The word *maize,* originally recorded from

Arawak-speaking Taíno Indians, means "life-giving seed" (Fussel 1999:42; Keegan 2000:1261). "In Guatemala," Super and Vargas (2000:1248) tell us, "one Quiché Maya word for maize is *kana,* which means 'our mother.'" Maize (in the form of tamales), choco-late, and human blood were crucial ritual offerings to the nobility and supernatural deities. Further, the Aztecs (Mexica) "called babies 'maize blossoms,' young girls were 'tender green ears,' and a warrior in his prime represented 'Lord Corn Cob'" (Pilcher 1998:18). Variations of the Mesoamerican tamal appear elsewhere in contemporary Latin America: in Argentina, Ecuador, parts of northern Chile, Bolivia, and Peru tamales are called *humintas,* while in Venezuela, Colombia, and adjoining areas they are referred to as *hallacas.* In Cen-tral America—Nicaragua, for example—tamales are called *nacatamal,* which, unlike their Mesoamerican counterparts, are wrapped not in corn husks but banana leaves (Downey 2001:1604).

Fermented, mildly alcoholic, and nutritious beverages were also part of the daily Mesoamerican diet. Of particular importance was *pozol,* made out of maize (Super and Vargas 2000:1250), as well as *pulque,* produced from the agave cactus plant. Similar per-mutations of maize-based beverages appear in Central America. In Nicaragua, for instance, the beverage *chichi* is made from fermented corn, while corn flour with water are the basis of *pinol,* and ground tortillas and cacao form the basis of *tiste* (Downey 2001:1604).

In the Andes, the food supply was likewise ample and nutritious. The bulk of the diet consisted of a wide spectrum of root crops, of which the potato was the most important. Thousands of varieties of potatoes, adapted to virtually every imaginable ecological niche across the vast Andean mountain region, have been identified. Although the loss of biodi-versity is an ever-present threat—Weismantel (1988) notes the few varieties currently sown in Ecuador—in many Andean valleys more than one hundred varieties are harvested (Brush 1992:163). As late as the mid 1980s, almost three dozen varieties of potatoes were culti-vated in a single Quechua-speaking community in Cochabamba, Bolivia (Sanabria 1993).

Maize also entered local diets and cuisines, and was symbolically significant in household and community rituals. Andeans also cultivated *quinoa* and *tarwi,* two espe-cially nutritious high altitude indigenous grains that are packed with proteins and oils. (The former is currently advertised as an important health food on dozens of Internet Web sites.) Due to the peculiarities of the landscape that allowed Andeans relatively easy access to a wide span of ecological niches (the ecological complementarity often noted by Andeanist ethnographers; see Chapter 2), nutritious sub-tropical foods such as peanuts and chili pep-pers often made their way into daily or seasonal cuisines. Chili peppers were (and still are) highly valued, forming the basis of a wide range of spicy sauces that complement potato and other root crop dishes to this day. The consumption of animal protein—particularly from llamas and guinea pigs—was often restricted to ritual occasions. As in Mesoamerica, fermented corn beer (*chicha* in Spanish; *aqa* in most Quechua languages) was widespread. In the eastern Andean slopes, especially in Ecuador, chicha may refer to a mild alcoholic beverage made out of manioc, a beverage also widespread throughout the Amazon. *Api* is a popular nonalcoholic, maize-based breakfast beverage that often abounds in present day Bolivian and Peruvian marketplaces.

In the tropical and sub-tropical regions—the Caribbean, coastal areas of northern South America, and large swaths of the Amazon Basin—the core pre-Columbian diet cen-tered on root crops, the most important of which was manioc, also known as cassava, or *yu[c]ca* (Peterson 1997). Other important crops cultivated by, for example, the Caribbean Taínos at the moment of the Spanish Conquest, included sweet potatoes, maize, peanuts, and, of course, the ubiquitous chili peppers (Keegan 2000:1263).

Chapter 4 emphasized that the European Conquest ushered in lasting transformations in indigenous Latin American and Caribbean societies as well as in Europe through the two-way flow and adoption of plants and animals (the Columbian Exchange). Related to these enormous changes is the fact that European colonialism was not merely a struggle over land and other resources, and the hearts and minds (and labor) of indigenous and, later, African peoples, but also a contest over taste, diet, and cuisine. Local foods and dishes were turned into cultural battlegrounds as Europeans strove to replace indigenous with European crops and cuisines. Wheat—the basis of bread, the European staple, and one with important symbolic and religious importance—was the spearhead in this struggle. Writing on Mexico—and the same argument could be made for many other parts of Latin America—Pilcher (1998:35) notes that for Europeans,

> wheat remained a religious necessity because it was the only grain recognized by the Roman Catholic Church for the Holy Eucharist . . . friars also launched campaigns against native festival foods that were identified with pagan practices.

These cultural and ideological campaigns to replace local crops with (especially) wheat largely failed, although it should be pointed out that barley and oats were two European-introduced grains that fared well and that eventually occupied an important position in local cuisines. Another important crop that grew well and was widely accepted was the fava bean (*haba*).

Although cultivated widely in Mesoamerica and the Andes, and despite making many inroads into local cuisines, wheat largely failed to displace the centrality of maize and the potato in local diets, or to undermine the symbolic and ritual importance that indigenous peoples attached to maize and potatoes. This does not mean, however, that wheat-based foodstuffs did not become symbolically important. The "baby breads" and other wheat-based offerings in the Mesoamerican and Andean ritual celebration of Todos Santos (Chapter 7), for example, almost certainly are an early colonial construction. Prior to the Conquest, tiny maize-based breads were offered (and consumed only) during important ritual celebrations (Weismantel 1991:871). Further, in contemporary indigenous communities where white bread is expensive and considered a luxury, "it is critically important in many social and ceremonial contexts" (Weismantel 1988:110).

Cattle, pigs, goats, and chickens (all introduced by Europeans) adjusted well to local conditions, thrived, and easily made their way into local cuisines. Of these, cattle became symbolically important. Soon into the colonial period, bull fights emerged in many locales as part and parcel of popular and ritual celebrations. For example, the celebration of Corpus Christi, "devoted to the living presence of Christ in the Eucharist" (Gutiérrez 1991:91), was often marked by the presence of dance troupes, processions, and bullfights when celebrated in colonial Mexico City (Curcio-Nagy 1994). Indeed, in some contemporary Ecuadorian Quichua-speaking communities, Corpus Christi is also referred to as the "fiesta of the *toros* [bulls]" (Weismantel 1988:206).

In Mesoamerica and the Andes, indigenous foodways and cuisines became an ideological marker of ethnic and class membership. For Europeans and Europeanized-elites, a Mexican "Indian" during the colonial and postcolonial periods was someone who attached importance to and subsisted on a diet largely consisting of maize, beans, and chilies. As late as 1845, well after independence, one Mexican cookbook "questioned the morals of any family that ate tamales—the food of the 'lower orders' " (Pilcher 1998:46). These class-based ideological associations became so deeply entrenched that, according to members of Hueyapán, a Nahuatl-speaking community in the Mexican state of Morelos, during the 1970s "*Indian* [italics added] food means 'ordinary things,' such as *tortillas, kidney beans, chiles, tamales,* calabash squash, pulque and a few fruits such as *tejocotes*" (Friedlander 1975:96). In the Andes, as late as the 1970s an analogous ideological pattern persisted, for there too an "Indian" was someone whose diet consisted largely of potatoes, chili peppers, and chicha (Van den Berghe and Primov 1977). Yet, many exceptions do exist, of course. Weismantel emphasizes that barley (a European-introduced crop) and not the potato is the key dietary staple in a Quichua-speaking community in central Ecuador, especially among the desperately poor. In this community, consuming potatoes is a sure sign "of a household's economic success" (1988:94). Europeans, although unable to fully impose their own versions of appropriate diets and cuisines, nevertheless played a role in influencing indigenous classificatory schemas, such as the hot and cold food classifications discussed later in this chapter.

Unable to be successfully and widely cultivated in the Caribbean or Amazonia, wheat fared even worse compared to root crops such as manioc. Further, importing European foodstuffs was often quite impractical. The cuisines of Europeans and Europeanized elites—especially on the slave-based sugar plantations—did not therefore differ significantly from that of their slave laborers. As a result, in these areas other more important markers of identity emerged. The Caribbean, Mintz (1985a:136–137) states in his characteristically straightforward way:

> Was an arena for the encounter of different foods, as it was for the encounter of different peoples; over time, new cuisines emerged, now typically Caribbean, though wearing older pedigrees. In food, as in all else, the islands took on their distinctive individual character—part African, part Asian, part Amerindian, part European . . . this manner of crops, tastes, dishes, and cuisines is intimately tied to the growth of peasantries. In this world area, cuisine was not so much a matter of the food of the elite classes percolating downward, but rather of the choicest plates of the poor becoming the quaint and colorful fare of the privileged. Much as happened with other aspects of culture in this region, "refinement" began with imitation, more than with innovation, at the top.

A good example of the blurring of elite and popular boundaries is the Brazilian dish *feijoada,* a post–nineteenth century "hearty concoction consist[ing] of rice, black beans, dried meats, sausage, and toasted manioc flour, and . . . garnished with kale and orange slices" (Gade 2000:1257). The feijoada which, as Margolis, Bezerra, and Fox (2001:291–292) note, means "big bean stew" and is Brazil's national dish:

*slave foods
legitimized
when elites
consume
them*

Is said to have originated during slave times. Traditionally, the feijoada contained inexpensive and less desirable cuts of meat such as tripe and pigs feet, Brazilian slaves having concocted the dish from the leftovers of the master's table.

Bananas (including what are now known as plantains [*plátanos* in Spanish]) and rice were two crops introduced by Europeans (see Crosby 1972) that thrived and had an astonishing impact on local foodways and cuisines, because they were better adapted to tropical and sub-tropical growing conditions than wheat. Mangos, brought to the Caribbean by the British in the late eighteenth century, also made their way into local cuisines but, with the possible exception of slave-worked plantations, did not emerge as a key food staple elsewhere (Pilcher 2000:1281). Bananas and plantains, coupled with root crops, formed the basis of popular diet and cuisines throughout much of the Caribbean, Central America, and parts of South America. In Puerto Rico and the Dominican Republic, for example, *pasteles*—prepared with a dough made out of root crops, stuffed with either beef, chicken, or pork (or simply with condiments), wrapped in banana leaves, and either roasted or boiled—were a common cuisine of peasants and sugar plantation workers.

*banana
plantation*

Bananas and plantains had even more far-reaching consequences, for these, along with coffee, were crucial in the transformation of the political economy and eventual underdevelopment of Central American nation-states (Bulmer-Thomas 1987). Cultivated in large-scale plantations often under conditions of extreme labor oppression, bananas and plantains have also been key crops and commodities that have played a powerful role in the forging of ethnic and class discrimination and identities. Bourgois' fieldwork among the Guaymí and Kuna working on a United Fruit Company banana plantation is a contemporary example (1989).

*rice
(slave
food)*

The social history of the spread and consumption of rice in Latin America and the Caribbean has yet to be written. Nevertheless, certain trends are clear. Rice was already growing in Peru's eastern lowlands a generation after the Conquest (Crosby 1972:70) and probably was expanding throughout the Mesoamerican and Central American lowlands as well. Super and Vargas (2000:1250) note that after the Conquest, wheat expanded into Mexico and the highlands of Central America, but it was rice that

> had the most success of any of the imported grains among all ethnic and social groups in Middle America . . . In Mexico, Indians came to depend on rice as a complement to or substitute for maize. . . . *Morisqueta,* rice prepared by a technique supposedly introduced by the Japanese, became common in the rural Mexican diet in the 1940s, and rice achieved even more fame as the basis for a drink known as *horchata,* prepared with rice, flour, sugar, cinnamon, and ice.

Early in the colonial period, Spaniards also introduced rice into their prized Caribbean possessions of Cuba and Puerto Rico. Some evidence (Pilcher 2000:1281) suggests that as sugar production expanded during the nineteenth century, cane planters began importing rice and jerked beef (called *carne vieja* [old meat] or *tasajo* in Puerto Rico and elsewhere in the Spanish-speaking Caribbean), suggesting how crucial rice had become in the diet of plantation workers. In Puerto Rico, rice did not become the cornerstone of local diet and cuisine until at least the mid-1920s, when United States–controlled corporate sugar plantation agriculture on the island reached its zenith. The growing dependence on ever-greater quantities of rice from the United States was paralleled by massive investments and technological innovations in rice production, making Louisiana one of the most important rice-producing regions in the Western hemisphere (Mintz 1956; Dietz 1986). The dependence of many Caribbean islands on imported food goes much further back in time, though, for "as early as the 1880s, the small island of St. Pierre had become so dependent on canned food from the United States that an American steamer was called 'food ship'" (Pilcher 2000:1285).

Along the way (the times and places varied considerably, and this story has also yet to be fully told), rice met, mingled with, and forged a lasting relationship with beans. Both currently constitute the most significant part of the diet and cuisine of most peoples in the Caribbean, Central America, northern South America, and Brazil. As with maize, beans eaten with rice are nutritionally wholesome, for "neither beans nor rice alone yields a high-quality protein because the former lacks the essential amino acids methionine and crytine, while the latter is deficient in lysine" (Pilcher 2000:1286).

Delicious combinations of rice and beans found in the Caribbean may be flaunted as "typical" or "traditional" cuisine in government publications aimed at the tourist market and dollar—Puerto Rico's *Qué Pasa!* magazine is a good example—but in fact, this "tradition" is of relatively recent origins. In multi-ethnic countries with a long history of ethnic and class discrimination, "typical," "authentic," or "traditional" dishes may embody different, contradictory meanings for the elites: "emphasizing their nation's cultural heritage . . . [while at the same time] . . . stand[ing] for the poor, the ignorant, and the non-white: people with whom the elite, for the most part, do not wish to identify" (Weismantel 1988:122). Puerto Rico again provides a good example: the delicious *gazpacho*—fresh avocados combined with tomatoes, onions, olive oil, and salted cod fish—is also portrayed as a "typical" dish in Puerto Rican cookbooks and government publications. Yet, the crucial ingredient in gazpacho—salted cod fish—was originally imported to the Hispanic and non-Hispanic Caribbean by European colonial elites wanting to feed primarily plantation workers and, as such, was often disdained by the elites themselves.

Further, elite foods and popular cuisines may shape each other and may both be molded by transnational processes.[1] *Tres leches,* widely considered a "typical" Nicaraguan dessert (but also enjoyed in other parts of the Central America and the Caribbean) is a good example:

> The Carnation Concentrated Milk Company wanted to boost its sales of canned milk. The company's home economists developed recipes, including one for a three-milk dessert, that appeared on can labels. During the 1920s, Carnation began exporting to Central America, especially Nicaragua, where housewives, wishing to introduce a foreign delicacy to the dinner table, began offering *tres leches* for dessert. Nicaraguans adopted the popular sweet as the national dessert. Today, chic Miami Caribbean–Central American restaurants offer it as a dessert to elites as Nicaraguan taramisu. (Beezley and Curcio-Nagy 2000a:xiv)

Elsewhere, the "new" and "old" come together, providing important insights into culture, history, and the imagination and resilience of Latin American and Caribbean peoples:

> Elements of the past combine everywhere with those of the present on Mexican tables. Old Mesoamerican foods such as chillies, squash, beans, avocados, and all kinds of maize derivatives are considered necessary in a meal. These are enriched with foods from the Old World such as pork, beef, lettuce, rice, oranges, and coffee. Some of the old foods still have a special place in social gatherings. For instance, a traditional wedding deserves a *mole de guajalote* just as the typical breakfast on the day of the child's first communion is unthinkable without hot chocolate and *tamales*. Families going out at night patronize restaurants specializing in *pozole*, a stew with grains of corn, meat, and old and new spices. New foods appear continually: Coca-Cola is already a staple; hamburgers and hot dogs are everywhere; new Chinese restaurants and pizza parlors open every day. It is interesting to note that many of these foods become "Mexicanized." For example, the large hamburger restaurants offer chillies and Mexican sauces, and one can order a *pizza poblana* with long strands of green chilli and mole on it. (Super and Vargas 2000:1253)

Food, Consumption, and Ritual

Mintz and Dubois (2002:107) remind us of the relationship between food and cuisine, and rituals and symbols, that often underpin social interactions. This is the case of guinea pigs and rituals in the Andes, and the idea of food pollution in Trinidad.

Guinea Pigs and Ritual in the Andes

The guinea pig, popularly known by its Spanish term *cuy* (*cuyes* or *cuys,* plural) and the Quechua word *quwi* (*quwis,* plural), has historically loomed as an important component of indigenous Andean diet, cuisine, and ritual settings. An Andean domesticate introduced to Europe in the sixteenth century, the cuy is currently raised from southern Colombia to northern Chile and Argentina, although prior to the Conquest its geographic distribution was much wider. Considerable ethnohistorical evidence suggests that in pre-Columbian times cuyes were consumed almost exclusively in household and community-level ceremonies (Gade 1967; Bolton 1979).

One would be hard pressed to find a Quechua- or Aymara-speaking household in the rural Andes that does not own and raise cuys, who typically huddle in the kitchen to shield themselves from freezing temperatures that periodically puncture the night. Cuys are remarkably easy to raise and even the poorest of households can afford to do so. They are also very nutritious: pound for pound, cuy flesh has a higher percentage of protein and the lowest fat content compared to poultry, beef, lamb, and pork (Morales 1995:50). Small wonder, then, that many development projects have centered on increasing the quantity and quality of guinea pig husbandry among Andean households (Archetti 1997a). Considered a delicacy, restaurants offering cuy abound in Andean urban areas, especially in and around marketplaces (see Photo 9.1).

PHOTO 9.1   *Roasting guinea pigs in Pillaro, Ecuador.*

To this day, cuys loom important in religious and healing rituals, and they are especially prized and consumed in virtually any significant household or community ceremony, secular or otherwise (Gade 1967; Bolton 1979; Morales 1995).

In rare instances, entire ritual celebrations center around the cuy. For example, in the Department of Ancash, Peru, a celebration called *jaca tsariy* ("to collect cuys" in the local Quechua language) marks the beginning of a celebration honoring local patron saints (Morales 1995:101-12). In charge of the celebration is a *mayordomo* or *prioste* (sponsor) who coordinates the gathering and preparation of food and drink for the guests. Assisted by a *sirvinti* (from the Spanish *sirviente,* or servant), an important responsibility of the sponsor is to keep track of those who have committed to offering cuys for the festivity. Such an offering, Morales states, "is a symbol of both personal reciprocity and community support" (1995:104). Several women—referred to by the Quechua kin term *llumtsuy* (daughter-in-law)—assist the sponsor and the sirvinti. These women recruit their own *jaca toreros* (cuy toreros, or cuy "bullfighters")—always men or young boys—whose playful dances with cuys held with an attached string figure prominently in this celebration.

Two days before the patron saint's day, the sponsor serves a community-wide meal, the *comun micuy,* marking the formal opening of the jaca tsariy. Shortly thereafter,

the sponsor, along with his own musical band, leaves for the llumtsuys' houses to invite them to join him in the inauguration of the festivities. The mayor, or first llumtsuy, is always the first one to be invited to join . . . then they go to each and every llumtsuys' door to dance and whistle to the rhythm of the songs played by the band and to drink chicha, alcohol, and *huarapo* (fermented sugarcane drink). The llumtsuys come out of their houses proudly holding a tray of cuy meal (*jaca pichu*) and showing an elegantly adorned live cuy held by an appointed torero. (Even if the llumtsuys' offering is a live animal other than a cuy, her tray always consists of cuy meal.) (Morales 1995:103–105)

Laughter, humor, and especially satire, have historically permeated popular rituals and celebrations through which anger and discontent have been expressed and "alternative visions of the social order" publicly conveyed (Beezley et al. 1994b:xxv; Goldstein 2003; see also Chapter 11). The jaca tsariy—in which the symbolic importance of the cuy looms so prominently—is an example of such a popular celebration, or **ritual of resistance,** and not merely a colorful or quaint Andean performance. The social commentaries embodied in the public staging of the jaca tsariy unmistakably surface when we learn what happens at the sponsor's house:

> Once all the llumtsuys have displayed their cooked cuys, the . . . master of ceremonies appoints a judge, an attorney general, a physician, and witnesses to read the will of the deceased, which the *jaca pichus* (cuy dishes) represent. The . . . master of ceremonies picks a jaca pichu and calls the dead cuy by the name of a local authority, politician, or anyone whom . . . [he] . . . wishes to satirize. He then summons the judge, the attorney general, and the witnesses for them to declare the death of a nearby hacendado . . . and to legitimize the terms of the will. The physician declares the death whom the cuy represents and turns the body of the hacendado over to the witness, who hands it to the sponsor for its proper disposition. A group of women cut[s] the cuy into pieces to serve the audience. (Morales 1995:106–107)

Juthaa: Sharing Polluting Food in Trinidad

Documenting **food taboos** and explaining why they exist—why it is that in some cultures consuming certain foods is prohibited while in others relished—have long attracted the attention of anthropologists (Grivetti 2000). In some societies, such as India, food taboos are linked to the idea of pollution, whereby certain foods or substances are avoided by some groups because they have been tainted, or made "unclean," by having come into contact with members of other groups who are themselves considered unclean.

The Indian (and specifically Hindu) cultural influence is prominent in Trinidad, Jamaica, Suriname, Guiana, and some Caribbean coastline areas to which large numbers of Indian indentured laborers were transported by the British in the mid-nineteenth century to labor in the sugarcane plantations. Khan's research (1994) focuses on **food pollution** (*juthaa*)—the idea that certain foods are "unclean" or polluted and should be avoided—in Trinidad, the largest island of the twin-island nation-state of Trinidad and Tobago. His analysis reveals how a cultural concept can acquire new, multiple, and seemingly contradictory meanings in a radically different historical and cultural milieu from which it originally derived.

Juthaa, which refers to "food and drink that have become polluted by being partially consumed by others" (Khan 1994:245), is a significant dimension of local belief, daily discourse, and social relationships in Trinidad. Yet, it was early on detached from the caste stratification system with which, in India, it was tightly intertwined. This was because caste, as a complex system of social inequality partially rooted and justified in religious ideology, never took root in the Caribbean (see also Braithwaite 1971). However, juthaa is still closely associated with the consumption and sharing of food, as well as to the notion of pollution. Yet, in contemporary Trinidad, this ideological construct reveals less about hierarchy and inequality at the level of social relationships and much more about the ways in which Trinidadians attempt to relate to each other on a more equal footing, as well as their attempts to refashion the concept to make it more relevant to contemporary contexts.

Juthaa is invariably linked to the cooking and sharing of food, because it "is both a principle conduit of pollution in India and a key medium of social relations in Trinidad" (Khan 1994:249). Sharing food is extraordinarily important in Trinidadian culture and social relations. Throughout Trinidad, food conveys multiple messages. It is closely related to *obeah* (magic) as well as to *maljo* (evil eye, *najar* in Hindi; see also Chapter 8). Food looms prominently in calypso music and conveys different messages in multiple social contexts:

> Through food, one can convey trust and equality by acceptance, or the obverse through refusal; one can inadvertently invite maljo by showing (off) too freely the possession of food, particularly something special. Eating food is a point of vulnerability engineered through obeah, either physical (one can become ill) or psychological/emotional (one's will can be conquered). In fact, a common Trinidadian folk aphorism, "What don't kill does fatten," is applied equally to a variety of food contents and implies a general recognition that food transactions or food itself can have either beneficial (positive) or malevolent (negative) capacities . . . [A]lthough polluted food per se is not desirable, the act of sharing it—offer and acceptance—often involves a negotiation of power and a degree of persuasion and capitulation among the persons involved; that is, an assertion of the positive aspect of demonstrated nonsuperiority versus the negative ones of refusal. (Khan 1994:250)

The social tensions and insecurities involved in food sharing are not exclusively Trinidadian but also surface in many others parts of Latin America. In the Brazilian northeast, for example, one cultural norm is that guests should be offered food and drink; to not do so is considered extremely antisocial behavior. Yet, in the context of deprivation and poverty that afflict this region of Brazil, the sharing and offering of food can be risky indeed, for the sumptuous display of food can spark envy and jealousy on the part of the guests. As a result, the hosts fear that they might come down with evil eye sickness (Rebhun 1994:371; see also Chapter 8).

The cardinal norm in Trinidadian society—that the sharing of food is important, that one shares food with equals, and that "to attend an event or visit someone's home and not eat is as bad, or worse, than not attending at all" (Khan 1994:254)—takes place against the backdrop of juthaa. How do Trinidadians reconcile the prime value they attach to the commensality of food with the ever-lurking and real danger of pollution, which often manifests itself in the appearance of illness? According to Khan, they do so by reconfiguring some of the original meanings of juthaa so that individuals and social contexts have a greater say in determining the likelihood or potential of pollution. As Khan states:

> Exposure to pollution among Indo-Trinidadians is something that the individual can, in a sense, regulate, through decisions as to whose juthaa can be

shared. That is, the question for each person becomes: Among which other individuals, and within which contexts, can polluting substances be risked? (1994:254)

It is widely accepted that juthaa is not a danger if food is shared with someone one trusts, or with whom someone has a close bond and who, therefore, is a "clean" person. A clean person is also someone who is a good person, especially important in a context in which "living good with people" is attached considerable importance (Khan 1994:256). In Trinidad, it is the social context, recreated in everyday behavior, that determines the potential negative or positive outcome of juthaa—and not the other way around. Rather than constituting a cultural construct of exclusion, juthaa provides, almost paradoxically, an idiom through which social relationships can be forged, for individuals "can decide . . . how and with whom they will establish bonds through sharing juthaa" (Khan 1994:262).

In many ways juthaa is a cultural idiom that in the present Trinidadian context says more about equality—or the striving toward equality—than hierarchy, more about sharing than exclusion, and more about identity than religion. In Trinidad, juthaa is not associated with class differences—it is not the case that low-income or lower-status people are tarnished with juthaa while wealthy, "higher"-class folks are not. Neither is it the case that juthaa is rigidly identified with Indian (Hindu) cultural heritage, for

what is notable is that among Indo-Trinidadian Muslims and Hindus alike, use of the word juthaa is not associated exclusively with Hinduism or the caste system. Indo-Trinidadian Muslims use juthaa as an overt term as often and in the same way as do Hindus. While certainly many are aware of its caste-based origins, both Muslims and Hindus relate . . . to the concept . . . as an index of Indian identity, not as that which definitively denotes any discrete ethnic or religious entity. (Khan 1994:256)

Communicating Gender and Sexuality Through Food

What kind of food is prepared by and for whom also provides a significant prism through which to understand gender and sexuality:

In many cultures, eating is a sexual and gendered experience . . . Food and sex are metaphorically overlapping . . . there are associations between eating, intercourse, and reproduction . . . Maleness and femaleness . . . are associated with specific foods, and rules often exist to control the consumption of those foods . . . [M]ale power and female subordination are reproduced through food and body beliefs and practices . . . Between men and women . . . food is both a means of differentiation and a channel of connection. By claiming different roles in regard to food and distinct attributes through identification with specific foods, men and women define their masculinity and femininity, their similarity and difference. (Counihan 1999:9-12)

As Weismantel notes, ethnic identity is likewise often conveyed and re-affirmed through food and cuisine, especially in ethnically and class stratified societies, for "the act of cooking food, and thus transforming [food] is a means of expressing what a people think of themselves, who they are, where they live, and what their place is in the natural and social world and in the political and economic systems of the nation" (1988:194). The following pages focus on how food expresses statements on gender and ethnic ideologies and relationships in highland, rural Ecuador; urban Jamaica; and northeastern Brazil.

Highland Ecuador

Weismantel carried out fieldwork in Zumbagua, a Quichua speaking community in the Ecuadorian highland basin (*sierra*) region. One of her most interesting arguments is that rather than simply denoting female subordination and powerlessness, laboring in the kitchen—cooking and serving food—enables women to assert, in the private and public spheres, their clout:

> The domain of the kitchen provides . . . women with . . . a . . . feminine sort of political power. In the kitchen, even more than in pasture and field, a woman exerts her control over her subordinates: mother over children, mother-in-law over daughters-in-law. A woman with recently married sons has direct control over the lives and labor of several strong, young adults and is answerable only to her husband, who considers cooking to lie outside his domain. The young women sometimes bear an onerous burden, but the passing of time will eventually bring them into the position of power . . . The symbolism of serving food . . . is ambiguous. . . . on the surface . . . [it] . . . seems to place the woman serving at the bottom of the social hierarchy. She ladles soup into bowls and hands them to her young daughter with whispered instructions that grandfather must be served first, then uncle, while she herself eats last. Despite this apparent powerlessness . . . cuisine and etiquette provide delicate instruments for communicating messages about social position and relative power and even create opportunities to readjust the status quo. . . . [T]his "symbol of women's subordination" provides the woman who wields the ladle the chance smugly to hand out excruciating insults while meekly proclaiming her utter lack of political power. (Weismantel 1988:26–29)

In Zumbagua, there are many gendered ways in which women once in the kitchen—a realm which, as Weismantel reminds us, is largely "unmediated by men" (1988:177)—can assert themselves publicly through the practices entailed in preparing and serving food. One way is by refusing to follow prescribed gender obligations, as when the "disaffected wife signals her displeasure not just with soup but with cold, leftover soup," or when she fails to have ready food for her spouse when he returns from work, as when "an angry spouse, surrounded by a phalanx of supportive same-sex kin, decides to indulge in a full-fledged, public airing of grievances, [with] accusations that *she* has no food ready when he is hungry" (Weismantel 1988:168, 181).

Yet, other, clever ways exist for women to rebuff their male spouses' behavior in ways that do not directly or openly challenge prevailing gender expectations. Weismantel recounts the story of a woman whose husband went out drinking and returned late at night quite drunk. The woman, understandably angry, decided to retaliate by in fact offering (and not denying) food to her husband when he arrived:

> When her husband arrived home many hours later, drunk and sleepy and ready for bed, she informed him that he must be very hungry: as an obedient wife she had prepared a nice dinner for him. Almost unconscious, he forced himself to sit upright long enough to eat two enormous bowls of soup under her reproachful eyes. The meal over, he crept off to bed, but his ordeal had only begun. The next day he found himself in an extremely delicate physical state, such that the three very elaborate meals she had prepared for him, which he dutifully consumed, resulted in several hasty exits from the kitchen to the bushes outside. She appeared to enjoy cooking for him very much that day, smugly playing the virtuous wife in front of her in-laws, who watched with some amusement and did not interfere. (1988:181)

In this example, the "virtuous" wife not only played along with the customary gender conventions that say she is expected to cook for her husband, but also followed and used to her benefit two central food conventions in Zumbagua culture: that the serving of food constitutes a gift, and that food that is offered must be consumed when it is offered and how it is cooked.

Women laboring in kitchens also have other ways of asserting themselves by conveying statements on hierarchy and status. For example, if guests are present, the order in which guests are served, the kinds of bowls and spoons that they are served their meals with, and, finally, what exactly the women puts from the cooking pot into the bowls for specific people—whether she puts more or less beef or potatoes, for example—suggest her ability to almost literally construct hierarchy and status among those present (Weismantel 1988:179-80).

Food serves not only as a medium through which gender relations are expressed, and through which women can assert themselves. Some foods are **gender-inflected foods** in that they convey culturally construed notions of gender identity associated with femaleness (femininity) or with maleness (masculinity). The prized hot chili sauce (*uchu* in the local Quichua dialect; *llaqwa* in much of Peru and Bolivia) is consumed mainly by men, and many women state that for them it is too strong (*chinchi*) or bitter (*jayaj*). When women state that uchu is jayaj, they are linking it with masculinity and strength. A similar association between maleness and jayaj exists in relation with the hallucinogen ayahuasca (see Chapter 8) because it is associated with the male domain of shamanism. Drinking *trago* (cane alcohol) is also associated with maleness, not only because it is usually drunk by males, but also because of the public and symbolic statements made when men blow "mouthfuls of *trago* over the bulls during Corpus Christi to make them more *bravo*" (Weismantel 1988:136).

Food also expresses ethnic identity and perhaps more importantly, the place of indigenous peoples at the bottom of Ecuador's social, economic, and political hierarchy. The diet in Zumbagua mainly consists of barley, onions, potatoes, and some vegetables. Most meals are cooked in the form of soups (*sopas*)—*yanuna*, the Quichua verb to cook, also means to boil. Yet, white (bleached) rice and bread, considered special treats or luxuries (*wanlla*), are highly valued and sought after.

Three reasons explain the widespread desire for rice and bread, and the symbolic importance attached to both. The first is that few community members can afford to purchase them on a regular basis, and therefore these two foods surface only sporadically in meals. Second, rice and bread happen to be two important staples (in addition to beef and seafood) in the diet of many if not most nonindigenous ("White") Ecuadorians who are at the top of the national hierarchy. The third is the semantic and ideological link between *white* bread and rice (as opposed to unbleached rice and whole wheat bread, neither of which are consumed widely in Ecuador regardless of ethnic or class background) and "White" Ecuadorians. As was (and still is) the case of white, refined sugar in the Caribbean (Mintz 1985b), scarcity and "whiteness" have worked hand in hand to justify, construct, and express inequality.

These symbolic as well as material associations not only reveal why bread and rice are longed for but also communicate important messages regarding ethnic and class discrimination. For example, many younger community members striving to include white rice—far less nutritious than barley—in their meals do so in an attempt to "construct an identity for themselves in contradistinction to what they see as old and ignorant lives" (Weismantel 1988:147). These associations, as well as the real and ongoing ethnic and class prejudice that indigenous peoples in Ecuador are subjected to, explains why

> white rice [has emerged] as a topic of discourse . . . where it stands for the class of people, "whites," who customarily eat it, and for "Indians" who aspire to be like them. Derogatory comments about those who "pretend to eat rice every day" are heard . . . White rice . . . functions metalinguistically in the indigenous food system as a symbol of the alien "white" system. (Weismantel 1988:147)

Jamaica

Sobo's fieldwork (1993) illustrates the manifold meanings of food preparations, exchanges, and consumption among poor, urban Jamaicans. In particular, food is an important medium through which different modes of sociality are expressed, feelings of well-being conveyed, and gender and social relations articulated.

In Jamaican society and culture, sharing and consuming food prepared by others is highly valued and at the same time considered potentially dangerous. It is valued because it binds people to each other in webs of reciprocity and obligations; and yet, consuming food prepared by others is viewed with great suspicion because it is an important medium through which others can inflict evil and harm. This important paradox—the need to share and consume food prepared by others and the strong likelihood that the offering of food is anything but an altruistic undertaking—generates considerable tension in everyday life and is bound up with Jamaican ways of conceptualizing the body as an entry point of good and evil. As Sobo explains:

> Food paranoia is common, runs deep, and is more than a matter of simple hygiene. Saying a person's "hands are dirtied," their cooking "unclean," or their food is full of "dirt" carries much more meaning than a non-Jamaican might think . . . Jamaicans truly fear that those wishing to harm them will do so through their food. A meal is something taken into the body, and poison can be

ingested along with it by an unsuspecting eater . . . Some people, adamant about taking food only in their own yards, will sit "empty" in others' yards for hours. No matter how much gas the empty "belly" generates and despite the unpleasant sensation of hunger "twisting" the "tripe," they never consider eating. But it is quite rude to refuse food when offered. Refusal signifies suspicion and distrust, which are bound to cause offense. Sensitive hosts realize this and may allow their guests easy escape by phrasing offers as negative assumptions, like "You don't want fe me [any of my] dinner?" (1993:112–113)

The suspicion surrounding the potentially manipulative uses of food—and its relationship to what Cohen (1971:416) years ago called "anxiety in interpersonal relationships" in Jamaica—spills over into different arenas of social life. It is especially noticeable between those sharing a kinship relationship and who, therefore, can make and justify multiple claims on each other. The ambivalence surrounding family and kin networks—these are an important source of support in the everyday struggle to survive and yet are potential breeding grounds of competition and manipulation—is probably not unique to Jamaicans. This potential ambiguity is also expressed through the seemingly mundane acts of offering and eating meals—and consuming meals offered by others without question or hesitation is a reflection of supreme trust.

Commensality is also an important medium through which gender relations are expressed, solidified, or ruptured. (One other important means is, of course, sexual intercourse.) The ambiguity and potential pitfalls that inhere in the relationships between men and women are often expressed through food. Men are often suspicious of women using food as a way of "tying" them for ulterior motives. One Jamaican man tells of a woman who offered him cake but secretly added "a little something" so he would fall madly in love with her. He considered himself lucky that the cake did not set too well—he vomited afterwards—and he quickly broke off this potentially disastrous relationship into which his lover had attempted to "trick" him (Sobo 1993:120).

Food, gender, and cultural constructions of the body overlap considerably. In a societal context in which common-law, transient unions prevail (Bolles 1996; Prior 2005; see also Chapter 6), men are constantly concerned about the possibility of being locked into binding relationships by manipulative lovers. Males are also quite fearful of menstrual blood, which they consider a highly polluting and dangerous substance—and "the most potent means of 'compellance' " (Sobo 1993:230). As a result, in their interactions with women, men are often worried about lovers combining menstrual blood with food in an attempt to "trick" or "bind" them. Sometimes the kind of food that is prepared and offered by a lover—its smell, taste, color, or consistency—provides clues as to whether she has ulterior, mischievous motives. For example:

The most commonly adulterated food is rice and peas, a reddish-brown dish. A woman can steam herself directly over the pot as she finishes cooking for this. Red pea soup, carrot juice, "stew-peas," and potato pudding are also known as potential menses carriers. All are the correct color and are commonly eaten. Some men are so frightened of ingesting menses that they refuse even red herring, a dried fish which they say takes its color from having been killed when menstruating. As careful as men are, menstrual blood diluted in food cannot be tasted. As one woman said, laughing about the small amount needed to compel, 'Cho—you think that little bit can flavor pot?' (Sobo 1993:230)

Brazil

Food, sexuality, and gender overlap considerably and in diverse ways in different societal and cultural contexts. In the Brazilian shantytown studied by Goldstein (2003), sexuality, gender relations, and differential power relations are often conveyed through **consumption metaphors** in which male and female identities are partly constructed and defined through the type of agency displayed in the act of sexual intercourse.[2] Brazilian male identity is partly constructed, symbolically and otherwise, by taking the lead, active sexual role (the inserter)—regardless of whether intercourse is with a woman or another man (see also Chapter 6). This active role is linguistically expressed as haven "eaten" someone else:

> The standard understanding of maleness and male identity in the Brazilian construction of sexuality—more common among the popular classes—is that a man who eats other men and assumes the public status as the active sexual partner can maintain a firm male identity as an homem, while the passive partner, the bicha or viado, considered the recipient of anal sex, loses status. (2003:236)

Although males who "eat" many others (males or females) solidify their identity, status, and power over them, such a path is not available to women. If women are especially voracious "eaters" (have many sexual partners), they are "referred to as *galinhas* (chickens) and *piranhas* (piranas or meat-eating fish), and both of these animal metaphors have negative connotations" (Goldstein 2003:236). Eating metaphors and the construction of sexuality and gender identity are firmly related to the differential and unequal access to economic resources between men and women in the domestic domain (see Chapter 6). Consumption metaphors, then, function as a linguistic and discursive medium through which gender inequality and power struggles are communicated.

The symbolic importance of food in the realm of gender and sexuality surfaces in other contexts as well. Statements on the kinds of foods typically eaten by whom often convey class-specific commentaries on sexuality and sexual potency. Goldstein notes that shantytown dwellers, who are otherwise wretchedly poor, pride themselves in having a lot of enjoyable sex which, unlike many other things necessary and desirable in life, is readily available and free. "Good sex" is one of those preciously few domains of life in which favela residents have an edge over *os ricos* (the rich). Favela women are quite clear that sexual potency is a class-specific attribute, and that this potential in turn is very much related to the kinds of food consumed. Consider, for example, the following statement by a favela woman:

> The poor man eats well, a *feijão* [bean soup] with meat inside, a *mocotó* [soup made from the hoof of a cow], *carne seca* [beef dried in the sun] inside the feijão . . . What I ask is the following, "Is the rich person going to eat all this?" He eats only jelly and cheese. Bread and butter. What strength does that have?

For this reason, they lose their potency early. At times, the poor man is feeling weak and he sends me to make mocotó . . . It makes you strong. I know because I am from Bahia. I make it. The rich person doesn't eat feijão. The iron is there. The bed [sex] of the poor person is better. Because of the food. (Goldstein 2003:243)

Cuisine, Cookbooks, and Nation-Building

Food and cuisine also have a particular capacity to evoke feelings of shared belonging and community—what Turner called **communitas.** That is, "A strong, total communal experience of oneness in which an individual senses . . . a merging of awareness" (1969:182). An important theme in the study of food and cuisine has therefore to do with the coalescence of national identity, in elucidating "the roles of gender, class, and geography in forging nations" (Pilcher 1998:3). In the case of Mexico, "Connections between cuisine and identity—what people eat and who they are—run deep into Mexican history," so much so that the prized chili peppers "now form part of the national identity, captured in the popular Mexican refrain: '*Yo soy como el chile verde, picante pero sabroso*' (I am like the green chile, hot but tasty)" (Pilcher 1998:163). Indeed, the construction of a national identity—a crucial cultural underpinning of the modern nation-state—that would overshadow regional, ethnic, or class identities and affiliations, has been a difficult challenge faced by Latin American and Caribbean elites since independence. The production and dissemination of national cuisines was one way this challenge was met and overcome. The ways in which the direct political intervention in the distribution of food staples has functioned to consolidate national political factions should not be overlooked (Ochoa 2000). How and why food and national cuisines were and have been important in the forging of national identities in Belize and Mexico are illustrated in the following sections.

Globalization and National Cuisine in Belize

Belize (formerly British Honduras) is a particularly interesting country with which to explore the connections between food, cuisine, and national identity. This is so because it achieved independence from Great Britain quite recently; because it has a complex mix of ethnic groups, languages, and regions with different historical and cultural trajectories; and because a sense of national identity—of nationhood—has only recently (and tenuously) emerged. The four most important languages spoken in Belize are English, Spanish, Maya, and Garifuna, and censuses list seven major ethnoracial categories—Creole, Mestizo, Maya, Garifuna, White, East Indian, and Chinese. During the past two decades, many Maya, fleeing the violence in Guatemala (see Chapter 12), have crossed into and settled in Belize (Stone 2000).

In a witty statement, Wilk says that "Belizeans know their flag, anthem, capital, and great founding father, and they now know that they should have a culture to go with them" (1999:244). He argues that the forging of a national cuisine so central to the coalescence of a Belizean national identity was in fact largely influenced by recent external or foreign economic forces and cultural influences—what many call globalization (see Chapter 10)—with the "paradoxical result that in an increasingly open, global society like Belize, tastes and preferences are now more deeply localized than ever before" (1999:253).

Wilk begins with an account of cuisine he was offered at two different moments of his research stays in Belize. In 1973, hoping to enjoy "something authentically Belizean," he was offered a meal that local Belizeans thought he would like: canned corned beef and sardines, stale Mexican bread, and a Seven-Up. In 1990, he was offered a rather different meal, one which, he and his wife were told,

> was produced in Belize and cooked to Belizean recipes. We had tortillas (from the Guatemalan-owned factory down the road), stewed beans (which I later found were imported from the United States . . .), stewed chicken (from nearby Mennonite farms), salad (some of the lettuce was from Mexico) with bottled French dressing (Kraft from England), and an avocado with sliced white cheese (made locally by Salvadoran refugees). (1999:245)

Further, the first self-proclaimed "Belizean Restaurant" opened that same week, and an "advertisement asked customers to 'Treat yourself to a Belizean feast. Authentic Belizean dishes—Garnachas, Tamales, Rice and Beans, Stew Chicken, Fried Chicken.'" As Wilk notes, these foods and cuisines, already widely available and consumed in Belize during his first research period in the early 1970s, were publicly recognized as part of the national cuisine only a decade later. The central (and perhaps obvious) question that Wilk poses is "How is it that British and Mexican dishes, and global standards like stewed and fried chicken, emerged so quickly as an emblematic Belizean cuisine?" (1999:246)

A great deal in fact had happened in Belize in the seventeen years between the two meals, the most important perhaps being the extent to which Belize and Belizeans had come into contact (through travel but particularly through the media) with external influences, tourists, and images, especially from the United States. This growing and intensifying influence of the global on the local has been met by a growing and ongoing public debate over what constitutes, or ought to constitute, "authentic" or "traditional" Belizean culture, one that was largely absent when Wilk visited Belize the first time. The emergence of an "authentic" Belizean cuisine in 1990 had much to do with how these external influences provided the context, rationale, and even ideological justification for the need for such authenticity. The Lambeys, who provided Wilk and his wife with the second meal in 1990,

> know how to play this game properly. They are Belizean nationalists who know that they are supposed to have something authentic and local to offer. They have been abroad and have learned to perceive and categorize differences as "national" and "cultural." They have learned that foreigners expect them to be Belizean, and they know how to do the job. They are . . . busy creating traditions and national culture . . . [Further], serving an authentic Belizean meal . . . is performance of modernity and sophistication. (1999:247)

This seemingly paradoxical juxtaposition of authentic and traditional, and modern and sophisticated, is also better understood by understanding how it radically contrasts with the colonial-era **hierarchy of taste and cuisine.** During the colonial era, diet was highly stratified by class, so that the elite favored imports from Europe, while wage laborers preferred any type of food they could afford in stores, and both disdained the diet of the peasantry, largely consisting of roots crops, rice, fruits and vegetables and, occasionally, wild game. Cuisines currently construed as "authentic" or "traditional" not only sharply contrast with but almost represent an inversion of the colonial stratification of cuisines. Lobster, for example, now highly valued, was "eaten by the poor because it was cheap, by the elite because it was prized in Europe, but shunned by the middle class as 'trash fish'" (1999: 249). Further, the transformation of Mexican foods and cuisines from the northern part of the country had a great deal to do with how the middle class—which has spearheaded the construction of "authentic" national cuisine—views these foods as a "safely exotic option—associated neither with the class below nor the class above" (1999:249).

In a matter of a few decades, an "authentic" cuisine—one reconstituted remarkably quickly from a variety of disparate sources—had come to loom at the forefront of Belizean national consciousness and sense of national identity. This became painfully clear to England's Queen Elizabeth when she visited Belize in 1985. During that visit, Belizean officials did their best to offer the monarch of the British empire a host of local delicacies. The decision was made to offer as the principal meat dish at the queen's banquet a large rodent (called *gibnut* or *paca*), whose flesh, according to rural dwellers, is quite tasty—but disdained and rarely eaten by middle-class Belizeans. The British tabloids reacted quickly and in a characteristically ferocious way, accusing Belizeans of insulting the queen's dignity. One British tabloid front page stated that the queen was "Served Rat by Wogs." This in turn provoked an immediate, decided, and nationalist response by Belizeans:

> Most Belizeans saw this as an example of British arrogance and racism. For the first time, a Belizean dish became a matter of public pride. Nationalist chefs and nutritionists defended the Belizean gibnut as tasty, healthful, and nutritious, Reinterpreted as a national delicacy, today it often appears on restaurant menus as "Royal Rat," and its high price and legitimacy in national cuisine place heavy hunting pressures on remaining populations. (1999:251)

Cookbooks, Tamales, and Mexican Nation-Building

Maize, beans, chilies, and squash were cornerstones of Aztec and Mesoamerican diet and cuisine prior to the European Conquest. Five hundred years later, recipes similar to those that Aztec women prepared during pre-Conquest festivals surfaced in 1992 at the "First Annual Week of the Tamal, sponsored by the National Museum of Popular Culture" (Pilcher 1998:1; see also Photo 9.2).

The Mexico that the Creole and Europeanized-elites assumed control of after the protracted wars of independence was a huge country with imposing geographic barriers and inaccessible or virtually nonexistent communications; pronounced linguistic diversity; and hundreds of ethnic groups whose members were convinced on an everyday basis that they were something other than Mexicans. National, Spanish-speaking elites therefore faced the daunting task of governing and converting Mexico into a modern nation-state, and of

PHOTO 9.2 *A typical working class family in Mexico eating tamales in the kitchen.*

instilling a national identity, a sense of being "Mexican." There were many ways of over-coming these obstacles—for example, incorporating indigenous peoples into the cash economy, or constructing schools—but one especially important strategy was to develop and have most Mexicans identify with a national cuisine through the writing and dissemination of national cookbooks.

As occurred elsewhere, changing diet and cuisine were linked to other concerns, such as fomenting "a stable domestic environment" and promoting "patriotism within the home" (Pilcher 1998:48). The drive against "lower" class foods and diets was also part and parcel of a wider, more inclusive cultural effort aimed at overhauling health, hygiene, and sexual norms; instilling a capitalist work ethic; and spreading the use of the Spanish language. In fact, by the early twentieth century, national elites viewed Mexico's poverty and underdevelopment as a direct consequence of a popular diet made up principally of maize, beans, and chilies. The "debility" of the Mexican "Indian"—and the inability of Mexico to become an "advanced" nation—was supposedly caused by a popular diet virtually devoid of milk, meat, and bread. Such a diet, furthermore, was perceived as a threat to the social order:

> Even more dreadful to the . . . elite was the threat to public order posed by popular cooking. In the countryside poor diets led to nothing more serious than indolence, but in the cities the lack of adequate nutrition provoked defiant behavior, lawlessness, and alcoholism. (Pilcher 1998:83)

The colonial and postcolonial drive against maize did not wholly succeed because of three reasons. The first was the concerted and stubborn resistance by Mexico's popular classes at altering their diet. Second, there was a pronounced change in elite attitudes toward maize, from disdain to recognizing its significance. This was because by the mid-1940s, Mexican and United States scientists began underscoring the extraordinary nutritional value of the maize, bean, and chilies complex, and were widely disseminating the results of their scientific studies. The third reason accounting for maize's resilience had to do with the rapid proliferation of cookbooks drawing on different regional recipes, national cuisines that would be identified with *lo mexicano* by most Mexican citizens. These cookbooks and their accompanying recipes were primarily written and disseminated by women and, in this sense, the development of a national cuisine and the forging of a national identity were profoundly gendered affairs:

> The formation of a national community in the kitchen grew out of the basic sociability of Mexican women, for housewives carried out a brisk market in recipes as well as gossip . . . Cookbooks inspired national loyalty less by any didactic content than by fostering a sense of community among women . . . The transformation of household practices into national symbols encouraged women to take more active roles in the national life . . . As the rise of nationalism transferred sacred ground from church to state, domestic roles also offered women a voice in this new religion of the people. (Pilcher 1998:66, 148–149)

Controversies: "Hot" and "Cold" Foods

A consistent theme in the anthropology of food in Latin America and the Caribbean, and one overlapping with medical anthropology, has been the distinction between **hot and cold foods** (Messer 1981, 1987; Mathews 1983; Boster and Weller 1990; Harwood 1998; Foster, G. M. 1998). The dichotomy between hot and cold has little to do with thermal temperatures, either in a raw or cooked state, and much more with specific qualities ascribed to certain foods and food categories, especially their effects on emotional and somatic well-being and overall health. For example, in a Oaxacan Mexican community, chocolate, sugar, and honey are almost always classed at hot, while *amarillo* (a sauce dish laced with chili peppers) and *caldo* (a soup or broth) are most often conceptualized as cold. Some Puerto Ricans in New York City place white and lima beans in the cold category, while viewing kidney beans, evaporated milk, and alcoholic beverages as hot. Furthermore, hot and cold classifications vary significantly across and within countries, regions, and communities. Thus, New York City Puerto Ricans view sugarcane as cold but Mexican Oaxacans believe it is a hot substance, while in Mexico bananas are viewed by some Tlaxcalans as cold and by Oaxacans as hot. And even within the same community—in Oaxaca, Mexico, or Jamaica, for example—there may exist an even split of opinions about whether a food (tea, for example), is hot or cold (Mathews 1983:830–831; Harwood 1998:253; Boster and Weller 1990:177; Sobo 1993:46). Further, sometimes even finer distinctions are made—

Messer (1981:135) records seven hot and cold terms in a Zapotec-speaking community in Oaxaca—along what is often a cultural continuum rather than a categorical dichotomy.

But how do anthropologists explain how and why some food are classed as cold or hot, and what do they have to say about the cultural and social implications of this classification? The debate between Mathews (1983) and Boster and Weller (1990) provides some useful insights. Mathews' position is that

> investigators have been more concerned with describing the shared content of humoral categories than they have with analyzing how individuals actively go about classifying items and assigning them to categories in the first place . . . [and that] . . . hot/cold values are not fixed in one shared system of classification. Rather, several conceptual systems underlie humoral classification, and these systems are differentially invoked depending on context. (1983:828)

Thus, individuals within the same community may vary in their food classifications, for these are context-dependent and yet at the same time the underlying process of decision-making (including criteria and contexts) whereby they go about classifying food is broadly shared. This tension and seeming contrast is superficial at best. In the community studied by Mathews, foods are alternatively classed at hold or cold along three dimensions. The "danger" dimension alludes to negative effects on the body when foods are ingested, so that, for example, foods that cause bloatedness or constipation are generally classed as cold, while hot foods cause diarrhea or gas. This is why meal preparation emphasizes a balance between hot and cold foods to "neutralize" their potential harmful effects. Yet, general statements are consistently context-specific, so that someone who consumes gelatin (a cold food that causes stomachaches) but who develops some other symptom may also class gelatin, in that specific context, as "hot."

The second dimension along which foods are classified is what Mathews calls "neutralization." Through this dimension and classification, the idea is not to offset the effects of cold foods but to neutralize the intrinsic "hot" and "cold" states of individuals and their bodies. This is particularly important in the sexual realm because of the widespread belief that

> some individuals are born abnormally "hot" or . . . "cold" . . . "[H]ot" individuals . . . suffer a disproportionate number of "cold" illnesses and have abnormally strong sexual drives as reflected in "promiscuous" sexual behavior before marriage and adulterous behavior after marriage. "Cold" individuals . . . suffer a disproportionate number of "hot" illnesses and have weak sexual drives demonstrated by sexual disinterest, and the failure to marry, have sexual liaisons, and produce offspring. (Mathews 1983:833)

Given this classification of bodily (and sexual) states, food classifications will again vary, depending on whether hot or cold individuals (or significant others) attempt to deal with their cold or hot illnesses. Thus, men and women may class gelatin as cold during food preparation and as being along the danger dimension (see previous text), but wives, attempting to control the adulterous behavior of their "hot" spouses, will try to convince them to consume "cold" foods on certain occasions. Further, classifications may vary across the danger and neutralization dimensions: cucumbers, for example, are hot in the context of meals preparation but cold when attempting to deal with excessive sexual drive.

The third dimension has to do with the treatment of minor illnesses—the "healthful" dimension. Here the objective of food classification is to deal with common, ordinary illnesses, such as coughs or swollen stomachs. And within this category, foods are alternatively classed as either hot or cold, depending on the specific illness. Sobo (1993:45–46) raises an identical point in her study of a Jamaican community, and Messer's research, also in Oaxaca (1981, 1987), generally agrees with Mathews' overall results.

Boster and Weller's (1990) research was slightly different and had two objectives. The first was to dispute some research (e.g., Logan and Morrill 1979) suggesting that classificatory variations (lack of agreement) largely stem from intracultural variability, that is, the presence of subcultures with different belief systems or unequal access to the same store of cultural knowledge. Their second, related objective was to dispute Mathews' conclusions that if there is general disagreement on food classifications, it stems from their contextual underpinnings.

To substantiate their arguments, Boster and Weller worked with two very different groups—couples in Tlaxcala, Mexico, and undergraduates from a Pennsylvania college. The reason for comparing two such dissimilar groups had to do with critiquing a core assumption of Logan and Morrill's research: that two radically different cultures, groups, or subcultures would largely disagree on the classification of identical types of food. (Although Pennsylvania college students may agree on whether a specific food is "spicy," unlike Mexican Tlaxcalans, the hot/cold dichotomy is not an important part of their culture.) Both groups were presented with four identical questions on how they would classify eighty foods (seventy-five of which also appeared in Mathews' study) along the hot/cold continuum, and across Mathews' three dimensions. Using statistical techniques to measure associations between and among responses, and to control for statistical bias when dealing with small samples, Boster and Weller arrived at some surprising results. One was that Pennsylvania college students by and large agreed as much as the Tlaxcalans on the classification of most foods as hot or cold both in general terms and across Mathews' three dimensions.

Turning to the Tlaxcalan responses, Boster and Weller note that these responses were far less consistent across Mathews' danger, neutralization, and heath dimensions than those of the Oaxacans. They also addressed the possible objection that the differences in classification might simply stem from cultural differences between Tlaxcala and Oaxaca. They did so by undertaking statistical correlations between responses on the classifications of foods between Pennsylvania students, Tlaxcalans, and, based on Mathews' data, Oaxacans. One of the results of these analyses was that Tlaxcalans and Oaxacans were far more similar to each other than to the Pennsylvania students. They summarize their research in the following way:

> First, agreement alone does not . . . indicate the existence of a cultural system: here . . . Pennsylvanians display a very high degree of agreement in their responses . . . about the hot-cold valences of foods, even though they were chosen for their ignorance of this cultural system. Second, context does not always

explain away variation: in neither group is there a strong reduction of variation
when context is more narrowly specified. Third, context sensitivity is not necessarily the hallmark of expertise: the Pennsylvanians show a great deal of context sensitivity while the Tlaxcalans display virtually none. Fourth, the
Tlaxcalans and Oaxacans . . . share a cultural system of hot-cold classification . . .
because they agree with each other more often than with Pennsylvanians . . .
This suggests that the presence of context specificity is not good evidence for
the existence of a cultural system nor is the lack of it evidence for the absence
of one. (Boster and Weller 1990:176–177)

In the United States: Tamales, Gender, and Survival

The symbolic role of tamales in underpinning Mexican identity is not restricted to Mexico
but is also important for large numbers of itinerant Mexican farmworkers and their families
in the United States. Identity is partially expressed through practice—which may include
cooking food—and preparing tamales takes up considerable time and effort. Consider, for
example, the following depiction of the making of tamales among Mexican farm laborers
in Texas:

> In the array of artifacts by which Tejano migrant farm workers identify them-
> selves, the tamale has no serious rival. It is a complicated culinary treat
> demanding days of preparation, marking festive—sometimes sacred—occasions,
> signaling the cook's extraordinary concern for the diners, and requiring a spe-
> cial set of cultural skills and tastes to appreciate and consume appropriately.
> Tamales are served wrapped in corn husks which hold a soft outer paste of
> *masa harina* (a flour) and a rich inner mash prepared from the meat of a pig's
> head. (Williams 1984:113)

Further, preparing tamales is a quintessential gendered and social affair:

> Only women make tamales. They cooperate to do so with domestic fanfare
> which stretches through days of buying the pigs' heads, stripping the meat,
> cooking the mash, preparing the paste, and stuffing, wrapping, and baking or
> boiling the final tamale. Women shop together because the heads are very
> bulky; they gather around huge, steaming pots to cook together as well.
> Tamales are thus labor-intensive food items which symbolize and also exag-
> gerate women's routine nurturance of men. The ritual and cooperation of
> tamale cookery dramatically underscore women's shared monopoly of domes-
> tic tasks. (Williams 1984:113)

The time, effort, and money channeled to preparing tamales can be staggering, particularly
during ritual occasions that draw together dozens of extended family members scattered
across the United States, as well friends and acquaintances. In one Christmas celebration

documented by Williams, more than two thousand tamales were cooked, consumed, and distributed.

During her fieldwork with migrant families in Texas and Illinois, Williams learned that migrant women solidly accepted their roles in household affairs, especially in the domestic sphere of cooking (particularly tamales), few expressed doubts that their husbands were entitled to demand of them tamales, and all women agreed that it was their obligation to provide their husbands and families with tamales. But why?

One important foci of Williams' fieldwork was to dispel the notion that migrant women viewed their roles in domestic affairs as necessarily oppressive, and that they were submissive to their husbands. Williams explains:

> Because migrant women are so involved in family life and so seemingly submissive to their husbands, they have been described often as martyred purveyors of rural Mexican and Christian custom, tyrannized by excessively masculine, crudely domineering, rude and petty bullies in marriage, and blind to any world outside the family because they are suffocated by the concerns of kin. Most disconcerting to outsider observers is that migrant women seem to embrace such stereotypes: they argue that they *should* monopolize their foodways and that they should *not* question the authority of their husbands. If men want tamales, men should have them. But easy stereotypes can mislead. (1984:113)

Williams' fieldwork underscored the point that preparing and sharing tamales was crucially important far beyond the immediate confines of kitchen life, taste, and cuisine. Migrant farm life is distinguished by extreme poverty, poor health, low pay (often below minimum wage), seasonal hunger, erratic employment, and unpredictable income (see also Rothenberg 1998; Martínez 2001). As a result, migrant families are constantly on the move in search of work opportunities. Further, family members—young and old, male and female—are forced to contribute in their own ways to the economic well-being of their households, and males (including husbands) openly recognize the crucial importance of the work of their female kin and wives .

Poverty, unpredictability, necessarily flexible work roles, and a transient lifestyle go hand in hand with the importance that migrants attach to forging and maintaining social relationships, especially with extended kin living or working near or faraway. The great deal of time, effort, and money that migrant women devote to preparing and sharing tamales is crucial to the success of this broader strategy—and its importance is recognized by both women and men, wives and husbands. Because preparing tamales is so time and labor intensive, many women come together to share in the work.

Preparing tamales is thus a key opportunity for relatives and acquaintances to gather and share news about their lives, including work opportunities elsewhere. Sharing tamales also creates reciprocal obligations with those—family or friends—recently arrived from Mexico or elsewhere in the United States. Tamales loom important in accumulating and investing in **social capital**—"resources, actual or virtual, that accrue to an individual or a group by virtue of possessing a durable network of more or less institutionalized relationships of mutual acquaintance and recognition" (Bourdieu and Wacquant 1992:119; quoted in Aguilera and Massey 2003:672)—for the economic and social survival of migrant families. Recent research underscores that migrant farm families with wider and more enduring social networks (social capital) enjoy higher incomes and more secure work opportunities than those who do not (Aguilera and Massey 2003).

The sharing of food also is important in creating fictive kin relationships, thereby expanding the social field, which can be crucial at a moment of crisis. Williams' following vignette is telling:

> Each summer some two dozen of the Gomas' relatives arrive to work through the migrant season, and during that time Sra. Goma mobilizes on their behalf the resources of her Illinois networks—legal aid, public assistance, transportation, and a less formal example, a service station owner who will cash paychecks. She has worked hard to stretch and secure this network, often initially obligating friends through food. By sharing her . . . dinners, Illinois residents act as though they are kin, and through time she finds that she can call on them for help as if they really were. (Williams 1984:119)

Thus women's work—especially, but not limited to the kitchen domain and the preparing and sharing of food and tamales—is absolutely crucial in the lives of migrants, and in their attempts to build for themselves and their families a more viable, predictable, and decent life in the United States. Women—as well as their spouses and other male relatives—recognize and celebrate in various ways their importance in this undertaking. As a result, women command far greater prestige, status, and authority within their households and social networks—and vis-à-vis their spouses—than stereotypical images of domination and submissiveness may imply.

Summary

Eating and enjoying food may seem a mundane undertaking, but it is in fact culturally and socially important. Indigenous peoples enjoyed a wide spectrum of foods and cuisines, all significant in ritual and social interactions. After the Conquest, some European crops fared well while others did not, and widespread attempts to replace indigenous with European foods and cuisines largely failed. This chapter also highlighted ways in which food loomed important in ritual and social relationships in Ecuador and Trinidad. Another theme was that food and cuisine are key in gender identities and relationships, and this chapter explored these connections in highland Ecuador, Jamaica, and Brazil. Food and cuisine were also shown to be significant politically, especially in the forging of national identities, as in Belize and Mexico. Foods, like most aspects of culture, are classified in different ways, which in turn reveals much about health and sexuality: such is the case of the hot/cold dichotomy discussed in this chapter. Finally, this chapter also drew attention to the crucial cultural, social, and economic importance of tamales from the vantage point of migrant farmworkers in the United States.

ISSUES AND QUESTIONS

1. *Anthropology of Food.* What does the field of the anthropology of food consist of and what generalizations does it make about food, culture, and social relations? Are there ways that food and cuisine make different statements about culture and social relations than those statements raised in previous chapters?

2. *Inequality or Hierarchy.* Drawing on two separate examples, explain and illustrate how food and cuisine serve to convey statements about cultural, social, or economic inequality or hierarchy. Might there be examples in which they do not?

3. *Nationalism and National Identity.* This chapter underscored the relationship between food and culture, and nationalism and national identity. Drawing on the examples discussed in this chapter, explain what this relationship consists of. What other examples, either from Latin America and the Caribbean or other world regions, might also be relevant?

4. *Hot or Cold Foods.* The distinction between hot and cold foods is one that anthropologists have emphasized for many years. What does this distinction consist of? Which realms of culture does the hot/cold contrast shed light on? Might the hold/cold distinction be relevant to some groups or historical periods and not others?

KEY TERMS AND CONCEPTS

Anthropology of food   p. 251
Communitas   p. 270
Consumption metaphors   p. 269
Food pollution   p. 262
Food taboos   p. 262

Gender-inflected foods   p. 266
Hierarchy of taste and cuisine
    p. 272
Hot and cold foods   p. 274
Reservoirs of memory   p. 252

Ritual of resistance   p. 262
Social capital   p. 278
Peasants   p. 253

ENDNOTES

1 As noted in Chapter 8, globalization is generating a significant impact on diet and nutritional health.

2 Consumption metaphors of the type described by Goldstein are not restricted to Brazil or the Latin American and Caribbean context.

10 Perspectives on Globalization

This chapter centers on the contemporary flow of people and goods, and technology and production, across national boundaries, in what is known as globalization. After reviewing some debates on the economic and cultural dimensions of globalization, attention turns to ethnic tourism as an important cultural phenomenon and its potential transformative effects at the local level. Globalization also entails a continuous flow of investments and production, and an ever-tighter integration between countries. The cultural effects of such transnational linkages are taken up in the third section, which focuses on how the North American Free Trade Agreement (NAFTA) has spurred and intensified migration between Mexico and North America, and on cultural and gendered outcomes of the proliferation of maquiladora assembly and manufacturing plants. The chapter then turns to the relationship between global economic interests and deforestation. The controversies surrounding how some anthropologists represent Amazonian peoples, and how these representations may be endangering their livelihoods and resources, is the focus of the fifth section. Finally, this chapter provides a look into the lives of Hispanic/Latino domestic workers in the United States.

Globalization

Whereas fifty years ago most Latin American and Caribbean peoples lived in rural villages and earned a living by cultivating the land, today most live in urban areas and earn a living by engaging in a variety of nonagricultural, often "informal" occupations; whereas fifty years ago most had little knowledge and firsthand experience with cultural "others" (and their cultural messages) beyond their community, region, or country, that is not the case today when even the most "isolated," or "traditional," are likely to be intimately acquainted with worldwide events and come into direct contact with "Westerners" or other Latin Americans; despite the fact that Latin American and Caribbean economies have been embedded in one way or another in the world system for centuries, the transnational, global linkages of today are likely to have a far quicker and especially pronounced economic, cultural, and social impact than those of fifty years ago.

Globalization is one of the most popular and widely circulating terms today. It is also one of the most ill-defined and ambiguous social science concepts, partly because it overlaps with other, analogous ones. Hence, although the term appeared around 1960, among scholars "there is no agreement as to whether it was with Magellan and Mercator, James Watt and Captain Cook, Nixon and Kissinger, or Thatcher and Reagan that globalization started or, to be more precise, that the narrative of globalization ought to begin" (Guillén 2001:237–238). Inda and Rosaldo's volume (2002) provides a broad overview of issues and debates on globalization from the vantage point of anthropology.

Despite its ambiguity (or, perhaps, because of it) many agree that **globalization** is a wide ranging economic and cultural process swiftly connecting in manifold and intricate ways (and in forms unimaginable to many just a few decades ago) peoples, cultures, and societies throughout the globe. Guillén states that "intuitively, globalization is a process fueled by, and resulting in, increasing cross-border flows of goods, services, money, people, information, and culture . . . a 'compression' of space and time, a shrinking of the world" (2001:236); Appadurai associates globalization with a "shifting world" and "deterritorial- ization" expressed in a "loosening of the bonds between people, wealth, and territories" (1991:192–193); Foster talks about a "global ecumene" marked by an "interconnectedness of cultures brought about by global flows of images, objects, and people" (1991:236); while for Kearney (1995:548), quoting Giddens (1990:64), we are witnessing "the intensi- fication of world-wide social relations which link distant localities in such a way that local happenings are shaped by events occurring many miles away and vice versa." Part of the difficulty of defining globalization more precisely is that global connections are hardly new (Wolf 1997 [1982]). Yet, there are probably no historic parallels analogous to the speed, intensity, and pervasiveness of connections that characterize contemporary globalization.

One broad meaning of globalization centers attention on it as an economic phenome- non. Yet, the term has become so entrenched in everyday parlance and academic writings, and so solidified in commonplace understandings of the world, that it is often viewed as a "natural" part and parcel of everyday life, camouflaging the fact that the changes alluded to previously are manifestations of the "global triumph of capitalism" (Comaroff and Comaroff 2001:1). As an economic process, globalization is rooted in a fundamental transformation of the U.S. political economy in the early 1980s and the subsequent spread of what has been glossed as the "new economy" (Harms and Knapp 2003), the "emerging global factory" (Blim 1992), or the "rise of market economics" (Green 1995). The political–economic model is better known in Latin America and the Caribbean as **neoliberalism**—a model based on the belief that the (unregulated) market is a far better regulator of economic and social and cultural life than the state (Sanabria 1999).

Neoliberalism has two broad and related dimensions. The first is a retrenchment, or "retreat" (Gill 2000), of the state from the social sphere, an unraveling of the social contract between the state and its citizens. The effort to disengage the state and make it "leaner" and more "efficient" manifests itself in cutbacks in social spending, as in pensions, health, edu- cation, basic infrastructure, and transportation. In Latin America and the Caribbean, this effort has been paralleled by a sharp decline in state economic investments (such as agri- culture, price supports, and subsidies) and the privatization of state enterprises, such as railroads, airlines, telecommunications, banks, and (formerly nationalized) oil and mining companies. For example, between December 1982 and April 1991, 75 percent of Mexico's almost twelve hundred state-owned enterprises were privatized or "liquidated" (Moody 1995:101). The second major dimension of neoliberalism is that of creating conditions favoring above all the accumulation of capital and investment, and easing the flow of goods and profits across national boundaries. Sharply restraining wage increases; undermining job security ("labor flexibility"); shedding tariffs and other restrictions to investment, imports, and exports; being able to extract natural resources (oil, lumber, minerals) relatively free of environmental regulations; being able to easily close down manufacturing plants and then resurrecting them elsewhere where resources are less expensive and/or labor costs are lower ("outsourcing"); and eroding environmental and labor laws are some ways this second objective is achieved.

Globalization is also a cultural process that has several dimensions (Appadurai 1996). The first is that different peoples throughout the world are acquiring greater (although not necessarily more accurate) understandings and knowledge of others through the widespread circulation of images, symbols, and messages. This ability rests on the emergence and spread of technological innovations, especially in communications. Today, vast numbers of Latin Americans can communicate with each other via telephone, or television or cable programming (see also Chapter 11); or, as is the case among indigenous peoples, share news and events, or build alliances with faraway others, via the Internet (Becker and Delgado-P. 1998; Delgado-P. 2002; see also Chapter 12). That Guaraní and Quechua speakers can use Microsoft operating systems and other software in their native languages points to the extraordinary communicative potential of globalization. Another important venue through which cultural communication is taking place is through travel, primarily by Asian, European, and North American tourists. A rather different form of transnational travel experience is the diaspora of Central American war refugees, explored in Chapter 12.

The second major hallmark of globalization as a cultural process is that it is profoundly asymmetric—it is pervaded and partially made possible by unequal power relations. Thus, some indigenous peoples may have access to the Internet, but the capacity to generate this and other technological innovations (and the ability to distribute them) are not in their hands. And although ever-greater numbers of North American, European, and Asian tourists travel to Latin America and come into contact with indigenous peoples, comparatively few of the latter ever set foot in North America, Europe, or Asia. What this also means is that the direction of the content of cultural messages, symbols, and images is largely unidirectional. As a result, scholars are increasingly questioning whether a homogenous "global culture" is in the making, erasing cultural boundaries and undermining local cultures and identities. The answer is of course difficult and complex, but at least in the Latin American and Caribbean context, evidence and cases studies presented in previous pages (such as the rise of indigenist movements discussed in Chapter 5), as well as in this and subsequent chapters suggest that such a global culture is very far on the horizon.

Tourism, Crafts, and Cultural Authenticity

One indicator of globalization is the vast increase in global travel, especially by European and North American, and increasingly Asian, tourists, which has swelled threefold in the past twenty years (Guillén 2001:239). This increase has been matched by the growing importance of tourism in many Latin American and Caribbean countries. One recent research thrust has been on the relationship between tourism, prostitution, and sex work, especially in the Caribbean (Brennan 2004; Kempadoo 2004).

Tourists leave in their wake—often unnoticed by themselves—profound and sometimes contradictory changes in local communities and landscapes. Tourism, especially in major resort areas with international hotel chains and fast-food franchises, sometimes ushers in landscapes not dissimilar from those in tourists' home countries. Yet, other times tourism—especially undertaken by tourists wishing to experience "authentic" or "traditional" culture—invigorates local cultural traditions, or it leads to their reemergence or refashioning in novel contexts. This process, which often also spurs heightened pride in local or ethnic identity, is known as the **invention of tradition** (Hobsbawn 1983; Maddox 1993; Comaroff and Comaroff 1992). The **anthropology of tourism** focuses on these sorts of impacts and exchanges between tourists and those with whom they come across in their travels. (It is no coincidence that the emergence of this field of study dates to the early 1980s, or the onset of globalization.) Some of the major questions in this rapidly growing field include:

> What are the dynamics and impacts of inter-cultural contact between tourists and locals? . . . How is culture represented in tourist settings, and how is it perceived? . . . How are cultural traditions changed or reinvented over time to match tourist expectations . . . and what can distinguish the genuine from the spurious? . . . How do indigenous societies change as they become integrated with the tourism market? (Stronza 2001:262)

In Search of the "Authentic" and the Timeless

Many tourists are increasingly seeking out the "authentic," wishing to experience "the pristine, the natural, that which is as yet untouched by modernity" (Cohen 1988:374, quoted in Stronza 2001:265). This "modern" desire for the "traditional" or the "authentic"—which sharply contrasts with Latin American elites' views of the "traditional" as an obstacle or barrier to modernity—is both being shaped by and having a profound impact on local cultures and communities where tourists' expectations are being met. This process of **cultural negotiation**—which entails but is not limited to "playing up" to tourist expectations and desires—may have paradoxical outcomes, both changing and reviving values and traditions, including conceptions of self and national identity (Stronza 2001:271).

Because they embody and magnify a deep sense of timelessness, antiquity, and tradition, a principal tourist destination is archaeological sites. And few sites in South America rival the magnificence and sense of awe that tourists experience in Cusco, Peru, and its nearby ruins of Machu Picchu (see Chapter 3). Attracting half a million visitors yearly, tourism is the most important economic activity in Cusco, which has led to "selective re-creation and reconstruction of the past" (Silverman 2002:883)—especially the Inca past—by local government officials and elites, as well as by members of the popular classes. The attempt to convert Cusco into Peru's cultural capital reflect efforts to make the past more meaningful for those in the present—including but not limited to tourists. Elsewhere, Kaplan (1993) has underscored the role of Mexican museums in projecting coherent national images for the tourist market.

The privileging of and playing up to the Inca past has taken many forms. The Cusco municipality is funding the excavation and restoration of Incan structures, and has changed the name of the city to Qosqo to more closely adhere to Quechua pronunciation. The city is also referred to by honorific titles, such as "Imperial City," "Millennial City," or "Immortal Cusco" (Silverman 2002:885). And elite calls are made for more people to speak Quechua openly on the streets—despite the fact that speaking Quechua has historically been associated with "ignorant" and poverty-ridden "Indians." This attempt at refashioning the past to convey a timeless, essentialized present/past for tourists has been quite random. For example, Inca artifacts and stone structures are often placed in other parts of the city far from where they were excavated, and an emblem of one of Cusco's best hotels depicts coastal Nazca pottery—made one thousand years before the Incas.

Local people are involved in this selective process of historical reconstruction. For example, folkloric performances throughout the year take place in Cusco, and many local groups compete to participate in the Festival of Inti Raymi—the Inca winter solstice festival—turning it into one of the hottest tourist attractions. This selective reconstruction of the past can be contentious and reveal underlying tensions. The controversies surrounding the display of an "Inca flag" (most scholars believe that the Incas did not have such a flag), designed by a local engineer in 1971 and widely adopted by the Cusco municipality two years later, is an example:

> . . . in 2000 . . . officials realized that the invented "Inca flag" . . . is the same as the international gay community's seven-colored rainbow emblem . . . Indeed, in *El Comercio* [a leading newspaper], on July 9, 2000, Cusco's . . . mayor . . . complained that the Inca flag had been "usurped by the gay community" and needed to be replaced . . . [T]he lieutenant mayor . . . stated that replacement was imperative so as "to avoid the moral deterioration of Cusco society" . . . There were political ramifications as well . . . [The lieutenant mayor] worried that prestigious international guests were refusing to have their photographs taken in the municipality building next to the flag of Cusco for fear of being identified with the gay community. The Gay Movement of Lima . . . quickly publicized its offense that the official flag of Cusco would be changed to differentiate it from a gay symbol. (Silverman 2002:888–889)

Producing "Ethnic" Handicrafts

Tourists' search for the "traditional," their enormous purchasing power compared to those living in the communities and sites they visit, and their demand for and purchase of things "native," "ethnic," or "indigenous" to bring back home and display to others, often invigorate artisan-based craft and textile traditions (Nash 1993).

This has occurred in Panama, where highly decorated cloths called *molas*—"barely one hundred years old and clearly developed through contact with Europeans" (Sherzer 1994:902)—are the most distinctive trait of Kuna ethnic identity (Tice 2002). It was not until the 1960s and 1970s when Kuna began producing molas for sale. Although some molas are sold to tourists visiting Panama, most are sold to intermediaries who supply Europe, Japan, and the United States. Part of the impetus for producing molas for the international market stemmed from the growing number of visiting tourists and a decline in local income, but also because of the growing attention, visibility, and demand that molas garnered in international elite circles, such as museums and art galleries. And in a classic but not surprising display of how commoditization can have unintended consequences, by the late 1980s, molas "had become a well-recognized symbol of Panama" (Tice 2002:222).

Spurred by the growing tourist and ethnic market, analogous processes are occurring elsewhere. Guatemala, for instance, has experienced a surge in artisan and textile production. Ehlers documents the almost fortuitous circumstances that led to the creation of a prosperous textile cooperative in San Antonio Palopó, a Mayan-speaking community in highland Guatemala (1993). Textile weaving is, of course, a deeply rooted tradition in Guatemala, as in most of Mesoamerica. Palopó was no exception, where women weaved using backstrap looms. But the emergence of commercial weaving geared mainly to the tourist and ethnic market was set in motion by fortuitous circumstances and clever foresight. First came a road that linked the community to the Lake Atitlán area, where many tourists visited. Community members then decided to organize into a cooperative so they could weave the *cortes*—traditional skirts—that they had often bought in a nearby town and, perhaps, sell some to tourists. They then approached a Peace Corps volunteer in a neighboring village, who moved to Palopó and provided technical and management assistance, and recruited help from a master weaver, who taught community members how to use foot looms. The bishop of the Catholic Church provided money to build a cooperative building; local nuns furnished the foot looms; and the United States Agency for International Development (USAID) and Oxfam offered supplies. Getting the first shipments of cortes to ethnic and tourist shops in Guatemala City proved a challenge, but it was overcome when the owner of a small business firm in nearby Panachel that exported to the United States became interested in Palopó's cortes and agreed to purchase them on a consistent basis. Guatemala's civil war during the 1980s—which virtually shut down the tourist industry—barely affected the cooperative, for virtually all its weavings were destined for the U.S. market. Less than ten years after the first community members thought of mass producing cortes, weaving for export was a thriving business (Ehlers 1993).

Among the best known, successful, and affluent South American ethnic weavers are the Otavaleños, named after the town and region of Otavalo in northern Ecuador. Otavaleños are well-known for their weaving tradition—ethnohistorical documents suggest that they furnished high-quality textiles to the Inca state (Salomon 1981)—but they are especially famous for their entrepreneurial ability to supply weavings for the North American and European market by engaging in long-distance, transnational migration, while also maintaining their distinctive sense of identity and community (Meisch 1998; Colloredo-Mansfeld 1999; see also Photo 10.1). This successful mix of the modern and traditional, the local and transnational, along with the production for the global market is one of the most distinctive traits of Otavaleño society and culture:

> Native peoples must have the cash and commodities of the marketplace to reproduce the runa kawsay (native Andean life). To be sure, subsistence farming; livestock keeping; creating extensive, kin-based networks of mutual support; and other facets of indigenous production matter as much now . . . as they ever have. Yet, such practices . . . must adapt to widespread and often disjointed circulation of people and goods. Exporting Andean handicrafts, importing Italian fedoras for men, shipping locally made sweaters to Colombia (goods made according to U.S. Peace Corps designs), bringing English tweed cloth back from Europe for women's skirts . . . departing for the summer tourist season in

PHOTO 10.1   *Otavalo Weavers, Ecuador.*

Prague, returning for a child's baptism are the large and small acts producing Otavalo's social world. In all this flow, culture materializes itself not so much in fixed institutions and symbols but in rhythms of accumulation and consumption and in arrivals and departures. (Colloredo-Mansfeld 1999:5)

At any given moment, Otavaleño households have members and social networks in far-flung North American, European, and Asian locales selling their goods and, in so doing, reproducing their distinctive way of life. Otavaleños' sense of community and identity is continuously forged by participating in key events—baptisms, weddings, and other rituals—that solidify a sense of identity and community. One of the most interesting aspects of Otavalo's entrepreneurial ethnic culture is that already in the 1940s there were reports of Otavaleños selling their goods outside of Ecuador—which suggests that the emergence of the global "ethnic" market boosted, but did not create, the long-standing practice of contemporary far-flung commercial trading. Clearly, then, Otavaleño insertion into the contemporary global economy "does not signal the corruption of a more 'authentic' native Andean way of life. In fact, the absence of merchant Indians, long-distance exchange, and complex deals for 'foreign goods' represents a diminishing of indigenous society" (Colloredo-Mansfeld 1999:125).

Zorn (2004) has traced the fortunes of the Andean community of Taquile, a small island on the Peruvian side of Lake Titicaca, as it became progressively enmeshed with the global ethnic tourist market. Unlike Otavalo's long historic trajectory of long-distance, commercially oriented weaving, tourism and the marketing of ethnic weavings in Taquile is relatively recent. Prior to the early 1970s, virtually all of Taquile's weaving was destined for use and not sale. Thirty-five years ago, most households were primarily engaged in agriculture.

Like the Otavaleños, Taquileans actively embraced tourists and responded to their need to encounter (and purchase) the "authentic," including the *chumpi* (Quechua, *faja* in Spanish), exquisitely designed woven belts, one of the most characteristic Taquile weavings. And again like the Otavaleños, Taquileans maintained a strong emphasis on agriculture and variety of communal and social institutions. But, unlike the Otavaleños, Taquileans went far beyond merely expanding the household-based manufacture and marketing of textiles, for they channeled "the money earned from textile sales . . . to build community-based tourism businesses and services" (Zorn 2004:85).

Taquileans' initial ventures into the tourist market were partly triggered by the active involvement of a Peace Corps volunteer, who took it upon himself to market some of the island's weavings in Cusco during the early 1970s. These years coincided with an influx of tourists, and by 1981 Taquileans had founded a cooperative geared almost exclusively to those tourists. In a symbolically significantly move, Taquileans called their cooperative "Manco Capac Taquilean Crafts Association," after the first Inca monarch. They purchased boats to take tourists back and forth between their island and the Peruvian mainland, and founded restaurants and lodging houses for tourists wishing to stay overnight (Zorn 2004:85–91, 121–122).

Time-honored communal institutions have provided an organizational springboard enabling Taquileans to face up to the challenges of the tourist market. Taquileans have organized at least half a dozen different committees that have jurisdiction over some facet of the tourist sector (e.g., a committee on housing, one on food, and so forth). One of these committees applied for and received a grant from the Inter-American Foundation to purchase motors and boat parts necessary to transfer tourists to and from the island, and other grants have enabled community members to buy solar panels for their homes and restaurants. Taquileans have traveled to and performed "ethnic" dances in Washington, D.C., and have even built a museum that displays and sells local, "ethnic" handicrafts (some not actually from Taquile). And, in a classic (and recent) case of the invention of tradition, a "Festival Fair" emerged (Zorn 2004:117–125). Clearly, the spurring or reinvigoration of tradition has gone hand-in-hand with a global tourist market. In an example of the transnational connections that Taquileans and tourists have forged, Zorn recalls:

> I received soon after September 11, 2001, from Juan Quispe, who had traveled by boat to an Internet café [on the Peruvian mainland] . . . an email: "Please we want to know that you are well. We cry and suffer because of so many disappeared people in New York and in Washington. Please tell us that you are well." Because of tourism to their community, Juan and other Taquileans felt connected to people in the Unites States, through direct experiences not mediated either by Taquilean migration or through mass media. (2004:129)

Transnational Production and Labor

Globalization is about much more than the mere flow of people, images, or culture: it has much to do with the transnational, relatively unfettered flow of capital and investments, the production and distribution of goods, and the relentless drive to increase profits (Harms and Knapp 2003). These imperatives, coupled with inexpensive labor and other lower costs in Third World countries, as well as technological innovations that make it relatively simple for manufacturing plants to shut down at one site and re-open at another, account for the increasing production of goods in countries such as in Mexico primarily for consumers in industrialized countries.

The global economy is also, and unquestionably, "profoundly gendered" (Mills 2003:42). Regardless of country, region, political system, or ethnic or cultural boundaries, transnational factories and agribusiness enterprises mass-producing goods for First World consumers (such as the author or readers of this textbook) are overwhelmingly staffed by young women and even girls. Indeed, young women and girl workers, toiling ten or fourteen hours a day with low pay, and no job security or health benefits, almost certainly assembled (in Malaysia) the Dell laptop with which I have written this book; assembled (in Mexico) my television set and DVD player; and sewed (in Guatemala and Honduras) the jeans and tank top that I wear at this very moment. In the Caribbean, so profound and widespread has been the incorporation of women into the formal (i.e., extra-domestic) workforce, and so important is their labor and income for their households, that to still think of the "male breadwinner" is a myth (Safa 1995).

The highly **gendered distribution of global labor** is buttressed and ideologically justified by a global ideology stressing the "natural" aptitude of women in assembly and light manufacturing plants, and that these young female workers are also far more submissive—or potentially far more docile—than their male counterparts. This seemingly "natural" manual dexterity and an equally "natural" submissiveness, coupled with labor costs that are a mere fraction of those in the United States, Europe, or Japan, drives the incessant search for female labor in Third World countries. This transnational "affirmation of the body" (Stoler 1995:115) is a key metaphor and ideological linchpin structuring the gendered segmentation of global labor, perhaps overshadowing ethnicity or race as crucial cultural manifestations of contemporary global capitalism. The search for inexpensive and docile (mostly female) workers also generates circuits of mobile transnational labor Although migrant farm workers in the United States represent one example, another is that of the (often illegal) domestic workers providing services for (and hidden away in) the homes of the wealthy and influential in the United States (Mills 2003:45–46; for a more thorough discussion of Hispanic/Latina domestic workers, see the section "In the United States: Domestic Workers in the Midst of Affluence" later in this chapter).

The increasing participation of women in transnational production and service industries generates contradictory consequences for women and men. For example, although women are often wrenched away from family and home, transnational work provides them with more disposable income and sometimes a greater sense of autonomy, as is displayed in their ability to initiate courtship, or their decreased dependence on their male spouses. Yet, these same conditions often clash with entrenched gender roles and expectations at home. And males, often locked out of the labor market, and/or left behind, may experience "crises of masculinity" (Mills 2003:49–53). The following sections illustrate the role of class, ethnicity, and gender in underpinning transnational production.

The North American Free Trade Agreement

The **North American Free Trade Agreement** (NAFTA; Tratado de Libre Comercio de América del Norte, TLC), as well as the forthcoming Central American Free Trade Agreement (CAFTA; Harman 2005; Hitt and Davis 2005), are two examples of efforts at unraveling political and economic restrictions to the flow of investments and goods across national boundaries under the aegis of globalization. Signed by the United States, Mexico, and Canada in October 1992, and effective on January 1, 1994—the very day that the Zapatistas launched their uprising in the Mexican region of Chiapas (for more details see Chapter 12)—NAFTA called for tariff reductions on major goods and the lifting of most political and financial restrictions on transnational capital and financial investments (Green 1995:146–148). In the context of free-trade thinking, it was hoped that NAFTA would spur prosperity on both sides of the border.

From the eyes of the Mexican state and powerful allied corporate interests, NAFTA promised a host of economic and political benefits. Some of the economic advantages included consolidating an economic restructuring well underway as a response to the financial collapse of the early 1980s; lowering domestic inflation by importing less expensive goods; deflecting U.S. protectionist policies; attracting foreign investment; heightening corporate competitiveness, especially in manufactured exports; and, ultimately, creating countless jobs. The potential political gains were no less important: restoring national and international confidence and legitimacy in the Mexican government, particularly in the then-ruling Partido Revolucionario Institucional (PRI); and, by strengthening powerful corporate interests historically allied to the PRI, ensuring its dominance of the Mexican political system (Poitras and Robinson 1994). Although some labor leaders opposed NAFTA, the PRI's historical control of major labor organizations ensured that most opposition remained muted. Peasant organizations—fearful of the impact of a flood of less expensive grain (especially maize) and other agricultural imports—proved ineffective in mustering political opposition to NAFTA.

Like in Mexico, powerful economic and political interests in the United States also viewed NAFTA as an endless source of bounty and prosperity. NAFTA was supported by major industrial and manufacturing interests that envisioned an explosive growth of exports; greater competitiveness; and heightened profit margins, largely due to far lower wages in Mexico. Major agro-industrial corporations, especially those in the grain sector, which held a competitive edge over Mexican producers, also supported NAFTA because it promised a greater share of the grain market. NAFTA was also politically important because it was heralded as a sure way to jump-start a sluggish economy, create endless jobs, and legitimize the ideology of free trade. As in Mexico, there were opponents as well. These included major labor groups who feared a hemorrhage of jobs across the border, and some agricultural sectors—such as sugar producers, who enjoyed protectionist policies, or fruit and vegetable growers in California and Florida, who feared a flood of less-costly imports (Moody 1995; Avery 1998).

In a global investment game such as NAFTA, there are, of course, multiple winners and losers in all countries, as Green predicted shortly after NAFTAs formal onset (1995:151–152; see also Conroy and Glasmeier 1992–1993). He anticipated, for example, that Mexican peasants, faced with massive imports of maize and beans from far more efficient U.S. agribusinesses, would likely to lose out, while large-scale exporters to the United States would benefit from the liberalization of trade, as would large numbers of the un- or under-employed, who would find jobs in newly created plants and service industries. Green also predicted that U.S. and Canadian consumers would likely gain from imports of inexpensive, seasonally available fruits and vegetables (as well as other goods), while workers in North American manufacturing plants would take a hit as plants shut down and moved across the border to take advantage of lax labor and environmental laws, along with lower wages.

In the case of Mexico, it appears that many of Green's predictions have in fact come true. A surge in manufacturing, export-led jobs (most in the maquila industry, as well as in the financial sector) was an immediate result of NAFTA (Salas 2000:34). Yet, between 1993 and 1998, Mexico's economy generated less than 10 percent of jobs necessary to absorb new entrants into the workforce (Binford 2005:31). Further, LaFranchi (2003) notes that many plants originally set up in Mexico are now moving elsewhere in search of even lower wages.

As many predicted, NAFTA has led to massive imports of maize, almost certainly undermining many peasant farmers. In 1994, Mexico imported 2.7 million metric tons (MT) of maize; by 2003, this amount had more than doubled to 5.7 million MT (Food and Agriculture Organization 2005). In fact, the Mexican government began lifting corn subsidies long before NAFTA (Nash 1995:179; Salas 2000:35). Between 1991 and 1999, U.S. exports to Mexico surged 160 percent while Mexico's imports tripled. By 1999, more than 80 percent of Mexican exports were destined to the United States (Henwood 2000:50–51). Although exports of fruits and vegetables to North America rose rapidly after NAFTA, Mexico currently imports almost 40 percent of the food it consumes (Barndt 2002:175).

Salas suggests that NAFTA has led to a greater income disparity and, in absolute terms, an overall decrease in the purchasing power of wages (2000:34). Other sources partly support this view: between 1990 and 1999, Mexico's Gini coefficient of income distribution increased (suggesting greater income inequality), although in 2002 it edged slightly downward from .542 to .514 (Economic Commission for Latin America and the Caribbean 2004:12). Most average Mexicans have probably not benefited from NAFTA. Small wonder, then, that Gutmann encountered widespread cynicism about and resistance to NAFTA among Mexico's City's urban working class (see also Wise et al. 2003; Bacon 2004). This muted resistance took on a nationalist tone, as many made a "correspondence of transnationalism with rich *vendidos* (sell-outs) on the one hand, and of the Mexican nation with its poor *jodidos* (screwed) on the other" (Gutmann 2003c:410).

NAFTA has spurred the expansion of agribusinesses producing fruits and vegetables for the North American (U.S. and Canadian) markets, and Barndt (1999:67) considers this sector "one of the very few winners of NAFTA in Mexico." The tomato—a gloss of the Nahuatl word *tomatl* meaning "something round and plump" (Barndt 2002:11)—is especially prominent. Tomatoes, mainly cultivated in the Mexican states of Baja California, Sinaola, and Jalisco, constitute almost one-quarter of Mexico's fruit and vegetable production (Barndt 2002:13). The increasing investment in agribusiness tomato production has generated intense migrant (and especially female) labor streams within Mexico itself, the emergence of "moving maquila[s]" (2002:186). Work conditions of those laboring in the fields of Mexican agribusinesses that primarily satisfy North American demand are deplorable (see In Their Own Words 10.1).

IN THEIR OWN WORDS 10.1
Migrant Farm Workers in Mexico's Tomato Industry

A substantial portion of tomatoes harvested and packed in Mexico are destined for the United States and Canada. Itinerant farm workers—often entire families—make up the bulk of the labor force of agribusinesses that monopolize the production and exports of tomatoes in Mexico.

> We're from Guerrero. Contractors came to our town to find people to work here. After we finish our contract, they take us back in trucks. . . .
>
> In Guerrero, we grew our own vegetables at home. But not here.
>
> Some women carry their children on their backs while they're working, because they don't have anyone who can take care of them.
>
> We live with my parents; we're eleven brothers and sisters. Eight of us work, and we share the pay. My husband says that the younger ones should work, too. I'd like them at least to study a bit.
>
> We have only one room. How can they bring more people when [there] aren't enough rooms? We don't even have a kitchen, just a place to sleep.
>
> We earn twenty-eight pesos a day. It's never enough to save anything. Sometimes the children need shoes and it's not enough. They give us some clothes, because twenty-eight pesos is nothing. There's no union and no vacations.
>
> One day my husband came home with a stomachache and a headache, vomiting white foam. The doctor said that he had been intoxicated with the fertilizer and that he should cover his mouth with a handkerchief. (Barndt 2002:195–196)

Transnational Migrants in the United States and Canada

NAFTA's impact can also be assessed in other ways. Cohen et al. state that "no one would deny the long-term changes that NAFTA and neoliberal reforms brought to rural Mexico. In fact, urban and rural economies have suffered, and the traditional rural emigrant stream has been supplemented by large urban streams" (2005:90). NAFTA has not stemmed the tide of legal or illegal Mexican migrants working in the United States and, if anything, may have accelerated the flow of inexpensive labor to the North (*el norte*). People in the United States of Mexican birth or descent totaled 6.7 million in 1995; by early 2004, their numbers had almost doubled to 11.2 million. Net migration from Mexico to the United States increased from more than two hundred thousand between 1980 and 1984 to almost six hundred thousand in the period between 2000 and 2004 (Binford 2005:32). The proliferation of service sector jobs and the increasing demand for unskilled labor in other occupations are also attracting immigrant labor to the United States. The Pew Hispanic Research Center estimates that more than half of the almost twelve million unauthorized migrants in the United States are from Mexico (Passel 2006).[1]

Mexican immigration to the United States long precedes NAFTA. During World War II, large-scale growers in the agricultural sector, concerned about looming shortages of farmhands, petitioned for and received from the government permission to allow itinerant Mexican laborers into the United States to work as farmhands. This plan, known as the bracero program (from the Spanish word *brazo,* arm), lasted for twenty years, during which four to five million Mexicans worked in the United States. A separate yet analogous strategy of recruiting itinerant farm workers, from Mexico and elsewhere (the H-2 program), began after the end of World War II and continues to this day (Rothenberg 1998:36–40). *Crossing Over,* by Martínez (2001), and Rothenberg's *With These Hands* (1998) depict the hopes and aspirations of, and challenges faced by, Mexican and Mexican American families as they labor in the U.S. economy. Life is especially difficult for those men, women, and children who work in the fields, and whose labor produces fresh, canned, or frozen fruits and vegetables sold in supermarkets (see In Their Own Words 10.2).

Although in the past most Mexican immigrants worked as itinerant farmhands, today this is no longer the case. Indeed, Mexican workers at the lower end of the econominc and class hierarchy are in such demand throughout large swaths of the United States that their labor has become "structurally embedded" in the economy (Binford 2005:34). Further, the U.S. labor force is increasingly segmented by ethnic and class background, with ever greater percentages of jobs at the lowest spectrum of the pay scale taken up by Mexican immigrants and other Hispanics/Latinos. Most Mexican migrants send part of their earnings back to Mexico, and the total remittances can be enormous. From less than $1 billion in 1980, remittances surged to $5 billion in 1996, often constituting 75 to 90 percent of the disposable income of many Mexican rural communities (Binford 2003:306). Although the impact of this flow of migrant dollars back to Mexico is unquestionable, considerable debate centers on its economic and social consequences. Binford (2003) suggests that migrant dollars are generally not productively invested and, as a result, pull few Mexicans out of poverty and generate hardly any well-paying and lasting jobs; further, these remittances exacerbate social and economic inequality. This view has been contested by Cohen et al., who suggest that many poor rural communities are far better off with these remittances than without them, for "largely ignored in this equality-inequality debate are the multiple options available for remittances to be disbursed, to alleviate social distress, address immediate health concerns, reduce or off-set risk, broaden portfolios, invest in more migration and spread the impacts" (2005:92).

NAFTA has also spurred Mexican migration to Canada, where what Binford (2005:33–34) and others call "ethnic slotting" in the labor force also occurs. In Ontario, "many of the locally produced tomatoes are harvested by Mexican migrant farmworkers, men and women, who come north each summer . . . " (Barndt 2002:26). Between 1995 and 1997, the number of Mexican farm laborers working in Ontario increased by almost 30 percent (Barron 1999:120). NAFTA almost certainly will further the integration of Mexican and Canadian economies, especially in food production and distribution. As a result, Mexican workers are likely "to follow the crops and the demand for their cheap labor, feeding not only Mexicans and Canadians but also the global food system itself" (Barron 1999:123).

Labor and Gender in Mexican and Guatemalan Maquilas

Work and culture, as anthropologists and others have long recognized, are intimately related. Work rhythms, production schedules, and skills needed and tasks deployed, invariably generate a work culture, ethic, or worldview; conversely, culture itself—including

IN THEIR OWN WORDS 10.2
Work and Daily Life of Migrant Workers in the United States

For a year, Isabel Valle lived and traveled with a Mexican American migrant farmworker family. Her account provides a close-up of this family's daily life in search of seasonal harvest work (Valle 1991).

> Maria Elena Martinez and I are the first to wake up when the alarm goes off at 4 a.m. She heads for the kitchen to brew fresh coffee and make flour tortillas, scrambled eggs and refried beans. We'll make tacos and wrap them in foil to eat later during a break from the field work. We quickly put on our working clothes . . . Then we wake up the children. Calling their names out does not work. Neither does shaking them. The only thing that works with 10-year-old Jimmy is dragging him from under the covers and into the bathroom so he can wash his face and get dressed. With Billy, 7, we have a harder time. Maria Elena has to kneel beside him and dress him while he is still sound asleep on the floor. By this time it's usually 4:45 a.m., and we have to be in the fields at 5 to pick raspberries . . . The day is not unlike many such days the Martinez family experiences each time they travel the country in search of agricultural work.

Every spring, Raul, 61, and Maria Elena Martinez, 52, load their personal belongings and their children into the pickup. This year, along with the youngest of their 13 children, they decided to come to Washington state to work the fields picking asparagus . . . Raul and Maria Elena traveled with their sons Charlie, 15; Jimmy, 10; Billy, 7; Doris, their 20-year-old daughter; son Danny, 28, and his wife and two children . . . [María Elena] and the children found a job picking raspberries in Milton-Freewater, Ore. That's where we're headed at this early-morning hour. Once we get to the fields, everyone immediately goes to work. Picking raspberries is not hard physical labor, but it is tedious . . . In the five hours we work, we fill 14 flats. Two days later when we go to pick up our pay we find we earned $23 . . . Putting it in terms I'm familiar with, I divide the amount earned into the hours worked to find it comes out to about $4.60 an hour. However, there are four of us working, so it really adds up to only $1.15 an hour. This is how some migrant families live year after year.

---

constructed notions of gender—often sets limits on or shapes work practices. Some work sites or economic sectors—mining, for instance—generate distinct forms of masculinity, while others, such as domestic spheres, discussed more fully later in this chapter, surface as particularly female work domains (Thompson 1963; Willis 1981; Klubock 1997; Sanabria 2000). **Maquilas** or **maquiladoras,** transnational light manufacturing and assembly plants, are an example of the latter.

Maquilas appeared in Latin America and the Caribbean during the 1960s, shortly after the emergence of similar transnational implants in Asia (Ong 1987). Transnational corporations based primarily in the United States and Europe set up these plants as a way of lowering labor and other costs, while at the same time boosting productivity and profit margins. There, in the "Third World," loomed the prospect of recruiting a seemingly endless supply of workers who could be paid a mere fraction of what their counterparts in the United States and Europe would be willing to work for. Labor laws or unions protecting workers were lax or virtually nonexistent; and environmental legislation was practically absent. Those corporations also looked forward to employing countless "docile"—submissive and easily controlled—female workers, whose "natural" manual dexterity easily lent itself to the kinds of minute, tedious work required. In short, corporate interests sought out workers with suitable "feminine" somatic traits that could boost productivity. As noted earlier, the image and narrative of the "docile" and manually able female worker have been recurrent ideological justifications for corporate investment in maquila plants throughout the Third World.

Mexican maquilas, employing overwhelmingly female labor, have been no exception. There are more than 3,000 maquilas in Mexico, employing more than one million workers (Wright 2001:133). Four hundred of these maquilas are staffed by almost 250,000 laborers in Ciudad Juárez, across the United States–Mexico border from El Paso, Texas (Nathan 1999:24).

Salzinger's fieldwork (2003) in Ciudad Juárez maquilas suggests that "docile" feminine workers are not simply "out there" ready to be recruited. Rather, workers' femininity or masculinity—how workers come to view tasks as inherently "feminine" or "masculine" and how their own identity as "women" or "men" are shaped by these gendered views of work—are the result of concrete, ongoing labor practices. Salzinger's second important point is that the ideal of recruiting docile female workers notwithstanding, there is in fact considerable variability in the extent to which this goal is met. Salzinger worked in four maquilas (Panoptimex, Particimex, Andromex, and Anarchomex) that differed greatly in how feminine and masculine identities were shaped.

In Panoptimex, which employs virtually all women, plant managers were wedded to the ideal of docile, feminine workers, and were able to recruit them and forge a submissive "feminine" shop-floor production culture. Salzinger found a "remarkable accuracy in which its workers incarnate the image of an inviolably docile femininity," and the few male workers were considered "not-men," with "no standing in the game" (2003:30).

Most workers are young, single women living with parents or other kin, and are under the surveillance of mostly male supervisors. Managers have succeeded in creating a shop-floor culture where the productivity of work teams has been internalized as an important component of workers' sense of worth. One female worker told Salzinger (2003:63) that "when they start congratulating the other lines for having finished and we haven't, you feel bad." Other practices also contribute to the feminization of labor, as when managers refer to all workers, female or male, as *operadoras* (female operators) and employ the feminine pronoun *todas* (2003:69). Feminized productivity is also a powerful tool in disciplining male workers, as when managers threaten to move them into "female" work spaces or shift them to "womanly task[s]" (2003:73). The result is a highly productive maquila with an extremely feminized workforce and work culture.

The Particimex maquila employs predominantly female managers who have, nevertheless, a different version of the ideal "feminine" worker than at Panoptimex. Here, "She is a young woman willing to make decisions and able to take charge—understood to operate in explicit contrast to the submissive women of 'traditional Mexican culture' whom managers envision their workers to be outside the factory" (2003:31). This shift away from the stereotypical image of a submissive worker is partly the result of plant managers distancing themselves from the (equally stereotypical) image of the Mexican "macho" vis-à-vis their North American superiors, and adopting North American labor norms and practices that seem more "progressive." The playing down of gender differences in the public sphere is carried out in various ways. In this maquila, "Everyone in the factory wears the same light blue, short-sleeved smocks and ID tags adorned with underexposed black-and-white photos" (Salzinger 2003:84, 123). Further, management also foments teamwork and encourages women to be "collaborators" (and not mere workers) by assuming a greater responsibility for their own work.

In Andromex, where half of the plant's workers are men, the image and ideal of the docile, feminine worker does not even surface, concerns about "femininity" are replaced by an ambience of masculinity, and "managers . . . constitute women and men alike as 'workers'" (2003:32). Masculinity, not femininity, is touted, the feminization of work (and male labor) replaced by the masculinization of "feminine" work. Labor ideology on the shop floor emphasizes the ability of workers to earn a decent wage for their families, which underpins ideas regarding gender and masculinity—what it takes to be or become a real "man" (and worker). Hence, read an English translation of part of the front page of the plant newspaper:

> TO BE A MAN is not just to be male, a mere individual of the masculine sex . . .
> TO BE A MAN is to be the creator of something, a home, a business, a position
> . . . TO BE A MAN is to do things, not to look for reasons to show that they
> cannot be done. (2003:104.)

Various material and cultural reasons account for this particular gendered version of shop-floor culture. One is that Andromex requires a permanent and highly skilled labor force and cannot afford high turnover rates and the time to train new workers. Workers earn much more than in other maquilas, and managers are far less likely to fire insubordinate workers. Parallel cultural norms also operate on the shop floor. For example, a public discourse centered on respect (*respeto*) and autonomy permeates the shop floor—a message that also appeals to female workers. Earning decent wages to meet the needs of their families bolsters their self-respect and solidifies a sense of masculinity, all which in turn drives workers to produce even more. High wage earnings are also important for women in that they reinforce women's sense of autonomy, both on the shop floor and when they return home.

In Anarchomex, a uniform and consistent version of either femininity or masculinity has not been forged, leading to a great deal of resistance. Despite employing mostly males, plant managers "continue to address all workers through the trope of femininity, deprecating male workers . . . As a result . . . struggles over the meaning of masculinity and femininity and the appropriate gender of the work become the center of shop-floor contestation . . . " (2003:32–33). Here, ideology is radically divorced from productive practice and labor relations on the shop floor, because managements' insistence that (ideally) maquila labor is indeed feminine work runs contrary to the composition of a workforce that is predominantly male. Low pay further exacerbates labor tensions in Anarchomex. In such a context,

"Male workers enter on the defensive—their masculinity questioned outside the plant by popular images of feminine maquila workers and inside by the very managers who hired them" (2003:142).

The numerical and economic preponderance of Mexican maquilas has often over-shadowed the fact that many similar production sites exist in Central America. Green has explored how maquiladoras in Guatemala, staffed almost exclusively by Maya female and male youths, "may operate as new sites of exploitation by reinforcing and intensifying existing inequalities and intergenerational tensions, and manufacturing powerlessness" (2003:52). She notes that most Maya peasants in rural Guatemala are unable to provide for their families by engaging in agriculture because of exceedingly small plots of land (the result of partible inheritance), but also because free trade policies have led to a flood of less expensive maize and beans from the United States, which has undermined the value of crops produced locally. Further, work in maquila factories offers youths an opportunity to gain some income to help out at home, while at the some time instilling contradictory and sometimes unachievable desires and consequences:

> There is a newness for Mayan adolescents who work the factory lines—wages for consumption of items never imagined or within reach beforehand, leisure time and short-term freedoms with regard to their relations with young men before marriage. Yet, simultaneously, factory work reinforces the status quo in terms of exploitation of them as young women, as workers and as Indians. It reinforces their subordinate gender roles both at work and at home, and it insinuates them into the modern world, but only as the mirror image and inferior "Other." While the benefits of factory work expose them to the desires of and limited participation in "modern" consumption practices, which they cannot afford, they leave their jobs after five years or so with no marketable skills elsewhere and no further job training. They return home ill and exhausted, unemployed and disaffected. (Green 2003:63)

Lurking Danger on the Borderlands: Women, Maquilas, and Death

As in other historic moments of rapid economic and social change, swift transformations spurred by globalization generate conflictive (if not explosive) conditions, expectations, or life experiences—what Comaroff and Comaroff have called "*experiential* contradictions at the core of neoliberal capitalism" (2001:8). Some of these (gendered) contradictions have been dealt with previously in this chapter. And yet, these incongruities and ambiguities are not merely "good to think about"; they have real, life-or-death consequences—as is the case of young maquila workers in Ciudad Juárez, Mexico.

To be young, female, and living in Ciudad Juárez is dangerous. In 1993, the first bodies of young women—almost all maquila workers—were found in remote locations; all had been raped, and some tortured before being killed. In the past twelve years, more than four hundred young women have been murdered or kidnapped and presumed dead. Amnesty International published a special report to garner international outcry on the level of violence and terror that afflicts Ciudad Juárez (2003). Since then, Mexican federal police have arrested and convicted more than a dozen men on kidnapping and murder charges, and a special prosecutor has been appointed to oversee the murder investigations. And yet, the killings have not only not stopped but have become more brutal: in May 2005, the bodies of two young girls, seven and ten years old, were found raped and murdered, prompting massive demonstrations by tens of thousands of people clamoring for more security (Betancourt 2005; McKinley 2004; Wright 2001; Nathan 1999).

This ongoing and lethal sexual violence has to do with a social and cultural milieu generated by the maquila industry. Important are the pervasive and (for males) threatening perceptions of female sexuality and the transgression of gender boundaries. Wright (2001) calls attention to a widespread perception of maquila female workers as young women gone astray, no longer under the gaze and control of their parents (or husbands), whose morals and "traditional values" have been corrupted, and who lead "double lives"—appearing by day as "the dutiful daughter, wife, mother, sister, and laborer," but at nighttime revealing their "inner prostitute, slut, and barmaid" (2001:128–129). This image of "loose" women is also shared by maquila management, who blame maquila workers themselves for the climate of violence.

Wright calls this "death by cultural narrative," which absolves the industry of any responsibility. Further, Wright argues, this narrative is sustained by a wider and deeper view portraying maquila workers as lacking job loyalty (because they are prone to leave one job in search of another), and not worth the effort it takes to train them. The maquila female worker, then, is viewed as an easily interchangeable, disposable body, not worth much concern on management's part (2001:143–144).

Pondering the history of systemic violence perpetuated against indigenous peoples in Amazonian Colombia, Taussig has suggested that "cultures of terror are nourished by the intermingling of silence and myth" (1987:8). If this is correct, then prevailing gender ideologies and norms, as well as perceptions of maquila women leading double lives (*la doble vida*)—conforming during the day to expected gender roles but not doing so at night—may help us understand violence against women in Ciudad Juárez. Nathan (1999:26) suggests that maquilas have encouraged la doble vida, and have also placed males on the defensive. An important context providing fertile ground for male violence is women's greater autonomy—or greater attempts at autonomy—in and outside the home, and the economic marginalization of many men, which threatens their masculinity and their role as providers. Further, maquila women are ideologically and metaphorically linked to illicit sexuality and sexual perversion, feeding into a widespread sense of anger and rage, especially but not only among males, and symbolically transforming maquilas into brothels and maquila workers into prostitutes. Theses two distinct processes—maquilas workers' greater autonomy and maquilas' threat to male identity and masculinity, coupled with a broad-based view of maquila women as almost morally worthless—take place within and feed into a generalized state of terror and death.

Global Interests and the Environment

A critical issue and concern in the study of globalization concerns the impact on the environment as transnational corporations seek out and are often given wide latitude in extracting renewable and nonrenewable resources (Roberts and Thanos 2003; Vertovec and Posey 2003). Escalating environmental concerns have been paralleled by growing interest in sustainable development and biodiversity, and both have arisen partly as a result of widespread environmental degradation and deforestation. The following two sections review recent work on sustainable development and biodiversity in Latin America, and well as the widespread deforestation taking place in Amazonia and Central America.

Sustainable Development and Bioprospecting

Global concerns over the future of the planet's resources and, in Latin America, worries about the worldwide climatic effects from the possible devastation of Amazonia, have generated enormous interest in **sustainable development,** self-sustaining and environmentally nondestructive livelihood practices. Interest in and research on sustainable development has been expressed by international organizations, such as the United Nations' Division for Sustainable Development, whose motto is "Development that meets the needs of the present without compromising the ability of future generations to meet their own needs" (see www.un.org/esa/sustdev/publications/publications.htm for more information). This awareness of sustainable development has paralleled research on indigenous or "traditional" environmental knowledge and livelihood practices, often assumed by many nongovernmental organizations (NGOs), social scientists, and development organizations to be intrinsically self-sustaining and environmentally friendly (Brush and Stabinsky 1996). This knowledge has the great advantage of being

> relatively malleable . . . that is, finely tuned to the continually changing circumstances that define a particular locality. There are several comparative advantages enjoyed by local people. They are very astute about their local environment and have accumulated a lot of experience concerning those things that affect their existence. They have a keen awareness of the interconnectedness and ecology of plants, animals, and soils. They are ingenious at making do with the natural and mechanical resources at their disposal. (De Walt 1999:106)

This image of "ecologically noble Indians" living in harmony with nature (the Kayapo, discussed in Chapter 5, are a good example) has a long history in Western thought, but has only recently been resurrected in the light of global environmental and sustainable development concerns (Orlove and Brush 1996:335; Krech 1999). Despite research documenting that the "Ecological Indian" is a representation that rarely corresponds to reality (Orlove and Brush 1996:335–336), and in stark contrast to much development thinking of the 1960s and 1970s that portrayed such livelihood practices as backward and a barrier to development and modernity, it is now assumed that this knowledge can be put to use for furthering sustainable development. For instance, the United States Agency for International Development (USAID) now recognizes the value of "the natural resources knowledge and management practices of indigenous peoples" (2005:viii).

Examples abound on how essentialist representations of the indigenous undermine sustainable developments efforts. Swartley's analysis (2002) of a raised field project in Bolivia among Aymara peasants sheds light on unwarranted assumptions underlying sustainable development efforts, and on harnessing indigenous knowledge in alternative, self-sustaining livelihood practices. Raised fields are, potentially, extraordinarily productive and self-sustaining in the long run, requiring virtually no agricultural, technical, or capital inputs, their most important limiting factor being labor. Because they were also "native" to this region (and hence part of local culture), raised fields seemed an exemplary model of a sustainable "indigenous" or "traditional" practice that could, with proper "outside" incentives, be reinvigorated.

In a classic example of elite representations of the timeless "other" (Said 1979; Dirks 2001), Aymara peasants were portrayed as stuck in time, and supposedly agreeable to using only hand tools that, depicted in project pamphlets, bore a striking resemblance to those portrayed in *Nueva crónica y buen gobierno*, written by the Andean chronicler Felipe Guamán Poma de Ayala in the seventeenth century.

Misconstrued representations of the timeless "other" did not in and of themselves account for the failure of this Bolivian project. Contrary to initial expectations, the fields did not sustain continuously high yields and it was only when yields began to decline and project incentives discontinued that the fields were forsaken. The project also misconstrued contemporary Andean peasants as primarily interested and engaged in subsistence agriculture, and with plenty of free time (and available labor) on their hands. That many community residents migrated to and spent periods of time in La Paz or, further east, in the sub-tropical yungas region, or were engaged in a variety of nonagricultural occupations, was largely ignored by project funders and NGOs. Swartley concluded (2002:155–156) that interest in raised fields was "an invented tradition of . . . archaeologists and development workers" that did not concur with the contemporary reality of Aymara peoples.

Growing interest in and importance attached to sustainable development has been paralleled by mounting concerns over the global loss of plant and genetic biodiversity. In Latin America, Amazonia again occupies the center stage:

> In 2005, the . . . [agency] . . . is launching a new regional program to support conservation of biological diversity in the Amazon Basin . . . The Amazon Basin's biological diversity is staggering. It holds the largest area of contiguous and relatively intact tropical forest in the world. (United States Agency for International Development 2005:i)

Concerns over the disappearance of genetic biodiversity are, of course, nothing new. Anthropologists and others have long expressed similar apprehensions concerning the diminishing stock of Andean potato varieties as peasants opt for cultivating a narrower range of more lucrative varieties (Orlove 1987; Brush 1992). What *is* novel is the extent to which pharmaceutical corporations with an eye on uncovering new genetic material for the highly profitable North American prescription drug market have a stake in biodiversity research; the important role that governmental institutions and NGOs play; and that indigenous groups (and their knowledge) are progressively drawn into this search as potential "bioprospectors" (Escobar 1994a, 1994b; Orlove and Brush 1996; Smith, N. J. 1999; Greene 2004). Moran et al. (2001:505) outline some of the major questions and debates in the rapidly growing field of **bioprospecting:**

Is bioprospecting an innovative mechanism that will (a) help produce new therapeutics and preserve traditional medical systems, (b) conserve both biological and cultural diversity by demonstrating their medical, economic, and social values, and (c) bring biotechnology and other benefits to bio-diversity rich but technology poor countries? Or is bioprospecting yet another form of colonialism—"bioimperialism"—wherein the North rips off the South's resources and intellectual property rights?

The role of indigenous knowledge is crucial for successful bioprospecting—which is why indigenous groups are important "players" in these efforts. This recognition stems from growing awareness of the contributions of indigenous knowledge to modern medicine. Moran et al. (2001:512) note that "of the 120 active compounds isolated from higher plants and used today in Western medicine, 74% have the same therapeutic use as in native societies," while Brush (1993:661) notes that "almost half of promising anticancer compounds are from plants known to folk medicine." Often forgotten is that what is now known as indigenous knowledge has had anthropological forerunners in ethnobotany, cognitive anthropology, ethnoecology, and cultural ecology (Brush 1993:658–659). The role of ethnobiological knowledge documented by anthropologists should not be underestimated for, in Brazil and elsewhere, it was crucial in forging the image of the Amazonian Indian as a steward of the environment, and legitimizing environmental NGO alliances with indigenous groups (Conklin and Graham 1995:698–699; Greene 2004:214).

Closely related to the issue of bioprospecting are growing concerns about the possibilities of biopiracy—the usurpation by pharmaceutical interests of legal rights over the chemical properties of plants long cultivated or consumed by indigenous peoples for ritual or healing purposes (Conklin 2002; Greene 2004). Claims by Amazonian indigenous peoples (and supported by North American allies) that they have intellectual property rights over plants native to the region were acknowledged in a 1999 landmark decision by the U.S. Patent and Trademark Office (PTO) canceling a patent over the ayahuasca vine—crucial in shamanistic healing practices (see also Chapter 8)—issued to a United States citizen (Wiser 1999).

Deforestation and Degradation

With over 6.5 million square kilometers shared mainly between Brazil, Colombia, Venezuela, Peru, Bolivia, and Ecuador, South America's Amazon region is the largest contiguous area of sub-tropical and tropical forest in the world, and the planet's leading repository of plant biodiversity. Given that deforestation may play an important role in global warming trends, the potential disappearance of Amazonian forests is one of the foremost and controversial issues in the contemporary environmentalist movement, and one of the most significant and pressing foci of research in geography, ecology, and ecological anthropology (Fearnside 2001a, 2001b; Laurance et al. 2001, 2005a, 2005b; Laurance and Williamson 2001; Cámara et al. 2005).

There are good reasons for these concerns, for Amazonian deforestation is widespread and escalating. In Brazil, where the largest portion of the Amazonian forest is located, almost 175,000 square kilometers—about 1.5 times the size of the state of New

TABLE 10.1   Change in Forest Cover: South and Central America, Select Countries: 1990–2000

Region/Country	Total 1990	Total 2000	Loss 1990–2000	% Loss 1990–2000
South America	792,767	761,295	31,472	4.0
Brazil	566,998	543,905	23,093	4.1
Bolivia	54,679	53,068	1,611	2.9
Colombia	51,506	49,601	1,905	3.7
Peru	67,903	65,215	2,688	4.0
Venezuela	51,681	49,506	2,175	4.2
Central America	19,523	16,476	3,047	15.6
Costa Rica	2,126	1,968	158	7.4
El Salvador	193	121	72	37.3
Guatemala	3,387	2,850	537	15.9
Honduras	5,972	5,383	589	9.9
Nicaragua	4,450	3,278	1,172	26.3
Panama	3,395	2,876	519	15.3

Source: Adapted from Food and Agriculture Organization (2001:31–32). Numbers are in thousands of hectares.

York—were deforested between 1988 and 1998 (Wood 2003:4–5). Other data further underscore the devastation being wrought on Amazonia. According to the Food and Agriculture Organization (2001; see also Table 10.1), Brazil's Amazon region lost twenty-three million hectares of forest cover between 1990 and 2000. This number is equivalent to 73 percent of the almost thirty-two million hectares lost in all of Amazonia during this ten year period.

Amazonia is not the only region where widespread and accelerated deforestation is taking place. Although it occupies the center stage of global concerns because of its enormous size, the percentage of forest cover that Amazonia loses pales in comparison with the destruction of Central American forests (see Table 10.1). For example, although Amazonia lost 4 percent of its forests between 1990 and 2000, almost 16 percent vanished in Central America. El Salvador—which has "the most destitute [population] in all of Central America" (Williams 1986:170)—lost an astonishing one-third of its forests in a mere ten years; equally impoverished Nicaragua lost more than one-fourth. At the current rate of devastation—and despite attempts at reforestation, or the "swapping" of foreign debt for forest bioreserves (Kahn and McDonald 1995)—forests in Central America will be but a passing memory in a matter of decades.

In explaining how and why deforestation has occurred and what might be done to stem its onslaught, many scholars rely on an analytic framework known as **political ecology** (Schmink and Wood 1987; Stonich 1993; Durham 1995; Robbins 2004; Paulson and Gezon 2005) or the "new" ecology (Scoones 1999). This approach stresses conflictive relationships between members of different social groups with unequal access to productive resources and economic and political power, and who, therefore, are differentially positioned within the hierarchical order within which they find themselves. Examples of these social groups include settlers pushed to the frontier by poverty or political instability in their home communities; owners of large agribusiness estates or cattle ranches;

international financial institutions, such as the World Bank; national political or military elites; and consumers of sub-tropical and tropical commodities in the First World. It is precisely the ongoing—direct or indirect—interaction and competition between these social groups in a context marked by inequality and widespread poverty that set in hand and perpetuate the conditions underpinning deforestation. Painter (1995a:8–9) provides a useful summary:

> First, environmental destruction associated with . . . smallholding farmers is a consequence of their impoverishment . . . [which] . . . often has occurred together with loss of land and subjection to violence at the hands of wealthy individuals and corporate interests engaged in land speculation and of state authorities . . . Second, while easier access [to frontier land by] smallholders has meant that the environmental destruction associated with their productive systems has received the most attention, much more land has been degraded by the activities of wealthy individual and corporate interests . . . Third, the same policies and practices that result in wealthy interests receiving land on concessionary terms are responsible for the impoverishment of smallholders, because they institutionalize and exacerbate unequal access to resources. Thus, the crucial issue underlying environmental destruction in Latin America is gross inequality in access to resources.

The Amazon. By the early 1960s, governments encouraged migration to sparsely populated tropical and sub-tropical frontier regions. National security concerns often underpinned these attempts for, the rationale went, frontier regions would be less likely to fall to neighboring countries if large numbers of settled peasants were present. Equally important, colonization of frontier areas was also a way of defusing potential unrest in more heavily populated regions where poverty and unequal access to resources (especially land) were present (Foweraker 1981; Sanabria 1993).

Colonists or frontier settlers practice **swidden** or **shifting cultivation,** whereby trees are cut down and then burned to enhance soil fertility. After several years of continuous cropping, yields begin to decline, and colonists are forced to renew the process,which drives them deeper into virgin forests. As a result, early concerns about deforestation suggested that colonists were the ones to "blame" for—or were the prime movers behind—deforestation. These explanations were both misguided and premature. Many scholars now acknowledge that although shifting cultivation contributes to deforestation, the overwhelming loss of forest cover has to do with powerful vested interests.

Most research agrees that large-scale economic interests are largely responsible for the deforestation and degradation of Amazonia. Moran notes that road building facilitates entry into Amazonia by many settlers, but it also provides the opportunity for wealthy and privileged Brazilians to take advantage of favorable credit policies to accumulate land and convert it into pasture for cattle grazing. Interestingly enough, an overwhelming proportion of credit and other fiscal incentives is channeled not to small settlers but to cattle ranchers, whose enterprises would be unprofitable without these external subsidies. This in turn accelerates the conversion of land into pasture (1993:6). As Wood argues, "Much of the deforestation that has taken place in the Amazon was carried out by middle- and large-scale ranchers who converted the forest cover to pasture, often with the support of fiscal incentives" (2003:11).

Walker and Moran (2000) have alternatively suggested that the dichotomy between small-scale colonists or settlers, who engage in a variety of productive activities on land plots of between fifty to one hundred hectares, and ranchers, specializing in raising cattle herds on large (more than one thousand hectares) is misleading. They suggest that market conditions have also favored the pursuit of cattle farming by small-scale producers. Over the course of twenty years, prices—relative to beef—of major crops grown for the market (such as rice, cocoa, beans, and corn) have either remained stationary or have in fact declined. Colonist households also recognize the market incentives to herd cattle, and in some regions cattle ranching may provide one-third of a household's income (Walker and Moran 2000:685–686). Nevertheless, they agree with others who have noted the trend that "large landowners may be held accountable for a disproportionate share of the overall magnitude [of deforestation]." But it is also "important to emphasize the primacy of the cattle economy across all agrarian sectors" (Walker and Moran 2000:694, 696).

In other parts of Amazonia, similar trends can be detected. Although cattle ranching accounted for much of the forest loss in eastern lowland Bolivia until the 1970s, free-market policies and incentives have accelerated the growth of capital-intensive agribusiness, so that "the main cause of deforestation has been the rapid growth of mechanized soybean production" (Kaimowitz et al. 1999:512), coupled with growing timber exports. One important issue is the potential environmental devastation in Brazilian Amazonia wrought by dozens of major highway and infrastructure projects either planned for the near future or currently in place. Laurance et al (2001a, 2001b) suggest that the impact of these investments will be massive, a claim disputed by others (Cámara et al 2005).

Central America.   By many accounts, the expansion of cattle ranching for the production of beef to satisfy the appetites of North American consumers has been one of the main culprits of the widespread deforestation in Central America. This had led many to suggest that the insatiable demand by North American consumers for hamburgers is the principal cause of Central American deforestation—this has been called the "hamburger thesis."

Edelman suggests that this is a one-sided, partial explanation. In his case study on Costa Rica, Edelman says that the "popular image of voracious cattlemen bulldozing ever-greater expanses of virgin forest" (1995:29) is mistaken. Although cattle ranching may have been the prime cause of deforestation during the 1960s and 1970s, this is no longer the case: since the 1980s, North American demand for Central American beef has fallen (along with cattle prices), while domestic consumption has risen. In any case, the debt crises of the 1980s, coupled with a retrenchment of state subsidies for cattle ranching, has reduced the profitability of this sector, at least in Costa Rica. Although Edelman seems hesitant to explain why deforestation continues apace in a context in which the cattle ranching sector is in "crisis," he does note that reforestation efforts will not succeed because large-scale cattle ranchers have, ironically, taken advantage of their privileged position to monopolize fiscal incentives provided by the United States Agency for International Development (USAID). The monies have not been well spent, for after getting their hands on USAID monies, ranchers have invested little in reforestation.

Elsewhere, remarkably similar processes driving deforestation, pasture expansion, poverty, and political instability have been at work. Williams (1986:129–134, 170–174) notes that in the Matagalpa region of Nicaragua, more than 90 percent of the forest cover disappeared in slightly over twelve years, during which time cattle ranchers expanded their herds and drove peasants off their lands. A few years later, Matagalpa became a major bastion of the Frente Sandinista de Liberación Nacional, which toppled the dictatorship of Anastasio Somoza in 1979 (see Chapter 12). In nearby El Salvador, widespread deforestation and landlessness began accelerating with the spread of large-scale, mechanized and capital-intensive cotton enterprises in the 1960s, a trend aggravated by the expansion of cattle ranching in the 1970s. In less than a decade, rural landlessness almost doubled.

Stonich's research in Honduras focused on the relationship between the expansion of nontraditional exports and "heightened social differentiation, deepened human impoverishment, and escalating environmental destruction" (1995:63). She notes that in southern Honduras it is not cattle but the growth of large-scale cotton enterprises during the 1960s and 1970s, often with state and international incentives, that spurred deforestation. As in Costa Rica, El Salvador, and elsewhere in Central America, on the heels of cotton came the ranchers and their cattle. Herds multiplied, with significant impacts on the environment, for "the percentage of land in pasture, the percentage of total cattle owned, and the mean number of cattle owned are positively related to the size of landholdings" (Stonich 1995:77). The result of these two "booms," as well as the growth of new exports crops such as melons, has been a marked concentration of land, and a rural landlessness rate surpassing 80 percent.

Strikingly similar processes are recorded in Petén, in northern Guatemala. Until the 1960s, the economy of this sparsely populated and heavily forested region was based on swidden or shifting agriculture and, second, on the tree tapping of chicle, a latex used for making bubble gum. (*Chicle* is what bubble gum is called in much of Spanish-speaking Latin America and the Caribbean.) In the ensuing three decades, the population of Petén multiplied and almost half of the forest cover disappeared. Many who migrated to Petén during the 1960s and 1970s were poor Maya-speaking peasants fleeing poverty and raging civil war in the southern highlands. Yet, lured by state and international tax breaks, subsidies, and other incentives, "multinationals and middle-class Guatemalans were also drawn north," investing in mineral and petroleum exploration, logging, and cattle ranching, and gobbling up huge tracts of land. This forced "poor householders to enter undisturbed forests, where the process may be repeated in ever larger, counterproductive cycles" (Schwartz 1995:107, 116).

Controversies: Global Interests and Ethnographic Representations in the Amazon

Anthropologists are currently paying more attention to the thorny issue of the political and economic repercussions of **ethnographic representation**—how they describe and mold an image about the culture and social practices of the peoples they study. The issue is not so much the questioning of ethnographic fieldwork but of recognizing that some representations may bolster unsubstantiated stereotypical thinking on indigenous peoples, and therefore

PHOTO 10.2   *Yanömamo warriors celebrating Rehao, an annual ceremony honoring the memory of recently deceased. At dawn, the ashes of the dead will be consumed.*

provide further justifications for far more powerful groups and political and economic interests to trample on indigenous rights and livelihoods. This awareness of the down-to-earth—and sometimes life-and-death—consequences for indigenous peoples of how they are portrayed in ethnographic writings is especially important in Amazonia, where powerful global political–economic interests are and have been historically vying for its rich resources. These concerns also loom particularly relevant since the publication of Tierney's *Darkness in El Dorado: How Scientists and Journalists Devastated the Amazon* (2000). Tierney's book, focusing on the South American Yanömamo, ignited a firestorm within and outside of anthropology (see Photo 10.2). In fact, "In many ways, but obviously not all, this is the most important book ever written about the Yanomami. None of some 60 books previously published on the Yanomami . . . was subjected to a panel discussion and open forum at any AAA [American Anthropological Association] convention . . . investigations in three countries . . . [and] . . . Brazilian anthropological critics of . . . Chagnon never began to have such an impact as Tierney" (Sponsel 2002:149).

One important reason for the controversy surrounding *Darkness in El Dorado* is Tierney's accusation that Chagnon and his colleagues, either through neglect or by privileging their research goals over the safety of their informants, directly or indirectly contributed to, or failed to take the necessary measures to stem, a measles outbreak that killed many Yanömamo (2000:36–82). On this specific point, Tierney's accusations have been strongly refuted by Chagnon and his colleagues as well as by major scholarly associations (Hagen et al. 2001; American Anthropological Association 2000a, 2000b).

Tierney devotes far more attention (8 entire chapters) to Chagnon's analysis of Yanömamo warfare and his representations of Yanömamo as inherently violent and "fierce." Tierney focuses on these themes to make two related arguments: that Chagnon is mistaken about the causes and extent of Yanömamo war-making, and that by depicting the Yanömamo as intrinsically fierce, he has provided a further ideological justification for powerful economic interests to continue appropriating and ravaging Yanömamo territories (Tierney 2000:149–256).

One of Chagnon's central ideas—that access to women and future wives is an important catalyst of Yanömamo violence—has been partly dealt with in Chapter 6 in this book. Yet, there may be alternate explanations for such violence. Other anthropologists believe that Yanömamo aggression is best understood as the result of wider webs of violence inflicted on them by Western, nonindigenous outsiders, a point also stressed by Taussig for indigenous peoples in the Colombian Pacific lowlands (1987). Such webs of violence include introduction of prized Western goods (a practice that, incidentally, Chagnon repeatedly used during his fieldwork); raging diseases; encroachments on Yanömamo land by miners; development projects that threaten their landscapes; and massacres inflicted upon them by Brazilian nationals coveting their lands and natural resources. Rejecting a socio-biological basis for Yanömamo warfare, Ferguson proposes instead a historical and political–economic explanation:

> Only by putting Yanomami society in historical perspective can we understand their warfare, and only by understanding the causes of their warfare can we understand what Western contact has meant to them and how they have acted as agents in shaping their own history. Although some Yanomami really have been engaged in intensive warfare and other kinds of bloody conflict, this violence is not an expression of Yanomami culture itself. It is, rather, a product of specific historical situations: the Yanomami make war not because Western influence is absent but because it is present, and present in certain specific forms. All Yanomami warfare *that we know about* occurs within . . . a "tribal zone," an extensive area beyond state administrative control, inhabited by nonstate people who must react to the far-flung effects of state presence. (1995:6)

Further, in addition to the possibility that the Yanömamo studied by Chagnon are less violent than he portrays them to be, some anthropologists have stressed that other Yanömamo groups are far less aggressive (Smole 1976; Alés 2000a). Nevertheless, these alternate accounts—including a caveat by Chagnon himself in the third edition (1983) of his ethnography—have been largely clouded by Chagnon's publications, which have solidified the widespread view that "the" Yanömamo are intrinsically fierce and violent.

And fierce they certainly seem to be, with a propensity toward killing others a seemingly overriding and structural feature of Yanömamo's culture and society. Despite the absence of "The Fierce People" from the title of the fifth (1997) edition of Chagnon's ethnography, terms such as *ferocity*, *treachery*, *killings*, and *fierce* are repeatedly used to characterize contemporary Yanömamo. As a result of Chagnon's depictions stressing revenge killings, incessant warfare and raiding, violence against women, and the use of

hallucinogenic drugs, the Yanömamo have acquired the (unenviable) reputation of being
the most warlike (and perhaps disliked) of all Amazonian tribal groups. Indeed, violence
appears such an overriding dimension of Yanömamo society and culture that readers,
before learning much else about this society, are introduced to a detailed account of a
revenge killing as early as the second page in the fifth edition of Chagnon's ethnography. A
few pages later, readers learn that the Yanömamo "have lived in a chronic state of warfare"
(Chagnon 1997:9). One of his goals in writing *The Fierce People* was to put an end to "all
the garbage about the Noble Savage" (Golden 1997, quoted in Tierney 2000:42).

Shortly after the appearance of Tierney's book, the American Anthropological Association entrusted a committee—the El Dorado Task Force—to investigate Tierney's accusations (American Anthropological Association 2002a, 2002b). The Task Force took up the
twin issues of Chagnon's representations of the Yanömamo and their possible consequences
(2002a:31–39). The Task Force concurred with the "allegations that his [i.e., Chagnon's]
representations of Yanomami ways of life were damaging to them and that he made insuffi-
cient effort to undo this damage" (2002a:31). The Task Force also singled out the widespread use of disparaging epithets that surface in some early editions of Chagnon's classic
ethnography—such as "brutal," "cruel," "treacherous," "fierce"—although it also noted
that in the fourth (1992) edition Chagnon raised the concern that "students . . . might falsely
conclude that the Yanömamo are 'animal-like.'" Further, the Task Force took issue with
Chagnon for not doing enough to offset what it called "vulgarized representations" of the
Yanömamo. For example, during a 1995 interview with the Brazilian magazine *Veja*,
Chagnon was asked, "What is the real Indian like?" Part of his response was that "Real
Indians sweat, they smell bad, they take hallucinogenic drugs, they belch after they eat, they
covet and at times steal their neighbor's wife, they fornicate, and they make war"
(2002a:37). Many anthropologists believe that the lasting impression that legions of readers of the multiple editions of Chagnon's ethnography have come away with is that the
Yanömamo are bloodthirsty, cruel, vicious, untrustworthy, filthy—in effect, ghastly and not
quite human. And the implications are real and disturbing:

> The problem faced by advocates of the Yanomami in Venezuela and especially
> Brazil is, unfortunately, not to combat romantic images of Indians, but to deal
> with a public—and, most importantly, powerful national and regional politi-
> cians and businessmen—that sees Indians as worthless savages who block the
> development of Brazil. Chagnon's remarks about sweating, smelling, belching,
> and fornicating, in this context used precisely the terms of this popular image,
> which can be found reproduced in films, television programs, cartoons, and
> other sites where the most vulgar images of Indian "savagery" are reproduced
> for public consumption. And, most unfortunately, much of the rest of the inter-
> view attacked NGO's, other anthropologists, and missionaries who have advo-
> cated for the Yanomami. (2002a:37)

The Task Force also questioned Chagnon's repeated depictions of the Yanömamo as a
"Stone Age" society, somehow frozen in time, which also does little to undermine views
of their purported savagery. It noted the multiple characterizations of the Yanömamo as
"unacculturated," "primitive," "our contemporary ancestors," and the like. Worse, "The
elaboration of the discourse of 'antiquity' of the Yanomami sometimes takes startling

forms. For instance, in the fifth edition [of his ethnography, 1997], Chagnon amends his discussion of personal cleanliness among the Yanomami as follows: 'It is difficult to blow your nose gracefully when you are stark naked and the invention of handkerchiefs is millennia away' " (2000a:38).

Chagnon's role as a "fierce interpreter," Salamone (1997) suggests, has endangered the survival of the very people he has studied for decades. Cognizant of the ethical responsibility that anthropologists have toward the people they study—what Scheper-Hughes has called the "Primacy of the Ethical" (1995)—other anthropologists, following the footsteps of Smole (1976), have attempted to provide alternate views of the Yanömamo. For example, in reflecting on "the fighting and bellicosity for which [the Yanomami] have for so long been (in)famously caricatured," Alés focuses instead on the "affective" dimensions of conviviality and sociality, their "capacity for melancholy and sadness after the death of their number [and their] . . . ability to feel distress . . ." (Alés 2000:133, 148). Speaking for many anthropologists, Coronil (2001:266) states that "our gift, our responsibility, is to work to produce forms of understanding that make intolerable the conditions that maintain injustice in any form, including our use of the privilege of science itself." Whether this kind of work will in time shift the tide of public opinion in favor of the Yanömamo remains to be seen.

In The United States: Domestic Workers in the Midst of Affluence

The transformation of national and international economies spurred by globalization creates special labor niches in Latin America and elsewhere. One of these niches, at the intersection of class, gender, and ethnicity, is domestic labor or service, which anthropologists working in Latin America and the Caribbean (Gill 1994) and Asia (Constable 1997) are increasingly paying attention to. Female Mexican and other Latin American legal and undocumented workers are in high demand and fill similar niches in the U.S. economy.

In the witty film *A Day Without a Mexican,* "Anglo" homemakers in Los Angeles are thrown into a frenzy as they frantically attempt to take care of daily house chores without their Mexican domestic helpers. In one especially amusing scene, a homemaker is unable to remember where her domestic worker stored what she needs to prepare breakfast and suddenly remembers that she is out of orange juice. She realizes that for the first time in quite a while she needs to purchase groceries, and darts around the house trying to do laundry. "Latina immigrant labor," Hondagneu-Soleto (2001:ix) tells us, "constitutes a bedrock of . . . contemporary U.S. culture and economy, yet the work and the women who do it remain invisible and disregarded." In her book, Hondagneu-Soleto highlights the life experiences of these women in the United States and the challenges they face as they go about carving out a future for themselves and their families.

Hispanics/Latinos, many of them immigrants, make up a substantial portion of California's population, especially in Los Angeles. For example, almost half of the five hundred thousand Salvadorans in the United States live in the greater Los Angeles area (Mahler 1995:5). The vast majority of Salvadoran, Mexican, and Guatemalan immigrants in Los Angeles work in the low pay service sector, and many of these are women, as Hondagneu-Soleto (2001:7) reminds us:

Twice as many gardeners and domestic workers were working in Los Angeles in 1990 as in 1980. Mexicans, Salvadorans, and Guatemalans perform these . . . jobs; and by 1990 those three groups, numbering about two million, made up more than half of the adults who had immigrated to Los Angeles since 1965. Hundreds of thousands of Mexican, Salvadoran, and Guatemalan women sought employment in Los Angeles during the 1970s, 1980s, and 1990s.

The overwhelming number of women employed in the domestic sector as housekeepers, cleaners, or nannies are originally from El Salvador and Guatemala, having fled the civil wars of the 1970s and 1980s that raged in their home countries. Often they are single or, if mothers, have left their children behind to be taken care of by extended family members. In California, the strong demand for domestic work means that women can more easily and quickly find employment than their male counterparts (Hondagneu-Soleto 2001:52–64). *Domésticas* (female domestic workers) who work as housekeepers are usually also assigned the responsibility of taking care of their employers' children. This, as we shall see, is a source of considerable tension between domésticas and their employers.

Adjusting to their new life in the United States is often a painful experience, partly because immigrant domésticas leave behind friends and family, including, often, their own children. They also have to cope with discrimination, loneliness, low wages, and job insecurity. But it is also difficult because of the wide cultural gap—and possibilities of ongoing cultural misreading—between themselves and their (invariably "Anglo") employers. This is especially the case with live-in domésticas. Hondagneu-Soleto discusses several examples of cultural misunderstandings that live-in domésticas are forced to understand and cope with.

Food and culture are intertwined in many ways (see Chapter 9 for more details). In the case of domestic workers and their employers, food and eating meals is one domain where significant cultural mismatches often take place, and this frequently leads to considerable tension. What Hondagneu-Soleto calls the "indignities of food" that many domésticas experience have much to do with the different meanings and expectations that they and their employers attach to the job as well as to food and meals. Live-in domésticas often expect that their employers have a plentiful, wide selection of food readily available, an expectation that often clashes with day-to-day reality:

> In some of the homes where they work, the employers are out all day. When [they] return home, they may only snack, keeping on hand little besides hot dogs, packets of macaroni and cheese, cereal, and peanut butter for the children. Such foods are considered neither nutritious nor appetizing by Latina immigrants, many of whom are accustomed to sitting down to meals prepared with fresh vegetables, rice, beans, and meat. (Hondagneu-Soleto 2001:33)

Who eats with whom and when are also cultural understandings and expectations that are often unclear and hence need to be resolved on the job. For example, although some employers may invite their domésticas to join them at the dinner table, many often refuse (to the dismay of their employers), because "sitting down to share a meal symbolizes membership in a family, and Latina employees, for the most part, know they are not just like one of the family" (Hondagneu-Soleto 2001:34). On the other hand, sitting down to share a meal with employers can also backfire, as when one doméstica sat down, uninvited, to have dinner with her employer's family. The outraged homemaker's husband (she didn't "know her place") fired her. In this case, the doméstica "crossed an invisible boundary by joining the family and the in-laws at the table" (Hondagneu-Soleto 2001:191).

Regardless of whether domésticas sit down to eat with their employers or their families, they prefer warm and close relationships with those for whom they work. This too may be a source of considerable disappointment—if not tension—for often employers favor maintaining personal distance with their employees. For their part, domésticas may prefer employers who pay less but who treat them warmly and with respect. They are aware that

> employers can use personalistic relations as a strategy to mask low salaries, lack of benefits, and long hours of work without overtime pay, but for the most part, Latina housecleaners and nanny/housekeepers see cold, impersonal employer-employee relations as blatant reminders of the low regard in which society holds them. (Hondagneu-Soleto 2001:208)

Differing expectations about appropriate behavior by children and how they should be raised are also a source of misunderstandings. For instance, some domésticas are appalled at what they consider disrespectful behavior by and lack of proper disciplining of children, as "when parents, after witnessing a child scratch or bite or spit at them, simply shrug their shoulders and ignore such behavior" (Hondagneu-Soleto 2001:41). Adolescent pranks or the wasting of food are also examples of behavior that domésticas have difficulty understanding and grappling with. At the same time, though, many domésticas experience considerable ambiguity when it comes to child rearing practices:

> Some women openly admire American middle-class parents for setting limits on television viewing, or for punishing their children with "time-outs" rather than spanking, and are eager to learn these child-rearing strategies. Other[s] criticize what they see as American parents' indulgence and coddling of children. (Hondagneu-Soleto 2001:153)

Children are crucial in many other ways in structuring labor relations between employers and their domésticas, and in establishing the symbolic boundaries of work. Indeed, the emotional bonds that many domésticas establish with the children they take care of are a strategic arena in and through which labor and labor control issues are played out, for

> these emotional attachments do not remain "outside" the labor process, but are often used by both employers and employees to get what they want [and] both parents and care providers may exploit the emotional bond between the nanny/housekeeper and the children for their own benefit. (Hondagneu-Soleto 2001:150)

Many housekeepers are also hired to look after and, hopefully, provide loving care for their employers' children. This is an important source of tension and confusion because employers often resist the idea that this "intimate" kind of work should entail monetary compensation, that love cannot and should not be measured through money. The view that "labors of love do not really constitute employment" (Hondagneu-Soleto 2001:120) is of course resisted by domésticas.

Further, both employers and domésticas use emotions toward children as a lever to negotiate some of the terms of work, the former trying to get more work out of their domésticas, the latter often resisting. One doméstica (a former lawyer in Peru), apparently overwhelmed by increasing demands that she keep the house clean and take better care of her employer's children, "relied not on her emotional bond with the children but on concern for the children's safety and social development to redefine her job so that her 'nanny' duties outweighed 'housekeeping' chores" (Hondagneu-Soleto 2001:151).

Nevertheless, many domésticas become attached to the children they care for, especially those domésticas who have left behind children of their own, and the "loving care that they cannot give their own children is sometimes transferred to their employers' children" (Hondagneu-Soleto 2001:152). These bonds can be difficult to deal with when they leave their employment (or are fired), and one way of minimizing this painful experience is to try to distance themselves from the children. As one woman told Hondagneu-Soleto (2001:123):

> Now I stop myself from becoming too close. Before, when my own children weren't living here [in the United States], I gave all my love to the children I cared for . . . When the job ended, I hurt so much. I can't let that happen again.

Summary

This chapter focused attention on contemporary globalization, an economic and cultural process linking peoples in ever-tighter, manifold ways. It focused first on how ethnic tourism and the incessant search for "authenticity" is spurring cultural creativity, traditions, and ethnic pride and consciousness. The North American Free Trade Agreement was then examined, with particular attention placed on its impact on migration, and on the cultural, social, and gendered changes brought about by the surge of maquiladora assembly plants. This chapter then turned to the important relationships between global economic interests, inequality, and massive deforestation in Amazonia and Central America. A related issue subsequently raised centered on the dangers posed to Amazonian peoples, and their livelihoods and environments, of some anthropological works depicting them as savage or primitive. Finally, this chapter called attention to the often-hidden lives of immigrant domestic workers employed by affluent North American households.

ISSUES AND QUESTIONS

1. *Globalization.* What are some of the meanings associated with the concept of globalization, and which examples from this chapter illustrate these different meanings? Is contemporary globalization distinct from other economic and cultural processes that have in the past linked different peoples in manifold ways?

2. *Cultural Homogeneity and Heterogeneity.* One important debate centers on whether globalization is ushering in a more uniform, Western-dominated, global culture, and thereby erasing or undermining local cultural differences. Which examples from this and other chapters of this book can be used to illustrate whether this concern is justified?

3. *North American Free Trade Agreement.* Why might NAFTA be a good example of globalization? Which examples illustrate how NAFTA and maquiladoras have both economic and cultural consequences? Are there perhaps others not mentioned in this book?

4. *Impact on the Environment.* How and in what ways is globalization having an impact on the environment? Why might this be so? Are there ways suggested in this chapter that might curb or stem globalization's environmental consequences? Might these be effective? Why? Why not?

KEY TERMS AND CONCEPTS

Anthropology of tourism   p. 284
Biopiracy   p. 301
Bioprospecting   p. 300
Cultural negotiation   p. 284
Ethnographic representation
   p. 305
Gendered distribution of global
   labor   p. 289

Globalization   p. 282
Invention of tradition   p. 284
Maquilas or maquiladoras
   p. 284
Neoliberalism   p. 282
North American Free Trade
   Agreement   p. 290
Political ecology   p. 302

Sustainable development
   p. 299
Swidden or shifting cultivation
   p. 303

ENDNOTE

1 An "unauthorized migrant" is someone "who resides in the United States but who is *not* a U.S. citizen, has *not* been admitted for permanent residence, and is *not* in a set of specific authorized temporary statuses permitting longer-term residence and work" (Passel 2006: i).

11 Manifestations of Popular Culture

Manifestations of popular culture are the focus of this chapter. After examining some conceptual and methodological issues in defining popular culture, attention turns to sports, especially soccer and baseball. The significance of Carnaval is the focal point of the third section. Dance and music—tango, salsa, and reggae—are taken up in the fourth section. The powerful cultural role of mass media, in particular television and telenovelas (soap operas), is subsequently examined. One controversy related to dance and music—the relationship between tango and sexuality—is then raised. The final part of this chapter probes the meanings of the widely popular teenage ritual of the quinceañera—the celebration of a girl's fifteenth birthday—in the United States.

What Is Popular Culture?

The study of popular culture is very much in vogue. For example, a conference on Latin American popular culture is held periodically; an academic journal—*Studies in Latin American Popular Culture*—is published yearly; and several major edited volumes have recently appeared (Beezley et al. 1994a; Bueno and Caesar 1998a; Beezley and Curcio-Nagy 2000b; Aching 2002). Despite this interest, scholars disagree on what precisely popular culture means, and how to conceptually and methodologically delimit the "popular" from other dimensions of culture. Part of the reason may be that, as Canclini (1996:62) suggests, **popular culture** is not a scientific construct but, rather, "a field of dispute and negotiation over social meaning." In a summary of presentations of the fourth Conference on Latin American Popular Culture (1994) Mahan states that "the papers assembled in this volume of *Studies in Latin American Popular Culture* [suggest] that what scholars mean by popular culture—and what they should study when they wish to understand it—remains without a single, satisfactory answer" (1996:5).

There have been different attempts to grapple with the meaning and scope of popular culture. Some scholars attempt to quantify the pervasiveness of a popular cultural expression by, for example, ascertaining the percentage of a country's population that watches prime-time soap operas (telenovelas; see also the section "Television and Telenovelas" later in this chapter). Others approach popular culture by attempting to contrast it with what is not popular, such as "elite," "dominant," or "high" culture. Webster's Third New International Dictionary (Gove et al. 1986) defines *popular* as "relevant to any of the people," "relating to the general public," or "involving participation by the common people as distinguished from a specific class or group."

These definitions resonate with scholarly approaches, such as Hinds' interpretation of popular culture as "culture which is widely disseminated and consumed by large numbers of people" (1996:1). Beezley and Curcio-Nagy's portrayal is comparable:

> Popular culture, as the term appears throughout this book, defines everyday culture. It identifies a set of behavioral practices with pervasive, ordinary character and acknowledges the general acceptance of these practices, their roots in common knowledge, and their frequent expression in nonwritten form . . . oral traditions, music, visual imagery, dance, and family food represent the unique community character that forms much of popular culture. (2000a:xi)

Ordinary, pervasive, common, and *widespread* are some keywords used to demarcate popular culture. Much of popular culture is also nonwritten and transmitted through verbal or visual means. This peculiarity partly has to do with the fact that until recently most Latin American and Caribbean culture has been grounded in oral tradition. But perhaps more importantly, many contemporary innovations in popular culture have been spurred by nonwritten technological advances, such as television and cinema. Hence, popular culture ought not be construed as opposed to or incompatible with modern life ways. Many expressions of popular culture certainly exhibit African or indigenous elements—in music and dance (merengue, bomba, or samba in Puerto Rico, the Dominican Republic, or Brazil), or Carnaval in Brazil or Bolivia—that lend a particular "flavor" to Latin American and Caribbean popular culture. It would be a mistake, though, to assume that these expressions of culture are static or "traditional" (Chasteen 2000, 2004).

Further, overtly or covertly, popular culture often displays resistance to domination (Handler 1994). That is, popular culture repeatedly questions and challenges—through parody, satire, and gossip—the socio-cultural and political–economic hierarchy and stratification that has existed in Latin America and the Caribbean since the European Conquest. Research on popular celebrations—public displays which often have religious undercurrents and are celebrated by wide segments of a population—is one example of the ways that popular culture often questions and challenges hierarchy and stratification (Beezley et al 1994a; Beezley and Curcio-Nagy 2000a). Further, popular culture is not only interesting and fun to study, but it is important in the construction of local senses of identity. Lastly, popular culture is an important cultural repertoire from which national elites have attempted to forge a sense of national consciousness and identity crucial for the coalescence of modern nation-states (Geddes González 1996; Austerlitz 1997; Vianna 1999; Holton 2000; Wade 2000).

Most scholars studying popular culture are not anthropologists. The relatively recent interest by cultural anthropologists in popular culture mainly stems from recognizing cultural heterogeneity in stratified, culturally diverse societies and, as a result, acknowledging finer distinctions such as working-class, peasant, or popular culture. Anthropologists have also begun to attach importance to technological advances in communications and the constant flow of information, ideas, and images across cultural and political boundaries (see Chapter 10). Most nonanthropological studies of popular culture have focused on **texts.** These refer to means through which ideas, values, and norms are transmitted to a wider audience, and include books, magazines and newspapers, television and cinema, and even sports events. Yet, there is a role for anthropologists and ethnographic fieldwork, cultural anthropology's methodological hallmark:

> How can one be sure that actions one construes as resistance are experienced or intended as such by those engaged in them? . . . In the absence of ethnographic fieldwork—or some other method to engage directly with the people "out there" who are creating and consuming the cultural products being analyzed by scholars—the discourse of cultural studies on resistance remains . . . profoundly elitist. (Handler 1994:4)

Sports

Sports, or "gamelike activity having rules, a competitive element, and requiring some form of physical exertion" (Blanchard 1995:9), are part and parcel of the culture of all societies. Soccer and baseball—extraordinarily popular in Latin America and the Caribbean—are examples of what Guttman (1994) calls modern sports, distinguished by being highly competitive secular activities in which rules are the same for all players regardless of ascriptive traits (such as ethnicity or race), and marked by specialized roles, an emphasis on training and efficiency, oversight by national or international bureaucracies, and importance attached to record keeping.

Soccer

Soccer is such a passionate sport in South America that Lever has called it a "madness" (1983), and Galeano states that

> few things happen in Latin America that do not have some direct or indirect relation with soccer. Whether it's something we celebrate together, or a shipwreck that takes us all down, soccer counts in Latin America, sometimes more than anything else. (2004:42; see also 2003)

Soccer's direct antecedents can be traced to medieval peasant villages in England and France. By the eighteenth and nineteenth centuries, this type of popular football was altered and adopted by middle and elite sectors of British society. Subsequently portrayed and envisioned as a "higher" class sport, it was quickly and widely emulated by working-class sectors, "quickly diffus[ing] downward through the social strata" (Guttman 1994:42–43). The spread of soccer to and its popularity in South America was one result of the enormous cultural and economic influence of Great Britain during the nineteenth century, especially in Chile, Argentina, and Uruguay, where soccer clubs appeared by the mid-1800s. By 1902, São Paulo, Brazil, had a soccer team, and by 1914 the sport "had developed . . . rapidly among all classes in the urban centers" (Guttman 1994:62). In Brazil, the rapid spread of soccer's popularity from an elite to a genuinely popular, mass sport, reveals a great deal about changing race and class relationships and ideologies in Brazilian society (Daflon and Ballvé 2004).

The Central American Soccer War. There are many reasons why men and women, young and old, play or view sports, or why they back one club or team and not another. Yet, regardless of the explanations people themselves may profess, modern sports in contemporary societies often serve as a medium and even catalyst through which nationalistic and political tensions and conflicts are channeled. The 1969 **soccer war** between El Salvador and Honduras is one example of how nationalism and political economy can become enmeshed in the playing of such a popular sport (Durham 1979).

On June 15, 1969, Salvadoran and Honduran teams, vying for the World Cup, played their third match. The Salvadoran team beat Honduras, a near riot ensued and Honduran spectators were beaten up. Shortly thereafter, Honduras began to forcibly expel thousands of Salvadoran migrants living in Honduras. Days later, El Salvador invaded Honduras, precipitating a three month war that left thousands dead and many more refugees in Central America's two poorest countries. Because this war occurred just after a soccer match, journalists quickly labeled it a soccer war, and some journalistic accounts questioned the rationality of the "Latin" mind or culture. It is, after all, one thing to brawl after a crucial soccer match, as so often happens in Europe, but quite another thing to go to war over the outcome of a soccer game.

Others also pondered the war and its causes. One early explanation emphasized the role of overpopulation, for when the match was held, hundreds of thousands of Salvadorans were living and working in Honduras; El Salvador historically has been the poorest and most densely populated country of Central America. Dubbed a "demographic" war, the idea was that the Salvadoran presence was leading to an unsustainable pressure on land and other resources in Honduras, which would partly explain why it began expelling Salvadorans (see Durham 1979 and Anderson 1981 for detailed bibliographies).

Durham (1979) disagreed with this ecological-demographic theory, favoring instead a political–economic explanation focusing on inequality and conflicts within and between El Salvador and Honduras. Prior to the 1969 soccer match that ignited the conflict, tensions between the countries were already high. This was because their borders had been hotly contested for more than one hundred years, but also because Honduras was reaping far fewer benefits than El Salvador from a common market agreement signed a decade earlier.

But the war had much to do with other kinds of tensions and contexts. For example, in El Salvador the close correlation between high demographic densities, land scarcity, and widespread poverty was primarily a result of increasing concentration of land and other productive resources by large landowners, which left many in the countryside landless. In turn, many of these landless ended up crossing the border and working in Honduras. Political agitation and class conflict were also present in Honduras, where landowners, especially cattle ranchers, were also despoiling peasants of their land.

There is no evidence that the war was sparked by landless Honduran and Salvadoran peasants, imbued with nationalistic fervor, competing against each other for land in Honduras. In fact, rather than divided by ethnically-charged animosity, peasants from both countries joined hands in an attempt to halt the spread of cattle ranches and other landed estates in Honduras itself. Responding to escalating and increasingly dangerous agitation, local landowners organized themselves into a cattle ranching association that "succeeded in translating an internal problem of resource competition into an external one" (Durham 1979:165). One way they did so was by casting the conflict in nationalist terms, blaming

Salvadorans for the agrarian problems and conflicts in Honduras. Through different channels—newspapers, radio, and political and sports events—the landed elite spurred the creation of a new nationalism and inflamed nationalist tensions that were latent but ever-present during that fateful soccer match of June 15, 1969.

Nationalism, Masculinity, and Party Politics in Argentine Soccer.   In Argentina, what soccer means is intimately tied to nationalistic fervor as well as to national identity, the construction of male identities (masculinity), and competing party politics. How soccer is important for Argentine national identity is nicely captured in the following statements provided to Archetti:

> *Los argentinos somos una raza futbolística* ("We Argentinians are of the football breed") . . . You know what I mean. We must learn to think as a united people, as a society. Argentinians are very individualistic, with little national feeling . . . except when the national football teams plays. Then our patriotism emerges, including many . . . who feel that football is not important. (1999:161)

Yet, anthropologists, feminist scholars, and others have also often commented on how in Latin America and elsewhere nationalism is profoundly gendered and male centered (Martínez-San Miguel 1997; Caulfield 2000, 2001; de Moya 2004; Dore 2000a). This idea is especially relevant in Argentina, where soccer is not only important for national but also masculine identity, so that victory

> is intimately associated with the deployment of some male virtues: courage, physical strength, tactical rational planning and moral endurance. In addition, these virtues are seen . . . as constitutive of paternity and relations of father [the winning team] and son [the losing team]. (Archetti 1999:168)

The Argentine film *Evita Capitana* conveys how soccer has historically been associated with competing party politics, class conflicts, and deep ideological divisions. The film is set in 1951, during the last stage of Juan Domingo Perón's first government (he was up for re-election), and before his Peronismo social movement coalesced into Argentina's most powerful political force. *Evita Capitana* centers the audience's attention on the final match of the national soccer championship, played between Racing (a team comprised of and favored by elite sectors) and the newer Banfield soccer team, mainly consisting of working-class youths. This class divide was also mirrored, politically and ideologically, within Perón's government. The elite Racing team, for example, was favored and sponsored by Perón's finance minister, while the working-class Banfield team was the favorite of Peron's wife, the legendary Evita, who campaigned on behalf of the disenfranchised *descamisados* (shirtless ones). The film nicely illustrates ways that deep social and political divisions are enacted on the soccer field, and how and why soccer matches are often emotionally-charged mediums through which ideological and political conflicts are played out.

The multi-faceted links between soccer and politics in Argentine society are as strong as when Evita Perón rooted for the Banfield team in 1951. Alabarces (2004) reminds us that the military junta that seized power in 1976 (see Chapter 12) used the 1978 World Cup match, played in Argentina, to divert attention from the fierce repression underway; that in the 1980s former president Menen appeared at the national stadium wearing the national team's soccer jersey shortly after taking power; and that in 2001—under the grinding poverty, growing unemployment, and escalating social unrest that led to the resignation of President De la Rúa—street protests bore an uncanny resemblance to the brawls that soccer fans often employed against police after a soccer match. Indeed, Alabarces (2004:35) states that the

> practices learned at soccer stadiums—the spontaneous creation of chants and the tactics of resistance against police repression—became purely political when crossbred with popular mobilization.

Popular Discontent and Soccer in Urban Chile. How soccer serves as a public expressive medium through which popular discontent is channeled has been stressed by Lemebel (1998). As in Argentina, soccer in Chile is a national passion. Lemebel, however, focuses attention on how and why soccer is an especially important vent for young, disenfranchised youths of Santiago's urban shantytowns. "During the 1980s," Lemebel tells us, "Santiago's poor barrios were the cradle of the intense struggle against the [Augusto] Pinochet regime" (1998:37). A decade later, after the return to democracy, these same shantytowns are the site of intense resistance against the widening gap between the poor and rich. The links between soccer and politics in Chile—as in Argentina—are multiple: General Pinochet, Galeano (2004:41) tells us, thought it was important to name himself president of Colo-Colo, Chile's most popular soccer club.

Santiago's barrios are teeming with soccer fan clubs called **barras bravas** (fierce fan clubs). These are "fierce" not only because of the passion that their young working-class and marginalized members exhibit at soccer matches, but also because of the intensity with which these youths display a more general nonconformist, rebellious attitude toward Chilean society and dominant social expectations:

> The two most important *barras*— famous for their devotion to their teams—are La Garra Blanca (The White Claw) and Los de Abajo (The Ones from Below). The former is devote[d] to the Colo-Colo soccer team . . . named after a heroic indigenous warrior who has been mystified in Chile's official histories for defending the territory against the Spaniards during the Conquest. La Garra Blanca appropriated the hero's epic narrative and translated it into the social and economic idioms of its members. The members of La Garra, mostly young men from Santiago's peripheries, refer to themselves as "Indios, Proletarios, y Rebolucionarios" (Indians, Proletarians, and Revolutionaries), contradicting the narrative of upward social mobility so pervasive in contemporary Chilean society. (Lemebel 1998:38)

Profoundly angry and disenchanted, the youthful barras are teeming with rage, which is openly and often bitterly expressed during and after soccer matches:

> During games, wooden stadium bleachers are set ablaze, and sticks, rocks and bottles rain on the playing field. As the fans make their way back to their neighborhoods, dozens of windshields are left shattered. The buses of the

barras transport their pubescent mayhem throughout the country, following their team wherever it may go as they sing:

I was born in a neighborhood made of tin and cardboard
I have smoked pot and I have felt love
I have been to jail many times, and many times I have lost my voice
Now with democracy everything remains the same
We ask ourselves how long we can put up with it
Now that I am from below [referring to the name of the *barra*]
I understand the situation
There are only two options—to be a hell-raiser and join the "rebolución"
(Lemebel 1998:39)

The film *Barras Bravas* provides a gripping look into barras in Santiago. The film is important because it provides insights not furnished by Lemebel, such as that barras claim their own territorial boundaries, that their members display an intense loyalty to each other, and that barras often engage in bloody feuds against each other.

Baseball

Internationally, baseball is associated with the United States, which spawned and popularized the modern version of this sport by the end of the nineteenth century. Yet, baseball is extraordinarily popular and important in the Spanish-speaking Caribbean and Central America, a fact reflecting more the history and political economy of these regions—and especially their long-time relationships with the United States—than the playing of the sport itself. Like soccer, devotion to baseball is also intimately related to politics: Fidel Castro is not only a lifelong baseball fan but so were many Sandinistas at the height of the armed conflict in Nicaragua (see Chapter 12):

> Daniel Ortega, the former Sandinista president of Nicaragua, is an avid follower of the Baltimore Orioles, and he is often photographed wearing a Mets cap. That contras and Sandinistas should be able to agree on anything is noteworthy, but baseball has always proven to be the cultural form that crosses political lines. When Nicaragua lost in a recent international baseball competition, one Sandinista felt the loss so deeply that he remarked, "It was so sad, even the contras cried." (Klein 1991:96)

The Dominican Republic.   "To the average Dominican," Klein states,

> baseball is a major source of cultural pride. The country's identification with the game is deep and its signs are pervasive . . . *pelota* (baseball) is an opportunity to escape a life of poverty; while to the major league franchises there, the country is a seemingly endless source of cheap and genuine talent. In the Dominican Republic baseball has become much more than a game, even more

than a national pastime: it is a crucial arena of intercultural relations, in which significance attaches to everything about the game, its symbols, and its players . . . There is nothing comparable to it in the United States, nothing as central, as dearly held as baseball is for Dominicans. Americans may love the game of baseball as much as Dominicans do, but they do not need it as much. For Dominicans baseball is a wide-ranging set of symbols: every turn at bat is a candle of hope, every swing is the wave of a banner, the sweeping arc of a sword. (1991:1)

The emergence of baseball in the Caribbean and the Dominican Republic is intimately related to sugar plantation agriculture and the political–economic dominance by the United States—baseball "followed" the United States' flag just as soccer trailed Britain's Union Jack. Baseball was first introduced in the Dominican Republic during the 1860s by elite wealthy émigrés from Cuba who were fleeing slave revolts and who invested in sugar plantations. In a few decades, baseball's popularity crossed class boundaries and became especially popular in closely knit working-class communities in and around sugar plantations (Klein 1991:15–25). The potential political ramifications of the cultural importance attached to baseball by nonelite Dominicans was not overlooked by the United States ambassador, who in 1913 stated in a memo to the State Department that

I deem it worthy of the Department's notice that the American national game of base-ball is being played and supported here with great enthusiasm. The remarkable effect of this outlet for the animal spirits of the young men, is that they are leaving the plazas where they were in the habit of congregating and talking revolution and are resorting to the ball fields where they become wildly partizan each for his favorite team. The importance of this . . . interest . . . should not be minimized. It satisfies a craving in the nature of the people for exciting conflict, and is a real substitute for the contest in the hill-sides with rifles. (Klein 1991:110)

Perhaps the ambassador was wrong on this point, or perhaps he spoke too early. Either way, three years later (in 1916), United States Marines invaded the Dominican Republic.

There are several related reasons why baseball has loomed so culturally significant in the contemporary Dominican Republic. One has to do with the country's widespread poverty and scarcity of jobs, and the few alternatives that members of the popular classes have to improve their living standards. Further, most Dominicans know at least someone who has "made it" in the U.S. major leagues. The fantastic salaries that major league players earn when playing for U.S. teams—when compared to what the average Dominican earns—also has much to do with the powerful significance attached to baseball. That playing and succeeding in baseball is viewed by so many as perhaps the only legitimate road out of poverty also dovetails with many cultural and social expectations. For example, a player's success in the U.S. major league baseball is a victory not only for himself but also for his immediate family and home community. This explains the intense social pressures to succeed and avoid the painful shame of failure.

Yet, baseball is also so important for so many Dominicans because it is closely tied to national pride *and* because playing baseball is viewed by many as perhaps the only arena in which the Dominican Republic has an edge over the historic economic, political, and military superiority of the United States. A cultural activity (playing baseball) is therefore catapulted onto the front stage of historically unequal Dominican–United States relationships and provides a way of leveling the "playing field" in a contest that otherwise cannot be won. This explains why the Dominican team Licey is so revered: it beat the team comprised of members of the United States Marines occupying the Dominican Republic between 1916 and 1924 (Klein 1991:116–117). This is also why well-known players, especially those who play in U.S. major leagues and therefore succeed, are also venerated and imbued with national pride. This is important for, as Klein (1991:58) has aptly noted, there are few "cultural heroes with a machete [for the cutting of sugar cane] in their hand."

Cuba.   As in the case of the Dominican Republic, the historical relevance of baseball in Cuba cannot be fully understood without underscoring the powerful economic and political influence of the United States in the latter half of the nineteenth century. While the 1898 Spanish American War consolidated the United States' economic, political, and cultural clout in Cuba, in fact commercial ties between the Spanish colony and the United States were widespread prior to 1898, and Cuban elites (still Spanish subjects) often traveled between Cuba and the United States. Landowning elites—especially those with widespread investments in sugarcane plantation agriculture—adopted the sport by the 1860s, and a decade later the first professional sports teams and matches appeared (González Echevarría 1999:75–89). To members of this elite class, baseball was an important symbol of modernity and progressive North American culture, which sharply contrasted with the old and decaying Spanish order, best represented in the sports sphere by bullfighting. A description of baseball and bullfighting in late 1880s in the city of Matanzas by a Cuban novelist captures the thrust of this cultural and political gulf—and the emerging link between baseball and nationalism:

> That afternoon, besides the game of baseball—civilized, manly, healthy—there was a bullfight, that savage entertainment that never took hold in the noble and progressive Antillean milieu. In the glorietas and stands of the baseball stadium there swarmed a creole [native Cuban] crowd . . . In the barbaric ring there thronged an important crowd [Spaniards], and among them, naturally, the city's entire police force, among whose members, also naturally, there wasn't a single native of the nation. (quoted in González Echevarría 1999:96)

Indeed, one important legacy of nineteenth-century baseball was the strong link forged between baseball and Cuban nationality through the following century:

> Growing up Cuban meant growing up with baseball as an integral part of one's life. Baseball was played since the beginning of the nation; hence it was part of the nation. In the countryside, playing baseball was as quotidian as eating black beans and rice and roasting a pig on Christmas Eve. (González Echevarría 1999:110)

Revolutionary ideology notwithstanding, baseball in contemporary Cuba continues to be its national game—just as it had been prior to Fidel Castro's 1959 revolution. This suggests not only the extent to which baseball had become widely entrenched in Cuban popular culture and national consciousness prior to 1959, but how it also left a deep influence on future revolutionaries. In fact, the continuing popularity of baseball after Castro's revolution is less a paradox than an example of how a cultural artifact or activity (playing baseball) is imbued with new messages and meanings in a radically different political and economic context.

Fidel Castro not only has been an avid baseball fan all his life, but after the 1959 revolution he aggressively sponsored baseball on a scale not seen before: many new stadiums were built; amateur provincial leagues were established; national championships were organized; racial and other barriers to club membership were torn down; and professional training on an island-wide basis, backed by state institutions such as the Instituto Nacional de Deportes, Educación Física y Recreación (National Institute of Sports, Physical Education, and Recreation), became widespread. Cuba also strongly sponsored participation of its athletes and players in Olympic and Pan American games, and other kinds of matches between Cuban, North American, European, and Latin American and Caribbean teams (González Echevarría 1999:352–363).

The powerful role of Fidel Castro and the Cuban state in promoting baseball can only partly be explained by its widespread popularity among most Cubans (including Fidel himself). Political ideology and commitment to the goals of the revolution also played an important role for, as González Echevarría (1999:354) notes, "To the revolutionaries the notion of beating the United States at its own game became a cherished dream, even if it meant perpetuating an undeniable American influence." Excelling in baseball—especially against the United States—became one way of legitimating the superiority of the socialist order and its values, of defending the revolution and the motherland, and, as a result, the sport became "an arena for ideological confrontation with capitalist powers" (González Echevarría 1999:365).

Carnaval and Popular Celebrations

A major expression of popular culture in much of Latin America is Carnaval (also spelled Carnival). In many ways a **secular-religious ritual,** or sets of highly ritualized activities, Carnaval is intimately linked to popular Catholicism because of its links to the Christian liturgical calendar and partial origins in medieval European Christianity (Harris 2003).

The Origins of Carnaval

What is known and celebrated as Carnaval in Latin America and the Caribbean today has deep roots, partially originating in Europe at the dawn of the medieval period and partially a resulting syncretism of Christian and pre-Christian beliefs and practices. Pre- and non-Christian spring festivals celebrating the first harvests after long and bitter winters, auguring upcoming bounty and the end of famine, and linked to fertility and feminine fertility deities, were widespread and continued after the spread of Christianity.

In Europe, much Christian thought and practice centering around the death and resurrection of Jesus Christ (between Good Friday and Easter Sunday) eventually overlapped with non-Christian spring festivals. Prior to 325 A.D., Easter was timed to Passover (the Jewish spring harvest festival), and in what may have been a move to separate Christianity and Judaism, in 325 A.D., a Catholic Church Council ruled that Easter be celebrated on the first Sunday after the first full moon in spring, preceded by forty days of fasting, abstinence, and meditation. In 1091, Pope Gregory the Great decreed that Carnaval celebrations be limited to the six days immediately prior to the beginning of this forty day fasting period, or Lent. Indeed, the word *Carnaval* comes from Latin *carne vale,* meaning "take away the meat" (Da Matta 1992:104). Carnaval, then, takes place during the week prior to Ash Wednesday—the beginning of Lent—and most celebrations are on the preceding Saturday and Sunday:

Carnaval ◄─────► Ash Wednesday ◄─────► Good Friday/Easter Sunday
       ◄── 40 days (Excluding Sundays) ──────────►

The masks, dancing, tricksters, sexual overtures, representations of demons, ghosts, devils, and other prominent features of the celebration of Carnaval in Mesoamerica and the Andes probably have their origins in both pre- and post-Christian Europe. By about the tenth to eleventh century A.D., the beliefs, practices, and celebrations of Carnaval had become solidly entrenched in European popular culture and religion. It is this complex of beliefs and practices that was brought over to the Americas by the Spanish and Portuguese.

But Europeans did not merely force Carnaval onto Latin American societies, for there too structurally analogous festivals celebrating and marking the end of one agricultural season and the beginning of the next were widespread. This was particularly the case in heavily populated areas where intensive agriculture was practiced, such as Mesoamerica and the Andes (Grigsby and Cook de Leonard 1992; MacCormack 1998), and perhaps parts of central and northern South America. Where intensive agriculture was not practiced—that is, where crops and other resources were easily available year-round—such as the Caribbean, Amazonia, and much of what is now Brazil—such festivals were rare. Yet, even in these regions, the quick acceptance and entrenchment of the European Carnaval had much to do with the slave experience, most likely because of the presence of analogous festivals in African regions from which slaves were forcibly abducted (Andrews 2004:123). Thus, European beliefs and practices revolving around Carnaval resonated and blended with local indigenous as well as African cultures.

Understanding Carnaval

Not all Carnaval celebrations in Latin America are exactly the same; the music, costumes, pageantry, public activities, and meanings varying widely. In some countries or regions Carnaval looms especially prominent and visible, while in others it is barely present. Nevertheless, where Carnaval *is* an important public and mass cultural event, it is also a:

1. *Ritualized popular celebration.* Carnaval is often a mass ritual, or a **ritualized popular celebration.** That is, it is a highly stylized, choreographed public performance, despite that to an outsider its celebration may come across as chaotic and lacking in structure. It is celebrated in specific, well-determined times and places, and how it is celebrated—such as the kinds of music played, costumes displayed, or dances performed—varies little from year to year.

   2. *National ritual.* In some countries, Carnaval is often a huge and spectacular celebration that is national in scope, drawing together many people, regardless of class or ethnic background. Some of the best examples are the Bahia or Rio de Janeiro Carnavals (Brazil) or the Oruro Carnaval in Bolivia. These celebrations, the Brazilian anthropologist Da Matta tells us, "dramatiz[e] crucial, encompassing, global values of . . . society" (1992:26–27). As a result, they reflect and embody a great deal of national culture, of a society's values and norms. As national rituals, they are also important for national identity: would Brazilians view themselves as Brazilians without participating in Carnaval? Probably not. Can they envision Brazil without Carnaval? Probably not, for it "has become in Brazil something fundamentally and richly Brazilian" (Turner 1987:76). "Carnival," Linger (1992:8) states, "[is] acknowledged within [Brazil] and without as the chief and most eloquent expression of Brazilian popular culture." With the goal of fomenting tourism, Carnaval's role in underpinning and forging national identity has often been the result of elite-centered policies to market Carnaval as an "authentic" representation of national culture, such as in Trinidad and Tobago (Green 2002).

   3. *Ritual of inversion.* Carnaval is intrinsically a **ritual of inversion.** This means that for a few days, the social order is symbolically and metaphorically turned upside down and social roles are reversed. As a result, that which is normally proscribed is now sanctioned and encouraged, and that which is impossible in daily life is possible. The poor can become rich; the powerless can turn powerful; fantasies are no longer restricted to the realm of the unachievable; that which is normally hidden from everyday view now surfaces in the public sphere; that which is forbidden is now encouraged. In commenting on the pervasiveness of Brazilian Carnaval, Turner notes that "the secret of Brazilian culture perhaps . . . lies in that it has created a 'palace of Carnaval' . . . out of fantasies suppressed through the rest of the year by immersion in industrial labor, by submission to an autocratic regime, by tenacious vestiges of feudal attitudes in the relations between men and women, young and old" (1987.88).

   This also means that implicit in Carnaval is a public and popular commentary and questioning of the social order. Little wonder, then, that during and after colonial times, Carnaval was often viewed with deep suspicion and fear by elites (Linger 1992: 10–12). The African experience in Latin America and the Caribbean provides many examples of how Carnaval was repeatedly construed as a mass public celebration potentially dangerous to the social order. Andrews tells us, for example, that during the nineteenth century

> Brazilian and Cuban authorities sought to eliminate the African content of Carnaval, the annual "festival of the flesh" that precedes Lent. Throughout Afro–Latin America, these festivities had deep African roots. During the first half of the 1800s, slaves and free blacks in Buenos Aires, Montevideo, Rio de Janeiro, Cartagena, Havana, and other cities gathered for riotous dancing and drumming contests . . . Carnaval was also an occasion through which members of the lower class could briefly turn the tables on their social betters by pelting

them with eggs, balloons, and other small missiles filled with water, flour, honey, or cruder substances . . . So enthusiastically did poor and working-class celebrants embrace this opportunity to upend the social hierarchy that by the 1840s and 1850s many municipal governments had banned or placed severe limits on Carnaval. (2004:123; for other examples, see Chasteen 2000:48–49)

Colonial elites often had good reasons to be fearful of Carnaval, because many times popular celebrations stepped beyond the **private transcript**—that is, that facet of life often hidden from the gaze of elites and power holders (Scott 1985, 1990)—and bordered on public, outright rebellion. During the 1858 Carnaval season in Trinidad, for example, British soldiers fought running skirmishes with thousands of masked Africans "armed with hatchets, woodmen's axes, cutlasses, bludgeons, and knives" (Pearse 1971:544). One terrified eyewitness, a member of the planter class, recounted the following:

> In our towns . . . commencing with the orgies on Sunday night, we have the fearful howling of a parcel of semi-savages emerging God knows from where, exhibiting hellish scenes and the most demoniacal representation of the days of slavery as they were 40 years ago; then using the mask the two following days as a mere cloak for every species of barbarism and crime. (quoted in Pearse 1971:544)

At the same time, although a streak of resistance is part and parcel of all popular celebrations, we should also be wary of the potential transformative effects of Carnaval:

> It could be argued that Carnival may well reinforce the dominant social structure simply because the inversions that take place during that week are temporary and ultimately take place only with elite approval . . . On the other hand, the carnivalesque aesthetics that permeate everyday life—rather than a week during the year—may provide a fruitful opening for witnessing the more durable forms of resistance existing the other fifty-one weeks of the year. (Goldstein 2003:34)

4. *Channel that embodies memory.* Carnaval celebrations either at the community or national levels often function as a reminder—as a sort of memory history book—harking back to events and collective experiences deemed relevant for understanding the present. In this way, although played out in the present, Carnaval has deep links with the past, but often these links are continuously reinterpreted to make sense of a changing present. The Bolivian Carnaval of Oruro, discussed later in the section "Fertility, Community, and the Supernatural in Bolivian Carnaval," is a good example.

5. *Medium that stresses cohesion and solidarity.* Carnaval is celebrated not only in major and national spectacles, but also at the local, community level. As such, and like other kinds of secular and religious local rituals, community-level celebrations of Carnaval instill cohesion and solidarity by indirectly stressing the importance of being a member of a specific community, or sharing community interests or values. The fostering of a **collective**

sense of identity is a key function of Carnaval. In the case of Brazil, "Carnival . . . is one of those perpetual institutions that has enabled Brazilians to sense and feel . . . their specific continuity as a distinct social and political entity" (Da Matta 1992:15).

6. *Major drama and public spectacle.* National Carnaval celebrations, such as those in Bahia and Rio in Brazil, are major, intensely dramatic, public spectacles. As an exaggerated public dramatization (Da Matta 1992:23), Carnaval appeals to and conveys messages through sight and sound, smell and taste, and physical sensuality and experience, thereby instilling a visible and lasting imprint. The sensuality and overt sexual displays, some of the most visible manifestations of Brazil's Bahia and Rio de Janeiro Carnavals, serve as one example of dramatic public spectacles meant to leave a lasting imprint on memory. The belief and saying that "sin . . . does not exist beneath the equator" has been around for a long time, but still resonates well with the fact that "all-encompassing sensuality . . . is . . . fundamental to the whole meaning of the festival" (Parker 2003a:213, 225), and especially the massive display of sexual imagery. According to one Brazilian:

> The parade has become a type of stage for sensuality, with its floats . . . in their tropical, sensual frenzy . . . The bodies are . . . semi-nude, showing the energy of hot, happy, virile bodies . . . The in and out movements of their legs, bellies, sexes, and buttocks give the connotation of an external sexual climax. (Parker 2003a:225)

Tourism and Violence in Brazilian Carnaval

The film *Carnaval in Bahia*, centered in the city of Salvador, capital of the Brazilian state of Bahia, vividly illustrates the major features of Carnaval outlined previously. Second only in magnitude to Rio de Janeiro, Bahia's Carnaval is a spectacular event dominating everyday life well before and after its celebration. Examples of ritualized inversion abound: economic and social stratification are reversed, as when the poor and marginalized are transformed into kings, queens, and other popular celebrities; and racial and political hierarchies are temporarily overturned, as when "White" Brazilians appear as poor and downtrodden while "Blacks" assume politically powerful roles. (The state of Bahia is the most heavily African, or Black, of Brazil.) Further, the boundaries between the private and public, home and street, are temporarily erased; there is a heightened emphasis on sexuality and the transgression of sexual mores and identities; and satire and parody directed at political authorities abound. (Green [1999] has emphasized the role of Carnaval as a venue and catalyst for the expression of male homosexuality and other sexual identities.) The African influence is also quite noticeable in music and dance, as in the samba, or in candomblé rituals (see Chapter 7) that protect against evil and ensure the success of dance and music troupes or organizations (see Photo 11.1).

Bahia's Carnaval is also an event of international scope, attracting countless overseas tourists, often European. Yet, they are not mere tourist/spectators with little impact on Bahia's Carnaval and the context within which it takes place, because their presence, and especially what they long for, has important cultural consequences (Armstrong 1999). Many tourists attending Bahia's Carnaval differ from those who prefer Rio de Janeiro's Carnaval celebrations in that they often are less wealthy, are younger, and they stay for

PHOTO 11.1   *Brazilian actress Paula Burlamaqui dances atop a float during Carnaval celebrations in Rio de Janerio.*

considerably longer periods of time. Further, rather than remaining at the margins as mere distant spectators, many foreign tourists thrive in forging relationships with local Brazilians. As noted in Chapter 10, many of these tourists are often in search of "authentic" culture, in this case authentic Afro Brazilian culture. For these tourists, a major attraction of Salvador (and the state of Bahia) is its pervasive African influence, which is touted and proudly advertised by government officials:

> The two central photographic icons of Bahian tourist brochures are the beach scene and the Afro-Brazilian female street vendors of Bahian cuisine, known as *baianas* . . . The *baianas's* elaborate attire of white cotton and lace flocks, corsets and turbans, is that of a domestic slave from the plantation era . . . The food . . . of ritual procedures derived from Candomblé is specifically Afro-Bahian. (Armstrong 1999:140)

This combination of tourists seeking to experience "authentic" Afro Brazilian culture, coupled by its flaunting by government officials, has had a profound impact on Carnaval and on the local cultural and social context. Participation in Carnaval is through formally registered associations called **blocos.** An important effect of the search for cultural authenticity by tourists has been to spur Afro Brazilian blocos and a renewed sense of pride in the African (and slave) legacy, a "revitalization of things African" (Armstrong 1999:154). Tourists are therefore a powerful force legitimizing African heritage, stimulating an increased participation in Carnaval by the politically and economically marginalized Afro

Brazilian population, and undermining the influence of local elites—who are overwhelmingly wealthy and "White." This in turn has led government officials and local elites to restore decaying segments of the city where Afro Brazilian blocos are especially prominent, and to pay increasing attention to the needs of local residents. As Armstrong concludes:

> In Salvador, the Afro-Brazilian heritage has been gradually rehabilitated at the aesthetic level, and, at least implicitly, at a moral level, affording a social legitimacy that can only become more significant in an era where the rhetoric of democracy prevails. The international tourist, specifically young European enthusiasts of Bahia's vibrant syncretic *negritude,* has influenced the new power-relationship between the *negro-mestiço* and the local elite. (1999:155–156)

Yet, Carnaval is not all fun and gaiety but also a potentially dangerous setting, or a social and cultural context in which violence or the prospect of violence looms ever-present (Linger 1992). This capacity stems from Carnaval's inherent quality as a channel for social discontent and hence its potential for confrontation. Indeed, many activities and performances are borderline aggressive, or they minimally mimic aggression toward others. As Linger explains in his analysis of Carnaval in São Luis, capital of the Brazilian state of Maranhao:

> In its treatment of aggression, Carnival employs a common but sometimes fragile ironic device—mimicry. Imitation aggression, more or less stylized, is and always has been a fixture of Carnival . . . Carnival urges one to perform aggressive acts, but only in play, and to tolerate aggressions from others as if they were play. It burlesques the violence in society, denying that aggression has serious causes and consequences. (1992:14)

Ideally, then, Carnaval allows the opportunity to channel anxiety, frustrations, and aggression, or the potential for aggression, in a socially acceptable way, expressed by the phrase "anything goes." Carnaval is a prime opportunity for the venting of aggression:

> Carnaval permits . . . "venting," or . . . the banishing from one's interior world of accumulated frustrations, irritations, resentments, spiritual maladies, anger and psychological pains in general . . . [This is expressed as] botar para fora, to cast out . . . This may be done by getting roaring drunk, shouting, or—and this is where the problems arise—provoking or attacking another person. (Linger 1992:77–78)

Person-to-person provocations called **entrudos** are a distinct trait of Carnaval, and "during the nineteenth century, in Brazil as in Portugal, Carnival was known as entrudo. Its hallmark was a stylized provocation—a form of ritualized aggression" (Linger 1992:59). Entrudos easily degenerate into direct physical confrontations between two persons called **brigas** that often end in murder. Hence, the inherent paradox of and uncertainty in Carnaval: ideally it is supposed to channel aggression and frustrations but at the same time it is

Playing, Provoking, and Aggression in Brazil's Carnaval

Carnaval is a unique milieu for venting anxieties, frustrations, and fantasies and, as such, it is ideal for provocations and potential aggression, as the following statements conveyed to Linger (1992) illustrate:

> She came up to me sticking her hand in my face. I grabbed and sticked her, I said, "Did you come here to play or fight? [Você veio pra brincar ou pra brigar?] . . . Sometimes . . . a lot of things happen during Carnival . . . sometimes a person has already left home with bad intentions, wanting to fight . . . Sometimes people really try to get rid of a lot of things [during Carnival] . . . Sometimes. In the case of a woman, she's with a guy, maybe she knows he's with the police and she

starts to bug somebody . . . so that the other person will strike back. (p. 71)

> Carnival is an expenditure of energy. It's when you discharge all the rotten stuff that you've been holding in. I think it's the discharge of a wretched, impoverished people who [want] moments to breathe. (p. 80)

> The facet of Carnaval that I like the best is to be playing, understand? Not working . . . The pleasure of knowing today I don't have a *patrão* [boss], everybody's here, even the patrão is here . . . *I even give him an elbow and so on while I'm dancing* . . . On this day I don't even look at him as a patrão, although he doesn't stop being one. You don't feel like his employee. (p. 81)

a context that is "singularly conducive" for "brigas and even murder" (Linger 1992:59, 72; see also In Their Own Words 11.1).

Fertility, Community, and the Supernatural in Bolivian Carnaval

In many Andean communities, Carnaval is a joyous and propitious time of the year to celebrate impending crop harvests and pay homage to supernatural deities who have assured the fertility of the land and bountiful crops. Among the Yura in southern Bolivia, Carnaval

> falls in late summer, about the time when the crops are beginning to ripen. The Yura think of Carnaval, then, as a first-fruits celebration, and their satisfaction at the end of the threat of hunger adds to the significance of the event. Indeed, the most common Quechua name for the festival is Pujllay, "to play." The scene of fertility fulfilled is an underlying theme of Carnaval. (Rasnake 1988:242)

But Carnaval is also about symbolically renewing and accentuating social relationships between villages, forging community cohesion, and underscoring Yuras' ethnic identity and autonomy vis-à-vis the wider Bolivian society. Each community is represented by a music and dance troupe, headed by senior leaders. These begin by visiting all of the dispersed households within each community or ayllu, thereby reaffirming its distinctiveness vis-à-vis other Yura ayllus. Ayllu-wide troupes then visit and play music and dance with other ayllu groups until members of all of Yuras' ayllus have collectively participated. Further, this collective participation also entails walking to and playing music and dancing at landmarks, or "*mojones,* the mountain peaks which mark the boundaries of the entire ethnic region" (Rasnake 1988:245). Carnaval in Yura is a **cultural performance,** or a ritualized cultural spectacle, that accomplishes the "sacralization of land and territorial boundaries . . . identification of spiritual power with the ayllu order and its authorities, and . . . the . . . propiation of the symbols of outside power" (Rasnake 1988:259).

The enormous cultural and ethnic heterogeneity within most Latin American and Caribbean countries leads to different meanings, interpretations, and displays of Carnaval even within the same country. Among Bolivian miners, Carnaval too is a season of joy, and it is intensely celebrated with dances, costumes, and dance troupes almost identical to those in the national Carnaval festivities of Oruro (Nash 1979). In the context of the historically dangerous task of underground mining, Carnaval serves to bond miners with the supernatural forces to whom miners turn for protection and good luck. Carnaval dances, costumes, dancers, and pageantry also dramatize the all-important role of Christian and non-Christian supernatural forces in the everyday lives of miners, and remind miners of their past by especially magnifying past events and injustices. In many ways, both the present and the past are recreated in the course of enacting Carnaval. As Nash explains:

> Carnaval is associated with historical precedents relating to the pre-conquest or early post-conquest days. The traditions of the indigenous and Spanish populations are woven together but as distinctive strands, not as homogenized elements, and appear in the dances and dramas that interpret past and present. There are two main dramas: The first is the triumph over the monsters sent by Huari [a pre-Conquest, overarching deity], which took place sometime before the conquest but which, over the centuries, incorporated post-conquest spirits and powers. The second is the conquest of the Indians by the Spaniards and their subjugation in the labor force of the mines and the vineyards. The first drama is played out in the Devil dance . . . The second is enacted by the Children of the Sun on the plaza on Sunday of Carnaval, as well as in the dances, especially that of the *Diablada* and the *Morenada.* (1979:127–128)

The *Diablada* (Devil dance) is one of the most colorful and culturally significant dances during Carnaval in Oruro, among Bolivian miners, and elsewhere (see Photo 11.2).

Dancers wear large, heavy masks made out of plaster with "three serpents springing from [the Devil's] forehead between two arching horns, representing the monsters that threatened to devour the Uru Urus who inhabited the town before the arrival of the Spaniards" (Nash 1979:129). The dance itself

> captures the essence of Carnival in Oruro. According to legend, the dance began when a miner fell asleep after the ch'alla [ritual offering] to the devil in the mine. As he woke up, he saw the devil himself dancing and he followed

PHOTO 11.2   *A Bolivian Diablos (Devils) dance group performs during the
Oruro Carnaval.*

him, dancing out of the mine. After that, the miners continued to dance in the
streets following the ch'alla on the Friday of Carnival. (Nash 1979:129–130)

Music and Dance

Cross-culturally, music is studied by ethnomusicologists who seek to understand how and
why lyrics express individual and social experiences from the vantage points of gender,
class, and age; how the differential distribution of power and knowledge structure the production of musical genres, or how and why certain lyrics are sung; and ways that music and
songs convey and instill a sense of "time, place, feeling, style, belonging, and identity"
(Feld and Fox 1994:31–38). Although dance can be carried out in the absence of music, and
music in the absence of dance, they generally go hand in hand. The result is that "in many
ways dance is simply part of music, to which it is integrally related" (Kaeppler 1978:32).
Tango, to which we now turn, is not merely an example of such a unified musical and dance
genre, but also exemplifies, as does rumba in contemporary Cuba (Daniel 1995), the
"power of dance as national symbol" (Reed 1998:513).

Tango

During the colonial period, Buenos Aires and Montevideo received thousands of African
slaves later sent to other parts of South America, especially to Bolivian mines (Andrews
2004). By the early 1800s, about 20 percent of the population of Buenos Aires was African

or of African descent. The highly distinctive, stylized, and choreographed dance known as tango in Argentina—the country many consider the most "White" and "Europeanized" of Latin America—has its roots in this slave experience.

Tango appears as place names (toponyms) in Angola and Mali, and during colonial times the word tango, in Argentina and elsewhere, meant a locale where slaves or free Africans danced, "an African dance hall" (Collier et al 1995:41). Tango also referred to kinds of dancing that, like in Africa, "one did to drums" (Chasteen 2000:44). Tango was also often used interchangeably with *candombé* and *milonga,* permutations of African words referring to dance and music styles. Candombé as a music and dance genre, and Candomblé as a religious system (discussed in Chapter 6), almost certainly have similar roots. According to Castro, *milonga*—originally *mulonga*—was an African term meaning "words." It reached Buenos Aires through Montevideo, and "the dance . . . came to be called tango . . . due to the sound made by the drum . . . and indeed the drum itself was called 'tango'. . . This dance was popularized by the Afro-Argentine *candombé*" (1991:95–96; see also Andrews 2004:121).

By the mid-1800s, Buenos Aires' African population had virtually disappeared and tango lost its association with African slaves and heritage. But the dance style was appropriated by working-class Argentine youths, many of them first- or second-generation European (especially Italian and Spanish) immigrants. As late as the 1800s, to "do tango" (*tanguear*) was considered "barbaric" by elites, and it was associated with the "lower," disreputable, "criminal" sectors (Castro 1991:91–92). This association also had a linguistic basis, for one peculiarity of Argentine Spanish after the waves of European immigration was the emergence of **lunfardo,** a linguistic argot forged primarily from Spanish and Italian loan words largely unintelligible to elite speakers of standard Spanish (see Table 11.1).

TABLE 11.1   Examples of Late Nineteenth Century Buenos Aires Lunfardo

Lunfardo words	Meaning	Spanish translation
Trabajo	To rob	Robar
Pillo	Thief	Ladrón
Lunfardo	Criminal/thief	Criminal/ladrón
Beaba	Armed robbery	Robo armado
El bobo	Wallet	Cartera
Mina	Girl	Muchacha
Bacán	Man, can be a robber	Hombre
Michos	Poor people	Personas pobres
Chancletas	Doors	Puertas
Bolines	Rooms	Cuartos/habitaciones
Chúa	Key	Llave
Vaiven	Knife	Cuchillo
Bufosa	Pistol	Pistola
Encanado	Jail	Cárcel

Source: Castro 1991: 42–43. Spanish translations provided by author. Readers should note that the word and meaning of *pillo* is identical in many other Spanish-speaking countries.

Lunfardo's first written description dates to 1879 in the context of describing what was perceived as urban "criminal" life, and elite rejection of tango was part of wider concerns of the "specter of the future of Argentina with crowded crime ridden cities and unassimilated foreigners" (Castro 1991:17–18). By the early 1900s, tango had evolved into the "dance and musical vehicle of the urban poor, the socially unacceptable, the disenfranchised, and the disinherited" (Castro 1991:90), and lyrics centered on themes such as the hard realities of slum life, exploitation of the poor by the rich, and urban violence. The wretched health and living conditions of the slums were propitious to the spread of disease, especially tuberculosis. Through the early twentieth century literature and other media, tuberculosis eventually became ideologically linked to slum inhabitants who embraced tango (Armus 2003).

In 1920, tango began to acquire middle- and elite-class respectability. Sheet music and the advent of recording, record production, and radio enabled tango lyrics to be translated into more standard Spanish as well as disseminated (and understood) by more people of different class backgrounds. Equally important, prior to World War I, tango had become a fad in Europe—a musical and dance hit—especially in Paris. Tango's European popularity paved the way for its legitimacy among Argentina's elite classes (Castro 1991:92). By the 1930s, tango was no longer an isolated expression of the Buenos Aires' "lower" classes: it was national, cut across class lines, included the "homemaker," and was "popular" (Castro 1991:141). Its meanings also changed, depicting less slum and marginalized life, immigrant experiences, and working-class struggles. The transformation of tango lyrics into what they are largely today—mainly emphasizing romance, infidelity, and the importance of self-sacrificing (marianist) mothers—took place in the 1940s under the early presidency of Juan Domingo Perón, who founded a populist, working-class movement (*Peronismo*) that has had an enormous influence in Argentine society and politics. One of Perón's goals was to change "public morals," emphasize Argentina as a Catholic country, and to "purify" Argentine Spanish. One obvious objective was to instill "good morals" into tango lyrics and suppress lunfardo, which had the added benefit of "protecting youth from [the lyrics'] corrupting influence" (Castro 1991:209–210). Equally important, tango themes dealing with social issues were deemed incompatible with the new social order, and those tangos that

> had themes of hunger, poverty, unfair working conditions could no longer exist in the Argentina of Perón. Perón had brought dignity to the worker, better working conditions, holidays, and better pay . . . the tangos that portrayed women as prostitutes, deceivers, connivers, betrayers were no longer valid. The conditions that made women so no longer existed in the "new" Argentina. (Castro 1991:229–230)

Contemporary tango lyrics and dance choreography are punctuated by three themes (Taylor 1976, 1987). One is how lyrics evoke profound (individual and perhaps national) feelings of melancholy, sadness, and introspection, often expressed in the lunfardo term *mufarse,* which

> indicates not only anger and unhappiness, but also denotes indulging oneself in surrender to these feelings. It is the entire complex of actions and emotions

sitting alone at a table with a drink, sipping it slowly while contemplating the totality of one's misfortunes . . . and *enjoying oneself.* (Taylor 1976:277)

Such feelings come across vividly in the tango *Cafetín de Buenos Aires* (Taylor 1976:277).

The second theme centers on ways in which tango lyrics evoke nostalgia and are existentially important for a collective sense of identity. In a nation in which the immigrant experience is underscored in a myriad of publications and official discourses (while the native indigenous history and experience is played down), tango lyrics evoke a sort of homesickness, a longing for places or symbolic landscapes that anchor memories and experiences of the past, real or imagined. Two landscapes loom symbolically important as anchors to the past and as bedrocks of the present. The first are the slums (*arrabales, barrios*) of Buenos Aires, where most of the millions of immigrants settled, and where working-class identity and tango coalesced. Tango laments "the lost neighborhood or *barrio* on the edge of Buenos Aires, where the sophisticated but disillusioned tango singer spent his youth" (Taylor 1987:483). One example is *Mi Buenos Aires Querido* (My Beloved Buenos Aires). The second symbolically charged landscape important for memory and identity are the vast plains of the Pampas, where the gaucho and the gaucho culture were forged. The tango *Adios, Pampa Mía* (Farewell, My Pampa) nicely captures this longing.

The third overarching theme of tango lyrics and dance choreography is gender and sexuality, which is taken up in the "Controversies" section later in this chapter.

Salsa

Tango was popular elsewhere in Latin America during the 1920s and 1930s, especially in northern South America and the Caribbean, but its influence largely remained circumscribed to Argentina and Uruguay. Such has definitely not been the case with **salsa,** a varied musical and dance genre which since the 1960s has enjoyed tremendous popularity among Hispanics/Latinos in the United States, as well as in the Spanish-speaking Caribbean, Venezuela, Colombia, Panama, and the Caribbean coastlines of Mexico and Central America (Manuel 1994; Duany 1990, 1996; Aparicio 1998; Washburne 1998; Waxter 2000). Salsa has also "become part of the visible presence of Latin American cultural practices in many countries around the globe such as Britain, France, Germany, Holland, Ireland, Japan, Norway, Spain and Switzerland among others" (Román-Velázquez 1999:115).

Some years ago Bilby, in commenting on the cultural variability and miscegenation of the Caribbean, noted that it "has become a major exporter of culture" (1985:181). He was writing specifically about music and dance, stressing how both have loomed crucial in the everyday lives of Caribbean peoples since colonial times, their strong African influence, and, in the Spanish-speaking Caribbean, the key role of Cuban, Puerto Rican, and Dominican music and dance. These insights are important for understanding the emergence and cultural roots of salsa, as well as its broad appeal.

Salsa is a Caribbean cultural creation. Scholars agree that salsa emerged in Puerto Rico and the Hispanic/Latino neighborhoods of New York City in the early 1960s, roughly a decade after tens of thousands of Puerto Ricans began migrating there (Manuel 1994:271–273; Washburne 1998:162; Waxer 2000:118). Typically, salsa bands (*conjuntos*) are comprised of six to ten musicians playing percussion and bass instruments, sometimes with the use of electronic synthesizers, and always with a lead singer. Dancers often accompany the conjunto musicians. There is in fact a wide variety of salsa styles and assemblages, ranging from fast-moving, hit-pitch, full conjuntos (Puerto Rico's El Gran Combo is a well-known example), to the softer, low-keyed melodies of Panamanian-born Rubén Blades.

Although it is clear that what is now known as salsa emerged in the 1960s among Puerto Ricans, scholars continue to debate the question of whether different Caribbean musical traditions were either the forerunners of or were refashioned into contemporary salsa. Some think that salsa—in terms of musical melodies, pitch, tone, instrumentation, and the like—is largely an appropriation and transformation of Cuban musical genres. A strong proponent of this view is Manuel (1994) who, after emphasizing the powerful influence in Puerto Rico of Cuban music, argues that salsa is a Puerto Rican "home-grown transplant" of Cuban genres such as guaracha and ruma and not Puerto Rican ones such as plena, bomba, and the seis. Duany (1990, 1996), although recognizing the broad similarities between some Cuban and Puerto Rican musical genres, argues that Puerto Rican salsa owes much more to national musical traditions.

Salsa is a broad musical category, encompassing multiple styles that are each influenced by national and transnational genres. Waxer's analysis of the emergence of Colombian salsa bands in Cali is a case in point. Although salsa music appeared in Colombia in the 1960s, it was not until the 1980s that it displaced the popular national *música tropical*—which Waxter defines as "a cosmopolitan room sound based on the traditional *cumbias, gaitas,* and *porros* of Colombia's Atlantic Coast" (2000:120). In the intervening twenty years, Colombian bands engaged in a continuous process of selection and experimentation, generating a wide span of salsa styles drawing on Cuban and Puerto Rican tunes and styles, North American rock, and Colombian genres (such as música tropical and cumbia). In this process of cultural innovation, Colombians even adapted elements of *salsa romántica* (romantic salsa) which, although developed in Puerto Rico, "was promoted by the Miami-based Latin music industry during the late 1980s as a commercial style fusing romantic pop ballads and salsa rhythms" (Waxter 2000:163).

Music is fun and enjoyable to listen to—but it is much more than that. Like other aspects of culture, music and dance are key symbolic vehicles through which different peoples recapitulate their version of history and simultaneously forge and communicate their sense of cultural or ethnic identity. In the Caribbean,

> music has been an important cultural marker in the process of identity construction, consolidation, and transformation, whether based on racial, ethnic, class, or national discourses . . . Caribbean music has always helped to define the boundaries between "us" and "them." Folk and popular music, in particular, have articulated the cultural identity of many Caribbean groups, including runaway slaves, peasants, plantation workers, urban artisans, labor migrants, and middle-class intellectuals. (Duany 1996:177)

The role of salsa in the forging of a Hispanic/Latino identity is especially prominent in New York City and other northeastern U.S. cities:

> Since the late 1960s, salsa has emerged as a musical expression of the aesthetics, values, and identity of Puerto Ricans, Nuyoricans, and others. Its aspira-

> tions to pan-Latino popularity are explicit in many of its song texts calling for Latino solidarity, and in the statements of musicians and aficionados, who celebrate it as a challenge to the hegemony of Anglo-American music and culture. Salsa's significance as a vehicle for Puerto Rican, Nuyorican, and pan-Latino identity is also inherent in its appeal across a broad spectrum of Latino nationalities, age groups, and social classes. (Manuel 1994:264)

Among Latin Americans living abroad, playing salsa is also a key medium through which a pan-Hispanic/Latino identity is articulated and reaffirmed regardless of country of origin. In her analysis of salsa bands in London, Román-Velázquez (1999) notes that the construction of this identity has as much to do with music as with the ways in which the bodies of singers and dancers are expected to be in sync with musical rhythms. That is, a culturally acceptable rendering of salsa not only requires the mastery of instruments and rhythms but also acceptably stylized bodily movements. Unlike other musical genres (such as rap), salsa is always sung in Spanish, and some songs may allude to broad Latin American and Caribbean themes and motifs. Yet, what also makes salsa in London a quintessential Latino genre are the specific ways through which "bodies are experienced through music . . . and . . . music . . . experienced through . . . bodies." Playing and dancing salsa, therefore, gives rise to a construction of a "Latinised" body, which in turn is part of a broader cultural repertoire underpinning Hispanic/Latino identity in London (Román-Velázquez 1999:116).

Each country in which salsa is popular either has developed or is best represented by specific styles. That these are often hybrid creations means that a great deal of cultural information flows through the constant adaptation and re-adaptation of styles and motifs from different countries. This in turn may be bolstering a pan-Hispanic/Latino sense of community or camaraderie across national boundaries. One example is the salsa tune *Buenaventura y Caney* from the Colombian Grupo Niche, which addresses a message to Puerto Ricans in Puerto Rico and New York City, and to Panamanians and Venezuelans (Waxer 2000:132).

Reggae

Internationally, reggae music is invariably associated with Jamaica and Bob Marley, Jamaica's best known reggae artist. Twenty-five years after Marley's death (in 1981) fans continue to purchase his music: in 2000, more of Marley's music collections were sold "than at any time during his life," and his collection *Legend* sold fifteen million copies (Weber 2000:258–259).

Like salsa, reggae refers to a broad musical genre that is comprised of different styles and the product of diverse musical traditions (Bilby 1985:206–207; Prahlad 2001). The term *reggae* and the music it stands for emerged in the early to mid-1960s. In Jamaica, the immediate musical precursor to reggae was, in the 1940s and 1950s, the *mento* style, partly influenced by Trinidadian ballads known as *calypso*. In the late 1950s and early 1960s, *ska* emerged when Jamaican musicians began playing U.S. blues; later, influences from U.S. soul music influenced the rise of *rock steady* music; shortly thereafter, reggae appeared on the scene (Bilby 1985:206–207).

Interpreting these musical genres (including reggae) as a mere result of external influences would be mistaken for, as with other aspects of culture, these genres emerged in a specific historical context and were a product of both local and external factors. The first part of the 1960s was especially volatile, politically and culturally, in Jamaica, throughout the Americas, and in other parts of the globe. For example, these years coincided with Jamaica's independence from England (in 1962) and marked political and economic conflicts; in the United States, with the civil rights and Black Power movements; and in Africa with many liberation movements struggling against European colonialism.

The reggae music represented by Marley and best known among international fans— what is known as "roots reggae"—is a heavily politicized musical genre, committed to social justice, and the lyrics deeply identify with the poor, oppressed, and downtrodden worldwide. The names of some artists or groups highlight the political or oppositional underpinnings of roots reggae: Wailing Souls, Burning Spear, Meditations, Gladiators. All are part of what Prahlad (2001:33) has called the "warrior/priest persona" dimension of roots reggae artists and Rastarfari religious identity. This dimension of roots reggae was the result of the broader political and cultural context of the 1960s *as well as* the growth of Rastarfari religious ideology in Jamaica during this period. Rastarfari—members of which are called *rastas* or *rastafarians*—emerged on the Jamaican cultural scene in the shanty-towns of Kingston (Jamaica's capital) during the 1930s; at the time they were considered social outcasts by elites and British colonial officials. Rather than a "cult" (Kitzinger 1969), Rastafari is better described as a political–religious worldview.

Because Rastarfari heavily influenced roots reggae musical style, lyrics, and political commitment, it is important to sketch some basic tenets of this religious system or worldview. (This overview of Rastarfari and all following quotations are drawn from Prahlad [2001:11–49].) One is the idea of *anciency,* the belief that rastas represent the "original man," or "first from creation," originating in Africa, and specifically Ethiopia.[1] There is, therefore, a strong association between Rastarfari and Africa, a reaffirmation of the past that is linked to Africa, and an underscoring of African cultural heritage. As such, Rastarfari is an "Afro-centric ideology," buttressed by constant references to the Biblical passages; many rastas have viewed themselves as Biblical prophets. This African-centered ideology partly explains why roots reggae became popular in parts of southern Africa, and it also explains attempts by Marley to speak to the historical experience of African Americans in the United States. One example of the latter is the composition *Buffalo Soldiers,* which appeared in the 1983 album *Confrontation,* and which alluded to African American soldiers of the U.S. cavalry during the nineteenth century.

A second important concept of Rastarfari is that of *ital,* which although specifically suggesting a vegetarian diet and a preference for raw over cooked foods, more broadly connotes a deeper natural relationship with the world. The important idea underlying *ital*— "whatever is natural is better"—partly explains, for example, dreadlocks and other aspects of rasta behavior and appearance. A third Rastafarian tenet is that of *knowing,* which contrasts with *believing,* or European/Western false knowledge. *Knowing* implies spirituality, meditation, an inward search for the truth—a search that is enhanced or made possible by the smoking of *ganja,* or marijuana (see Chapter 8), in meditation groups called reasonings or groundings.

Another key precept of Rastarfari—and one with a more immediate connection to reggae as a musical genre—is the idea that one should "Chant Down Babylon." It implies an obligation to work against the forces of evil through the use of music and words. In fact, a question that Marley posed in one of his compositions was: "Can we free the people with music?" To "Chant Down Babylon" also denotes a powerful connection made in Rastafari thought between words, sound, and power. Indeed, one cannot "appreciate either the lyrical or the instrumental elements of roots reggae until one can approach the songs with an awareness that this fundamental outlook informs every facet of this genre" and that it "assumes the power of sounds to effect change in the corporeal world." This "ritual sound" also has healing properties, which means that playing and hearing reggae music is a form of "sacred healing."

Finally, it is important to underscore that the popularity of reggae music, both in Jamaica and abroad, which was exemplified by Bob Marley, also had much to do with the use of proverbs, a widespread characteristic of Jamaican popular culture. The images and metaphors embedded in proverbs made them superb mediums of communication, and their brevity allowed musicians to easily incorporate them into reggae lyrics. Further, the use of some widespread and semantically flexible proverbs (e.g., "What goes around comes around") enabled reggae musicians to communicate with wider, international audiences, who could interpret these proverbs in multiple and still meaningful ways (Prahlad 2001:58–59). Reggae artists also used specifically Jamaican proverbs, the meanings of which were easily understood by most Jamaicans, such as "Cause iron sharpeneth iron" (implying a connection or similarity between events or people), or "Dog more than bone" (suggesting scarcity or that life is hard). Other proverbs, such as "A hungry man is an angry man," could easily be understood by both Jamaican and non-Jamaican audiences (Prahlad 2001:79–80).

Television and Telenovelas

Telenovelas, television soap operas, are a ubiquitous and pervasive mass cultural phenomenon in Latin America and the Caribbean, much of which is gripped by a "telenovela mania" (Hippolyte Ortega 1998:71). One author states that "telenovelas are the basic staple of all Latin American TV programming (day and prime time), of Spanish language programming in the [United States], and, to a lesser degree, of TV programming in Spain" (quoted in Hippolyte Ortega 1998:64).

This "mania" is recent, dating from about the late 1960s and early 1970s (Rowe and Shelling 1991:108). The popularity of telenovelas has partly rested on increasing purchasing power of the popular classes, and the expansion of television and technology. Mexico, Venezuela, Colombia, and Brazil are the major producers and exporters of telenovelas (Morrissey 2002:221). Miami and Los Angeles, home to large numbers of Hispanics/Latinos as well as to Univisión and Telemundo, the two leading Spanish language media conglomerates, may someday become major producers and exporters of telenovelas in the United States (Gates 2000; Porter 2002; Ahrens 2003a, 2003b; Ballvé 2004).

But how popular *are* telenovelas? When they effectively tap into widespread sentiments and reflect and convey social realities, telenovelas are viewed by enormous audiences. Rowe and Schelling note that the 1980s Mexican telenovela *Cuna de Lobos* (Cradle of the Wolves) was regularly watched by forty million Mexicans, or almost 50 percent of the population, and "when the last episode was shown, the city [Mexico City] came to a standstill; the underground drivers refused to work, and everyone stayed at home" (1991:110–111). In Brazil, the television programming of Rede Globo, "the world's most watched commercial TV network" (Kottak 1990:9), every night attracts an audience of between sixty to eighty million people, or between 30 and 50 percent of all Brazilians. One anecdote has it that during the 1970s, then U.S. Secretary of State Kissinger arrived earlier than expected in Brazil and found no Brazilian officials to greet him; he subsequently learned that his official greeting party was somewhere else watching the final chapter of an especially popular telenovela (Kottak 1990:40–41).

Why are Telenovelas so Popular?

Hippolyte Ortega notes that "the telenovela is an important expression of Latin American popular culture not only because of its success with the public, but also because it reflects this public's symbolic and affective world" (1998:64). It does so because it takes the form of a melodrama dramatizing central events that common people face in their ordinary, everyday lives. Watching a telenovela

> is a family ritual organized to maintain the attention of the spectators. Typically, everybody feels involved in the telecast. The story is discussed during and after the performance. Later, viewers even offer possible solutions to the conflicts presented in the drama by writing letters to authors and actors. All feel affected by the world created in the telenovelas, as long as it raises problems they believe they have gone through themselves. (Hippolyte Ortega 1998:67)

And yet, although it may be partially true that "all [may] feel affected by the world created in the telenovelas," not all viewers are alike nor do they interpret the worldview conveyed by telenovelas in precisely the same way. To simply allude to "viewers" implicitly suggests cultural homogeneity—a position that contrasts sharply with the one taken by many anthropologists and other critical scholars that in stratified societies (such as in Latin America and Caribbean nation-states), culture is largely segmented across gender, class, racial, and ethnic fault lines. In northeastern Brazil, for example, La Pastina has emphasized how the meanings of the telenovela *The Cattle King* were intertwined with changing gender expectations and roles:

> Established gender norms, attitudes, and the changing political economy of Macambira structured in many ways the levels of interaction between viewers and text. Women's increasing economic power, due to their work as embroiderers, and the increasing dependence of men on women's income, have created a fracture in the traditional male-female domination patterns. This has allowed women to question their roles and men's roles in the household and community. The telenovela seemed to be one way through which women observed alternatives, which were then appropriated to assess their own lives and the life of the community in relation to that of the characters in the south. (2004:177)

Also in northeastern Brazil, shantytown residents viewing telenovelas do so for rather different reasons than the wealthy, and the meanings they ascribe to the messages conveyed are also different. Goldstein tells us that watching telenovelas "transported" favela viewers "into the lives and problems of people distant from their own lives and problems" (2003:101). Although others may be "transported" for analogous (but not identical) reasons, the ways that favela viewers interpret and react to what they see clearly reflects their position within Brazil's class and racial hierarchy:

> Watching television in Felicidade Eterna, which was always a group activity, there would often be a scene that any other audience would perceive as tragic. Yet here, among a collection of people who live in absurd conditions, the tragedies of the elites depicted in the telenovelas tended to fall on deaf ears. These scenes were much more often poked fun at rather than wept about. (Goldstein 2003:101)

The telenovela is a powerful expressive medium for other reasons (Hippolyte Ortega 1998; Morrissey 2002). Unlike U.S. soap operas, which may last for years, telenovelas are broadcast for four to six months. Hence, central issues and conflicts—between good and evil, rich and poor, fortune and misfortune—are resolved more rapidly, and the telenovela can far more easily and quickly incorporate novel themes and plots. For example, although romance and love across the class spectrum have historically constituted the core telenovela plot, telenovelas have become thematically more specialized, with historical, political, cultural, and ecological themes. Further—and again unlike U.S. soaps—telenovelas are always broadcast in prime time and on major television stations, therefore reaching wider and more diverse audiences. Finally, although U.S. soaps largely target women, telenovelas are designed to appeal to both men and women.

The flexibility of telenovelas to encapsulate new themes and plots, and to engage their audiences in novel ways, is illustrated by two popular telenovelas: the first, *Tres Mujeres* (Three Women), captivated Mexican audiences by explicitly focusing on gender and sexuality in ways that at the time were unknown in Mexican television programming; the second, *Por Estas Calles* (Through These Streets), set in Venezuela, portrayed the corruption scandal that eventually led to the downfall of former Venezuelan president Carlos Andrés Pérez.

Tres Mujeres was exceptional because it lasted far longer than other telenovelas, and because it explicitly portrayed contemporary, urban women's lives and challenged customary gender and sexuality expectations in Mexican culture (Morrissey 2002). For example, in line with customary gender expectations, a major theme in many telenovelas is that of a heroine (and virgin) who eventually has sexual intercourse with the man of her dreams, who she hopes will marry her. The main female protagonist in *Tres Mujeres,* however, was not only not a virgin, but she openly expressed her sexual needs and engaged in multiple sexual liaisons. And also contrary to marianist ideology (see Chapter 6), she neither remarried nor remained chaste after her husband's death. Homosexuality, domestic violence, and rebellious behavior by women against abusive spouses were discussed openly, "making it clear to viewers that women must not allow themselves to be abused by husbands and lovers" (Morrissey 2002:225). Women's health issues—often a publicly taboo subject—were also candidly talked about. One scene depicted a conversation about the difficulties of maintaining a love affair after a woman's hysterectomy; another focused the audience's attention on how premarital pregnancies often result in the woman's lover abandoning her. *Tres Mujeres* also depicted women's economic status and career roles in new ways: rather than portraying them in bipolar ways—either rich and spoiled, or as poor servants or marginalized street vendors—the key female protagonists were economically mobile white collar business workers, artists, models, and the like.

Por Estas Calles was a sensation in Venezuela and a new mode of telenovela programming. Rather than indirectly and diffidently alluding to contemporary political, economic, and social conditions, it put them on view each and every night for an audience of millions (Hippolyte Ortega 1998; see also the video *Telenovelas: Love, TV, and Power*). The context of this telenovela was Venezuela between the big oil boom of the 1970s and the country's economic collapse in the early 1990s. It explicitly dealt with crime, drug trafficking, youth violence and slum life, political instability, and corruption at the highest levels of government. One crucial variation was how it publicly dealt with the corruption and bribery scandal that enveloped the government of President Carlos Andrés Pérez. Daily journalistic accounts of the official inquiry and subsequent congressional investigations immediately made their way into that night's telenovela plot, with live actors mimicking top government officials (including Andrés Pérez) and their supposed illegal dealings. *Por Estas Calles* represented contemporary social reality, the lived experience of millions of Venezuelans in ways not ever seen:

> Until this telenovela, no other television program in Venezuela had so successfully exposed the national reality as, in effect, an extravagant melodrama consisting of juvenile delinquency, drug trafficking, money laundering, and . . . corruption, among other things. The plot did not invent a totally imaginary country. In other words, it did not represent Venezuela's political and social chronicle through imaginary characters with imaginary problems; rather, it situated the action of the telenovela precisely in the heart of Caracas, and its characters lived out dramas that were shared with the whole Venezuelan population. (Hippolyte Ortega 1998:72)

The Cultural Impact of Telenovelas and Television Programming

Telenovelas and major network television programming are produced in a handful of countries but viewed by tens of millions of Latin American and Caribbean peoples. As a result, both are having far-reaching cultural consequences. Two examples come immediately to mind: the forging of a continent-wide Latin American identity, and the fostering of a more homogenous national culture and sense of identity.

Despite idiomatic and lexical differences in spoken Spanish, the content of telenovelas is easily understood by most Spanish speakers regardless of the country in which they reside. (Brazilian telenovelas are often dubbed into Spanish, although the reverse occurs less often). And despite the pan-Hispanic/Latino plots of most telenovelas, they invariably transmit culturally specific information on the country in which they are produced. For example, a woman in Puerto Rico who has never traveled to Mexico but views a Mexican telenovela is exposed to images of new people and landscapes, as well as a great deal of information on Mexican society and culture. That Puerto Rican viewer is in some ways "in" and learning about Mexico. Thus, by putting huge numbers of people of different class and cultural backgrounds into brief but intimate and effortless contact— people who otherwise would have little opportunity to be in cultural touch with each other—telenovelas may be contributing to the forging of a pan-Hispanic/Latino identity and sense of community.

Cable network programming may be performing the same task. Among Hispanic/ Latinos in the United States, one extraordinarily popular program reaching forty countries and tens of millions of viewers is *Don Francisco Presenta,* produced in and transmitted from Miami on Wednesday and Saturday evenings (eastern standard time) through the Univisión network. This two-to-three hour program brings together singers, musical groups, celebrities, and ordinary citizens from a wide spectrum of Latin American class and cultural backgrounds. The program even has its own Web page, which can be accessed through the Univisión Web site. In addition to games and comedy shows, one of the most important and appealing aspects of this program is that it presents segments reflecting everyday life experiences and perceived needs of Hispanics/Latinos in the United States. These may include interviewing itinerant Mexican farmworkers in the United States, or highlighting the personal, economic, or legal plight of immigrants. The following are some examples that appeared Saturday evenings:

- A couple that has lived in the United States for many years is torn between wishing to remain in the United States and returning to Latin America. The Mexican husband wishes to return to Mexico with his family, but his Honduran wife adamantly refuses to leave. Their children, the wife states, have more "future" in the United States (where they were born). Most of her family has moved from Honduras to the United States. (Perhaps there are other unstated reasons for the woman's reluctance to leave the United States, for "studies of Mexican and Caribbean women in the United States often find that they are much more reluctant than their male compatriots to return to the home country, believing that it would likely entail a parallel return to the more patriarchal household relations" [Mills 2003:49]).

- An immigrant couple has been in the United States for more than twenty years, and the wife has not been in contact with her parents since she left home. This particular evening, Don Mario arranged for her to see and speak with her mother and father via satellite.

- Two persons have established a two-year intense relationship through Univision's *Amor y Amigos* (Love and Friends) Web site. After two years, they finally meet in person.

- A case of domestic violence is dealt with openly. The husband admits to beating his wife, is admonished by Don Francisco, and agrees to undergo therapy. His wife forgives him and agrees to return home.

The second cultural role and consequence of telenovelas, and television programming generally, is leveling regional and cultural differences within specific countries. That is, by transmitting and reconstructing national traditions (such as Carnaval), mass media may be forging a more uniform national culture across geographic and other boundaries, and perhaps a more cohesive sense of national identity. Twentieth century mass media may be facilitating the emergence of a more cohesive national community analogous to how the printed press did so in nineteenth century Europe (Anderson 1983). In Brazil, for example, Rede Globo (Brazil's largest and most important television network) has become politically powerful partly because for decades the Brazilian federal government has recognized its role in spurring national integration:

> Millions of Brazilians . . . formerly excluded by isolation and illiteracy now have joined in a single national communication system. They now have better access than ever to distinctive Brazilian themes and representations . . . Working hand in hand with the federal government, Brazilian television has helped spread a changing image of the nation—*from rural-regional to urban-national* . . . The theme of national integration was a central point of agreement between military government policies and Globo's objectives of undermining regional traditions and stimulating national mass consumption. (Kottak 1990:15–16, 36–37)

To what extent are Latin American and Caribbean peoples culturally influenced by Western images and messages transmitted via television? Is television programming a vehicle of cultural imperialism? These are, of course, difficult questions to answer. What *is* clear is that telenovelas especially, and probably the greater part of television programming produced in and transmitted throughout Latin America, are local creations, designed to meet the local needs and cultural specificity of local societies and communities. As Kottak (1990:16) suggests for Brazil—and the argument is equally compelling for other countries: "It isn't North American culture but a new pan-Brazilian national culture that Brazilian TV is propagating . . . The programs . . . are made by Brazilians, for Brazilians."

Controversies: Tango and Sexuality

Tango lyrics and choreography overwhelmingly center attention on males. Lyrics—particularly after the shift away from themes emphasizing social life in the slums of Buenos Aires at the turn of the twentieth century—largely emphasize the sad plight of the male who cannot escape falling in love or the need to forge a meaningful relationship with a woman—who, invariably, spurns his love or betrays him. The tango ¡*Uno!* (One!) poignantly captures the theme of male torment and female betrayal.

The key plot of male suffering and anguish at the hands of unfaithful, untrustworthy, betraying women is paralleled by a motif underscoring the comfort, understanding, and lifelong camaraderie that males receive from their male friends in tango clubs and cafés. The tango *Cafetín de Buenos Aires* is a good example of this second motif underscoring male friendship (Foster, D. W. 1998:179).

Tango dance choreography also underscores the pivotal position of men vis-à-vis women:

> The relationship of man and woman . . . as an encounter between the active, powerful, and completely dominant male and the passive, docile, and completely submissive female . . . The male dancer in the tango seldom recedes. The advance of the man slightly inclined over the woman so that she is forced to recede is characteristic of the tango . . . The female shows no will of her own . . . She is never allowed as in other dances to escape the man's embrace and must execute the most complex figures of the legs with her upper body immobile in a stylized, tense embrace, totally overpowered by the male. (Taylor 1976:281–282; see also Photo 11.3)

Tango lyrics and choreography invariably convey a "resolutely heterosexist" message (Foster, D. W. 1998:170) that emphasizes the less-than-moral qualities of women as well as male centrality, sexual dominance, and compulsory heterosexuality as key dimensions of male identity—especially in the public sphere. Sensual (heterosexual) love, paralleled by male companionship and heterosexual sexual pleasure are important motifs, according

PHOTO 3.3   *Tango street dancers at Dorrego Square in the old San Telmo district of Buenos Aires, Argentina.*

to E. P. Archetti (1997b:200–203), in the construction of one version of Argentine masculinity.

Yet, what kinds of sexualities are conveyed, displayed, or partially implied by tango lyrics and choreography are anything but clear, and they may convey more than an expression of entrenched heterosexuality. Relying on textual sources and interviews, Savigliano (1995) suggests that tango dance especially has expressed different and conflictive versions of machismo and maleness; of the relationship between machismo, homosociality, and heterosexuality; and of latent homosexuality or at least homoeroticism. She notes that early twentieth century tango dance and lyrics centered on males (all male dance partners were not uncommon): *male* virility, friendships and male bonding, and pride. Twentieth century sources and contemporary lyrics point to a common plot: "The fall of a pristine and dignified male whose nature somehow became compromised by erotic, heterosexual concerns" (Savigliano 1995:40). She concludes that "tango is not about sex—at least not about heterosexuality," and that it could be viewed as a "struggle . . . waged between men but carried out through women" (1995:45–46).

Savigliano's interpretation has been echoed by others. In *Tango and the Sandal of Homosocial Desire* Tobin (1998:84) suggests that

> the original tango, repeatedly described by the historians of Argentine music as a simulation or a choreographic representation of sexual intercourse, is a cultural expression with significant homoerotic and homosexual connotations that today are deeply embedded in the imagined national identity of the large Argentine middle class.

Tobin not only reminds readers of evidence that early tango was primarily danced by all-male pairs, but rejects two widespread explanations for the prevalence of all-male dancing: the marked gender imbalance in Buenos Aires at the turn of the nineteenth century (most immigrants who arrived in Argentina were male) and the idea that men danced (and continue to dance) with men to learn to lead dancing with women. He perceptively asks:

> What if a man practiced tango with other men one hour for every five minutes he danced with a woman? Is it a question of how much time he spent practicing tango with other men and how much time with women, or is it a question of his motives for dancing with men? (1998:82)

He notes that his fieldwork revealed that "many men continue[d] to spend much of their time on the dance floor in the arms of other men despite the availability of female partners" (91). With this ethnographic insight, and informed by feminist scholarship, he suggests that

> The primary relation in tango is not between the heterosexual dance partners, but is between the man who dances with a woman and the other men who watch . . . In tango . . . I find that homosocial desire is not expressed through the *exchange* of women . . . but . . . through the *display* of women. (Tobin 1998:90)

In The United States: Quinceañeras, Gender, and Tradition

A widespread, popular, yet sorely under-researched celebration among many Latin Americans in the United States is the **quinceañera** (from the Spanish *quince* [fifteen] and *años* [years]), a public ritual marking a young woman's fifteenth birthday. The quinceañera, which typically entails a Catholic Church service followed by a reception, is often preceded by months of preparation, is quite costly, and usually involves the participation of dozens of people, especially extended family members. Quinceañeras are also widespread in Latin America, especially in urban areas and among nonindigenous groups. Napolitano (2002:128–153) emphasizes the importance of this ritual for notions of the female body and family relations among young migrants to Mexico City. The following vignette presents one Mexican American quinceañera:

> The young girl . . . has an escort and a group of attendants for the day. The latter . . . is called a *corte de honor* and is composed of fourteen pairs of *chambelanes* [young men] and *damas* [ladies] . . . who escort the young girl, [who] also has an escort for the day, making a total of fifteen pairs . . . each . . . symboliz[ing] a year of the girl's life . . . She arrives [at the Church] dressed in an elaborate white dress . . . [There] the fourteen pairs of *damas* and *chambelanes* walk down the church aisle, followed by the young girl and her parents . . . The parents present the girl with gifts . . . During the service, the girl reaffirms and promises to continue her faith by restating her baptismal and confirmation vows . . . and offering roses [to] the Virgin Mary . . . After the service, everyone goes to a hall where the reception is held . . . At the hall, the *corte de honor* enters the dance area through an archway and forms a corridor for the young woman and her escort. The couples are followed by the girl's parents who carry a pair of white high-heeled shoes. The young woman then sits on an elevated chair, where the father places the white shoes on his daughter's feet. She rises from the chair and proceeds to dance with her father . . . continuing her rite of passage from childhood to adulthood. (Watters 1998:147).

But why celebrate a quinceañera? What meanings or statements are conveyed by those who sponsor and agree to partake of this celebration? The quinceañera has typically been interpreted as a **rite of passage,** a phrase coined by Van Gennep (1960) to refer to rituals (highly stylized and choreographed patterns of behavior) that signal marked transitions in the life cycle, such as marriage or death. As a rite of passage, some scholars have interpreted the quinceañera as a crucial shift and marker from the role and status of young girl to that of a full-fledged, socially defined adult woman associated with marriage, motherhood, and dependence on a spouse. Small wonder, then, that many Mexican American women refusing to accept quinceañeras attach quite different meanings to it: "Oppression of the woman, limiting her choices and potential growth in . . . society" (Watters 1998:149). Further, much of the popular press (and probably more than one serious scholar) often portrays quinceañeras among Mexican Americans as a "traditional" and fundamental aspect of Mexican culture—a "A 500-Year Old Tradition," according to one account—often going as far as noting striking resemblances to Aztec or Maya cultural practices (La Voz de Colorado 2001; La Prensa 2004).

Inspired by feminist scholarship, Dávalos approached quinceañeras from a different perspective, emphasizing instead the multiplicity of meanings and the "different voices and discourses" embedded in them (2003:145). She notes that despite the fact that Catholic clergy often do not agree on what exactly constitutes a "traditional" quinceañera, there is nevertheless a concerted and near-unanimous effort to construe it as a "traditional"—and therefore a fundamental—dimension of Mexican American culture. The emphasis placed on the ongoing construction of such "traditional" culture is not without religious and other ideological underpinnings:

> According to Catholic officials and journalists, the *quinceañera* is an extension of baptism, an opportunity for conversion, and a chance to encourage young girls to begin a life of service. Church officials emphasize the role the *quinceañera* plays in bringing people to the church and in teaching gender roles and cultural traditions. Through the *quinceañera,* Catholic priests provide instruction to parents on how to educate their daughters about gender roles, "female" behavior, and sexuality . . . *Mexicanas* and their families who refuse to follow Church requirements or who practice the *quinceañera* in ways not approved by their pastor are referred to as untraditional, pagan, amoral, unfit parents, or "lacking [cultural] identity." (Dávalos 2003:149)

One important point raised by Dávalos is that many Mexican American women partake of the quinceañera not because they wholeheartedly accept the idea that it signals the transition to full womanhood—and eventual marriage, motherhood, and subordination to future spouses—but because it is important for their sense of identity as *Mexican American* women. That is, quinceañeras are often far more important for the construction of cultural rather than gender identity. Indeed, many women view participation in quinceañeras as a medium of cultural affirmation:

> Although the *quinceañera* is described and practiced in several ways, mothers and daughters spoke most often about the *quinceañera,* as "something that has to be done because of who we are" and as a way of "holding onto your roots." I interpret these expressions as an imperative to practice one's ethnic culture in any event that *makes* a girl into a woman, but more importantly *makes* her into a Mexican woman. (2003:151)

One would be mistaken, Dávalos believes, to think that when these women claim that the quinceañeras are "traditional" they are sharing similar understandings of the meanings of *traditional* professed by the Catholic clergy:

> Though the *quinceañera* is framed as a "tradition," the category takes different meaning than the one constructed in public discourse. *Mexicanas* do not value the *quinceañera* because they can locate its origins in a specific ancient civilization. Rather, they claim that the *quinceañera* is important because it transforms and physically connects a person to "Mexican culture"—a time and place that has particular meaning to each individual . . . Following more than a temporal connection, most women link the *quinceañera* to a specific person, to a specific memory, or to a specific place—that is, to a sister, to *una quinceañera en el año pasado* [a *quinceañera* last year], or to the *rancho* of their childhood . . . In this way, "tradition" is a bodily experience authenticated by memory and practice. (2003:153–154)

It may also be the case that quinceañeras are culturally and socially far more important for those who attend the ceremony than for the young girl for whom the ceremony takes place. In the course of fieldwork among poor Mexican American migrant farm families in Texas and Illinois, Williams found that quinceañeras provide a singular opportunity for dispersed extended family members to come together and solidify bonds and reciprocal ties to each other—all essential for the survival of desperately poor and itinerant farm working families:

> The *quinceañera* feast does signal the importance of her life to *them* [i.e., extended kin], and the lavish ritual expressions which surround such occasions such as this work to bind kin, recreate obligations, and promise reciprocity. Most people know that they too will be commemorated at the appropriate times, and that their lives are significant to others as well. Further, through ritual, migrants dramatically defy the degrading "total institutions" in which they spend half of their lives: the monotonous surroundings and crowded, unsanitary conditions which tacitly proclaim their worthlessness. (1984:121)

Summary

Although difficult conceptually to define, popular culture is a ubiquitous dimension of everyday life. This chapter surveyed some aspects of popular culture. It focused first on sports, illustrating how soccer and baseball both spark and channel political rivalries, nationalist fervor, popular discontent, and national identity. Carnaval was shown to be a powerful expression of popular culture, a multi-faceted ritual with numerous political, cultural, and social undercurrents and manifestations. This chapter also drew attention to various musical and dance genres, and how these are important expressions of popular longings. They also express and consolidate ethnic, class, and other identities. Mass media, and particularly the extraordinarily popular telenovelas, were shown to also express widespread sentiments and longings. The final section centered attention on the cultural importance in the United States of the quinceañera ritual.

ISSUES AND QUESTIONS

1. *Popular Culture.* Why is "popular" culture difficult to define and circumscribe? What other important anthropological concepts might face a similar dilemma? Because this chapter has surveyed some expressions of popular culture, might the question of definition really be a nonissue? How? Why?

2. *Nationalism, and National Identity.* One theme of this chapter has been that expressions of popular culture are important symbolic mediums through which nationalist tendencies flare up, and through which national and local identities coalesce. Which examples can you discuss that appear to substantiate this point? Might there be others not discussed in this chapter?

3. *Resistance or Challenges to the Social Order.* Examples discussed in this chapter suggest that expressions of popular culture may be ways through which the social order is resisted or challenged. Is this an adequate interpretation of the examples appearing in this chapter? Might there be alternate interpretations and, if so, what are they and which examples can be used to substantiate them?

4. *Gender and Sexuality.* Different forms of popular culture appear to be related to gender and sexuality. Which two examples from this chapters can be used to illustrate how and why this may be so?

KEY TERMS AND CONCEPTS

Barras bravas   p. 319
Blocos   p. 328
Brigas   p. 330
Cultural performance   p. 331
Entrudo   p. 329
Lunfardo   p. 333
Popular culture   p. 314

Private transcript   p. 326
Quinceañera   p. 347
Rite of passage   p. 347
Ritual of inversion   p. 325
Ritualized popular celebration
    p. 324
Salsa   p. 335

Secular-religious ritual   p. 323
Soccer war   p. 317
Telenovelas   p. 339
Texts   p. 315

ENDNOTE

1 *Rastafari* stems from *Ras Tafari*, the name of Haille Selassie before he was crowned Ethiopian emperor in 1930 (Kitzinger 1969).

CHAPTER

12

Violence, Memory, and Striving for a Just World

This final chapter turns to case studies of mass violence and social conflicts in Central America, Mexico, and South America to understand some of their causes and explore their current and future legacies, cultural or otherwise. The first section explores why studies of mass violence and conflicts have not occupied a prominent place in cultural anthropology. It then focuses on the relationship between mass violence, death, and memory, underscoring the latter's powerful role—remembering or, in the cases of others, forgetting—through which individuals interpret and make sense of past traumatic events, and why such memories are important. The subsequent sections center on the Central American civil wars of the 1980s (Nicaragua, El Salvador, and Guatemala); the 1971 coup against Chilean president Salvador Allende led by General Pinochet; Argentina's dirty war; the widespread violence in Colombia; the Zapatista uprising in Chiapas, Mexico; and Peru's Shining Path insurgency. These sections are followed by a critical examination of the acrimonious controversy surrounding the publication of Rigoberta Menchú's quasi-autobiography on events during the Guatemalan civil war. The last part of this chapter draws attention to ways that Central American refugees—especially Guatemalan Mayas—are striving to rebuild their lives and sustain their culture in the United States.

Violence and Memory

"Massive trauma," Robben (2005:125) tells us,

> is more than the sum total of individual suffering because it ruptures social bonds, destroys group identities, undermines the sense of community, and entails cultural disorientation when taken-for-granted meanings become obsolete. A social trauma is thus a wound to the social body and its cultural frame.

Yet, anthropologists have devoted little time and effort to studying mass violence and death, despite the fact that in the 1960s some were at the forefront in the study of revolutionary wars (Wolf 1969). When widespread terror broke out in Central America during the 1970s and 1980s, even Adams, whose landmark book *Crucifixion by Power* (1970) underscored the history of repression in Guatemala, stated that anthropologists " . . . [were] not . . . in the forefront in the study of violence, terror and war" (1988:275). Wilson (1991:33) also noted that "anthropology has historically ignored the harsh realities of modern wars among the people being 'anthropologized' . . . Anthropologists have usually been the last to respond to armed confrontation between the modern nation-state and social groups." But why has this been so? Scheper-Hughes and Bourgois suggest that

> anthropologists were too slow, too hesitant, too reflective; and the ethnographic knowledge that was produced was too local. Political events were altogether too fast and unstable, so that by the time the anthropologist had something to say it was usually long after the fact . . . [and] . . . the characteristic avoidance of violence by most twentieth-century anthropologists was based on a legitimate fear that study and analyses of *indigenous* forms of human cruelty and mass killing (which certainly exist) would only exacerbate Western stereotypes of primitivity, savagery, and barbarism that took modern anthropology more than half a century to dislodge. (2004:4–6).

Recently, anthropologists *have* grappled with mass violence and terror as legitimate concerns of study (Nagengast 1994; Wolf 1999; Aretxaga 2003; Richards 2005). Yet, still "to this day most early-warning signs concerning genocidal sentiments, gestures, and acts come from political journalists rather than from ethnographers . . . In all, anthropology is a late arrival to the field" (Scheper-Hughes and Bourgois 2004:5).

Despite increasing research on violence, scholars still have trouble defining it, perhaps because, like most social science concepts, it is so "slippery" (Scheper-Hughes and Bourgois 2004:1; Nagengast 1994:111). Despite the difficulties of drawing neat conceptual boundaries around forms of violence, the following case studies draw attention to overlapping types, including **genocide** (the purposeful targeting and killing of people on the basis of presumed cultural and/or racial differences), **dirty wars** (illegitimate or illegal state violence against citizens), **revolutionary violence** (armed popular uprisings with the intention of overhauling the political, economic, and social institutions of society) (Nagengast 1994; Scheper-Hughes and Bourgois 2004; Bourgois 2004; Aretxaga 2003), and **structural violence** (Farmer 2004a, 2004b; defined in Chapter 8).

Unlike mass violence and terror, memory or **memory work** *has* occupied an important place in anthropology, such as research carried out in the context of genocide in different world regions (Hinton 2002). It is at the interstices of anthropology, history, and violence that some of the most significant research on memory in Latin America and the Caribbean has been undertaken (Jelin 1997; Hale 1997; Stern 2004). Forensic anthropologists—led by the almost-legendary Clyde Snow—have played a unique role in forging memory work by painstakingly locating mass hidden graves, identifying victims, bolstering the ability of victims' relatives to keep alive the memories of their loved ones, and providing information to Latin American truth commissions investigating war crimes and prosecuting war criminals (Gibbons 1992; McEvoy and Conway 2004; Robben 2005; see also Photo 12.1).

Literary writers—especially poets—also reflected on and conveyed the pains suffered by so many during the tragically violent periods of war and violence, thereby also leaving their mark on Latin American and Caribbean memory work. Such is the example of Ernesto Cardenal—priest and Nicaragua's most renown poet—who, in his famous 1973 *Canto*

PHOTO 12.1   *Forensic anthropologists dig out bodies of victims of the Dirty War, at an Argentine cemetery.*

Nacional (National Chant), intertwined history, cosmic outlook, revolution, and liberation theology (Beverley and Zimmerman 1990:84). Others, such as those in El Salvador, forged their poetry in the midst of guerilla combat (see In Their Own Words 12.1).

The Central American Civil Wars

Understanding the social history and political economy of Central America—the expansion of export agriculture, the appropriation of peasant land and labor, coalescence of powerful national elites, and forging of strong, repressive states—is crucial for appreciating how and why civil strife riddled this region in the 1970s and 1980s.

Export crops had long been grown in Central America—cacao, and indigo and cochineal (both used for dying) in El Salvador and Guatemala are good examples. Yet, it was coffee that paved the way for social strife. The increasing demand for coffee by the late 1800s in Europe and the United States (Jiménez 1995) had a rippling effect in Central America. With the possible exception of Honduras, by 1900 coffee was furnishing Central American countries with most of their export earnings, a trend that continued through the mid-twentieth century. The expansion of coffee cultivation required an active role by the state, which provided large coffee growers with infrastructural and financial support, such

IN THEIR OWN WORDS   **12.1**

Guerilla Poetry from El Salvador

I'll Die Gladly
(by Delfy Góchez Fernández, 1979)
they're going to kill me
when?
I don't know . . .
what I do know clearly is that I'll die
that way, assassinated by the enemy.
and my blood will water our land
and the flowers of freedom will grow . . .
with the child that yesterday wept for a crust of
bread
and who today grows like a river

Those Who Stopped Halfway
(by José María Cuellar, undated)
Those who stopped halfway
with their eyes lost in the fog.
those who gazed for the last time at night
or in the semi-darkness of the tin shanty
at the sad dress of their mother,
their father's stricken features,
those who had the bad luck
to run into drunken National Guardsmen
and were beaten, wounded or jailed,
those who witnessed the rape of their mother,
or the decapitation of their father
and joined up with the man who sold cloth bolts
on credit,
the peasant, the shoeshine boy, the slum
dweller, the orphan,
and they join up in memory of those who fell . . .

(*Source*: From *On the Front Line: Guerilla Poems of El Salvador* edited and translated by Claribel Alegría and Darwin J. Flakoll. Curbstone Press, 1989. Distributed by Consortium. Reprinted with permission.

---

as road building, improvements of port facilities, and credit. In turn, the state itself prospered and grew from taxes on coffee exports (Bulmer-Thomas 1987:8–13, 92–110; Fowler 1987; McCreery 1994:113–129).

This convergence between specialized, large-scale coffee elites and the state underpinned political cohesiveness as elites largely shed aside their intra-class quarrels to create a stable climate conducive to sustained growth of the coffee sector, and state institutions grew in size and complexity. The ability of states to enhance their coercive power by increasing police and army forces was largely derived from taxes levied on exported coffee. Unlike coffee, bananas, the second most important export crop in the 1930s and 1940s, were largely cultivated on coastal plains distant from peasant communities and by transnational corporations (such as the United Fruit Company), over which national elites and states had little control. Further, elites and states, especially in El Salvador, Guatemala, and Nicaragua, dislodged peasants from their lands and appropriated their labor through "vagrancy" laws, forced labor drafts, and debt peonage, and they channeled this labor into large-scale coffee estates (Bulmer-Thomas 1987:11–29, 74–77; McCreery 1994:236–264; Williams 1994:220–232).

By the 1950s, cotton began to rival coffee in economic importance, and by the 1960s, most cotton cultivation was concentrated in large estates controlled by a handful of elite families. By the 1970s, for instance, one-fourth of the entire Salvadoran cotton crop was controlled by eighteen families. Cotton expansion stimulated deforestation, especially along the coastal plains, and the conversion of land formerly cultivated in subsistence crops (such as maize) into cotton. By 1963, in some coastal regions of Nicaragua, cotton fields had engulfed three-fourths of all cropland (Williams 1986:32–54). After cotton came cattle, which also deepened economic and political marginalization. By the 1970s, poverty and inequality in much of Central America reached startling levels, and in El Salvador, Nicaragua, and Guatemala especially, where "the state did not ameliorate growing inequality and employed heavy repression," rebellions broke out (Booth 1993:321–325). Only Costa Rica and, to a lesser extent, Honduras, were spared the conflicts of the 1970s and 1980s.

Nicaragua and El Salvador

Nicaragua. The July 1979 victory of the Frente Sandinista de Liberación Nacional (FSLN, named after Augusto Sandino, who fought United States Marines occupying Nicaragua in the 1920s) over the regime of Anastasio Somoza was a watershed event in Central and Latin American history. Six years after a Chilean military coup toppled the presidency of Salvador Allende (see the section later in this chapter titled "Chile's Pinochet"), in Nicaragua a broad-based coalition promising sweeping social changes had overthrown the Somoza regime, one of Latin America's most entrenched family dynasties. Of the three Central American countries that became embroiled in civil war, only in Nicaragua did a revolutionary movement succeed—albeit temporarily—in seizing political power.

Three important conditions contributed to the Sandinista victory in Nicaragua. There was, first, a long historical trajectory of peasant and working-class activism and political consciousness in rural and urban areas. Second, the spread of a revolutionary ideology was enhanced by radical Catholicism in an overwhelmingly Catholic country. In organizing community study groups, reading and explaining the Bible in ways that peasants and working-class members could understand, and stressing social inequality, activist Catholic clergy and lay workers raised political consciousness and laid the groundwork for imagining an alternate future (Lancaster 1988; Gould 1990:272–276). The famous song *Misa Campesina* (Peasant Mass) illustrates the fusion of popular aspirations and activist Catholic preachings (Gould 1990:277).

By violently repressing Catholic activists, the National Guard fused the message of social justice with the Sandinista call for revolutionary change and drove many Catholic lay leaders into the FSLN. Further, after the 1974 earthquake that devastated Managua, the Catholic Church hierarchy openly turned against Somoza, calling for "structural changes and changes of governmental authorities" (quoted by Gould 1990:272).

Third, during much of its history, the Somozas had ruled Nicaragua as a piece of family property, in no way representing the political and economic interests of all elites. Political favoritism and crony nepotism had turned many elite members of Nicaraguan society against the Somoza family. Repression against opposition leaders—such as the 1978 assassination of Pedro Joaquín Chamorro, editor of *La Prensa* newspaper—further alienated many Nicaraguan elites from the Somoza family (Gould 1990:281).

In the context of civil unrest elsewhere in Central America, the United States viewed the Sandinista victory as an open road to instability and communism. Faced with a possible "domino-effect"—one country after another "falling" to "communism"—the administration of former U.S. President Ronald Reagan organized and financed a counter-insurgency movement against the Sandinistas during what was widely known as the **contra war.** With an economy in shambles; the need to be on a constant war footing to fend off contra attacks, especially from neighboring Honduras; and with Nicaraguans weary of war, the deeply divided Sandinistas called for general elections in 1990. They lost to Violeta Chamorro, widow of the slain newspaper editor. Rigid ideology and an inability to come to terms with profound ethnic, cultural, and regional differences within Nicaragua also contributed to the Sandinista defeat. Along the ethnically and linguistically diverse Atlantic coast, for instance, Sandinistas encountered considerable resistance by the Miskitu and other indigenous groups (Diskin 1991:163).

El Salvador.   In some ways, the violence that gripped tiny El Salvador in the 1970s and 1980s actually began forty years earlier. By 1931, conditions were ripe for a social explosion for, as the U.S. military attaché at the time noted, "90 percent of the wealth of the Nation is held by about half of 1 per cent of the population . . . [and] . . . thirty or forty families own nearly everything in the country" (quoted in Pérez Brignoli 1995:234).

The 1932 rebellion was the "largest peasant uprising" Central America had so far experienced (Browning 1971:207, quoted by Pérez Brignoli 1995:243). Important characteristics underpinned this rebellion. First, it was primarily concentrated in a few coffee-producing regions. Second, these areas were also the last strongholds of the few remaining indigenous communities with strong communal institutions, such as the cofradías. Third, most indigenous land had been appropriated by the turn of the century by the country's coffee elite. Lastly, the Salvadoran Communist party was especially active in these regions prior to the outbreak of violence (Kincaid 1993).

The rebellion itself lasted only three or four days, during which at least twenty-five thousand indigenous peasants perished, a tragedy movingly conveyed by Alegría and Flakoll's gripping novel (1989b). The speed and ruthlessness with which the indigenous population was exterminated cannot be explained by any real threat that rebels posed, because only a fraction of those killed actually participated in the rebellion. In February 1932, shortly after the uprising had been crushed, a coffee plantation owner published in a regional newspaper his views—no doubt shared by other members of the elite class—of El Salvador's "Indians." These furnish insights into the ethnic, racial, and class fears that fueled the ensuing genocide (see In Their Own Words 12.2).

By early 1980—shortly after the 1979 overthrow of the Somoza dictatorship in Nicaragua—a full-blown insurrection was underway in El Salvador. Although the political and economic context of El Salvador proved ripe for popular revolt, an important social catalyst was the presence in rural areas of what Kincaid (1993:133) called the "Catholic Left." As in Nicaragua and Guatemala, liberation theology provided a moral and ideological justification (and organizing skills) that later proved crucial for guerrilla organizations. The widely publicized killings of Jesuit priests and Catholic nuns, as well as the astonishing 1980 public assassination of Archbishop Arturo Romero as he celebrated mass in the capital's Cathedral, illustrate how elements of the Catholic Church were viewed as dangerous "others" by Salvadoran security forces (Franco 2004).

Years of fighting left thousands of Salvadorans dead and many others as refugees. The main guerilla organization—the Farabundo Martí National Liberation Front (FMLN), named after a founder of the Salvadoran Communist party who died in the 1932 revolt—was unable to stem the armed forces' onslaught, which was backed by billions of dollars of

---

IN THEIR OWN WORDS   **12.2**

Elite Views on El Salvador's Indian "Problem," 1932

Shortly after the 1932 massacre of tens of thousands of Salvadoran indigenous peasants, a coffee planter expressed these views on his country's "Indians":

> [They are] a horde of wild savages . . . They, who are crafty by nature, and who come from a race inferior to ours, a conquered race, need little to ignite their deep-felt passions against the Mestizos, because they hate us and always will. Our most serious mistake was to grant them civil rights. This was bad for the country. They were told that they were free, that the nation was also theirs, and that they were entitled to elect their own leaders and act as they saw fit. Of course, they took this to mean that they could steal, destroy property and kill their employers . . . It is our wish that this race be exterminated. If it is not, it will come back even stronger, more experienced and less stupid, and ready, in future attempts, to do away with all of us . . . They did the right thing in the United States, getting rid of them, with bullets, rather than letting them stop progress. They killed the Indians first because they were never going to change. Here, we have treated them as if they were part of our family, shown them every consideration, but you should see them in action! Their instincts are savage. (Perez Brigndi 1995:255)

U.S. military assistance. In a classic divide-and-conquer strategy, the armed forces pitted peasants against each other through intimidation and gruesome massacres. One of the worst atrocities took place in El Mozote, where more than one thousand civilians, including 135 children, were slaughtered by security forces (Binford 1996). Factional disputes and intra-guerilla violence also weakened resistance to the army. One of the most tragic consequences of the conflict in El Salvador is the

> enduring normalization of internecine violence in the broader context of political violence, [which] makes sense if the extent of the pain and terror that political repression causes is fully appreciated as a "pressure cooker" generating everyday violence through the systematic distortion of social relations and sensibilities. It also helps explain why El Salvador had the highest per capita homicide rate in the western hemisphere during the 1990s *after* the end of the Civil War. 6,250 people per year perished from direct political violence during the civil war in the 1980s, compared to 8,700 to 11,000 killed every year by criminal violence in the 1990s following the peace accords of New Year's Eve of 1990/1. (Bourgois 2004:431)

Guatemala's Despotic State

The violence in Guatemala—the most atrocious of all in Central America—pitted an increasingly militarized state against predominantly Maya guerillas and civilians, resulting in the slaughter of 150,000 Maya and the displacement of one million Guatemalans

(Loucky and Moors 2000:3). Most fighting occurred in the heavily Maya western highlands, especially in the departments of Quiché, Alta Verapaz, and Quezaltenango. There, two Marxist guerilla organizations, the Guerilla Army of the Poor (*Ejército Guerillero del Pueblo,* EGP) and the Revolutionary Organization of People in Arms (*Organización Revolucionaria del Pueblo en Armas,* ORPA) emerged in the late 1960s. This conflict was preceded by a long history of uprisings, as well as ethnic and class inequality between the Maya rural population and the minority Ladino\Mestizo political and economic elites (Carmack 1988; Smith 1990a, 1990b; McCreery 1994).

Scholars disagree whether guerilla attacks initially provoked the fierce response by the armed forces, and whether Maya peasants initially supported the guerilla organizations or did so after the start of the army's counterinsurgency campaign (Wilson 1991; Hale 1997; see also the Stoll-Menchú controversy later in this chapter). Nevertheless, the military unleashed a wave of terror and brutality unknown in recent Guatemalan history and memory. Years later, declassified U.S. intelligence documents showed that the

> C.I.A. station in Guatemala City knew that the Guatemalan army was massacring entire Mayan villages while Reagan administration officials publicly supported the military regime's human rights record. (Krauss 1999)

In 1990, the Guatemalan Catholic Church's Human Rights Office commissioned an inquiry into the civil war. Two years after the signing of the Guatemalan Peace Accords, the Church's 1998 final report—"Guatemala, Never Again! Recovery of Historical Memory Project (REMHI)"—detailed the human rights abuses by both the Guatemalan army *and* its guerilla adversaries, and described some of their tragic and lasting consequences (Archdiocese of Guatemala 1999). (The 1999 edition alluded to in the following pages is an abridged English version of the eight volume report published in Spanish in 1998.)

At the height of the conflict, the military, unable to defeat the guerillas, turned its eyes on the Maya civilian population. As Wilson (1991:40) has aptly put it, "Acting on Mao-Tse-Tung's famous dictum that guerillas depended on the population like fish on the sea, the army set about draining the sea." Major hallmarks of the army's campaign were widespread and grizzly massacres of unarmed men, women, and children, part of a systematic scorched-earth campaign—*operativo de tierra arrasada* (Danner 2004:334). Guerillas too committed atrocities. Nevertheless, the REMHI inquiry notes that the armed forces and its paramilitary civil patrols were responsible for more than 90 percent of the massacres (Archdiocese of Guatemala 1999:133–134). The methodic targeting of unarmed children and women was one of the most hideous aspects of army repression, a carefully planned strategy verging on genocide:

> Half of the massacres [carried out by the army] included the collective murder of children . . . In many massacres . . . violence against children was not only part of the violence against the community in general but also had a deliberate purpose. In the testimonies gathered by REMHI, soldiers or patrollers frequently refer to the killing of children as a way of eliminating the possibility of rebuilding the community. (Archdiocese of Guatemala 1999:30–31)

The roots of the Guatemalan conflict were undeniably political and economic inequality between Ladino elites and the largely Mayan-speaking indigenous population. Yet, the need to understand violence and mass death is both deep and an eminently cultural affair. And in their need to make sense and cope with sudden and seemingly arbitrary violence and death, most people draw on existing cultural repertoires, including religious beliefs, that hark back to analogous events through the juxtaposing of the past and the present. In this ongoing creation of cultural memory, the Guatemalan Maya were no different. Green notes, for example, that

> when speaking of la violencia of the 1980s, I was struck by how frequently people used the metaphor of conquest to describe it. "Lo mismo cuando se mat[ó] a Tecum Uman" (it is the same when they killed Tecum Uman), doña Marta said when describing the recent whirlwind of death, alluding to the Maya-K'iche hero who died valiantly in battle against the Spaniards. (2004:188)

Analogous statements were ushered by others trying to give meaning to the tragedy unfolding around them. Elsewhere in the department of Quiché:

> An Indian shaman . . . announced that Tecum . . . had returned to earth . . . "to bring justice to Guatemala." Significantly, he is said to have brought two million "warriors" (read "guerillas") with him . . . The tale suggests that the more traditional Indians have, in fact, seen that the . . . war is analogous to the Spanish conquest. The guerillas too have taken note of the parallel. One Indian guerilla, an avowed Catholic, now searches for images in *Popol Vuh* to help her understand the violence. Because the evil power in that book takes the form of gods who resided in an underworld called Xibalbá, she believes that evil is "when repression came to the Quiché. Since we were all born here, how can those men [the soldiers] do this killing . . . [And bury them] in clandestine cemeteries! Those men, those soldiers who killed us . . . that is what we call Xibalbá." (Carmack 1988:69; for other examples, see Danner 2004)

Religion was inexorably bound up in the Guatemalan conflict. In the late 1960s, Catholic priests and lay activists involved with the Quiché Maya were espousing liberation theology and establishing grassroots cooperatives, and health and literacy programs. Many lay activists eventually assumed positions of moral authority and prestige in Maya communities, embracing an image of an egalitarian social order through the teachings of the Bible; they often were the first to join the guerilla movement, calling for "The Kingdom of God on Earth" (Wilson 1991:39). Some Catholic clergy sided ideologically with the military's offensive to stamp out "communism." Others joined the guerillas—and also become targets of the army's wrath (Archdiocese of Guatemala 1999:169). By 1980, the Catholic Church in Quiché was, in the eyes of the Guatemalan military, the enemy. After the murder of several Catholic priests, and with his own life threatened, the Catholic Bishop of Quiché ordered his priests to flee the dioceses (Carmack 1988:44–45). One Catholic nun told Wilson:

> We couldn't just abandon them up there fleeing in the mountains. I was forced out of the country but came back in to be with my people. We carried out baptisms and masses and helped in the organization of food. We preached about

the reality of what was happening. We said that the Q'eqchi' were like the Israelites in the desert, fleeing the soldiers of Egypt. (1991:48)

Catholics were not the only ones to take sides with the guerillas or the Maya civilians fleeing for their lives. Protestant missionaries also died attempting to shield civilians. But the role of radical evangelical sects in legitimizing violence against civilians has been well documented. Most sided with the military, for in

> a Latin America . . . considered to be lost in the darkness of folk Catholic idolatry, and now stalked by Communist wolves in the sheep's clothing of liberation theology, Guatemala was to become a beacon of light. It would serve as a model of biblical righteousness for other countries threatened by the same satanic forces; it was to become a theological "New Israel" of the Americas. (Stoll 1988:91; for similar claims, see Archdiocese of Guatemala 1999:47)

During and after the conflict, culture and religion loomed prominently in other ways. Some religious beliefs and rituals simply could not be retained in the midst of war. For example, the Q'eqchi of Alta Verapaz believe in the *tzuultaq'a*, bigendered, capricious mountain spirits, intermediaries between God and mortals, between this world and the afterworld. If presented with proper offerings, the tzuultaq'a will insure the well-being of one's crops, livestock, and health. Further, the tzuultaq'a are highly localized, residing in mountains near the villages that they look after and from which they receive homage, and the Q'eqchi only recognize those tzuultaq'a living closest to their communities. The effect of war on the devotion to the tzuultaq'a appears to have been disastrous: rituals to appease the spirits could not be carried out under a nomadic existence in the forests where guerillas and villagers fled. Cultural materials needed for the tzuultaq'a—such as incense and candles—were not available, which also meant that, in the absence of these rituals, the tzuultaq'a were no longer bound to protect the villagers against danger and assure the fertility of their crops. For most Q'eqchi, the reciprocal ritual and social relations with their tzuultaq'a simply could not be sustained (Wilson 1991).

To not be able to bury one's loved ones in a culturally acceptable way is a major affront to cultural sensibilities and a tragic experience to undergo. Among the Maya it was no different:

> The disappeared are among what Robert Hertz (1960) has called the "unquiet dead," referring to those who have died violent or unnatural deaths. Hertz has argued that funeral rituals are a way of strengthening the social bond. The Mayas believe that without proper burial souls linger in the liminal space between earth and the afterlife, condemned in time between death and the final obsequies. And yet these wandering souls may act as intermediaries between nature and the living, buffering as well as enhancing memories through the imagery of their violent deaths. (Green 2004:194)

Maya villagers were not alone in interpreting and grounding everyday experiences of warfare through cultural and religious lens. The Guatemalan army was also adept at manipulating Q'eqchi culture and religion for its purposes:

> In Chajul, Quiché, two of the religious icons on the alter are dressed in the uniform of the elite army counterinsurgency troops. In many parts of the Guatemalan highlands, the civil patrols march with their rifles in the local saint processions . . . The army has manipulated Q'eqchi culture deftly to fit its own requirements. The system of social contract which the military has imposed could not have worked so effectively if it did not have resonance in the indigenous culture itself. The army has attempted to appropriate for its own ends the . . . Tzuultaq'a. The sign at the entrance of the Cobán army headquarters reads, "Cobán Military Base—Home of the Soldier Tzuultaq'a." (Wilson 1991:51)

The "use of sacred sites as killing fields" and turning churches "into detention and torture centers" were other ways the army seized on cultural symbols to undermine Maya resistance (Archdiocese of Guatemala 1999:19, 47).

Living with apprehension and terror is one of the lasting and traumatic consequences of the war. Whether it is someone walking down the street who happens to stare, or an unexpected knock at the door or telephone ring, Guatemalans face and have to deal with constant fear. Yet, and as in Chile and Argentina, many Guatemalans have overcome and courageously stood up against fear, and have emphasized the importance of not forgetting. Following the footsteps of the Argentine Mothers of the Plaza de Mayo (see the section on Argentina later in this chapter), they have organized the Grupo de Apoyo Mutuo (mutual support group, GAM) representing the more than fifty thousand who disappeared during Guatemala's violence (Green 2004:190; REMHI 1999:9). The rise of pan-Maya activism has been one of the most important social and cultural consequences of this period of violence (Warren 1999).

Adams has reflected on the past violence inflicted on and future prospects of the Guatemalan Maya:

> If the relatively mild repression following the 1954 conservative victory brought in its train the revolutionary activity of the 1960s and 1970s, one cannot ignore what may be harvested from this decade of violence. What will be the future thoughts of the thousands of children, whose numbers will doubtless exceed 100,000 before the present era ends, growing up with the knowledge that their . . . families were . . . killed by the army? . . . And, finally, what is the . . . future of a population that first learned about democratic participation in the revolutionary decade of 1944–54, only to have it snatched away by a CIA-backed coup, and to have been brought by frustration into active revolt, only to have it result in the slaughter of 1975–85? (1988:291)

Chile's Pinochet

In 1970, a coalition of left-wing parties called the Unidad Popular (Popular Unity, UP) led by Salvador Allende won the presidential elections, inaugurating the first popularly elected Marxist government in Latin American and Caribbean history. Three years later, on September 11, 1973, the armed forces led by General Augusto Pinochet staged a violent coup and launched one of the most enduring (1973–1990) and repressive military regimes in Latin America and the Caribbean. Twenty-five years later, in October 1998, while visiting London, the retired General Pinochet was arrested by British police following up on an international arrest warrant issued by a Spanish judge charging Pinochet of murdering Spanish citizens during his regime. These three pivotal events spanning almost thirty years have defined the political, social, and cultural landscapes of Chile, and will almost certainly continue to do so for many years to come (Brody 1999; Moulian 1999; Faiola 2000a).

The 1970 election of Allende was symbolically and politically significant because it signaled, for the first time, the *real* possibility of a Marxist government carrying out profound structural changes in a peaceful, nonviolent way. Given Latin America's long tradition of authoritarian rule and political culture, and especially after the 1954 CIA-backed coup that overthrew the popularly elected, reformist Guatemalan government of Jacobo Arbenz, this type of peaceful change was a prospect that few could envision. What proved crucial in the electoral success of the UP was Chile's tradition of electoral politics and military subordination to civilian control; an equally strong and lengthy trajectory of labor activism and union organizing; political divisions within the political and economic elites; and strong support from progressive elements of the Catholic Church (Stern 2004).

By 1973, major forces were undermining Chile's experiment in peaceful, radical change and laying the groundwork for the upcoming military coup. Although Allende had won the presidency in fair and open elections, he captured only one-third of the popular vote. Facing stiff parliamentary opposition, Allende turned to technical legalities to undertake his program, thereby reducing his legitimacy vis-à-vis his opponents. The United States also worked against Allende by sponsoring economic sabotage and covert, CIA-directed operations to foment political opposition and dissent. Further, although Allende was enormously popular among his supporters, his economic program of rapid economic changes led to unpopular scarcities, high inflation, rationing, and black market profiteering. The UP experiment also led to land invasions, factory takeovers, and work stoppages that neither he nor his government were willing or able to fully control. Lastly, parliamentary and legal opposition gave way to overt hostility and, more importantly, the possibility of a violent overthrow of the UP soon loomed in the imagination of many (Stern 2004:20–27). By the end of 1973, then, many opponents of the UP—including the top military leadership—were convinced that Chile was edging toward a deep abyss and that a violent change of course was the only way to avoid the steep plunge. The coup was an exceptionally violent and haunting spectacle, as tanks and fighter planes bombarded, and troops stormed, the presidential palace (La Moneda) after Allende refused to surrender (see Photo 12.2).

The Pinochet-led military, encountering particularly stiff resistance in urban shanty-towns (Schneider 1992), relentlessly hunted down, imprisoned, exiled, abducted, tortured, or killed tens of thousands of UP members, sympathizers, or for that matter, anyone suspected of being a threat. In so doing, it generated a culture of fear that

> was embodied in individualized abductions, political cleansings of key institutions such as schools and universities, and massive sweeps of targeted neighborhoods to search homes and arrest suspects. Danger and violence would be so pervasive and intimidating that potential critics would presumably be frightened into apathy, a kind of active rejection of political knowledge and concern as legitimate activity. (Stern 2004:32)

PHOTO 12.2   *The Chilean presidential palace La Moneda under fire during the September 11, 1973 coup. September 11 is a date that was burned into the Chilean psyche long before the 2001 World Trade Center attacks turned that day into a symbol for the United States.*

The Chilean military widely and systematically kidnapped, tortured, and subsequently and secretly murdered (and hid the bodies of) opponents as an instrument of state terror. It is in Chile that the verb **desaparecer** (to disappear) first became synonymous with military repression, and the category of **desaparecidos** (the disappeared) first emerged. Both also later loomed important in Argentina. For most of us, it is very difficult to cope with the death of a loved one and to keep alive his or her memory. Yet *not knowing* what exactly happened, when, and where—When was she killed? How and by whom? Did she suffer? Where might her remains lie? How can she be remembered and honored if her remains are never found?—is an especially traumatic experience. It is this moving quest to find out what happened to and remember and not forget the desaparecidos that propels much of memory work in contemporary Chile, Argentina, and Guatemala.

Memory—what of the past one remembers (or decides to forget), and how it is deciphered—is contentious. In Chile, as well as in Argentina and Guatemala, there are different ways of constructing the past, different types of memories, and diverse imaginings of a collective future filtered through individual and socially significant experiences, longings, and fears. For those who believed that the 1973 coup had "saved" Chile from the brink of disaster, "memory as salvation" looms large. For those who experienced persecution and suffered personal loss—as those still in search of loved desaparecidos—memory of the past is experienced and remembered as a traumatic, ongoing, unresolved "rupture" (Stern 2004:24–67). Such is the case of Señora Herminda, whose two sons, Ernesto and Gerardo, are among the desaparecidos:

> Not only does Señora Herminda remember the military period as a time that brought a deep and continuing rupture, a cruel wound that fails to heal, to her life. She also has reorganized much of her life around the idea of memory and rupture—the struggle to honor and maintain the memory of her missing sons. As remembered people who really existed, they must be found, if only to give them a decent burial. (Stern 2004:49–50)

For others who did not directly experience personal loss and anguish but either saw first-hand what others had experienced and/or were concerned about their own safety, the military period is remembered as a time of "persecution and awakening" (Stern 2004:51–67). For those Chileans who would rather "forget" the past—or at least not openly talk about it—memory is a sort of "closed box," that comes with an understanding that "some themes and some remembrances [are] so explosive—conflictive and intractable—that little [can] be gained from a public opening and airing of the contents inside" (Stern 2004:89).

Pinochet spent sixteen months under house arrest in London while British authorities decided whether to extradite him to Spain. The political ramifications of the international arrest warrant against Pinochet were enormous (and especially vexing for the United States), for on the horizon loomed the prospect that others also accused of gross violations of human rights— former Argentine, Salvadoran, and Guatemalan military officers living in the United States, for example—would no longer enjoy safe havens. The United States has consistently opposed the legitimacy of the International Criminal Court in The Hague to try crimes against humanity, arguing that it would undermine national sovereignty, and has cut foreign aid to Latin American countries that have refused to sign immunity agreements shielding U.S. soldiers and officials from arrest (Brody 1999:20; Forero 2005). In the end, and after much political and legal maneuvering and intrigue, the British government allowed Pinochet to return to Chile in March 2000, arguing that because of his poor health he was unfit to stand trial (Faiola 2000a). Interestingly enough, Chile's civilian government had sided with Pinochet's lawyers in opposing his extradition to Spain, perhaps because, as Moulian (1999:14–15) suggests, it feared a backlash from the military.

After the return of parliamentary democracy in 1990—and under the guidelines of a constitution written under his rule—Pinochet became a senator for life and enjoyed legal immunity. Yet, by the time he returned to Chile in late 2000, the political and cultural climate had changed enormously. The Chilean judiciary—perhaps spurred on by the relentless efforts of human rights activists and others who refused to forget the desaparecidos—began demonstrating increasing independence from the legal constraints imposed by the constitution. By the end of 2004, Pinochet was stripped of his immunity, under house arrest, and facing trial for kidnapping and murder. And in a strange twist of ironic fate, Chile's desaparecidos played an unexpected role in Pinochet's outcome: prosecutors argued that unaccounted bodies were those of victims presumably kidnapped, a crime not covered under the amnesty laws promulgated during the last years of military rule (Faiola 2000b; Harman 2004; Rohter 2005).

Argentina's Dirty War

In 1990, Adolfo Scilingo, a disgruntled ex-naval officer, wrote a letter to former General Videla, who headed the military junta that seized power in 1976. In it Scilingo provides chilling details into some of the methods that he and others employed in dealing with "subversives" in the mid-1970s:

> In 1977, as a lieutenant stationed at the Naval School of Mechanics . . . I participated in two aerial transports, the first with thirteen subversives aboard . . . and the second with seventeen terrorists . . . The prisoners were told they were being taken to a prison in the south and for that reason had to receive a vaccination. They received an initial dose of anesthetic, which was reinforced by another larger dose during the flight. Finally . . . they were stripped naked and thrown into the waters of the South Atlantic from the planes during the flight. (quoted in Verbitsky 1996:8)

Years later, in the summer of 1982, I returned to La Plata, capital of the province of Buenos Aires, to visit Atilio, an Argentine student whom I had befriended in the early 1970s while attending the Universidad Nacional de La Plata and whom I had not seen since 1976. Entering his home, I greeted his mother Mama Martínez—as she was affectionately known—a sweet and fragile woman. When I approached and said hello, she failed to recognize me. I then reminded her who I was and asked for the whereabouts of Atilio. Looking extremely tired and frazzled, she told me *se ha ido* (he has left). Not immediately understanding what precisely she meant, I asked her when he would be returning home. Mama Martínez told me again, this time in tears, that *Atilio se ha ido,* quickly adding that *se lo llevaron* (they took him away). That afternoon, I understood that Atilio had been one of the thousands "disappeared" during the military regime. Several months after returning to Pittsburgh, I received an anonymous letter from Argentina explaining that while undergoing his compulsory military service, Atilio had been accused of being a *subversivo* (subversive), tortured, and thrown off a helicopter into the Atlantic Ocean. His body was probably never found.

But before I left La Plata for Pittsburgh, Mama Martínez invited me to accompany her to the weekly vigil that she and dozens of other mothers of desaparecidos were participating in at Buenos Aires' Plaza de Mayo demanding to know the fate of their loved ones. Upon returning to her house several days later, Mama Martínez got together her purse—and quickly and in a matter-of-fact way placed a revolver in it. Quite nervous, I meekly asked what she planned to do with the revolver. Her answer was forthcoming, calm, and unambiguous: *no me van a llevar como se llevaron a Atilio* (they will not take me [away] as they took Atilio). That morning, we hopped on a train to Buenos Aires and joined the *Madres de la Plaza de Mayo,* under the watchful eyes of uniformed (in addition to, almost certainly, undercover) police. Mama Martínez died shortly after I returned to Pittsburgh, spared, hopefully, the details of the death of her son, and my friend.

After the military government agreed to general elections, in September 1973, Juan Domingo Perón, accompanied by his wife María Estela ("Isabelita") Martínez de Perón, returned to Argentina after eighteen years of exile in Spain to assume the presidency of a deeply divided country. Less than ten months later (October 1974) Perón died and Isabelita—Argentina's vice-president—was sworn in as president. The period between Perón's return and Isabelita's presidency was marked by escalating social and economic unrest, runaway inflation, scarcity and hoarding of basic food staples, general strikes and—ominously—mounting guerilla assassinations of key police and military leaders, along with prominent businessmen and labor leaders. Unable to contain the mayhem, and facing isolated military revolts, the Peronist government was overthrown by the armed forces in March 1976. In an official announcement, the military junta promised that "the action of the Government will be characterized by the respect of the law within a framework of order and respect for human dignity. The fundamental objective will be to restore the essential values that guide the State" (de Onis 1976:1). Widespread and unrelenting terror soon was underway.

Several characteristics set Argentina apart from other cases of violence analyzed in this chapter. First, the conflict was overwhelmingly centered in cities. Second, the predominantly middle-class guerilla groups that took up arms in the late 1960s and early 1970s— the *Ejército Revolucionario del Pueblo* and the Peronist *Montoneros*—were not large, broad-based social movements with significant support and legitimacy. Further, most of their armed actions involved spectacular kidnappings and assassinations and not open, frontal confrontations with the armed forces. Third, although guerilla groups initially surfaced in the context of widespread labor agitation and active resistance to the military regime, most Argentines neither openly sided with guerillas nor condoned the ferocious and unbridled military repression that followed. Most citizens were predominantly "uncommitted undecidables" who would have rather wished "simply to carry on with their lives" (Robben 2004:200–204). The fact that the guerilla groups acted largely at the margins of an overwhelmingly unresponsive Argentine society may explain why by 1976 they had already been routed by the military.

Although by 1976 guerilla groups posed no threat to the military, it mattered little. Like cancerous cells that quietly multiply and make their way through the human body until it is too late, the specter of "subversives" and "subversive" ideas spreading through Argentine society was a haunting threat that could not be easily ignored. Small wonder that those in the military, as former naval officer Scilingo related years later in an interview, viewed themselves as "saviors of the fatherland" (quoted in Verbitsky 1996:9). The missionary— almost fanatical—zeal with which the military went about exterminating perceived enemies of the fatherland (*patria*) is captured in a chilling 1976 statement by the military governor of the province of Buenos Aires:

> First we will kill all the subversives; then we will kill their collaborators;
> then . . . their sympathizers, then . . . those who remain indifferent; and finally
> we will kill the timid. (quoted in Robben 2004:204)

In 1983, shortly after the return to democratic rule, the government formed a commission to investigate the disappearances that had taken place under military rule. The commission's report—*Nunca Más* (Never Again)—documented the disappearance of at least nine thousand men, women, and children, although some have suggested that between fifteen and thirty thousand could have been disappeared (Suárez-Orozco 2004:380). These numbers do not include the many thousands who died and whose bodies were recovered and accounted for. Even for a country long accustomed to military regimes, the mass, systematic disappearance and torture of tens of thousands, and the intensity of silence that was imposed through outright fear, was a watershed, unparalleled episode in Argentine history. Fear and silence were so pervasive during those years that most in Argentina who experienced this tragedy firsthand (including this author) would only years later fully realize the full scope of the atrocities that had taken place. Widespread terror had ramifying cultural effects, even generating a distinctive lexicon of terror (Feitlowitz 1998).

It was in this period characterized by extreme fear and anxiety that some women in the mid-1970s mustered the courage to publicly demand news of the whereabouts of their loved ones. Robben (2005:131) reminds us that "the military had had a head start in the politics of memory by obliterating the bodies of the assassinated disappeared, thus attempting to confine the traces of their repression purely to the discursive domain." Nevertheless, the **Mothers of the Plaza de Mayo** represent and have represented the most important and highly charged symbolic rallying point around which the memories of the desaparecidos have been kept alive. Coupled with the final report of Argentina's truth commission and a subsequently nationally televised documentary based on *Nunca Más,* the Mothers were instrumental in paving the way for the 1985 trials of former junta members. A series of military mutinies after 1985 revealed, though, the continuing importance of the military, a point that was not lost on former president Menem, who "pardoned 277 military officers and former guerrillas in October 1989, and in December 1990 decreed a pardon for the incarcerated military commanders as a final turning of the page in pursuit of national reconciliation" (Robben 2005:141).

Monuments have of course been erected in Argentina—as in other countries and repressive contexts analyzed in this chapter—to remember and honor the dead (Jelin 1997:26–28). Yet, nothing rivals the symbolic and emotional impact and legacy of chanting mothers (many of whom are by now grandmothers, joined by the children and grandchildren of the disappeared) circling the Plaza de Mayo with placards and photographs in direct view of buildings that house the principal institutions of government and state power (see Photo 12.3). Their emotionally gripping and heart-breaking stories, widely circulated

PHOTO 12.3 *Demonstration by Mothers of the Plaza de Mayo in Buenos Aires, Argentina.*

IN THEIR OWN WORDS   1 2 . 3

Madres de la Plaza de Mayo Remember

The following are two examples of mothers narrating the abduction and disappearance of their loved ones, and how they strive to keep their memories alive:

> Leticia . . . had finished high school a few months before they took her away . . . She was very decisive . . . [and] . . . did not agree to stop her activities in the union in spite of the times in which we were living; she considered it to be a just cause . . . Does teaching one's children love for others, justice, and freedom deserve this reward? Wasn't this the practice of the purest beliefs of Christianity, Judaism, and Humanism? . . . Leticia . . . was going with her fellow students to a union meeting at one of the girl's houses; she did not get there . . . Nine years later, I learnt that they had killed her together with two other kids, 17 and 18 years old, students at

the National High School of Buenos Aires. (Mellibovsky 1997:8–10)

> My daughter . . . Mónica lived with us and her brothers in an apartment downtown . . . They took her from . . . our own home, with all of us present. An armed forces team came . . . at five o'clock in the morning . . . [Mónica] undertook missionary work with all her heart. But her major giving of herself was at the Bajo Flores shantytown . . . She simply loved the villagers . . . understood them . . . and felt them to be her equals. And she devoted herself to the children because she loved justice above any personal interest . . . That's why . . . they took her away . . . The only thing that gives me some consolation is to repeat the Gospel's phrase: "Happy be they who are hungry and thirst for justice, for they shall be satisfied." (Mellibovsky 1997: 103–104)

---

in publications and other media—and, more recently, through the Mothers' Web site—have also kept alive the memories of the disappeared (see In Their Own Words 12.3).

Colombia's Violencia

For decades, Colombia has been engulfed in a protracted, seemingly never-ending conflict that has left tens of thousands dead, and millions displaced from their homes. The systemic, pervasive, unrelenting violence is grimly represented by murder rates that, depending on the source one consults, can easily fluctuate between seven and fifty times that of the United States or western Europe (Jimeno 2001:225; Taussig 2003:87–88). If a state is a political entity with a sufficient degree of legitimacy and organizational capability to successfully negotiate competing claims from different social classes, as well as establish effective rule over a national territory, then the Colombian state is fragile indeed. Its lack of hegemony explains why it has been unable to grapple with the historical and structural conditions underpinning mass violence, establish a monopoly over the use of lethal force, protect its citizens from wanton violence, and acquire legitimacy. The result is a "war system" (Richani 2003:11) or "war machine" (Taussig 2003:23) in which the Colombian state, the police and armed forces, leftist guerillas, paramilitaries, drug trafficking cartels, and criminal street gangs are locked in a struggle that, at present, cannot be won by any one sector.

The two major leftist guerilla organizations are the Fuerzas Armadas Revolucionarias de Colombia (FARC) and the Ejército de Liberación Nacional (ELN), both founded in the 1960s. Between 1985 and 1995 FARC (the main guerilla group) expanded its operations in many Colombian municipalities. In areas they solidly control, guerillas, as do paramilitaries, levy *vacunas* (literally "vaccinations"), that is, protection money. Although it is a predominantly rural movement, FARC has established a foothold in some urban shantytowns where residents "are either first-generation recent migrants from rural areas or their children" (Richani 2003:28–79). FARC's attempt at participating in legal electoral politics in 1985 proved disastrous when thousands of its members were assassinated (Taussig 2003:133). The current stalemate between FARC and the Colombian state was aptly demonstrated when the latter ceded control to FARC of more than forty thousand square kilometers of national territory (Richani 2003:90–91).

Paramilitary organizations representing elite interests were officially sanctioned in 1965 and 1968 when civil defense organizations were legalized to combat leftist insurgents. In 1987, Colombia's defense minister (an army general) said that these organizations were "legitimate" for the "defense of property and lives" (Richani 2003:104). A "clandestine wing of the army and police" (Taussig 2003:xii), paramilitaries (*paras*) are hired by large-scale cattle ranchers and landowners to protect them against guerillas and fight against peasants; by drug traffickers to fight off guerillas and the Colombian army; and by multinational corporations to protect them against guerillas and as a way of forcing peasants off their land, especially where oil and mining are significant. Union leaders are favorite targets of paramilitaries. Taussig notes that different kinds of paramilitaries

> grow out of local circumstances and are not necessarily formalized. There is the local merchant . . . who decides to go on a killing spree at night along with his drunk buddies in the pickup of SUV—the favored vehicle of death squads in the Americas—so as to take out a few transvestis downtown, some rateros in the barrio, or the glue-sniffing kids huddled under the bridge. There are also the goon squads assembled by large landowners, and all manner of local self-defense organizations, formed against the guerilla many years, even decades, ago. Some of these are officially recognized by the government as legitimate . . . "Private security forces" now abound in Colombia, employing far more people than the national police and army combined. A strange hybrid, paramilitarization drifts into an obscure no-man's-land between the state and civil society. (2003:10)

Paramilitaries have a great deal of national-level political clout. They control large segments of three Colombian states and, recently, have been acquiring huge tracts of the country's best agricultural lands through a combination of intimidation and money payments. Further, a substantial number—perhaps 30 percent—of Colombia's Congressional legislators support the paramilitaries, one of whose top commanders delivered a speech to the Colombian Congress after flying into Bogotá's military airport (Forero 2004b, 2004c). In another poignant example of the paramilitaries' power—and of the inability of the Colombian state to exercise political hegemony—the government has passed, with strong U.S. backing, a "Justice and Peace Law." The law's main objective is to entice paramilitary organizations to disarm and surrender the territories they now control, and a key provision is that paramilitary leaders will be legally immune to serious legal charges, such as murder. Further, leaders of paramilitary organizations—which control the largest share of cocaine flowing into the United States—will be shielded from extradition to the United States on drug trafficking charges (Forero and Trujillo 2005). The *New York Times* (2005) has suggested that Colombia's Justice and Peace Law should perhaps be renamed "Impunity of Mass Murderers, Terrorists and Major Cocaine Traffickers Law." Drug traffickers and trafficking organizations—the main targets of the U.S. "war on drugs"—are also responsible for a great deal of Colombia's violence, which is particularly acute in cities such as Cali and Medellín. The emergence of youth criminal gangs has been one of the most insidious consequences of drug trafficking (Ceballos Melguizo 2001).

In Colombia's "reign of warlords," most citizens feel unable to control events leading up to violent acts, and "understand authority as being an unpredictable, menacing entity, as being arbitrary authority" (Jimeno 2001:221–222). Pervasive violence accompanied by an equally omnipresent lack of legitimacy leads to a situation where competing claims of truth—what precisely occurred, when, why, and by whom—is up for grabs, for "as soon as such a thing [massacre or kidnapping] has happened, many versions can be found. The institutional version is not received as being the truth; it is seen as just one among many and has little credibility" (Jimeno 2001:228). Although Colombians of all backgrounds have suffered from violence, it is the poor, common folk who suffer the most from and are often caught in the middle of the worst atrocities—what some Colombians call being in a "sandwich" (Taussig 2003:93; Jimeno 2001:232).

In 2001, Taussig spent two weeks in a town "taken over by paramilitaries imposing law and order through selective assassinations—what Colombians call a **limpieza** [social cleansing]" (2003:xi). Leftist guerillas, as Taussig and others have noted, also carry out limpiezas. In this town, and elsewhere in Colombia, generalized fear and competing versions of reality have led to a culture of fear and terror in which

> nobody seems to have a clear idea of who they [paramilitaries] are, what they are, or what they want. Nobody knows what to do. People here are much too scared to confront them, organize against them, or join them. What's more, they . . . disappear and appear at will within the town itself, like phantoms. (Taussig 2003:21–22; see also Margold 1999)

One of Taussig's arguments is that despite the violence and fear inflicted on this town and its people, paramilitaries (also called *paras, pistoleros* [gunmen] or *autodefensas* [self-defense groups]) in fact appear to enjoy substantial support and legitimacy, given the "chaos, mayhem and murders" that are part and parcel of daily life (Taussig 2003:15). That is, it is the basic lack of security and predictability—which the Colombian state is unable to provide—that underlies the sympathy (if not support and legitimacy) that the paras seemingly enjoy. This support may explain why the Autodefensas Unidas de Colombia (United Self-Defense Groups of Colombia), the largest paramilitary organization, has it own Web site and why the autobiography written by its founder has been reprinted several times. Both paramilitaries and guerillas invoke similar rationales for their existence—the inability of the Colombian state to provide security. Taussig returned seventeen months later to the town he had briefly visited in 2001 and notes that

> The paras were killing two to three "delinquents" a week. Some people suspect many murders are actually carried out by the army's intelligence service as well. However, most assassinations are done *en frente*—openly in public view—while the police and army kill you from behind, *a espaldas,* and out of town. Nobody dares to protest. At the most, people just whisper to one another at the funerals for the victims. Vandalism has disappeared; there is no breaking of windows or smashing of signs, the kids who make a living pushing carts to and from the market no longer fight among themselves, and there are no disputes in the streets . . . the paras have subcontracted some of their security operations to gang members who have joined them. The central plaza was full of smart new yellow taxis with two-way radios. The drivers make two to three trips a day to the Cali airport for businessmen and engineers traveling to the new factories in the tax-free industrial park . . . [Townspeople] . . . now sometimes [leave] the front door open during the day, something I have never once seen in thirty years. The *limpieza* is over. The *limpieza* was a success. (2003:188–189)

Mexico's Zapatistas

On January 1, 1994, an armed rebellion broke out in Chiapas, one of the most heavily indigenous (and Maya) regions of southeastern Mexico. Emerging from the eastern lowland Lancandón forest, insurgents of the Ejército Zapatista de Liberación Nacional (EZLN, popularly known as Zapatistas, named after Emiliano Zapata, a popular leader of the Mexican Revolution; see Stephen 2002) seized several towns, including the Chiapas state capital of San Cristóbal de Las Casas, and attacked a nearby army garrison. In the ensuing two weeks, Chiapas was an open battleground as thousands of Mexican soldiers fought pitched battles to recapture Chiapas, while rebels retreated into the Lancandón forest. In the most intense mobilization of the Mexican army in recent memory, seventy thousand troops had encircled Chiapas by 1997, but not before the Zapatistas had wrested from the Mexican government, in 1996, a large measure of autonomy over dozens of municipalities.

The Zapatista uprising has been a watershed event in Mexican and Latin American politics for several reasons. It reveals the skillful use of politics and political maneuvering by Zapatistas to take advantage of global political–economic conditions to further their cause and almost literally force the Mexican state to the negotiating table. Second, the uprising has demonstrated the Zapatistas' ability to convey their message to a wide public audience, and work with and gain widespread support from broad segments of the Mexican population, including many indigenous peoples. Third, the Zapatistas have demonstrated a deft capacity to harness modern media and communications—through, for example, radio and its Web site—to attract the worldwide attention of international human rights organizations and NGOs, as well as indigenous organizations outside of Mexico. As a result, the Zapatista movement is important for understanding how contemporary economic and cultural globalization can simultaneously undermine indigenous communities *and* spur the emergence and coalescence of politically significant social movements.

By the 1990s, a number of conditions had paved the road for the Zapatista rebellion. Chiapas was not only one of the poorest and most backward of Mexico's states, but had "remained a conservative state controlled by its landowning oligarchy, which had survived the Mexican revolution" (Maybury-Lewis 2002 [1997]:15). And, analogous to what occurred in other countries analyzed in this chapter, Catholic clergy and lay workers had been in Chiapas for decades preaching the message of liberation theology and organizing activist-based Christian communities (Nash 2001:164–168). Further, Chiapas' Mayan speaking peoples had been working in lowland plantations since the 1920s and colonizing the eastern Lancandón forest in greater numbers since the 1970s. By the 1980s, more than 40 percent of highland Mayas in some communities were without access to land. Political and religious persecution also drove many highland Maya peoples into the Lancandón. The Lancandón ethnic group itself did not participate in the rebellion (anonymous reviewer).

In the Lancandón itself, most of the land had historically been concentrated in the hands of large-scale cattle ranchers and plantation owners, where there are also rich oil and timber reserves. Further, neoliberal economic reforms during the Salinas presidency threatened to further undermine indigenous livelihoods and thwart hopes for a better future. Some of these included the lifting of subsidies for small-scale cultivators and reduction of credit and technical assistance programs for small-scale peasant cultivators. Even more menacing was the controversial 1992 law privatizing communal lands (*ejidos*), one of the most distinctive legacies of the Mexican Revolution. Although this law endangered the integrity of many indigenous communities throughout Mexico, in the Lancandón area it quickly "dashed the hopes of the colonizers for gaining title to the lands they had cleared and cultivated for the past twenty-five years" (Nash 1995:179; Rus and Collier 2003:36–51, 2001:124; Cancian and Brown 1998). As Maybury-Lewis states, the economic and social policies of the Salinas administration "threatened to replicate, one century later, what happened after the reform laws under President Porfirio Díaz. At that time, indigenous communities were broken up and many Indians were forced into the rural proletariat while the large estates grew bigger and the great landlords prospered" (2002 [1997]:17). The Zapatista revolt also coincided with the implementation of the North American Free Trade Agreement (see Chapter 10 for more details), pointing to an important undercurrent of opposition to trade policies that are a distinctive hallmark of contemporary economic globalization.

Although the Zapatistas' charismatic, masked leader subcomandante Marcos may not be of indigenous background, the Zapatistas represent an indigenous grassroots movement rooted in Maya culture (Maybury-Lewis 2002 [1997]:16). Their communiqués, for example, reflect a poetic use of the Mayan language, such as in "repeated references to what the heart says reflect a belief that true language (known in Maya as *batzil k'op*) issues from the heart" (Nash 1995:178). Some Maya consider Marcos to be "'*Rey Cha'uk*,' or King of Lightning, a term applied to outstanding curer-diviners who had powerful *nahwales* or animal spirits" (Nash 2001:129). The EZLN has also garnered considerable support from women, who constitute almost half of its membership. Indeed, it was a high-ranking female EZLN leader who led the initial assault on San Cristóbal de Las Casas (Nash 2001:180; Kampwirth 2002:83).

The Zapatistas have been adept at forging alliances with multiple civil society groups and NGOs. There was an enormous swelling of support across Mexico, such as large scale demonstrations and hunger strikes in Mexico City's *zócalo* (main square). Chiapas' Catholic bishop also took an active role in pressing the government for a negotiated settlement (Nash 1995; 2001:122–131). The mass and visible presence of a wide spectrum of national and international NGOs and civil society groups "may have made the difference between the Mexican's army's low-intensity warfare and the Guatemalan war of extermination in the 1980s" (Nash 2001:139). A good example of the Zapatistas' attempt to mobilize national and public opinion to their side through the use of modern communications happened in 1995 when they "called upon 'the citizens of Mexico and the world' to participate in a plebiscite concerning the new relation between indigenous people and the state . . . The plebiscite was . . . enacted by email, fax, and plebiscite tables within Mexico" (Nash 2001:145).

The Zapatistas have also been clever at timing their political activities to draw a great deal of attention. For example, they sponsored a "National Democratic Convention" in San Cristóbal de Las Casas two weeks before the 1994 national presidential elections, which "drew over 6000 representatives of the press, intellectuals, along with indigenous as well as leaders of grassroots movements throughout the Hemisphere" and the 1995 International Day of Women in San Cristóbal de Las Casas within easy sight of the Mexican military (Nash 1995:184–185). And in a stunning public relations display and show of political strength widely publicized on Mexican television, twenty-three masked Zapatista commanders walked from Chiapas to Mexico City in March 2001, their safety guaranteed by President Fox. Their leader, comandante Esther, a Maya woman, spoke for two hours before Mexico's National Congress demanding constitutional changes that would benefit indigenous peoples. Yet, several months later, only some watered-down versions of the Zapatista demands were ratified by Mexico's Congress, resulting in a continuing standoff between the Mexican state and the Zapatistas (Thompson 2001; Thompson and Weiner 2001; Patterson 2001). More importantly, the Mexican Congress and most state legislatures approved constitutional changes that rolled back the autonomy of EZLN controlled areas and communities (Stahler-Sholk 1995).

The 1996 San Andrés peace accords included greater control over Chiapas' natural resources, the power to pass laws independent of the Mexican state, a redistribution of land, and educational reforms, including the teaching of indigenous history and the inclusion of local languages in the school curriculum (Nash 2001:123–154). Despite the 1996 peace agreement, the Zapatista uprising has unfortunately led to the emergence in the Chiapas highlands and the Lancandón of paramilitary groups under the direction of local political and economic elites, and deepening political and religious divisiveness and conflicts between Catholics and Protestants. In 1997, forty-five Christian catechists (thirty-six of them women and children) were massacred in the small highland hamlet of Acteal; their killers were indigenous people from the same municipality (Nash 2001:184–197; Rus and Collier 2003:54). Hernández Castillo (2003) provides other examples of the growing divisiveness and "militarization" of the Chiapas highlands.

The stalemate in Chiapas is political and not military, for the Mexican state surely has the firepower to overwhelm the Zapatistas. But in fact it has been unwilling to do so, and this reluctance stems from broader political–economic concerns. The financial consequences of a politically unstable Mexico no doubt played a part in the decision by then-President Zedillo to resolve the conflict peacefully. One month after the Zapatistas emerged onto the political front stage, the Mexican stock market took a plunge and billions of dollars flowed out of the country. The widely publicized assassination of Luis Colosio during the 1994 electoral campaign—the presidential candidate of the Partido Revolucionario Institucional (PRI) which, until Fox's election, had dominated Mexico since the Mexican Revolution—also contributed to a sense of growing political instability (Nash 1995:172–173). In a 2001 speech, President Fox stated that "Peace . . . is the only starting point for our country to pay this enormous debt we have to 10 million indigenous who live in extreme poverty" (quoted in Patterson 2001). Significantly, he delivered this speech to members of Mexico's Chamber of Transport and Tourism.

Peru's Shining Path

On the eve of the 1980 general elections—the first after seventeen years of military rule—masked individuals belonging to what later would be known as Sendero Luminoso (Shining Path; henceforth SL) burned ballots in Chuschi, a small town in the indigenous southern highlands region of Ayacucho. This seemingly innocuous act hardly captured the attention or imagination of most Peruvians, least of all those in Lima, Peru's capital. Yet, a decade later, Lima itself was besieged by SL, which had evolved into a powerful movement setting off the bloodiest armed conflict in recent Peruvian history. This brutal war—so terrifying that it is widely remembered in the southern highlands as *manchay tiempo* (time of fear, Quechua; Manrique 1990–1991:38)—claimed the lives of almost seventy thousand Peruvians and turned hundreds of thousands into refugees (Forero 2003a).

For fifteen years, SL had been organizing in the southern highlands, where for decades cultural anthropologists had been carrying out detailed fieldwork. Yet, it appears that SL's emergence took them by surprise and they were unable to predict—as most others were also not able to do—that "self-styled revolutionaries from an extremely impoverished and largely Indian highland region could effectively spread a ruthless war through much of the national territory, sustain it into the 1990s, then provoke a sense of imminent government and social collapse in Lima by 1992" (Stern 1998a:2).

That cultural anthropologists were unable to anticipate the rise of SL despite their intimate knowledge of Andean communities in this region raises the issue of theory and method on the ethnographic "gaze," or what anthropologists "see" on the ground. Starn believes that anthropologists' inability to anticipate the rise and spread of SL had to do with a prevailing theoretical lens that he has called **Andeanism,** which encouraged viewing Andean peoples' life ways as largely nonmodern, frozen in time, and largely detached from the wider Peruvian reality and its contradictions and conflicts (1991, 1994; Said 1979). This essentialized focus discouraged an emphasis on politics and political conflicts, resulting in fieldwork and an ethnographic focus privileging stability rather than change, cooperation instead of conflict, continuity in place of rupture, and downplaying broader contexts of change.

The historical background is important for understanding how and why SL emerged, because since the Conquest, the southern Peruvian highlands has been the most backward and poorest region of Peru, with the majority of its Quechua- and Aymara-speaking peoples dominated politically and economically by a small number of "White" and Mestizo Peruvians. The tumultuous decades of the 1960s and 1970s witnessed massive agrarian reform, large-scale land invasions of hacienda lands, the flowering of regional peasant and labor organizations and activism, and the rise of the first guerilla groups inspired by the Cuban revolution. By the 1980s, rampant inflation and free market policies had led to widespread poverty, which many Peruvians responded to by participating in nationwide general strikes (Smith 1989; Degregori 1990–1991:12).

The blossoming of left-wing political and academic activism was also important. Universities became centers of reflection, critical thinking, and writing on the poverty and inequality in Peru and Latin America, as well as foci of political activism (Stern 1993). These events coincided with the 1959 opening of the San Cristóbal de Huamanga University in Ayacucho. It is precisely from the ranks of university professors and students that SL's leadership emerged (Isbell 1992:79). SL's leader Abimael Guzmán—the "fourth sword of Marxism" after Marx, Lenin, and Mao (Degregori 1990–1991:11)—was a professor of philosophy at Huamanga, and SL rank-and-file followers were mainly provincial Mestizo youths of peasant origins. (SL received considerable support from women, an issue discussed at the end of this section.) SL's aim was the complete destruction of Peruvian society, and the only way to achieve this goal was to wage war mercilessly. SL "rejected the primacy of politics in favor of the primacy of violence; violence is the essence of revolution; war is it principal task" (Degregori 1990–1991:11). Its scope of action centered in the southern highlands, mainly in Ayacucho, the northeast Mantaro valley that supplied foodstuffs and other goods to Lima, and the eastern lowland coca producing zones, from which it received funds and arms from drug traffickers.

SL was never a peasant army, although it did initially center war efforts in the countryside, especially in Ayacucho. SL garnered support from indigenous communities by pursuing strategies that resonated culturally in many villages. Although SL's brutal violence may have also alienated many, the savage repression that the southern highlands experienced from the armed forces "deflected wrath and discouraged open rupture with Sendero" (Stern 1988b:121–123), at least during the early years of the conflict.

One of SL's early strategies was to focus on local elites: by intimidating and assassinating merchants, landowners, political officials, and policemen in public "popular trials," SL targeted and underscored the vulnerability of those representatives of the social order responsible for the marginality and poverty of Andean peasants. The symbolic effect was unmistakable, for "by shaking to its underpinnings the supposed eternal stability of traditional highland society, Sendero overturn[ed] the long-internalized conviction that the [elites] are fundamentally superior beings" (Manrique 1990–1991:36). Another strategy was to forcibly redistribute resources, as when in Chuschi SL slaughtered and redistributed sheep from neighboring communities. "Moralization" campaigns, in which, for example, thieves and cattle rustlers were publicly executed, were also popular in many communities. SL strategists were also particularly adept at taking sides in and capitalizing on long-standing animosities between neighboring villages (Isbell 1992).

With time, peasant support for SL waned. One reason had to do with SL's strategy of attacking deeply entrenched Andean cultural institutions in an attempt to forge a "new" society free of the vestiges of the (capitalist) past. For example, efforts at abolishing fiestas (and the heavy drinking that normally took place during these celebrations) as well as community civil and religious hierarchies were met with considerable resistance. Andean peasants also fiercely resisted SL attempts at closing marketplaces and enforcing a strict subsistence strategy (the idea here was to sever peasant ties with the wider capitalist economy), for many of the goods they required on a daily basis were obtained through market exchanges. Many village-level popular celebrations such as *"Vida Michy,* the adolescent competitive games accompanied by song duels, riddle games, dancing and drinking" (Isbell 1992:85) were staunchly defended. SL efforts to bolster its political control by undermining village political autonomy—an important stalwart of Andean community life—were also resisted.

Other factors contributed to the eventual waning of peasant support, such as the very real possibility of being attacked by either SL or the army: the armed forces viewed as *terrucos* (terrorists) villagers intimidated into tolerating SL presence, or providing it with goods and supplies. The armed forces then unleashed against these villagers ferocious repression. SL mistakenly assumed that Peruvian soldiers would not fire on highland peasants, but most troops deployed in the southern highlands were from coastal and eastern jungle areas, and they displayed deep prejudices against Quechua- and Aymara-speaking villagers. Many villages that agreed to organize self-defense committees (*montoneras* or *rondas campesinas*)—and thus convince the army that they were not harboring terrucos—were in turn attacked by SL. Caught in the middle between SL and the army, hundreds of villages were destroyed or abandoned (Manrique 1990–1991:32–36; Starn 1999).

SL's atrocities—its "glorification of violent suffering" (Stern 1988b:123)—both backfired and were interpreted through an Andean cultural lens. In some communities, SL members were viewed as a "new form of *ñaqa,* the supernatural being that robs body fat" and in "many versions of Sendero's atrocities, [SL] was equated with a ñaqa who cuts the flesh of victims to feed the Sendero armies" (Isbell 1992:92). As one villager explained:

> We are more afraid of Sendero than we are of the army or of the police. Let me tell you something that happened. I have a friend who is a health worker . . . In a meeting of the five communities . . . which he attended, they told about one thousand Sendero militants who entered the region and killed the young and old. They carried off flesh; that is to say, they cut off the flesh with knives and carried it off in sacks. They left behind only bones and skeletons." (Isbell 1992:93)

This interpretation of savage, beastly beings who illegitimately appropriate fat runs deep in Andean culture. During the "Great Rebellions" of 1780–1782—which almost succeeded in toppling the Spanish colonial order in Bolivia and Peru (see Chapter 4)—Andean "insurrectionaries placed the Spaniards in the Andean category of *ñak'aq,* a Quechua term for humanoid beings considered criminal, beastly, and demonic. The human status of such beings was ambiguous, for they stood apart from normal humanity . . . [for their] . . . well-being was predicated on destroying human life" (Stern 1987b:145).

In the early 1990s, SL took its war to Peru's capital, home to one-third of all Peruvians. There, control of and support from shantytowns was crucial in its strategy to seize power, for, according to an SL document, "Lima and the surrounding shantytowns are the scenario in which the final battle of the popular war will be defined" (Burt 1998:267). Because of its strategic location near the Pan American highway, its enormous size (more than 250,000 inhabitants) and its history of left-wing political organizing, SL's offensive early on targeted the shantytown of Villa El Salvador. SL was in fact able to initially gain a foothold in Villa El Salvador. Working on its behalf were the devastating effects of free market policies that reduced the purchasing power of citizens almost 80 percent between 1986 and 1991, and doubled the number of Peruvians living in extreme poverty. The April 1992 self-coup (*autogolpe*) of then-president Alberto Fujimori who, with the backing of the armed forces, assumed dictatorial powers, also played into the hands of SL by deepening the distrust of the state by shantytown dwellers and highlighting its repressive nature. A few days later, SL began its assault on Lima (Burt 1998:268–294).

SL employed strategies similar to those it had followed in the highlands. It took advantage of the fact that most shantytown dwellers viewed the state as intrinsically illegitimate, corrupt, and unable or unwilling to meet their needs (such as providing basic services and security). The fear and loathing shantytown residents had of the military and police further delegitimized the state. SL also capitalized on conflicts and ideological divisions within left-leaning political organizations (some of which expressed ambiguity toward SL's violent methods), who confronted the dilemma of how to oppose SL without allying themselves with the Peruvian state, police, and military, whom they considered the real enemies. SL's "moralizing" campaigns—selective assassinations of thieves, drug addicts and dealers, and the like—garnered much sympathy. SL also took an active part in popular struggles at the local level—land invasions, land reclamations, acquisition of land titles, provision of local services—which enabled it to gain legitimacy. Further, SL played popular organizations against each other, undermining the possibility of an early united front against it. And, as in the highlands, SL relied on selective (but highly visible) assassinations of popular leaders to instill terror and forestall open opposition. In a particularly gruesome example of this strategy, SL targeted María Elena Moyano, vice-mayor of Villa El Salvador, head of the most important woman's organization, and a leading advocate of peace. She paid the consequences of leading a demonstration against SL and, with white flags, calling for peace. On the following day she was assassinated and her body blown up with dynamite in front of her children (Burt 1998:272–291).

Learning about María Elena Moyano's assassination is important not only because it highlights the risks that women faced if they opposed SL, but also because in a context of all-out war where most men—fathers, husbands, lovers, and sons—were either fighting, dead, imprisoned, or in hiding, it was women who bore the burden of caring for children, protecting the lives of surviving family members, and providing for their households. As a result, they played a crucial role in organizing local and regional women's clubs for mutual support and as a visible platform for mobilizing public opinion and support for peace. For example, by 1995, the Federation of Mothers' Clubs in Ayacucho had one thousand four hundred clubs, and women organized the first nationwide march for peace in 1988 (Cordero 1998:359–360).

SL received considerable support from, and many of its senior and field commanders were women (Andreas 1990–1991; Tarazona-Sevillano 1992; Cordero 1998). According to Andreas (1990–1991:22–23) SL's quest to destroy all political and social institutions also meant the destruction of male–dominated institutions; that its emphasis on protecting the subsistence economy resonated well with women because of their crucial role in the house-hold economy and because they headed over one-third of all Peruvian households; and that SL's resolve of doing away with male rape, abuses, and adultery, as well as severely punishing men who abandoned their wives and children, conveyed a liberating message to women. Cordero (1998) provides a slightly different argument, claiming that although true that SL's ideology appealed to many women because it promised to unshackle them from male-dominated institutions, in practice SL itself was patriarchal. Although SL recruited large numbers of women, and many were among the top leaders and field com-manders, most were involved in logistical and support tasks resembling "domestic" chores or tasks. Further, SL never really attempted to seriously question prevailing gender expecta-tions and roles. Ideologically, gender interests were subordinated to the larger interests of the revolution.

SL's leader Guzmán was captured in Lima in September 1992. His conviction by a secret military tribunal was later declared unconstitutional, and he is currently being tried in a civilian court. Guzmán's capture was one of several factors that greatly diminished SL's ability to wage war on a sustained basis. By this time, its support in the highlands had thinned and, despite—or perhaps because of—its terror tactics, most shantytown dwellers mustered the courage to openly oppose it. Another important factor was that shortly after his arrest, Guzmán called for peace talks, an offer that was accepted by only some of his followers, effectively splitting the SL. Alas, this tale is still not over. A decade after its supreme leader was captured, SL continues to mount attacks, although on a vastly reduced scale. And, in an ominous sign, SL has reappeared in Lima, most notably in critical shanty-towns such as Villa El Salvador, carrying out selective assassinations and bombings (Burt 1998:295; Chauvin 2002; Forero 2003b, 2004a).

Controversies: Rigoberta Menchú, and the Politics of Memory and Culture

In 1982, Rigoberta Menchú, a twenty-three-year-old Maya woman, related a tape-recorded tale of the Guatemalan conflict in Paris to Elizabeth Burgos, a Latin American anthropolo-gist and writer—an account that included details of the deaths of several family members. The English translation, published in 1984 with the title *I, Rigoberta Menchú: An Indian Woman in Guatemala* (Menchú 1984), immediately became a sensation in- and outside of Guatemala. For the first time, North Americans could read an intimate, extraordinarily mov-ing and, because it was narrated by a native Guatemalan Maya, seemingly authoritative, eye-witness account of the terror taking place in Guatemala. (Spanish-speakers had an edge, because Menchú's story had been published in Cuba a year earlier.) Menchú's narrative became a landmark work in Latin American studies and testimonial (*testimonio*) literature (Beverley 2004), won her immediate and lasting acclaim, and her book has been published into several languages.

Based on fieldwork in Guatemala and a close re-reading and corroboration of Menchú's narrative, fourteen years later anthropologist David Stoll published *Rigoberta Menchú and the Story of All Poor Guatemalans* (1999a), a stinging critique of Menchú's story. Aware of the controversy that might surround his book—but perhaps not anticipating such an outcry—Stoll began telling readers why he wrote his text by asking: "What if much of Rigoberta's story is not true?" (1999a:viii). One starting point for writing his book is in fact to question of the accuracy and truthfulness of details of Menchú's account. In any case, he does still acknowledge that Menchú's narrative "is fundamentally right about what the army did" and that "her story expresses a larger truth" (Stoll 1999a:ix). Stoll's claims have been succinctly summarized by Rus (1999:6):

> Contrary to what Rigoberta has claimed, her father had been not a traditional villager who had lost his fields to predatory landlords but a progressive and fairly well-off man whose land fights had mostly been with his in-laws; that her immediate family had not been forced by poverty to become migrant workers on Guatemala's coastal plantations, where one of her brothers died of malnutrition, but had managed to make a living in the highlands, where her supposed deceased brother still lived; that she herself had not been monolingual in K'iche and unlettered until she joined the revolutionary movement but had finished her secondary education in a Catholic boarding school; and, finally, that when she and her family joined the revolutionary movement at the beginning of the 1980s, it appears to have been not so much because that was the next logical step from having been leaders of local struggles for peasant rights as because they had been swept up in a factional fight within their village to which the army had overreacted. In short, Rigoberta's testimony of deprivation, racial discrimination, and repression, eventually leading to redemption through the act of taking up arms against her people's oppressors, appeared to have been at least partly fictionalized. The most renowned modern document of Native Americans' resistance to conquest and disappearance seemed not to be true.

Stoll stated that he wrote his book to question three widespread misconceptions to which he believes *I, Rigoberta Menchú* contributed:

1. That most Mayas voluntarily supported the guerillas. Stoll says that those who apparently did were forced to do so because the guerillas placed them in a situation that would justify massive retaliation by the army, a point that some scholars believe has some merit.

2. That it is a mistake to solely blame the Guatemalan army for its indiscriminate massacres of Maya peasants. Stoll says that the guerrillas should not be romanticized or mythologized, because they consciously lured peasants into situations knowing that they would be slaughtered by the army, did so to further their own political agendas, and hence bear much of the responsibility for the deaths of thousands of Maya peasants. Some scholars also agree with Stoll on this point.

3. That accounts by native voices (such as by Rigoberta Menchú) are more authoritative or credible than those of non-native interpreters (e.g., anthropologists). A related goal is to critique academic trends that, according to Stoll, do not seriously grapple with issues of veracity or stress enough the empirical gathering of facts.

The ongoing Stoll–Menchú debate is certainly one of the most acrimonious academic disputes to have surfaced in recent years—nor will it wither away anytime in the near future. This is not only because many believe, correctly or incorrectly, that Stoll has unjustly attacked Menchú (a revered icon) for perhaps unknown, ulterior motives, but also because this debate and Stoll's book lies squarely within five other broader, contentious, and overlapping academic firestorms about the politics of culture and the production of knowledge (Hale 1997; Gossen 1999; Smith, C. A. 1999; Arias 2001; Beverley 2001, 2004; Lovell and Lutz 2001; Pratt 2001; Warren 2001).

1. Issues of **representational authority.** The issue is whether anthropologists or other scholars can assign to themselves the privileged role of speaking for "others" and on what grounds. "The argument between Menchú and Stoll," Beverley tells us, "is not so much about what really happened as it is about who has the authority to narrate" (2001:221). Some of Stoll's critics suggest that by attacking Menchú he undermines her ability to represent the needs and aspirations of many Guatemalans and Mayas, and thereby diverts attention away from other, serious lapses in his own evidence and interpretations (Hale 1997; Smith, C. A. 1999).

2. The pivotal role of **positionality.** The concern here is whether anthropologists or other scholars can avoid allowing their class, gender, or ethnic backgrounds to "filter" or interpret what they "see" or how they interpret what they think they "see" or "hear" in the course of their fieldwork. Many scholars, including those critical of Stoll's book, believe that they cannot, and that to therefore aspire to (much less achieve) scientifically "valid" or "bias-free" gathering and interpretations of "facts"—as Stoll claims is possible and that he himself has done—is illusory. For example, Carol Smith emphasizes that

> The "postmodern and/or postcolonial" move to add new voices to our experience is not an attempt to restrict the repertoire of perspectives but an attempt to expand it to include voices never before represented . . . [Further], . . . One reason we now emphasize the complexity of truth and the need to hear many voices rather than a single "objective" one is that the facts do not speak for themselves—they always have to be interpreted. (1999:25)

3. The thorny (and perhaps irresolvable) issue of whether there exist **single or multiple truths,** that is, whether single or multiple renderings or interpretations of a single "fact" are plausible or possible. Many scholars believe that because of positionality, multiple truths are possible—which does not necessarily mean that they are "wrong" or "untrue." As Beverley notes:

> There is no one universal standard for truth . . . [and] . . . claims about truth are contextual: they have to do with how people construct different understandings of the world and historical memory from the same set of facts in situations of gender, ethnic, and class inequality, exploitation, and repression. (2001:226)

4. The **political consequences of ethnographic work** or, more generally, the production of knowledge. Does a scathing critique of Rigoberta Menchú damage her ability to speak for, and mobilize public opinion on behalf of, Guatemala's Mayas? Might a book such as Stoll's be interpreted and used by Guatemalans who sided with the military to claim

that Menchú "lied," and what might this mean for the vast majority of Guatemala's Mayan-speaking people? This is precisely Menchú's point when she claims that those who "attack her" also "humiliate the victims" of the Guatemalan genocide (Menchú 2001). Many are concerned that

> inevitably, the exposé of an indigenous leader would be used by the right in its attempts to undercut the momentum for reforms, discredit congressional adversaries, and sideline indigenous issues in the peace process. (Warren 2001:210)

   5. The **interpretation of testimonies** such as *I, Rigoberta Menchú* and the role of veracity or "truth." Most scholars—including Stoll (1999b; Warren 2001:199)—agree that Menchú never intended her account to be a strict autobiography, although scholars have faulted her for never openly admitting this point. Her narrative is best understood, Stoll's critics argue, as a composite and collective rendering of the traumatic experiences and memory of a large number of Mayas during Guatemala's war, the product of a strategic literary move designed attract attention to the trauma of conflict. As an "epic narrative"—of which, as Gossen (1999) reminds us, there are many examples in Western culture—little is to be gained by questioning the veracity of certain details, as Stoll has done, for such an account is neither pure "fact" nor entirely "fiction" representing, as it does, "larger truths."

   Also, Menchú's account emerged from within, or at least had deep similarities with, a long tradition of native Mayan language texts and oral historical accounts, which include features such as

> (1) factual discrepancies or contradictions; (2) questions of authority and representation; (3) the purposeful act of simplifying, embellishing, improvising, and orchestrating what is being said in order to emphasize specific points and to downplay or conceal others, but not to alter the substance of what actually happened; and (4) political protest that is both conscious and overt, fueled by the need to speak out against injustice and repression in an attempt to have one's rights respected. (Lovell and Lutz 2001:172)

In the United States: Fleeing War and Reconstituting New Lives

The Central American civil wars led to a massive diaspora of peoples from El Salvador, Guatemala, and Nicaragua. Many fled to neighboring countries, such as Belize, Mexico, and, to a lesser extent, Costa Rica. Many others, such as Guatemalan Mayas, sought refuge in the United States and Canada. A million or more Guatemalans have emigrated to the United States and Canada, most of them Maya war refugees. In the United States, they are concentrated in California (especially in Los Angeles), Texas, and Florida, although many also live and work in Alabama, Colorado, North Carolina, Kansas, and other states (Loucky and Moors 2000:3–9). Heartbreaking as it is to leave family and friends behind, Lutz and Lovell (2000:33) remind us that migration has historically been a deeply entrenched Maya survival strategy.

The challenges Maya peoples face as they reconstitute their lives and those of their family members in the United States—as well as the opportunities presented to them—partly depend on where they live and work. Many moved to Los Angeles, which has one of the highest concentrations of Mayas in the United States. Similar to the experience of other immigrants, the Maya arrived in different stages. The earliest settled in the early 1970s (i.e., prior to the onset of the Guatemalan civil war), some first working as agricultural laborers in Mexico. The second stage came in the 1980s, at the height of the Guatemalan conflict. Mayas who arrived during this time were assisted in many ways by those who had arrived earlier. Lastly are the economic refugees, who have migrated to Los Angeles to improve their lives in light of the dismal economic conditions in Guatemala after the conclusion of the war (Loucky 2000:216).

Most Mayas live in crowded apartments in poor neighborhoods (barrios), with entire families sometimes sharing a single bedroom. Most work in the garment industry (*la costura*), often in low-paid sweatshops. Life in the United States is sometimes viewed as a struggle (*lucha*) and an ever-present worry is to become lost (*perdido*) in such an enormous city. Yet, what they have going for them is "a deep-seated strength associated with shared experiences of hardship and hard work as corollaries of life in highland Guatemala" (Loucky 2000:214–219).

Mayas adapt in Los Angeles by relying on deeply cohesive social networks. A recently arrived migrant will seek out family or kin who provide him/her with housing, help in getting around the city, and obtaining a job. Mayas—like many other immigrant groups—attach enormous importance to building and sustaining social relationships and networks through which resources (information on jobs or housing, the pooling of money to attract others from Guatemala, and so forth) flow. This in turn strengthens ethnic and community cohesiveness, which is also bolstered by a lending hand from institutions such as church congregations. Establishing mutual aid associations is important because these are crucial for surviving in a strange land, and also because they cut across linguistic and geographical places of origin (e.g., those speaking different Mayan languages or those from ethnically different communities in Guatemala). One of these mutual aid associations pools money for repatriation of the remains of those who have died in Los Angeles (Loucky 2000:220).

Guatemalan Maya immigrants in Los Angeles also organize themselves into quasi-religious groups or fraternities that are associated with the parishes they belonged to in Guatemala. These groups raise money for their former Guatemalan parishes and sponsor fiestas in honor of the patron saint of their home communities, as well as music and dance festivities, all of which serve to promote ethnic and community cohesion and ease the transition and adaptation to life in the United States (Wellmeir 1998).

Mayas have also settled in much smaller cities. Fink and Dunn (2000) explore Maya experiences and adaptations in Morgantown, South Carolina, as they labor in the poultry plants, one of the most rapidly expanding industries in the southern United States in which immigrant laborers (such as the Maya) have found a niche. As in Los Angeles, Mayas have forged strong community organizations. In Morgantown, these include pan-Hispanic/Latino soccer teams and a Maya mutual aid society, which as in Los Angeles, pays for funeral expenses in Guatemala for those who have died in Morgantown (Fink and Dunn 2000:186).

During the economic boom of the 1980s, the poultry industry faced labor shortages—precisely when many Guatemalans were fleeing their country. This fortuitous coincidence led to "Mexicans and Central Americans, especially Guatemalans," becoming "the employees of choice" in poultry plants (Fink and Dunn 2000: 176), despite the fact that not one of the hundreds of Maya who eventually staffed Morgantown's poultry plant—the town's largest industry—ever had experienced factorylike work conditions. Due to changes in immigration policies in 1986, thousands of other Maya unable to acquire legal work permits labor as undocumented workers harvesting fruits and vegetables in Florida (Camposeco 2000).

The poultry industry is significant for understanding Maya migration to the south because it "stands as a symbol of an exploding new wave of low-wage domestic food-processing industries . . . [that is] . . . generally bitterly resistant to unionization and collective bargaining." Further, and at least in Morgantown, 80 percent of workers in this industry are Hispanic/Latino males, and 90 percent of these are Maya (Fink and Dunn 2000:175). Andrés' life history reveals the complex set of circumstances leading to his arrival in Morgantown:

> His uncle was killed by the army . . . and he himself had been abducted . . . and questioned in the middle of the night by guerillas. Fleeing his home, Andrés hid out in other pueblos before crossing the border to Mexico in 1984. For months he worked construction jobs while slipping back and forth across the border to see his family. Later that year, he was summoned by a friend in Indiantown [Florida]. After weeks of walking across the country, he crossed the U.S. border in a van at Nogales, Arizona, and went straight to Indiantown, where his wife [Juana] joined him a year later. Four years later a call from Juana's sister . . . already in Morgantown, invited them to come to North Carolina. (Fink and Dunn 2000:179)

Low pay and appalling work conditions led plant workers (again, overwhelmingly Maya) to initiate in 1991 work stoppages, culminating in a 1995 strike. Although forced to return to work after management threatened to break the strike by hiring replacements, workers managed to obtain some concessions from the plant's management. That same year, workers voted to unionize, a step approved by the National Labor Relations Board. However, shortly after this vote, the company backed away from labor negotiations and closed the plant.

Despite the dismal outcome of attempts to organize a union and improve working conditions, these efforts reveal much of Maya culture. For example, Maya workers demonstrated a great deal of cohesion and solidarity during their labor disputes, in no small measure because of their shared ethnic identity. The 1991 dispute highlighted the importance attached to age hierarchies, for "at the prompting of a community 'elder,' Francisco José, whom the workers respectfully call 'Don Pancho,' the entire night shift not only departed the plant but quickly dispersed from Morgantown back to their Florida roots (from which they had to be summoned by a company anxious to settle an issue blamed on miscommunication)" (Fink and Dunn 2000:183). All Maya participated in the work stoppages and strike, but it was the younger, more acculturated youths—some political activists in Guatemala before arriving in the United States—who spearheaded the work actions. Interestingly enough, although several of the Maya elders called the strike a *huelga* (the standard Spanish translation for strike), some of younger Maya preferred a more politicized term: *levantamiento* or uprising (Fink and Dunn 2000:185–186).

Regardless of where they live or the kinds of work they do, Mayas have to face up to the issue of ethnic identity in a rapidly changing cultural milieu. New identities ("Guatemalan," "Central American," or "Latino") may be emerging among the Maya in Los Angeles (Loucky 2000:222). In Morgantown, distinctions between the Maya Awakatekos and Chalchitekos—distinctions that proved important in Guatemalan rural villages—seem less important in the collective enterprise to survive (Fink and Dunn 2000:186-7). One Maya living in Florida reflects on what this all may mean:

> As we now look ahead to the future, we are questioning our identity. What will the future of the Maya in Florida be like? There are already many different groups here. In the beginning there was unity, but now factions have divided the community. One faction wants to Americanize, to give up their Maya iden-tity and become more American . . . Ladinos, on the other hand, pressure us to reach equality not as Maya but in a different, more Guatemalan, way. Given these problems, adaptation to our new home in the United States is not easy for us. What are we going to do? (Camposeco 2000:173)

Summary

This chapter has focused on themes that rarely receive much attention in introductory cul-tural anthropology courses and texts or, for that matter, in cultural anthropology itself as an academic discipline: mass violence, terror, and death, as well as their social, cultural, and political consequences. The preceding pages have also underscored ways in which these events are interpreted and remembered, for interpretation and memory are eminently cul-tural undertakings.

Although painful and unsettling, systematic and pervasive violence and death on a mass scale has been an excruciating dimension of life experiences of millions of Latin Americans that should not be ignored, minimized, or shoved away. Further, most who have directly experienced such traumatic events—the disappearance of a father or mother, the wanton murder of a spouse or child, the massacre of fellow villagers, or pervasive fear—have had to cope with their consequences and memories. These issues are not merely wor-thy of attention in their own right. Perhaps by understanding how and why mass, systemic violence has taken place, underscoring its tragic toll on so many, and how and why "to remember a terrible, traumatic past is to help heal its wounds" (Hale 1997:817), anthropol-ogists can help in constructing a more just and humane future. The peoples that anthropolo-gists have devoted their careers to studying deserve no less.

ISSUES AND QUESTIONS

1. *Violence, Terror, and Death.* A central theme of this chapter is that cultural anthropology has largely side-stepped the issue of mass violence, terror, and death. What were some of the reasons for largely steering clear of such unpleasant topics? Are there perhaps other reasons not raised in this chapter?

2. *The Importance of Memory.* This chapter has argued that memory—remembering or forgetting past traumatic events—is culturally very important. But why and how? Which examples illustrate how and why memory is culturally important and/or filtered through cultural lens? Might there be other, non–Latin American examples, that these can be compared with?

3. *Rigoberta Menchú–Stoll Controversy.* Controversies are hardly new in cultural anthropology. But why is the Menchú–Stoll debate so controversial and acrimonious? What specifically is learned about cultural anthropology by focusing on this debate? Might the issues and questions stemming from this debate also be relevant for other cases of mass violence analyzed in this chapter?

KEY TERMS AND CONCEPTS

Andeanism   p. 374
Contra war   p. 356
Desaparecer   p. 363
Desaparecidos   p. 363
Dirty wars   p. 352
Genocide   p. 352
Interpretation of testimonies p. 381

Limpieza   p. 370
Memory work   p. 352
Mothers of the Plaza de Mayo p. 367
Political consequences of ethnographic work   p. 380
Positionality   p. 380

Representational authority p. 380
Revolutionary violence   p. 352
Single or multiple truths   p. 380
Structural violence   p. 352

BIBLIOGRAPHY

Abercrombie, T. A. 1998. Pathways of Memory and Power: Ethnography and History Among an Andean People. Madison: University of Wisconsin Press.

Aching, G. 2002. Masking and Power: Carnival and Popular Culture in the Caribbean. Minneapolis: University of Minnesota Press.

Adams, R. N. 1970. Crucifixion by Power: Essays on Guatemalan National Social Structure, 1944–1966. Austin: University of Texas Press.

———. 1988. Conclusions: What Can We Know About the Harvest of Violence? In Harvest of Violence: The Maya Indians and the Guatemalan Crisis. Carmack, R. M., ed. pp. 274–292. Norman: University of Oklahoma Press.

Adelaar, W. F. H. 1991. The Endangered Languages Problem: South America. In Endangered Languages. Robins, R. H. and Uhlenbeck, E. M., eds. pp. 45–91. New York: St. Martin's Press.

Adovasio, J. M. 2002. The First Americans: In Pursuit of Archaeology's Greatest Mystery. New York: The Modern Library.

Aguilera, M. B. and Massey, D. S. 2003. Social Capital and the Wages of Mexican Migrants: New Hypotheses and Tests. Social Forces 82(2):671–701.

Ahrens, F. 2003a. FCC Clears Univision-Hispanic Broadcasting Deal; Republicans in Favor, Democrats Opposed; Merger to Create Spanish-Language Media Giant. Washington Post. Sep. 23, p. A5.

———. 2003b. Spanish-Language Paper Seeks Independence; L.A. Family Aims to Buy Tribune Co. Share. Washington Post. Oct. 10, p. E2.

Aizenman, N. C. 2002. Campaigns Take on an Ethnic Flavor; Candidates Respond to Growing Numbers. Washington Post. Nov. 2, p. B1.

———. 2003. Pr. George's Reaches out to Hispanics; Bilingual Workers, Translated Documents, Spanish-Language Radio Show Reflect Shift. Washington Post. Nov. 28, p. B3.

Alabarces, P. 2004. Soccer and the Return of Argentine Politics. NACLA Report on the Americas 37(5):33–37.

Albó, X. 1981. The Future of Oppressed Languages in the Andes. In Cultural Transformations and Ethnicity in Modern Ecuador. Whitten, N. E., ed. pp. 267–288. Urbana: University of Illinois Press.

———. 1995. Bolivia: Toward a Plurinational State. In Indigenous Perceptions of the Nation-State in Latin America. Giordani, L. and Snipes, M. M., eds. pp. 39–60. Williamsburg, VA: College of William and Mary.

Alcorn, J. B. 1990. Evaluating Folk Medicine: Stories of Herbs, Healing, and Healers. Latin American Research Review 25(1):259–270.

Alegría, C. and Flakoll, D. J. 1989a. On the Front Line: Guerilla Poems of El Salvador. Willimantic, CT: Curbstone Press.

———. 1989b. Ashes of Izalco. Willimantic, CT: Curbstone Press.

Alés, C. 2000. Anger as a Marker of Love: The Ethic of Conviviality Among the Yanomami. In The Anthropology of Love and Anger: The Aesthetics of Conviviality in Native Amazonia. Overing, J. and Passes, A., eds. pp. 133–151. London and New York: Routledge.

Allaire, L. 1997. The Caribs of the Lesser Antilles. In The Indigenous People of the Caribbean. Wilson, S. M., ed. pp. 177–185. Gainesville: University Press of Florida.

———. 1999. Archaeology of the Caribbean Region. In The Cambridge History of the Native Peoples of the Americas (Vol. III [South America], Part 1). Salomon, F. and Schwartz, S. B., eds. pp. 668–733. Cambridge: Cambridge University Press.

Allen, C. 1988. The Hold Life Has: Coca and Cultural Identity in an Andean Community. Washington, D.C.: Smithsonian Institution Press.

Alvarez, R. R. Jr. 1995. The Mexican-US Border: The Making of an Anthropology of Borderlands. Annual Review of Anthropology 24:447–470.

American Anthropological Association. 2002a. El Dorado Task Force Papers (Vol. I). www.aaanet.org/edtf/ index.htm.

———. 2002b. El Dorado Task Force Papers (Vol. II). www .aaanet.org/edtf/index.htm.

Amnesty International. 2003. Intolerable Killings: 10 Years of Abductions and Murder of Women in Ciudad Juárez and Chihuahua. http://web.amnesty.org/library/pdf/Amr410262 003english/$file/amr4102603.pdf.

Anderson, B. 1983. Imagined Communities: Reflections on the Origin and Spread of Nationalism. New York: Verso.

Anderson, R. N. 1996. The Quilombo of Palmares: A New Overview of a Maroon State in Seventeenth-Century Brazil. Journal of Latin American Studies 28(3): 545–566.

Anderson, T. 1981. The War of the Dispossessed: Honduras and El Salvador 1969. Lincoln: University of Nebraska Press.

Andreas, C. 1990–1991. Women at War. NACLA Report on the Americas 24(4):20–27.

Andrews, G. R. 1994. Afro-Latin America: The Late 1900s. Journal of Social History 28(2):363–379.

———. 2004. Afro-Latin America: 1800–2000. New York: Oxford University Press.

Annis, S. 1987. God and Production in a Guatemalan Town. Austin: University of Texas Press.

Aparicio, F. R. 1998. Listening to Salsa: Gender, Latin Popular Music, and Puerto Rican Cultures. Hanover, NH: University Press of New England.

Appadurai, A. 1988. Putting Hierarchy in Its Place. Current Anthropology 3(1):36–49.

———. 1991. Global Ethnoscapes: Notes and Queries for a Transnational Anthropology. In Recapturing Anthropology: Working in the Present. Fox, R. G., ed. pp. 191–210. Santa Fe, NM: School of American Research Press.

———. 1996. Modernity at Large: Cultural Dimensions of Globalization. Minneapolis: University of Minnesota Press.

Appelbaum, N. P. 2003. Muddied Waters: Race, Region and a Local History in Colombia, 1846–1948. Durham, NC: Duke University Press.

———. et al. 2003. Introduction: Racial Nations. In Race and Nation in Modern Latin America. Appelbaum, N. P. et al., eds. pp. 1–31. Chapel Hill: University of North Carolina Press.

Archdiocese of Guatemala. 1999. REMHI (Recovery of Historical Memory Project); The Official Report of Human Rights, Office, Archdiocese of Guatemala. Maryknoll, NY and London: Orbis Books; Latin America Bureau.

Archetti, E. P. 1997a. Guinea-Pigs: Food, Symbol, and Conflict of Knowledge in Ecuador. Oxford: Berg.

———. 1997b. Multiple Masculinities: The Worlds of Tango and Football in Argentina. In Sex and Sexuality in Latin America. Balderston, D. and Guy, D. J., eds. pp. 199–216. New York: New York University Press.

———. 1999. Masculinities: Football, Polo, and the Tango in Argentina. Oxford: Berg.

Archive of the Indigenous Languages of Latin America. n.d. (a). The Indigenous Languages of Latin America. www.ailla. utexas.org/site/la_langs.html.

———. n.d. (b). Information About the Indigenous Languages of Latin America. www.ailla.utexas.org/ site/lg_info.html.

———. n.d. (c). Mesoamerican Languages. www.ailla.utexas.org/ site/ma_lg_tbl.html.

———. n.d. (d). Information About the Indigenous Languages of Latin America. www.ailla.utexas. org/site/lg_info.html.

Aretxaga, B. 2003. Maddening States. Annual Review of Anthropology 32:393–410.

Arias, A. 2001. Rigoberta Mechú's History within the Guatemalan Context. In The Rigoberta Menchú Controversy (with a Response by David Stoll). Arias, A., ed. pp. 3–28. Minneapolis University of Minnesota Press.

Arias, E. and Palloni, A. 1999. Prevalence and Patterns of Female Headed Households in Latin America. Journal of Comparative Family Studies 30(2):257–279.

Armstrong, P. 1999. The Cultural Economy of the Bahian Carnaval. Studies in Latin American Popular Culture 18:139–158.

Armus, D. 2003. Tango, Gender and Tuberculosis in Buenos Aires, 1900–1940. In Disease in the Historiography of Modern Latin America. Armus, D., ed. pp. 101–129. Durham, NC: Duke University Press.

Arnold, D. Y. 1988. Matrilineal Practice in a Patrilineal Setting: Rituals and Metaphors of Kinship in an Andean Ayllu. Ph.D. dissertation. University of London.

Arnold, P. P. 1999. Eating Landscape: Aztec and European Occupation of Tlalocan. Boulder: University Press of Colorado.

Ashburn, F. D. 1947. The Ranks of Death: A Medical History of the Conquest of America. New York: Coward-McCann.

Atkinson, J. M. 1992. Shamanisms Today. Annual Review of Anthropology 21:307–330.

Austerlitz, P. 1997. Merengue: Dominican Music and Dominican Identity. Philadelphia: Temple University Press.

Avery, W. P. 1998. Domestic Interests in NAFTA Bargaining. Political Science Quarterly 113(2):281–305.

Axtell, J. 1992. Columbian Encounters: Beyond 1992. William and Mary Quarterly 49:335–360.

———. 1995. Columbian Encounters: 1992–1995. William and Mary Quarterly 52(4):649–696.

Ayala, C. J. 1999. American Sugar Kingdom: The Plantation Economy of the Spanish Caribbean, 1898–1934. Chapel Hill: University of North Carolina Press.

Bacon, D. 2004. The Children of NAFTA. Labor Wars on the US/Mexico Border. Berkeley: University of California Press.

Baer, R. D. and Bustillo, M. 1993. Susto and Mal de Ojo Among Florida Farmworkers: Emic and Etic Perspectives. Medical Anthropology Quarterly 7(1):90–100.

Bakewell, P. J. 1987. Mining. In Colonial Spanish America. Bethell, L., ed. pp. 203–249. Cambridge: Cambridge University Press.

Ballvé, M. 2004. Battle for Latino Media. NACLA Report on the Americas 37(4):20–25.

Barndt, D. 1999. Whose "Choice"?: "Flexible" Women Workers in the Tomato Food Chain. In Women Working the NAFTA Food Chain: Women, Food and Globalization. Barndt, D., ed. pp. 61–80. Ontario: Second Story Press.

———. 2002. Tangled Routes: Women, Work, and Globalization on the Tomato Trail. Lantham, MD: Rowman and Littlefield.

Barrett, R. et al. 1998. Emerging and Re-Emerging Infectious Diseases: The Third Epidemiologic Transition. Annual Review of Anthropology 27:247–71.

Barrios de Chungara, D. 1978. Let Me Speak: The Autobiography of a Bolivian Mining Woman (edited by M. Vieser). New York: Monthly Review Press.

Barron, A. 1999. Mexican Women on the Move: Migrant Workers in Mexico and Canada. In Women Working the NAFTA Food Chain: Women, Food and Globalization. Barndt, D., ed. pp. 113–126. Ontario: Second Story Press.

Barth, F. 1969. Ethnic Groups and Boundaries: The Social Organization of Cultural Difference. Oslo: Universitetsforlaget.

Basso, E. B., ed. 1977. The Carib-Speaking Indians: Culture, Society, and Language. Tucson: University of Arizona Press.

Basso, K. 1988. "Speaking with Names": Language and Landscape Among the Western Apache. Cultural Anthropology 3(2):99–130.

Bastien, J. W. 1985. Qollahuaya-Andean Body Concepts: A Topographical-Hydraulic Model of Physiology. American Anthropologist 87(3):595–611.

———. 1992. Drum and Stethoscope: Integrating Ethnomedicine and Biomedicine in Bolivia. Salt Lake City: University of Utah Press.

———. and Donahue, J. M., eds. 1981. Health in the Andes. Washington, D.C.: American Anthropological Association.

Becker, M. and Delgado-P., G. 1998. Latin America: The Internet and Indigenous Texts. Cultural Survival Quarterly 21(4): 23–28.

Beezley, W. H. et al. 1994a. Rituals of Rule, Rituals of Resistance: Public Celebrations and Popular Culture in Mexico. Wilmington, DE: Scholarly Resources.

———. 1994b. Introduction: Constructing Consent, Inciting Conflict. In Rituals of Rule, Rituals of Resistance: Public Celebrations and Popular Culture in Mexico. Beezley, W. H. et al., eds. pp. xiii–xxxii. Wilmington, DE: Scholarly Resources.

Beezley, W. H. and Curcio-Nagy, L. A. 2000a. Introduction. In Latin American Popular Culture: An Introduction. Beezley, W. H. and Curcio-Nagy, L. A., eds. pp. xi–xxiii. Wilmington, DE: Scholarly Resources.

———. eds. 2000b. Latin American Popular Culture: An Introduction. Wilmington, DE: Scholarly Resources.

Behar, R. 1987. Sex and Sin, Witchcraft and the Devil in Late-Colonial Mexico. American Ethnologist 14(1):34–54.

Berger, M. T. 2004. Workable Sisterhood: The Political Journey of Stigmatized Women with HIV/AIDS. Princeton, NJ: Princeton University Press.

Bermann, M. 1994. Lukurmata: Household Archaeology in Prehispanic Bolivia. Princeton, NJ: Princeton University Press.

Bernstein, J. 1991. Quincentenary: U.S. Commission Adrift. NACLA Report on the Americas 35(3):9–11.

Betancourt, A. 2005. Mexico: New Prosecutor for Rampant Murders. New York Times. May 31, p. A6.

Béteille, A. 1998. The Idea of Indigenous People. Current Anthropology 39(2):187–192.

Bethell, L., ed. 1987. Colonial Spanish America. Cambridge: Cambridge University Press.

Beverley, J. 2001. What Happens When the Subaltern Speaks: Rigoberta Menchú, Multiculturalism, and the Presumption of Equal Worth. In The Rigoberta Menchú Controversy (with a Response by David Stoll). Arias, A., ed. pp. 219–236. Minneapolis: University of Minnesota Press.

———. 2004. Testimonio: On the Politics of Truth. Minneapolis: University of Minnesota Press.

———. and Zimmerman, M. 1990. Literature and Politics in the Central American Revolutions. Austin: University of Texas Press.

Bilby, K. M. 1985. The Caribbean as a Musical Region. In Caribbean Contours. Mintz, S. W. and Price, S., eds. pp. 181–218. Baltimore: The Johns Hopkins University Press.

———. 1996. Ethnogenesis in the Guianas and Jamaica: Two Maroon Cases. In History, Power, and Identity: Ethnogenesis in the Americas, 1492–1992. Hill, J. D., ed. pp. 119–141. Iowa City: University of Iowa Press.

———. 2000. Making Modenity in the Hinterlands: New Maroon Musics in the Black Atlantic. Popular Music 19(3):265–292.

Binford, L. 1996. The *El Mozote* Massacre: Anthropology and Human Rights. Tucson: University of Arizona Press.

———. 2003. Migrant Remittances and (Under) Development in Mexico. Critique of Anthropology 23(3):305–336.

———. 2005. A Generation of Migrants: Why They Leave, Where They End Up. NACLA Report on the Americas 39(1):31–37.

Blanchard, K. 1995. The Anthropology of Sport: An Introduction. South Hadley, MA: Bergin & Garvey.

Blim, M. L. 1992. Introduction: The Emerging Global Factory and Anthropology. In Anthropology and the Global Factory: Studies of the New Industrialization in the Late Twentieth Century. Rothstein, F. A. and Blim, M. L., eds. pp. 1–32. New York: Bergin & Garvey.

———. 2000. Capitalisms in Late Modernity. Annual Review of Anthropology 29:25–38.

Bliss, K. E. 2001. The Sexual Revolution in Mexican Studies: New Perspectives on Gender, Sexuality, and Culture in Modern Mexico. Latin American Research Review 36(1):247–268.

Blouet, B. W. and Blouet, O. M., eds. 2002. Latin America and the Caribbean: A Systematic and Regional Survey. New York: John Wiley and Sons.

Blustein, P. and Faiola, A. 2002. Argentine Defaults on Debt Payment; Action Widens Split with Global System. Washington Post. Nov. 15, p. E1.

Bolin, I. 1998. Rituals of Respect: The Secret of Survival in the High Peruvian Andes. Austin: University of Texas Press.

Bolles, A. L. 1996. Sister Jamaica: A Study of Women, Work, and Households in Kingston. Lanham, MD: University Press of America.

Bolton, R. 1979. Guinea Pigs, Protein, and Ritual. Ethnology 18:229–252.

———. et al. 1991. AIDS Literature for Anthropologists: A Working Bibliography. The Journal of Sex Research 28(2):307–346.

Booth, J. A. 1993. Inequality and Rebellion in Central America. In Development and Underdevelopment: The Political Economy of Inequality. Seligson, M. A. and Passé-Smith, J. T., eds. pp. 315–330. Boulder: Lynne Rienner.

Borah, W. 1992. The Historical Demography of Aboriginal and Colonial America: An Attempt at Perspective. In The Native Population of the Americas in 1492. Denevan, W. M., ed. pp. 13–34. Madison: University of Wisconsin Press.

Boster, J. S. and Weller, S. C. 1990. Cognitive and Contextual Variation in Hot-Cold Classification. American Anthropologist 92:171–179.

Bourdieu, P. 1984. Distinction: A Social Critique of the Judgement of Taste. Cambridge, MA: Harvard University Press.

———. and Wacquant, L. 1992. An Invitation to Reflexive Sociology. Chicago: University of Chicago Press.

Bourgois, P. I. 1989. Ethnicity at Work: Divided Labor on a Central American Banana Plantation. Baltimore: John Hopkins University Press.

———. 1995. In Search of Respect: Selling Crack in El Barrio. Cambridge: Cambridge University Press.

———. 2004. The Continuum of Violence in War and Peace: Post-Cold War Lessons from El Salvador. In Violence in War and Peace. Scheper-Hughes, N. and Bourgois, P., eds. pp. 425–434. Malden, MA and Oxford: Blackwell.

Brading, D. A. 2001. Mexican Phoenix: Our Lady of Guadalupe: Image and Tradition Across Five Centuries. Cambridge: Cambridge University Press.

———. and Cross, H. E. 1985. Colonial Silver Mining: Mexico and Peru. In Readings in Latin American History: Volume I, The Formative Centuries. Bakewell, P. J. et al., eds. pp. 129–156. Durham, NC: Duke University Press.

Braithwaite, L. E. 1971. Social Stratification and Cultural Pluralism. In Peoples and Cultures of the Caribbean: An Anthropological Reader. Horowitz, M. M., ed. pp. 95–116. Garden City, NY: Natural History Press.

Brandes, S. H. 1997. Sugar, Colonialism, and Death: On the Origins of Mexico's Day of the Dead. Comparative Studies in Society and History 39(2):270–299.

Brass, T. 1986. Cargos and Conflict: The Fiesta System and Capitalist Development in Eastern Peru. Journal of Peasant Studies 13(3):45–62.

Brennan, D. 2004. What's Love Got To Do With It?: Transnational Desires and Sex Tourism in The Dominican Republic. Durham, NC: Duke University Press.

Briggs, C. L. 2003. Stories in Time of Cholera: Racial Profiling During a Medical Nightmare. Berkeley: University of California Press.

Briggs, L. 2002. Reproducing Empire: Race, Sex, Science, and U.S. Imperialism in Puerto Rico. Berkeley: University of California Press.

Brodwin, P. 1996. Medicine and Morality in Haiti: The Contest for Healing Power. Cambridge: Cambridge University Press.

Brody, R. 1999. The Pinochet Precedent: Changing the Equation of Repression. NACLA Report on the Americas 37(6):18–20.

Brown, A. D. 1992. Otras Voces: A Case for Multiple Perspectives on El Quinto Centenario. Hispania 75(3):732–733.

Brown, K. M. 1991. Mama Lola: A Vodou Priestess in Brooklyn. Berkeley: University of California Press.

Brown, M. F. 1998. Can Culture Be Copyrighted? Current Anthropology 39(2):193–222.

Brown, P. J. et al. 1998. Medical Anthropology: An Introduction to the Fields. In Understanding and Applying Medical Anthropology. Brown, P. J., ed. pp. 10–19. London and Toronto: Mayfield Publishing Company.

Browning, D. 1971. El Salvador: Landscape and Society. New York: Oxford University Press.

Brumfiel, E. M. 2001. Asking about Aztec Gender: The Historical and Archaeological Evidence. In Gender in Pre-Hispanic America: A Symposium at Dumbarton Oaks 12 and 13 Oct.

1996. Klein, C. F. and Quilter, J., eds. pp. 57–86. Washington, D.C.: Dumbarton Oaks Research Library and Collection.

Brush, S. B. 1992. Ethnoecology, Biodiversity, and Modernization in Andean Potato Agriculture. Journal of Ethnobiology 12:161–185.

———. 1993. Indigenous Knowledge of Biological Resources and Intellectual Property Rights: The Role of Anthropology. American Anthropologist 95(3):653–671.

———. and Stabinsky, D. 1996. Valuing Local Knowledge: Indigenous People and Intellectual Property Pights. Washington, D.C.: Island Press.

Buechler, H. C. and Buechler, J.-M. 1996. The World of Sofia Velázquez: The Autobiography of a Bolivian Market Vendor. New York: Columbia University Press.

Bulmer-Thomas, V. 1987. The Political Economy of Central America Since 1920. Cambridge: Cambridge University Press.

Burchard, R. E. 1992. Coca Chewing and Diet. Current Anthropology 33(1):1–24.

Burkhart, L. M. 2001a. Before Guadalupe: The Virgin Mary in Early Colonial Nahuatl Literature. Albany: State University of New York. Institute for Mesoamerican Studies.

———. 2001b. Gender in Nahuatl Texts of the Early Colonial Period: Native "Tradition" and the Dialogue with Christianity. In Gender in Pre-Hispanic America: A Symposium at Dumbarton Oaks 12 and 13 Oct. 1996. Klein, C. F. and Quilter, J., eds. pp. 87–108. Washington, D.C.: Dumbarton Oaks Research Library and Collection.

———. and Gasco, J. 1996a. The Colonial Period in Mesoamerica. In The Legacy of Mesoamerica: History and Culture of a Native American Civilization. Carmack, R. M. et al., eds. pp. 154–195. Upper Saddle River, NJ: Prentice Hall.

———. 1996b. Mesoamerica and Spain: The Conquest. In The Legacy of Mesoamerica: History and Culture of a Native American Civilization. Carmack, R. M. et al., eds. pp 122 153. Upper Saddle River, NJ: Prentice Hall.

Burkholder, M. A. and Johnson, L. L. 2004. Colonial Latin America. New York: Oxford University Press.

Burt, J.-M. 1998. Shining Path and the "Decisive Battle" in Lima's *Barriadas*: The Case of Villa El Salvador. In Shining and Other Paths: War and Society in Peru, 1980–1995. Stern, S. J., ed. pp. 267–306. Durham, NC: Duke University Press.

Butzer, K. W. 1992. The Americas Before and After 1492: An Introduction to Current Geographical Research. Annals of the Association of American Geographers 82(3):345–368.

———. and Williams, B. J. 1992. Addendum: Three Indigenous Maps from New Spain Dated ca. 1580. Annals of the Association of American Geographers 82(3):536–542.

Cadaval, O. 1998. Creating a Latino Identity in the Nation's Capital: The Latino Festival. New York: Garland Publishing.

Cahill, D. 2002. The Virgin and the Inca: An Incaic Procession in the City of Cuzco in 1692. Ethnohistory 49(3):611–649.

Calvo, T. 1989. The Warmth of the Heart: Seventeenth-Century Guadalajara Families. In Sexuality and Marriage in Colonial

Latin America. Lavrin, A., ed. pp. 286–312. Lincoln: University of Nebraska Press.

Cámara, G. et al. 2005. Amazonian Deforestation Models. Science 307 (February 18):1043–1044.

Camposeco, J. 2000. A Maya Voice: The Refugees in Indiantown, Florida. In The Maya Diaspora: Guatemalan Roots, New American Lives. Loucky, J. and Moors, M. M., eds. pp. 172–174. Philadelphia: Temple University Press.

Cancian, F. 1965. Economics and Prestige in a Maya Community: The Religious Cargo System in Zincantan. Stanford: Stanford University Press.

———. 1990. The Zinacantan Cargo Waiting Lists as a Reflection of Social, Political, and Economic Changes, 1952–1987. In Class, Politics, and Popular Religion in Mexico and Central America. Stephen, L. and Dow, J., eds. pp. 63–76. Washington, D.C.: American Anthropological Association.

———. and Brown, P. 1998. Who Is Rebelling in Chiapas? In Crossing Currents: Continuity and Change in Latin America. Whiteford, M. B. and Whiteford, S., eds. pp. 341–345. Upper Saddle River, NJ: Prentice Hall.

Canclini, N. G. 1996. Popular Culture: From Epic to Simulacrum. Studies in Latin American Popular Culture 15:61–71.

Canin, E. 1997. "Work, a Roof, and Bread for the Poor": Managua's Christian Base Communities in the Nicaraguan "Revolution from Below." Latin American Perspectives 24(2):80–101.

Carlson, P. 2004. Hey, Professor, Assimilate This. Washington Post. March 9, p. C1.

Carmack, R. M. 1988. The Story of Santa Cruz Quiché. In Harvest of Violence: The Maya Indians and the Guatemalan Crisis. Carmack, R. M., ed. pp. 39–69. Norman: University of Oklahoma Press.

———. et al. 1996. Introduction. In The Legacy of Mesoamerica: History and Culture of a Native American Civilization. Carmack, R. M. et al., eds. pp. 1–38. Upper Saddle River, NJ: Prentice Hall.

Carneiro, R. L. 1970. A Theory of the Origin of the State. Science 169:733–738.

Carrasco, P. 1961. The Civil-Religious Hierarchy in Mesoamerican Communities: Pre-Spanish Background and Colonial Development. American Anthropologist 63(3):483–497.

Carreño, M. A. 2004. Manual de urbanidad y buenas maneras: De consulta indispensable para niños, jóvenes y adultos. Bogotá: Panamericana.

Carrera, M. M. 2003. Imagining Identity in New Spain: Race, Lineage, and the Colonial Body in Portraiture and Casta Paintings. Austin: University of Texas Press.

Carrillo, H. 2002. The Night Is Young: Sexuality in Mexico in the Time of AIDS. Chicago: University of Chicago Press.

———. 2003. Neither Machos nor Maricones: Masculinitiy and Emerging Male Homosexual Identities in Mexico. In Changing Men and Masculinities in Latin America. Gutmann, M. C., ed. pp. 351–369. Durham, NC: Duke University Press.

Carter, W. E., ed. 1980. Cannabis in Costa Rica: A Study of Chronic Marihuana Use. Philadelphia: Institute for the Study of Human Issues.

Casanueva, F. 1991. Smallpox and War in Southern Chile in the Late Eighteenth Century. In "Secret Judgements of God": Old World Disease in Colonial Spanish America. Cook, D. N. and Lovell, W. G., eds. pp. 183–212. Norman: University of Oklahoma Press.

Caspar, F. 1956. Tupari. London: Bell.

Castañeda, C. 1968. The Teachings of Don Juan: A Yaqui Way of Knowledge. Berkeley: University of California Press.

Castro, D. S. 1991. The Argentine Tango as Social History, 1880–1955: The Soul of the People. Lewiston, NY: E. Mellen Press.

Caulfield, S. 2000. In Defense of Honor: Sexual Morality, Modernity, and Nation in Early-Twentieth-Century Brazil. Durham, NC: Duke University Press.

———. 2001. The History of Gender in the Historiography of Latin America. Hispanic American Historical Review 81(3–4):449–490.

Ceballos Melguizo, R. 2001. The Evolution of Armed Conflict in Medellín. Latin American Perspectives 28(116):110–131.

Chagnon, N. A. 1997. Yanömamo (5th ed.). Fort Worth: Harcourt Brace College Publishers.

Chambers, S. C. 2003. Little Middle Ground: The Instability of Mestizo Identity in the Andes, Eighteenth and Nineteenth Centuries. In Race and Nation in Modern Latin America. Appelbaum, N. P. et al., eds. pp. 32–55. Chapel Hill: University of North Carolina Press.

Chance, J. K. 1990. Changes in Twentieth-Century Mesoamerican Cargo Systems. In Class, Politics, and Popular Religion in Mexico and Central America. Stephen, L. and Dow, J., eds. pp. 27–42. Washington, D.C.: American Anthropological Association.

Chant, S. 2002. Researching Gender, Families and Households in Latin America: From the 20th into the 21st Century. Bulletin of Latin American Research 21(4):545–575.

Charney, P. J. 1991. Holding Together the Indian Family During Colonial Times in the Lima Valley, Peru. Milwaukee: The University of Wisconsin–Milwaukee, Center for Latin American Studies. Discussion Paper No. 86.

———. 2001. Indian Society in the Valley of Lima, Peru 1532–1824. Lanham, MD: University Press of America.

Chase, J. 2002. Introduction: The Spaces of Neoliberalism in Latin America. In The Spaces of Neoliberalism: Land, Place and Family in Latin America. Chase, J., ed. pp. 1–21. Bloomfield, CT: Kumarian Press.

Chasteen, J. C. 2000. Black Kings, Blackface Carnival, and Nineteenth-Century Origins of the Tango. In Latin American Popular Culture: An Introduction. Beezley, W. H. and Curcio-Nagy, L. A., eds. pp. 43–59. Wilmington, DE: Scholarly Resources.

———. 2004. National Rhythms, African Roots: Deep History of Latin American Dance. Albuquerque: University of New Mexico Press.

Chauvin, L. O. 2002. Rebel Group's Presence Growing Near Peru's Capital; The Mayor of a Lima Suburb has Received Death Threats that He Says are from the Shining Path. Christian Science Monitor. Apr. 12, p. 7.

Chinchilla, N. S. 1990. Revolutionary Popular Feminism in Nicaragua: Articulating Class, Gender, and National Sovereignty. Gender and Society 4(3):370–397.

Chinni, D. 2004. The New Economy's Biggest Product: An Enduring Underclass? Christian Science Monitor. Apr. 27, p. 9.

Chollett, D. 1998. Culture, Sweetness, and Death: The Political Economy of Sugar Production and Consumption. In Crossing Currents: Continuity and Change in Latin America. Whiteford, M. B. and Whiteford, S., eds. pp. 368–378. Upper Saddle River, NJ: Prentice Hall.

Christian Science Monitor. 2004. Mexico in U.S. Politics. Christian Science Monitor. Mar. 8, p. 8.

Chungara, D. and Yañez, A. 1992. The Owners of This Land: An Interview with Domitila Chungara. Latin American Perspectives 19(3):92–95.

Clawson, D. L. 2004. Latin America and the Caribbean: Lands and People. Boston: McGraw-Hill.

Clendinnen, I. 1987. Ambivalent Conquests: Maya and Spaniard in Yucatán, 1517–1570. Cambridge: Cambridge University Press.

Cline, S. L. 2000. Native Peoples of Colonial Central Mexico. In The Cambridge History of the Native Peoples of the Americas (Vol II [Mesoamerica], Part 2). Adams, R. E. and MacLeod, M. J., eds. pp. 187–222. Cambridge: Cambridge University Press.

Cohen, E. 1988. Authenticity and Commoditization in Tourism. Annals of Tourism Research 15:371–386.

Cohen, J. et al. 2005. Why Remittances Shouldn't Be Blamed for Rural Underdevelopment in Mexico. Critique of Anthropology 25(1): 87–96.

Cohn, B. S. 1996. Colonialism and Its Forms of Knowledge: The British in India. Princeton, NJ: Princeton University Press.

Cohodas, M. 2002. Multiplicity and Discourse in Maya Gender Relations. In Ancient Maya Gender Identity Relations. Gustafson, L. S. and Trevelyan, A. M., eds. pp. 11–54. Westport, CT: Bergin & Garvey.

Coleman, K. M. et al. 1993. Protestantism in El Salvador: Conventional Wisdom Versus the Survey Evidence. In Rethinking Protestantism in Latin America. Garrard-Burnett, V. and Stoll, D., eds. pp. 111–142. Philadelphia: Temple University Press.

Collier, J. 1986. From Mary to Modern Woman: The Material Basis of Marianismo and Its Transformation in a Spanish Village. American Ethnologist 13:100–107.

Colloredo-Mansfeld, R. 1999. The Native Leisure Class: Consumption and Cultural Creativity in the Andes. Chicago: University of Chicago Press.

Comaroff, J. L. and Comaroff, J. L. 1992. Ethnography and the Historical Imagination. Boulder, CO: Westview.

———. 1993. Modernity and Its Malcontents: Ritual and Power in Postcolonial Africa. Chicago: University of Chicago Press.

———. 2001. Millennial Capitalism: First Thoughts on a Second Coming. In Millennial Capitalism and the Culture of Neoliberalism. Comaroff, J. and Comaroff, J. L., eds. pp. 1–56. Durham, NC: Duke University Press.

Comerford, M. 2002. Haiti. In HIV and AIDS: A Global View. McElrath, K., ed. pp. 87–96. Westport, CT: Greenwood Press.

Conkey, M. W. and Gero, J. M. 1997. Programme to Practice: Gender and Feminism in Archaeology. Annual Review of Anthropology 26:411–37.

Conklin, B. A. 1997. Body Paint, Feathers, and VCRs: Aesthetics and Authenticity in Amazonian Activism. American Ethnologist 24(4):711–737.

———. 2001. Women's Blood, Warriors' Blood, and the Conquest of Vitality in Amazonia. In Gender in Amazonia and Melanesia: An Exploration of the Comparative Method. Gregor, T. A. and Tuzin, D., eds. pp. 141–174. Berkeley: University of California Press.

———. 2002. Shamans Versus Pirates in the Amazonian Treasure Chest. American Anthropologist 104(4):1050–1061.

———. and Graham, L. 1995. The Shifting Middle Ground: Amazonian Indians and Eco-Politics. American Anthropologist 97:695–710.

Conrad, G. W. and Demarest, A. A. 1984. Religion and Empire: The Dynamics of Aztec and Inca Expansion. Cambridge: Cambridge University Press.

Conroy, M. E. and Glasmeier, A. K. 1992–1993. Unprecedented Disparities, Unparalleled Adjustment Needs: Winners and Losers on the NAFTA "Fast Track." Journal of Interamerican Studies and World Affairs 34(4):1–37.

Constable, N. 1997. Maid to Order in Hong Kong: Stories of Filipina Workers. Ithaca, NY: Cornell University Press.

Cook, N. D. 1998. Born to Die: Disease and New World Conquest, 1492–1650. Cambridge: Cambridge University Press.

Cook, S. and Binford, L. 1990. Obliging Need: Rural Petty Industry in Mexican Capitalism. Austin: University of Texas Press.

Cooper, F. and Stoler, A. L., eds. 1997. Tensions of Empire: Colonial Cultures in a Bourgeois World. Berkeley: University of California Press.

Cooperman, A. 2005. Robertson Calls for Chávez Assassination. Washington Post. Aug. 24, p. A2.

Cordero, I. C. 1998. Women in War: Impact and Responses. In Shining and Other Paths: War and Society in Peru, 1980–1995. Stern, S. J., ed. pp. 345–374. Durham, NC: Duke University Press.

Coronil, F. 1996. Beyond Occidentalism: Toward Nonimperial Geohistorical Categories. Cultural Anthropology 11(1): 51–87.

———. 1997. Magical State: Nature, Money and Modernity in Venezuela. Chicago: University of Chicago Press.

———. 2001. Perspectives on Tierney's Darkness in El Dorado. Current Anthropology 42(2):265–276.

Counihan, C. M. 1999. The Anthropology of Food and Body: Gender, Meaning, and Power. New York: Routledge.

Crain, M. M. 1991. Poetics and Politics in the Ecuadorian Andes: Women's Narratives of Death and Devil Possesion. American Ethnologist 18(1):67–89.

Crandall, R. 2001. Explicit Narcotization: U.S. Policy Toward Colombia During the Samper Administration. Latin American Politics and Society 43(3):95–120.

Crandon-Malamud, L. 1993. Blessings of the Virgen in Capitalist Society: The Transformation of a Rural Bolivian Fiesta. American Anthropologist 95(3):574–596.

Crehan, K. A. 2002. Gramsci, Culture and Anthropology. Berkeley: University of California Press.

Crocker, J. C. 1985. Vital Souls: Bororo Cosmology, Natural Symbolism, and Shamanism. Tucson: University of Arizona Press.

Crosby, A. W. 1972. The Columbian Exchange: Biological and Cultural Consequences of 1492. Westport, CT: Greenwood Press.

———. 1985. Conquistador y Pestilencia: The First New World Pandemic and the Fall of the Great Indian Empires. In Readings in Latin American History: Volume I, The Formative Centuries. Bakewell, P. J. et al., eds. pp. 35–50. Durham, NC: Duke University Press.

Cueto, M. 2003. Stigma and Blame During an Epidemic: Cholera in Peru, 1991. In Disease in the History of Modern Latin America: From Malaria to AIDS. Armus, D., ed. pp. 268–289. Durham, NC: Duke University Press.

Curcio-Nagy, L. A. 1994. Giants and Gypsies: Corpus Christi in Colonial Mexico City. In Rituals of Rule, Rituals of Resistance: Public Celebrations and Popular Culture in Mexico. Beezley, W. H. et al., eds. pp. 1–26. Wilmington, DE: Scholarly Resources.

Da Matta, R. 1992. Carnivals, Rogues, and Heroes: An Interpretation of the Brazilian Dilemma (translated from the Portuguese by John Drury). Notre Dame, IN: University of Notre Dame Press.

Daflon, R. and Ballvé, T. 2004. The Beautiful Game? Race and Class in Brazilian Soccer. NACLA Report on the Americas 37(5):23–26.

Daniel, Y. 1995. Rumba: Dance and Social Change Contemporary Cuba. Bloomington: Indiana University Press.

Danner, M. 2004. The Massacre at El Mozote: A Parable of the Cold War. In Violence in War and Peace. Scheper-Hughes, N. and Bourgois, P., eds. pp. 334–338. Malden, MA, and Oxford: Blackwell.

Dávalos, K. M. 2003. La Quinceañera: Making Gender and Ethnic Identities. In Velvet Barrios: Pop Culture and Chicana/o Sexualities. de Alba, A. G., ed. pp. 141–162. New York: Palgrave Macmillan.

Davis, D. L. and Guarnaccia, P. J. 1989. Introduction to Health, Culture and the Nature of Nerves. Medical Anthropology 11:1–13.

Davis, W. 1985. Hallucinogenic Plants and Their Use in Traditional Societies: An Overview. Cultural Survival Quarterly 9(4):2–5.

De Genova, N. 1998. Race, Space, and the Reinvention of Latin America in Mexican Chicago. Latin American Perspectives 25(6):87–116.

de la Cadena, M. 1996. The Political Tensions of Representations and Misrepresentations: Intellectuals and Mestizas in Cuzco (1919–1990). Journal of Latin American Anthropology 2(1):112–147.

———. 2000. Indigenous Mestizos: The Politics of Race and Culture in Cuzco, Peru, 1919–1991. Durham, NC: Duke University Press.

de la Fuente, A. 1999. Myths of Racial Democracy: Cuba 1900–1912. Latin American Research Review 34(3):39–73.

de los Ríos, R. 1993. Gender, Health, and Development: An Approach in the Making. In Gender, Women and Health in the Americas. Gómez, E., ed. pp. 3–17. Washington, D.C.: Pan American Health Organization.

de Moya, E. A. 2004. Power Games and Totalitarian Masculinity in the Dominican Republic. In Interrogating Caribbean Masculinities: Theoretical and Empirical Analyses. Reddock, R. E., ed. pp. 68–104. Kingston, Jamaica: University of the West Indies Press.

de Onis, J. 1976. Mrs. Perón Overthrown by Military in Argentina and Reported Arrested. New York Times. Mar. 24, p. 1.

De Vos, S. 1987. Latin American Households in Comparative Perspective. Population Studies 41(3): 501–517.

Dean, C. 2001. Andean Androgyny and the Making of Men. In Gender in Pre-Hispanic America: A Symposium at Dumbarton Oaks 12 and 13 Oct. 1996. Klein, C. F. and Quilter, J., eds. pp. 143–182. Washington, D.C.: Dumbarton Oaks Research Library and Collection.

Deans-Smith, S. 1994. The Working Poor and the Eighteenth-Century Colonial State: Gender, Public Order, and Work Discipline. In Rituals of Rule, Rituals of Resistance: Public Celebrations and Popular Culture in Mexico. Beezley, W. H. et al., eds. pp. 47–76. Wilmington, DE: Scholarly Resources.

Debert-Ribeiro, M. B. 1993. Women and Chronic Disease in Latin America. In Gender, Women and Health in the Americas. Gómez, E., ed. pp. 82–89. Washington, D.C.: Pan American Health Organization.

Degregori, C. I. 1990–1991. A Dwarf Star. NACLA Report on the Americas 24(4):10–16.

Delgado-P., G. 2002. Solidarity in Cyberspace: Indigenous Peoples Online. NACLA Report on the Americas 35(5):49–51.

Denevan, W. M. 1966. The Aboriginal Cultural Geography of the Llanos de Mojos of Bolivia. Berkeley: University of California Press.

———. 1980. Latin America. In World Systems of Traditional Resource Management. Klee, G. A., ed. pp. 217–256. New York: Halsted Press.

———. 1992a. The Aboriginal Population of Amazonia. In The Native Population of the Americas in 1492. Denevan, W. M., ed. pp. 205–234. Madison: University of Wisconsin Press.

———. 1992b. The Pristine Myth: The Landscape of the Americas in 1492. Annals of the Association of American Geographers 82(3):369–385.

———. 2001. Cultivated Landscapes of Native Amazonia and the Andes. New York: Oxford University Press.

Descola, P. 1994. In the Society of Nature: A Native Ecology in Amazonia. Cambridge: Cambridge University Press.

Deshon, S. K. 1963. Compadrazgo on a Henequen Hacienda in Yucatán: A Structural Re-Evaluation. American Anthropologist 65(3):574–583.

Devine, T. L. 1999. Indigenous Identity and Identification in Peru: Indigenismo, Education and Contradictions in State Discourses. Journal of Latin American Cultural Studies 8(1):63–74.

DeWalt, B. R. 1979. Review of "The Fiesta System and Economic Change." American Ethnologist 6(1):201–204.

———. 1999. Combining Indigenous and Scientific Knowledge to Improve Agriculture and Natural Resource Management in Latin America. In Traditional Modern Natural Resource Management in Latin America. Pichon, F. J. et al., eds. pp. 101–102. Pittsburgh: University of Pittsburgh Press.

Diehl, R. A. 2000. The Precolumbian Cultures of the Gulf Coast. In The Cambridge History of the Native Peoples of the Americas (Volume II [Mesoamerica], Part 1). Adams, R. E. and MacLeod, M. J., eds. pp. 156–196. Cambridge: Cambridge University Press.

Dietz, J. L. 1986. Economic History of Puerto Rico: Institutional Change and Capitalist Development. Princeton, NJ: Princeton University Press.

Dillehay, T. D. 2000. The Settlement of the Americas: A New Prehistory. New York: Basic Books.

Dinerstein, A. C. 2003. ¡Que se Vayan Todos! Popular Insurrection and the Asambleas Barriales in Argentina. Bulletin of Latin American Research 22(2):187–200.

Dirks, N. B. 1992. Introduction: Colonialism and Culture. In Colonialism and Culture. Dirks, N. B., ed. pp. 1–27. Ann Arbor: University of Michigan Press.

———. 1996. Is Vice Versa? Historical Anthropologies and Anthropological Histories. In The Historic Turn in the Human Sciences. McDonald, T. J., ed. pp. 17–52. Ann Arbor: University of Michigan Press.

———. 2001. Castes of Mind: Colonialism and the Making of Modern India. Princeton, NJ: Princeton University Press.

———. et al. 1994. Introduction. In Culture, Power, History: A Reader in Contemporary Social Theory. Dirks, N. B. et al., eds. pp. 3–45. Princeton, NJ: Princeton University Press.

Diskin, M. 1991. Ethnic Discourse and the Challenge to Anthropology: The Nicaraguan Case. In Nation-States and Indians in Latin America. Urban, G. and Sherzer, J., eds. pp. 156–180. Austin: University of Texas Press.

Dixon, E. J. 2000. Bones, Boats, and Bison: Archaeology and the First Colonization of Western North America. Albuquerque: University of New Mexico Press.

Dixon, R. M. W. and Aikhenvald, A. Y. 1999. Introduction. In The Amazonian Languages. Dixon, R. M. W. and Aikhenvald, A. Y., eds. pp. 1–22. Cambridge: Cambridge University Press.

Dobkin de Ríos, M. 1972. Visionary Vine: Hallucinogenic Healing in the Peruvian Amazon. Prospect Heights, IL: Waveland Press.

Dobyns, H. F. 1993. Disease Transfer at Contact. Annual Review of Anthropology 22:273–291.

Dodson, M. 1979. Liberation Theology and Christian Radicalism in Contemporary Latin America. Journal of Latin American Studies 11(1):203–222.

Dore, E. 1997. The Holy Family: Imagined Households in Latin American History. In Gender Politics in Latin America. Dore, E., ed. pp. 101–117. New York: Monthly Review Press.

———. 2000a. One Step Forward, Two Steps Back: Gender and the State in the Long Nineteenth Century. In Hidden Histories of Gender and the State in Latin America. Dore, E. and Molyneux, M., eds. pp. 3–32. Durham, NC: Duke University Press.

———. 2000b. Property, Households, and Public Regulation of Domestic Life: Diriomo, Nicaragua, 1840–1900. In Hidden Histories of Gender and the State in Latin America. Dore, E. and Molyneux, M., eds. pp. 147–171. Durham, NC: Duke University Press.

——— and Molyneux, M., eds. 2000. Hidden Histories of Gender and the State in Latin America. Durham, NC: Duke University Press.

Douglas, M. 1987. A Distinctive Anthropological Perspective. In Constructive Drinking: Perspectives on Drink from Anthropology. Douglas, M., ed. pp. 3–15. Cambridge: Cambridge University Press.

Dow, J. 1977. Religion in the Organization of a Mexican Peasant Economy. In Peasant Livelihood: Studies in Economic Anthropology and Cultural Ecology. Halperin, R. and Dow, J., eds. pp. 215–226. New York: St. Martin's Press.

Dow, J. W. and Van Kemper, R. 1991. Middle America and the Caribbean. In Encyclopedia of World Cultures (Vol. VIII). Levinson, D., ed. pp. xxi–xxxiv. Boston: G.K. Hall & Co.

Downey, S. B. 2001. Nicaragua. In Countries and Their Cultures (Vol. III). Ember, M. and Ember, C. R., eds. pp. 1601–1611. New York: Macmillan Reference USA.

Dreher, M. C. 1982. Working Men and Ganja: Marihuana Use in Rural Jamaica. Philadelphia: Institute for the Study of Human Issues.

Drennan, R. D. 1987. Regional Demography in Chiefdoms. In Chiefdoms in the Americas. Drennan, R. D. and Uribe, C. A., eds. pp. 307–324. Lanham, MD: University Press of America.

———. and Uribe, C. A. 1987a. Part II. Central America. In Chiefdoms in the Americas. Drennan, R. D. and Uribe, C. A., eds. pp. 59–62. Lanham, MD: University Press of America.

———. 1987b. Part III. South America. In Chiefdoms in the Americas. Drennan, R. D. and Uribe, C. A., eds. pp. 141–145. Lanham, MD: University Press of America.

———., eds. 1987c. Chiefdoms in the Americas. Lanham, MD: University Press of America.

Duany, J. 1990. "Salsa," "Plena," and "Danza": Recent Materials on Puerto Rican Popular Music. Latin American Music Review 11(2):286–296.

———. 1996. Rethinking the Popular: Recent Essays on Caribbean Music and Identity. Latin American Music Review 11(2):286–296.

Dufour, D. L. 1994. Diet and Nutritional Status of Amazonian Peoples. In Amazonian Indians from Prehistory to the Present: Anthropological Perspectives. Roosevelt, A. C., ed. pp. 151–175. Tucson: University of Arizona Press.

Dunkerley, J. 1984. Rebellion in the Veins: Political Struggle in Bolivia, 1952–1982. London: Verso.

Durham, W. H. 1979. Scarcity and Survival in Central America: Ecological Origins of the Soccer War. Stanford: Stanford University Press.

———. 1995. Conclusion: Political Ecology and Environmental Destruction in Latin America. In The Social Causes of Environmental Destruction in Latin America. Painter, M. and Durham, W. H., eds. pp. 249–264. Ann Arbor: University of Michigan Press.

Eagleton, T. 1991. Ideology: An Introduction. London: Verso.

Eber, C. 2000[1995]. Women and Alcohol in a Highland Maya Town: Water of Hope, Water of Sorrow (rev. ed.). Austin: University of Texas Press.

Economic Commission for Latin America. 2004. Social Panorama of Latin America (Briefing Paper). www.eclac.org/publicaciones/DesarrolloSocial/0/LCL2220PI/PSI2004_Summary_Web.pdf.

———. 2005. Statistical Yearbook for Latin America and the Caribbean, 2004. www.eclac.org/publicaciones/Estadisticas/4/LCG2264PB/p0_i.pdf.

Edelman, M. 1994. Landlords and the Devil: Class, Ethnic, and Gender Dimensions of Central American Peasant Narratives. Cultural Anthropology 9(1):58–93.

———. 1995. Rethinking the Hamburger Thesis: Deforestation and the Crisis of Central America's Beef Exports. In The Social Causes of Environmental Destruction in Latin America. Painter, M. and Durham, W. H., eds. pp. 25–62. Ann Arbor: University of Michigan Press.

Ehlers, T. B. 1991. Debunking Marianismo: Economic Vulnerability and Survival Strategies Among Guatemalan Wives. Ethnology 30(2):1–16.

———. 1993. Belts, Business, and Bloomingdale's: An Alternative Model for Guatemalan Artisan Development. In Crafts in the World Market: Impact of Global Exchange on Middle American Artisans. Nash, J. C., ed. pp. 181–198. Albany: State University of New York Press.

Eiss, P. K. 2002. Hunting for the Virgin: Meat, Money, and Memory in Tetiz, Yucatán. Cultural Anthropology 17(3): 291–330.

Elliott, J. H. 1987. The Spanish Conquest. In Colonial Spanish America. Bethell, L., ed. pp. 1–58. Cambridge: Cambridge University Press.

England, N. C. 2003. Mayan Language Revival and Revitalization Politics: Linguists and Linguistic Ideologies. American Anthropologist 105(4):733–743.

Escobar, A. and Alvarez, S. E., eds. 1992. The Making of Social Movements in Latin America: Identity, Strategy, and Democracy. Boulder, CO: Westview.

Eubanks, M. W. 2001. The Mysterious Origin of Maize. Economic Botany 55(4):492–514.

Evans, B. 1990. Migration Processes in Upper Peru in the Seventeenth Century. In Migration in Colonial Spanish America. Robinson, D. J., ed. pp. 62–85. Cambridge: Cambridge University Press.

Fagan, B. M. 2000. Ancient North America: The Archaeology of a Continent. London: Thames and Hudson.

Faiola, A. 2000a. Pinochet Returns to Chile; Flight from Britain Ends 16-Month Extradition Crusade. Washington Post. Mar. 3, p. A1.

———. 2000b. Pinochet Indicted for Chilean Atrocities: Ex-Dictator Put Under House Arrest for Killings and Kidnappings. Washington Post. Dec. 2, p. A1.

Farmer, P. 1992. AIDS and Accusation: Haiti and the Geography of Blame. Berkeley: University of California Press.

———. 1996. Social Inequalities and Emerging Infectious Diseases. Emerging Infectious Diseases 2(4):259–269.

———. 1997a. Social Scientists and the New Tuberculosis. Social Science and Medicine 44(3):347–358.

———. 1997b. Ethnography, Social Analysis, and the Prevention of Sexually Transmitted HIV Infections Among Poor Women in Haiti. In The Anthropology of Infectious Disease: International Health Perspectives. Inhorn, M. C. and Brown, P. J., eds. pp. 413–438. Sydney, Australia: Gordon and Breach Publishers.

———. 2004a. An Anthropology of Structural Violence. Current Anthropology 45(3):305–325.

———. 2004b. On Suffering and Structural Violence: A View from Below. In Violence in War and Peace. Scheper-Hughes, N. and Bourgois, P., eds. pp. 281–289. Malden, MA and Oxford: Blackwell.

Faron, L. C. 1968. The Mapuche Indians of Chile. New York: Holt, Rinehart and Winston.

Farriss, N. 1984. Maya Society Under Colonial Rule. Princeton, NJ: Princeton University Press.

Fearnside, P. M. 2001a. The Potential of Brazil's Forest Sector for Mitigating Global Warming Under the Kyoto Protocol. Mitigation and Adaptation Strategies for Global Change 6:355–372.

———. 2001b. Saving Tropical Forests as a Global Warming Countermeasure: An Issue That Divides the Environmental Movement. Ecological Economics 39:167–184.

Feinsilver, J. M. 1993. Healing the Masses: Cuban Health Politics at Home and Abroad. Berkeley: University of California Press.

Feitlowitz, M. 1998. A Lexicon of Terror: Argentina and the Legacies of Torture. New York: Oxford University Press.

Feld, S. and Aaron A. Fox. 1994. Music and Language. Annual Review of Anthropology 23:25–53.

Ferguson, R. B. 1995. Yanomami Warfare: A Political History. Santa Fe, NM: School of American Research Press.

Fernández Olmos, M. and Paravisini-Gebert, L. 2003. Creole Religions of the Caribbean: An Introduction from Vodou and Santería to Obeah and Espiritismo. New York: New York University Press.

Ferrándiz, F. 2003. *Malandros*, María Lionza and Masculinity in a Venezuelan Shantytown. In Changing Men and Masculinities in Latin America. Gutmann, M. C., ed. pp. 115–133. Durham, NC: Duke University Press.

Field, L. 1991. Ecuador's Pan-Indian Uprising. NACLA. Report on the Americas 25(3):39–44.

Fink, L. and Dunn, A. 2000. The Maya of Morganton: Exploring Worker Identity Within the Global Marketplace. In The Maya Diaspora: Guatemalan Roots, New American Lives. Loucky, J. and Moors, M. M., eds. pp. 175–196. Philadelphia: Temple University Press.

Finkler, K. 1994. Women in Pain: Gender and Morbidity in Mexico. Philadelphia: University of Philadelphia Press.

———. 1998. Sacred Healing and Biomedicine Compared. In Understanding and Applying Medical Anthropology. Brown, P. J., ed. pp. 118–128. London and Toronto: Mayfield Publishing Company.

Food and Agriculture Organization. 2001. State of Forestry in the Region-2000. www.fao.org/Regional/LAmerica/prior/recnat/pdf/sfor15i.pdf.

———. 2005. Key Statistics of Food and Agriculture External Trade. Imports: Mexico. www.fao.org/es/ess/toptrade/trade.asp.

Ford, P. 2001. Europe Shifts out of Drug-War Mode: Belgium, Britain, France, and Portugal Are Among Those Moving Toward the Dutch Model of Teatment, Not Arrest. Christian Science Monitor. Mar. 12, p. 1.

Forero, J. 2003a. Peru Report Says 69,000 Die in 20 Years of Rebel War. New York Times. Aug. 29, p. A3.

———. 2003b. Shining Path Rebels Are Spreading Terror Again in Peru. New York Times. July 23, p. A4.

———. 2004a. Peru: Rebel Leader's Trial Off Again. New York Times. Nov. 16, p. A6.

———. 2004b. Rightist Militias Force in Colombia's Congress. New York Times. Nov. 10, p. A3.

———. 2004c. Colombia's Landed Gentry: Coca Lords and Other Bullies. New York Times. Jan. 21, p. A4.

———. 2005. Bush's Aid Cuts on Court Issue Roil Latin American Neighbors. New York Times. Aug. 19, p. A1.

———. and Trujillo, M. 2005. New Colombia Law Grants Concessions to Paramilitaries. New York Times. June 23, p. A3.

Foster, D. W. 1998. Tango, Buenos Aires, Borges: Cultural Production and Urban Sexual Regulation. In Imagination Beyond Nation: Latin American Popular Culture. Bueno, E. P. and Caesar, T., eds. pp. 167–194. Pittsburgh: University of Pittsburgh Press.

Foster, G. M. 1998. How to Stay Well in Tzintzuntzan. In Crossing Currents: Continuity and Change in Latin America. Whiteford, M. B. and Whiteford, S., eds. pp. 290–304. Upper Saddle River, NJ: Prentice Hall.

Foster, R. J. 1991. Making National Cultures in the Global Ecumene. Annual Review of Anthropology 20:235–260.

Foweraker, J. 1981. The Struggle for Land: A Political Economy of the Pioneer Frontier in Brazil From 1930 to the Present Day. Cambridge: Cambridge University Press.

Fowler, W. R. 1987. Cacao, Indigo, and Coffee: Cash Crops in the History of El Salvador. Research in Economic Anthropology 8:139–167.

Franco, J. 2004. Killing Priests, Nuns, Women, Children. In Violence in War and Peace. Scheper-Hughes, N. and Bourgois, P., eds. pp. 196–199. Malden, MA and Oxford: Blackwell.

Franke, R. W. 1987. The Effects of Colonialism and Neocolonialism on the Gastronomic Patterns of the Third World. In Food and Evolution: Toward a Theory of Human Food Habits. Harris, M. and Ross, E. B., eds. pp. 455–479. Philadelphia: Temple University Press.

Friedlander, J. 1975. Being Indian in Hueyapán: A Study of Forced Identity in Contemporary Mexico. New York: St. Martin's Press.

———. 1981. The Secularization of the Cargo System. Latin American Research Review 16(2):131–143.

Furst, P. T. 1987. South American Shamanism. In The Encyclopedia of Religion (Vol. xiii). Eliade, M., ed. pp. 219–223. New York: Macmillan.

Fussell, B. 1999. Translating Maize into Corn: The Transformation of America's Native Grain. Social Research 66(1):41–65.

Gade, D. W. 1967. The Guinea Pig in Andean Folk Culture. Geographical Review 57(2):213–224.

———. 1979. Inca and Colonial Settlement, Coca Cultivation and Endemic Disease in the Tropical Forest. Journal of Historical Geography 5(3):263–279.

———. 1992. Landscape, System, and Identity in the Post-Conquest Andes. Annals of the Association of American Geographers 82(3):460–477.

———. 2000. South America. In The Cambridge World History of Food (Vol ii). Kiple, K. F. and Ornelas, K. C., eds. pp. 1254–1259. Cambridge: Cambridge University Press.

———. and Escobar, M. 1982. Village Settlement and the Colonial Legacy in Southern Peru. Geographical Review 72(4):430–449.

Gailey, C. W. 1987. Kinship to Kingship: Gender Hierarchy and State Formation in the Tongan Islands. Austin: University of Texas Press.

Galeano, E. 1997[1973]. Open Veins of Latin America: Five Centuries of the Pillage of a Continent (25th anniversary edition; foreword by Isabel Allende; translated by Cedric Belfrage). New York: Monthly Review Press.

———. 1986. Memoria del fuego III. El siglo del viento. Bogotá: Siglo Veintiuno.

———. 2003. Soccer in Sun and Shadow. New York: Verso.

———. 2004. Soccer: Opiate of the People? NACLA Report on the Americas 37(5):38–42.

Gandy, M. and Zumla, A. 2002. The Resurgence of Disease: Social and Historical Perspectives on the "New" Tuberculosis. Social Science and Medicine 55:385–396.

Garza Cuarón, B. and Lastram, Y. 1991. Endangered Languages in Mexico. In Endangered Languages. Robins, R. H. et al., eds. pp. 93–134. New York: St. Martin's Press.

Garzón, S. 1998a. Case Study Three: San Juan Comalapa. In The Life of Our Language: Kaqchikel Maya Maintenance, Shift, and Revitalization. Garzón, S. et al., eds. pp. 129–154. Austin: University of Texas Press.

———. 1998b. Introduction. In The Life of Our Language: Kaqchikel Maya Maintenance, Shift, and Revitalization. Garzón, S. et al., eds. pp. 1–8. Austin: University of Texas Press.

———. 1998c. Indigenous Groups and Their Language Contact Relations. In The Life of Our Language: Kaqchikel Maya Maintenance, Shift, and Revitalization. Garzón, S. et al., eds. pp. 9–43. Austin: University of Texas Press.

Gasco, J. and Smith, M. E. 1996. Origins and Development of Mesoamerican Civilization. In The Legacy of Mesoamerica: History and Culture of a Native American Civilization. Carmack, R. M. et al., eds. pp. 40–79. Upper Saddle River, NJ: Prentice Hall.

Gaspar, D. B. and Hine, D. C., eds. 2004. Beyond Bondage: Free Women of Color in the Americas. Urbana: University of Illinois Press.

Gates, A. 2000. A TV Family That Happens to Be Latino. New York Times. June 25, p. 13.59.

Geddes González, H. 1996. Mass Media and Cultural Identity Among the Yucatec Maya: The Constitution of Global, National, and Local Subjects. Studies in Latin American Popular Culture 15:131–153.

Géliga Vargas, J. A. 1996. Expanding the Popular Culture Debates: "Puertorriqueñas," Hollywood, and Cultural Identity. Studies in Latin American Popular Culture 15:155–173.

Gibbons, A. 1992. Scientists Search for "The Disappeared" in Guatemala. Science 257(5069):479.

Gibson, C. 1964. The Aztecs Under Spanish Rule: A History of the Indians of the Valley of Mexico, 1519–1810. Stanford: Stanford University Press.

———. 1987. Indian Societies Under Spanish Rule. In Colonial Spanish America. Bethell, L., ed. pp. 361–399. Cambridge: Cambridge University Press.

Gibson, C. and Jung, K. 2002. Historical Census Statistics on Population Totals by Race, 1790 to 1990, and by Hispanic Origin, 1970 to 1990, for the United States, Regions, Divisions, and States. Washington, D.C.: U.S. Census Bureau. Population Division. Working Paper No. 56.

Giddens, A. 1990. The Consequences of Modernity. Stanford: Stanford University Press.

Gieryn, T. E. 2000. A Space for Place in Sociology. Annual Review of Sociology 26:663–496.

Gilbert, A., ed. 1996. The Mega-City in Latin America. Tokyo and New York: United Nations University Press.

Gill, L. 1994. Precarious Dependencies: Gender, Class, and Domestic Service in Bolivia. New York: Columbia University Press.

———. 2000. Teetering on the Rim: Global Restructuring, Daily Life, and the Armed Retreat of the Bolivian State. New York: Columbia University Press.

Gledhill, J. 2000. Power and Its Disguises: Anthropological Perspectives on Politics. London: Pluto Press.

Golden, F. 1997. Scientist a Fierce Advocate for a Fierce People. Los Angeles Times. May 15.

Goldin, L. R. 1999. Rural Guatemala in Economic and Social Transition. In Globalization and the Rural Poor in Latin America. Loker, W. M., ed. pp. 93–110. Boulder and London: Lynne Rienner Publishers.

Goldstein, D. M. 2003. Laughter Out of Place: Race, Class, Violence, and Sexuality in a Rio Shantytown. Berkeley: University of California Press.

González, D. 2001. Panel Urges Legalization of Marijuana. New York Times. Sep. 30, p. A19.

González, N. L. 1988. Soujourners of the Caribbean: Ethnogenesis and Ethnohistory of the Garifuna. Urbana: University of Illinois Press.

———. 1997. The Garifuna of Central America. In The Indigenous People of the Caribbean. Wilson, S. M., ed. pp. 197–205. Gainesville: University Press of Florida.

González Echevarría, R. 1999. The Pride of Havana: A History of Cuban Baseball. New York: Oxford University Press.

Goodstein, L. and Forero, J. 2005. Robertson Suggests U.S. Kill Venezuela's Leader. New York Times. Aug. 24, p. A10.

Gordon, R. 1992. The Bushman Myth: The Making of a Namibian Underclass. Boulder, CO: Westview.

Gose, P. 1994. Deathly Waters and Hungry Mountains: Agrarian Ritual and Class Formation in an Andean Town. Toronto: University of Toronto Press.

Gossen, G. H. 1996. The Religious Traditions of Mesoamerica. In The Legacy of Mesoamerica: History and Culture of a Native American Civilization. Carmack, R. M. et al., eds. pp. 290–320. Upper Saddle River, NJ: Prentice Hall.

———. 1999. Rigoberta Menchú and Her Epic Narrative. Latin American Perspectives 26(109):64–69.

Gould, J. L. 1990. To Lead As Equals: Rural Protest and Political Consciousness in Chinandega, Nicaragua, 1912–1979. Chapel Hill: University of North Carolina Press.

Gove, P. B. 1986. Webster's Third New International Dictionary of the English Language, Unabridged. Springfield, MA: Merriam-Webster.

Gow, P. 1991. Of Mixed Blood: Kinship and History in Peruvian Amazonia. Oxford: Clarendon Press.

———. 1994. River People: Shamanism and History in Western Amazonia. In Shamanism, History, and the State. Thomas, N. and Humphrey, C., eds. pp. 90–114. Ann Arbor: The University of Michigan Press.

Green, D. 1995. Silent Revolution: The Rise of Market Economics in Latin America. London: Cassell (published in association with The Latin American Bureau).

Green, G. L. 2002. Marketing the Nation: Carnival and Tourism in Trinidad and Tobago. Critique of Anthropology 22(3): 283–304.

Green, J. N. 1999. Beyond Carnival: Male Homosexuality in Twentieth-Century Brazil. Chicago: University of Chicago Press.

Green, L. 1993. Shifting Affiliations: Mayan Widows and Evangélicos in Guatemala. In Rethinking Protestantism in Latin America. Garrard-Burnett, V. and Stoll, D., eds. pp. 159–179. Philadelphia: Temple University Press.

———. 2003. Notes on Mayan Youth and Rural Industrialization in Guatemala. Critique of Anthropology 23(1):51–73.

———. 2004. Living in a State of Fear. In Violence in War and Peace. Scheper-Hughes, N. and Bourgois, P., eds. pp. 186–195. Malden, MA and Oxford: Blackwell.

Greene, S. 2004. Indigenous People Incorporated? Culture as Politics, Culture as Property in Pharmaceutical Bioprospecting. Current Anthropology 45(2):211–237.

Gregor, T. A. and Tuzin, D. 2001. Comparing Gender in Amazonia and Melanesia: A Theoretical Orientation. In Gender in Amazonia and Melanesia: An Exploration of the Comparative Method. Gregor, T. A. and Tuzin, D., eds. pp. 1–16. Berkeley: University of California Press.

Griffin, K. and Vermelho, L. L. 2002. Brazil. In HIV and AIDS: A Global View. McElrath, K., ed. pp. 17–41. Westport, CT: Greenwood Press.

Griffiths, N. 1996. The Cross and the Serpent: Religious Repression and Resurgence in Colonial Peru. Norman: University of Oklahoma Press.

Grigsby, T. L. and Cook de Leonard, C. 1992. Xilonen in Tepoztlan: A Comparison of Tepoztecan and Aztec Agrarian Ritual Schedules. Ethnohistory 39(2):108–147.

Grinevald, C. 1998. Language Endangerment in South America: A Programmatic Approach. In Endangered Languages: Current Issues and Future Prospects. Grenoble, L. A. and Whaley, L. J., eds. pp. 124–159. Cambridge: Cambridge University Press.

Grivetti, L. E. 2000. Food Prejudices and Taboos. In The Cambridge World History of Food (Vol II). Kiple, K. F. and Ornelas, K. C., eds. pp. 1495–1512. Cambridge: Cambridge University Press.

Gros, C. 1999. Evangelical Protestantism and Indigenous Populations. Bulletin of Latin American Research 18(2):175–197.

Guarnaccia, P. J. et al. 1989. The Multiple Meanings of Ataques de Nervios in the Latino Community. Medical Anthropology 11:47–63.

———. 1990. A Critical Review of Epidemiological Studies of Puerto Rican Mental Health. The American Journal of Psychiatry 147:1449–1456.

———. 1996. The Experience of Ataques de Nervios: Towards an Anthropology of Emotion in Puerto Rico. Culture, Medicine and Psychiatry 20:343–367.

Gudeman, S. 1975. Spiritual Relationships and Selecting a Godparent. Man 10(2):221–237.

———. and Schwartz, S. B. 1984. Cleansing Original Sin: Godparenthood and the Baptism of Slaves in Eighteenth-Century Bahia. In Kinship Ideology and Practice in Latin America. Smith, R. T., ed. pp. 35–58. Chapel Hill: University of North Carolina Press.

Guerra, F. 1988. The Earliest American Epidemic: The Influenza of 1493. Social Science History 12(3):305–325.

Guillén, M. F. 2001. Is Globalization Civilizing, Destructive or Feeble?: A Critique of Five Key Debates in the Social Science Literature. Annual Review of Sociology 27:235–260.

Guilmartin, J. F. 1991. The Cutting Edge: An Analysis of the Spanish Invasion and Overthrow of the Inca Empire, 1532–1539. In Transatlantic Encounters: Europeans and Andeans in the Sixteenth Century. Andrien, K. J. and Adorno, R., eds. pp. 40–72. Berkeley: University of California Press.

Guss, D. M. 1996. Cimarrones, Theater, and the State. In History, Power, and Identity: Ethnogenesis in the Americas, 1492–1992. Hill, J. D., ed. pp. 180–192. Iowa City: University of Iowa Press.

Guthmann, J. P. 1995. Epidemic Cholera in Latin America: Spread and Routes of Transmission. Journal of Tropical Medicine and Hygiene 98:419–427.

Gutiérrez, R. A. 1991. When Jesus Came, the Corn Mothers Went Away: Marriage, Sexuality, and Power in New Mexico, 1500–1846. Stanford: Stanford University Press.

Gutmann, M. C. ed. 1996. The Meanings of Macho: Being a Man in Mexico City. Berkeley: University of California Press.

———. 1997. Trafficking in Men: The Anthropology of Masculinity. Annual Review of Anthropology 26:385–409.

———. 2003a. Changing Men and Masculinities in Latin America. Durham, NC: Duke University Press.

———. 2003b. Introduction: Discarding Manly Dichotomies in Latin America. In Changing Men and Masculinities in Latin America. Gutmann, M. C., ed. pp. 1–26. Durham, NC: Duke University Press.

———. 2003c. For Whom the Taco Bell Tolls: Popular Responses to NAFTA South of the Border. In Perspectives on Las Américas: A Reader in Culture, History, and Representation. Gutmann, M. C. et al., eds. pp. 404–417. Malden, MA and Oxford: Blackwell.

Guttman, A. 1994. Games and Empires: Modern Sports and Cultural Imperialism. New York: Columbia University Press.

Hagen, E. H. et al. 2001. Preliminary Report. www.anth. ucsb.edu/ucsbpreliminaryreport.pdf.

Hale, C. R. 1997. Consciousness, Violence, and the Politics of Memory in Guatemala. Current Anthropology 38(5):817–838.

Hamilton, S. 1998. The Two-Headed Household: Gender and Rural Development in the Ecuadorean Andes. Pittsburgh: University of Pittsburgh Press.

Hammond, N. 2000. The Maya Lowlands: Pioneer Farmers to Merchant Princes. In The Cambridge History of the Native Peoples of the Americas (Volume II [Mesoamerica], Part 1). Adams, R. E. and MacLeod, M. J., eds. pp. 197–249. Cambridge: Cambridge University Press.

Hanchard, M. G. 1994. Orpheus and Power: The Movimento Negro of Rio de Janeiro and São Paulo, Brazil, 1945–1988. Princeton, NJ: Princeton University Press.

Handler, R. 1994. Romancing the Low: Anthropology vis-à-vis Cultural Studies vis-à-vis Popular Culture. Political and Legal Anthropology Review 17(2):1–6.

Handwerker, W. P. 1989. Women's Power and Social Revolution: Fertility Transition in the West Indies. Newbury Park, CO: Sage Publications.

Harding, R. E. 2000. A Refuge in Thunder: Candomblé and Alternative Spaces of Blackness. Bloomington: Indiana University Press.

Harley, J. B. 1992. Rereading the Maps of the Columbian Encounter. Annals of the Association of American Geographers 19(3):522–536.

Harman, D. 2004. In Chile, Pace of Justice Quickens. Christian Science Monitor. Dec. 15, p. 6.

———. 2005. Outsourcing Moves Closer to Home; A New Trade Agreement with Central America to Take Effect Jan. 1 Tempts More US Companies to Try "Nearsourcing." Christian Science Monitor. Nov. 28, p. 13.

Harms, J. B. and Knapp, T. 2003. The New Economy: What's New, What's Not. Review of Radical Political Economy 35(4):413–436.

Harner, M. J. 1973. The Jívaro People of the Sacred Waterfalls. Garden City, NY: Anchor Press/Doubleday.

Harris, M. 1969[1956]. Town and Country in Brazil. New York: AMS Press.

———. 1964. Patterns of Race in the Americas. New York: Walker and Company.

———. 1968. The Rise of Anthropological Theory. New York: Columbia University Press.

Harris, M. 2003. Carnival and Other Christian Festivals: Folk Theology and Folk Performance. Austin: University of Texas Press.

Harris, O. 2000. To Make the Earth Bear Fruit: Essays on Fertility, Work, and Gender in Highland Bolivia. London: University of London. Institute of Latin American Studies.

Harvey, D. 1990. Between Space and Time: Reflections on the Geographical Imagination. Annals of the Association of American Geographers 80(3):418–434.

Harvey, P. 1994. Domestic Violence in the Peruvian Andes. In Sex and Violence: Issues in Representation and Experience. Harvey, P. and Gow, P., eds. pp. 66–89. New York: Routledge.

Harwood, A. 1998. The Hot-Cold Theory of Disease: Implications for the Treatment of Puerto Rican Patients. In Understanding and Applying Medical Anthropology. Brown, P. J., ed. pp. 251–258. London and Toronto: Mayfield Publishing Company.

Hassig, R. 1994. Mexico and the Spanish Conquest. London: Longman.

Heath, D. B. 2002. Latin America: Image and Reality. In Contemporary Cultures and Societies of Latin America: A Reader in the Social Anthropology of Middle and South America (3rd Ed.). Heath, D. B., ed. pp. 1–6. Prospect Heights, IL: Waveland Press.

Hemming, J. 1970. The Conquest of the Incas. New York and London: Harcourt Brace Jovanovich.

Henman, A. 1985. Cocaine Futures. In Big Deal: The Politics of the Illicit Drugs Business. Henman, A. et al., eds. pp. 118–189. London: Pluto Press.

Henwood, D. 2000. Profiteering in the Hemisphere. NACLA Report on the Americas 34(3):49–54.

Hern, W. M. 1994. Health and Demography of Native Amazonians: Historical Perspective and Current Status. In Amazonian Indians from Prehistory to the Present: Anthropological Perspectives. Roosevelt, A. C., ed. pp. 123–149. Tucson: University of Arizona Press.

Hernández Castillo, R. A. 2003. Between Civil Disobedience and Silent Rejection: Differing Responses by Mam Peasants to the Zapatista Rebellion (translated by Francine Cronshaw). In Mayan Lives, Mayan Utopias: The Indigenous Peoples of Chiapas and the Zapatista Rebellion. Rus, J. et al., eds. pp. 63–83. Lanham, MD: Rowman & Littlefield.

Herskovits, M. J. 1937a. African Gods and Catholic Saints in New World Negro Belief. American Anthropologist 39(4):635–643.

———. 1937b. Life in a Haitian Village. New York: Alfred A. Knopf.

Hill, J. D. 1993. Keepers of the Sacred Chants: The Poetics of Ritual Power in an Amazonian Society. Tucson: University of Arizona Press.

———. 1996. Introduction: Ethnogenesis in the Americas, 1492–1992. In History, Power, and Identity: Ethnogenesis in the Americas, 1492–1992. Hill, J. D., ed. pp. 1–19. Iowa City: University of Iowa Press.

———. 2001. The Variety of Fertility Cultism in Amazonia: A Closer Look at Gender Symbolism in Northwestern Amazonia. In Gender in Amazonia and Melanesia: An Exploration of the Comparative Method. Gregor, T. A. and Tuzin, D., eds. pp. 45–68. Berkeley: University of California Press.

——— and Santos-Granero, F. 2002. Introduction. In Comparative Arawakan Histories: Rethinking Language Family and Culture Area in Amazonia. Hill, J. D. and Santos-Granero, F., eds. pp. 1–22. Urbana: University of Illinois Press.

Hill, K. and Hurtado, M. 1996. Ache Life History: The Ecology and Demography of a Foraging People. New York: Aldine De Gruyter.

Hill, R. M. I. 1992. Colonial Cakchiquels: Highland Maya Adaptation to Spanish Rule 1600–1700. Fort Worth, TX: Harcourt Brace Jovanovich.

Hinds, H. E. Jr. 1996. A Holistic Approach to the Study of Popular Culture: Context, Text, Audience, and Recoding. Studies in Latin American Popular Culture 15:11–29.

Hinton, A. L. ed. 2002. Annihilating Difference: The Anthropology of Genocide. Berkeley: University of California Press.

Hippolyte Ortega, N. 1998. Big Snakes on the Streets and Never Ending Stories: The Case of Venezuelan Telenovelas. In Imagination Beyond Nation: Latin American Popular Culture. Bueno, E. P. and Caesar, T., eds. pp. 64–80. Pittsburgh: University of Pittsburgh Press.

Hirsch, E. and O'Hanlon, M., eds. 1995. The Anthropology of Landscape: Perspectives on Place and Space. New York: Oxford University Press.

Hirsch, J. S. 2003. A Courtship After Marriage: Sexuality and Love in Mexican Transnational Families. Berkeley: University of California Press.

Hitt, G. and Davis, B. 2005. Bush Reaches Out to Democrats on Trade; Close CAFTA Vote Leads Republicans Soul-Searching. Wall Street Journal. Dec. 2, p. A4.

Hobsbawn, E. 1983. Introduction: Inventing Traditions. In The Invention of Tradition. Hobsbawn, E. and Ranger, T., eds. pp. 1–14. Cambridge: Cambridge University Press.

Hoetink, H. 1985. "Race" and Color in the Caribbean. In Caribbean Contours. Mintz, S. W. and Price, S., eds. pp. 55–84. Baltimore: Johns Hopkins University Press.

Hoffman, K. and Centeno, M. A. 2003. The Lopsided Continent: Inequality in Latin America. Annual Review of Sociology 29:363–390.

Holton, G. E. L. 2000. Oil, Race, and Calypso in Trinidad and Tobago, 1909–1990. In Latin American Popular Culture: An Introduction. Beezley, W. H. and Curcio-Nagy, L. A., eds. pp. 201–212. Wilmington, DE: Scholarly Resources.

Hondagneu-Soleto, P. 2001. Doméstica: Immigrant Workers Cleaning and Caring in the Shadows of Affluence. Berkeley: University of California Press.

Hornberger, N. H. 1997a. Introduction: Indigenous Literacies in the Americas. In Indigenous Literacies in the Americas: Language Planning from the Bottom Up. Hornberger, N. H., ed. pp. 3–16. Berlin and New York: Mouton de Gruyter.

———. 1997b. Language Planning from the Bottom Up. In Indigenous Literacies in the Americas: Language Planning from the Bottom up. Hornberher, N.H., ed. pp. 257–366. Berlin and New York: Mouton de Gruyter.

———. 1997c. Quechua Literacy and Empowerment in Peru. In Indigenous Literacies in the Americas: Language Planning from the Bottom Up. Hornberger, N. H., ed. pp. 215–236. Berlin and New York: Mouton de Gruyter.

Horowitz, M. M., ed. 1971a. Peoples and Cultures of the Caribbean. Garden City, NY: Natural History Press.

———. 1971b. A Decision Model of Conjugal Patterns in Martinique. In Peoples and Cultures of the Caribbean: An Anthropological Reader. Horowitz, M. M., ed. pp. 476–488. Garden City, NY: Natural History Press.

Huber, B. R. and Sandstrom, A. R., eds. 2001. Mesoamerican Healers. Austin: University of Texas Press.

Hulme, P. 1986. Colonial Encounters: Europe and the Native Caribbean 1492–1797. London: Methuen & Co.

———. and Whitehead, N. L., eds. 1992. Wild Majesty: Encounters with Caribs from Columbus to the Present Day. New York: Oxford University Press.

Huntington, S. P. 2004. The Hispanic Challenge. Foreign Policy 141:30–45.

Hurley, D. 2005. Medicinal Marijuana on Trial. New York Times. Mar. 29, p. F5.

Hutchison, E. Q. 2001. Labors Appropriate to Their Sex: Gender, Labor and Politics in Urban Chile. Durham, NC: Duke University Press.

Inciardi, J. A. ed. 1999. The Drug Legalization Debate. Thousand Oaks, CA: Sage Publications.

Inda, J. X. and Rosaldo, R., eds. 2002. The Anthropology of Globalization: A Reader. Malden, MA and Oxford: Blackwell Publishers.

Ingham, J. M. 1986. Mary, Michael, and Lucifer: Folk Catholicism in Central Mexico. Austin: University of Texas Press.

Inhorn, M. C. and Brown, P. J. 1990. The Anthropology of Infectious Disease. Annual Review of Anthropology 19:89–117.

Isbell, B. J. 1992. Shining Path and Peasant Responses in Rural Ayacucho. In The Shining Path of Peru. Palmer, D. S., ed. pp. 77–99. New York: St. Martin's Press.

Jackson, J. E. 1975. Recent Ethnography of Indigenous Northern Lowland South America. Annual Review of Anthropology 4:307–340.

Jacob, C. 1996. Toward a Cultural History of Cartography. Imago Mundi 48:191–198.

James, P. E. 1950[1942]. Latin America. New York: The Odyssey Press.

Jaquith, C. and Kopec, R. 1987. Advances, Challenges for Women in the New Nicaragua. The Militant. Nov. 20.

Jelin, E. 1997. The Minefields of Memory. NACLA Report on the Americas 37(2):23–29.

———. 1991. Family, Household and Gender Relations in Latin America. London and New York: Kegan Paul International (in association with UNESCO).

Jimeno, M. 2001. Violence and Social Life in Colombia. Critique of Anthropology 21(3):221–246.

Jiménez, M. F. 1995. "From Plantation to Cup": Coffee and Capitalism in the United States, 1830–1930. In Coffee, Sociey, and Power in Latin America. Roseberry, W. et al., eds. pp. 38–64. Baltimore: Johns Hopkins University.

Johnson, H. B. 1987. Portuguese Settlement, 1500–1580. In Colonial Brazil. Bethell, L., ed. pp. 1–38. Cambridge: Cambridge University Press.

Johnsson, M. 1986. Food and Culture Among Bolivian Aymara: Symbolic Expressions of Social Relations. Stockholm: Uppsala.

Jolly, M. 1998. Introduction: Colonial and Postcolonial Plots in Histories of Maternities and Modernities. In Maternities and Modernities: Colonial and Postcolonial Experiences in Asia and the Pacific. Ram, K. and Jolly, M., eds. pp. 1–25. Cambridge: Cambridge University Press.

Jones, G. D. 2000. The Lowand Maya, from the Conquest to the Present. In The Cambridge History of the Native Peoples of the Americas (Volume II [Mesoamerica], Part 2). Adams, R. E. and MacLeod, M. J., eds. pp. 346–391. Cambridge: Cambridge University Press.

Joralemon, D. 1982. New World Depopulation and the Case of Disease. Journal of Anthropological Research 38:108–127.

———. 1993. Sorcery and Shamanism: Curanderos and Clients in Northern Peru. Salt Lake City: University of Utah Press.

———. 1999. Exploring Medical Anthropology. Boston: Allyn and Bacon.

Joseph, G. M. 1988. Forging the Regional Pastime: Baseball and Class in Yucatán. In Sport and Society in Latin America: Diffusion, Dependancy, and the Rise of Mass Culture. Arbena, J. L., ed. pp. 29–61. New York: Greenwood Press.

Joyce, R. A. 2001. Negotiating Sex and Gender in Classic Maya Society. In Gender in Pre-Hispanic America: A Symposium at Dumbarton Oaks 12 and 13 October 1996. Klein, C. F. and Quilter, J., eds. pp. 109–142. Washington, D.C.: Dumbarton Oaks Research Library and Collection.

Kaeppler, A. 1978. Dance in Anthropological Perspective. Annual Review of Anthropology 23:31–49.

Kahn, J. R. and McDonald, J. A. 1995. Third-World Debt and Tropical Deforestation. Ecological Economics 12(2):107–123.

Kaimowitz, D. et al. 1999. The Effects of Structural Adjustment on Deforestation and Forest Degradation in Lowland Bolivia. World Development 27(3):505–520.

Kampwirth, K. 2002. Women and Guerilla Movements: Nicaragua, El Salvador, Chiapas, Cuba. University Park: Pennsylvania State University Press.

Kanaiaupuni, S. M. et al. 2005. Counting on Kin: Social Networks, Social Support, and Child Health Status. Social Forces 83(3):1137–1164.

Kaplan, F. S. 1993. Mexican Museums in the Creation of a National Image in World Tourism. In Crafts in the World Market: Impact of Global Exchange on Middle American Artisans. Nash, J. C., ed. pp. 103–125. Albany: State University of New York Press.

Karlsson, B. G. 2003. Anthropology and the "Indigenous Slot": Claims to and Debates About Indigenous Peoples' Status in India. Critique of Anthropology 23:(4):403–423.

Katzew, I. 2004. Casta Paintings: Images of Race in Eighteenth Century Mexico. New Haven, CT: Yale University Press.

Kearney, M. 1991. Borders and Boundaries of State and Self at the End of Empire. Journal of Historical Sociology 4(1):52–74.

———. 1995. The Local and the Global: The Anthropology of Globalization and Transnationalism. Annual Review of Anthropology 24:547–565.

———. 1996. Reconceptualizing the Peasantry: Anthropology in Global Perspective. Boulder, CO: Westview.

Keegan, W. F. 1992. The People Who Discovered Columbus: The Prehistory of the Bahamas. Gainesville: University Press of Florida.

———. 1997. "No Man [or Woman] is an Island": Elements of Taino Social Organization. In The Indigenous People of the Caribbean. Wilson, S. M., ed. pp. 109–117. Gainesville: University Press of Florida.

———. 2000. The Caribbean, Including Northern South America. In The Cambridge World History of Food (Vol. II). Kiple, K. F. and Ornelas, K. C., eds. pp. 1260–1277. Cambridge: Cambridge University Press.

Keesing, R. M. 1974. Theories of Culture. Annual Review of Anthropology 3:73–97.

Kelekna, P. 1994. Farming, Feuding, and Female Status: The Achuar Case. In Amazonian Indians from Prehistory to the Present: Anthropological Perspectives. Roosevelt, A., ed. pp. 225–248. Tucson: University of Arizona Press.

Kellog, S. 1991. Histories for Anthropology: Ten Years of Historical Research and Writing by Anthropologists, 1980–1990. Social Science History 15(4):417–455.

Kempadoo, K. 2004. Sexing the Caribbean: Gender, Race, and Sexual Labor. New York: Routledge.

Kerns, V. 1997. Women and the Ancestors: Black Carib Kinship and Ritual. Urbana: University of Illinois Press.

Khan, A. 1994. *Juthaa* in Trinidad: Food, Pollution, and Hierarchy in a Caribbean Disapora Community. American Ethnologist 21(2):245–269.

Kincaid, A. D. 1993. Peasants into Rebels: Community and Class in Rural El Salvador. In Constructing Culture and Power in Latin America. Levine, D. H., ed. pp. 119–154. Ann Arbor: University of Michigan Press.

Kirk, R. 2003. More Terrible than Death: Massacres, Drugs, and America's War in Colombia. New York: Public Affairs.

Kirtsoglou, E. and Theodossopoulos, D. 2004. "They are Taking our Culture Away": Tourism and Culture Commodification in the Garifuna Community of Roatan. Critique of Anthropology 24(2):135–157.

Kitzinger, S. 1969. Protest and Mysticism: The Rastafari Cult of Jamaica. Journal for the Scientific Study of Religion 8(2):240–262.

Klaiber, J. L. 1989. Prophets and Populists: Liberation Theology, 1968–1988. The Americas 46(1):1–15.

Klein, A. M. 1991. Sugarball: The American Game, the Dominican Dream. New Haven, CT: Yale University Press.

Klein, C. F. 2001. Conclusions: Envisioning Pre-Columbian Gender Studies. In Gender in Pre-Hispanic America: A Symposium at Dumbarton Oaks 12 and 13 Oct. 1996. Klein, C. F. and Quilter, J., eds. pp. 363–386. Washington, D.C.: Dumbarton Oaks Research Library and Collection.

——— and Quilter, J., eds. 2001. Gender in Pre-Hispanic America: A Symposium at Dumbarton Oaks, 12 and 13 Oct. 1996. Washington, D.C.: Dumbarton Oaks Research Library and Collection.

Klein, C. H. 2002. "Making a Scene": Travestis and the Gendered Politics of Space in Porto Alegre, Brazil. In Gender's Place: Feminist Anthropologies of Latin America. Montoya, R. et al., eds. pp. 217–236. New York: Palgrave Macmillan.

Klein, H. S. 1986. African Slavery in Latin America and the Caribbean. New York: Oxford University Press.

Klubock, T. M. 1997. Morality and Good Habits: The Construction of Gender and Class in the Chilean Copper Mines, 1904–1951. In Gendered Worlds of Latin American Women Workers: From Household and Factory to the Union Hall and Ballot Box. French, J. D. and Daniel, J., eds. pp. 232–263. Durham, NC: Duke University Press.

Knauft, B. M. 1997. Gender Identity, Political Economy and Modernity in Melanesia and Amazonia. The Journal of the Royal Anthropological Institute 3(2):233–259.

Knight, A. S. 1990. Racism, Revolution and Indigenismo: Mexico, 1910–1940. In The Idea of Race in Latin America, 1870–1940. Graham, R., ed. pp. 71–113. Austin: University of Texas Press.

Kottak, C. P. 1990. Prime-Time Society: An Anthropological Analysis of Television and Culture. Belmont, CA: Wadsworth Pub. Co.

———. 1999. Assault on Paradise: Social Change in a Brazilian Village. New York: McGraw-Hill.

Krauss, C. 1999. The C.I.A. and Guatemala: The Spies Who Never Came in from the Cold. New York Times. Mar. 7, Section 4, p. 1.

Krech, S. I. 1999. The Ecological Indian: Myth and History. New York: W.W. Norton & Co.

Krieger, N. et al. 1993. Racism, Sexism, and Social Class: Implications for Studies of Health, Disease, and Well-Being. American Journal of Preventive Medicine 9:82–122.

Kuhn, T. S. 1962. The Structure of Scientific Revolutions. Chicago: University of Chicago Press.

Kulick, D. 1997. The Gender of Brazilian Transgendered Prostitutes. American Anthropologist 99(3):574–585.

———. 1998. Travesti: Sex, Gender, and Culture among Brazilian Transgendered Prostitutes. Chicago: University of Chicago Press.

Kurtz, D. V. 1996. Hegemony and Anthropology: Gramsci, Exegeses, Reinterpretations. Critique of Anthropology 16(2):103–135.

Kuznesof, E. A. 1992. The Construction of Gender in Colonial Latin America. Colonial Latin American Review 1(1–2): 253–270.

La Pastina, A. C. 2004. Telenovela Reception in Rural Brazil: Gendered Readings and Sexual Mores. Critical Studies in Media Communication 21(2):162–181.

La Prensa. 2004. Giving Latinas the Quinceañera of their Dreams. La Prensa (Denver, CO). May 16, p. A3.

La Rosa Corzo, G. 2003. Runaway Slave Settlements in Cuba: Resistance and Repression. Chapel Hill: University of North Carolina Press.

La Voz de Colorado. 2001. A 500-Year-Old Tradition Meets Cyberspace: The Celebration of a Quinceañera. La Voz de Colorado (Denver, CO). Sep. 5, p. 6.

Lafaye, J. 1974. Quetzalcoatl and Guadalupe: The Formation of Mexican National Consciousness 1531–1813. Chicago: University of Chicago Press.

LaFranchi, H. 2003. A Decade Later, A Tempered Vision of NAFTA. Christian Science Monitor. Dec 30, p. 2.

Lancaster, R. N. 1988. Thanks to God and the Revolution: Popular Religion and Class Consciousness in the New Nicaragua. New York: Columbia University Press.

———. 1992. Life Is Hard: Machismo, Danger, and the Intimacy of Power in Nicaragua. Berkeley: University of California Press.

———. 1997. Sexual Positions: Caveats and Second Thoughts on "Categories." The Americas 54(1):1–16.

Landers, J. 2004. Maroon Women in Colonial Spanish America: Case Studies in the Circum-Caribbean from the Sixteenth Through the Eighteenth Centuries. In Beyond Bondage: Free Women of Color in the Americas. Gaspar, D. B. and Hine, D. C., eds. pp. 3–18. Urbana: University of Illinois Press.

Langdon E. J. and Baer, G., eds. 1992. Portals of Power: Shamanism in South America. Albuquerque: University of New Mexico Press.

Langer, E. D. 1985. Labor Strikes and Reciprocity on Chuquisaca Haciendas. Hispanic American Historical Review 65(2):255–277.

Langer, E. D. and Muñoz, E., eds. 2003. Contemporary Indigenous Movements in Latin America. Wilmington, DE: Scholarly Resources.

——— and Jackson, R. H., eds. 1995. The New Latin American Mission History. Lincoln and London: University of Nebraska Press.

Langley, L. D. 1989. America and the Americas: The United States in the Western Hemisphere. Athens: University of Georgia Press.

Larson, B. 1988b. Colonialism and Agrarian Transformation in Bolivia: Cochabamba, 1550–1900. Princeton, NJ: Princeton University Press.

——— and Harris, O., eds. 1995. Ethnicity, Markets, and Migration in the Andes: At the Crossroads of History and Anthropology. Durham, NC: Duke University Press.

Larson, C. S. 1994. In the Wake of Columbus: Native Population Biology in the Postcontact Americas. Yearbook of Physical Anthropology 37:109–154.

Larvie, P. 1997. Homophobia and the Ethnoscape of Sex Work in Rio de Janeiro. In Sexual Cultures and Migration in the Era of AIDS: Anthropological and Demographic Perspectives. Herdt, G., ed. pp. 143–164. Oxford: Clarendon Press.

———. 1999. Natural Born Targets: Male Hustlers and AIDS Prevention in Urban Brazil. In Men Who Sell Sex: International Perspectives on Male Prostitution and HIV/AIDS. Aggleton, P., ed. pp. 159–178. Philadelphia: Temple University Press.

———. 2003. Nation, Science, and Sex: AIDS and the New Brazilian Sexuality. In Disease in the History of Modern Latin America: From Malaria to AIDS. Armus, D., ed. pp. 290–314. Durham, NC: Duke University Press.

Lassalle, Y. M. and O'Dougherty, M. 1997. In Search of Weeping Worlds. Economies of Agency and Politics of Representation in the Ethnography of Inequality. Radical History Review 69:243–260.

Laurance, W. F. et al. 2001a. The Future of the Brazilian Amazon. Science 292(5503 January 19):438–439.

———. 2005a. A Delicate Balance in Amazonia. Science 307 (February 18):1044–1045.

———. 2005b. Response. Science 307 (February 18):1044.

Laurance, W. F. and Williamson, G. B. 2001b. Postive Feedbacks Among Forest Fragmentation, Drought, and Climate Change in the Amazon. Conservation Biology 15(6):1529–1535.

Lavallée, D. 2000. The First South Americans: The Peopling of a Continent from the Earliest Evidence to High Culture (translated by Paul G. Bahn). Salt Lake City: University of Utah Press.

Lederman, R. 1998. Globalization and the Future of Culture Areas: Melanesianist Anthropology in Transition. Annual Review of Anthropology 27:427–449.

Lee, H. and Bobadilla, J. L. 1994. Health Statistics for the Americas. Washington, D.C.: The World Bank. World Bank Technical Paper Number 262.

Lemebel, P. 1998. Soccer and Devotion in the Barrios of Santiago (translated by NACLA). NACLA Report on the Americas 32(1 July–Aug. 1998):36–42.

Lever, J. 1983. Soccer Madness. Chicago: University of Chicago Press.

Levine, D. H. 1992. Popular Voices in Latin American Catholicism. Princeton, NJ: Princeton University Press.

———. 1993. Popular Groups, Popular Culture, and Popular Religion. In Constructing Culture and Power in Latin America. Levine, D. H., ed. pp. 171–226. Ann Arbor: University of Michigan Press.

Lewis, O. 1961. The Children of Sánchez: Autobiography of a Mexican Family. New York: Vintage Books.

———. 1965. La Vida: A Puerto Rican Family in the Culture of Poverty: San Juan and New York. New York: Vintage Books.

Linger, D. T. 1992. Dangerous Encounters: Meanings of Violence in a Brazilian City. Stanford: Standford University Press.

Lipsett-Rivera, S. 2002. Mira lo que hace el diablo: The Devil in Mexican Popular Culture, 1750–1856. The Americas 59(2):201–219.

Locke, M. 1993. Cultivating the Body: Anthropology and Epistemologies of Bodily Practice and Knowledge. Annual Review of Anthropology 22:133–155.

Lockhart, J. 1969. Encomienda and Hacienda: The Evolution of the Great Estate in the Spanish Indies. Hispanic American Historical Review 49(3):411–29.

———. 1992. The Nahuas After the Conquest: A Social and Cultural History of the Indians of Mexico, Sixteenth Through Eighteenth Centuries. Stanford: Stanford University Press.

Logan, M. H. and Morrill, W. T. 1979. Humoral Medicine and Informant Variability: An Analysis of Acculturation and Cognitive Change among Guatemalan Villagers. Anthropos 74:785–802.

Lombardi, C. et al. 1983. Latin American History: A Teaching Atlas. Madison: Published for the Conference on Latin American History and University of Wisconsin Press.

López, R. L. 2002. The Devil, Women, and the Body in Seventeenth-Century Puebla Convents. The Americas 59(2):181–199.

López-Vicuña, I. 2004. Approaches to Sexuality in Latin America: Recent Scholarship on Gay and Lesbian Studies. Latin American Research Review 39(1):238–253.

Loucky, J. 2000. Maya in a Modern Metropolis: Establishing New Lives and Livelihoods in Los Angeles. In The Maya Diaspora: Guatemalan Roots, New American Lives. Loucky, J. and Moors, M. M., eds. pp. 214–222. Philadelphia: Temple University Press.

———. and Moors, M. M. 2000. The Maya Diaspora: Introduction. In The Maya Diaspora: Guatemalan Roots, New American Lives. Loucky, J. and Moors, M. M., eds. pp. 1–10. Philadelphia: Temple University Press.

Lovell, W. G. 1992a. Conquest and Survival in Colonial Guatemala: A Historical Geography of the Cuchumatan Highlands, 1500–1821. Montreal: McGill-Queen's University Press.

———. 1992b. "Heavy Shadows and Black Night": Disease and Depopulation in Colonial Spanish America. Annals of the Association of American Geographers 82(3):426–443.

———. and Lutz, C. H. 1994. Conquest and Population: Maya Demography in Historical Perspective. Latin American Research Review 29(2):133–142.

———. 1995. Introduction. In Demography and Empire: A Guide to the Population History of Spanish Central America, 1500–1821. Lovell, W. G. and Lutz, C. H., eds. pp. 1–17. Boulder, CO: Westview.

———. 2001. The Primacy of Larger Truths: Rigoberta Menchú and the Tradition of Native Testimony in Guatemala. In The Rigoberta Menchú Controversy (with a response by David Stoll). Arias, A., ed. pp. 171–197. Minneapolis: University of Minnesota Press.

Lowenthal, I. P. 1984. Labor, Sexuality, and the Conjugal Contract in Rural Haiti. In Haiti—Today and Tomorrow: An Interdisciplinary Study. Foster, C. R. and Valdman, A., eds. pp. 15–33. New York: University Press of America.

Lumbreras, L. 1999. Andean Urbanism and Statecraft, (C.E. 550–1450). In The Cambridge History of the Native Peoples of the Americas (Volume III [South America], Part 1). Salomon, F. and Schwartz, S. B., eds. pp. 518–576. Cambridge: Cambridge University Press.

Lunenfeld, M. 1992. What Shall We Tell the Children? The Press Encounters Columbus. History Teacher 25(2):137–144.

Lutz, C. H. and Lovell, G. W. 2000. Survivors on the Move: Maya Migration in Time and Space. In The Maya Diaspora: Guatemalan Roots, New American Lives. Loucky, J. and Moors, M. M., eds. pp. 11–34. Philadelphia: Temple University Press.

Lynch, T. F. 1999. The Earliest South American Lifeways. In The Cambridge History of the Native Peoples of the Americas (Volume III [South America], Part 1). Salomon, F. and Schwartz, S. B., eds. pp. 188–263. Cambridge: Cambridge University Press.

MacCormack, S. 1998. Time, Space, and Ritual Action: The Inka and Christian Calendars in Early Colonial Peru. In Native Traditions in the Postconquest World. Boone, E. H. and Cummins, T., eds. pp. 295–343. Washington, D.C.: Dumbarton Oaks Research Library and Collection.

Macintyre, S. 2001. Inequalities in Health: Is Research Gender Blind? In Poverty, Inequality, and Health: An International Perspective. León, D. A. and Walt, G., eds. pp. 283–293. New York: Oxford University Press.

MacKenzie, J. C. 2005. Maya Bodies and Minds: Religion and Modernity in a K'iche' Town. Ph.D. dissertation. State University of New York at Albany.

MacLeod, M. J. 2000. Mesoamerica Since the Spanish Invasion: An Overview. In The Cambridge History of the Native Peoples of the Americas (Volume II [Mesoamerica], Part 2). Adams, R. E. and MacLeod, M. J., eds. pp. 1–43. Cambridge: Cambridge University Press.

MacQueen, K. M. 1994. The Epidemiology of HIV Transmission: Trends, Structure and Dynamics. Annual Review of Anthropology 23:509–526.

Maddox, R. 1993. El Castillo: The Politics of Tradition in an Andalusian Town. Urbana: University of Illinois Press.

Mahan, E. 1996. What Is Popular Culture?: More Answers to an Old Question. Studies in Latin American Popular Culture 15:1–10.

Mahler, S. J. 1995. Salvadorans in Suburbia: Simbiosis and Conflict. Boston: Allyn and Bacon.

Mallon, F. 1992. Indian Communities, Political Cultures, and the State in Latin America, 1780–1990. Journal of Latin American Studies 24 (Quincentenary Supplement):35–53.

———. 1995. Peasant and Nation: The Making of Postcolonial Mexico and Peru. Berkeley: University of California Press.

Manrique, E. 1990–1991. Women at War. NACLA Report on the Americas 24(4):28–38.

Manuel, P. 1994. Puerto Rican Music and Cultural Identity: Creative Appropriations of Cuban Sources from Danza to Salsa. Ethnomusicology 38(2):249–280.

———. (with Kenneth Bilby and Michael Largey). 1995. Caribbean Currents: Caribbean Music from Rumba to Reggae. Philadelphia: Temple University Press.

Marcus, G. E. 1995. Ethnography in/of The World System: The Emergence of Multi-Sited Ethnography. Annual Review of Anthropology 24:95–117.

———. and Fischer, M. 1986. Taking Account of World Historical Political Economy: Knowable Communities in Larger Systems. In Anthropology as Cultural Critique: An Experimental Moment in the Human Sciences. Marcus, G. E. and Fischer, M., eds. pp. 77–110. Chicago: University of Chicago Press.

Margold, J. 1999. From "Cultures of Fear and Terror" to the Normalization of Violence. Critique of Anthropology 10(1):63–88.

Margolis, M. L. et al. 2001. Brazil. In Countries and Their Cultures (Vol. I). Ember, M. and Ember, C. R., eds. pp. 283–301. New York: Macmillan Reference USA.

Marks, J. 2003. Human Genome Diversity Project: Impact on Indigenous Communities. In Nature Encyclopedia of the Human Genome (Vol. III). Cooper, D. N., ed. pp. 335–338. London: Macmillan Publishers.

Martínez, R. 2001. Crossing Over: A Mexican Family in the Migrant Trail. New York: Henry Holt and Company.

Martínez-Alier, V. 1989. Marriage, Class and Colour in Nineteenth-Century Cuba: A Study of Racial Attitudes and Sexual Values in a Slave Society. Ann Arbor: University of Michigan Press.

Martínez-San Miguel, Y. 1997. Deconstructing Puerto Ricanness Through Sexuality: Female Counternarratives on Puerto Rican Identity (1894–1934). In Puerto Rican Jam: Rethinking Colonialism and Nationalism. Negrón-Munataner, F. and Grosfoguel, R., eds. pp. 127–139. Minneapolis: University of Minnesota Press.

Mathews, H. F. 1983. Context-Specific Variation in Humoral Classification. American Anthropologist 85(4):826–847.

———. 1985. "We Are Mayordomo": A Reinterpretation of Womens' Roles in the Mexican Cargo System. American Ethnologist 12(2):285–301.

Matthei, L. M. and Smith, D. A. 2004. Globalization, Migration and the Shaping of Masculinity in Belize. In Interrogating Caribbean Masculinities: Theoretical and Empirical Analyses. Reddock, R. E., ed. pp. 267–285. Kingston, Jamaica: University of the West Indies Press.

Maybury-Lewis, D. 2002[1997]. Indigenous Peoples, Ethnic Groups, and the State. Boston: Allyn and Bacon.

McAlister, E. 1998. The Madonna of 115th Street Revisited: Vodou and Haitian Catholicism in the Age of Transnationalism. In Gatherings in Diaspora: Religious Communities and the New Immigration. Warner, R. S. and Wittner, J. G., eds. pp. 123–160. Philadelphia: Temple University Press.

McCallum, C. 1996. The Body that Knows: From Cashinahua Epistemology to a Medical Anthropology of Lowland South America. Medical Anthropology Quarterly 10(3):347–372.

———. 2001. Gender and Sociality in Amazonia: How Real People Are Made. Oxford: Berg.

McClintock, A. 1995. Imperial Leather: Race, Gender and Sexuality in the Colonial Contest. New York: Routledge.

McCreery, D. 1994. Rural Guatemala 1760–1940. Stanford: Stanford University Press.

McDonald, T. J., ed. 1996. The Historic Turn in the Human Sciences. Ann Arbor: University of Michigan Press.

McGee Deutsch, S. 1991. Gender and Sociopolitical Change in Twentieth-Century Latin America. The Hispanic American Historical Review 71(2):259–306.

McKinley, J. C. 2004. Little Evidence of Serial Killings in Women's Deaths, Mexico Says. New York Times. Oct. 26, p. A8.

McNeill, W. H. 1999. How the Potato Changed the World's History. Social Research 66(1):67–83.

Meggers, 1971. Amazonia: Man and Culture in a Counterfeit Paradise. New York: Aldine.

———. 1979. Prehistoric America: An Ecological Perspective. New York: Aldine.

Meisch, L. 1998. The Reconquest of Otavalo, Ecuador: Indigenous Economic Gains and New Power Relations. Research in Economic Anthropology 19:11–30.

Mellibovsky, M. 1997. Circle of Love over Death: Testimonies of the Mothers of the Plaza de Mayo. Willimantic, CT: Curbstone Press.

Meltzer, D. J. 1995. Clocking the First Americans. Annual Review of Anthropology 24:21–45.

———. 1997. On the Plesitocene Antiquity of Monte Verde, Southern Chile. American Antiquity 62(4):659–663.

Melville, E. G. K. 1992. The Long-Term Effects of the Introduction of Sheep into Semi-Arid Sub-Tropical Regions. In Changing Tropical Forests: Historical Perspectives on Today's Challenges in Central and South America. Stern, H. and Tucker, R., eds. pp. 144–153. Durham, NC: Vienna, Austria: Forest History Society and IUFRO Forest History Group.

Menchú, R. 1984. I, Rigoberta Menchú: An Indian Woman in Guatemala (edited and introduced by Elizabeth Burgos-Debray; translated by Ann Wright). New York: Verso.

———. 2001. Those Who Attack Me Humiliate the Victims (interview by Juan Jesús Aznárez). In The Rigoberta

Menchú Controversy (with a response by David Stoll). Arias, A., ed. pp. 109–120. Minneapolis: University of Minnesota Press.

———. and Yañez, A. 1992. The Quincentenary, A Question of Class, Not Race: An Interview with Rigoberta Menchú. Latin American Perspectives 19(3):96–100.

Menegoni, L. 1996. Conceptions of Tuberculosis and Therapeutic Choices in Highland Chiapas. Medical Anthropology Quarterly 10(3):381–401.

Merbs, C. F. 1992. A New World of Infectious Disease. Yearbook of Physical Anthropology 35:3–42.

Merrifield, A. 1993. Place and Space: A Lefebvrian Reconciliation. Transactions of the Institute of British Geographers 18(4):516–531.

Meskell, L. 2002. The Intersections of Identity and Politics in Archaeology. Annual Review of Anthropology 31:279–301.

Messer, E. 1981. Hot-Cold Classification: Theoretical and Practical Implications of a Mexican Study. Social Science and Medicine 15B:133–145.

———. 1987. The Hot and Cold in Mesoamerican Indigenous and Hispanicized Thought. Social Science and Medicine 25:346–399.

Mignolo, W. D. 2005. The Idea of Latin America. Malden, MA and Oxford: Blackwell.

Miles, A. 1994. Helping out at Home: Gender Socialization, Moral Development, and Devil Stories in Cuenca, Ecuador. Ethos 22(2):132–157.

Miller, B. D. 2005. Cultural Anthropology. Boston: Allyn & Bacon.

———, ed. 1993. Sex and Gender Hierarchies. Cambridge: Cambridge University Press.

Mills, M. B. 2003. Gender and Inequality in the Global Labor Force. Annual Review of Anthropology 31:41–62.

Mintz, S. W. 1956. Cañamelar: The Subculture of a Rural Sugar Plantation Proletariat. In The People of Puerto Rico: A Study in Social Anthropology. Steward, J. S., ed. pp. 314–417. Urbana: University of Illinois Press.

———. 1971. The Caribbean as a Socio-Cultural Area. In Peoples and Cultures of the Caribbean: An Anthropological Reader. Horowitz, M. M., ed. pp. 17–46. Garden City, NY: Natural History Press.

———. 1985a. From Plantation to Peasantries in the Caribbean. In Caribbean Contours. Mintz, S. W. and Price, S., eds. pp. 127–154. Baltimore: Johns Hopkins University Press.

———. 1985b. Sweetness and Power: The Place of Sugar in Modern History. New York: Viking Penguin.

———. 1989. Caribbean Transformations. New York: Columbia University Press.

———. 1994. Eating and Being: What Food Means. In Food: Multidisciplinary Perspectives. Harriss-White, B. and Hoffenberg, R., ed. pp. 102–115. Malden, MA and Oxford: Blackwell.

———. 1996a. Enduring Substances, Trying Theories: The Caribbean Region as OIKOUMENE. Journal of the Royal Anthropological Institute (NS) 2:289–311.

———. 1996b. Tasting Food, Tasting Freedom. Boston: Beacon Press.

———. and Du Bois, C. M. 2002. The Anthropology of Food and Eating. Annual Review of Anthropology 31:99–119.

Mintz, S. W. and Price, S., eds. 1985. Caribbean Contours. Baltimore: Johns Hopkins University Press.

Molyneux, M. 2000a. State, Gender, and Institutional Change. The Federación de Mujeres Cubanas. In Hidden Histories of Gender and the State in Latin America. Dore, E. and Molyneux, M., eds. pp. 291–321. Durham, NC: Duke University Press.

———. 2000b. Twentieth Century State Formations in Latin America. In Hidden Histories of Gender and the State in Latin America. Dore, E. and Molyneux, M., eds. pp. 33–81. Durham, NC: Duke University Press.

Montoya, R. 2002b. Women's Sexuality, Knowledge, and Agency in Rural Nicaragua. In Gender's Place: Feminist Anthropologies of Latin America. Montoya, R. et al., eds. pp. 65–88. New York: Palgrave Macmillan.

Moody, K. 1995. NAFTA and the Corporate Redesign of North America. Latin American Perspectives 22(1):95–116.

Moore, A. and LeBaron, R. 1986. The Case for a Haitian Origin of the AIDS Epidemic. In The Social Dimensions of Aids: Method and Theory. Feldman, D. and Johnson, T., eds. pp. 77–93. New York: Praeger.

Morales, E. 1995. The Guinea Pig: Healing, Food, and Ritual in the Andes. Tucson: University of Arizona Press.

Moran, E. F. 1987. Environmental and Social Systems. In Latin America: Perspectives on a Region. Hopkins, J. W., ed. pp. 3–18. New York and London: Holmes & Meier.

———. 1993. Deforestation and Land Use in the Brazilian Amazon. Human Ecology 21(1):1–21.

———. 2000. Human Adaptability: An Introduction to Ecological Anthropology. Boulder, CO: Westview.

Moran, K. et al. 2001. Biodiversity Prospecting: Lessons and Prospects. Annual Review of Anthropology 30:505–526.

Moreno Fraginals, M. 1976. The Sugar Mill (translated by Cedric Belfage). New York: Monthly Review Press.

Mörner, M. 1973. The Spanish American Hacienda: A Survey of Recent Research and Debate. Hispanic American Historical Review 53(2):183–216.

Morrissey, M. 2002. Tres Mujeres: Reclaiming National Culture in the Post-Colonial Telenovela. Studies in Latin American Popular Culture 21:221–232.

Moulian, T. 1999. The Arrest and Its Aftermath. NACLA Report on the Americas 37(6):12–17.

Mukhopadhyay, C. C. and Higgins, P. J. 1988. Anthropological Studies of Women's Status Revisited: 1977–1987. Annual Review of Anthropology 17:461–495.

Muratorio, B. 1981. Protestantism, Ethnicity, and Class in Chimborazo. In Cultural Transformations and Ethnicity in Modern Ecuador. Whitten, N. E., ed. pp. 506–534. Urbana: University of Illinois Press.

Murphy, D. E. 2005. California Patrol Won't Seize Marijuana Used as Medicine. New York Times. Aug. 30, p. A15.

Murphy, J. M. 1994. Working the Spirit: Ceremonies of the African Diaspora. Boston: Beacon Press.

Murra, J. V. 1998. Litigation over the Rights of "Natural Lords" in Early Colonial Courts in the Andes. In Native Traditions in the Postconquest World. Boone, E. H. et al., eds. pp. 55–62. Washington, D.C.: Dumbarton Oaks Research Library and Collection.

Myerhoff, B. G. 1974. Peyote Hunt: The Sacred Journey of the Huichol Indians. Ithaca, NY: Cornell University Press.

Myers, F. D. 1988. Critical Trends in the Study of Hunters-Gatherers. Annual Review of Anthropology 17:261–282.

Nagengast, C. 1994. Violence, Terror, and the Crisis of the State. Annual Review of Anthropology 23:109–136.

Nahas, G. G., ed. 1999. Marihuana and Medicine. Totowa, NJ: Humana Press.

Napolitano, V. 2002. Migration, Mujercitas, and Medicine Men: Living in Urban Mexico. Berkeley: University of California.

Nash, J. C. 1979. We Eat the Mines and the Mines Eat Us: Dependency and Exploitation in Bolivian Tin Mines. New York: Columbia University Press.

———. 1980. Aztec Women: The Transition from Status to Class in Empire and Colony. In Women and Colonization: Anthropological Perspectives. Etienne, M. et al., eds. pp. 134–148. Brooklyn: J. F. Bergin Publishers.

———. 1981. Ethnographic Aspects of the World Capitalist System. Annual Review of Anthropology 10:393–423.

———. 1989. Gender Studies in Latin America. In Gender and Anthropology: Critical Reviews for Research and Training. Morgen, S., ed. pp. 228–246. Washington, D.C.: American Anthropological Association.

———. 1992. I Spent My Life in the Mines: The Story of Juan Rojas, Bolivian Tin Miner. New York: Columbia University Press.

———. 1993. Introduction: Traditional Arts and Changing Markets in Middle America. In Crafts in the World Market: Impact of Global Exchange on Middle American Artisans. Nash, J. C., ed. pp. 1–25. Albany: State University of New York Press.

———. 1995. The New World Dis-Order: A View from Chiapas, Mexico. In Indigenous Perceptions of the Nation-State in Latin America (Studies in Third World Societies, #56). Giordani, L. and Snipes, M. M., eds. pp. 171–198. Williamsburg, VA: College of William and Mary.

———. 2001. Mayan Visions: The Quest for Autonomy in an Age of Globalization. Albany: State University of New York Press.

Navarro, M. 2002. Against *Marianismo*. In Gender's Place: Feminist Anthropologies of Latin America. Montoya, R. et al., eds. pp. 257–272. New York: Palgrave Macmillan.

Nazzari, M. 1996. Concubinage in Colonial Brazil: The Inequalities of Race, Class and Gender. Journal of Family History 21(2):107–124.

Nesvig, M. 2001. The Complicated Terrain of Latin American Homosexuality. Hispanic American Historical Review 81(3–4):689–729.

New York City. 2000. Table SF# SB P-1 Part 2 of 2: Country of Birth for the Foreign-born Population, New York City, Boroughs and Census Tracts, 2000. www.nyc.gov/html/dep/pdf/census/sf3bp1pt2.pdf.

New York Times. 2005. Colombia's Capitulation (Editorial). New York Times. July 4, p. A12.

Newson, L. A. 1986. The Cost of Conquest: Indian Decline in Honduras Under Spanish Rule. Boulder, CO: Westview.

——— 1991. Old World Epidemics in Early Colonial Ecuador. In "Secret Judgements of God": Old World Disease in Colonial Spanish America. Cook, D. N. and Lovell, W. G., eds. pp. 84–112. Norman: University of Oklahoma Press.

———. 1995. Life and Death in Early Colonial Ecuador. Norman: University of Oklahoma Press.

Norget, K. 1997. The Politics of Liberation: The Popular Church, Indigenous Theology, and Grassroots Mobilization in Oaxaca, Mexico. Latin American Perspectives 24(5):96–127.

Nuñez Sarmiento, M. 2003. Gender Studies in Cuba: Methodological Approaches, 1974–2001. Gender and Society 17(1):7–32.

Nurse, K. 2004. Masculinities in Transition: Gender and the Global Problematique. In Interrogating Caribbean Masculinities: Theoretical and Empirical Analyses. Reddock, R. E., ed. pp. 3–37. Kingston, Jamaica: University of the West Indies Press.

Nutini, H. G. 1988. Todos Santos in Rural Tlaxcala. Princeton, NJ: Princeton University Press.

O'Brien, T. 1999. The Century of U.S. Capitalism in Latin America. Albuquerque: University of New Mexico Press.

O'Nell, C. W. 1975. An Investigation of Reported "Fright" as a Factor in the Etiology of Susto, "Magical Fright." Ethos 3(1):41–63.

Ocasio, R. 2002. Gays and the Cuban Revolution: The Case of Reinaldo Arenas. Latin American Perspectives 29(2):78–98.

Ochoa, E. C. 2000. Feeding Mexico: The Political Uses of Food Since 1910. Wilmington, DE: Scholarly Resources.

Olavarría, J. 2003. Men at Home? Child Rearing and Housekeeping Among Chilean Working-Class Fathers. In Changing Men and Masculinities in Latin America. Gutmann, M. C., ed. pp. 333–350. Durham, NC: Duke University Press.

Olwig, K. R. 1996. Recovering the Substantive Nature of Landscape. Annals of the Association of American Geographers 86(4):630–653.

Ong, A. 1987. Spirits of Resistance and Capitalist Discipline: Factory Women in Malaysia. Albany: State University of New York Press.

Orlove, B. S. 1977. Integration Through Production: The Use of Zonation in Espinar. American Ethnologist 4(1):84–100.

——— 1987. Stability and Change in Highland Andean Dietary Patterns. In Food and Evolution: Toward a Theory of Human Food Habits. Harris, M. and Ross, E. B., eds. pp. 481–515. Philadelphia: Temple University Press.

———— and Brush, S. B. 1996. Anthropology and the Conservation of Biodiversity. Annual Review of Anthropology 25:329–352.

Orlove, B. S. and Custred, G. 1980. The Alternative Model of Agrarian Society in the Andes: Households, Networks, and Corporate Groups. In Land and Power in Latin America: Agrarian Economies and Social Processes in the Andes. Orlove, B. and Custred, G., eds. pp. 31–53. New York: Holmes and Meiir.

Orlove, B. S. and Guillet, D. W. 1985. Theoretical and Methodological Considerations on the Study of Mountain Peoples: Reflections on the Idea of Subsistence Type and the Role of History in Human Ecology. Mountain Research and Development 5(1):3–18.

Ortíz, A. T. and Briggs, L. 2003. The Culture of Poverty, Crack Babies, and Welfare Cheats: The Making of the "Healthy White Baby Crisis." Social Text 21(3):39–57.

Ortíz, F. 1970. Cuban Counterpoint. New York: Vintage Books.

Ortner, S. B. 1984. Theory in Anthropology Since the Sixties. Comparative Studies in Society and History 26:126–167.

Osborn, A. 1968. Compadrazgo and Patronage: A Colombian Case. Man 3(4):593–608.

Padden, R. C. 1957. Cultural Change and Military Resistance in Araucanian Chile, 1550–1730. Southwestern Journal of Anthropology 13:103–121.

Padula, A. 1996. Gender, Sexuality, and Revolution in Cuba. Latin American Research Review 31(2):226–235.

Paluzzi, J. E. 2004. A Social Disease/A Social Response: Lessons in Tuberculosis from Early 20th Century Chile. Social Science and Medicine 59:763–773.

Pan American Health Organization. 1998. Health in the Americas (Vol. I). Washington, D.C.: Pan American Health Organization. Scientific Publication No. 569.

————. 2001a. HIV and AIDS in the Americas. Washington, D.C.: Pan American Health Organization and World Health Organization. Joint United Nations Programme on HIV/AIDS.

————. 2001b. Regional Core Health Data Initiative. Washington, D.C.: Pan American Health Organization. Special Program for Health Analysis. www.paho.org/english/sha/coredata/tabulator/newsq.

Pardo, O. F. 2004. The Origins of Mexican Catholicism: Nahua Rituals and Christian Sacraments in Sixteenth-Century Mexico. Ann Arbor: University of Michigan Press.

Parker, R. G. 1991. Bodies, Pleasures, and Passions: Sexual Culture in Contemporary Brazil. Boston: Beacon Press.

————. 1995. Changing Brazilian Constructions of Homosexuality. In Latin American Male Homosexualities. Murray, S. O., ed. pp. 241–255. Albuquerque: University of New Mexico Press.

————. 1997. Migration, Sexual Subcultures, and HIV/AIDS in Brazil. In Sexual Cultures and Migration in the Era of AIDS: Anthropological and Demographic Perspectives. Herdt, G., ed. pp. 55–69. Oxford: Clarendon Press.

————. 2003a. The Carnivalization of the World. In Perspectives on Las Américas: A Reader in Culture, History, and Representation. Gutmann, M. C. et al., eds. pp. 213–228. Malden, MA and Oxford: Blackwell.

————. 2003b. Changing Sexualities: Masculinity and Male Homosexuality in Brazil. In Changing Men and Masculinities in Latin America. Gutmann, M. C., ed. pp. 307–332. Durham, NC: Duke University Press.

Passel, J. S. 2006. The Size and Characteristics of the Unauthorized Migrant Population in the U.S.: Estimates Based on the March 2005 Current Population Survey. http://pewhispanic.org/files/reports/61.pdf.

Patterson, W. 2001. Masked Rebels Grab Spotlight in Mexico's Congress. Christian Science Monitor. Mar. 30, p. 7.

Paulsen, A. C. 1981. The Archaeology of the Absurd: Comments on "Cultural Materialism, Split Inheritance, and the Expansion of Ancient Peruvian Empires." American Antiquity 46:31–37.

Paulson, S. and Gezón, L. L., eds. 2005. Political Ecology Across Spaces, Scales, and Social Groups. New Brunswick, NJ: Rutgers University Press.

Paz, O. 1985. The Labyrinth of Solitude, the Other Mexico, and Other Essays. New York: Grove Press.

Pearse, A. 1971. Carnival in Nineteenth Century Trinidad. In Peoples and Cultures of the Caribbean: An Anthropological Reader. Horowitz, M. M., ed. pp. 528–552. Garden City, NY: Natural History Press.

Pedraza Gómez, Z. 1999. En cuerpo y alma: Visiones del progreso y de la felicidad. Bogotá: CORCAS Editores.

Pels, P. 1997. The Anthropology of Colonialism: Culture, History, and the Emergence of Western Governmentality. Annual Review of Anthropology 26:163–183.

Pérez, B. E. 2003. Power Encounters. In Histories and Historicites in Amazonia. Whitehead, N. L., ed. pp. 81–105. Lincoln: University of Nebraska Press.

Pérez Brignoli, H. 1995. Indians, Communists, and Peasants: The1932 Rebellion in El Salvador. In Coffee, Sociey, and Power in Latin America. Roseberry, W. et al., eds. pp. 232–261. Baltimore: Johns Hopkins University.

Pérez, G. M. 2002. "La tierra's Always Perceived as Woman": Imagining Urban Communities in Chicago's Puerto Rican Community. In Transnational Latina/o Communities: Politics, Processes, and Cultures. Vélez-Ibán´ez, C. G. and Sampaio, A., eds. pp. 181–202. Lanham, MD: Rowman & Littlefield.

Pérez y Mena, A. I. 1991. Speaking with the Dead: Development of Afro-Latin Religion Among Puerto Ricans in the United States. New York: AMS Press.

Petersen, J. 1997. Taino, Island Carib, and Prehistoric Amerindian Economies in the West Indies: Tropical Forest Adaptations to Island Environments. In The Indigenous People of the Caribbean. Wilson, S., ed. pp. 118–130. Gainsville: University Press of Florida.

Phillips, M. M. et al. 2002. A Global Journal Report: Brazil's Election Sparks Concerns for Its Neighbors—Left Leaning da

Silva's Victory Engenders Worries for a Default That Could Affect Entire Region. Wall Street Journal. Oct 28, p. C1.

Pilcher, J. M. 1998. Que Vivan los Tamales! Food and the Making of Mexican Identity. Albuquerque: University of New Mexico Press.

———. 2000. The Caribbean from 1492 to the Present. In The Cambridge World History of Food (Vol. II). Kiple, K. F. and Ornelas, K. C., eds. pp. 1278–1287. Cambridge: Cambridge University Press.

Piperno, D. and Pearsall, D. 1998. The Origins of Agriculture in the Lowland Neotropics. San Diego: Academic Press.

Platt, T. 1993. Simón Bolívar, the Sun of Justice and the Amerindian Virgin: Andean Conceptions of the Patria in Nineteenth-Century Potosí. Journal of Latin American Studies 25:159–185.

Plowman, T. 1984. The Ethnobotany of Coca (*Erythroxylumm spp., Erythroxylaceae*). Advances in Economic Botany 1:62–111.

———. 1986. Coca Chewing and the Botanical Origins of Coca (*Erythroxylum spp.*) in South America. In Coca and Cocaine: Effects on People and Policy in Latin America. Pacini, D. and Franquemont, C., eds. pp. 5–33. Cambridge, MA: Cultural Survival and LASP, Cornell University.

Poitras, G. and Robinson, R. 1994. The Politics of NAFTA in Mexico. Journal of Interamerican Studies and World Affairs 36(1):1–35.

Population Reference Bureau. 2003. 2003 World Population Data Sheet. www. prb.org/pdf/WorldPopulationDS03_Eng.pdf.

Porter, E. 2002. Univisión Seeks A Bigger Pie for Spanish TV. Wall Street Journal. Jan. 14, p. B1.

Portes, A. 1972. Rationality in the Slum: An Essay on Interpretive Sociology. Comparative Studies in Society and History 14(3):268–286.

———. 1989. Latin American Urbanization during the Years of the Crisis. Latin American Research Review 24(3):7–44.

———, et al 1989. The Informal Economy: Sudies in Avanced and Less Developed Countries. Baltimore: John Hopkins University Press.

Potthast-Jutkeit, B. 1991. The Ass of a Mare and Other Scandals: Marriage and Extramarital Relations in Nineteenth-Century Paraguay. Journal of Family History 16(3):215–240.

Powers, K. 1995. Andean Journeys: Migration, Ethnogenesis, and the State in Colonial Quito. Albuquerque: University of New Mexico Press.

Prahlad, Sw. A. 2001. Reggae Wisdom: Proverbs in Jamaican Music. Jackson: University Press of Mississippi.

Pratt, M. L. 2001. Rigoberta Mechú and the "Culture Wars." In The Rigoberta Menchú Controversy (with a response by David Stoll). Arias, A., ed. pp. 29–57. Minneapolis: University of Minnesota Press.

Price, R. 1979. Maroon Societies: Rebel Slave Communities in the Americas. Baltimore: John Hopkins University Press.

Prieur, A. 1996. Domination and Desire: Male Homosexuality and the Construction of Masculinity in Mexico. In Machos,

Mistresses, Madonnas: Contesting the Power of Latin American Gender Imagery. Melhuus, M. and Stolen, K. A., eds. pp. 83–107. London and New York: Verso.

Prior, M. 2005. Matrifocality, Power, and Gender Relations in Jamaica. In Gender in Cross-Cultural Perspective. Brettell, C. and Sargent, C., eds. pp. 372–380. Upper Saddle River, NJ: Prentice Hall.

Proctor, J. D. 1998. The Social Construction of Nature: Relativist Accusations, Pragmatist and Critical Realist Responses. Annals of the Association of American Geographers 88(3):352–376.

Ramos, A. R. 1994. The Hyperreal Indian. Critique of Anthropology 14(2):153–171.

———. R. 1998. Indigenism: Ethnic Politics in Brazil. Madison: University of Wisconsin Press.

———. Forthcoming. The Commodification of the Indian. In Human Impacts on Amazonia: The Role of Traditional Ecological Knowledge in Conservation and Development in Brazil. Posey, D. A., ed. New York: Columbia University Press.

Randall, V. and Waylen, G., eds. 1998. Gender, Politics and the State. New York: Routledge.

Rappaport, J. 1994. Cumbe Reborn: An Andean Ethnography of History. Chicago: University of Chicago Press.

Rasnake, R. 1988. Domination and Cultural Resistance: Authority and Power Among an Andean People. Durham, NC: Duke University Press.

Rebhun, L. A. 1994. Swallowing Frogs: Anger and Illness in Northeast Brazil. Medical Anthropology Quarterly 8(4):360–382.

Reddock, R. E. 2004a. Interrogating Caribbean Masculinities: An Introduction. In Interrogating Caribbean Masculinities: Theoretical and Empirical Analyses. Reddock, R. E., ed. pp. xiii–x. Kingston, Jamaica: University of the West Indies Press.

———. ed. 2004b. Interrogating Caribbean Masculinities: Theoretical and Empirical Analyses. Kingston, Jamaica: University of the West Indies Press.

Redmond, E. M. ed. 1998. Chiefdoms and Chieftaincy in the Americas. Gainesville: University Press of Florida.

Reed, N. 2001. The Caste War in Yucatán. Stanford: Stanford University Press.

Reed, S. A. 1998. The Politics and Poetics of Dance. Annual Review of Anthropology 27:503–532.

Reichel-Dolmatoff, G. 1971. Amazonian Cosmos: Sexual and Religious Symbolism of the Tukano Indians. Chicago: University of Chicago Press.

———. 1975. The Shaman and the Jaguar: A Study of Narcotic Drugs Among the Indians of Colombia. Philadelphia: Temple University Press.

Renteln, A. D. 1988. Relativism and the Search for Human Rights. American Anthropologist 90(1):56–72.

Rey, T. 1999. Our Lady of Class Struggle: The Cult of the Virgin Mary in Haiti. Trenton, NJ: Africa World Press.

Richani, N. 2002. Systems of Violence: The Political Economy of War and Peace in Colombia. Albany: State University of New York Press.

Richards, J. B. and Richards, M. 1997. Mayan Language Literacy in Guatemala: A Socio-Historical Overview. In Indigenous Literacies in the Americas: Language Planning from the Bottom Up. Hornberger, N. H., ed. pp. 189–211. Berlin and New York: Mouton de Gruyter.

Richards, P., ed. 2005. No Peace, No War: An Anthropology of Contemporary Armed Conflicts. Athens: Ohio University Press.

Richardson, B. C. 1989. Caribbean Migrations, 1838–1985. In The Modern Caribbean. Knight, F. W. and Palmer, C. A., eds. pp. 203–228. Chapel Hill: University of North Carolina Press.

Richardson, J. B. 1994. People of the Andes. Montreal and Washington D.C.: St. Remy Press and Smithsonian Books.

Rigdon, S. M. 1988. The Culture Facade: Art, Science, and Politics in the Work of Oscar Lewis. Urbana: University of Illinois Press.

Rivera Ayala, S. 1994. Lewd Songs and Dances from the Streets of Eighteenth-Century New Spain. In Rituals of Rule, Rituals of Resistance: Public Celebrations and Popular Culture in Mexico. Beezley, W. H. et al., eds. pp. 27–46. Wilmington, DE: Scholarly Resources.

Rivera, M. A. 1999. Prehistory of the Southern Cone. In The Cambridge History of the Native Peoples of the Americas (Volume III [South America], Part 1). Salomon, F. and Schwartz, S. B., eds. pp. 734–768. Cambridge: Cambridge University Press.

Robben, A. 2004. The Fear of Indifference: Combatants' Anxieties About the Political Identity of Civilians During Argentina's Dirty War. In Violence in War and Peace. Scheper-Hughes, N. and Bourgois, P., eds. pp. 200–206. Malden, MA and Oxford: Blackwell.

———. 2005. How Traumatized Societies Remember: The Aftermath of Argentina's Dirty War. Cultural Critique 59 (Winter):120–164.

Robbins, P. 2004. Political Ecology: A Critical Introduction. Malden, MA and Oxford: Blackwell.

Roberts, J. T. and Thanos, N. D. 2003. Trouble in Paradise: Globalization and Environmental Crises in Latin America. New York: Routledge.

Rodman, M. C. 1992. Empowering Place: Multilocality and Multivocality. American Anthropologist 94(3):640–656.

Rogers, N. 1992. The Anthropological Turn in Social History. In Approaching the Past: Historical Anthropology Through Irish Case Studies. Silverman, M. and Gulliver, P. H., eds. pp. 352–370. New York: Columbia University Press.

Rohter, L. 2005. Pinochet Under House Arrest. New York Times. Jan. 6, p. A8.

Roosevelt, A. C. 1999. The Maritime, Highland, Forest Dynamic and the Origins of Complex Culture. In The Cambridge History of the Native Peoples of the Americas (Vol. III [South America], Part 1). Salomon, F. and Schwartz, S. B., eds. pp. 264–349. Cambridge: Cambridge University Press.

———, ed. 1994. Amazonian Indians from Prehistory to the Present: Anthropological Perspectives. Tucson: University of Arizona Press.

———, et al. 1996. Paleoindian Cave Dwellers in the Amazon: The Peopling of the Americas. Science (New Series) 272(5260):373–384.

Roper, J. M. et al. 2003. Introduction to Special Issue: "Indigenous Transformational Movements in Contemporary Latin America." Latin American Perspectives 30(1):5–22.

Roseberry, W. 1988. Political Economy. Annual Review of Anthropology 17:161–185.

———. 1989. Anthropologies and Histories: Essays in Culture, History, and Political Economy. New Brunswick, NJ: Rutgers University Press.

Rosenbaum, B. 1996. Women and Gender in Mesoamerica. In The Legacy of Mesoamerica: History and Culture of a Native American Civilization. Carmack, R. M. et al., eds. pp. 321–352. Upper Saddle River, NJ: Prentice Hall.

Rosenberg, M. J. 2001. Jamaica's Marijuana Industry Withering; Globalization, U.S. Erradication Effort Hammer Island's Once-Lucrative Crop. Washington Post. Apr. 1, p. A21.

Rosenthal, E. et al. 2003. Why Marijuana Should be Legal. New York: Thunders Mouth Press.

Rostow, W. W. 1960. The Stages of Economic Growth: A Non-Communist Manifesto. Cambridge: Cambridge University Press.

Rothenberg, D. 1998. With These Hands: The Hidden World of Migrant Farmworkers Today. Berkeley: University of California Press.

Rouse, I. 1992. The Tainos: Rise and Decline of the People Who Greeted Columbus. New Haven, CT: Yale University Press.

Rowe, W. and Schelling, V. 1991. Memory and Modernity: Popular Culture in Latin America. New York: Verso.

Rubel, A. J. 1977. The Epidemiology of a Folk Illness: Susto in Hispanic America (originaly published in 1964 in the journal Ethnology). In Culture, Disease, and Healing: Studies in Medical Anthropology. Landy, D., ed. pp. 119–128. New York: Macmillan Publishing.

Rubin, V. D. and Lambros, C. 1975. Ganja in Jamaica: A Medical Anthropological Study of Chronic Marihuana Use. The Hague: Mouton.

Rus, J. 1999. Introduction to Special Issue "If Truth Be Told: A Forum on Stoll and Menchú." Latin American Perspectives 26(109):5–14.

——— and Wasserstrom, R. 1980. Civil-Religious Hierarchies in Central Chiapas: A Critical Perspective. American Ethnologist 7(3):466–478.

Rust, S. P. 2001. The Garifuna: Weaving a Future from a Tangled Past. National Geographic 200(3):102–113.

Safa, H. I. 1974. The Urban Poor of Puerto Rico: A Study in Development and Inequality. New York: Holt, Rinehart and Winston.

———. 1995. The Myth of the Male Breadwinner: Women and Industrialization in the Caribbean. Boulder, CO: Westview.

Sagas, E. 2000. Race and Politics in the Dominican Republic. Gainesville: University Press of Florida.

Said, E. W. 1979. Orientalism. New York: Vintage Books.

Salamone, F. A. 1997. The Yanomami and their Interpreters: Fierce People or Fierce Interpreters? Lanham, MD: University Press of America.

Salas, C. 2002. Mexico's Haves and Have-Nots: NAFTA Sharpens the Divide. NACLA Report on the Americas 35(4):32–41.

Salles-Reese, V. 1997. From Viracocha to the Virgin of Copacabana: Representation of the Sacred at Lake Titicaca. Austin: University of Texas Press.

Salomon, F. 1981. Weavers of Otavalo. In Cultural Transformations and Ethnicity in Modern Ecuador. Whitten, N. E., ed. pp. 420–449. Urbana: University of Illinois Press.

———. 1995. The Beautiful Grandparents: Andean Ancestor Shrines and Mortuary Ritual as Seen Through Colonial Records. In Tombs for the Living: Andean Mortuary Practices. Dillehay, T. D., ed. pp. 315–354. Washington, D.C.: Dumbarton Oaks Research Library and Collection.

———. 1999. Testimonies: The Making and Reading of Native South American Historical Sources. In The Cambridge History of the Native Peoples of the Americas (Volume III [South America], Part 1). Salomon, F. and Schwartz, S. B., eds. pp. 19–96. Cambridge: Cambridge University Press.

Salzinger, L. 2003. Genders in Production: Making Workers in Mexico's Global Factories. Berkeley: University of California Press.

Sanabria, H. 1993. The Coca Boom and Rural Social Change in Bolivia. Ann Arbor: University of Michigan Press.

———. 1997. The Discourse and Practice of Repression and Resistance in the Chapare. in Coca, Cocaine, and the Bolivian Reality. Léons, M. B. and Sanabria, H., eds. pp. 169–194. Albany: State University of New York Press.

———. 1999. Consolidating States, Restructuring Economies, and Confronting Workers and Peasants: The Antinomies of Bolivian Neo-Liberalism. Comparative Studies in Society and History 41(3):535–562.

———. 2000. Resistance and the Arts of Domination: Miners and the Bolivian State. Latin American Perspectives 27(1):56–81.

———. 2001. Exploring Kinship in Anthropology and History: Surnames and Social Transformations in the Bolivian Andes. Latin American Research Review 36(2):137–155.

———. 2004. The State and the Ongoing Struggle over Coca in Bolivia: Legitimacy, Hegemony, and Exercise of Power. In Dangerous Harvest: Drug Plants and the Transformation of Indigenous Landscapes. Steinberg, M. K. et al., eds. pp. 153–166. New York: Oxford University Press.

Sandstrom, A. R. 1991. Corn is Our Blood: Culture and Ethnic Identity in a Contemporary Aztec Indian Village. Norman: University of Oklahoma Press.

Santino, J. 1983. Halloween in America: Contemporary Customs and Performances. Western Folklore 42(1):1–20.

Satel, S. 2005. A Whiff of "Reefer Madness" in U.S. Drug Policy. New York Times. Aug. 15, p. F6.

Sauer, C. 1969(1925). The Morphology of Landscape. In Land and Life: A Selection from the Writings of Carl Ortwin Sauer. Leighly, J., ed. pp. 315–350. Berkeley: University of California Press.

Savigliano, M. 1995. Tango and the Political Economy of Passion. Boulder, CO: Westview.

Sawyer, S. 2004. Crude Chronicles: Indigenous Politics, Multinational Oil, and Neoliberalism in Ecuador. Durham, NC: Duke University Press.

Scarre, C. and Fagan, B. M. 2002. Ancient Civilizations. New York: Prentice Hall.

Scheinsohn, V. 2003. Hunter-Gatherer Archaeology in South America. Annual Review of Anthropology 32:339–361.

Scheper-Hughes, N. 1992. Death Without Weeping: The Violence of Everyday Life in Brazil. Berkeley: University of California Press.

———. 1995. The Primacy of the Ethical. Current Anthropology 36(3):409–440.

——— and Bourgois, P. 2004. Introduction: Making Sense of Violence. In Violence in War and Peace. Scheper-Hughes, N. and Bourgois, P., eds. pp. 1–31. Malden, MA and Oxford: Blackwell.

Schmink, M. and Wood, C. H. 1987. The "Political Ecology" of Amazonia. In Lands at Risk in the Third World: Local-Level Perspectives. Little, P. D. and Horowitz, M., eds. pp. 38–57. Boulder, CO: Westview.

Schneider, C. 1992. Radical Opposition Parties and Squatters Movements in Pinochet's Chile. In The Making of Social Movements in Latin America: Identity, Strategy, and Democracy. Escobar, A. and Alvarez, S. E., eds. pp. 260–275. Boulder, CO: Westview.

Schwartz, N. B. 1990. Forest Society: A Social History of Petén, Guatemala. Philadelphia: University of Pennsylvania Press.

Schwartz, S. B. 1978. Indian Labor and New World Plantations: European Demands and Indian Reponses in Northeastern Brazil. American Historical Review 83(1):43–79.

———. 1987. Plantations and Peripheries, c.1580–c.1750. In Colonial Brazil. Bethell, L., ed. pp. 67–144. Cambridge: Cambridge University Press.

Scoones, I. 1999. New Ecology and the Social Sciences: What Prospects for a Future Engagement? Annual Review of Anthropology 28:479–507.

Scott, J. C. 1976. The Moral Economy of the Peasant: Rebellion and Subsistence in Southeast Asia. New Haven, CT: Yale University Press.

———. 1985. Weapons of the Weak: Everyday Forms of Peasant Resistance. New Haven, CT: Yale University Press.

———. 1990. Domination and the Arts of Resistance. New Haven, CT: Yale University Press.

Scott, J. W. 1986. Gender: A Useful Category of Historical Analysis. The American Historical Review 91(5):1053–1075.

Seed, P. 1988. To Love, Honor, and Obey in Colonial Mexico: Conflicts over Marriage Choice, 1564–1821. Stanford: Stanford University Press.

Seligmann, L. J. 1993. To Be in Between: The *Cholas* as Market Women. In Constructing Culture and Power in Latin America. Levine, D. H., ed. pp. 267–310. Ann Arbor: University of Michigan Press.

Service, E. R. 1955. Indian-European Relations in Colonial Latin America. American Anthropologist 57:411–425.

———. 1962. Primitive Social Organization: An Evolutionary Perspective. New York: Random House.

Sharer, R. J. 1994. The Ancient Maya (5th ed.). Stanford: Stanford University Press.

Shaw, R. 1991. Christopher Columbus: Hero or Villain? Columbia (February).

Shelton, B. L. and Marks, J. 2001. Genetic Markers Not a Valid Test of Native Identity. Gene Watch 14(5):6–8.

Sherzer, J. 1994. The Kuna and Columbus: Encounters and Confrontations of Discourse. American Anthropologist 96(4):902–924.

Shimada, I. 1999. Evolution of Andean Diversity: Regional Formations (500 B.C.E.–C.E. 600). In The Cambridge History of the Native Peoples of the Americas (Volume III [South America], Part 1). Salomon, F. and Schwartz, S. B., eds. pp. 350–517. Cambridge: Cambridge University Press.

Sigal, P. 2000. From Moon Goddess to Virgins: The Colonization of Yucatecan Maya Sexual Desire. Austin: University of Texas Press.

Silverblatt, I. 1987. Moon, Sun, and Witches: Gender Ideologies and Class in Inca and Colonial Peru. Princeton, NJ: Princeton University Press.

———. 1988. Women in States. Annual Review of Anthropology 17:427–460.

———. 1988. Family Values in Seventeenth-Century Peru. In Native Traditions in the Postconquest World. Boone, E. H. and Cummins, T., eds. pp. 63–89. Washington, D.C.: Dumbarton Oaks Research Library and Collection.

———. 1995. Lessons of Gender and Ethnohistory in Mesoamerica. Ethnohistory 42(4):639–650.

Silverman, H. 2002. Touring Ancient Times: The Present and Presented Past in Contemporary Peru. American Anthropologist 104(3):881–902.

Silverman, M. and Gulliver, P. H. 1992. Historical Anthropology and the Ethnographic Tradition: A Personal, Historical, and Intellectual Account. In Approaching the Past: Historical Anthropology Through Irish Case Studies. Silverman, M. and Gulliver, P. H., eds. pp. 3–72. New York: Columbia University Press.

Silverman, S. 1979. The Peasant Concept in Anthropology. The Journal of Peasant Studies 7(1):49–69.

Singer, M. 2001a. Health, Disease, and Social Inequality. In Cultural Diversity in the United States: A Critical Reader. Susser, I. and Patterson, T. C., eds. pp. 77–99. Malden, MA and Oxford: Blackwell.

———. 2001b. Toward a Bio-Cultural and Political Economic Integration of Alcohol, Tobacco, and Drug Studies in the Coming Century. Social Science and Medicine 53:199–213.

Slatta, R. W. 1983. Gauchos and the Vanishing Frontier. Lincoln: University of Nebraska Press.

Sluyter, A. 2001. Colonialism and Landscape in the Americas: Material/Conceptual Transformations and Continuing Consequences. Annals of the Association of American Geographers 91(2):410–428.

Smith, C. A. 1990a. Introduction: Social Relations in Guatemala over Time and Space. In Guatemalan Indians and the State: 1540–1988. Smith, C. A., ed. pp. 1–34. Austin: University of Texas Press.

———. 1990b. Conclusion: History and Revolution in Guatemala. In Guatemalan Indians and the State: 1540–1988. Smith, C. A., ed. pp. 258–286. Austin: University of Texas Press.

———. 1999. Why Write an Exposé of Rigoberta Menchú? Latin American Perspectives 26(109):15–28.

Smith, G. 1989. Livelihood and Resistance: Peasants and the Politics of Land in Peru. Berkeley: University of California Press.

Smith, N. J. H. 1999. Biodiversity and Agroforestry Along the Amazon Floodplain. In Traditional and Modern Natural Resource Management in Latin America. Pichón, F. J. et al., eds. pp. 233–254. Pittsburgh: University of Pittsburgh Press.

Smith, R. T. 1970. Social Stratification in the Caribbean. In Essays in Comparative Social Stratification. Plotnicov, L. and Tuden, A., eds. pp. 43–76. Pittsburgh: University of Pittsburgh Press.

———. 1971. Culture and Social Structure in the Caribbean: Some Recent Work on Family and Kinship Studies. In Peoples and Cultures of the Caribbean: An Anthropological Reader. Horowitz, M. M., ed. pp. 448–475. Garden City, NY: Natural History Press.

———. 1992. Race, Class, and Gender in the Transition to Freedom. In The Meaning of Freedom: Economics, Politics, and Culture after Slavery. McGlynn, F. and Drescher, S., eds. pp. 257–290. Pittsburgh: University of Pittsurgh Press.

Smole, W. J. 1976. The Yanomama Indians: A Cultural Geography. Austin: University of Texas Press.

Sobo, E. J. 1993. One Blood: The Jamaican Body. Albany: State University of New York Press.

Socolow, S. M. 1989. Acceptable Partners: Marriage Choice in Colonial Argentina, 1778–1810. In Sexuality and Marriage in Colonial Latin America. Lavrin, A., ed. pp. 209–251. Lincoln: University of Nebraska Press.

Solien, N. L. 1971. West Indian Characteristics of the Black Carib. In Peoples and Cultures of the Caribbean: An Anthropological Reader. Horowitz, M. M., ed. pp. 133–142. Garden City, NY: Natural History Press.

Solomon, D. 2004. Three Cheers for Assimilation. New York Times Magazine. May 2, p. 21.

Spalding, K. 1984. Huarochirí: An Andean Society Under Inca and Spanish Rule. Stanford: Stanford University Press.

———. 1985. Social Climbers: Changing Patterns of Mobility Among the Indians of Colonial Peru. In Readings in Latin American History: Volume I, The Formative Centuries. Bakewell, P. J. et al., eds. pp. 157–173. Durham, NC: Duke University Press.

Spedding, A. L. 1997. The Coca Field as a Total Social Fact. In Coca, Cocaine, and the Bolivian Reality. Léons, M. B. and Sanabria, H., eds. pp. 47–70. Albany: State University of New York Press.

Spencer, C. S. and Redmond, E. M. 2004. Primary State Formation in Mesoamerica. Annual Review of Anthropology 33:173–199.

Spielmann, K. A. and Eder, J. F. 1994. Hunters and Farmers: Then and Now. Annual Review of Anthropology 23:303–323.

Spiro, M. E. 1986. Cultural Relativism and the Future of Anthropology. Cultural Anthropology 1(3): 259–286.

Sponsel, L. E. 1992. The Environmental History of Amazonia: Natural and Human Disturbances and the Ecological Transition. In Changing Tropical Forests: Historical Perspectives on Today's Challenges in Central and South America. Stern, H. and Tucker, R., eds. pp. 233–251. Durham, NC; Vienna, Austria: Forest History Society and IUFRO Forest History Group.

Sponsel, L. E. 2002. On Reflections on *Darkness in El Dorado*. Current Anthropology 43:149–152.

Stanish, C. 2001. The Origin of State Societies in South America. Annual Review of Anthropology 30:41–64.

Starn, O. 1991. Missing the Revolution: Anthropologists and the War in Peru. Cultural Anthropology 6(1):63–91.

———, 1994. Rethinking the Politics of Anthropology: The Case of the Andes. Current Anthropology 35(1):13–38.

———. 1999. Nightwatch: The Politics of Protest in the Andes. Durham, NC: Duke University Press.

Stavig, W. 1995. "Living in Offense of Our Lord:" Indigenous Sexual Values and Marital Life in the Colonial Crucible. Hispanic American Historical Review 75(4):597–622.

Stearman, A. M. 1987. No Longer Nomads: The Sirionó Revisited. Lanham and New York: Hamilton Press.

Stebbins, K. R. 1998. Tobacco or Health in the Third World: A Political Economy Perspective with Emphasis on Mexico. In Crossing Currents: Continuity and Change in Latin America. Whiteford, M. B. and Whiteford, S., eds. pp. 319–331. Upper Saddle River, NJ: Prentice Hall.

———. 2001. Going Like Gangbusters: Transnational Companies "Making a Killing" in South America. Medical Anthropology Quarterly 15(2):147–170.

Steckel, R. H. et al. 2002. Skeletal Health in the Western Hemisphere from 4000 B.C. to the Present. Evolutionary Anthropology 11:142–155.

Stein, S. J. and Stein, B. H. 1970. The Colonial Heritage of Latin America: Essays on Economic Dependence in Perspective. New York: Oxford University Press.

Steinberg, M. K. 2004. The Marijuana Milpa: Agricultural Adaptations in a Postsubsistence Maya Landscape in Southern Belize. In Dangerous Harvest: Drug Plants and the Transformation of Indigenous Landscapes. Steinberg, M. K. et al., eds. pp. 167–181. New York: Oxford University Press.

Stephen, L. 1992. Zapotec Women. Austin: University of Texas Press.

———. 2002. Zapata Lives! Histories and Cultural Politics in Southern Mexico. Berkeley: University of California Press.

———. et al. 2003. Introduction: Understanding the Américas: Insights from Latina/o and Latin American Studies. In Perspectives on *Las Américas*: A Reader in Culture, History, and Representation. Gutmann, M. C. et al., eds. pp. 1–30. Walden, MA and Oxford: Blackwell.

Stephen, L. and Dow, J. 1990. Introduction: Popular Religion in Mexico and Central America. In Class, Politics, and Popular Religion in Mexico and Central America. Stephen, L. and Dow, J., eds. pp. 1–26. Washington, D.C.: American Anthropological Association.

Stepick, A. 1998. Pride Against Prejudice: Haitians in the United States. Needham Heights, MA: Allyn and Bacon.

Stern, A. M. 2003. From Mestizophilia to Biotypology: Racialization and Science in Mexico, 1920–1960. In Race and Nation in Modern Latin America. Appelbaum, N. P. et al., eds. pp. 187–210. Chapel Hill: University of North Carolina Press.

Stern, S. J. 1982. Peru's Indian Peoples and the Challenge to Spanish Conquest: Huamanga to 1640. Madison: University of Wisconsin Press.

———. 1987a. The Age of Andean Insurrection, 1742–1782: A Reappraisal. In Resistance, Rebellion, and Conciousness in the Andean Peasant World, 18th to 20th Centuries. Stern, S. J., ed. pp. 34–93. Madison: University of Wisconsin Press.

———. 1987b. Introduction to Part Two. In Resistance, Rebellion, and Conciousness in the Andean Peasant World, 18th to 20th Centuries. Stern, S. J., ed. pp. 143–147. Madison: University of Wisconsin Press.

———. 1988. Feudalism, Capitalism, and the World-System in the Perspective of Latin America and the Caribbean. The American Historical Review 93(4):829–872.

———. 1993. Africa, Latin America, and the Splintering of Historical Knowledge: From Fragmentation to Reverberation. In Confronting Historical Paradigms: Peasants, Labor, and the Capitalist World System in Africa and Latin America. Cooper, F. et al., eds. pp. 3–22. Madison: University of Wisconsin Press.

————. 1995. The Secret History of Gender: Women, Men, and Power in Late Colonial Mexico. Chapel Hill: University of North Carolina Press.

————. 1998a. Beyond Enigma: An Agenda for Interpreting Shining Path and Peru, 1980–1995. In Shining and Other Paths: War and Society in Peru, 1980–1995. Stern, S. J., ed. pp. 1–9. Durham, NC: Duke University Press.

————. 1998b. Introduction to Part Two. In Shining and Other Paths: War and Society in Peru, 1980–1995. Stern, S. J., ed. pp. 13–21. Durham, NC: Duke University Press.

————. 2004. Remembering Pinochet's Chile: On the Eve of London 1998. Durham, NC: Duke University Press.

Stevens, E. P. 1973. Marianismo: The Other Face of Machismo in Latin America. In Female and Male in Latin America. Pescatello, A., ed. pp. 89–101. Pittsburgh: University of Pittsburgh Press.

Stevenson, R. W. 2004. Bush Is Considering Waiver for Mexicans Entering U.S. New York Times. Mar. 6, p. A4.

Steward, J. H. ed. 1946–1959. Handbook of South American Indians (7 Volumes). Washington, D.C.: General Printing Office (Smithsonian Instututution, Bureau of American Ethnology).

Stillwaggon, E. 1998. Stunted Lives, Stagnant Economies: Poverty, Disease, and Underdevelopment. New Brunswick, NJ: Rutgers University Press.

Stolcke, V. 1988. Coffee Planters, Workers and Wives: Class Conflict and Gender Relations on São Paulo Plantations 1850–1980. New York: St. Martin's Press.

Stoler, A. L. 1995. Race and the Education of Desire: Foucault's History of Sexuality and the Colonial Order of Things. Durham, NC: Duke University Press.

————. 2002. Carnal Knowledge and Imperial Power: Race and the Intimate in Colonial Rule. Berkeley: University of California Press.

Stoll, D. 1988. Evangelicals, Guerillas, and the Army: The Ixil Triangle Under Ríos Montt. In Harvest of Violence: The Maya Indians and the Guatemalan Crisis. Carmack, R. M., ed. pp. 90–118. Norman: University of Oklahoma Press.

————. 1993. Introduction: Rethinking Protestantism in Latin America. In Rethinking Protestantism in Latin America. Garrard-Burnett, V. and Stoll, D., eds. pp. 1–19. Philadelphia: Temple University Press.

————. 1999a. Rigoberta Menchú and the Story of All Poor Guatemalans. Boulder, CO: Westview.

————. 1999b. Rigoberta Menchú and the Last-Resort Paradigm. Latin American Perspectives 26(109):70–80.

Stone, M. C. 2000. Becoming Belizean: Maya Identity and the Politics of Nation. In The Maya Diaspora: Guatemalan Roots, New American Lives. Loucky, J. and Moors, M. M., eds. pp. 118–140. Philadelphia: Temple University Press.

Stonich, S. C. 1993. "I Am Destroying the Land!": The Political Ecology of Poverty and Environmental Destruction in Honduras. Boulder, CO: Westview.

————. 1995. Development, Rural Impoverishment, and Environmental Destruction in Honduras. In The Social Causes of Environmental Destruction in Latin America. Painter, M. and Durham, W. H., eds. pp. 63–100. Ann Arbor: University of Michigan Press.

Stowers, S. L. 2003. Hungry for the Taste of El Salvador: Gastronomic Nostalgia, Identity, and Resistance to Nutrithink in an Immigrant Community. Ph.D. dissertation. University of Massachussetts–Amherst.

Strobel, M. 2002. Women's History, Gender History, and European Colonialism. In Colonialism and the Modern World: Selected Studies. Blue, G. et al., eds. pp. 51–67. New York: M. E. Sharpe.

Strobele-Gregor, J. 1994. From Indio to Mestizo . . . to Indio: New Indianist Movements in Bolivia. Latin American Perspectives 21(2):106–123.

Stronza, A. 2001. Anthropology of Tourism: Forging New Ground for Ecotourism and Other Alternatives. Annual Review of Anthropology 30:261–283.

Super, J. C. and Vargas, L. A. 2000. Mexico and Highland Central America. In The Cambridge World History of Food (Vol. II). Kiple, K. F. and Ornelas, K. C., eds. pp. 1248–1253. Cambridge: Cambridge University Press.

Sutton, D. E. 2001. Remembrance of Repasts: An Anthropology of Food and Memory. Oxford: Berg.

Suárez Findlay, E. J. 1999. Imposing Decency: The Politics of Sexuality and Race in Puerto Rico 1870–1920. Durham, NC: Duke University Press.

Suárez-Orozco, M. M. 2004. The Treatment of Children in the "Dirty War": Ideology, State Terrorism, and the Abuse of Children in Argentina. In Violence in War and Peace. Scheper-Hughes, N. and Bourgois, P., eds. pp. 378–388. Malden, MA and Oxford: Blackwell.

Swartley, L. 2002. Inventing Indigenous Knowledge: Archaeology, Rural Development, and the Raised Field Rehabilitation Project in Bolivia. New York: Routledge.

Szeminski, J. 1987. Why Kill the Spaniard? New Perspectives on Andean Insurrectionary Ideology in the 18th Century. In Resistance, Rebellion, and Conciousness in the Andean Peasant World, 18th to 20th Centuries. Stern, S. J., ed. pp. 166–192. Madison: University of Wisconsin Press.

Tandeter, E. 1991. Crisis in Upper Peru, 1800–1805. Hispanic American Historical Review 71(1):35–71.

Tarazona-Sevillano, G. 1992. The Organization of Shining Path. In The Shining Path of Peru. Palmer, D. S., ed. pp. 189–208. New York: St. Martin's Press.

Tate, W. 2000. Repeating Past Mistakes: Aiding Counterinsurgency in Colombia. NACLA Report on the Americas 34(2):16–22.

Taussig, M. 1980. The Devil and Commodity Fetishism in South America. Chapel Hill: University of North Carolina Press.

————. 1987. Shamanism, Colonialism, and the Wild Man: A Study in Terror and Healing. Chicago: University of Chicago Press.

———. 2003. Law in a Lawless Land: Diary of a *Limpieza* in Colombia. New York: New Press.

———. 2004. My Cocaine Museum. Chicago: University of Chicago Press.

Tax, S. 1937. The Municipios of the Midwestern Highlands of Guatemala. American Anthropologist 60:433–441.

Taylor, J. 1976. Tango: Theme of Class and Nation. Ethnomusicology 20(2):273–291.

———. 1987. Tango: Ethos of Melancoly. Cultural Anthropology 1(4):481–493.

Taylor, W. B. 1974. Landed Society in New Spain: A View from the South. Hispanic American Historical Review 54(3): 387–413.

———. 1987. The Virgin of Guadalupe in New Spain: An Inquiry into the Social History of Marian Devotion. American Ethnologist 14(1):9–33.

Terto, V. Jr. 2000. Male Homosexuality and Seropositivity: The Construction of Social Identities in Brazil. In Framing the Sexual Subject: The Politics of Gender, Sexuality, and Power. Parker, R. et al., eds. pp. 60–78. Berkeley: University of California Press.

Thompson, E. P. 1963. The Making of the English Working Class. New York: Vintage.

Thompson, G. 2001. Added Rights for Indians Are Ratified in Mexico. New York Times. July 13, p. A4.

Thompson, S. 2002. We Alone Will Rule: Native Andean Politics in the Age of Insurgency. Madison: University of Wisconsin Press.

Thurner, M. 1997. From Two Republics to One Divided: Contradictions of Postcolonial Nationmaking in Andean Peru. Durham, NC: Duke University Press.

Tice, K. E. 2002. Kuna *Molas* and the Global Economy. In Contemporary Cultures and Societies of Latin America (3rd ed.). Heath, D. B., ed. pp. 219–224. Prospect Heights, IL: Waveland.

Tierney, P. 2000. Darkness in El Dorado: How Scientists and Journalists Devastated the Amazon. New York: W. W. Norton & Company.

Tobin, J. 1998. Tango and the Scandal of Homosocial Desire. In The Passion of Music and Dance: Body, Gender and Sexuality. Washabaugh, W., ed. pp. 79–102. Oxford: Berg.

Todorov, T. 1984. The Conquest of America (translated by Richard Howard). New York: Harper & Row.

Tosi, J. A. 1964. Climatic Control of Terrestrial Ecosystems: A Report on the Holdridge Model. Economic Geography 40(3):173–181.

Trevelyan, A. M. and Gustafson, L. S. 2002. Introduction. In Ancient Maya Gender Identity Relations. Gustafson, L. S. and Trevelyan, A. M., eds. pp. 1–10. Westport, CT: Bergin & Garvey.

Trexler, R. C. 1995. Sex and Conquest: Gendered Violence, Political Order, and the European Conquest of the Americas. Ithaca, NY: Cornell University Press.

Troll, C. 1968. The Cordilleras of the Tropical Americas: Aspects of Climatic, Phytogeographical and Agrarian Ecology. In Geo-Ecology of the Mountainous Regions of the Tropical Americas. pp. 15–56. Bonn: Ferd. Dummlers Verlag (Colloquim Geographicum. Band 9).

Trouillot, M.-R. 1992. The Caribbean Region: An Open Frontier in Anthropological Theory. Annual Review of Anthropology 21:19–42.

———. 1995. Silencing the Past: Power and the Production of History. Boston: Beacon Press.

Turner, T. 1989. Kayapo Plan Meeting to Discuss Dam. Cultural Survival Quarterly 13(1):20–22.

———. 1992. Defiant Images: The Kayapo Appropriation of Video. Anthropology Today 8(6):5–16.

Turner, V. 1969. The Ritual Process: Structure and Anti-Structure. Chicago: Aldine.

———. 1987. Carnival, Ritual and Play in Rio de Janeiro. In Time out of Time: Essays on the Festival. Falassi, A., ed. pp. 76–90. Albuquerque: University of New Mexico Press.

Twinam, A. 1999. Public Lives, Private Secrets: Gender, Honor, Sexuality, and Illegitimacy in Colonial Spanish America. Stanford, CA: Stanford University Press.

U.S. Census Bureau. 1993. Population Projections of the United States by Age, Sex, Race, and Hispanic Origin: 1995–2050. www.census.gov/prod/1/pop/p25–1130/p251130a.pdf.

———. 2000a. Profile of Selected Social Characteristics: 2000 (Census 2000 Summary File [SF 3]—Sample Data). http://factfinder.census.gov/servlet/QTTable?_ts=59668064734.

———. 2000b. Race and Hispanic or Latino: 2000 (Census 2000 Summary File 1 [SF 1] 100-Percent Data). http://factfinder.census.gov/servlet/QTTable?_ts=59669342593.

———. 2000c. Profile of Selected Social Characteristics: 2000 (Census 2000 Supplementary Survey Summary Tables). http://factfinder.census.gov/servlet/QTTable?_ts=5966885 3046.

———. 2000d. Language Spoken At Home: 2000 (Census 2000 Summary File 3 [SF 3]—Sample Data). http://factfinder.census.gov/servlet/QTTable?_ts=59668322781.

———. 2001. The Hispanic Population: Census 2000 Brief. www.census.gov/prod/2001pubs/c2kbr01–3. pdf.

Ubelaker, D. H. 1995. Status and Diet in Precontact Highland Ecuador. American Journal of Physical Anthropology 97:403–411.

UNAIDS. 2004a. 2004 Report on the Global AIDS Epidemic: Executive Summary. www.unaids.org/bangkok2004/GAR2004_pdf/GAR2004_Execsumm_en.pdf.

———. 2004b. 2004 Report on the Global AIDS Epidemic. www.unaids.org/EN/resources/epidemiology.asp.

United Nations. 1998. The State of the World's Children 1998. www.unicef.org/sowc98/sowc98.pdf.

———. 1999. World Population Prospects (The 1998 Revision; Vol. I: Comprehensive Tables). New York: United Nations. Department of Economic and Social Affairs.

———. 2002. World Population 2002 (Data Sheet). www.un.org/ esa/population/publications/wpp2002/POP-R2002-DATA_ Web.xls.

Unwin, T. 2000. A Waste of Space? Towards a Critique of the Social Production of Space: Transactions of the Institute of British Geographers 25(1):11–29.

Uzzell, D. 1977. *Susto* Revisited: Illness as Strategic Role. In Culture, Disease, and Healing: Studies in Medical Anthropology. Landy, D., ed. pp. 402–408. New York: Macmillan Publishing.

Valentine, C. A. 1968. Culture and Poverty: Critique and Counter-Proposals. Chicago: University of Chicago Press.

Valle, I. 1991. Migrant Workers Toil and Suffer for Little Return. Seattle Times. Aug. 11.

Van Cott, D. L. 2003. Andean Indigenous Movements and Constitutional Transformation: Venezuela in Comparative Perspective. Latin American Perspectives 30(1):49–69.

Van den Berghe, G. and Van den Berghe, P. L. 1966. Compadrazgo and Class in Southeastern Mexico. American Anthropologist 68(5):1236–1244.

Van den Berghe, P. L. and Primov, G. P. 1977. Inequality in the Peruvian Andes: Class and Ethnicity in Cuzco. Columbia: University of Missouri Press.

Van Gennep, A. 1960. The Rites of Passage. Chicago: University of Chicago Press.

Vargas Meza, R. 2000. Biowarfare in Colombia? NACLA Report on the Americas 34(2):20–22.

Vásquez, G. L. 1996. Conquistadores, Criollos, and Cholos: Manuel González Prada and the Birth of Peruvian Indigenismo. In Beyond Indigenous Voices: LAILA/ALILA 11th International Symposium on Latin American Indian Literatures (1994). Preuss, M. H., ed. pp. 167–178. Lancaster, CA: Labyrinthos.

Verbitsky, H. 1996. The Flight: Confessions of an Argentine Dirty Warrior. New York: New Press.

Vertovec, S. and Posey, D. 2003. Globalization, Globalism, Environment, and Environmentalism: Consciousness of Connections. New York: Oxford University Press.

Vianna, H. 1999. The Mystery of Samba: Popular Music and National Identity in Brazil (edited and translated by J. C. Chasteen). Chapel Hill: University of North Carolina Press.

Vidal, S. M. 2002. Secret Religious Cults and Political Leadership: Multiethnic Confederacies from Northwestern Amazonia. In Comparative Arawakan Histories: Rethinking Language Family and Culture Area in Amazonia. Hill, J. D. and Santos-Granero, F., eds. pp. 248–268. Urbana: University of Illinois Press.

Villamarín, J. A. and Villamarín, J. 1999. Chiefdoms: The Prevalence and Persistence of "Señoríos Naturales" 1400 to European Conquest. In The Cambridge History of the Native Peoples of the Americas (Vol. III [South America], Part 1). Salomon, F. and Schwartz, S. B., eds. pp. 577–667. Cambridge: Cambridge University Press.

Vinh-Kim, N. and Peschard, K. 2003. Anthropology, Inequality, and Disease: A Review. Annual Review of Anthropology 32:447–474.

Visweswaran, K. 1997. Histories of Feminist Ethnography. Annual Review of Anthropology 26:591–621.

Viveros Vigoya, M. 2003. Contemporary Latin American Perspectives on Masculinity. In Changing Men and Masculinities in Latin America. Gutmann, M. C., ed. pp. 27–57. Durham, NC: Duke University Press.

Voeks, R. S. 1997. Sacred Leaves of Candomblé: African Magic, Medicine, and Religion in Brazil. Austin: University of Texas Press.

Wachtel, N. 1977. The Vision of the Vanquished: The Spanish Conquest of Peru Through Indian Eyes 1530–1570. New York: Harper and Row.

Wade, P. 2000. Music, Race, and Nation: Música Tropical in Colombia. Chicago: University of Chicago Press.

Walker, R. et al. 2000. Deforestation and Cattle Ranching in the Brazilian Amazon: External Capital and Household Processes. World Development 28(4):683–699.

Warren, K. B. 1998. Indigenous Movements as a Challenge to the Unified Social Movement Paradigm for Guatemala. In Cultures of Politics, Politics of Cultures: Re-visioning Latin American Social Movements. Alvarez, S. E., ed. pp. 165–195. Boulder, CO: Westview.

———. 1999. Indigenous Movements and Their Critics: Pan-Maya Activism in Guatemala. Princeton, NJ: Princeton University Press.

———. 2001. Telling Truths: Taking David Stoll and the Rigoberta Menchú Exposé Seriously. In The Rigoberta Menchú Controversy (with a response by David Stoll). Arias, A., ed. pp. 198–218. Minneapolis: University of Minnesota Press.

Washburne, C. 1998. Play It "Con Filin!": The Swing and Expression of Salsa. Latin American Music Review 19(2):160–185.

Washington Post. 2002. The Problem Is Pot Prohibition (Editorial). Washington Post. May 4, p. A19.

———. 2004. Too Predictable. Washington Post. Jan. 19, p. A20.

Wasserstrom, R. 1978. The Exchange of Saints in Zinacantan: The Socioeconomic Bases of Religious Change in Southern Mexico. Ethnology 17(2):197–210.

Watanabe, J. M. 1990. Enduring Yet Ineffable Community in the Western Periphery of Guatemala. In Guatemalan Indians and the State: 1540–1988. Smith, C. A., ed. pp. 183–204. Austin: University of Texas Press.

Watson, H. A. 1994. The Caribbean in the Global Political Economy. Boulder, CO: L. Rienner Publishers.

Watters, B. 1988. Quinceañera: The Mexican-American Initiation Ritual of Young Women. In The American Ritual Tapestry: Social Rules, Cultural Meanings. Deegan, M. J., ed. pp. 145–158. Westport, CT: Greenwood.

Watters, D. 1997. Maritime Trade in the Prehistoric Eastern Caribbean. In The Indigenous People of the Caribbean. Wilson, S., ed. pp. 88–99. Gainsville: University Press of Florida.

Wauchope, R. ed. 1964–1976. Handbook of Middle American Indians (16 Volumes). Austin: University of Texas Press.

Waxter, L. 2000. "En Conga, Bonga y Campana": The Rise of Colombian Salsa. Latin American Music Review 21(3):118–168.

Wayland, C. 2001. Gendering Local Knowledge: Medicinal Plant Use and Primary Care in the Amazon. Medical Anthropology Quarterly 15(2):171–188.

Weaver, M. P. 1993. The Aztecs, Maya, and Their Predecessors: Archaeology of Mesoamerica. New York: Academic Press.

Weber, T. J. 2000. Likkle But Talawah (Small But Mighty): Reggae Music, Globalization, and the Birth of a Social Movement. Ph.D. dissertation. Bowling Green State University.

Weeks, J. M. and Ferbel, P. J. 1994. Ancient Caribbean. New York: Garland Publishing.

Weismantel, M. J. 1988. Food, Gender, and Poverty in the Ecuadorian Andes. Philadelphia: University of Pennsylvania Press.

———. 1991. Maize Beer and Andean Social Transformations: Drunken Indians, Bread Babies, and Chosen Women. MLN [Modern Language Notes] 106(4):861–879.

——— and Eisenman, S. F. 1998. Race in the Andes: Global Movements and Popular Ontologies. Bulletin of Latin American Research 17(2):121–142.

Wellmeier, N. J. 1998. Santa Eulalia's People in Exile: Maya Religion, Culture, and Identity in Los Angeles. In Gatherings in Diaspora: Religious Communities and the New Immigration. Warner, R. S. and Wittner, J. G., eds. pp. 97–122. Philadelphia: Temple University Press.

Whitehead, N. L. 1994. The Ancient Amerindian Polities of the Amazon, the Orinoco, and the Atlantic Coast: A Preliminary Analysis of Their Passage from Antiquity to Extinction. In Amazonian Indians from Prehistory to the Present: Anthropological Perspectives. Roosevelt, A., ed. pp. 33–54. Tucson: University of Arizona Press.

———. 1996a. Amazonian Archaeology, Searching for Paradise? A Review of Recent Literature and Fieldwork. Journal of Archaeological Research 4(3):241–264.

———. 1996b. Ethnogenesis and Ethnocide in the European Occupation of Native Suriname. In History, Power, and Identity: Ethnogenesis in the Americas, 1492–1992. Hill, J. D., ed. pp. 20–35. Iowa City: University of Iowa Press.

———. 2002. Dark Shamans: Kanaimà and the Poetics of Violent Death. Durham, NC: Duke University Press.

———. 2003. Introduction. In Histories and Historicites in Amazonia. Whitehead, N. L., ed. pp. vii–xxi. Lincoln: University of Nebraska Press.

Whitmore, T. M. and Turner II, B. L. 1992. Landscapes of Cultivation in Mesoamerica on the Eve of the Conquest. Annals of the Association of American Geographers 82(3):402–425.

———. 2001. Cultured Landscapes of Middle America on the Eve of Conquest. New York: Oxford University Press.

Whitten, N. E. 1976. Ecuadorian Ethnocide and Indigenous Ethnogenesis: Amazonian Resurgence Amidst Andean Colonialism. Journal of Ethnic Studies 4(2):1–22.

Wightman, A. M. 1990. Indigenous Migration and Social Change: The Forasteros of Cuzco, 1520–1720. Durham, NC: Duke University Press.

Wilbert, J. 1991. South America. In Encyclopedia of World Cultures. Levinson, D., ed. pp. xxiii–xll. Boston: G. K. Hall & Co.

Wilford, J. N. 2003. "Lost City" Yielding Its Secrets. New York Times. Mar. 18: p. D1.

Wilk, R. R. 1999. "Real Belizean Food": Building Local identity in the Transnational Caribbean. American Anthropologist 101(2):244–255.

Wilkie, J. W. et al. 1999. Statistical Abstract of Latin America (Vol. XXXV). Los Angeles: University of California. Committee on Latin American Studies.

———. 2001. Statistical Abstract of Latin America (Vol. XXXVII). Los Angeles: University of California. Committee on Latin American Studies.

Williams, B. 1984. Why Migrant Women Feed Their Husbands Tamales: Foodways as a Basis for a Revisionist View of Tejano Family Life. In Ethnic and Regional Foodways in the United States: The Performance of Group Identity. Keller Brown, L. and Kay, M., eds. pp. 113–126. Knoxville: University of Tennessee Press.

Williams, R. 1977. Marxism and Literature. New York: Oxford University Press.

Williams, R. G. 1986. Export Agriculture and the Crisis in Central America. Chapel Hill: University of North Carolina Press.

———. 1994. States and Social Evolution: Coffee and the Rise of National Governments in Central America. Chapel Hill: University of North Carolina Press.

Willis, P. 1981. Learning to Labor: How Working Class Kids Get Working Class Jobs. New York: Columbia University Press.

Wilson, F. 2004. Indian Citizenship and the Discourse of Hygiene/Disease in Nineteenth-Century Peru. Bulletin of Latin American Research 23(2):165–180.

Wilson, P. C. 2003. Ethnographic Museums and Cultural Commodification: Indigenous Organizations, NGOs, and Culture as a Resource in Amazonian Ecuador. Latin American Perspectives 30(1):162–180.

Wilson, R. 1991. Machine Guns and Mountain Spirits: The Cultural Effects of State Repression Among the Q'eqchi of Guatemala. Critique of Anthropology 11(1):33–61.

Winkelman, M. J. 1990. Shamans and Other "Magico-Religious" Healers: A Cross-Cultural Study of Their Origins, Nature, and Social Transformations. Ethos 18(3):308–352.

Wise, T. et al., eds. 2003. Confronting Globalization: Economic Integration and Popular Resistance in Mexico. Bloomfield, CT: Kumarian Press.

Wiser, G. M. 1999. PTO Rejection of the "Ayahuasca" Patent Claim: Background and Analysis. www.ciel.org/Biodiversity/ptorejection.html (Center for International Environmental Law).

Wolf, E. R. 1997[1982]. Europe and the People Without History. Berkeley: University of California Press.

————. 1955. Types of Latin American Peasantry: A Preliminary Discussion. American Anthropologist 57(3):452–470.

————. 1957. Closed Corporate Peasant Communities in Mesoamerica and Central Java. Southwestern Journal of Anthropology 13(1):1–18.

————. 1959. Sons of the Shaking Earth: The People of Mexico and Guatemala; Their Land, History, and Culture. Chicago: University of Chicago Press.

————. 1966. Peasants. Upper Saddle River, NJ: Prentice Hall.

————. 1969. Peasant Wars of the Twentieth Century. New York: Harper & Row.

————. 1986. The Vicissitudes of the Closed Corporate Peasant Community. American Ethnologist 13(2): 325–329.

————. 1999. Envisioning Power: Ideologies of Dominance and Crisis. Berkeley: University of California Press.

————. and Hansen, E. C. 1972. The Human Condition in Latin America. New York: Oxford University Press.

Wolf, E. R. and Mintz, S. 1957. Haciendas and Plantations in Middle America and the Antilles. Social and Economic Studies 6(3):380–412.

Wood, C. H. 2003. Introduction: Land Use and Deforestation in the Amazon. In Deforestation and Land Use in the Amazon. Wood, C. H. and Porro, R., eds. pp. 1–38. Gainesville: University Press of Florida.

World Health Organization. 2001–2002. Core Health Indicators. Comparison on Core Health Indicators Within the WHO Region. www.who.int/whois/country/compare.

Wright, M. W. 2001. The Dialectics of Still Life: Murder, Women, and Maquiladoras. In Millennial Capitalism and the Culture of Neoliberalism. Comaroff, J. and Comaroff, J. L., eds. pp. 125–146. Durham, NC: Duke University Press.

Wright, W. R. 1990. Café Con Leche: Race, Class, and National Image in Venezuela. Austin: University of Texas Press.

Zavella, P. 2003. "Playing with Fire": The Gendered Construction of Chicana/Mexicana Sexuality. In Perspectives on *Las Américas*: A Reader in Culture, History, and Representation. Gutmann, M. C. et al., eds. pp. 229–244. Malden, MA and Oxford: Blackwell.

Zentella, A. C. 2003. Returned Migration, Language, and Identity: Puerto Rican Bilinguals in Dos Worlds/Two Mundos. In Perspectives on *Las Américas*: A Reader in Culture, History, and Representation. Gutmann, M. C. et al., eds. pp. 245–258. Malden, MA and Oxford: Blackwell.

Zietilin, R. N. and Zeitlin, J. F. 2000. The PaleoIndian and Archaic Cultures of Mesoamerica. In The Cambridge History of the Native Peoples of the Americas (Vol. II [Mesoamerica], Part 1). Adams, R. E. and MacLeod, M. J., eds. pp. 45–121. Cambridge: Cambridge University Press.

Zorn, E. 2004. Weaving a Future: Tourism, Cloth, and Culture on an Andean Island. Iowa City: University of Iowa Press.

Zulawski, A. 1995. They Eat from Their Labor: Work and Social Change in Colonial Bolivia. Pittsburgh: University of Pittsburgh Press.

GLOSSARY

Altiplano Plateau lying between the eastern and western Andean mountain ranges.

Amazon (also Amazonia, Amazon Basin) Tropical forest region in South America primarily drained by the Amazon River.

Andean Mountains Mountain ranges of the Western Alpine System mainly located in Chile, Bolivia, and Peru.

Andean Rebellions Large-scale, eighteenth century insurrections in Peru and Bolivia.

Andeanism Perspective that interprets Andean peoples and their cultures in an essentialized way, as largely unchanging through time.

Anthropology of Food Subdiscipline of cultural anthropology that centers on the socio-cultural dimensions of food and cuisine.

Anthropology of the Body Field of cultural anthropology concerned with how the human body is culturally and socially construed.

Anthropology of the Emotions Subdiscipline of cultural anthropology that focuses on how the body is a metaphor expressing personal and collective emotional states.

Anthropology of Tourism Field of cultural anthropology concerned with the cultural consequences of tourism.

Archaeology Field of general anthropology concerned with the appearance, spread, and disappearance of social groups over long periods of time, and the transition from small-scale and egalitarian to large, stratified societies.

Archaic Period Archaeological period marked by sedentary lifestyles, rise in population, emergence of pottery, incipient agriculture, and appearance of chiefdoms.

Atacama Desert Long stretch of desert on the Chilean Pacific coast.

Bands Political and economic egalitarian societies mainly subsisting by hunting and gathering (foraging).

Barras Bravas Chilean soccer clubs comprised of rebellious youths.

Big Game Specialization Subsistence based on the hunting of large mammals; once viewed as the key characteristic of the Paleo-Indian archaeological phase.

Biomedicine Medical system prominent in Western societies that privileges biological over cultural explanations of sickness.

Biopiracy Usurpation by commercial interests of legal rights, through the awarding of patents, over the chemical properties of plants cultivated or consumed by indigenous peoples for ritual or healing purposes.

Bioprospecting Searching for commercially useful plant genetic material for the North American prescription drug market.

Black Carib Caribbean and coastline social groups that emerged out of the fusion of runaway African slaves and Carib-speaking indigenous peoples.

Blocos Afro Brazilian associations that represent neighborhoods participating in Brazilian Carnavals.

Brigas Personal physical encounters between two persons during Brazilian Carnaval.

Cabildo Colonial term referring to a town council.

Campaigns against Idolatry European efforts to stamp out indigenous "pagan" beliefs and practices.

Candomblé (see also Santería, Vodou) One of three major Afro–Latin religious systems in Brazil and the Caribbean.

Cargo (see also Civil–Religious Hierarchies) Ranked post, office, or position in the civil–religious systems.

Central American Volcanic Axis Physiographic region in Central America consisting of volcanic ranges, plateaus, and valleys.

Central Lowlands Major structural zone from northern South America to Argentina.

Central Plateau Physiographic region (also Mesa Central) in Mexico between the Western and Eastern Sierra Madre Mountain ranges.

Chaco Arid physiographic region in western Paraguay, southeastern Bolivia, northern Argentina, and western Brazil.

Chiefdoms Societies marked by initial economic and political stratification, including institutionalized formal political leaders or chiefs.

Chinampas Type of raised platform agricultural fields in Mexico.

Cimarrones Colonial-era Spanish term referring to runaway slaves.

Civil–Religious Hierarchies (see also Cargo) Hierarchically ranked system in which community members occupy alternate political and religious posts or cargos.

Coastal Plains Narrow stretches of primarily tropical plains facing the Atlantic, Pacific, and Caribbean seas.

Cofradías Colonial-era religious brotherhoods that sponsored religious celebrations, often for community patron saints.

Colonialism   Political–economic, social, and cultural subjugation of one people over another.

Columbian Exchange   Flow of animals and plants between the New and Old Worlds and the consequences of this two-way exchange.

Communitas   Intense feelings of shared belonging to and identification with a community.

Companionate Marriage   Type of marriage emerging in Mexico predicated on more balanced gender ideologies, relationships, and expectations.

Conquest Hierarchy   Process whereby religious and gender systems of conquered societies were symbolically subordinated to Inca control.

Constructive Drinking (see also Ritual Intoxication)   Idea that cross-culturally, seemingly excessive alcohol drinking is a sanctioned complement to ritual celebrations.

Consumption Metaphors   Metaphors equating eating with sexual intercourse.

Contra War   The war in Nicaragua during the 1980s that the United States financed and directed.

Critical Cultural Relativism (see also Cultural Relativism)   Idea that cultural relativism should take into account internal cultural differences and contrasting views of what are acceptable behaviors and norms.

Critical Medical Anthropology   Approach in medical anthropology stressing political and economic inequality in the study of health, illness, and disease.

Cultural Diversity or Variability   Perspective that focuses on how and why different peoples think and behave differently from others.

Cultural Negotiation   Refers to how tourists and those they encounter respond to each other's expectations and views of the other.

Cultural Performance   Ritualized and public cultural display.

Cultural Relativism (see also Critical Cultural Relativism)   Idea that cultural norms or practices should not be judged from the vantage point of one's own culture.

Cultural Similarities   Perspective that focuses on what and why diverse peoples around the globe share, or have in common, despite their seeming differences.

Culturalist Approach   In medical anthropology, the view that beliefs, values, and attitudes—and not inequality—are the causes of poor health.

Culture   Symbolic and material repertoire with which people make sense of the world around them, claim a sense of identity, and furnish the means with which to cope with changing circumstances.

Culture Area   Perspective that associated cultures or cultural traits with geographic or ecological areas.

Culture of Poverty   Viewpoint emphasizing that the poor have their own cultural system stemming from poverty.

Desaparecer   Spanish verb meaning "to disappear"; refers to the act of kidnapping, murdering, and hiding the bodies of opponents by army or police forces.

Desaparecidos   Spanish term referring to those who have been "disappeared."

Dirty War   Illegitimate or illegal state violence against citizens.

Disease   Biomedical concept equating sickness with the role of biological pathogens.

Domestication   Active and conscious supervision and control of plants and animals by social groups.

Eastern Highlands   Major structural zone in South America consisting of high altitude, eroded lands.

Egalitarian Societies   Societies characterized by the absence of economic and political inequality.

Encomendero   Colonial-era individual awarded a Spanish crown grant over indigenous labor (encomienda) in return for ensuring their well-being and conversion to Christianity.

Encomienda   Spanish crown grant over indigenous labor.

Endangered Languages   Languages that are on the verge of extinction.

Entrudo   Ritualized and aggressive provocations between two persons during Brazilian Carnaval.

Environmental Determinism   Idea that geography, or physical features of the environment, play a prominent role in shaping culture.

Estancias   Landed estates used primarily for cattle and sheep ranching.

Ethnicity   Shared group identity based on the common association of key cultural elements.

Ethnocentrism   Judging of other people's cultural beliefs and behaviors from the vantage point of one own's culture.

Ethnogenesis   Process whereby new societies and cultural identities emerge as a result of sudden political or economic changes.

Ethnographic Analogy   Approach that views contemporary societies as though they are representative of those existing in past times.

Ethnographic Representation   The process whereby anthropologists describe and form an image of the culture and social practices of the peoples they study.

Ethnography   A description or portrait of the culture and everyday life of the people studied.

Ethnomedicine   The medical systems in non-Western societies that stress social and cultural factors in diagnosing and treating culturally specific sickness.

Everyday Forms of Resistance   Forms of resistance or non-compliance that are often hidden from the view of elites and power holders.

Fazenda (see also Hacienda)   Large landed estate, often owned by absentee landlords, and worked by tenants (Portuguese).

Fazendeiro   Owner of an hacienda (Portuguese).

Food Pollution   Idea that certain foods are "unclean" or polluted and should be avoided.

Food Taboos   Prohibition on consuming certain foods.

Foraging Subsistence Mode   Way of earning a livelihood based on gathering and consuming undomesticated plants, and occasional reliance on hunting.

Formative Period   Archaeological period marked by increasing societal complexity and initial appearance of state societies.

Gender   Differences and similarities in roles, beliefs, and attitudes that are related to physical sexuality.

Gender Complementarity and Parallelism   Part of Mesoamerican and Andean gender systems in which women and men complemented each other and held important economic, political, and religious roles.

Gender Division of Labor   Productive tasks typically ascribed to and undertaken by males and females.

Gendered Distribution of Global Labor   Refers to how labor and productive activities at the global level are segmented along gender lines.

Gender-Inflected Foods   Foods that convey culturally construed notions of gender identity associated with femaleness (femininity) or with maleness (masculinity).

Gender-Inflected Societies   Societies in which gender roles and ideas concerning sexuality pervade multiple domains of culture.

General Anthropology   Also known as anthropology, comprises four subfields, of which cultural or socio-cultural anthropology is part.

Genocide   Deliberate targeting and killing of people on the basis of presumed cultural and/or racial characteristics.

Geographical Bias   Perspective that assumes that tropical environments work against the development of complex societies.

Globalization   Contemporary economic and cultural process swiftly linking peoples, cultures, and societies throughout the globe.

Godparenthood   Ritual in which sponsors of an infant's baptism, or a couple's marriage, became godparents of their godchildren and coparents of the baptized infant's or the groom or bride's parents.

Gulf Coastal Plains/Gulf Region   Physiographic region of tropical forest terrain and low-lying coastal plains facing the Caribbean Sea, Gulf of Mexico, and the Atlantic Ocean.

Hacendado (see also Fazendeiro)   Owner of an hacienda (Spanish).

Hacienda (see also Fazenda)   Large landed estate, often owned by absentee landlords, and worked by tenants (Spanish).

Haiti's Slave Revolution   Eighteenth-century slave uprising that led to the independence of the first country in Latin America and the Caribbean.

Hegemonic Racism   Process in which indigenous peoples partially adopted and reproduced the racial hierarchies imposed upon them by the White dominant society.

Hegemony   Refers to consent and allegiance toward, and a sense of legitimacy of, a political and economic order.

Hierarchy of Taste and Cuisine   Foods, cuisines, and tastes that parallel and are associated with hierarchically ranked social classes.

Homosociality   Feelings for and need of intense all-male bonding and companionship.

Honor   Norm stipulating that a women's reputation is based on premarital (female) chastity, church sanctioned marriage, and the siring of legitimate children.

Horizon Period   Archaeological period marked by the spread of regional states and the emergence and spread of the Aztec and Inca empires.

Hot and Cold Foods   Classification of foods as "hot" or "cold," each associated with emotional and somatic well-being, and overall health.

House/Street Divide   Norm stipulating that the proper domain of honorable women is the home, while that of men is the street, or outside the domestic domain. Also called the public/private dichotomy.

Identification   Meanings that quasi-racial categories acquire in social settings and partly through a process of ascription.

Illness   Culturally specific sickness or ailment.

Imperial Religious Cult   State religion forged during Aztec and Inca times that legitimated their imperial expansion.

Indigenismo   Social theories that posited that the redemption of indigenous peoples would be found in a return to a pure, Indian past, uncorrupted by the negative impacts of Spanish colonialism.

Indigenistas   Elites who advocated the ideals of indigenismo.

Informal Economy   Range of economic activities outside the control or monitoring of the state.

Intellectual Property Rights   The legal control over raw materials/resources and their subsequent transformations as well as over the entitlement to any benefits as a result of these changes.

Interior Mountain Ranges   Northern prolongation of the Western Alpine System that in the Greater Antilles surface as interior mountain ranges.

Interpretation of Testimonies   Different ways of understanding and reading quasi-biographical statements.

Intracultural Variability   Idea that suggests that cultures are not homogenous.

Invention of Tradition   The process whereby cultural traditions are refashioned in novel contexts.

Ladinos   Members of the Guatemalan landed-elite; roughly equivalent to Mestizo.

Landscape   Concept that alludes to the physical environment as profoundly shaped by human agency.

Latin America and the Caribbean as Concepts   Idea that Latin America and the Caribbean are social or cultural constructions.

Liberation Theology   Movement within the Catholic Church stressing the relationship between teachings of the Bible and social justice.

Life's Lesions   Adversities and unresolved contradictions that result in psychosomatic illnesses.

Liminality   A solemn state in which ordinary, everyday expectations and behaviors are temporarily suspended and others undertaken.

Limpieza   In Colombia, refers to the physical extermination of criminals and social outcasts.

Linguistic Anthropology   Subfield of general anthropology concerned with learning about societies and their cultures from the vantage point of language.

Llanos   Physiographic region in South America consisting of low-lying grasslands and savannas in northern Venezuela, southeastern Colombia, and eastern Bolivia.

Lunfardo   Linguistic argot or code that appeared in Buenos Aires in the nineteenth century from the fusion of Spanish, Italian, and African words.

Machismo   Model that associates masculinity with drinking, fearlessness, bravado behavior, and sexual potency.

Mal de Ojo   Illness attributed to direct eye contact with someone who is envious, jealous, or has a grudge.

Maquilas or Maquiladoras   Assembly plants, staffed primarily by women, whose goods are mainly destined for the North American market.

Marianismo   Gender ideology that construes women as passive, self-sacrificing, and submissive to men.

Maritime Coastal Adaptation   Subsistence strategy based on the exploitation of marine/sea resources.

Maroon Societies   Societies spawned by runaway slaves and a mix of indigenous, European, and African cultures.

Matrifocal Households   Female-headed households consisting mainly of women and children.

Matrilineal Descent   Rule specifying that rights and obligations pass through the female line.

Medical Anthropology   Field of cultural anthropology concerned with the cross-cultural study of the social, cultural, and biological dimensions of health and illness.

Medical System   Beliefs, values, practices, and knowledge for the diagnosis, treatment, and explanation of health and illness.

Memory Work   Research on collective memory of past traumatic events and its consequences.

Merced, Composición   Colonial-era land grant that often accompanied the awarding of encomiendas.

Mesa Central (Central Plateau)   Physiographic region in Mexico ringed by the Western and Eastern Sierra Madre mountain ranges.

Mesa del Norte   Hot and arid northern segment of the Mesa Central.

Mestizaje   Process of racial mixing between those viewed as White or European and Indian or indigenous.

Mestizo   Quasi-racial category intermediate between Indian and White.

Mitas   Colonial-era mandatory labor quotas or drafts.

Mothers of the Plaza de Mayo   Association of mothers of Argentina's "disappeared" during the 1970s and 1980s.

Mulatto   Quasi-racial category intermediate between Black and White.

Multi-Sited Ethnography   Ethnographic research in more than one site or locale.

Neoliberalism   A model based on the belief that the unregulated market is a better regulator of economic and social and cultural life than the state.

Neo-Local Residence   Residence rule in which couples set up their own independent household.

Neovolcanic Range   Physiographic region extending from the southeastern edge of Mexico's Central Plateau through most of Central America.

Nervios   Culturally specific illness marked by symptoms that include loss of emotional and bodily control.

North American Free Trade Agreement (NAFTA)   Agreement signed by Mexico, the United States, and Canada designed to reduce restrictions on trade.

Palenques (see also Quilombos)   Free slave communities formed by runaway slaves (Spanish).

Paleo-Indian Period   Earliest of the archaeological periods into which the prehistory of Latin America and the Caribbean is divided; marked by presence of small foraging bands.

Pampas   Physiographic region, mainly in Argentina, of almost treeless flat plains and grasslands with moderate, Mediterranean-type climate.

Parallel Descent   Rule specifying that rights and obligations pass from women to women, and men to men.

Participant Observation Methodological strategy in sociocultural anthropology emphasizing long-term, personal, face-to-face contact and living with the peoples studied.

Patagonia Arid, desertlike region in central and southeastern Argentina, extending in an eastern and southeastern direction from the Pampas to the western Andean Mountains.

Peasants Subsistence-oriented rural cultivators economically, politically, and socially subordinated to elites.

Personal Identity Meanings that quasi-racial categories acquire for the people who self-identify with them.

Physical/Biological Anthropology Subfield of general anthropology concerned with the evolution of the human species (homo sapiens sapiens) and the relationship between biology and cultural behavior.

Physiographic Regions Sizeable terrains exhibiting distinctive and circumscribed topographic, climatological, altitudinal, soil, and vegetative features.

Place Physical area or locale associated with or in which significant cultural life or interactions take place.

Plantation Highly capitalized estate, worked mainly by wage laborers producing goods for the world market.

Political Consequences of Ethnographic Work The awareness that ethnographic research and how indigenous peoples are represented by anthropologists have serious political consequences.

Political Ecology Approach emphasizing the interaction of political and economic forces in ecological changes.

Polytheistic Religious Systems Religious systems that incorporate new deities and stress their presence and active role in everyday life.

Popular Catholicism Widespread syncretic religious system that emerged out of the fusion of European medieval Catholicism and indigenous religious beliefs and practices.

Popular Culture Cultural beliefs and practices in stratified societies that are widely shared.

Positionality Debate on whether class, gender, or ethnic backgrounds of anthropologists influence the interpretation of their research.

Prehistory Historical development of societies prior to the European Conquest.

Primary State Formation When a state emerges in a context free of contact with other states.

Private Transcript Concept that emphasizes opposition and noncompliance far from the purvey of elites or power holders.

Public Commemorations Public, visible mediums through which historical events are remembered and different claims of truth emerge and are disputed.

Quilombos (see also Palenques) Free slave communities formed by runaway slaves (Portuguese).

Quinceañera Ritual celebration of a young girl's fifteenth birthday.

Race Concept that groups people on the presumption that biological differences separate human groups into distinct populations.

Racial Passing Process by which an individual comes to move from one position on a racial hierarchy to another.

Reducciones (also Congregaciones) Colonial-era policy that forced resettlement of indigenous peoples into villages, towns, or urban areas.

Religion System of beliefs and ritualized behaviors centered on supernatural beings and forces above and beyond nature and humankind.

Religious Pluralism Co-existence and overlap between different religious traditions.

Religious Syncretism Blending of Catholic, indigenous, and African religious traditions.

Repartimiento Colonial-era policy in which indigenous communities were grouped into administrative units providing labor to Europeans under crown supervision.

Repartimiento de Mercancías Colonial-era policy in which indigenous communities were forced to purchase European goods.

Representational Authority Whether anthropologists can or should assume the privileged role of speaking for the peoples they study.

Reservoirs of Memory How the past is recalled; memories of common heritage generated; and the past, present, and future interpreted.

Revolutionary Violence Armed violence or uprising with the objective of overhauling an economic, political, and social order.

Rite of Passage Rituals that signal and commemorate marked transitions in the life cycle.

Ritual Intoxication (see also Constructive Drinking) Alcohol intoxication that takes place as part of ritualized celebrations.

Ritual of Inversion Ritual behavior that temporarily and symbolically inverts the social order.

Ritual of Resistance Ritual behavior that expresses opposition to a social order.

Ritual Power Ability of rituals or ritual behavior to harness authority or legitimacy.

Ritualized Popular Celebration Highly stylized, choreographed public performance.

Rituals of Rule Rituals that publicly express and legitimate domination of one group over another.

Salsa Musical genre that appeared in Puerto Rico and Puerto Rican neighborhoods in New York City during the 1960s.

Santería (see also Candomblé and Vodou) One of three major Afro Latin religious systems found mainly in Brazil and the Caribbean.

Secular–Religious Ritual Ritual or ritual behavior that has both religious and nonreligious components.

Sertão Brazilian northeastern region renowned for its severely eroded and arid landscape.

Sex Wars The controversies surrounding the origins and functions of warfare among Amazonian societies centered on the capture of women.

Sexuality How erotic and physical desires toward others are shaped, internalized, challenged, and practiced by men and women.

Shamanism Religious system in which individuals have power to directly communicate with the supernatural through a trance or possession experience.

Shantytowns Urban slums on the periphery of major cities.

Single or Multiple Truths Controversy on whether more than one interpretation of reality (what occurred) is possible.

Soccer War War between Honduras and El Salvador sparked by the 1969 World Cup soccer match.

Social Capital Resources, symbolic or otherwise, that an individual garners through social networks.

Societal or Cultural Complexity Process through which societies increased their capacity to harness resources from their environments, sustain larger populations, and achieve a greater degree of political integration.

Socio-Cultural (Cultural) Anthropology Subfield of general anthropology that centers attention on the study of the culture of contemporary social groups.

Southern Highlands Physiographic region of high-altitude volcanic ranges and intermontane basins in southern Mexico and northern Central America.

Space A construct with spatial (i.e., geographic) coordinates or boundaries with which a landscape is set apart from others based on assumed commonalities or differences.

States Societies that display concentration of political and coercive power, political hierarchies, armies, and entrenched socioeconomic differentiation.

Structural Violence The effects of broad and pervasive patterns of poverty, inequality, and oppression that cut across cultural, ethnic, class, and gender boundaries.

Structural Zones Large swaths of distinct landforms sharing analogous topography, climatic, altitudinal, and geological characteristics into which Latin America and the Caribbean are divided.

Sustainable Development Self-sustaining and environmentally nondestructive livelihood practices.

Susto Popular illness sparked by a sudden and unexpected occurrence that startles, frightens, or produces anxiety.

Swidden or Shifting Cultivation Agricultural strategy typical of sub-tropical and tropical environments that entails cutting down and burning trees to enhance soil fertility.

Syncretism Process whereby different cultural traditions come into contact and merge in different ways to form novel ones.

Telenovelas Latin American and Caribbean soap operas.

Terra Firme Interior, upland, and slightly elevated area comprising 98 percent of Amazonia's land mass.

Texts Means through which ideas, values, and norms are transmitted to a wider audience.

Todos Santos Ritualized celebration of All Saints and All Souls day, October 31 and November 1.

Tribes Societies comprised of distinct segments, whose members claim a kinship or genealogical link to each other.

Várzea Narrow strip of seasonally flooded plains along the Amazon River.

Vodou (see also Santería and Candomblé) One of three major Afro Latin religious systems found mainly in Brazil and the Caribbean; typically associated with Haiti.

Western Alpine System One of three structural zones into which Latin America and the Caribbean are divided.

Witchcraft The malignant use or deployment of supernatural powers.

Yucatán Caste War Major rebellion between 1847 and 1901 in the Yucatán Peninsula.

Yucatán Peninsula Physiographic region in northeastern Mexico.

INDEX